----------- An

International

Dictionary

----------- of -----------

Accounting & Taxation

MW00961031

SAN JACINTO COLLEGE LIBRARY-CENTRAL

WITHDRAWN

----------- An -----------

International

Dictionary

----------- of -----------

Accounting & Taxation

12,000 + Entries on

Accounting, Auditing & Taxation

in the

USA, Canada, UK & Australia

Ref.
HF
5621
W3
2004

Clear One Sentence Definition

Right to the Point

Guy Wanjialin

iUniverse, Inc.
New York Lincoln Shanghai

b# 220136

An International Dictionary of Accounting & Taxation
12,000 + Entries on Accounting, Auditing & Taxation in the USA, Canada, UK & Australia

Copyright © 2004 by Guy Wanjialin

All rights reserved. No part of this book may be used or reproduced by any means, graphic, electronic, or mechanical, including photocopying, recording, taping or by any information storage retrieval system without the written permission of the publisher except in the case of brief quotations embodied in critical articles and reviews.

iUniverse books may be ordered through booksellers or by contacting:

iUniverse
2021 Pine Lake Road, Suite 100
Lincoln, NE 68512
www.iuniverse.com
1-800-Authors (1-800-288-4677)

ISBN-13: 978-0-595-31018-0 (pbk)
ISBN-13: 978-0-595-75844-9 (cloth)
ISBN-13: 978-0-595-75841-8 (ebk)
ISBN-10: 0-595-31018-4 (pbk)
ISBN-10: 0-595-75844-4 (cloth)
ISBN-10: 0-595-75841-X (ebk)

Printed in the United States of America

Contents

Preface

A world without accounting means confusion and chaos. Accounting is not only used in the business world, but rather it is used by everyone in all types of situations. Tax touches every aspect of our lives. People are talking about tax on the TV, the radio, newspaper, and the Internet. Life has grown, as a whole, toward higher levels of complexity. The language of accounting and taxation is also expanding: More and more new words are created, and new meanings are added to the old words.

Do you know these words: ad hoc, bath, below-water, blackout, brainstorming, capex, carve-out, e-tax, plugging, postil, Sarbanes-Oxley, strata......? Each term has its unique meaning you may not be able to find a definition in an ordinary dictionary.

Accounting and taxation are dynamic areas with a vocabulary that is constantly changing. It is this dictionary's purpose to present an up-to-date vocabulary. More than 12,000 entries have been drawn from accounting, auditing and taxation in the USA, Canada, UK and Australia.

This dictionary has a brand new design, and is very easy to use. Almost all terms are defined in one clear and simple sentence right to the point.

The author sincerely hopes that this dictionary will be a handy accessible guide to everyone from the layman to the expert in accounting, auditing and taxation.

Whether you are an accountant, CPA, tax professional and amateur, you will find this dictionary of immeasurably help.

To this end, this dictionary features:

Inclusive: more than 12,000 words and phrases are included. Acronyms and slang terms are also included.

International: The dictionary covers terms used in the United States, Canada, Australia and the United Kingdom.

Up-to-date: This dictionary covers all new words currently used in the USA, Canada, UK and Australia such as Bahamian trust, boodle, cyberlaundering, deadwood effect, Sarbanes-Oxley Act, etc.

Tax Planning Strategies: This dictionary contains many tax-planning strategies (e.g. incorporated talent).

Full Cross Reference: All related terms are cross referenced by three signals as "***Also***", "***See***" and "***Opp.***" in bold and italic type.

How to Use the Dictionary

Alphabetization: All entries are alphabetized by letter rather than by word. For example, **account day** follows **accountant**, and **Form W-4** follows **formula budget.**

Abbreviations: Abbreviation of an entry is placed inside a parenthesis "()". Abbreviation is also treated as a main entry, followed by the words and phrases it represents.

Antonym: Antonymous words are introduced by "***Opp***:"

Bold Type: Bold type is used to highlight main entries.

Cross References: Related entries are crossed referenced by "*See*:".

Definitions: Definitions follow the entries. If an entry has more than one definition, each definition will be marked and separated by <1>, <2>, <3>....

Foreign Words: Foreign words will be marked by "<UK>", "<Canada>", "<Australia>", "<French>", etc. For example:

carrot equity <UK><slang>, an equity investment with the benefit of an opportunity to buy additional shares if the company reaches certain financial objectives.

Italics: Italic type is used to indicate that italicized words and phrases will have a definition under that entry.

Old terms: Old terms and old names are introduced by "***Formerly called:***".

Parenthesis: Abbreviation of an entry will be placed inside a parenthesis.

Parts of Speech: All entries without special indications are nouns. All verbs are indicated by "<verb>".

Synonym: Definition of synonymous entries will be placed on the most frequently used entry. And all other synonymous entries will be introduced by "***Also***:". No definition will be given under the synonymous entry, but linked to the italicized entry with definition by a mark "=".

Word Order: Symbols, such as $, % are listed before numbers, and numbers are listed before alphabets.

$

$100 floor a threshold amount for casualty loss deduction.

$250 rule a rule under which no deduction is allowed for charitable contribution of $250 or more unless the taxpayer substantiates it.

$500 rule a rule that requires a taxpayer to file Form 8283 to substantiate charitable contribution of $500 or more.

$2,500 rule a rule that requires a company to pay the withheld payroll tax with Form 941 without making deposits if the tax liability is less than $2,500 for a quarter.

$5,000 rule a rule that requires a taxpayer to have a qualified appraisal for each donated property of $5000 or more.

2% floor = *2%-of-AGI floor.*

2% limit a limit on carryback or carryover of foreign extraction taxes which equals 2% of net extraction income for the year when the carryover or carryback arose.

2%-of-AGI floor the hurdle amount for claiming miscellaneous deduction. *Also*: 2% floor.

2-tier tax system taxation system that results in taxing the income going to shareholders twice.

2-to-1 current ratio the current ratio, where current assets are twice of current liabilities. *Also*: banker's ratio.

2-to-1 rule of thumb a general rule of appraising the liquidity of a firm by the 2-to-1 current ratio.

3-5-10-rule = *accelerated cost recovery system.*

3% rule <1> a rule under which itemized deduction of a taxpayer is reduced by 3% of AGI that exceeds a threshold amount. <2> a rule under which a participant's accrued benefit must be at least 3% of his or her normal retirement benefits for the year of participation.

3-year MACRS depreciable personal property with a class life of 4 years or less.

4-year rule four tax years beginning with the year of a change in accounting method.

5-year averaging = *5-year forward averaging.*

5-year forward averaging a method used to reduce income tax which requires distributions from qualified retirement plans must be done in 5 years following the year in which the individual dies. *Also*: 5-year averaging. *See*: *forward averaging.*

5-year MACRS property with a class life of more than 4 years and less than 10 years.

5-year rule = *7-year rule.*

7-pay test a test of a life insurance policy to see if the total premium paid at any time during the first 7 years exceeds the sum of the net level premium that would have been paid if the contract provided for paid-up future benefits after the payment of 7 level annual premiums.

7-year MACRS property with a class life of 10 years or more but less than 16 years.

7-year rule a rule under which if the basis of a partnership property is different from its fair market value within 7 years of the contribution, the property is treated as sold by the partnership at the FMV and the partner must realize the gain or loss. (It replaced 5-year rule since 6/9/1997).

8-column worksheet form worksheet where the post-adjustment trial balance columns are omitted.

9 by 4 layout the layout of nine columns and four rows used in process costing.

10% charitable deduction ceiling the maximum deduction amount of charitable contribution by a corporation, 10% of its taxable income.

10% guideline a rule that funded debt over 10% of the assessed valuation of taxable property for municipality is excessive.

10% method a method under which a taxpayer using percentage-of-completion method may elect not to recognize net income and allocate costs if less than 10% of the estimated total contract costs have been incurred. *Also*: modified percentage-of-completion method.

10%-or-more owner an owner who has at least 10% interest in a rental real estate activity.

10% rule of two companies before merger, investments between them of 10% or less of the total outstanding shares is considered independent.

10K = *Form 10K.*

10Q = *Form 10Q.*

10-year charge <UK> a 6% tax on trust assets charged every 10 years.

10-year forward averaging a method used to reduce income tax that requires distributions from qualified retirement plans must be done in 10 years following the year in which the individual dies. (Now replaced by *5-year forward averaging*).

10-year MACRS property with a class life of 16 years or more but less than 20 years.

15-year amortization the amortization of intangible assets over a 15-year period.

15-year MACRS property with a class life of 20 years or more but less than 25 years.

20-factor test IRS's test to determine employee or independent contractor.

20% cushion rule a rule under which that revenues from facilities financed by municipal bonds should exceed operating budget plus maintenance costs and debt service by at least 20% to allow for any unforeseen expenses.

20% margin = cushion.

20-year fixed average method a method of establishing deductions for additions to reserves for bad debts by banks and trust companies.

20-year MACRS property with a class life of 25.4 years or more.

20-day period = *cooling period.*

21-year deemed disposition rule <Canada> a rule requiring that trust assets be treated as if they were disposed of every 21 years for tax purposes.

21.5-year MACRS non-residential property, elevator and escalator in that type placed in service before May 12, 1993.

25% omission failure to report gross income exceeding 25% of the gross income shown on the tax return.

27.5-year MACRS residential rental property including manufacturing homes, elevators and escalators in that type.

30% bonus = *30% bonus depreciation.*

30% bonus depreciation *bonus depreciation* on *qualified property* purchased before Jan 1, 2005 up to 30% of the purchase price. *Also*: 30% bonus. *See*: *50% bonus depreciation.*

30% charities charitable organizations that are not *50% charities.*

30% rule a rule that disqualifies a mutual fund from income pass-through treatment if more than 30% of its gross income came from gains on positions held for less than three months. *Also*: short sale rule; short-short rule.

30% tax a flat rate tax imposed on interest, rents, and an extensive list of fixed or determinable annual or periodical gains, profits, and income from US sources paid to nonresidents and foreign companies on non-business income.

30/20 regulation <Australia> former rule that requires life insurance companies must hold 30% of their assets in public securities with at lease 20% of total assets in *commonwealth securities* in return for tax concessions.

30/360 a day count convention that uses 30 days in a month and 360 days in a year in calculating interest.

30-day letter a letter from the IRS of proposed adjustments of tax, stating that failure to respond in 30 days will result in a statutory notice of deficiency.

30-day wash rule = *wash sale rule.*

39-week rule a rule for claiming moving expense deduction, the individual who is an employee must be employed at the new place of employment for at least 39 weeks out of the 12 months following the move.

39-year MACRS non-residential property, elevator and escalator in that type placed in service after May 12, 1993.

50% bonus = *50% bonus depreciation.*

50% bonus depreciation *bonus depreciation* on *qualified property* up to 50% of the purchase price placed in service after May 5, 2003. *Also*: 50% bonus. *See*: *30% bonus depreciation.*

50% bonus depreciation property = *50% bonus property.*

50% bonus property *qualified property* under the 2003 Tax Act to claim the 50% bonus depreciation. *Also*: 50% bonus depreciation property. *See*: *qualified property.*

50% charities charitable organizations the contribution to which is deductible only up to 50%, e.g. churches, tax-exempt educational organizations, hospitals, trusts for colleges and universities, and certain private foundations.

50% method a method of amortizing a fixed asset in which half of the asset cost is transferred to expense when bought, and the second half will be charged to expense when replaced.

50% ownership test a taxpayer making a gift or business interest to someone else must have 50% ownership of the business.

50% pricing method a method, by which the parent DISC sales price is such that the DISC earns 50% of the combined taxable income of the parent and its DISC on the export sale plus 10% of the DISC's export promotion expenses attributable to the sale.

50% rule a rule under which only 50% of the meals and entertainment expenses are deductible.

50-employee/40% test a test under which a defined benefit plan is qualified only when it benefits the lesser of 40% of the employees or 50 employees.

50-mile rule a rule for moving expense deduction, the new place of work must be at least fifty miles farther from the old residence than the old place of work was from the old residence.

52-week tax year a tax year of 52 weeks and ends on the same day of the week.

53-week tax year a tax year of 53 weeks and ends on the same day of the week

60/40 treatment a tax rule that gains on broad-based index options or futures positions are reported as 60% long-term gains and 40% as short-term gains.

70% dividend-received deduction a 70% deduction allowed for dividend received from a domestic C corporation.

75% combined revenue test = *75% test.*

75% test a test to see if at least 75% of unaffiliated revenue is reported by the reportable segment. *Also*: 75% combined revenue test.

78-week rule a rule for moving expense deduction, a self-employed taxpayer must be self-employed 78 weeks during the 24 months following the move.

80% dividend-received deduction an 80% deduction allowed for dividend received from a 20%-owned company. *Also*: 80% exclusion.

80% exclusion = *80% dividend-received deduction.*

85% exclusion 85% of the cash dividends received by one company from another to be exempted from taxable income. *See*: *dividend exclusion; eligible dividend.*

90% test a test of the condition of adopting pooling of interest method, if the merger is under exchange of common stocks, the acquiring company must acquire at least 90% of the total outstanding shares of the acquired company.

90-day letter a letter from the IRS to a taxpayer who did nothing after receiving a 30 day letter. *Also*: deficiency letter; notice of deficiency; statutory notice of deficiency.

100% apportioned cost driver cost driver that relies entirely on the judgement of an informed estimator's of how much cost should be traced to each cost object and to which cost object.

100% balance sheet = *common-size balance sheet.*

100% dividend-received deduction a 100% deduction allowed for dividend received from members of an affiliated group, or from a foreign subsidiary.

100% income statement = *common-size income statement.*

100% profit and loss statement = *common-size income statement.*

133 1/3 rule a rule the gist of which is that a later year's accrual rate of benefits based on employer contributions must not be more than 133 1/3% of the current year's accrual rate.

144 stock = *restricted stock.*

150% declining balance method declining balance method under which the depreciation rate is 150% of that under the straight line method.

183-day rule <Canada> a rule under which if a person has stayed in Canada for 183 days and more in a year, he or she is subject to income tax.

200%-declining-balance method = *double declining balance method.*

360-days-per-year basis a basis for calculating annual interest on 30 days per month for twelve months. *See*: *Boston interest.*

365-days-per-year basis a basis for calculating annual interest on the exact days of the calendar months. *See*: *New York interest.*

401(k) employee investment plan which allows employees to put part of their gross earnings into a tax deferred plan. *Also*: salary reduction plan; section 401(k) plan.

403(b) annuity = *tax-sheltered annuity.*

403(b) plan employee retirement plan for non-profit organizations. *Also*: section 403(b) plan.

412(i) plan defined benefit plan

457 plan a non-qualified retirement plan for government employees only, similar to 401(k), except there are no employer matching contributions. *Also*: 457(b) plan; section 457 plan; section 457(b) plan.

457(b) plan = *457 plan.*

529 college savings plan = *qualified state tuition program.*

529 plan = *qualified state tuition program.*

1035 exchange an exchange of cash value from one life insurance policy to another, allowing a taxpayer to avoid capital gains or losses in the first policy as long as the second policy is of greater or equal cost.

1244 stock = *small business investment company stock.*

2053 trust a trust the child beneficiary of which can not get money until age 21.

A a

A <1> account. <2> adverse variance. <3> annuity. <4> asset. <5> audit.

A. total average dollar inventory

A&E <1> analysis and evaluation. <2> appropriation and expense.

A&P administrative and personnel.

AA active account

A & A accounting and auditing

AAA <1> accumulated adjustments account. <2> American Accounting Association.

AAPA American Association of the Public Accountants

AAR average annual return

AAUIA American Association of University Instructors in Accounting

ABA <1> Accredited Business Accountant. <2> Accredited Business Advisor.

abandoned asset an asset given up by the owner, and can be removed from the balance sheet.

abandoned bank account = *unclaimed bank account.*

abandoned property = *escheat property.*

abandonment <1> the writing off of an asset. <2> an option holder's choice not to exercise his right to buy or sell shares. *Also*: release.

abandonment loss the loss resulting from the relinquishment of an interest in worthless assets.

abandonment loss deduction a tax deduction for *abandonment loss.*

abandonment value the amount that can be realized immediately by selling an asset. *Also*: liquidation value.

abatement = *tax abatement.*

abatement cost = *environmental pollution-control cost.*

ABB activity-based budgeting

abbreviate account <UK> = *condensed balance sheet.*

abbreviated financial statement = *condensed financial statement.*

ABC activity-based costing

ABC classification = *usage value classification.*

ABC control system = *ABC method.*

ABC method a method whereby inventory items are classified into three groups according to whether the cost is relatively high, medium or low. *Also*: ABC control system. *See*: *selective control.*

ABC transaction a transaction that called for A, the operator, to convey his working interest to B, A then reserved a production payment larger than the cash paid by B, later A sold it to C for cash..

ABI adjusted business income

ABIL allowable business investment loss

ability to pay a person or entity's present and future ability to generate enough net income to meet its liabilities.

ABM activity-based management

abnormal depreciation extra depreciation caused by abnormal factors e.g. natural disaster. *Also*: extraordinary depreciation; special depreciation.

abnormal dividend <UK> a dividend that exceeds the amount on a normal return.

abnormal loss = *abnormal spoilage.*

abnormal retirement the retirement of an asset for reasons not contemplated when the rate of depreciation is fixed, e.g. a result of casualty or obsolescence.

abnormal return the return that is above those predicted by market movement.

abnormal spoilage loss of physical units due to abnormal factors e.g. production breakdown. ***Also***: abnormal loss.

ABO accumulated benefit obligation

abode <UK> = *principal residence.*

aboriginal cost = *original cost.*

above-the-line <1> above the line that separates income and expense, or assets and liabilities. <2> above the total amount crossing line in a T-account. <3> above the line that separates the annual revenue and annual expenditure, or the current and non-current budget items. <4> above the AGI where deductions are claimed by taxpayers in a tax return.

above-the-line deduction a deduction to arrive at adjusted gross income. ***Also***: adjustment; adjustment to gross income; deduction for AGI.

above-water an asset the value of which is greater than book value. ***See***: *below-water.*

ABS asset-backed security

abs. abstract.

absolute cash flow total cash inflows less cash outflows less depreciation.

absolute cost <1> the minimum cost that a firm must bear to remain as a going concern. <2> = *actual cost.*

absolute cost advantage the ability to obtain raw materials at lower costs, or to manufacture a product at lower cost.

absolute income = *real income.*

absolute income hypothesis a theory that holds expenditures and savings are a function of income.

absolute interest <1><UK> a trust beneficiary's interest in both the capital and income of trust assets. ***See***: *limited interest.* <2> = *substantial interest.*

absolute liability a form of liability without fault, such as product liability. ***Also***: liability without regard to fault; strict liability.

absolute priority rule (APR) the idea that creditors' claims take precedence over the shareholders' claim in the event of bankruptcy, liquidation or reorganization.

absolute return = *total return.*

absolute revenue the revenue that would be earned if there were no present process.

absolute value = *intrinsic value.*

absorbed overhead the overhead cost that has been charged to cost units.

absorbing cost = *cost absorption.*

absorption <1> = *cost absorption.* <2> = *merger.* <3> = *overhead absorption.*

absorption account = *contra account.*

absorption cost a cost including both fixed and variable costs. ***Also***: complete cost; full absorption cost; full cost; full product cost; single all inclusive unit cost figure; total absorption cost; total cost. ***See***: *partial cost.*

absorption costing assigning all costs, fixed and variable, to a product. ***Also***: conventional absorption costing; conventional costing; full costing; full-price costing; total absorption costing; total costing; traditional costing. ***See***: *partial costing.*

absorption costing income statement an income statement the cost in which is expressed in absorption cost, and shows the gross profit only. ***Also***: conventional income statement; function form income statement. ***See***: *direct costing income statement.*

absorption cost system cost system that uses absorption costs in the financial statements. ***Also***: conventional cost system; total cost system; traditional cost system.

absorption rate the rate at which properties are able to be leased or sold in a given area.

absorption ratio the ratio of section 263A cost to the section 471 cost.

absorption rule a rule which states that net operating losses first may be carried back to the third taxable year, then used to offset taxable income in the third year.

absorption standard costing = *standard absorption costing.*

absorption variance cost variance from budgeted absorption costing.

abstract (abs) = *trial balance.*

abstract account an account that is closed monthly.

abstract of account description of transactions in an account.

abstract of posting a table listing entries to be posted and the cross reference of them.

abusive shelter = *abusive tax shelter.*

abusive tax shelter limited partnership, investment plan or arrangement, deemed by the IRS to be claiming depreciation deduction based on the inflated value of assets. ***Also***: abusive shelter.

abusive trust a trust created for the purpose of avoiding tax.

ABV Accredited in Business Valuation

AC <1> active capital. <2> actual cost.

A/C <1> account. <2> account current.

ACA <1> <UK> associate of the Institute of Chartered Accountants in England and Wales. <2> Association of Certified Accountants.

ACAT Accreditation Council for Accountancy and Taxation

ACB adjusted cost base

ACC annual capital charge

acc <1> acceptance. <2> accepted. <3> account. <4> accountant.

ACCA <1> <UK> associate of the Chartered Association of Certified Accountants. <2> Association of Certified and Corporate Accountants.

accelerated cost recovery system (ACRS) a method that uses a time period shorter than an asset's useful life, over which a firm may take depreciation on the asset. ***Also***: 3-5-10 rule.

accelerated depreciation a depreciation that results in greater depreciation cost in the early years of a plant's useful life and lesser amounts in later years. ***Also***: amortization; emergency amortization.

accelerated method a method used in calculating accelerated depreciation, e.g. declining balance method, sum-of-the-years'-digits method, etc.

acceptable upper precision limit = *upper precision limit.*

acceptance <1> writing across the face of a bill by which the drawee agrees to pay. ***Also***: promise to pay. <2> agreement by a shareholder to accept the company's changes in his or her rights.

acceptance error = *beta risk.*

acceptance payable = *bill payable.*

acceptance receivable = *bill receivable.*

acceptance sampling <1> a sampling method that leads to a conclusion that the actual error rate in a population does not exceed certain level. <2> sampling used by internal auditors to test the compliance of the information channels of a firm.

acceptilation = *cancellation of debt.*

accession tax an inheritance tax on what the beneficiaries receive on the death of a person. ***Also***: capital acquisition tax. ***See:*** *estate tax.*

acc. ex. accrued expense

accidental loss financial loss caused by an accident.

accident year a 12-month period during which premiums and losses relating to an accident occurred.

accommodating account an account used by the balance of payments accounting for balancing gaps between autonomous accounts. ***Also***: compensating account; financing account. ***See***: *reconciliation account.*

accompanying note = *footnote.*

accompanying statement a statement accompanying the financial statements, such as the consolidated statement of income and retained earnings.

accompt = *account.*

account (a/c)(acc)(acct)(act) <1> a device used in recording and summarizing the increases and decreases in a revenue, an expense, asset, liability, or owner's equity item. ***Also***: account note. <2> the figures recorded in an account. <3> money value shown by a current account. <4> special item in the balance of payments. <5> = *accounting record.* <6> = *account period.* <7> = *ledger sheet.* <8> = *statement.*

accountability <1> the responsibility to perform a certain function. <2> the ability of a system to track the responsibility of an individual or institution uniquely.

accountable plan = *accountable reimbursement plan.*

accountable receipt a receipt given for money or for goods, coupled with an obligation, which must be accounted for subsequently, such as a deposit receipt.

accountable reimbursement plan a plan set up so that the employees can receive business expense reimbursements and not be required to include them in their gross income. ***Also***: accountable plan.

account adjustment the adjustment at the end of a period in order to show end-of-period balances for preparing statements.

account analysis = *account method.*

accountant (acc.)(acct) a person trained to post book entries and to balance books or to prepare financial statements.

accountant-client privilege shielding of the confidential information provided by a client to an accountant from being released to outsiders. ***Also***: accountant's privilege.

accountant in charge = *in-charge auditor.*

accountant's certificate = *auditor's report.*

accountants for the public interest (API) organizations serving the public welfare, such as technical support to nonprofit organizations.

accountant's letter = *comfort letter.*

accountant's liability potential legal obligation of an accountant who commits fraud or gross negligence in performing service. ***See***: *accountant's responsibility.*

accountant's liability insurance an insurance for accountants covering liability lawsuits arising from their professional activities.

accountant's method = *mercantile method.*

accountant's opinion = *comfort letter.*

accountant's privilege = *accountant-client privilege.*

accountant's profit = *pre-tax accounting income.*

accountant's report <1> = *auditor's report.* <2> = *management letter.*

accountant's responsibility ethical obligation to those who rely on the accountant's work. ***See***: *accountant's liability.*

account attached words on a dishonored check meaning the drawer's account has been attached to a court judgement.

account audit inspection of accounts to see whether they have been properly maintained.

account balance = *balance.*

account bill = *bill.*

account book = *book.*

account classification <1> the separation of accounts into meaningful groups. <2> = *chart of accounts.*

account closed words on a dishonored check meaning the drawer's account has been closed. ***See***: *no account.*

account code = *account code number.*

account code number a code to identify the name of an account and its classification in financial statements. ***Also***: account code; account number; accounts code; code of accounts.

account control the controlling of the subsidiary books by the general ledger.

account creditor a person to whom the balance of an open account is owed.

account current (A/C) statement issued by the insurance company on a monthly basis to its agents showing his or her commissions earned, premium written, cancellations of policy, and endorsements.

account debtor a person to who owes the balance of an open account.

account distribution a process by which debits and credits are identified to the correct accounts.

account distribution memo a memo for posting certain entries into a specified account.

account en route = *account in transit.*

account equity the amount a client's margin account would be worth if all open positions were liquidated. *Also*: equity.

account form <1> organization of an account, e.g. T-account, balance-column account, etc. *Also*: account pattern; form of account. <2> a form of listing items in two sides, the left-hand side and the right-hand side. *Also*: balancing form; two sided form. *See*: *financial position form; report form.*

account form balance sheet balance sheet format in which assets are listed on one side, while liabilities and capital are balanced against them on the other side. *Also*: balance sheet in the account form; horizontal balance sheet; two-sided balance sheet.

account form income statement income statement format in which income and disbursements are separately listed in two sides, and net income will be listed on the disbursements side, and net loss on the income side. *Also*: balance form income statement; technical form income statement.

account heading = *account title.*

account in balance an account of which the debit totals and the credit totals are equal. *Also*: closed account.

accounting (acct)(acctg) the art of recording, classifying, reporting, and interpreting the financial data.

accounting alternatives different methods selected under different situations according to the same accounting principle.

accounting and audit fee <UK> a fee paid to outside accountants and auditors.

accounting and review service = *review.*

accounting assumption an assumption serving as a guide to the accounting behavior, such as valuation of assets and liabilities.

accounting audit = *audit.*

accounting base <UK> = *measurement base.*

accounting based on value-to-the-firm = *current cost accounting.*

accounting basis variations in applying accounting assumptions, often produce balance sheet figures whose significance is difficult to interpret.

accounting bath heavy losses in an accounting period. *Also*: bath; big bath; blood bath; great loss; plenty red; shock loss.

accounting capital = *net worth.*

accounting change a change in accounting assumptions, principles, reporting entity or periods.

accounting concept an idea that serves as a basis in the interpretation of accounting information. *Also*: fundamental accounting concept.

accounting control <1> procedures that monitor the receipt and disbursement of funds and the recording of business transactions. *Also*: internal accounting control. *See*: *internal control.* <2> procedures and records concerned with the safeguarding of the assets and the reliability of financial records.

accounting convention procedures or methods employed by accounting practitioners generally.

accounting cushion overestimating allowance for an expense. *See*: *income smoothing.*

accounting cycle procedures from the records made in the books of original entry to posting to ledger accounts, making closing entries and adjusting entries and taking a trial balance. *Also*: bookkeeping cycle; cycle of accounting.

accounting date <UK> the date on which an accounting period ends.

accounting depreciation = *book depreciation.*

accounting disclosure = *full disclosure.*

accounting distribution the determination of debit and credit side of an entry.

accounting document = *supporting document.*

accounting earnings = *pre-tax accounting income.*

accounting entity business or other entity being accounted for separately.

accounting entity principle = *business entity principle.*

accounting entry = *entry.*

accounting equation the basic idea on which all accounting depends: assets = capital + liabilities (and sometimes + revenue - expenses - dividend). *Also*: accounting formula; balance sheet equation; balance sheet identity; bookkeeping equation; bookkeeping formula; capital equation; ownership equation; proprietorship equation. *See*: *basic accounting equation; expanded accounting equation.*

accounting error an error in the published financial statements about accounting principle or method.

accounting event a transaction entered in the books of a business.

accounting exemption the exemption of small business from rendering financial statements.

accounting exposure the risk that a company's equity, assets, or income will change in value as a result of exchange rate changes. *Also*: balance sheet exposure; translation exposure.

accounting firm a firm that renders accounting, auditing, taxation and management consultant services.

accounting for changes in general and specific prices = *constant dollar accounting.*

accounting for changes in the purchasing power of money = *constant dollar accounting.*

accounting for changing money value = *constant dollar accounting .*

accounting for defeasance procedure that allows a company to remove debt from its financial statements without retiring the debt formally.

accounting for derivatives the procedures under which an entity must recognize all derivatives as either assets or liabilities in the statement of financial position and measure those instruments at fair value.

accounting for external reporting = *stewardship accounting.*

accounting for internal reporting = *management accounting.*

accounting for investment properties = *depreciation accounting.*

accounting for liquidation accounting procedures for the liquidation of a firm. *Also*: liquidation accounting; termination accounting.

accounting formula = *accounting equation.*

accounting for price changes = *constant-dollar accounting.*

accounting for price level changes = *constant dollar accounting.*

accounting for stewardship = *stewardship accounting.*

accounting gain = *book gain.*

Accounting Hall of Fame = *Hall of Fame.*

accounting identity a relation that 2 numeral things such as asset and liability (and capital), credit and debit etc. are equal by accepted definitions.

accounting income <1> the difference between revenues after providing for historical costs of inventories and fixed assets consumed in the revenue process. *Also*: ex post income; periodic income. <2> = *pre-tax accounting income.*

accounting information system (AIS) a systematic device and methods used for gathering, processing and reporting the accounting information.

accounting insolvency = *deficiency.*

accounting job employment in accounting position.

accounting liquidity = *liquidity.*

accounting manual a handbook which contains policy guidelines, procedures and standards of accounting of a company or an individual.

accounting measurement accounting values in the form of money or other units.

accounting method a method used by accountants to report income and loss either on an overall basis, or with respect to any material item. *Also*: method of accounting.

accounting model = *standard accounting procedures.*

accounting on the accrual basis = *accrual basis accounting.*

accounting period (A/P) <1> a period at the end of which accounts are made up, balances are struck, and a profit or loss is arrived at. *Also*: audit period; fiscal period; period. <2> a period for which an income distribution is due. <3> period for determining personal tax liability.

accounting period assumption the artificial periods set in order to match the income and expenses. *Also*: periodicity assumption.

accounting period problem the difficulty of assigning revenues and expenses to short periods of time such as months or years, related to the *accounting period assumption.*

accounting policy a policy that consists of methods selected by management from the available alternatives.

accounting postulate basic assumption or axioms, generally accepted by virtue of their conformity to the objectives of the financial statements, which portray the economic and legal environment in which the accounting must operate.

accounting practice practical application of accounting to the accumulation and reporting needs of a client.

accounting price = *opportunity cost.*

accounting principles general rules derived from both the objectives and the concepts of accounting which govern the development of accounting techniques.

Accounting Principles Board (APB) committee formed in 1959 to formulate the accounting principles related to financial reporting based on underlying research, replaced by FASB in 1973.

accounting procedure method used to uncover, record or summarize financial data.

accounting profit = *pre-tax accounting income.*

accounting profit equation = *profit and loss statement equation.*

accounting rate of return rate of return determined by dividing income shown in the financial statements by the initial investment. *Also*: book rate of return; book value rate; cost of equity capital; financial rate of return; mercantile rate of return; simple rate of return; unadjusted rate of return. *See*: *average rate of return; internal rate of return.*

accounting rate of return method = *mercantile method.*

accounting record including journal, ledger, invoice, and financial statements, now the computer files. *Also*: account.

accounting reference period <UK> a selected period for the income statement by a limited company.

accounting risk the risk loss resulting from inappropriate signals given by an accounting or financial reporting requirement.

accounting standard a principle that achieves more uniformity practices and consistency of the accounting treatment of activities.

Accounting Standards Board (ASB) <UK> an official body for issuing accounting standards.

Accounting Standards Executive Committee (AcSEC) AICPA committee whose objective is to determine Institute technical policies regarding financial accounting and reporting standards.

accounting statement = *financial statement.*

accounting surplus = *book surplus.*

accounting system structure of records and procedures for recording, classifying, and reporting information on the financial position and operating results of an entity.

accounting techniques specific rules derived from the accounting principles to account for specific transactions and events faced by the accounting entity.

accounting timing difference = *temporary difference.*

accounting to employer = *adequate accounting.*

accounting transaction internal transfer transaction required by accounting methods. ***Also***: bookkeeping transaction; book transaction; paper transaction.

accounting unit a unit for calculating and recording fixed assets.

accounting valuation the valuation of an asset by an accounting professional.

accounting valuation assumption an assumption of cost basis for the valuation of assets, such as cost price, retail price, lower of cost or market, etc. ***Also***: valuation assumption.

accounting year accounting period consisting of twelve consecutive months. ***Also***: account year; annual accounting period; audit year; business year; commercial year; financial year; fiscal year; yearly accounting period.

account in transit an entry not recorded in an account yet. ***Also***: account en route.

account matrix = *spread sheet.*

account method a method of determining cost behavior by analyzing cost accounts. ***Also***: account analysis; accounts classification method; title of accounts method.

account name = *account title.*

account note = *account.*

account number (acc. no.)(a/c no.)(AN)(A/N) = *account code number.*

account numbering scheme = *accounts code system.*

account of business = *income statement.*

account of executor the record of estate receipts and expenditures kept by an executor. ***Also***: account of proceedings.

account of payments a list of all payments made in a period.

account of proceedings = *account of executor.*

account pattern = *account form.*

account payable (a/c pay.)(ac. pay.)(A/P) money owed by the business to someone else. ***Also***: payable.

account payee only words added to the crossing on a check telling the bank to credit the amount to the named payee's account.

account period a credit period of 14 calendar days during which the settlement of securities transactions between members of the stock exchange is deferred. ***Also***: account; account period of trading; stock exchange account.

account period of trading = *account period.*

account receivable (acct rec)(a/c rec)(A/R) money due to be received from someone else. ***Also***: account to receive; book debt; debit; debtor; debt receivable; receivable; receivable account.

account rendered = *statement of account.*

accounts classification method = *account method.*

accounts clerk = *bookkeeper.*

accounts code = *account code number.*

accounts code system a coding plan for not only identifying accounts but also telling their classifications in the accounting statements. ***Also***: account numbering scheme; account symbol system; symbolization of accounts; symbol system of account.

accounts payable days = *days purchases in accounts payable.*

accounts payable ledger a ledger maintaining separate accounts payable to every creditor. *Also*: creditors' ledger.

accounts payable to purchases ratio the ratio of the sum of accounts payable to the total amount of purchases within certain period.

accounts payable turnover the ratio of cost of goods sold for the year divided by the accounts payable balance at the end of that year.

accounts receivable days outstanding = *number of days' sales in receivables.*

accounts receivable factor a person or a company who purchases the accounts receivables of a customer at a discount. *Also*: factor.

accounts receivable factored accounts receivable sold to the factor. *Also*: discounted accounts receivable.

accounts receivable financing cash advance that uses accounts receivable as collateral. *Also*: discount factoring; factorage; factoring; financing receivables; invoice discounting.

accounts receivable insurance coverage when business records are destroyed by an insured peril and the business cannot collect money from its debtors.

accounts receivable ledger a ledger that maintains separate accounts for accounts receivable from each customer. *Also*: customers' ledger; debtors' ledger; receivables ledger.

accounts receivable turnover a ratio arrived at by dividing cash sales or credit sales by ending or average accounts receivable. *Also*: ratio of sales to debtors; receivables turnover.

account stated <1> a *statement of account* upon which parties agree. *Also*: stated account. <2> an account which arises when the IRS issues a certificate of overassessment to a taxpayer for his overpayment of taxes.

account statement a statement which summarizes all the transactions, and shows the status of a margin account with a broker.

account symbol system = *accounts code system.*

account title (act tit.) the name given to an account. *Also*: account heading; account name; caption of account; name of account.

account to pay = *giving account.*

account to receive = *account receivable.*

account type identification used to distinguish regulated and non-regulated brokerage accounts within the same account number, e.g. 01 for domestic commodities 02 for foreign commodities.

account year = *accounting year.*

Accreditation Council for Accountancy and Taxation (ACAT) a non-profit organization established in 1973 which accredits professionals in independent accounting practice as ABA or ABT.

Accredited Business Accountant (ABA) a professional title accredited by ACAT.

Accredited in Business Valuation (ABV) Designation in business valuation awarded by the AICPA to those who have met prescribed requirements and passed an examination.

accredited investor a person having a net worth of at least $1 million or an annual income of at least $200,000 or putting at least $150,000 into the deal, and the total investment is less than 20% of his net worth.

Accredited Tax Advisor (ATA) a professional title accredited by ACAT.

accreted value <1> theoretical price a bond would sell at if market interest rates were to remain at current levels. <2> the current value of a *zero-coupon bond*, including interest that has accumulated and reinvested. *Also*: compound accreted value.

accretion (acc.) <1> the adjustment of the difference between the cost price of a bond bought at an original discount and the par value of it. *Also*: accumulation. <2> increase in the asset value through internal expansion or acquisition.

accretion account a ledger account for recording the increase between the acquisition value and the face value of bonds bought at a discount.

accretive increasing in earnings per share by acquisition.

accrual an accounting procedure of recognizing income and expense earned or incurred but not yet received or paid. *Opp*: *deferral.*

accrual accounting = *accrual basis accounting.*

accrual asset an asset that is considered acceptable by a banker as collateral. *See*: *non-accrual asset.*

accrual basis a system by which the matching concept is applied. *Also*: accrual-deferral system; accrued basis.

accrual basis accounting the accounting procedures that adopt accrual basis. *Also*: accounting on the accrual basis; accrual accounting.

accrual basis income statement an income statement the income and cost figures of which are calculated under accrual basis.

accrual concept = *matching concept.*

accrual-deferral system = *accrual basis.*

accrual of discount annual addition to the book value contributed by bonds bought below par.

accrual option an option that gives the holder the right to receive daily interest when the underlying stock price trades within a specified range. *Also*: corridor option; fairway option.

accrual period the period during which the an underlying stock's price is monitored to determine the payout of an accrual option.

accrued asset interest, commissions, services, and items of revenue neither received nor past due but earned.

accrued basis = *accrual basis.*

accrued benefit <1> for a defined benefit plan, annual benefit in the form of an annuity. <2> for a defined contribution plan, the balance in the employee's account.

accrued-benefit-cost method = *unit credit method.*

accrued cost the cost of goods and services used up or employed during the period, whether paid for or not.

accrued depreciation <1> the difference between replacement cost-new and the current appraised value of a plant asset. <2> = *accumulated depreciation.*

accrued dividend regular dividend that is considered to be earned but not declared or payable.

accrued-expenditures basis a method by which all costs and expenses incurred are presented in the income statement.

accrued expense (acc. ex.) the same as accrued cost but limited to overhead only.

accrued interest an interest that has been accumulated between the most recent payment and the sale of a bond or fixed interest security. *Also*: interest accrued.

accrued interest adjustment an adjustment that reduces your taxable interest income by any interest that you reported and paid tax on as it was earned.

accrued interest payable amount of interests accumulated on a debt, e.g. the fixed income bond, but not yet paid.

accrued inventory purchased goods which have been received in the warehouse, but for which a vendor invoice has not yet arrived.

accrued liability (AL) <1> liability arising from accrued cost or accrued expenses that have been incurred but have not yet been paid. *Also*: reserve. <2> obligation that comes to existence as the result of a past contractual commitment or as the result of the tax laws.

accrued market discount an increase in the market price of a discounted bond resulting from an approaching maturity date.

accrued pension cost amount by which net periodic pension cost exceeds the amount contributed by the employer. ***Also***: unfunded accrued pension cost. ***See***: *prepaid pension cost.*

acct <1> *account.* <2> *accountant.* <3> *accounting.*

acctg accounting

acct no. account number

acct pay account payable

acc't pay account payable

acct rec account receivable

accum depr accumulated depreciation

accumulated adjustments account (AAA) an account for the S corporations, which consists of the taxable income for the period when the subchapter S election was in force, taxable income is modified by and adjustments made by shareholders to their basis in their stock. ***See***: *other adjustments account.*

accumulated amortization cumulative amortization against the intangible assets.

accumulated amount total amount of both the principal and its interest after a period of time. ***Also***: amount; both principal and interest; capital and interest; future amount; maturity value; principal and interest; terminal value; termination amount.

accumulated benefits actuarial approach an approach that uses actuarial estimate as the obligations to present employees and retirees assuming immediate termination of a pension plan

accumulated benefit obligation (ABO) the actuarial present value of benefits attributed by a pension benefit formula to employee services rendered before a date, based on employee services and compensation prior to that date. ***Also***: accumulated post-retirement benefit obligation. ***See***: *projected benefit obligation.*

accumulated contribution mandatory contribution of an employee plus interest stated under the plan.

accumulated cost total manufacturing costs of a product accumulated after several steps of processing.

accumulated deferred investment tax credit (ADITC) investment tax credit that has been accumulated by some public utility companies.

accumulated deficit = *deficiency.*

accumulated depreciation (acc depre) (accum. depr.) <1> total sum of all the amounts so far written off the value of a plant asset. ***Also***: accrued depreciation; accumulated provision for depreciation; aggregate depreciation; difference between cost and book value; property reserved; total depreciation. <2> = *allowance for depreciation.*

accumulated dividend a dividend not paid when due and carried as a liability. ***See***: *dividend in arrears; omitted dividend.*

accumulated earnings = *unappropriated retained earnings.*

accumulated earnings credit a deduction permitted in determining accumulated taxable income.

accumulated earnings tax (AET) a tax on corporations that pile up earnings without distributing them to the stockholders. ***Also***: accumulated profit tax; surplus accumulation tax.

accumulated income = *unappropriated retained earnings.*

accumulated ledger = *Boston ledger.*

accumulated post-retirement benefit obligation (APBO) = *accumulated benefit obligation.*

accumulated profit tax = *accumulated earnings tax.*

accumulated provision for depreciation = *accumulated depreciation.*

accumulated taxable income (ATI) a tax base on which accumulated profits tax is levied, the taxable income less dividends paying deduction and the accumulated earnings credit.

accumulation <1> adding the income from interest and dividends to the fund's principal. <2> the deliberate assembling of blocks of stock without necessarily bidding up prices. <3> the profit that has not been distributed as dividends, but are instead added to the company's capital account. <4> = *accretion.*

accumulation account an account used to record accumulated amounts such as accumulated depreciation, accumulated discount on bonds, etc.

accumulation and maintenance trust <UK> a trust that operates in a similar manner to a *discretionary trust*, then switches to a *fixed interest trust.*

accumulation distribution the distribution from a complex trust allocated to ordinary income accumulated in prior years.

accumulation method <1> an accounting method for recording discount on bonds as a separate item, and the bonds are recorded at their face value. <2> under process costing, the method by which the costs of previous process are added to the next period as the input costs.

accumulation trust = *complex trust.*

accumulation unit policyholder's interest in a variable annuity prior to the annuity date.

accuracy preciseness of accounting information in disclosing the business.

accuracy-related penalty a penalty on underpayment of tax due to clerical errors.

accurate presentation the presentation of accounting data without error.

ACE adjusted current earnings

ACE **adjustment** an adjustment to AMTI by adjusted current earnings.

ACFE Association of Certified Fraud Examiners

achieved upper precision limit = *upper deviation limit.*

acid-test ratio the ratio of a company's quick assets to its current liabilities. ***Also***: cash ratio; current assets ratio; doomsday ratio; liquidity ratio; liquid ratio; quick ratio; quick test.

a/c no. account number

a/c pay. account payable

acquired company a company whose controlling interest is held by another corporation. ***Also***: victim company.

acquired obligation amount allocated to the proceeds of an issue of governmental bonds while such issue is outstanding.

acquired surplus <1> surplus that has been gained by means other than regular trading. <2> under pooling of interests method, the uncapitalized portion of the net worth of the acquiring company. ***Also***: at acquisition retained earnings.

acquiring company a company holding the controlling interest of another through purchase or exchange of assets or shares. ***Also***: predator company; raider; raider company; successor company. ***See***: *target company.*

acquisition purchase of 50% or more of the controlling interest in another company. ***See***: *merger; consolidation.*

acquisition adjustment any adjustment between the acquisition costs of public utility assets and their original costs.

acquisition borrowing = *home acquisition debt.*

acquisition charge = *prepayment penalty.*

acquisition cost <1> the expenses incurred in order to obtain an asset. ***Also***: invested cost. <2> immediate cost of selling, underwriting and issuing a new insurance policy including clerical costs, agents' commission, advertising, and medical inspection fees. <3> = *purchase cost.*

acquisition cost method = *historical cost approach.*

acquisition discount the excess of stated redemption price of a short-term bond over the taxpayer's basis in it. ***See***: *market discount; original issue discount.*

acquisition fee a fee paid to a real estate agent for the purchase of property.

acquisition indebtedness <1> a debt incurred by an exempt organization in acquiring or improving property. <2> = *home acquisition debt.*

acquisition of assets <1> the acquisition of the target company's assets in a merger. ***Also***: *asset acquisition; exchange of assets.* <2> purchase of an asset from the general fund of a government.

acquisition of shares acquisition of the shares of another company in order to take over it. ***Also***: stock acquisition.

acquisition premium <1> difference between the actual cost for acquiring a target company versus the estimate made of its value before the acquisition. <2> the amount in excess of the original issue price plus OID required to be included in the gross income of previous holders of a debt instrument.

acquisition target = *target company.*

acquisitive D reorganization company A's transfer of assets to B, followed by A's distribution to its shareholders what is received from B, then A liquidates. ***See***: *divisive D reorganization; type D reorganization.*

acquittance = *debt repayment.*

a/c rec. account receivable

across the board budget = *master budget.*

ACRS accelerated cost recovery system

ACS automated collection system

AcSEC Accounting Standards Executive Committee

ACT advance corporate tax

act. account

act 360 a convention that uses the actual number of days in a month and 360 days in each year in calculating interest.

act 365 a convention that uses the actual number of days in a month and 365 days in each year in calculating interest.

active account (AA)(A/C a/c) an account which has frequent entries.

active asset (AA) an asset which is used in actual operations and earns income. ***Also***: earning asset; live asset; productive asset.

active bad debt a bad debt formerly written off but now is considered to be collectible.

active balance of payments amount by which a country's receipts from abroad exceed its total payments to foreign countries within one year. ***Also***: credit balance; favorable balance. ***See***: *unfavorable balance of payments.*

active business <Canada> a business carried on by a taxpayer other than an investment business or a personal service business.

active business income <Canada> income of the taxpayer for the tax year from an active business.

active capital (AC) = *working capital.*

active income personal income from wages, tips, salaries, commissions, and a trade or business in which a taxpayer materially participates. ***Also***: nonpassive income. ***See***: *earned income; passive income.*

active participant an individual who is eligible to participate in an employer-sponsored retirement plan.

active participation the participation in an activity in a significant and bona fide manner.

active premium annualized return of an investment minus annualized return of a chosen benchmark.

active return the return relative to a benchmark, e.g. if a portfolio's return is 7%, benchmark is 5%, then active return is 2%.

active risk a risk incurred by an investment manager when he tries to add value to a portfolio relative to a benchmark, usually it is the annual standard deviation of the *active return.* ***Also***: tracking error.

active trust a trust in which the trustee has some duty to perform.

activity a trade or business with income and expense.

activity account line of work performed by one or more components of a government unit.

activity accounting = *responsibility accounting.*

activity analysis approach an approach to identify direct costs by analyzing activities in the production process under unit costing.

activity-based budgeting (ABB) approach to budgeting which involves quantitative expression of the activities.

activity-based cost a cost the amount of which varies as the volume of activity varies.

activity-based costing (ABC) a costing method which divides cost of production into many cost pools and then allocates costs to products based on the activities which divide the costs.

activity-based depreciation a depreciation the amount of which is based on the actual volume of production or output. ***Also***: actual depreciation.

activity center pool of costs of two or more activities.

activity cost the cost in order to perform a specific function. It includes policy cost, and engineering cost. ***Also***: running cost.

activity cost driver = *cost driver.*

activity costing = *direct costing.*

activity cost pool grouping of all cost elements associated with an activity. ***Also***: cost pool.

activity driver = *cost driver.*

activity driver analysis identification and evaluation of the cost drivers to trace cost of activities to a cost object.

activity ratio measure of how well a firm manages its assets, usually calculated as volume of activity allowed ÷ volume of activity budgeted; or units of product × unit standard time ÷ budgeted hours. ***Also***: asset activity ratio; asset management ratio; operating efficiency ratio; turnover ratio.

activity sequence-sensitive calculation of the time-based process cost taking into consideration of sequential relationships among activities.

activity time variance = *capacity variance.*

activity variance the variance in costs due to the actual volume of activity differing from the practical volume of activity, including capacity variance and idle time variance.

act no. account number

actual absorption costing = *historical absorption costing.*

actual articles = *merchandise inventory.*

actual cash balance = *book balance.*

actual cash value cost of replacing damaged or destroyed property minus depreciation. ***Also***: replacement cost less depreciation.

actual cost (AC) <1> cost actually incurred. ***Also***: absolute cost; incurred cost. <2> = *actual cost of work performed.*

actual costing = *historical costing.*

actual cost of work performed (ACWP) the real costs of the work charged against the completed activities of a project. ***Also***: actual cost.

actual depreciation = *activity-based depreciation.*

actual expected standard cost = *expected standard cost.*

actual fraud the tort of obtaining money or property by means of a false portrayal of fact. ***Also***: fraud; fraud in fact. ***See***: *constructive fraud.*

actual inventory = *physical inventory.*

actually expected standard cost = *expected standard cost.*

actual normal cost system a method of determining the costs of production by examining the number of units produced, the actual direct material consumed, the actual labor used and a share of overhead calculated on the basis of typical schedule of production.

actual overhead the overhead cost actually incurred. ***Also***: spent overhead.

actual return on plan asset an increase in the fair market value of the assets of a retirement plan over the period plus any pension benefit paid minus contribution.

actual value method = *economic basis method.*

actual yield = *current yield.*

actuarial basis of accounting used in calculating the amount of contributions to be made periodically to a pension plan.

actuarial cost method a method used to determine periodic payments to be made to the pension plan and periodic pension expense, such as the unit credit method. *Also*: actuarial funding method; actuarial method.

actuarial equivalent a condition in which two or more payment streams have the same present value based on appropriate actuarial assumptions.

actuarial funding method = *actuarial cost method.*

actuarial gains or losses periodic adjustment made under pension plans to reflect the invalid estimates of future events or experience.

actuarial liability <UK> the liability of a retirement pension plan up to a valuation date measured by using the *projected unit method.*

actuarial margin amount of money retained by a life insurance company operating a separate account minus the amount of investment expense.

actuarial method = *actuarial cost method.*

actuarial rate <1> = *assumed rate of return.* <2> = *internal rate of return.*

actuarial report = *actuarial statement of valuation.*

actuarial statement of valuation a report of financial position of a qualified benefit plan. *Also*: actuarial report.

ACV actual cash value

ACWP actual cost of work performed

ADB adjusted debit balance

add-back to add a *non-deductible expense* back to expenses accounts, so that the profit and loss appropriation account may show the correct taxable profit.

added contribution margin = *incremental contribution margin.*

added cost <1> the costs incurred in the previous process but added to this process as an input. *Also*: cost added. <2> = *incremental cost.*

added risk asset <UK> bank asset other than cash and marketable securities.

added years <UK> extra pension benefits based on additional years of pensionable service.

addition <1> extra charge to the cost of a fixed asset. <2> a new and separate asset or an extension of an existing asset.

additional 263A cost = *section 263A cost.*

additional age-related allowance <UK> additional amount of personal allowance available to taxpayers aged 65 or over. *Also*: age-related allowance.

additional assessment further assessment for a tax of the same character previously paid in part.

additional bonds test a test to ensure that bond issuers meet the requirements of debt service.

additional capital <1> additional costs incurred in rectifying by-products. <2> total costs incurred to make a new asset available for use. *Also*: supplement cost. <3> = *additional paid-in capital.*

additional credit <Canada> a tax credit allowed in addition to basic tax credit, such as mental or physical impairment credit. *Also*: supplemental credit.

additional depreciation <1> extra depreciation allowed by tax laws under certain conditions. <2> amount by which the depreciation under current cost approach exceeds the depreciation under the historical approach.

additional first year depreciation = *bonus recovery.*

additional income extra income produced by obtaining one extra unit of product. ***Also***: marginal income.

additional liability a liability of a pension plan that must be reported, which is the minimum liability plus prepaid pension cost or minus accrued pension cost.

additional net income = *marginal profit.*

additional overhead = *marginal overhead.*

additional paid-in capital (APIC) capital paid in by stockholders in excess of the par value or stated value. ***Also***: additional capital; capital in excess of legal capital; capital surplus; contributed surplus; other contributed capital; paid-in capital in excess of par or stated value; paid-in surplus; premium on capital stock; share premium.

additional paid-in capital in excess of par = *contributed capital in excess of par value.*

additional paid-in capital in excess of stated value = *contributed capital in excess of stated value.*

additional personal allowance <UK> additional personal allowance available to a taxpayer who is single, separated, divorced or widowed and has a child. ***Also***: allowance for care of invalid spouse and child. ***See***: *invalid care allowance.*

additional share bonus share or rights issue allocated to outstanding stockholders.

additional standard deduction extra standard deduction for aged and blind taxpayers.

additional tax <Canada> the excess of the minimum amount over the total of the taxpayer's regular tax.

additional tax on excessive elections <Canada> = *Part 3 tax.*

additional voluntary contribution (AVC) <1><UK> extra contribution to a pension plan not exceeding 15% of an employee's annual earnings. <2><Canada> additional contribution to a registered pension plan made by a member to provide benefits under a money purchase provision.

addition cost = *incremental cost.*

addition to tax = *civil tax penalty.*

add-on yield = *assumed rate of return.*

adequacy of coverage a test that measures the extent to which the value of an asset is protected from potential loss.

adequate accounting submission to an employer of accounts with evidence that satisfies the IRS. ***Also***: accounting to employer.

adequate disclosure the disclosure of financial data at least in a set of financial statements.

adequate disclosure rule a rule preventing the IRS from including a questionable item in determining whether the taxpayer has omitted more than 25% of the gross income.

adequate stated interest stated interest of a debt if the sum of the present values equals or exceeds the stated principal amount.

ad hoc tax <Australia> a tax with a particular purpose.

ADITC accumulated deferred investment tax credit

adjudication <UK> judicial procedure for determining the stamp duty.

adjunct account an account that receives additions e.g. interest from or subtraction to another account. ***Opp***: *contra account.*

adjustable rate preferred stock (ARP)(ARPS) <1> *equity security* paying dividend at rates which change monthly or quarterly, based on the changes on US Treasury bill rate. ***Also***: controlled adjustable rate preferred stock; floating rate preferred. <2> = *auction rate preferred stock.*

adjusted account balance the balance of an account after the adjusting entries have been entered.

adjusted acquisition cost the acquisition cost of an asset adjusted by a chosen price index. ***Also***: adjusted historical cost.

adjusted balance method a method under which finance charge is based on the remaining balance on an account.

adjusted bank balance the new balance of a bank account after adding collections and subtracting any outstanding checks.

adjusted base amount threshold for provisional income to determine if social security benefits are taxable, $44,000 for married filing jointly, zero for married filing separately, or $34,000 for all other individuals.

adjusted base price a base price used to determine the windfall profits tax, the fixed price of a barrel of crude oil sold plus the price multiplied by an inflation adjustment factor.

adjusted basis the base price used to judge capital gains or losses upon the sale of a capital asset, usually the cost price plus broker's commissions.

adjusted book balance the new balance of the depositor's cash register after adding the unrecorded deposits and subtracting charges for services and uncollectible items.

adjusted book value the book value on a company's balance sheet after assets and liabilities are adjusted to market value. *Also*: modified book value.

adjusted business income (ABI) <Canada> income minus losses from active business carried on in Canada.

adjusted contribution margin in variable standard costing, the new contribution after adding or subtracting cost variances caused by variable costs.

adjusted cost base (ACB) <Canada> cost of a property or partnership interest plus the expenses incurred to acquire it.

adjusted cost basis change in an asset's book value due to improvement, calculated as the original cost plus additions to capital less depreciation.

adjusted cost method = *economic basis method.*

adjusted current cost of supplies earnings = *current cost of supplies income.*

adjusted current earnings (ACE) alternative minimum taxable income after adjustments, calculated as AMTI before NOL and ACE adjustments plus net tax exempt income +/- depreciation expense computed under §168(g), plus disallowed E&P items.

adjusted debit balance (ADB) position of a margin account after subtracting the amount owing the broker from the credit balance on the special miscellaneous account.

adjusted discounted future wages method a method of calculating human resource value by multiplying present value of the staff's future salaries and wages by an efficiency factor.

adjusted disposable income disposable income minus social transfers in kind.

adjusted earnings <1> income adjusted by inflation rate or by replacement cost. <2> of an insurance company, the earnings including the underwriting income, net investment income, equity in the changes in the unearned premium reserve, not including gain or loss from trading securities.

adjusted entry = *adjusting journal entry.*

adjusted excess deductions account an account for recording the beginning balance in the excess deductions a/c less current year's farm net income.

adjusted financial statement = *constant dollar financial statement.*

adjusted gain or loss the gain or loss from the sale or exchange of business property adjusted by using AMT tax basis rather than the regular tax basis.

adjusted gross estate gross estate minus nondiscretionary deduction.

adjusted gross income (AGI) a taxpayer's gross income minus above-the-line deductions. *Also*: net income.

adjusted gross profit under standard absorption costing, the net sales minus the standard cost of goods sold, then plus or minus cost variances.

adjusted historical cost = *adjusted acquisition cost.*

adjusted income method a method of presenting adjusted earnings as income figure in the income statement.

adjusted investor equity cash invested in a project increased by cost-of-living adjustment.

adjusted issue price the issue price of discount bonds plus daily OID interest additions.

adjusted itemized deductions the itemized deductions that exceed 60% of the adjusted gross income.

adjusted liability of insurance companies, the statutory liabilities minus interest maintenance reserve minus asset valuation reserve.

adjusted net minimum tax net minimum tax increased by any credit not allowed.

adjusted net worth of a business, it equals capital plus surplus plus an estimated value of the business on its book.

adjusted ordinary gross income (AOGI) adjusted gross income of a personal holding corporation.

adjusted premium net level premium of a policy plus the modification of acquisition expense for the first year.

adjusted premium method a method of calculating the cash surrender value of an insurance policy, by subtracting adjusted premium from the net level premium used in the computation of the prospective reserve.

adjusted present value (APV) net present value of an asset financed by equity, plus the present value of cash flows from financing.

adjusted rate of return = *internal rate of return.*

adjusted rate of return method = *internal rate of return method.*

adjusted reserve rate the lower of the average earnings rate or the current earnings rate.

adjusted retail book value the ending retail book value corrected to reflect the inventory shortages and overages.

adjusted sales value predetermined price minus after-cost.

adjusted selling price method a method used in pricing the ending inventory, by subtracting a profit from the adjusted sales value.

adjusted surplus statutory surplus plus the interest maintenance reserve plus asset valuation reserve.

adjusted tax the amount of income taxes that would have been paid if the company's pretax income were equal to its operating income.

adjusted taxable estate *taxable estate* reduced by death tax of $60,000.

adjusted trial balance the trial balance taken right after the adjusting entries are posted. *Also*: trial balance after adjustment.

adjusted value the value of the property less debt described in.

adjusting entry = *auditor's adjusting entry.*

adjusting event <UK> post balance sheet event that provides additional evidence of conditions existing at the balance sheet date.

adjusting journal entry (AJE) an accounting entry used at the close of a fiscal period to record income and expenses in the proper period and make the profit and loss statement show the correct income. *Also*: adjusted entry.

adjustment (adj.) <1> changes in the account due to adjusting entries. <2> the reinstatement of financial statement items in order to show the changes in price level. <3> the adjustment of financial statements for tax purposes. <4> a change in the tax return record. <5> = *above-the-line deduction.*

adjustment account <1> = *controlling account.* <2> = *valuation account.*

adjustment account method a method under which the branch inventory is recorded at selling price, and mark on is recorded in the Branch Adjustment account, the balance of which, called the unrealized profit of branch, is deducted from the inventory in the balance sheet.

adjustment entry = *auditor's adjusting entry.*

adjustment income the income payable to a surviving spouse or other beneficiary upon the death of the primary wage earner.

adjustment to gross income = *above-the-line deduction.*

administration cost the cost of controlling, directing and managing a business which can not be directly charged to the production, distribution and selling of its products. ***Also***: firm-wide cost.

administration expense the expense associated with the compensating and supporting of personnel who are involved in managing the activities of a business. ***Also***: general administration cost; general and administrative expense.

administration expense/administration cost ratio a ratio of the administration expenses to the budgeted administration costs.

administration period the period from the date of death to the completion of the administration of an estate.

administrative accounting the accounting procedures for the administrative budget, expenditure, control, appraisal, etc.

administrative and selling expense = *selling and administrative expense.*

administrative audit <1> = *internal audit.* <2> = *operating audit.* <3> = *preemptive audit.*

administrative charge group employee benefit plan administration charge.

administrative control organization plan and the procedures and records that are concerned with the decision process that leads to management authorization of transactions.

administrative expense the expense incurred in the process of administering an estate. ***Also***: general expense.

administrative expense budget a budget about the administrative expense.

administrative expense variance difference between planned and actual administrative expense.

administrative pricing rule an IRS rule used to allocate income on export sales to a foreign sales corporation.

administrative review a process for reviewing an IRS's denial or sanction by an applicant or an authorized e-file provider.

administrative working paper audit working paper designed to help the auditors in planning and administration of the engagement.

administrator a court-appointed person to manage the estate of a deceased person without a will. ***See***: *executor.*

admissible asset an asset which can be treated as an invested asset by the excess profits tax rules.

admitted asset the asset of an insurer that is taken into account by an examining body in determining his financial status.

admitted to dealings = *listed security.*

adoption cost credit = *adoption credit.*

adoption credit first $10,000 in 2003 for expenses paid to adopt a qualifying child. ***Also***: adoption cost credit; credit for adoption expenses.

adoption-related expense any expense related to adoption of a child.

adoption taxpayer identification number (ATIN) a number assigned temporarily by the IRS for a child who is in domestic adoption process.

ADR <1> asset depreciation range. <2> automatic dividend reinvestment plan.

ADRS asset depreciation range system

ADS alternative depreciation system

ad valorem penalty = *civil tax penalty.*

ad valorem tax a tax imposed on the basis of the value of the property.

advance child tax credit a child tax credit paid to a qualified taxpayer in advance.

advance corporate tax (ACT) <UK> tax paid by UK companies on the dividends they pay.

advanced earned income credit payment of earned income credit in advance to eligible employees by an employer in addition to their wages.

advance from customers payment made by customers in advance of performance by the seller.

advance funded pension plan a pension plan in which funds are set aside before the retirement of an employee.

advance pricing agreement a private tax ruling from two countries' tax agencies on how profit and earnings from a financial transaction will be allocated between the countries for tax purposes.

advance rent any amount received from the tenant before the period that it covers.

advance to affiliates advance made to affiliated corporations.

advance to employees = *employee advance.*

advance to vendors money paid to a vendor before shipment of goods.

adverse development risk of loss resulting from contracts concluded in the past.

adverse minimum the sum of capital recovery cost of the asset and the expenditures saved by using that asset.

adverse opinion an auditor's opinion stating that the financial statements do not present fairly in conformity with GAAP or inadequate disclosure of essential data.

adverse ruling a ruling issued by the IRS to a taxpayer, taking a position adverse to the conclusion sought by the taxpayer with respect to a transaction.

adverse variance (A.) = *unfavorable variance.*

advertising reserve amount set aside for future advertising expenditures.

advertising-sales ratio total advertising expenditure divided by total sales over some time period. ***Also***: advertising to sales ratio.

advertising to sales ratio = *advertising/sales ratio.*

advice of audit an advice from an auditor to adjust some accounts at the end of an audit process.

advisory fee compensation paid to investment advisors. ***Also***: management fee.

AET accumulated earnings tax

AFC average fixed cost

AFD allowance for depreciation

affiliate <1> a relationship between two companies when one owns substantial interest but less than a majority of another company. <2> = *control person.*

affiliated corporation a corporation that is an affiliate to the same parent company. ***Also***: associated company; connected company; related company.

affiliated group a group of companies that elects to file a consolidated tax return. ***See***: *controlled group.*

affiliated person = *control person.*

afflux of capital = *capital inflow.*

AFR applicable federal rate

AFS available-for-sale securities

after-acquired property any property coming to the bankrupt after the date of the adjudication order.

after-closing after closing the book or after distributing the net income. ***Also***: post-closing.

after-closing trial balance trial balance prepared after the closing entries have been entered. ***Also***: closing trial balance; out-of-balance-post-closing trial balance; post-closing trial balance after closing; trial balance after closing.

after-cost any cost that occurs after the deal but relates to the income in the deal.

after-purchase cost the cost incurred after the purchase of a product.

after-sales cost the cost incurs when providing after-sales service.

after-separation cost the cost incurring after the main product and the by-product are separated. *Also*: subsequent cost; subsequent processing cost.

after-tax basis a basis for comparing the returns on a corporate taxable bond and municipal tax-free bond.

after-tax contribution the contribution to a retirement plan that is subject to tax. *Also*: voluntary contribution.

after-tax cost of capital = *net-of-tax cost of capital.*

after-tax financing <Canada> financing whereby the lender can offer reduced rate of interest to eligible corporate borrowers.

after-tax profit net profit after deduction of income taxes. *Also*: profit after tax; taxed profit.

after-tax profit margin ratio calculated by taking net income after taxes and dividing it by net sales.

after-tax rate of return after-tax profit divided by the average investment.

after-tax real rate of return after-tax rate of return minus rate of inflation.

after-tax return <1> the return from an investment after all income taxes have been deducted. *Also*: return after tax. <2> rate of return of a mutual fund calculated at the highest marginal federal tax rate for dividends, interest income and short-term capital gains and at the maximum rate for long-term capital gains.

after-the-fact accounting the accounting without forecasting, planning, or budgeting.

AGA Association of Government Accountants

age allowance <UK> an allowance that can replace personal allowance with higher amount if a taxpayer reaches age. *Also*: fixed age allowance; personal age allowance.

age credit <Canada> a tax credit available to Canadians age 65 and over.

aged trial balance = *aging schedule.*

age-life method of depreciation = *straight-line method of depreciation.*

agency audit assessment of an advertising agency's performance by the client.

agency cost reduction in the value of a business when an agent pursues his interest to the detriment of the business's interest.

agency cost view a theory which holds that various agency costs will create a complex environment in which total agency costs are at a minimum with debt financing.

agency current account a current account maintained with an agency.

agency fund a custodial fund for another government agency. *See*: *trust fund.*

agency risk premium an additional return to cover the risks associated with the control of an enterprise by agents.

agency worker <UK> a person hired by an employment agency and sent to work for a third party. *See*: *employee leasing firm.*

age-related allowance <UK> = *additional age-related allowance.*

age-weighted plan a retirement plan characterized by the fact that both the age and compensation level of an employee are used to determine benefits.

aggregate accounting the accounting methods and procedures for the recording and reporting economic activities of a whole country. *Also*: lot accounting; macro accounting. *See*: *micro accounting.*

aggregate balance sheet = *consolidated balance sheet.*

aggregate cash flow = *total cash flow.*

aggregate cost <1> total cost of an investment portfolio. <2> prime cost plus variable overhead. <3> = *total cost.*

aggregate depreciation = *accumulated depreciation.*

aggregate expense the expense of all divisions combined for the entire year.

aggregate income = *gross national income.*

aggregate level cost basis actuarial method of calculating benefits and their costs for all the employees as a group rather than for each individual employee. *See*: *individual level cost basis.*

aggregate levy <UK> a £1.60 per ton levy on rock, gravel or sand together with incorporated substances.

aggregate limit maximum amount of coverage in force under a health insurance policy, a property damage policy or a liability policy.

aggregate method a method for projecting costs for a whole pension or insurance plan rather than for each individual in the plan. *Also*: modified aggregate method. *See*: *individual level-premium method; projected benefit cost.*

aggregation combination of assets or cash flows, for analytical or financial reporting purposes.

AGI adjusted gross income

aging <1> the classification of assets lives. <2> = *aging accounts receivable.*

aging accounts receivable accounting check that analyzes the time interval between the date of sale and the current report date. *Also*: aging; analysis of aging of accounts receivable.

aging method a method that applies different percentage to different aging groups to calculate allowance for bad debts. *Also*: aging of accounts receivable method. *See*: *balance sheet approach; percentage of accounts receivable method.*

aging of accounts receivables method = *aging method.*

aging schedule a list that shows how long accounts receivable have been owed and past due items. *Also*: aged trial balance; schedule of accounts receivable by age.

AGM annual general meeting

agreed case a taxpayer's return audited by the IRS, the adjustments to which the tax payer agrees.

agreed-upon procedure audit procedure that results in an audit report providing a summary of work performed and findings.

agricultural buildings allowance <UK> balancing allowance that is applicable to agricultural buildings when a balancing event occurred.

agricultural property <UK> agricultural land or building used for intensive fish-farming or live-stock rearing, and 100% free of inheritance tax.

agricultural value <UK> the value of a property if it were subject to perpetual covenant prohibiting its use otherwise than as agricultural property.

AICPA American Institute of Certified Public Accountants

AIMR Association for Investment Management and Research

air passenger duty (APD) <UK> a duty levied on passengers traveling by air from a UK airport.

AIS accounting information system

AISG Accountants International Study Group

AJE adjusting journal entry

a.k.a. also known as

ALAE allocated loss adjustment expense

alcohol credit = *alcohol fuels credit.*

alcohol fuels credit a 60 cents per gallon tax credit allowed for using alcohol as a fuel. *Also*: alcohol credit; alcohol mixture credit.

alcohol mixture credit = *alcohol fuels credit.*

alcohol tax an excise tax on alcohol manufacturers.

algebraic method a method under which costs of the service departments that serve each other are allocated by using simultaneous algebraic methods and equations. *Also*: mathematical solution allocation; simultaneous allocation; simultaneous equations method. *See*: *multi-step cost reassignment; reciprocal service cost allocation.*

alienation transfer of asset from one entity to another.

alien corporation a company incorporated under the laws of a foreign country. ***See***: *foreign corporation.*

alien property the property owner by a foreigner.

alimony <1> money paid for the support of a separated spouse or ex-spouse. ***Also***: separate maintenance payment; spousal support. <2> = *living cost.*

alimony recapture occurs if payments sharply decline in the second or third years, the amount must be reported from the first and second year as income in the third year.

"A" list <UK> a list of the present members of a company in the course of liquidation. ***See***: *"B" list.*

all capital earnings rate a ratio calculated as (net income + interest + minority stock) ÷ asset value. ***Also***: rate of return on total capital. ***See***: *return on total assets.*

all current accounting a method in which assets and liabilities items are all adjusted in their current market value.

all earnings and profits amount earnings and profits attributable to the stock in a foreign corporation that was liquidated into a domestic parent corporation.

all-events test under the accrual method, income must be included in gross income when all the events have occurred that fix the right to receive the income and the amount thereof can be determined with reasonable accuracy.

all financial resources concept a concept which states that the statement of changes in financial position should include not only cash and working capital but also other assets.

all in a bond issuer's interest rate net of commissions and related expenses.

all inclusive concept a concept which states that the income statement should include not only operating but also non-operating items. ***Also***: clean surplus concept; earning power concept. ***Opp***: *current operating performance theory.*

all-inclusive income statement an income statement including both operating and non-operating income. ***Also***: statement of income and profit and loss.

all-in cost total cost, explicit and implicit, of an investment. ***See***: *total cost.*

allocable costs all depreciation deductions with respect to the taxpayer's assets.

allocable parental tax income tax on child's earnings at the parents' rate if they were included in the parents' income.

allocated cost the cost arbitrarily assigned on a basis other than a cause/effect relationship. ***Also***: apportioned cost.

allocated loss adjustment expense (ALAE) an expense incurred in investigating and settling claims that are assigned to specific claims or groups of claims as prescribed in statistical data reporting plans or financial accounting rules.

allocation <1> distributing income or expense to the cost object. <2> segregating item with tax significance to transactions or assets with which they can be associated on a fair basis. <3> crediting a payment to one account when it is not specifically marked when that client has two accounts. <4> charging to a cost center the overhead that results solely from the existence of that center.

allocation of difference the allocation of a portion of the *differential* after acquisition of a subsidiary into a specific asset and liability.

allocation of income rule a tax rule that defines how income and deductions are to be allocated between domestic and foreign sources.

allocation of tax dollars = *tax allocation.*

allocation period the period required for the acquiring company to obtain all existing information necessary for recording the business combination.

all other current assets any current assets which do not belong to a main category.

all other current liabilities any other current liabilities which do not belong to a main category.

all other expenses miscellaneous expense and other expenses not included in general and administrative expenses.

allotment (allot) <1> charging of costs to cost units or cost centers. <2> = *allotment of shares.*

allotment of shares the allocation of new issue of shares among subscribers. ***Also***: allotment; distribution of shares.

allowable business expense <UK> = *deductible business expense.*

allowable business investment loss (ABIL) <Canada> *business investment loss* that can be deducted against taxable income.

allowable capital loss <Canada> capital loss that is tax deductible, which equals capital loss multiplied by the *inclusion rate* (50% in 2002).

allowable cost <1> items or elements of a cost that is reimbursable under a payment formula. <2> depreciation tax deductions with respect to plant assets.

allowable deduction <UK> = *tax deduction.*

allowable depreciation the amount of depreciation a taxpayer is entitled to claim for property written off under tax law and regulations.

allowable exemption unadjusted personal exemption amount minus the *personal exemption phase out* amount.

allowable expense <1> an expense which can be deducted from wages by an individual in calculating his or her taxable income. <2> = *tax deductible expense.*

allowable loss = *deductible loss.*

allowable medical expense <Canada> medical expense that is deductible for income tax purpose.

allowable risk auditor's allowable risk of incorrect acceptance.

allowance <1> amount paid by an employer to cover anticipated costs. <2> = *provision.*

allowance audit the audit procedure to check if the provisions are correctly recorded.

allowance for bad debts estimated amount of accounts receivable to be uncollectible. ***Also***: allowance for uncollectible accounts; bad debt loss provision; bad debt reserve; loan loss provision; provision for bad and doubtful debts; provision for bad debts; reserve for bad debts; reserve for doubtful debts.

allowance for care of invalid spouse and child <UK> = *additional personal allowance.*

allowance for deficiency in base stock an estimated amount of loss due to changes in the fair market prices of the stock when reimbursing the deficiency in base stock in the previous period.

allowance for depreciation (AFD) reserve for depreciation the value of fixed assets. ***Also***: accumulated depreciation; capital allowance; depreciation allowance; depreciation and diminution provision; depreciation reserve; property reserve; reserve for wear, tear, obsolescence and inadequacy.

allowance for inflation = *indexation allowance.*

allowance for inventory price decline reserve for loss caused by future decline in the value of inventory. ***Also***: inventory allowance.

allowance for loss due to market decline of inventory = *allowance for reduction of inventory to market.*

allowance for obsolescence = *reserve for obsolescence.*

allowance for reduction of inventory to market an allowance for losses due to the decline in market price when reinstating the inventory items in market price. ***Also***: allowance for loss due to market decline of inventory; allowance to reduce inventory to market value.

allowance for sampling risk (ASR) the amount used to create a range, set by + or - limits from the sample results, in which the true value of the population characteristic being measured is likely to lie. *Also*: precision.

allowance for uncollectible accounts = *allowance for bad debts.*

allowance method a method whereby an estimate is made at the end of a period of the portion of that period's credit sales which will prove uncollectible, and an entry is made to an expense account, and to an allowance account. *Also*: indirect method. *See*: *direct method.*

allowance to reduce inventory to LCM reserve for compensating any loss incurred when reinstating stock cost at the lower of cost or market basis.

allowance to reduce inventory to lifo basis = *lifo reserve.*

allowance to reduce inventory to market value = *allowance for reduction of inventory to market.*

allowance to reduce marketable securities to market value reserve for loss realized as a result of further decline in the market value of current investment in securities.

allowed depreciation amount of depreciation actually claimed by a tax payer, whether or not legally exclusive.

all-purpose financial statement a financial statement form suitable for all types of business. *Also*: general-purpose financial statement. *See*: *general balance sheet.*

alpha risk <1> audit risk that the assessed level of control risk based on the sample is higher than the true operating effectiveness of the control structure or procedure. *Also*: risk of assessing control risk too high; type 1 error. *See*: *beta risk.* <2> audit risk that the sample supports the conclusion that the balance is materially misstated when it is not. *Also*: risk of incorrect rejection.

alter-ego theory a judicial approach to corporate transactions in which present and former corporations are treated as a single continuing entity.

alter-ego trust <Canada> a trust set up after 1999 by an individual aged 65 or over.

alternative asset an asset that has the potential to provide value to the owner but is not traditionally considered asset, such as collectible.

alternative cost <1> cost that should incur under different conditions. *Also*: imputed cost. <2> = *opportunity cost.*

alternative credit an alternative *research and development credit* calculated by applying a percentage to the extent that the research and development expenses exceed a base amount.

alternative depreciation system (ADS) a system used in computing AMTI, which provides for straight line depreciation over the property's ADS class life, 12 years for personal property with no ADS class life and 40 years for real property.

alternative fuel production credit a $3 per barrel tax credit allowed for the production of qualified fuels sold to an unrelated party.

alternative investment <1> investment in a non-security instrument by a professional money manager. <2> works of art, horses, antiques etc.

alternative itemized deduction a deduction subtracted from the sum of adjusted gross income and the specified items of tax preference to arrive at the base of AMT. *Also*: alternative tax itemized deduction.

alternative minimum cost method a method under which the normal cost is the lessor of the cost under the actuarial cost method of the employee pension plan or under the accrued benefit cost method without benefit projections.

alternative minimum funding standard a/c a complex minimum funding account used to determine whether an employer's contributions to qualified pension plans are adequate.

alternative minimum tax (AMT) tax designed to extract a minimum level of taxation in the event of extraordinary large deductions, it is the higher of *regular tax* or *tentative minimum tax*. ***Also***: minimum tax.

alternative minimum taxable income (AMTI) a taxpayer's AGI ignoring NOL, reduced by alternative tax net operating loss deduction, the alternative tax itemized deductions and any amount included in income under the trust *throwback rules* and increased by items of *tax preference*.

alternative tax a lower tax imposed by which a corporation's net capital gains are taxed at a rate not exceeding 28% if a higher tax would otherwise be imposed.

alternative tax itemized deduction = *alternative itemized deduction*.

alternative tax net operating loss deductions the net operating loss carryover or carryback deduction to the year for the alternative tax purpose.

alternative-use cost = *opportunity cost*.

alternative valuation date six months after the date of a decedent's death, the FMV of this date is used to determine the basis of the estate.

Altman Z-score an index that predicts whether or not a company is likely to enter into bankruptcy. ***Also***: Z-score.

amalgamated balance sheet = *consolidated balance sheet*.

amalgamation <UK> = *merger*.

amalgamation by absorption = *merger*.

amalgamation surplus = *credit differential*.

amateur athlete trust <Canada> a trust the assets of which must be administered by a Canadian amateur athlete association.

amended declaration a revised declaration of estimated tax that has been revised due to changes in the taxpayer's gross income, exemptions, or credits.

amended return a tax return filed as a corrective supplement to or a replacement of an original tax return, either to correct error or as the basis of a new claim for a tax refund or credit. ***Also***: corrective return.

American Accounting Association (AAA) an organization of college professors and of practicing accountants, founded in 1916. ***Formerly called***: American Association of University Instructors of Accounting.

American Association of Public Accountants (AAPA) = *American Institute of Certified Public Accountants*.

American Association of University Instructors in Accounting (AAUIA) = *American Accounting Association*.

American audit standpoint an audit viewpoint focusing on the financial statements, with all-inclusive concept as its condition. ***See***: *English audit standpoint*.

American Institute of Accountants (AIA) former name of the AICPA from 1917 to 1953.

American Institute of Certified Public Accountants (AICPA) the professional body of the practicing CPAs founded in 1887. In 1917, it changed its name to the American Institute of Accountants, merged with the ASCPA in 1936, and changed to its present name in 1957. ***Formerly called***: American Association of Public Accountants

American plan (AP) a hotel billing plan under which all three meals are included in the room price. ***See:*** *European plan*.

amortizable section 197 intangible = *section 197 property*.

amortization <1> the systematic recovery of the cost of an intangible or wasting asset for income tax purposes over its useful life. <2> = *accelerated depreciation*.

amortization factor the pool *factor* implied by the scheduled amortization assuming no prepayments, usually the present value of a $1 per year for a fixed number of years.

amortization gap the difference between the recorded accumulated depreciation and the amount that would have been obtained if the replacement cost of the asset had been at its current level since it is acquired.

Also: backlog depreciation; catch-up depreciation; make-up depreciation.

amortization method <1> the method for writing off an intangible asset over a period equal to its expected life. <2> the method for reducing a debt by periodic payments covering both interest and part of the principal until the whole debt has been paid off. <3> a method of recording bonds issue at their carrying value, and the discounts are amortized evenly through-out the period.

amortized cost = *carrying amount.*

amount = *accumulated amount.*

amount at interest = *principal.*

amount at risk <1> difference between the face value of a permanent life insurance policy and its accrued cash value. <2> the lessor of the policy limit or the maximum possible loss to the insured.

amount brought forward amount of an item brought forward from the previous period to this period.

amount carried forward amount of an item carried forward to the next period.

amount carried over amount of an item carried from this page to the next.

amount due the amount due the government when tax liability is greater than the tax paid. *See*: *tax liability.*

amount for an eligible dependent <Canada> = *dependency exemption.*

amount in figures the amount written in Arabic numerals.

amount in words amount written in words.

amount of 1 = *accumulated amount.*

amount recognized the amount of gain reportable and subject to tax.

AMPS auction market preferred stock

AMT alternative minimum tax

AMT basis tax basis in a stock calculated by adding adjustments in AMTI to the option price paid when the stock became vested.

AMT carryover <Canada> 7-year carryover for additional taxes that have been paid as a result of the AMT.

AMT credit previously paid AMT attributable to federal items only, not exclusion items.

AMT exemption $40,250 ($58,000 for married filing jointly) in 2003 and 2004, phased out if AMTI exceeds the threshold $150,000 and will become zero when AMTI reaches $273,500 ($382,000 for married filing jointly). *Also*: exemption amount.

AMTI alternative minimum taxable income

AMT rate a tax rate applied to AMTI, 26% on the first $175,000 ($87,500 for married filing separately) that exceeds the AMT exemption, and 28% on any AMTI above $175,000.

AN account number

analogy method a method of forecasting future behavior of costs by their historical behavior.

analysis <1> setting out the results of analyzing accounting records. <2> auditor's work of rechecking accounting records.

analysis of aging of accounts receivable = *aging of accounts receivable.*

analysis of financial statements = *financial statement analysis.*

analysis of variance determining whether a difference found in a dependent variable, when it is exposed to the influence of one or more experimental variables, exceed what may be expected by change. *Also*: variance analysis.

analytical accounting the procedures for the maximization of profit and earnings by using analytical methods.

analytical auditing audit procedures which focus on accounting information system and its outputs.

analytical journal = *columnar journal.*

analytical petty cash book a petty cash book ruled into a number of extra columns to allow figures for various costs to be filled in different columns and to be totaled separately, giving an analysis of the various kinds of costs.

analytical procedures (AP) the audit procedures consisting of evaluation of financial information made by a study of plausible relationships among financial and non-financial data. ***Also***: analytical review procedures.

analytical review procedures = *analytical procedures.*

analytical studies method a method for classifying fixed and variable cost pattern by analyzing cost data.

analytical work sheet = *columnar work sheet.*

analyzing entry adjusting entries used in preparing the statement of changes in financial position.

angel = *angel investor.*

angel investor an individual who provides capital to one or more startups. ***Also***: angel. ***See***: *invisible venture capital; venture capital firm.*

$a_{n|i}$ small a angle n at i, the amount of 1 formula $a_{n|i} = p^{<1+i>n}$ use for calculating future amount of a principal p which earns compound interest at a rate i for n periods.

annotated financial statement financial statement with annotations attached.

annotation = *footnote.*

announcement date = *declaration date.*

annual accounting concept a concept the gist of which is that events with tax significance should be recorded in and by reference to the present taxable year alone even though other disparities may result or their eventual outcome is doubtful, and the future events are left for future years.

annual accounting period = *accounting year.*

annual appreciation the annual increase in the value of a bond.

annual basis = *annualizing method.*

annual budget an annual plan for the coordination of revenues and expenditures.

annual capital cost the cost figure arrived at by determining and observing activities of a firm experiencing a constant yearly cash flow that could be compared with an annual capital charge.

annual cost of capital recovery calculated as: (invested capital - net salvage value) ÷ recovery years.

annual effective yield = *annual percentage yield.*

annual exclusion the maximum amount per year ($11,000 in 2003) that a person is allowed to give another person without gift tax. ***Also***: annual gift tax exclusion; gift tax exclusion. ***See***: *unified credit.*

annual exempt amount <UK> an amount of £7,100 per year free of capital gains tax, or £3,000 per year free of inheritance tax. ***Also***: annual exemption.

annual exemption = *annual exempt amount.*

annual financial audit = *external audit.*

annual general meeting (AGM) <UK> = *annual meeting.*

annual gift tax exclusion = *annual exclusion.*

annual GST information report <Australia> a GST report made at the end of a year for any information not reported each quarter.

annual GST return <Australia> a GST report that shows all GST information for the whole year.

annual interest total amount of interests for one year. ***Also***: interest annuity; interest per annum. ***See:*** *yearly interest.*

annualization of expenses converting the budgeted expenses for a period less than a year to a proportion to a yearly budgeted costs.

annualization of income accommodating certain short periods by hypothesizing an income tax computed as if the taxpayer's income for the short period reflected income for an entire year, and then reducing the tax to reflect the brevity of the period.

annualized earnings <Canada> earnings of an employee who worked for less than a year, converted to an annual number.

annualized gain monthly gain converted to that of 12 months, e.g. if monthly gain is 1.5%, it will be $[1 \times (1 + 1.5\%)]^{12-1} = 19.6\%$.

annualized holding period return the annual rate of return compounded for a given holding period.

annualized income method a method used by IRS to impose penalty for companies with seasonal income or zero tax liability or NOL in the previous tax year. (At least 25% of the tax on annualized income must be prepaid each quarter).

annualized method a method for calculating estimated quarterly tax payment based on income received up to the end of the latest quarter, annualized to a 12-month period.

annualized rate <Canada> a rate of change in a short period calculated to show what the change will be over one year.

annualized return the rate of return of a cumulative multi-year return or a fractional year return, after compounding and discounting.

annualizing method a method under which the gross income for a short year is multiplied by 12 and divided by the number of months in the short year. ***Also***: annual basis. ***See***: *optional look-back method.*

annual meeting once-a-year meeting of stockholders to hear the corporation's results and elect board of directors. ***Also***: annual general meeting; general meeting; stockholders' meeting.

annual non-payroll tax return = *Form 945.*

annual percentage rate (APR) rate that is charged for borrowing for a 12 month period including interest and fees.

annual percentage yield (APY) the rate actually earned or paid in one year, taking into account the effect of compounding. ***Also***: annual effective yield.

annual premium costing a method of determining pension costs by the premium costs of an insurance premium in one year. ***See***: *single premium costing.*

annual rate of return annual return divided by average investment.

annual report annual financial statements and summary of important information of a company. ***See***: *Form 10K.*

annual return <1> a tax return for a year. <2><UK> a summary of a company's capital, together with an up-to-date list of directors and members, number of shares held, and a balance sheet. <3><UK> a banker's return to the IR reporting his name, residence, and occupation, etc.

annual statement the annual statement filed by an insurance company reporting assets, liabilities, receipts, and disbursements.

annuity (A) series of fixed or variable payments (called *rents*) at some future time.

annuity certain an annuity the amounts paid and the payment dates of which are fixed and guaranteed by an insurance company.

annuity cost = *pension cost.*

annuity date the date on which the initial annuity payment is made.

annuity due an annuity under which a payment is made at the beginning of a period. ***See***: *deferred annuity.*

annuity factor present value of an annuity of $1 per year beginning at the taxpayer's age attained in the first distribution year and continuing for his life. ***See***: *discount factor; future value factor.*

annuity factor method a method for making penalty-free early withdrawals from retirement accounts, given an annuity factor of 12.00 the annual distribution of a $1 million account will be $83,333 ($1 million divided by 12).

annuity in arrears = *deferred annuity.*

annuity method <1> application of the annuity principal to obtain the amount, rate and time needed to liquidate an interest-bearing debt. <2> a depreciation method that makes regular annual charges which gradually get smaller until they become nothing when the value of the asset is reduced to zero. *Also*: equal annual payment method.

annuity starting date the first day of the first period for which an amount is paid or received under an annuity contract.

annuity trust a trust the trustee is required to pay some money annually to one or more beneficiaries.

anti-abuse rule a rule that permits the IRS to ignore regular standards and make a determination based on all the facts and circumstances

anti-churning rule a rule that limits the transferor's liability to the extent the basis of a property in the transferee's hands equals the transferor's adjusted basis.

anticipated discount = *instant interest.*

anticipated interest the interest earned on a savings account assuming there is no withdrawal before the end of the current interest period.

anticipation assigning or marking charges against income or profit before such gain is realized.

anti-dilutive security a security excluded when calculating the dilutive EPS because the per share effect of which is greater than the basic earnings per share effect.

anti-dumping duty an import duty applied to a particularly commodity selling at a very low price from a specified country.

AOGI adjusted ordinary gross income

AP <1> American plan. <2> analytical procedures.

A/P <1> accounting period. <2> account payable.

APB. Accounting Principles Board

APBO accumulated post-retirement benefit obligation

APD air passenger duty

API accountants for the public interest

APIC additional paid-in capital

appended footnote = *footnote.*

applicable amount <1> $3,000 income tax amount for taxable years beginning after 1977 ($1,500 for married taxpayers filing separately). <2><UK> amount a person needs to live on per week.

applicable corporation = *C corporation.*

applicable credit = *unified credit.*

applicable exclusion amount = *unified credit exemption.*

application <1> using *overpayment* of tax against tax liability in future periods. <2> = *cost application.*

application of overhead assigning overhead costs to an output unit on the basis of a predetermined rate.

applied cost a financial measure of resources consumed or applied within a given period to accomplish a specific purpose regardless of when ordered, received or paid for.

applied overhead the overhead cost which has been applied to the products or the departments.

applied overhead rate = *overhead application rate.*

apportioned cost = *allocated cost.*

apportionment <1> funds from a federal government. <2> = *cost allocation.* <3> = *overhead allocation.*

appraisal capital current value of an asset beyond its originally cost. *Also*: appraisal surplus; appreciation surplus; capital from adjustment; revaluation surplus; surplus from revaluation; surplus on appreciation of capital assets; unrealized appreciation from revaluation of assets; unrealized capital increment; valuation profit. *Opp*: *valuation loss.*

appraisal cost the cost of discovering which individual products do not conform to the specifications.

appraisal increment increase in value of an asset after appraisal.

appraisal loss decrease in value of an asset after appraisal.

appraisal method depreciation method by appraisals made at the beginning and end of each period, depreciation charges for that period being the difference between appraised values. ***Also***: indirect method; inventory method; valuation account practice; valuation method.

appraisal surplus = *appraisal capital.*

appreciated financial position a position in which there would be a gain should it be sold. ***See***: *positive carry*; *unrealized gain.*

appreciated property a property that has increased in value.

appreciation an increase in the value of an asset. *Opp: depreciation.*

appreciation surplus = *appraisal capital.*

appropriated retained earnings the retained earnings earmarked for a specific use as a means of informing stockholders that they are not available for dividends. ***Also***: common reserve fund; non-distributable asset; reserve; reserved surplus; retained earnings-appropriated; surplus reserve.

appropriate percentage <Canada> the lowest percentage applicable in determining income tax payable.

appropriation <1> the maximum amount of expenditures of a government unit that are amortized. <2> the distribution of the estate of a decedent. <3> application of a particular payment for a particular debt. <4> forecast of asset outflow of a fund.

approved discretionary share option <UK> option up to £30,000 granted to an employee under an *approved share option scheme.*

approved issuer levy <Australia> tax on interest paid by borrowers.

approved purpose <Canada> farming and the activities included in the definition of a qualified property.

approved savings-related share option <UK> the option granted to an employee under an *approved share option scheme* and is linked to a *save as you earn* scheme.

approved share <Canada> share of stock eligible for *labour-sponsored fund credit.*

approved share option scheme <UK> an employee share option scheme with Inland Revenue's approval. ***Also***: approved share scheme.

approved share scheme <UK> = *approved share option scheme.*

approximate rate of return method = *mercantile method.*

APR <1> absolute priority rule. <2> annual percentage rate.

APS Auditing Procedure Studies.

APV adjusted present value

APY annual percentage yield

AQL acceptable quality level

AR <1> account receivable. <2> annual return.

arbitrary method = *liberalized depreciation method.*

arbitrary percentage method a method of recognizing deferred revenue by applying an arbitrary percentage on the outstanding balance of receivables on installment sales. ***Also***: direct percentage method.

arbitrage pricing model an alternative to *capital asset pricing model*, which may specify returns as a linear function of more than a single factor.

arbl assets re-priced before liabilities

ARE accounting & reporting

argument in accounting an argument that characterizes fair values of assets as being more relevant but less reliable than the historical cost.

arising basis <1> a basis for recognizing taxable income on accrual basis regardless of the cash inflows. <2><UK> a tax on all world-wide income and gains based on the date when payment is due.

arithmetical average cost method a method that treats the costs arrived at by arithmetical methods as the cost of a product.

arithmetical progress method a method by which the depreciation amounts of every period are arranged in an arithmetical progress order.

arm's length of a transaction between two independent persons, one doe not have undue influence over the other.

arm's length allocation <Canada> an allocation of profit or loss that would have occurred between the parties if they had been dealing at arm's length with each other.

ARPS auction rate preferred stock

ARR average rate of return

Arrowsmith doctrine a doctrine requiring that restorations of income associated with prior closed transactions will take their tax character from the prior transactions.

ARSC Accounting and Review Services Committee

articles of association <UK> = *by-laws.*

articles of incorporation the primary legal document of a corporation filed with the state to begin corporate existence. ***Also***: certificate of incorporation; charter.

articles of organization a document that an LLC files with the proper state authorities to begin legal existence.

articulation statement a table showing the end-of-period debit and credit balances, used by *matrix bookkeeping*. ***Also***: spread sheet.

artistic income <UK> income from the sales of art work, such as paintings.

AS <1> account sales. <2> accumulated surplus.

as at words meaning that the dates of the financial statements are subject to change.

ASB <1> Accounting Standards Board. <2> Auditing Standards Board.

ascertainable useful life the useful life of an asset in the taxpayer's hands that is reasonably capable of estimation.

ASCPA American Society of Certified Public Accountants.

ASEC Assurance Services Executive Committee

as of adjustment a client's correction of telecommunication breakdown by referring to a bank's reserve records.

ASR allowance for sampling risk

as-reported earnings a public company's reported earnings obtained by applying generally accepted accounting principles.

ASSC Accounting Standards Steering Committee.

assembly order cost a job order cost system used by industries engaged in the assembly of completed parts into a finished product.

asserted liability a liability item that, absent a contest, could be deducted, e.g. a bill for services of a non-capital nature submitted to a firm.

assertion any declaration or set of declarations about whether the subject matter is based on or in conformity with the criteria selected. ***See***: *management assertion.*

assessable cost variance cost variance the amount of which can be estimated.

assessable income statutory income less deductions and exemptions. ***Also***: income for assessment.

assessable stock a stock whose holders can be assessed for further liability in the event of insolvency. ***Opp***: *nonassessable stock.*

assessed value the value of an item assessed by a government agency for property tax purpose. ***Also***: rateable value.

assessment <UK> the calculation of a taxpayer's tax by the Inland Revenue.

assessment period statutory period during which a deficiency can be assessed by the IRS.

asset (A) property or title held by a person or a company.

asset accretion improvement in the value of a corporation's assets through expansion, acquisition, or growth. ***Also***: resource accretion.

asset acquisition = *acquisition of assets.*

asset activity ratio = *activity ratio.*

asset adequacy tested reserve of an insurance company, the required reserve to satisfy all life insurance policy obligations and expenses.

asset allocation the allocation of assets into predetermined portions among several different types of securities.

asset allocation mutual fund a mutual fund that rotates among stocks, bonds and other money market instruments to maximize return and minimize risk.

asset and liability method a method under which a current or deferred tax liability or asset is recognized for both the current or deferred tax consequences, and the amount is measured based on the enacted tax law to determine the amount of tax payable or refundable currently or in future years. ***See***: *liability method.*

asset-and-liability statement = *balance sheet.*

asset availability the condition of an asset for usability.

asset-backed financing a method of financing in which lenders and equity investors look to the cash flow from a particular asset.

asset-backed security (ABS) a security collateralized by a particular asset, such as a loan, lease, real estate etc.

asset backing = *book value per share.*

asset class <UK> a category of assets: cash, equities, bonds, or property.

asset cost <1> the value of an asset expressed in cost. <2> = *depreciable cost.* <3> = *plant asset cost.*

asset cover extent to which assets as collateral for stockholders i.e. the ratio of all assets to all common stock. ***Also***: asset coverage; net asset cover.

asset coverage <1> calculated as: (net assets - preferred debts) ÷ preferred debts. <2> = *asset cover.* <3> = *asset-liability ratio.*

asset coverage test a bond indenture test that permits additional borrowing if the ratio of assets to debt does not fall below a minimum.

asset deficiency the market value of assets is lower than the original cost, or less than the money borrowed to buy them.

asset depreciation range (ADR) choice of life time the IRS will let you use when you claim depreciation on a particular asset.

asset depreciation range system (ADRS) system by which the asset depreciation range for an asset consists of a statutory midpoint (e.g. 10 years) bounded by a 40% range (the ADR is 8 to 12 years).

asset depreciation risk loss that an insurer may incur as the result of market crash.

asset dividend = *property dividend.*

asset earning power the ratio of earnings before taxes divided by the total assets of a business. ***Also***: ratio of earnings to total assets.

asset/equity ratio the ratio of a firm's assets to stockholders' equity. ***Also***: total assets to equity ratio. ***See***: *equity multiplier.*

asset expense allowance the amount of asset that may be expensed.

asset expiration = *depreciation.*

asset forfeiture law a law providing for forfeiture of property, particularly that used in a crime or derived from a crime.

asset guideline period the midpoint on the asset depreciation range.

asset income = *property income.*

asset-liability gap any projected shortfall in the ability of a financial institution to meet its contractual obligations from current holdings.

asset-liability person a person involved in the asset and liability management of a financial institution.

asset-liability ratio the ratio of assets to liabilities. ***Also***: asset coverage; asset-to-debt ratio.

asset-liability view a concept which holds that revenue and expense result only from change in the assets and liabilities. ***Also***: balance-sheet view; capital maintenance view. **See**: *net accretion concept; revenue expense view.*

asset life the period for which an asset can be used.

asset management ratio = *activity ratio.*

asset method <1> a method for recording prepayments as assets and, at the end of the period, determining the portion of the asset that was consumed in that period. ***Also***: increase and decrease method. <2> a method that recognizes the difference between beginning and ending values of the assets as the income of that period. ***Opp***: *expense method.*

asset out of accounts = *nonledger asset.*

asset out of books = *nonledger asset.*

asset premium the amount by which the depreciation based on the current value exceeds that based on the historical cost when the market price of the asset is rising.

asset ratio the ratio of net assets to net sales.

asset revaluation reserve = *revaluation reserve.*

asset reversion recovery by the sponsoring employer of any defined benefit pension fund of assets in excess of the amounts required to pay accrued benefits.

asset share value policyholder's equity share of the life insurance company's assets.

assets re-priced before liabilities (arbl) a rate used to measure the sensitivity of a bank or firm. If a bank has an arbl of 1 or higher, it is said to be asset sensitive.

asset tax of a life insurance company marginal tax effects caused by the use of earnings rates to determine tax deductions.

asset to be realized an asset to be realized at the beginning of a liquidation period.

asset-to-debt ratio = *asset-liability ratio.*

asset turnover number of times the assets are changed in form to obtain certain amount of sales, arrived at by dividing sales by assets. ***Also***: revenue generated per dollar of investment; total asset turnover.

asset utilization measure of how efficiently a corporation uses its assets to produce revenues and profits. **See**: *return on total assets.*

asset utilization ratio the ratio of net sales to total assets. ***Also***: ratio of sales to total assets.

asset valuation reserve (AVR) reserve for stocks, bonds, real estate, mortgages and similar types of invested assets.

asset value = *book value per share..*

asset value per share = *book value per share.*

assignment of income transfer of income from one person to another, the transferor is still liable for the income tax. ***Also***: income assignment; transfer of rights to income.

associated company <UK> = *affiliated corporation.*

associated cost = *related cost.*

associated operations <UK> two or more operations that affect one piece of property.

associating cost and effect a costing under which costs attached to a product become expense only when the unit to which they attach is sold. **See**: *immediate recognition; systematic and rational allocation.*

Association for Investment Management and Research (AIMR) <UK> an international non-profit organization for investment professionals, formed in 1990 by a merger between the ICFA and the FAF.

Association of Certified Accountants (ACA) an association incorporated by Royal Charter in 1904, now is the second largest accounting body in the UK.

Association of Certified Fraud Examiners (ACFE) an international, 28,000-member professional body dedicated to fighting fraud. **See**: *certified fraud examiner.*

assumed cost = *imputed cost.*

assumed debt a debt of an acquired firm that becomes an obligation of the acquirer.

assumed loss method a method in which a partner whose share of loss exceeds his capital plus his current account balance is assumed to be insolvent and his deficit is allotted to the solvent partners.

assumed rate of return the rate of return assumed by a retirement plan actuary in calculating liability coverage and coverage gaps. *Also*: actuarial rate; add-on yield.

assurance service independent professional services that improve the quality of information, or its context, for decision makers.

astronaut <UK> an individual who escapes taxation by not being resident in any territory.

ASWA American Society of Women Accountants

asymmetric taxes a transaction in which the participants have different net tax rates.

AT attestation standards

ATA <1> Accredited Tax Advisor. <2> American Taxation Association.

at acquisition retained earnings = *acquired surplus.*

ATI accumulated taxable income

ATII <UK> associate of the Chartered Institute of Taxation.

ATIN adoption taxpayer identification number

ATO Australian Taxation Office

at-risk adjustment <Canada> the amount or benefit that the taxpayer is entitled to receive whether by way of reimbursement, income guarantee, compensation, loan or other form of guarantee against the risk of loss.

at-risk amount <Canada> a limit partner's adjusted cost base plus share of current year's income minus amount owing to the partnership.

at-risk rule <1> shareholders of the S corporation is at risk with respect to an activity to the extent of his or her pro rata share of the basis of the property that is contributed to that activity. <2> provision in the tax code which states that a limited partner may only include debt as part of his basis in the partnership if he is personally liable for it. <3> a rule that states the loss from passive activities is deductible only to the extent that a taxpayer has at risk in the property allocated to that activity.

A trust = *marital deduction trust.*

attached account a bank account against which a court order has been issued permitting the disbursements of funds only with the consent of the court.

attainable good performance standard cost = *expected standard cost.*

attainable standard cost = *expected standard cost.*

attained age-normal method a method of determining pension expense by the normal ages of the employees. *See*: *projected benefit cost.*

attestation report = *attest report.*

attestation standards (AT) standards that enable CPAs to examine or review the nonfinancial statement information and to perform and report on the results of those engagements.

attest function audit an audit to attest the accounting records by obtaining evidence and evaluating the evidence.

attest report a written conclusion about the reliability of an assertion. *Also*: attestation report.

at the lower of cost or market = *cost or marker, whichever is lower.*

attributable cost = *product cost.*

attributable earnings income that is attributable to a member of a group of companies.

attributable profit <UK> that portion of profit attributable to the completed portion of a project.

attributes sampling audit sampling that reaches a conclusion in terms of a rate of occurrence. *See*: *variables sampling.*

attribution method a method used to assign benefit costs on a years-of-service basis, over the approximate service years of employees.

attribution period a period for accruing the expected post-retirement healthcare benefit obligation, which begins with the date of hire and ends at the full eligibility date.

attribution rate = *overhead application rate.*

attributions method a method for the post-retirement benefits that assigns costs on a years-of-service approach, and allocates the costs over approximate service years of employees.

attrition method = *continuous allotment method.*

AUC average unit cost.

auction market preferred stock (AMPS) = *auction rate preferred stock.*

auction rate preferred stock (ARPS) the *preferred stock* with dividend adjusted every seven weeks through a *Dutch auction*. ***Also***: adjustable-rate preferred stock; auction market preferred stock; Dutch auction rate transferable security; flexible auction rate preferred stock; market auction preferred stock; money market preferred; money market preferred stock; remarketed preferred stock; short-term auction rate.

auction value = *liquidating value.*

aud <1> audit. <2> auditor.

audit (a.)(aud) <1> an examination by the auditor of the books and accounts of a firm. ***Also***: accounting audit; auditing. <2> the investigation of a taxpayer's return in order to verify its accuracy. <3> = *balance sheet audit.*

audit adjustment entry = *auditor's adjusting entry.*

audit by comparison audit method by comparing current and past records.

audit by-product auditor's advice to the management.

audit certificate = *auditor's report.*

audit committee a committee appointed by the board of directors of a public company with supervisory and oversight responsibilities, especially in the area of accounting policy and audit policy.

audit cycle obtaining evidence - recording - first appraisal - proof - further appraisal - auditor's report.

audit documentation working paper, electronic files, audit evidence and significant audit findings or issues.

audited books = *certified financial statements.*

audited financial statements = *certified financial statements.*

audited net sales total amount of sales for the period minus returns and allowances.

audit equation underlying evidence + corroborating evidence = sufficient competent evidential matters.

audit evidence underlying accounting data corroborating available to the auditor. ***See***: *evidential matter.*

audit expectation gap the difference between an auditor's ability to detect fraud or other problems and the expectations users of financial statements have for the auditor's skills and powers.

audit file = *audit working paper.*

audit findings result of audit procedures. ***Also***: audit result.

audit hypothesis testing = *hypothesis testing.*

auditing = *audit.*

auditing by rotation auditing of the same firm by 2 auditors independently in order to avoid collusion.

auditing by test and scrutiny test audit with careful investigation.

auditing standard a standard applied by the auditors in auditing the client's accounting records and behavior. ***Also***: audit standard; basis of audit.

Auditing Standards Board (ASB) Board authorized by the AICPA to promulgate auditing and attest standards, procedures, and implementation guidance for AICPA members performing such services.

audit memo a memo used by auditors. ***Also***: memorandum of audit.

audit of financial statements = *financial statements audit.*

audit of returns = *final audit.*

auditor (aud.) <1> qualified person performing an audit. <2> = *independent auditor.*

Auditor General <Canada> an officer of the Parliament who is responsible for auditing all government agencies. ***See:*** *Comptroller and Auditor General; Comptroller General.*

auditor independence = *independence.*

auditor's adjusting entry a journal entry recommended by an auditor and expected to be used by the client. ***Also***: adjusting entry; adjustment entry; audit adjustment entry; auditor's entry. ***See***: *correcting journal entry; worksheet entry.*

auditor's certificate = *auditor's report.*

auditor's entry = *auditor's adjusting entry.*

auditor's liability <1> failure to uncover a fraud or defalcation being perpetrated against the client. <2> failure to complete the audit at an agreed-upon time.

auditor's opinion professional opinion of an auditor.

auditor's report a report by the auditor after performing an audit. ***Also***: accountant's certificate; accountant's report; audit certificate; auditor's certificate; audit report; certificate of audit; certificate of independent public accountants; opinion report; report of independent CPA.

auditor's standard report = *unqualified report.*

auditor's statement a brief statement made by an auditor in the annual report about the company's financial statements and operating results.

audit period <1> the time period from the audit contract to the audit report. <2> = *accounting period.*

audit plan a plan of the audit engagement, outlining the nature and characteristics of the client's business operations and the overall audit strategy.

audit program a detailed listing of the specific audit procedures to be performed in the course of an audit engagement.

audit report = *auditor's report.*

audit result = *audit findings.*

audit risk <1> the risk that an account and its related assertions may contain material misstatements and the risk that the auditor will not detect them, including *control risk, detection risk* and *inherent risk.* <2> the risk that a tax return may be audited by the IRS. <3> the risk stemming from unrealistic expectations of what an audit covers or what an auditor can be expected to detect.

audit risk alerts annual updates alerting auditors to current economic, regulatory, and professional developments in various industries.

audit sampling the sampling by an auditor to establish a basis for appraisal of the complete accounting records.

audit-sensitive position a position in which the activities are normally an element of or subject to *significant control.*

audit standard = *auditing standard.*

audit strategy a plan for audit issues before they are raised.

audit test verification activities that are performed during the sampling process. ***Also***: sampling audit; test; test audit; test basis examination; test checking; testing.

audit trail <1> a cross-reference from a record to its source to properly explain it, document it, or check its accuracy. <2> written records that document a process, activity, or event. ***Also***: paper trail.

audit trigger a factor that may trigger an IRS audit.

audit working paper the records kept by the auditor of the procedures followed, the tests performed, the information obtained, and the conclusion. ***Also***: audit file.

audit year <1> an audit period of 12 consecutive months. <2> = *accounting year.*

Aud. SEC Auditing Standards Executive Committee

AuSec Auditing Standards Executive Committee

Australian Taxation Office (ATO) <Australia> a federal government's principal revenue collection agency.

authorised unit trust <UK> an investment unit trust that invests its funds in fixed income securities.

authorized capital stock the amount of capital of which the company is authorized to raise, represented by the total face value or stated value of all shares. ***Also***: free capital; registered capital. ***See***: *nominal capital.*

authorized e-file provider a business authorized to participate in the IRS e-file program.

authorized shares maximum number of shares of stock that a company can issue. ***Also***: shares authorized.

authorized unit trust = *unit investment trust.*

automated collection system (ACS) IRS agency system that contacts taxpayers via telephone regarding delinquent taxes and tax returns.

automatic audit the audit performed without a plan. ***See***: *selective audit.*

automatic consent IRS approval of a change in accounting method by filing Form 3115.

automatic dividend reinvestment plan (ADR) a plan under which stockholders can get more shares instead of receiving dividends.

automatic extension the right of taxpayers to file tax returns 4 months later if they file for an extension and pay the tax in full by the due date.

automatic stay a provision of the bankruptcy code that prevents creditors from seizing collateral when a firm files for Chapter 11 bankruptcy.

autonomous account an account in the *balance of payments* that relates to the trade of goods and services, donation, capital transfer, etc.

auxiliary journal = *special journal.*

auxiliary ledger = *subsidiary ledger.*

availability float the time period, or the dollar amount, represented by checks that have been deposited but not cleared.

available balance <1> ending inventory balance calculated as the actual inventory + quantity ordered - reserved stock. <2> account balance calculated as carrying balance of bank deposits - reserves - uncollectibles - commitments.

available cash flow total cash sources less total cash uses before the payment of debt service.

available-for-sale securities (AFS) debt or equity securities not classified as either *held-to-maturity* or *trading securities.*

available-for-use rule <Canada> a rule under which capital cost allowance is allowed at the time it is first used by the taxpayer to earn income.

available surplus = *unappropriated retained earnings.*

AVC <1> additional voluntary contribution. <2> average variable cost.

AVCO average cost

averageable income the amount by which current year's taxable income exceeds 120% of average base period income.

average accounting return the average accounting rate of return of a set of investment projects.

average acquisition cost method a method of valuing increments of inventory under the dollar-value method by which cost of ending inventory of the current period is determined on the basis of average cost of acquisition or production over the year.

average adjusted basis an average of the adjusted basis at the beginning of each month in the taxable year during which the taxpayer held the property.

average age of accounts receivable = *number of days' sales in receivables.*

average age of inventory = *number of days' sales in inventory.*

average annual compound return <UK> annual return of investment taking into account the reinvestment of distributions.

average annual return (AAR) the annual return of a mutual fund stated after all fees have been deducted.

average base period income the taxpayer's average taxable income for the four years prior to the computation year.

average basis a taxpayer's basis in an asset after making additions or subtractions to reflect improvement and depreciation.

average basis method a method by which taxpayers who buy stock left in the hands of a custodian can use average cost method for determining the basis of stock bought at different prices.

"average book" method a method by which the rate of return on investment is equal to annual profit after depreciation divided by the average book value of assets. ***See***: *"original book" method.*

average cleared balance average balance on a credit account adjusted for the unclear effects used as the basis of an allowance made against the cost of keeping a current account before the charge is ascertained.

average collected balance calculated as: (sum of the daily balances of a deposit account - uncommitted deposits - uncollectibles) ÷ number of days in that period.

average collection period ratio = *number of days' sales in receivables.*

average cost (AVCO)(avg. cost) = *cost per unit.*

average cost flow assumption an assumption that the stages of completion of every process under process costing are equal.

average costing the costing that combines beginning inventory costs with current period production costs. ***Also***: weighted average costing.

average cost method a method of assigning costs to specific units of inventory on any of the following bases: simple average; weighted average; and moving average.

average cost of capital the required cost of capital paid in a period to bondholders and stockholders divided by total capital.

average daily balance the sum of all daily balances for the interest period divided by the number of days.

average days' sales uncollected = *number of days' sales in receivables.*

average debtor collection period = *number of days' sales in receivables.*

average earnings rate the average of the earning rates of the current and the four preceding taxable years.

average equity average daily balance of a customer's account, calculated by a broker.

average fixed cost (AFC) = *fixed costs per unit.*

average inventory investment period = *number of days' sales in inventory.*

average life method a depreciation method which uses the average life of an asset.

average number of shares outstanding average number of shares outstanding for a given year.

average overhead rate = *normal factory overhead rate.*

average period = *base period.*

average price method a method of pricing ending inventory by using the average price of the purchased items.

average price per share average cost per share of mutual fund. It equals total cost of the fund shares divided by total number of shares owned.

average rate of return (ARR) a rate of return calculated by using the average investment, 50% of the required initial investment. ***See***: *accounting rate of return.*

average remaining service life <UK> a weighted average of the expected future service of the current employees up to their retirement dates.

average settlement period = *number of days' sales in receivables.*

average standard cost = *normal standard cost.*

average tax rate <1> a taxpayer's tax liability divided by taxable income. ***Also***: effective income tax rate; effective tax rate; implicit tax rate.

average total cost = *total cost per unit.*

average variable cost (AVC) = *variable costs pre unit.*

averaging <1> = *constant dollar plan.* <2> = *income averaging.*

averaging convention a method for arbitrarily solving the problem of when to consider the depreciable assets placed in services, such as *half-year convention* and *full-year convention.*

averaging method a method under which actuarial gains and losses are recognized immediately if they arise from a single occurrence not directly related to the pension fund.

avg. cost average cost

avoidable cost amount of cost that can be reduced by making a decision, such as separable fixed cost. ***Also***: escapable cost.

avoidable fixed cost the cost that may or may not be incurred under certain conditions.

avoidance = *tax avoidance.*

avoidance of taxation = *tax avoidance.*

avoidance transaction = *tax avoidance transaction.*

avoided cost the cost that has to be spent if the project did not proceed.

AVR asset valuation reserve

award of legal costs <Canada> money that is awarded to a taxpayer by a court.

away from home IRS definition of being away from home substantially longer than a normal workday, for a period of time that would require sleep or rest.

away-from-home expense = *travel expense.*

B b

B <1> budget. <2> buffer stock.

b variable cost pre unit in the formula: y = a + bx.

B2B business to business

B2B stock business to business stock

B2C business to consumer

B2C stock business to consumer stock

BAC budget at completion

back duty = *back tax.*

back-end fee = *back-end load.*

back-end load charge by a mutual fund for selling or redeeming the shares. ***Also***: back-end fee; exit cost; exit fee; exit load. ***See***: *front-end load.*

back-flush costing a costing method that delays recording production charges until finished goods occur, thus eliminating work-in-process inventory. ***Also***: delayed costing; end-point costing.

back-in, farm-out a concept in oil and gas industry, which provides that the grantor's retained non-operating interest can later be changed into an undivided working or operating interest.

backlog accumulated items need to be processed by the accountant or auditor.

backlog depreciation = *amortization gap.*

back pay unpaid wage or salary.

back tax any tax owed and is past due. ***Also***: back duty; delinquent tax; past due tax; unpaid tax.

backup withholding tax withheld from investment income, such as interest and dividends, and *reportable payments.*

backwards spreading <UK> tax relief that allows authors and artists to spread their income backwards 2 or 3 years. ***See:*** *forwards spreading.*

bad account <1> <under direct charge off method> = *bad debt.* <2> <under allowance method> = *doubtful account.*

bad boy clause a clause which states if a top executive commits certain act, the benefit will be canceled.

bad check a check that is dishonored on presentation due to insufficient funds, forgery, or other defect. ***Also***: bounced check; dishonored check; dud cheque; kite; protest check; rejected check; returned check; return item; rubber check; rubber cheque; worthless check. ***See:*** *non-sufficient fund check.*

bad debt amount due on an open account that has been proved to be uncollectible. ***Also***: bad account; charge-off; dead account; dead loan; desperate debt; sleeping account; uncollectible account; worthless account.

bad debt loss = *loss on bad debts.*

bad debt loss provision = *allowance for bad debts.*

bad debt ratio a ratio of trade debts uncollectible to sales for a given period.

bad debt reserve = *allowance for bad debts.*

bad debts written off a customer's account that is removed from the books when the payment appears unlikely.

bad will = *negative goodwill.*

Bahamian trust a trust established in Bahamas where the grantor will retain any power over the trust or trustee.

bailout <1> to provide a public company with loans at low interest or tax concession by the government. <2> to relieve a person or a firm in financial trouble. <3> to provide payments to shareholders that are taxable at desirable capital gains rates.

bailout period = *payback period.*

bal. balance

balance (bal.) <1> net debit or credit amount in an account. *Also*: account balance; remainder. <2> the difference between debit and credit amounts, or between income and expense. <3> the credit sum equals the debit sum in a trial balance. <4> when the ledger balance equals the total of the balances of subsidiary accounts. <5> the balance of an input-output table. <6> = *break-even.*

balance account = *real account.*

balance book a book in which balances of accounts are entered in order to prove their accuracy with the ledger balance.

balance brought down <in T-account> = *balance brought forward.*

balance brought forward (bal b/f) the balance of an account that is brought from the previous period to the current period. *Also*: balance brought down; balance down.

balance brought over the balance brought from last page to this page in a ledger.

balance carried down (bal. c/d) <in T-account> = *balance carried forward.*

balance carried forward (bal. c/f) account balance carried from this period to the next period. *Also*: balance carried down; balance forward.

balance carried over the balance carried from this page to the next page in a ledger.

balance certificate the document to the shareholder certifying the unsold portion of shares.

balance column account an account having a balance column besides credit and debit columns. *Also*: balance form account; debit-credit-balance-form account; three-column account.

balance control check verification of the accuracy of account balances by using the formula: old balance + transactions = new balance.

balanced inventory ideal situation in which inventory items on hand or in transit are sufficient to meet anticipated production or sales needs for a period. *Also*: stockless purchasing. *See*: *just-in-time.*

balance down = *balance brought forward.*

balance due total amount needed to equalize the debit and credit sum of a current account.

balance-due date <Canada> the date on which a tax due must be paid. (for a trust and corporation, 90 days after the end of a tax year, for an individual April 30.)

balance due from the debit balance in a current account, i. e. the account receivable from others. *Also*: balance in our favor.

balance due to credit balance in a current account, i.e. sum payable to others. *Also*: balance in your favor.

balance form account = *balance-column account.*

balance form income statement = *account form income statement.*

balance for official financing <UK> the balance on current account plus the total of investment and other capital flow plus the balancing item.

balance forward = *balance carried forward.*

balance in our favor = *balance due from.*

balance in your favor = *balance due to.*

balance of autonomous transactions the transactions derived from changes in the reserves of domestic monetary agencies and the changes in liabilities to foreign official agencies.

balance of current account the net balance of country's international payments arising from exports and imports of goods and services, together with unilateral transfers, excluding capital flows.

balance of errors a balance of a country's international payments arising from errors or omissions.

balance of international indebtedness the difference between a nation's borrowings from abroad and its loans made to other countries.

balance of international payments (BIP) = *balance of payments.*

balance of payments (BOP)(bop) balance of trade plus other financial transactions such as loans made to other countries. ***Also***: balance of international payments; international balance of payments; payments balance.

balance of payments statement record of the economic transactions between the residents of a country and the residents of other countries in a given period.

balance of stockholders' equity owners' equity in a balance sheet after assets and liabilities are adjusted by a general price level index.

balance-of-stores system = *periodic inventory method.*

balance of trade the difference between a country's exports and its imports. ***Also***: balance on goods and services; trade balance; trading difference; visible balance.

balance on goods and services = *balance of trade.*

balance receipt = *balance ticket.*

balance sheet (B/S) a statement that lists assets and liabilities of a given firm to portray its net worth at a given point of time. ***Also***: asset-and-liability statement; statement of assets and liabilities; statement of condition; statement of condition of affairs; statement of financial position; statement of the sources and composition of company capital; static statement.

balance sheet account (B/S a/c) an account the balance of which is to be shown in the balance sheet. ***Also***: trial balance account. ***See***: *revenue and expense account.*

balance sheet approach <1> a method of estimating bad debts expense by applying a percentage on the accounts receivable balance. ***See***: *aging method*; *income statement approach.* <2> a method of preparing the statement of stockholders' equity based on the following equation: stockholders' equity = assets - liability. <3> = *balance sheet oriented.*

balance sheet audit an audit that focuses on the balance sheet only. ***Also***: audit.

balance sheet audit for credit purpose balance sheet audit for the purpose of rating borrowers' credit standing.

balance sheet date the specified day when the balance sheet is prepared.

balance sheet equation = *accounting equation.*

balance sheet expenditure = *capital expenditure.*

balance sheet exposure = *accounting exposure.*

balance sheet for credit purpose balance sheet that focuses on the credit standing of a firm, and is based on the equation: asset - negative asset = net asset.

balance-sheet format a form of presenting balance sheet, such as *account form, financial position form* and *report form.*

balance sheet identity = *accounting equation.*

balance sheet-income statement ratios financial ratios calculated by using the figures shown in the balance sheet and the income statement. ***Also***: bi-statement ratios.

balance sheet in the account form = *account form balance sheet.*

balance sheet laundering money laundering activity when the person parks the money in the company bank account. ***See***: *overstatement of reported revenues.*

balance sheet oriented an emphasis on the amount to be reported on a balance sheet as deferred tax asset or tax liability. *Also*: balance sheet approach.

balance sheet ratio a ratio calculated from figures in the balance sheet.

balance sheet reserve amount shown as a liability on the balance sheet of insurance companies payable to policyholders.

balance sheet restated a balance sheet the figures of which have been adjusted by a general price level index.

balance sheet total the total value of assets shown in a balance sheet.

balance sheet value the total value of assets shown on the balance sheet (the original costs minus accumulated depreciation).

balance sheet view = *asset-liability view*.

balance ticket a document given to a broker by a company for the remaining shares unsold after some shares have been sold. *Also*: balance receipt.

balance transferred (bal. tra.) a balance which is transferred from one account to another.

balancing account <1> account used to record changes of each period in every variable, when preparing the input-output table. <2> = *settlement account*.

balancing allowance <UK> amount that a taxpayer may deduct from taxable income when an asset is sold for less than its *tax written-down value*.

balancing charge <UK> amount added to the taxable trading profits of a taxpayer when an asset is sold for higher than its *tax written-down value*.

balancing event <UK> an event when the relevant interest is transferred and where the building is demolished, destroyed or ceases to exist.

balancing form = *account form*.

balancing item = *settlement account*.

balancing ledger = *self-balancing ledger*.

balancing the books a periodical closing up of accounts by bringing down a balance to make the totals of debit and credit sides in balance, and adjustment of ledger accounts to obtain profit or loss.

bal b/d balance brought down

bal b/f balance brought forward

bal c/d balance carried down

bal c/f balance carried forward

balloon interest the highest rate applying to a portion of serial bonds that matures late in the repayment schedule.

ballpark figure an estimate of a stock's financial prospectus based on preliminary information or incomplete data.

bankable asset the asset that a bank will receive or accept as pledge for a loan. *See*: *eligible asset*.

bank balance <1> the difference between banks after clearing. <2> checking account balance shown on the bank statement.

bank call a call from the federal or state government for a bank to render the financial statements.

bank charge service fee charged by a bank.

bank collection float = *collection float*.

bank cut-off statement a bank statement which covers a specified number of days following the close of a fiscal year, used by the auditor.

bank deposit method a method of determining a taxpayer's income whereby all deposits to bank accounts are totaled, and tall deposits from nontaxable sources and transfers between the taxpayer's accounts are subtracted.

bank discount (BD)(B/D) deduction of interest made in advance from the amount of a loan by the lender. *Also*: deduction; discount; discount interest; loan discount; rebate.

banker's book <UK> a copy of the entries in a bank's book serving as an evidence of the original record.

banker's ratio = *2-to-1 current ratio*.

banking institution = *financial institution*.

bank interest <1> interest charged by a bank on a loan. <2> interest paid by a bank on money deposited.

bank lockbox = *lockbox.*

bank prime interest rate an interest rate at which banks lend money to their largest and credit-worthy customers. ***Also***: bank rate; base rate; blue chip rate; concessional rate; fine rate; preferential rate; prime interest rate; prime rate; prime rate of interest.

bank rate = *bank prime interest rate.*

bank return <UK> weekly report of the financial position of the Bank of England. ***Also***: weekly return.

bankruptcy balance sheet a balance sheet showing the financial status of the bankrupt.

bankruptcy cost view a theory which holds that bankruptcy cost will offset the other benefits from leverage so that the optimal leverage is less than 100% debt financing. ***Also***: bankruptcy view.

bankruptcy remote entity a subsidiary or affiliate company the asset and liability structure and legal status of which make its obligations secure even in the event of the bankruptcy of its parent or guarantor.

bankruptcy reorganization = *type G reorganization.*

bankruptcy view = *bankruptcy cost view.*

bank statement balance the balance of cash shown on the bank's statement.

bank transfer schedule an audit schedule that shows the dates of all transfers of cash among the client's various bank accounts in order to detect kiting.

BAP Beta Alpha Psi

Bardahl formula a test to determine whether a company's accumulations of working capital are excessive for the purpose of imposing the accumulated profit tax.

bare trust <UK> a trust the grantor of which retains no rights to the assets and income will be taxable to the beneficiary. ***See***: *grantor trust.*

bargain purchase option (BPO) an option that allows the lessee to purchase leased property for an amount substantially lower than the expected fair market value.

bargain sale to charity selling property to a charity for less than the property's actually worth. Depending on the circumstances, this could result in a tax deduction or extra *taxable income.*

barter to trade by exchanging one commodity for another. ***Also***: *swap.*

Barth system <UK> a payment by results system in which a worker's payroll equals number of output units × standard time per unit × the number of hours actually worked × hourly rate.

base amount <1> amount for the purpose of calculating the *qualified research expense credit*, $25,000 in 2002. <2> amount used in calculating social security tax. ***See***: *first base amount; second base amount.* <3> the amount in determining the excess parachute payment, usually the average annualized compensation income included in the taxpayer's gross income in the five preceding tax years.

base calendar year the calendar year within which the 1st taxable year of the credit period ends.

base capital common shares plus additional paid-in capital and retained earnings.

base case a method for projecting the financial performance of a company on the basis of reasonable operating and financial projection assumptions. ***See***: *downside case.*

base currency = *reporting currency.*

base interest rate = *cut-off rate of return.*

base period <1> the three taxable years immediately preceding the year for which the credit for increasing research activities is determined. <2> the 4 years preceding the current taxable year for which income averaging is claimed. ***Also***: average period.

<3><Australia> the period prior to the *declared period* when declared period quotas have been imposed.

base period year any of the four years immediately preceding a tax year.

base probability of loss the probability of not achieving expected return.

base rate <UK> = *bank prime interest rate.*

base stock = *buffer stock.*

base stock method a method of inventory valuation under which the base stock appears in every stocktaking at its original cost, the excess stock above this base stock is valued using other methods such as lifo. ***Also***: cost of the oldest stock method; minimum stock method; normal stock method; perpetual stock method.

base-year cost aggregate cost of all items in an inventory pool, determined as of the beginning of the taxable year for which the lifo inventory method is first adopted.

basic accounting equation the simple form of accounting equation: assets = liabilities + capital. ***See***: *expanded accounting equation.*

basic balance sum of the balance of payments of the current account plus long-term capital movements.

basic cost a cost used to determine the asset value, such as the cost of production or the purchasing cost.

basic earning power (BEP) *profitability ratio* obtained by profit before taxes divided by net sales.

basic earnings per share (BEPS) = *primary earnings per share.*

basic exemption <Canada> $40,000 provided in computing taxable income subject to the minimum tax for individual and certain trust.

basic IRR rule a rule under which a project will be accepted if the *internal rate of return* is higher than the discount rate, and rejected if lower.

basic minimum inventory = *buffer stock.*

basic minimum tax credit <Canada> the aggregate of personal tax credit, charitable donation credit, medical expense credit, disability credit, education tax credit and UI and CPP contribution tax credit.

basic net income per share = *primary earnings per share.*

basic P/E the price/earnings ratio that has been discounted at the market rate.

basic period the 3 taxable years ending with the taxable year immediately preceding the 1st taxable year beginning after Dec 31, 1983.

basic precision in PPS sampling, it equals reliability factor multiplied by sampling interval.

basic profit = *contribution margin.*

basic rate of tax <1> an income tax rate that applies to all income remaining after personal exemptions have been deducted from the net statutory income. <2><UK> the 23% tax rate specified in the Finance Act each year charged on all income not subject to *higher rate, lower rate* or *starting rate.*

basic rate tax <UK> tax based on the basic rate of tax.

basic research investigation for the advancement of scientific knowledge not having specific commercial objective.

basic retirement pension <UK> state retirement pension paid to a single man aged 65 or a single woman aged 60. ***Also***: old person's pension.

basic standard cost an unchangeable cost, as long as the specifications of the product do not change significantly, against which all the future costs for an indeterminable period of time is measured. ***Also***: constant standard cost; index standard cost; measurement standard cost; permanent standard cost; static standard cost; yard-stick standard cost.

basic standard deduction standard deduction for regular taxpayers who are neither aged nor blind.

basic stock merchandise that is in constant demand, thus requiring perpetual inventory throughout the year.

basic wage the wage paid to an employee excluding payments for bonus, holiday pay, over time or insurance.

basic yield annual return produced by an investment which carried no risk. *Also*: risk-free return. *See*: *benchmark return.*

basis <1> the cost of a purchased asset less any depreciation previously allowed or allowable for tax purposes. <2> the face value of an installment less the income that would be reported if the obligation were paid in full. <3> the amount of money held by the partner plus the adjusted basis of assets contributed to a partnership. *Also*: partner's basis. <4> = *tax basis.*

basis adjustment adjustment of the basis in partnership assets on a distribution, sale or transfer of partnership interest.

basis limitation a shareholder's basis in the S corporation's stock and debt.

basis of apportionment <UK> = *basis of distribution.*

basis of audit = *auditing standard.*

basis of distribution a basis on which overhead costs are distributed, such as area, working hours, number of employees etc. *Also*: basis of apportionment; burden vehicle; overhead distribution basis.

basis period a period in which income from a particular source forms the basis of assessment.

batch a single transaction consisting of the electronic data from one or more tax returns. *Also*: job lot.

batch costing <1> allocating costs to a batch of identical items of production, treated as a single unit. *Also*: job lot costing. <2> = *process costing.*

batch posting the posting of entries at a fixed interval. *See*: *real-time posting.*

bath = *accounting bath.*

Bausch & Lomb doctrine a rule that a type C reorganization will be denied if a parent company first buys the stock of a company which has a subsidiary, then issued stock to the acquired company in exchange for the subsidiary's assets, and it liquidates the subsidiary.

B/B a/c back to back account

BCF broadcast cash flow

BCR benefit-cost ratio

BC ratio benefit-cost ratio

BCWP budgeted cost of work performed

BCWS budgeted cost for work scheduled

BD bank discount

B/D bank discount

b/d brought down

bearer form a form of security not registered on the issuer's book, payable to bearer.

bearer stock a stock the dividends of which are paid to those who hold the certificate. *Also*: floater; street certificate.

Beatles clause <UK> a clause that subjects to income tax a capital sum received for the sale of a taxpayer's future earnings.

B/E chart break-even chart

bed and breakfasting selling the securities which have fallen in value at the last day of a period, recording the loss for capital gains tax deduction, and then buying the securities back on the next morning.

Bedaux system a premium bonus scheme in which the incentive payment per unit of time saved is 75% the rate paid for the standard time.

before-separation cost the cost of joint-products before they are separated.

before-tax income = *pre-tax accounting income.*

beginning balance the beginning or the first balance of an account that is recorded. *Also*: opening balance; preceding balance.

beginning inventory the inventory at the beginning of a period. *Also*: opening inventory; stock at start.

behavioral accounting procedures assisting in the explanation and management of human behavior.

behavioral classification the classification of costs into fixed and variable cost portion according to their relations with the volume of activities.

behavioral cost pattern = *cost behavior pattern.*

below-market loan = *below-market-rate loan.*

below-market-rate loan interest-free loan or bargain-rate loan to a friend or relative. *Also*: below-market loan.

below the line <1> a non-operating items not taken into account when determining profit. <2> below the line that crosses the totals in a T-account. <3> a deduction in a tax return that is treated as an itemized deduction.

below the line balance the balance of a T-account which is written below the end-of-period crossing. *Also*: below the totals balance.

below-the-line deduction a deduction from AGI to arrive at taxable income, such as standard deduction and itemized deduction.

below the totals balance = *below the line balance.*

below-water an asset the actual value of which is lower than the book value. *See*: *above-water.*

below zero a situation when the market price of a stock is less than the paid-up value of a stock.

benchmark excess return = *benchmark return.*

benchmark return the return the benchmark investment index, such as the S&P 500. *Also*: benchmark excess return; benchmark timing return; risk-free return.

benchmark statistics comprehensive data used as a basis for developing and adjusting interim estimates.

benchmark surplus additional amount of surplus set aside by an insurance company to act as a supplement to the cash flow in the event contingencies occur.

benchmark timing return = *benchmark return.*

beneficial interest the right of substantial enjoyment or interest. *See*: *fiduciary estate.*

beneficial owner an investment firm's client who is the actual owner of a stock held, even though the stock is registered in the firm's name.

beneficiary a person who receives benefit from someone or something.

benefit <Canada> any amount paid under a pension plan.

benefit allocation method a method of funding a retirement plan under which a single payment is made to the fund for one year of recognized service.

benefit-cost analysis = *cost-benefit analysis.*

benefit-cost ratio (BCR) total cash inflows ÷ total cash outflows. *Also*: benefits-divided-by-costs ratio.

benefit earned <Canada> portion of a taxpayer's pension that is considered to have accrued during the year.

benefit in kind <UK> benefit received from a company other than cash, subject to tax.

benefit of carry = *negative carry.*

benefit offset a partial or complete loss of pension plan benefits that may result when an employee owes money to the plan or receives benefits from another source.

benefit principle a rule stating that taxes should be levied upon the taxpayers in proportion to the benefits they receive.

benefit received money or other benefit that a taxpayer received from the government.

benefits-divided-by-costs ratio = *benefit-cost ratio.*

benefits-years-of-service approach an approach that takes future salary levels into consideration in calculating service cost. *Also*: projected unit credit method. *See*: *projected unit method.*

benefit theory a theory, based on the *going concern*, which holds that expectations of future benefits give managers a forward-looking direction and motivate investors to commit capital to an enterprise.

benefit-to-cost text = *cost-benefit analysis.*

BEP <1> basic earning power. <2> break-even point.

bequest a gift of personal property by will. *Also*: legacy.

best-interest-of-creditors test a test that a stockholder who is voting against a plan of reorganization must receive at least as much as if the debtor were liquidated.

beta risk <1> the risk that the assessed level of control risk, based on the sample is less than the true operating effectiveness of the control structure or procedure policy. *Also*: acceptance error; risk of assessing control risk too low; type II error. <2> risk that the sample supports the conclusion that the account balance is not materially misstated when it is. *Also*: risk of incorrect acceptance. *See*: *alpha risk.*

betterment improvement of the service potential of a fixed asset. *Also*: improvement. *See*: *capital improvement.*

betterment tax a tax levied on the property owners whose property is benefited by the betterment.

b/f brought forward

bias a deviation in the process of searching, disclosing and utilizing the supporting documents.

big 3 three major professionals in tax practice: tax attorney, CPA and EA.

big 4 currently the four largest public accounting firms in the world: Deloitte & Touche LLP; Ernst & Young LLP; KPMG LLP and PricewaterhouseCoopers.

big 5 formerly the five largest public accounting firms before Anderson & Co. discontinued auditing public companies.

big 6 formerly the six largest public accounting firms before Coopers and Lybrand merged.

big 8 formerly the 8 largest public accounting firms: Arthur Anderson & Co.; Arthur Young & Co.; Cooper & Lybrand; Deloitte, Haskins & Sells; Ernst & Whinney; Peat, Marwick, Mitchell & Co.; Price Waterhouse; and Touch Ross & Co.

big bath = *accounting bath.*

BIL business investment loss

bill a list of charges sent to the client for the services provided. *Also*: account bill.

bill and hold transaction a transaction in which sales of merchandise are improperly billed to customers prior to delivery, with the goods being held by the business.

billed receivable account receivable for which the customer has been billed. *See*: *unbilled receivable.*

billing cycle the time between an invoice is sent to the client to the collection of cash.

bill obligatory = *promissory note.*

bill of costs an itemized list of the costs incurred by the winning party in a court case.

bill of debt = *promissory note.*

bill of sale a written instrument given to pass the property title from a seller to a buyer.

bill payable (BP)(B/P)(B. pay.) trade acceptance owed by a business to trade creditors. *Also*: acceptance payable; payable.

bill receivable (B/R)(B rec.) a trade bill of exchange given by the customers, which the drawer or acceptor must pay at maturity. *Also*: acceptance receivable.

bill single = *promissory note.*

bill-when-shipped method a revenue recognition method which recognizes revenues when a product has been shipped to the customer.

bin = *bucket.*

bi-statement ratios = *balance sheet-income statement ratios.*

black box a computer system, portfolio, balance sheet, or income statement that is not transparent to its users, and which consequently demands a high degree of trust in its creators.

blacked-out quiet period = *quiet period.*

black money net income that is unreported for tax purposes.

Black Motor formula a formula used to determine the reserve for bad debts by using a moving average that is based on the average receivables and bad debt losses for the prior 6 years.

blackout <1> the period during which the management will provide answers to only straight-forward factual questions from security analysts or the press because of a pending securities issuance. <2> a period during which a company's employees are restricted in their purchases and/or sales of company stock. ***See***: *restricted stock.*

blackout period an interval of more than three consecutive business days in which employees may not adjust the investments contained in the pension plans. ***Also***: pension fund blackout period.

blank check a signed check with the amount left blank.

blank check company = *shell company.*

blank check preferred stock authorization given to the management to issue preferred stock without further approval of the board or the stockholders.

blanket extension an extension of time for filing tax returns, up to and including the 15th day of the sixth month following the end of the taxable year.

blanket inventory lien a lender's lien against all the borrower's inventories.

blanket overhead rate = *single overhead allocation rate.*

blanket percentage method a method under which all assets are depreciated by one single rate.

blank form a type of *positive form* which requests that the recipient furnishes certain data. ***See***: *positive form.*

blank stock a stock the terms of which are not set forth in the company's articles of incorporation.

blended payment <Canada> payment of both income and capital combined.

blended presentation method a method under which component units the activities of which are so closely tied to the primary government as to be indistinguishable are combined with the primary government figures. ***See***: *discrete presentation method.*

blended tax rate <1> rate of tax on gains with long- and short-term characteristics, e.g. gains on trading broad-based index. <2> rate of tax that includes state and local taxes. <3> rate of tax for taxpayers who are in two tax brackets when a new tax law is in effect.

blind person who is totally bind, or can not see better than 20/200, or the field of vision is 20 degree or less.

blind count an internal control procedure by counting the actual quantity received by the receiving department independent of any quantity records.

blind entry a bookkeeping entry stating only the accounts and amounts debited and credited, but not giving other explanations for the entry.

blind person's allowance = *relief for blind person.*

blind person's relief = *relief for blind person.*

blind trust a trust in which the beneficiaries do not have knowledge of the trust's assets and how they are managed, usually for the management of a public official's assets.

"B" list <UK> a list of the past members of a company within the last 12 months before the liquidation. ***See***: *"A" list.*

blocked account = *frozen account.*

blocked income the income earned by a foreign taxpayer not subject to tax in the US because he is precluded in foreign country from converting to US dollar.

block method <1> a method of preparing consolidated balance sheet under which capital of the subsidiary is eliminated step by step by the actual investment rates incurred when investing in the subsidiary. *Also*: step-by-step method. <2> a method for controlling a large block of subsidiary accounts by establishing sub-control accounts.

block sampling a sample that consists of contiguous units (e.g. auditor selects four blocks of ten vouchers for examination) or a period of time (e.g. every March, May and September).

blood bath = *accounting bath.*

blotter <1> irregular book that records transactions as they incur. *Also*: waste book. <2> cash daybook used by securities dealers. *Also*: cash blotter. <3> = *book of original entry.*

Blue Book a publication of the Congressional Joint Committee on Taxation.

blue-chip rate = *bank prime interest rate.*

blue-skying stock = *worthless security.*

bobtail statement a simplified statement for a demand deposit account.

body corporate <UK> a *company* incorporated in UK or elsewhere.

BOE Board of Examiners

bona fide cost sharing arrangement the agreement between 2 or more members of a group of controlled entities providing for the sharing of the costs and risk of developing intangible properties in return for a specified interest in the intangible that may be produced.

bona fide selling price actual price at which goods are offered during the 30-day period after the date of the inventory.

bond conversion premium = *conversion premium.*

bond discount amount by which the bonds are sold below their face value. *Also*: debenture discount; debt discount; discount on creditors.

bond equivalent yield = *equivalent bond yield.*

bond interest rate = *coupon rate.*

bond premium amount by which the selling price of a bond is greater than face amount. *Also*: premium on bonds.

bond premium amortization the amortization of premium on tax-exempt bonds.

bond ratio total liability represented by bonds due after one year divided by the same figure plus stockholder's equity.

bond sinking fund assets accumulated to pay a bond issue at maturity. *Also*: fund for retirement of bonds.

bonds-outstanding method a method which results in a decreasing amount of premium or discount amortization of bonds each period in proportion to the decrease in the outstanding balance.

bonds payable liability incurred by the issuance of bonds.

bond stock ratio calculated as: bonds ÷ corporate earnings yield.

bond stripping = *coupon stripping.*

bond trust a *trust* the subject matter of which consists in bonds that yield interest income.

bond trustee a trustee for the holders of a bond.

bond value market value of the fixed-income element of a convertible bond.

bond washing selling bonds ex-interest before ex-date to nontaxable persons, and after ex-date buying them back at a price representing original price plus interest, thus the interest is not taxable.

bond yield calculated as present income of bonds ÷ current market value.

bonus <1> the difference between the amount contributed by the new partner and the capital allocated. <2> the difference between the capital account balance and the amount paid to a partner who withdraws from the partnership. <3><UK> extra reward paid by employers to employees.

bonus certificate a statement received by a policy holder from the insurance company on the occasion of a division of its profits to inform him of the amount accruing to him.

bonus depreciation extra depreciation allowed in the first year to taxpayers purchasing *qualified property*. ***See***: *30% bonus depreciation; 50% bonus depreciation.*

bonus dividend = *extra dividend.*

bonus issue = *bonus share.*

bonus method a method under which a partnership only recognizes identifiable asset, not unidentifiable ones. ***See***: *goodwill method.*

bonus recovery allowance that a taxpayer may write off up to $5,000 (gradually rising to $10,000 in and after 1986), of new or used recovery property which the taxpayer bought for use in a trade or business and qualifies for the investment tax credit. ***Also***: additional first year depreciation.

bonus share free additional share issued to existing shareholders as a *stock dividend.* ***Also***: bonus issue; bonus stock; capitalization issue; dividend share; dividend stock.

bonus stock = *bonus share.*

boodle money received through corruption in public service.

book (bk) <1> a book of account kept by accountants for recording transactions. ***Also***: account book. <2> preliminary indication of interest on the part of prospective buyers of an issue of new securities.

book audit = *paper audit.*

book balance cash balance shown on the depositor's account. ***Also***: actual cash balance.

bookbuld the way of conducting an issue of shares where the price is not fixed, but rather is determined by a process in which interested investors bid for the shares.

book cash = *ledger cash.*

book charge a charge to revenue without paying cash.

book closure the period during which a public company will not entertain any requests for transfer of shares from current owners to new owners.

book cost <1> a cost, such as depreciation, without paying cash. ***Also***: paper expense; transfer cost. <2> = *imputed cost.* <3> = *recorded cost.*

book debt = *account receivable.*

book depreciation amount that can be deducted for depreciation purposes from the cost of an asset as shown in the accounting statements. ***Also***: accounting depreciation. ***See***: *tax depreciation.*

book entry an accounting entry passed merely for the purpose of book adjustment.

book entry security a security not in the form of a certificate, but as an entry in an account at a bank. ***See***: *uncertificated share.*

book equity = *net worth.*

book gain sale of a non-current asset for more than book value. ***Also***: accounting gain; gain on disposal.

book income = *net income per book.*

book inventory = *perpetual inventory.*

book inventory method = *perpetual inventory method.*

bookkeeper (bkpr) a person responsible for making entries on the general ledger. ***Also***: accounts clerk; junior account.

bookkeeping (bkpg)(bkg) the art, practice or work involved in the systematic recording of the transactions affecting a business. ***Also***: write-up work.

bookkeeping cycle = *accounting cycle.*

bookkeeping entry = *entry.*

bookkeeping equation = *accounting equation.*

bookkeeping error an error in depositor's record, not in the bank statement.

bookkeeping formula = *accounting equation.*

bookkeeping in matrix form = *matrix bookkeeping.*

bookkeeping process entry → record keeping → calculating → adjusting → result.

bookkeeping profit = *fictitious profit.*

bookkeeping system books, documents, methods, procedures used in bookkeeping.

bookkeeping transaction = *accounting transaction.*

bookkeeping without book = *bookless accounting system.*

bookless accounting system the computer-aided accounting system or a system which uses original documents for posting items to ledger accounts. ***Also***: bookkeeping without book; direct posting; file posting; ledger less accounting; slip system.

book method a method of determining the internal rate of return by using book figures.

book of business total amount of insurance on an insurer's books at a particular time.

book of final entry a book in which are finally entered the debits and credits first recorded in the book of original entry. ***Also***: book of secondary entry.

book of first entry = *book of original entry.*

book of original entry book in which all business dealings of the concern are first recorded in the order in which they take place. ***Also***: blotter; book of first entry; book of prime entry; entry book; subsidiary book of account.

book of posting entry = *posting medium.*

book of prime entry = *book of original entry.*

book of secondary entry = *book of final entry.*

book profit (BP) <1> = *fictitious profit.* <2> = *pre-tax accounting income* <3> = *unconfirmed profit.*

book rate of return (BRR) = *accounting rate of return.*

book revaluation readjustment of book value by debiting the expense account and crediting contra account or allowance account.

books and papers = *books and records.*

books and records all financial and other records of a person or a business. ***Also***: books and papers.

book share = *uncertificated share.*

books of account books that must be verified by an auditor.

book surplus <1> profit under going concern concept. ***Also***: surplus. <2> profit before audit adjustments or before separating the capital surplus and earned surplus. ***Also***: accounting surplus.

book to bill ratio a ratio to measure the hi-tech industry's demand to supply ratio for orders on a company's book to number of orders filled.

book to market ratio a ratio of the book value to the *market value* of outstanding shares. ***See***: *price/book ratio.*

book transaction = *accounting transaction.*

book value (bv)(B/V) <1> amount of an asset recorded in the books. ***Also***: carrying value; initial cost of asset. <2> amount calculated as total assets - intangibles - current liabilities - long term liabilities - equity issues that have a prior claim. <3> the value of shareholders' equity less the book value of preferred stock, plus deferred taxes and investment tax. <4> = *net worth.* <5> = *written down value.*

book value basis a method in which the gain or loss from reduction of capital is directly credited or debited to the capital account.

book value method <1> a method of recording book value of assets acquired through non-monetary exchange, plus boot less loss as the new book value, no gain is recognized. ***See***: *fair value method.* <2> a method of recording conversion of convertible bonds to common stock, under which the paid-in capital is credited by the carrying amount of the bonds. ***See***: *market value method.* <3> = *economic basis method.* <4> = *mercantile method.*

book value of common stock calculated as net worth - book value of preferred stock.

book value of preferred stock paid-in capital from preferred stock plus preferred dividend.

book value of subsidiary stock in excess of cost = *credit differential.*

book value per common the book value of common stock divided by the number of outstanding common shares.

book value per share amount of net assets applicable to each share of outstanding stock. *Also*: asset backing; asset value; asset value per share; net assets per share; net asset value per share.

book value rate = *accounting rate of return.*

boot <1> amount of cash paid when an old asset is exchanged for a new asset in a like-kind exchange. <2> = *boot dividend.*

boot dividend money or the fair market value of property of a party to the reorganization that is received by the target company or by the shareholders in exchange for their stock. *Also*: boot.

bootstrap a start-up company with very little capital.

bootstrap acquisition a transaction in which the assets of the acquired entity of property are used to fund the merger.

bootstrapping creating a theoretical spot rate curve using a yield projection as the basis for the yield of the next maturity.

bootstrap sale using the assets of a newly acquired company to pay part of the cost of buying the company.

bop. balance of payment

borrowed capital <1> cash dividends declared by corporation and retired by it pursuant to agreement with stockholders for operating business. <2> = *debt capital.*

borrowed reserve fund borrowed from a Federal Reserve bank by a member bank to maintain the required reserve ratio.

borrowed stock the stock borrowed for the performance of a short sale.

borrowing expense an expense incurred in borrowing money in addition to interest.

borrowing power = *debt capacity.*

Boston interest the interest computed by using a 30-day month, not the exact number of days in the month. *Also*: ordinary interest. *Opp*: *New York interest. See*: *360-days-per-year basis.*

Boston ledger a ledger with columnar accounts and trial balance. *Also*: accumulated ledger; journal ledger; ledger journal; progressive ledger; tabular ledger; tabulated ledger; trial balance ledger.

both principal and interest = *accumulated amount.*

bottom bracket the income bracket with zero tax rate in a tax table. *See: first tax bracket.*

bottom line *profit* or *loss* as it is shown at the bottom line of an *income statement. Also*: operating results. *See*: *top line.*

bottom-line allocation overall allocation of profits and losses of a partnership.

bottom-line consolidation the merger of a life insurance company and a non-life insurance company, in which income or loss is computed separately, and then added for tax purposes.

bottom of the harbor a method in which corporate founders strip the assets, fail to pay accrued tax liabilities, and then transfer the remaining ownership to a third party.

bought ledger = *purchase ledger.*

bounced check = *bad check.*

bound book a book bound as compared with a loose leaf book.

box option investing in equity options that generate capital gains instead of investing in money market instruments which generate ordinary income.

BP book profit

B/P bill payable

B. pay. bill payable

BPO bargain purchase option

B/R bill receivable

bracket = *tax bracket.*

bracket creep gradual movement of income into higher tax brackets due to inflation.

brain power the research and development staff of a company.

brainstorming a problem-solving method under which auditors sit together, share each other's idea, and find possible solutions to a problem.

branch account with double money columns branch account with invoice price column and the actual price column.

branch adjustment account an account for recording the difference between the branch sales receipts and the balance of the branch account which is recorded at the invoice price.

branch ledger a book at the head office and contains an a/c for each branch into which accounts are posted all the transactions between the branches and the head office.

branch profit tax a tax on the dividends received from a branch.

breakeven (B/E) a situation where income from sales equals expenses of production. *Also*: *balance.*

breakeven analysis a method of studying the profitability of a business or of a product by showing at what level or production costs are just covered by income. *Also*: indifference analysis.

breakeven chart (B/E chart) a graph showing the level of costs incurred and profits related to the activities. *Also*: chart of cost and revenue behavior; cost-volume-profit chart; director diagram; profit planning chart; revenue cost graph.

breakeven chart with profit appropriation a breakeven chart in which the lines of the profit distribution are drawn in its profit area.

breakeven chart with variable costs at base a breakeven chart where the variable cost curve is drawn from the "0" point, then fixed cost line is added in order to obtain the total cost curve. *Opp*: *traditional breakeven chart.*

breakeven diagram formula a formula showing the relation of every factor in breakeven analysis.

breakeven lease payment the lease payment at which a party is indifferent between entering and not entering into a lease.

breakeven payment rate the repayment rate of a mortgage-backed security that will produce the same cash flow yield as that of a benchmark.

breakeven point (BEP) point of activity at which sales equals costs, no income is earned.

breakeven point in dollars level of sales dollars required to cover all cost during a given period.

breakeven tax rate a tax rate at which a prospective investor to a project is indifferent between entering into and not entering into the transaction.

breakeven time the time needed for convertible bond's yield advantage to cover the premium, calculated by dividing the premium over conversion value by a convertible's current yield advantage over the underlying.

breakeven units the number of units that must be produced and sold to generate revenue sufficient enough to cover costs exactly incurred.

break fee <1> fee paid by a target company to bidders (during an acquisition) if the pending deal is terminated. <2> fee paid by one party of a contract to another in order to terminate or cancel legal obligations.

break sheet <1> a sheet prepared by a clearing house that lists all trades that do not match the submissions from brokerage house or a floor broker. <2> a sheet prepared by a broker based on discrepancies between a firm's books and a clearing house report.

break-up value <1> in an investment fund or an issue of a holding company, the value of the assets available for the issue, taking all the marketable securities at their market value. <2> = *liquidating value.*

bright line test a clear division between what is acceptable and what is not from a professional, or regulatory perspective.

brokerage cost the price change from the moment an order is placed with a broker until a trade is complete.

bro't for'd brought forward

brother-sister group a group of companies each holds 50% of the ownership of each other. ***See:*** *parent-subsidiary group.*

brought down (b/d) = *brought forward.*

brought forward (B/F)(b/f)(bro't for'd)(brt fwd) at the top of an a/c to show a total sum which has been carried forward from the last period. ***Also:*** brought down.

brought over (b/o) describes an amount which is to be brought forward from an earlier page.

B/S <1> balance sheet. <2> bill of sale. <3> buffer stock.

BT before tax

B to B = *business to business.*

B trust = *family trust.*

bucket a category of financial instruments separated for the analysis and measurement of risk. ***Also:*** bin.

bucketizing the process of dividing contractual or expected cash flows from diverse financial instruments into categories called *buckets.*

budget (B)(bud.) formal statement of future plans expressed in monetary items.

budget accounting = *governmental accounting.*

budgetary account a *nominal account* used to record approved budgetary estimate of revenue or expenditure. ***See:*** *regular account.*

budgetary basis statement financial statement of a government fund or agency based on a budget. ***See:*** *GAAP basis statement.*

budgetary control management control by making detailed comparisons of actual income and expense in order to make sure that plans are being kept to.

budgetary fund entity a fund entity where the budget is part of the accounting records.

budgetary spending the expenditure that is controlled by a budget.

budgetary transaction a transaction that affects the net indebtedness of the government.

budget at completion (BAC) original budget of the cost to complete a project. ***See:*** *estimate at completion.*

budget cost variance the difference between actual cost and budget cost.

budget-day value <UK> the value of an asset on April 6, 1965, used in calculating capital gains tax.

budget deficit amount by which government spending exceeds revenues. ***Also:*** deficit.

budgeted balance sheet a balance sheet that shows the effects of planned operations and planned capital investments on assets and equities, in the financial resources budget.

budgeted capacity variance that part of capacity variance caused by the difference between activity at practical level and the activity budgeted.

budgeted cost a cost, projected in its operating plans.

budgeted cost for work scheduled (BCWS) = *planned budget.*

budgeted cost of work performed (BCWP) = *earned value.*

budgeted financial statement the financial statement based on the budget figures.

budgeted income statement the income statement that ties together the results of the profit budget, summarizes the expected effect of planned operations on revenues, expense and income.

budget loan a mortgage loan that requires certain tax, insurance and assessment to be held in escrow in addition to the principal and interest.

budget model financial model which an organization uses to plan the financial effects of its future activities.

budget surplus = *surplus.*

budget variance the difference between the actual amount of expense and the budgeted amount for the volume of activity attained. *Also*: expense variance; flexible budget variance; spending variance.

buffer stock (B)(BS) inventory maintained by a company to safeguard against unpredictable shortages in further deliveries or to meet exceptional demand. *Also*: base stock; basic minimum inventory; inventory cushion; margin of safety; minimum stock; perpetual stock; safety inventory.

bug false data contained in the prospectus or financial statements.

building lease a lease of land for a long term, the lessee covenanting to build on it.

build-up approach a sales budgeting approach under which an estimate of how much an average buyer will buy in a particular time is calculated then multiply this by the number of potential buyers to generate potential sales.

built-in deduction taxable deduction such as depreciation, interest, theft loss, etc. which accrued in an economic sense in a separate return limitation year, but recognized in, or carried over to, a year in which the company becomes a member of a group.

built-in gain <1> the excess of fair market value over the adjusted basis of a property. <2> = *recognized built-in gain.*

built-in gain tax a tax on an S corporation's *net recognized built-in gain.*

bulk handling financing of accounts receivables in bulk rather than one at a time.

bulk sale the sale of inventory of a taxpayer's line of business to one buyer in a transaction.

bulk sales escrow an examination process designed to protect a buyer of a business from unknown liabilities.

bullet loan a term loan that calls for no amortization.

bunched cost lump sum costs which are not identifiable.

burden = *overhead.*

burden credit = *overhead applied.*

burden of proof the taxpayer's responsibility to prove that a tax return is accurate, or the IRS' responsibility to provide convincing evidence that it is inaccurate.

burden pool a group of labors separated for each skill category. *Also*: overhead pool.

burden rate = *overhead rate.*

burden vehicle = *basis of distribution.*

burned-out tax shelter a tax shelter which has become burdensome to the investor. *See*: *cross the line.*

burning cost ratio the ratio of excess losses to premium income. *Also*: pure loss cost.

burning out the exhaustion of the benefit of a tax shelter.

burning ratio <1> actual fire loss divided by the total value of the property exposed to the peril of fire. <2> losses resulting from fire divided by the total fire amount of inforce business.

burn rate the rate of negative cash flow per month, used to measure how long it will take for a start up to reach positive cash flow. *See*: *defensive-interval ratio.*

business asset an item you own for your business that you expect to last several years, such as a car, computer equipment, or office furniture.

business associate a person with whom the taxpayer could reasonably expect to engage or deal with in the active conduct of business.

business bad debt bad debt that qualifies for the ordinary loss treatment. *See*: *non-business bad debt.*

business combination = *merger.*

business combination law legislation governing related party transactions and mergers.

business corporation a corporation organized to carry out activities for profit. *Also*: corporation for profit; for-profit corporation. *Opp*: *nonprofit corporation.*

business cost = *business expense.*

business entity principle a basic rule that a business firm has an existence of its own, and should be separated from the persons who own or run it. *Also*: accounting entity principle; enterprise theory; entity theory.

business exigencies rule a rule applied to travel expenses that requires the transportation to be appropriate and helpful to the taxpayer in order to qualify for deduction.

business expense cost or expense necessary for producing the income of a trade or business. *Also*: business cost; cost of doing business; establishment charge.

business income <UK> income derived from a business. *Also*: profit from business.

business income tax <1> tax on income from a business. <2><Canada> income tax paid by a taxpayer to a foreign government.

business investment loss (BIL) <Canada> loss resulting from the disposal of a *capital asset* owned by a small company after 1977.

business judgement rule a rule that directors and officers can not be held liable to investors for business decisions that turned out to cause losses to the investors.

business loss <UK><Canada> excess of business expenses over revenue. *Also*: non-capital loss; loss from business.

business number <Canada> a number assigned by the Minister to identify a corporation or partnership. *See*: *federal ID number*.

business property a property used the ordinary course of business.

business rate <UK> = *business tax*.

business-related credit a tax credit only available to a business.

business risk the risk associated with a company's survival and profitability.

business start-up expense = *organization cost*.

business start-up relief <UK> tax relief allowed to the dividend up to £10,000 of a new company which has just started business for less than a year.

business tax a tax on the business, such as local tax, state and federal taxes. *Also*: business rate.

business to business (B2B) business conducted between companies, rather than between a company and individual consumers. *Also*: B to B.

business to business stock (B2B stock) stock issued by a company that serves e-commerce companies with software solutions that enable them to transact business with e-vendors.

business to consumer (B2C) business conducted between a company and individual consumers.

business to consumer stock (B2C stock) stock issued by a company that serves e-commerce companies with software solutions that enable them to transact business with e-customers.

business transaction an exchange of goods, services, money, and/or the right to collect money.

business trust an entity organized as a trust serving the same purposes as a business. *Also*: common-law trust; Massachusetts business trust; Massachusetts trust.

business-type accounting system governmental accounting system which uses the accrual basis. *Also*: cost-type accounting system.

business valuation (BV) process by which a supportable opinion about the worth of a business or individual assets or liabilities is produced.

business voucher = *supporting document*.

business year = *accounting year*.

busy season = *tax season*.

but-for income an income derived from a favorable variance in a cost element.

butterfly transaction <Canada> = *divisive D reorganization*.

buy in to purchase partnership interest and become a partner.

buy out to sell partnership interest and retire.

BV <1> book value. <2> business valuation.

by-laws the procedures for the establishment of a new company, which cover such things as the issue and the transfer of shares, procedures of the annual meetings, the voting rights, etc. ***Also***: articles of association; company by-laws. ***See***: *memorandum of association.*

bypass trust <1> = *credit-shelter trust.* <2> = *family trust.*

byproduct accounting method a method for assigning cost to byproduct inventory or recognizing byproduct as an asset in the balance sheet.

Byrun doctrine a theory that holds the gross estate of the decedent does not include stock transferred to a trust, even though the decedent retained the right to veto.

C c

C <1> capital. <2> cash. <3> contribution. <4> cost.

C/A <1> capital account. <2> capital asset. <3> credit account. <4> current account. <5> current asset.

CA <1> capital appreciation. <2> cash account. <3> chartered accountant. <4> chief accountant.

CAA conventional absorption accounting

CAAT computer assisted audit technique

CACA Chartered Association of Certified Accountants

CAE Certified Association Executive

cafeteria plan employer-sponsored benefit package that offers employees a choice between taking cash and receiving qualified benefits.

CAF number Centralized Authorization File number

CAFR comprehensive annual financial report

CAGR compound annual growth rate

calculated income = *taxable income.*

calculation account a temporary account used in calculating profit and loss. ***Also***: contrast account. ***See***: *contra account.*

calendar variance calculated as (working days in actual month - working days in standard month) × total number of working hours per day × fixed overhead absorption rate per hour.

calendar year accounting incurred losses insurance company, losses paid plus positive or negative changes in the year-end loss reserves during that particular year.

callable capital that part of the company's capital not yet paid up and on which the company may call for payments.

callable preferred stock preferred stock for which the issuing company retains the right or option to call in and retire the stock at a specified price. ***Also***: callable stock.

callable stock = *callable preferred stock.*

called-up capital <UK> that portion of the *unpaid capital* called to be paid. ***See***: *contributed capital; partly paid shares; uncalled capital.*

calling back cross referencing the entries with the posting medium in order to check the errors in posting.

calling over daily calling out of the day book figures with the current ledger accounts and the other books to which the items have passed.

call on contributory <UK> demand made by a company on persons liable to contribute to the assets.

call premium <1> the amount by which the redemption price exceeds the issue price of a callable bond or a preferred stock. ***Also***: redemption premium. <2> amount that the buyer of a call option has to pay to the option seller for the call option.

call report a quarterly financial report filed by a bank in compliance with regulatory requirements.

Calmar ratio a ratio used to determine return relative to risk in a hedge fund, which equals compounded annual return divided by the maximum drawdown.

Canada child tax benefit (CCTB) = *child tax benefit.*

Canada Customs and Revenue Agency (CCRA) <Canada> federal agency created by the Canada Customs and Revenue Agency Act for supporting the administration and enforcement of tax legislation. ***Formerly called***: *Revenue Canada Taxation.*

Canada Health and Social Transfer (CHST) <Canada> federal transfer provided to province in support of health care and post-secondary education.

Canada Pension Plan (CPP) <Canada> a contributory, income-related social insurance program against the loss of income due to retirement, disability or death.

Canada-US Tax Convention a tax treaty between Canada and the US signed in 1980.

Canadian-controlled private corporation (CCPC) <Canada> a corporation controlled by a Canadian citizen, eligible for *small business deduction.*

Canadian corporation a corporation owned by Canadian shareholders.

Canadian film or video production tax credit <Canada> a refundable tax credit of up to 12% of the eligible cost of a certified Canadian film or video production.

Canadian Institute of Chartered Accountants (CICA) <Canada> a body created by provincial institutes of chartered accountants to set standards, make representations to the federal government and handle international affairs.

Canadian partnership <Canada> partnership all member of which are resident in Canada.

cancellation <UK> payment received from the cancellation of a share option.

cancellation of debt (COD) creditor's relief of an indebtedness. ***Also***: acceptilation; cancellation of indebtedness; debt cancellation; debt forgiveness; discharge of debt; exemption of debt; quittance; release from debt; remission of debt.

cancellation of debt income the discharge of a taxpayer's liability for less than the face amount of an obligation. ***Also***: COD income; income from discharge of indebtedness.

cancellation of indebtedness = *cancellation of debt.*

cancelled check a check that has been paid by the bank. ***Also***: paid check.

cancelled debt a debt that has been cancelled by the creditor. ***Also***: forgiven debt. ***See:*** *loan written off.*

CAO chief accounting officer

capability profile a result of the appraisal of an organization's assets and liabilities.

capacity cost fixed cost incurred to provide facilities such as space and equipment. ***Also***: committed cost. ***See***: *programmed cost.*

capacity ratio <1> ratio of marginal output to maximum attainable output. <2> ratio of actual hours worked to budgeted hours.

capacity usage variance the cost variance caused by the delay in actual working hours due to strike, etc.

capacity utilization rate the ratio of actual output to the output under normal capacity.

capacity variance <1> that part of the volume variance caused by the difference between practical capacity and normal capacity. ***Also***: activity time variance; capacity volume variance; volume variance. <2> that part of cost variance caused by the difference between actual capacity and normal capacity. ***Also***: utilization variance.

capacity volume variance = *capacity variance.*

CAPE cash adjusted price/earnings ratio

capex money spent to acquire new assets or upgrade physical assets. ***Also***: capital expense; capital spending.

capital (c.)(cap.) <1> money, plant, and skills used to produce economic output. <2> long term debt plus owner's equity. <3> =

net asset. <4> = *net worth.* <5> = *owner's capital.*

capital account (CA)(C/A)(C a/c) <1> account for recording owner's equity. <2> a taxpayer's records of long term assets. <3> record of the expenditures to be capitalized. <4> in the balance of payments, the net result of public and private international investment and lending activities.

capital account balance <1> balance of the capital accounts in the balance of payments. <2> current balance in the owner's capital account.

capital accounting = *equity accounting.*

capital account method a method of accounting under which the partners' invested capital is recorded in a separate account. ***Opp***: *fixed capital method.*

capital acquisition tax = *accession tax.*

capital adequacy ratio (CAR) measurement of a bank's credit exposures, it equals capital divided by risk-weighted assets.

capital allowance <1> that portion of the gross national income which consists of depreciation. <2> deduction allowed in a tax assessment for expenses on certain capital equipment used. ***Also***: writing-down allowance. <3><UK> = *allowance for depreciation.*

Capital Allowances Act <UK> a law enacted in 2001 setting forth tax rules for capital allowances of fixed assets.

capital and interest = *accumulated amount.*

capital arrangement arranging the balance sheet items in the order of "fixed assets - current assets, and fixed liabilities - current liabilities". ***Also***: fixed-first-order of arrangement. ***Opp***: *current arrangement.*

capital asset (CA) <1> an asset except any of the following: inventories, trade account receivables, real asset and depreciable assets used in business, copyright, and government obligations due in one year. ***Also***: capital property; personal capital asset. <2> = *plant asset.*

capital asset pricing model (CAPM) a model developed by James Tobin and Bill Sharps, which treats the risk inherent in any financial instruments as being made of 2 components: the systematic risk and unsystematic risk. ***See***: *arbitrage pricing model.*

capital bonus <1> bonus based on the invested capital of a partner. <2> = *stock dividend.*

capital budget a budget listing capital or investment outlays and also the sources of finances needed to sustain them.

capital charges interest on invested capital and depreciation.

capital consumption that part of a company's investment used in the process of production. (depreciation plus accidental damage to fixed capital). ***Also***: user cost.

capital consumption adjustment the difference between capital consumption amount claimed on income tax returns and *capital consumption allowances.*

capital consumption allowance (CCA) <1> the amount that is measured at straight line method of depreciation, consistent service life and replacement cost. ***Also***: depreciation. <2> in the National Income and Products Accounts, charges against gross business product for the consumption of durable goods consisting of depreciation, destruction and accidental loss of physical capital.

capital cost (CC) <1> = *cost of capital.* <2> <Canada> = *plant asset cost.*

capital cost allowance (CCA) <Canada> portion of the cost of a plant asset allowed to be deducted as depreciation for income tax purpose.

capital cut-off point rate of interest point at which a company can acquire capital economically.

capital distribution = *return of capital.*

capital dividend a dividend paid out of the corporation's capital. ***Also***: dividend out of

capital; interest out of capital; paid in dividend; tax-free capital dividend.

capital duty <UK> a tax charged when the contributed capital is increased.

capital employed (CE) <1> the capital that is unrecovered at any point in the life of a project or a firm. <2> total assets less current liabilities plus bank overdrafts. <3> UK = *net worth.*

capital equation = *accounting equation.*

capital equity = *partner's equity.*

capital expenditure (CE) an expenditure that results in the creation, or improvement of a capital asset, and must be added to the amount of net assets, rather than deducted from current income. ***Also***: balance sheet expenditure; capital investment; capital outlay; charge to capital; long-term expenditure. ***Opp:*** *revenue expenditure.*

capital expenditures budget part of a financial budget, a listing of the plant and equipment to be bought if the proposed production program is carried out. ***Also***: plant and equipment budget.

capital expense = *capex.*

capital flight movement of capital from one investment to another in search of greater stability or return. ***Also***: flight of capital.

capital formation <1> development and accumulation of capital goods or producer goods for use in future production. <2> = *capital increment.*

capital from adjustment = *appraisal capital.*

capital from consolidation = *credit differential.*

capital from conversion of preferred stock to common stock an increase in capital account due to excess of the recorded value of common stock after conversion over the original book value of preferred stock before conversion.

capital from defaulted subscriptions that portion of the capital subscribed and paid by a shareholder who fails to pay the remaining portion of capital.

capital from donation = *donated capital.*

capital from redemption of capital stock an increase in capital due to the excess of book value of redeemed stock over its redemption price.

capital fund of banks or insurance companies, capital paid in by stockholders plus accumulated surplus.

capital fund/receivables of banks or insurance companies, a ratio of paid-in capital plus accumulated surplus to debts owed to finance companies.

capital gain (CG) proceeds from the sale of a *capital asset* exceeding the basis of that asset. ***See***: *portfolio income.*

capital gain dividend = *capital gains dividend.*

capital gain net income excess of gains from all the sales or exchanges of capital assets.

capital gain property capital asset if sold at its fair market value would result in a long term capital gain.

capital gains distribution a distribution to the shareholders of a mutual fund out of earnings.

capital gains distribution per share of an investment trust, disbursements to stockholders per share.

capital gains dividend mutual fund dividend that represents a distribution of earnings from the capital gains realized. ***Also***: capital gain dividend.

capital gains expense <UK> cost incurred in buying and selling a capital asset.

capital gains exposure = *potential capital gains exposure.*

capital gains inclusion rate = *inclusion rate.*

capital gains indexation allowance <UK> = *indexation allowance.*

capital gains refund <Canada> refund that is equal to the lesser of 14% of the total of all capital gains dividend paid by an investment corporation and its refundable capital gains tax on hand at the end of a tax year.

capital gains tax (CGT) <1> a tax on a security held for longer than six-months and

sold at a profit. <2><UK> a tax on capital gains of individual taxpayers, for companies they pay *corporation tax on chargeable gains.*

capital gains yield return on a stock as a result of price change.

capital gearing <UK> short- and long-term debt as a percentage of *net tangible assets.*

capital improvement permanent structure added to a real property that increases its value. ***See***: *betterment.*

capital in cash = *free capital.*

capital increment the transfer of retained earnings into capital account by the articles of incorporation. ***Also***: capital formation.

capital in excess of legal capital = *additional paid-in capital.*

capital inflow the incoming of foreign money into a country. ***Also***: afflux of capital; inflow of capital.

capital instrument an instrument issued as a means of raising capital.

capital interest = *dividend.*

capital invested = *owner's capital.*

capital investment = *capital expenditure.*

capital item <1> capital which may produce capital gain. <2> a separate item in the capital account, such as drawings. <3> industrial goods that enter the finished product partially, e.g. equipment.

capitalizable cost the cost that must be capitalized under the capitalization rule.

capitalization (cap.) <1> using a given rate of interest, the estimation of the capital sum, representing the total sum lent or the periodic value. <2> conversion of a company's assets into share capital by issuing more shares. <3> estimating the capital required to produce a given profit. The required capital equals profit divided by average rate of return. <4> the sum of long term bond and stockholder's equity. <5> = *invested capital.* <6> = *market capitalization.*

capitalization issue = *bonus share.*

capitalization of earnings a method of determining the amount of goodwill by the excess of total *capitalized value* over net assets. ***Also***: income capitalization.

capitalization of income determining the value of a business by dividing the present value of the possible future income of the business by the average rate of return. ***Also***: capitalized earnings approach.

capitalization of income method a method of valuation under which the value of the business is the present value of all future income.

capitalization of net cash inflows method = *direct valuation.*

capitalization rate <1> it equals capitalized profit ÷ net income. <2> it equals present value ÷ estimated future net income. <3> = *discount rate.* <4> = *return on investment.*

capitalization ratios analysis of a company's capital structures showing what percentage of the total is debt, preferred stock, common stock, and other equity. ***Also***: financial leverage ratios.

capitalization rule a rule under which some overhead costs of manufacturers or wholesaler with $10 million gross annual revenue must be capitalized. ***Also***: Section 263A.

capitalization table a table showing the capitalization of a business, such as the amount of capital obtained from each source.

capitalized cost portion of the cost of a plant asset that has been written off.

capitalized earnings approach = *capitalization of income.*

capitalized interest <1> non-deductible portion (50%) of the interest expense on the money borrowed using appreciated stock as collateral. <2><Canada> interest on money borrowed to acquire a property that is added to the cost of that property.

capitalized method a method of estimating the value of a fixed asset by subtracting anticipated expenses from anticipated revenue of the asset.

capitalized tax property tax, mortgage interest, sales tax, etc. that have been capitalized other than expensed.

capitalized value <1> estimated value of an asset calculated by reference to its current annual earnings at the prevailing interest rate. ***Also***: economic value; present value. <2> the value of an acquired company which has been transferred into the acquiring company's capital account.

capital lease a lease the ownership of the leased asset is transferred to the lessee at the end of the base period. ***Also***: financial lease; financing lease; full payout lease. ***See:*** *operating lease.*

capital leverage the effect to earnings per common share when large sum of income must be paid for bond interest or preferred dividends. ***See***: *financial leverage; operating leverage; Wall Street leverage.*

capital liability <1> the fixed liability incurred in order to obtain capital or capital assets. <2> = *net worth.* <3> = *owner's capital.*

capital loss (CL) a loss from the actual or constructive sale or exchange of a capital asset when proceeds is less than the tax basis in it.

capital loss carryback process of treating the excess of current year's net losses from the sale or exchange of capital assets as short-term capital losses in prior year.

capital loss carryovers long-term and short term capital losses that are not absorbed in the present taxable year but can be applied against income in following taxable years.

capital maintenance a concept that recognize a provision or segregation of income and capital required to avoid erosion of invested capital.

capital maintenance view = *asset-liability view.*

capital outlay = *capital expenditure.*

capital owned = *net worth.*

capital position = *financial position.*

capital projects fund a government fund to acquire or build capital assets.

capital property = *capital asset.*

capital rationing placing limits on the new investment either by fixing the cost of capital or setting a maximum on the capital budget.

capital receipt <Canada> compensation for loss of a capital asset of an enduring nature.

capital reconciliation statement = *statement of changes in financial position.*

capital recovery concept a concept which holds that a taxpayer should not be taxed in a trade if the result was the receipt of consideration short of the taxpayer's capital investment in property being disposed of.

capital recovery cost <1> investment cost in capital assets that must be recovered each period. <2> = *depreciation cost.*

capital redemption reserve an account that represents the nominal value of shares which have been redeemed in so far as the redemption was not paid for by the proceeds of a new issue of shares and is not a payment out of capital.

capital redemption yield the profit made by holding a dated stock until redemption.

capital replacement = *economical depreciation.*

capital requirement financing required for the operation of a business, e.g. long term debt and working capital.

capital reserve <1> an allowance accounting for only deficiency. ***Also***: undistributable reserve. ***See***: *revenue reserve.* <2> = *revaluation reserve.*

capital reversing capital-labor ratio in an economy may not necessarily continue to rise indefinitely as the rate of profit falls.

capital share a share issued by a dual purpose fund the holder of which receives only the long term capital gains on that fund's investments. ***See***: *income share.*

capital spending = *capex.*

capital statement a statement showing the increase, decrease and end-of-period balance of partnership capital.

capital stock (CS) the ownership equity in corporation that results from the sale of the shares of its stock. ***Also***: real capital stock; stock of capital.

capital stock adjustment principle a rule which suggests that the level of net investment in a proportion of the difference between the desired capital stock and the actual capital stock.

capital stock certificate = *stock certificate.*

capital structure <1> the makeup of liabilities and owners' equities of a business. <2> the ratios of loan and equity capital to total capital. <3> = *equity-debt ratio.*

capital structure expenditure = *cost of flotation.*

capital surplus <1> calculated as: total assets - total liabilities - issued capital - paid-in surplus - revenue surplus. <2> = *additional paid-in capital.*

capital surplus statement a statement showing the calculation of capital surplus.

capital tax <Canada> a federal tax on the capital of large corporations and financial institutions. ***Also***: Part 6 tax.

capital transaction a transaction that gives rise to long-term or short-term capital gains or loss.

capital turnover = *equity turnover.*

capital turnover rate = *equity turnover.*

capital turnover ratio a ratio designed to indicate efficiency in the use of capital by measuring the amount of sales activity in relation to the amount of capital employed to support such activity.

capitation = *poll tax.*

capitation tax = *poll tax*

CAPM capital asset pricing model

cap rate <1> discount rate used to determine the present value of a stream of future earnings. <2> = *return on investment.*

caption of account = *account title.*

CAR <1> capital adequacy ratio. <2> cumulative abnormal return.

car allowance an allowance paid for the business use of an employee's car.

card accounting old accounting which used a lot of cards in recording.

caregiver <Canada> a taxpayer who maintains a dwelling and supports a dependent. ***See***: *head of household.*

caregiver credit <Canada> a credit allowed to a taxpayer who is qualified as a caregiver.

Caribbean trust an offshore trust created in countries in the Caribbean Island.

carr. frd carried forward

carr. fwd carried forward

carried down (c/d) = *carried forward.*

carried forward (carr. frd)(carr. fwd)(c/f)(cd. fwd)(c/d fwd)(CF/FWD) describing the amount which has been carried forward to the next period. ***Also***: carried down.

carried interest portion of any gains realized by a mutual fund to which the fund managers are entitled.

carried over (c.o.)(c/o) describing the amount that has been carried to the next page.

carrot equity <UK><slang> equity investment with an opportunity to buy additional shares if the issuing company reaches certain financial objectives.

carry the difference between cost of financing the purchase minus the cash yield from the securities. ***Also***: cost of carry; net financing cost. ***See***: *negative carry; positive carry.*

carry-back <1> matching current expense with the revenue of the previous periods. <2> = *loss carry-back.*

carry forward <1> to defer current purchase cost to be matched with the future revenue. <2> to defer a tax credit or deduction to future periods. ***Also***: carry over. <3> = *loss carry-forward.*

carry income and loss the difference between the interest yield of a dealer's portfolio and the cost of the funds which support that portfolio. ***Also***: running margin.

carrying amount par value of a bond issue less any unamortized discount or plus unamortized premium. *Also*: amortized cost.

carrying charge <1> timber industry terms, cost incurred for fire protection, insect and disease control, property taxes, and other maintenance expense. <2> amount charged customers in transactions involving extension of credit, e.g. credit card sales. <3> an ongoing expense of maintaining a property.

carrying cost <1> the cost which varies with the average quantity on hand in inventory during the year. *Also*: cost of carrying inventory; cost of "having"; holding cost; inventory carrying cost; stockholding cost. <2><UK> cost the amount of which increases as the investment in current assets increases.

carrying loss = *monetary loss.*

carrying on business <Canada> carrying on a profession, calling, trade, manufacture or undertaking an adventure or concern in the nature of trade.

carrying value <1> = *book value.* <2> = *written down value.*

carry over = *carry forward.*

carryover basis a basis in property in the hands of a transferee determined by reference to the transferor's basis.

carryover dividend a component of dividends paid deduction of a personal holding company consisting of the excess of dividends paid in the prior two years over the company's taxable income, as modified.

CART Committee-Appointed Review Team

carved-out income <Canada> a taxpayer's income from carved-out properties.

carved-out property <Canada> a property with a maximum production output, such as a mine, petroleum or natural gas well, etc.

carve-out = *partial spinoff.*

CASB Cost Accounting Standards Board

cash actual cash on hand and at bank accounts.

cash accounting <UK> accounting under which value added tax is based on the amounts paid and amounts received in a tax year.

cash account method a method of preparing cash budget like a cash account.

cash adjusted price/earnings ratio (CAPE) P/E ratio of a company with a lot of cash on hand, adjusted to reflect the cash portion of the stock is worth exactly that amount.

cash and carry a tax avoidance method in which an investor buys and holds a security, and sells short of the same security at a higher price for quite a long time and treats the interests as a deductible expense.

cash and equivalent = *cash asset.*

cash asset an asset represented by actual cash on hand and at bank in the balance sheet plus *cash equivalent*. *Also*: cash and equivalent; dollar asset; spot asset.

cash asset ratio cash and marketable securities divided by current liability.

cash balance plan a hybrid pension plan that provides for the employer to contribute annually a percent of employee's salary, and if the employee should change employment, the balance can be transferred to an IRA.

cash basis the basis in which revenues are reported as being earned when received in cash and expenses are deducted in the period in which cash is disbursed. *Also*: cash method; cash receipts and disbursements method.

cash blotter = *blotter.*

cash book (CN)(c.b.)(c/b) = *cash journal.*

cash budget financial budget for cash inflows and outflows of a future period, including beginning cash balance, planned cash receipts, planned cash payments and ending balance.

cash charge a charge or expense that results in the payment of cash. *Also*: out-of-pocket expense.

cash collateral account (CCA) a supplementary cash position account that underlies an asset backed security to facilitate meeting cash flow requirements on the securities if pool payments lag and to provide a small amount of additional collateral. ***Also***: collateral investment account.

cash collection basis a basis in which installment sales are recognized only when they are collected in cash. ***See***: *installment sales method.*

cash conversion cycle = *cash cycle.*

cash cost <1> <Canada> cost of inventory maintained by a farmer. <2> = *out-of-pocket cost.*

cash cycle the length of time from the purchase of raw materials to the collection of cash after selling the final products. ***Also***: cash conversion cycle.

cash debt coverage ratio the ratio of net cash provided by operations to total liabilities.

cash-deposit ratio = *cash ratio.*

cash disbursements journal (CDJ)(D.) a special journal used to record only transactions involving cash disbursements. ***Also***: payout journal.

cash discount = *purchase discount.*

cash dividend declared dividends payable in cash or by check. ***See***: *dividend in kind; property dividend.*

cash drawer method a method under which profit is the money left over in the cash drawer.

cash earnings cash revenue in excess of cash expenses.

cash EPS ratio derived from operating cash flow divided by diluted shares outstanding.

cash equivalent <1> marketable security, Treasury bill or banker's acceptance that is considered cash asset. <2> benefit received that is the equivalent of cash, hence considered gross income of a cash method taxpayer.

cash equivalents doctrine a doctrine under which cash basis taxpayers are required to report income even though no cash is actually received if the cash equivalent is received.

cash expenditures method a method for showing any under-statement of income by matching annual expenditures, other than capital expense, with reported income. ***Also***: cash flow method; source and application of funds method.

cash flow (CF) <1> charge that affects the cash account balance. <2> the difference between cash inflows and cash outflows, usually the gross profit after tax plus depreciation and other non-cash charges. ***Also***: income stream.

cash flow accounting = *modified accrual.*

cash flow after interest and taxes (CFAIT) net income after interest expense and taxes plus depreciation.

cash flow after taxes (CFAT) net income after taxes plus depreciation.

cash flow break-even the activity level at which the cash flow generated by a business is enough to cover its fixed costs.

cash flow coverage of debt service = *cash flow coverage ratio.*

cash flow coverage ratio number of times that liabilities are covered by *earnings before interest, taxes, depreciation, amortization* and *rent*. ***Also***: cash flow coverage of debt service.

cash flow depreciation the depreciation calculated on the cash proceeds approach.

cash flow from operations the sum of net income, depreciation, change in accruals, and change in accounts payable, minus change in accounts receivable, and change in inventories. ***Also***: operating cash flows.

cash flow hedge using derivative instruments to hedge the exposure to variability in expected future cash flow. ***See***: *fair value hedge.*

cash flow method <1> a method for appraising investment alternatives by comparing their cash flows. ***Also***: cash flow technique;

insider view point approach. <2> = *cash expenditures method.*

cash flow per common = *cash flow per share.*

cash flow per share amount determined by adding depreciation and amortization charges to net income and dividing the result by the actual number of shares of common stock outstanding. ***Also***: cash flow per common.

cash flow ratio <1> the ratio of cash flow to sales of a particular period. ***Also***: ratio of cash flow to sales. <2> financial measure utilized by lenders and investors to evaluate the borrower's cash flow relative to the total interest, fixed charges debt service, or total debt of the firm.

cash flow return on investment (CFROI) valuation model that assumes the stock market sets prices based on cash flow, not on earnings and corporate performance, calculated as cash flow divided by the market value of capital employed.

cash flow statement a statement that accounts for the increase or decrease in a corporation's cash during a period by showing where it got cash and the uses it made of cash. ***Also***: flow statement; statement of cash flows; statement of cash receipts and disbursements.

cash flow surplus the surplus resulting from an additional amount of capital necessary to act as a supplement to the reserves in the event of contingencies that would impair the insurance company's ability to make future payments.

cash flow technique = *cash flow method.*

cash flow time line a line depicting the relationship between operating activities and cash flows of a business over a period of time.

cash flow yield the ratio of cash flows from operating activities divided by net income.

cash fraction <UK> distribution to a shareholder from the proceeds of selling the fractional shares after a merger or takeover.

cash generated by operations cash asset obtained from normal operations, calculated as revenue minus cash cost and cash expense. ***Also***: cash provided from operations.

cash journal a journal used to record only those transactions that involve cash receipts and disbursements. ***Also***: cash book; day-book cash journal.

cash loss the loss that actually reduces the cash. ***See:*** *tax loss.*

cash method = *cash basis.*

cash-on-cash = *cash on cash return.*

cash on cash return the return on investment calculated when there is no secondary market, usually equals annual cash earnings divided by total investment in cash. ***Also***: cash-on-cash.

cash-on-cash yield comparative measure using the total amount of distributions paid upon an income trust divided by its market value.

cash-on-hand requirement the level of cash needed in a business for daily operations, such as the making of payments to trade creditors and employees.

cash-out law the law that allows stockholders to sell their shares to a majority stockholder at a premium price.

cash payable method = *payback method.*

cash payment a payment made in cash or cash equivalent. ***Also***: money payment.

cash proceeds approach a method for depreciation based on the proportion of cash proceeds of each period. ***See***: *time-adjusted revenue method.*

cash provided from operations = *cash generated by operations.*

cash ratio <1> ratio of a bank's cash holdings and liquid assets to its total deposit liabilities. ***Also***: cash-deposit ratio; reserve ratio. <2> = *acid-test ratio.*

cash receipts and disbursements method = *cash basis.*

cash receipts journal (CR)(C/R)(CRJ)(R.) journal used to record only transactions involving cash receipts.

cash reserve (CR) cash reserved by a bank to meet the demands of its customers. ***Also***: till money.

cash return on gross investment (CROGI) measure of financial performance calculated as gross cash flow after taxes divided by gross investment.

cash schedule a statement prepared by a cashier each day to show any increase, decrease and balance, over and short and of cash he holds.

cash surrender value (CSV) amount an insurance company will return to the insured person on cancellation of the policy. ***Also***: surrender value.

cash voucher = *payment voucher*.

cash wages cash wages include wages paid by check, cash, or money order.

casino gaming industry all activities related to legalized gambling and the operations.

CASTA Computerized Accounting Tool Services

casual audit = *surprise audit*.

casual earnings <UK> taxpayer's income from irregular work.

casual sales exemption a transaction by any person other than an issuer, underwriter, or dealer that is exempt from registration under 1933 Act.

casualty the complete or partial destruction of property resulting from an identifiable event of a sudden, unexpected or unusual nature.

casualty and theft loss a loss caused by a hurricane, earthquake, fire, flood or similar event that is sudden, unexpected, or unusual.

casualty loss financial loss from an unexpected or unusual event. ***See***: *disaster loss*.

CAT Competency Assessment Tool

catch-all rule a method that treats only the amounts in excess of a taxpayer's investment in the annuity contract as income.

catch-up contribution a additional contribution, $3,000 to SEP and $1,500 to SIMPLE in 2004, by a taxpayer aged 50 or above.

catch-up depreciation = *amortization gap*.

catch up rule a principle that allows an individual participating in an eligible state deferred compensation plan electively to defer amounts that could have been, but were not, deferred within the $7,500/33.5% limit of includable compensation.

category method a method that applies *cost or market, whichever is lower* to different categories of inventory.

cattle breeding shelter a tax shelter in which the investor buys an interest in a herd of cattle to be bred with a view to profitable sales of the progeny.

cattle feeding shelter a tax shelter that can offer substantial deferral opportunities, designed to provide major deductions for the cost of feed, with a reversal of the deduction when the cattle are sold.

cause and effect costing = *direct costing*.

C/B cash book

c. b. cash book

CBO Congressional Budget Office

CBT Computer Based Testing

C.C. <1> capital cost. <2> current cost.

CCA <1> capital cost allowance. <2> cash collateral account. <3> current cost accounting.

CCL climate change levy

C corporation any company other than an S corporation. ***Also***: applicable corporation; ineligible corporation.

CCPC Canadian-controlled private corporation

CCRA Canada Customs and Revenue Agency

CCS earnings = current cost of supplies income.

CCS income current cost of supplies income

CCTB Canada child tax benefit

CD cash disbursements journal

c.d. cum dividend

c/d carried down

C/D cash disbursements journal

CDC community development corporation

cd fwd carried forward

CDJ cash disbursements journal

CDTA current deferred tax asset

CE <1> capital expenditure. <2> cash earnings.

ceiling amount the amount not less than $20,000 under a tax rate category in a tax table.

ceiling limitation net realizable value of an inventory item, it equals selling price less selling cost and cost to complete. *See*: *floor limitation.*

cemetery care trust <Canada> a trust created for the care and maintenance of a cemetery. ***Also***: perpetual care fund.

center-ruled ledger a ledger with the amounts column in the center.

Centralized Authorization File number (CAF number) a number assigned by the IRS to a representative of a taxpayer.

cents column two small rows for recording cents in the amounts column.

cents less accounting an accounting practice in which the last two digits of dollar and cents are eliminated and amounts are recorded in whole dollars. ***Also***: whole dollar accounting.

cents per share dividend or a mutual fund's distribution that a shareholder receives for each share owned.

CEO chief executive officer

certainty equivalent amount received today in lieu of a chance to receive a possibly higher, but uncertain amount. *See*: *present value.*

certificate = *stock certificate.*

certificate of audit = *auditor's report.*

certificate of balance sheet auditor's certificate to balance sheet only.

certificate of capital stock = *stock certificate.*

certificate of incorporation = *articles of incorporation.*

certificate of independent public accountants = *auditor's report.*

certificate of stock = *stock certificate.*

certificate of tax clearance a certificate issued when evidence establishes that no debt is owed to the Department of Treasury. ***Also***: federal tax clearance certificate; tax clearance certificate.

certificate of tax deposit <UK> a certificate purchased from the Inland Revenue by a taxpayer to pay advance tax.

certificate of value <UK> a certificate stating that the consideration in a transfer of property does not exceed certain amount.

certified financial statements financial statements in which the auditor's question to doubts, limitations or disagreements over any item have been made. ***Also***: audited books; audited financial statements; qualified accounts.

certified fraud examiner (CFE) a member of the Association of Certified Fraud Examiners specialized in fraud examinations.

Certified Information System Auditor (CISA) professional designation in the area of computer system audits, conferred by the EDP Auditor Association.

Certified Internal Auditor (CIA) an international certification awarded by the IIA that reflects competence in the principles and practices of internal auditing.

Certified Management Accountant (CMA) <1> title bestowed by the IMA on persons meeting certain requirements, principally an exam covering economic theory, financial management, and cost accounting, etc. <2><UK> the title bestowed by the CIMA.

certified property <Canada> property that is a building or machinery and equipment used in a manufacturing or processing operation.

certified public accountant (CPA) a person who has met requirements as to education, experience, moral character, age etc. and has been licensed to practice public accounting. *Also*: chartered accountant; chartered public accountant.

CESG Canada education savings grant

CEV credit equivalent value

C/F <1> carried forward. <2> carry forward.

CFAIT cash flow after interest taxes

CFAT cash flow after taxes

CFC controlled foreign corporation

CFE certified fraud examiner

CFO chief financial officer

CFROI cash flow return on investment

CG capital gain

CGS cost of goods sold

CGT capital gains tax

chain liquidation the liquidations of parent and subsidiaries.

chance variances = *random variances.*

change fund an imprest fund used to facilitate the collection of money from customers.

change in accounting estimate <1> change of estimated financial statement amount based on new information or experience. <2> increase in the percentage used to estimate the doubtful accounts expense, a major write down of inventory due to obsolescence, a change in the estimated economic life of fixed assets, a change in the estimated recoverable units of natural resources, and a revision in the amount of estimated liability for product warranties.

change in accounting method a switch by a taxpayer from one overall method of accounting for income to a different method or a change in the treatment of a material item.

change in accounting principles the adoption of another alternative GAAP which is clearly preferable.

change in financial position a change in the cash flow, source of funds and capital expenditures etc.

change in reporting entity a change that results in the financial statements representing a different entity.

change of business a change in the continuity of a business, e.g. changes in employees, location, equipment, products, or other significant items.

changing percentage of cost less scrap method a depreciation method in which the cost less scrap value is used as the basis, and the rate of depreciation varies in different periods.

channel check method of independent stock analysis whereby company information is supplied by third parties.

channel stuffing deceptive business practice used by companies to artificially inflate sales and earnings figures.

Chapter 7 provisions of the Bankruptcy Reform Act under which the debtor firm's assets are liquidated by a court.

Chapter 11 provisions of the Bankruptcy Reform Act under which the debtor firm is reorganized by a court.

character subject to depreciation = *depreciable asset.*

chargeable asset <UK> an asset that is not exempt from capital gains tax on a disposal.

chargeable business asset <UK> an asset used for the purpose of a trade, profession of business that is subject to capital gains tax.

chargeable event <UK> an event that triggers income tax on the proceeds received from a life insurance policy, e.g. death, maturity, surrender or assignment of the policy etc.

chargeable premium <UK> taxable income received as a premium from a lease.

chargeable transfer <UK> for inheritance purpose, a transfer of value made by an individual that is not an exempt transfer.

charge and discharge statement summary of the principal and income associated with a fiduciary responsibility.

charge back provision a provision that requires allocations of income or gain to a partner with reference to losses or deductions previously allocated to that partner.

charge for credit = *interest.*

charge notice = *debit memorandum.*

charge-off <1> = *bad debt.* <2> = *write-down.*

charge-off method = *direct method.*

charge on income = *income deduction.*

charge side = *debit side.*

charge to capital = *capital expenditure.*

charge to income = *income deduction.*

charging profit and loss method charging an item to the profit and loss account rather than recognizing it as an income or expense.

charitable bail-out donation of shares in a closely-held corporation, which redeems them.

charitable contribution amount given to a charitable organization. ***Also***: contribution.

charitable donation credit <Canada> a tax credit allowed to a taxpayer who made some charitable donation during the tax year.

charitable gift annuity an annuity that guarantees a stream of lifetime payment to a taxpayer who made a gift to a charity.

charitable remainder trust a trust to be funded by the remainder of an estate.

charitable trust a trust the beneficiaries of which are charitable in nature. ***Also***: public trust. ***See***: *private trust.*

charter = *articles of incorporation.*

chartered accountant (CA) <UK> = *certified public accountant.*

Chartered Association of Certified Accountants (CACA) <UK> a professional body established in 1904. (www.acca.org.uk)

Chartered Institute of Management Accountants (CIMA) <UK> founded in 1919, a professional body for management accountants with designatory letters CMA.

Chartered Institute of Public Finance and Accountancy (CIPFA) <UK> founded in 1885, a professional body for members who have posts in central or local government. www.cipfa.org.uk

Chartered Institute of Taxation (CIOT) <UK> senior professional body in the UK specializing in taxation. (www.ciot.org.uk)

chartered public accountant = *certified public accountant.*

chart of accounts a complete listing of all the accounts used in the general ledger and their identifying number. ***Also***: account classification; classification of accounts.

chart of cost and revenue behavior = *breakeven chart.*

chattel = *personal property.*

cheap stock a stock which is sold at a price lower than its true value while the company is still in a stage of development or promotion.

cheat sheet financial document supplied to a prospective investor by a bank without reporting to the SEC.

check digit a digit appended to a number to assure its accuracy.

check income the income recognized when a cash-basis taxpayer receives a check from the solvent payer.

checking the accounts daily writing of all checks and creditors on a check ledger, the items then are called back against the ledger postings as a check on accuracy.

check in transit = *outstanding check.*

check kiting = ***kiting.***

check ledger a book used in an old system of hand-written bookkeeping whereby the debit and credit postings in the bank's current a/c ledgers were checked against similar items independently entered in books.

check-the-box regulations rules that permit an unincorporated entity to choose to be taxed as a partnership or a corporation by checking a box on Form 8832.

ChFC Chartered Financial Consultant

chief executive officer (CEO) the officer of a firm who is principally responsible for the activities.

chief financial officer (CFO) an executive officer in a firm responsible for handling funds, collecting and reporting financial data.

chief information officer (CIO) an executive officer in a firm responsible for information and related issues.

chief judge the judge of the Tax Court who is in charge.

chief operating officer (COO) senior manager whose responsibility is to manage the day-to-day operations of the company and then report this to the CEO.

child and dependent-care credit tax credit that offsets part of child care expense for a child under the age of 13 or disabled. ***Also***: child-care credit. ***See***: *child credit*.

child-care credit = *child and independent-care credit.*

child care expense money paid for someone to look after a taxpayer's child while he or she is working. ***Also***: child minding expense.

child care expense deduction <Canada> a tax deduction allowed to a taxpayer who has to pay child care expense. ***Also***: Section 8 deduction.

child care tax credit <UK> a tax credit available to taxpayers with a child under 11 years old.

child credit tax credit of $1,000 in 2003 for each child under age 17 as a dependent. ***Also***: child tax credit. ***See***: *child and dependent-care credit.*

child minding expense <UK> = *child care expense.*

child support payments made under a divorce or separation agreement for the support of a child.

child tax benefit <Canada> an annual tax credit to families with children, $2,372 for the first child and $2,172 for each additional child. ***Also***: Canada child tax benefit. ***See***: *national child benefit.*

child tax credit = *child credit.*

child with special needs a child with a medical condition or physical, mental or emotional handicaps.

China Trade Act corporation a company subject to special deduction for income derived from Taiwan and Hong Kong.

Chinese wall legal barrier between audit and non-audit operations within an audit client when a CPA provides both audit and non-audit services. ***Also***: ethical wall; firewall; green baize door.

CHST Canada Health and Social Transfer

churning transferring property in order to qualify it for cost recovery under accelerated cost recovery system.

CI compound interest

CIA <1> certified internal auditor. <2> collateral investment account.

CIAS Center for Investment Advisory Services

CIBT cash income before taxes

CIC cost improvement cost

CICA Canadian Institute of Chartered Accountants

CIMA Chartered Institute of Management Accountants

CIO chief information officer

CIOT Chartered Institute of Taxation

CIP construction in progress

CIPFA Chartered Institute of Public Finance and Accountancy

circulated financial statement = *published financial statement.*

circulating asset = *current asset.*

circulating capital = *working capital.*

circulating liability = *current liability.*

CISA Certified Information System Auditor

CITP Certified Information Technology Professional

civil damage money paid under judgements and out-of-court settlements.

civil tax penalty a penalty imposed by the IRS and which are not classified as being criminal in nature. *Also*: addition to tax; ad valorem penalty. *See*: *criminal tax penalty*.

CJJ completed job journal

CL <1> capital loss. <2> current liability.

claim expense cost incurred in adjusting an insurance claim.

claim for refund request for a refund of, or credit against any tax.

class a category of assets having a similar nature, function or use in the business.

class 1 national insurance contribution <UK> national insurance contribution deducted from an employee taxpayer's earnings.

class 1 property <Canada> a bridge, canal, dam, road, sidewalk etc. with a 4% capital cost allowance.

class 2 national insurance contribution <UK> national insurance contribution paid by a self-employed taxpayer weekly.

class 2 property <Canada> electrical generating equipment with a 6% capital cost allowance.

class 3 national insurance contribution <UK> national insurance contribution paid voluntarily by a taxpayer.

class 3 property <Canada> building or other structure with a 5% capital cost allowance.

class 4 national insurance contribution <UK> national insurance contribution paid by a taxpayer who runs a business.

class 4 property <Canada> a railway system with a 6% capital cost allowance.

class 5 property <Canada> property of a chemical pulp mill with a 10% capital cost allowance.

class 6 property <Canada> building of frame, log, corrugated metal etc. with a 10% capital cost allowance.

class 7 property <Canada> a canoe or rowboat with a 15% capital cost allowance.

class 8 property <Canada> manufacturer's plant asset with a 20% capital cost allowance.

class 9 property <Canada> electrical generating equipment with a 25% capital cost allowance.

class 10 property <Canada> automobile with a 30% capital cost allowance.

class 11 property <Canada> property used to generate rental income with a 35% capital cost allowance.

class 12 property <Canada> book, kitchen utensil, medical equipment etc. with a 100% capital cost allowance.

class 13 property <Canada> leasehold interest with a 100% capital cost allowance.

class 14 property <Canada> franchise, license or a patent with a 100% capital cost allowance.

class 15 property <Canada> timber cutting equipment with a 100% capital cost allowance.

class 16 property <Canada> aircraft and attached furniture or equipment with a 40% capital cost allowance.

class 17 property <Canada> telephone system with an 8% capital cost allowance.

class 18 property <Canada> motion picture film with a 60% capital cost allowance.

class 19 property <Canada> class 8 property acquired from Jun 13, 1963 to Jan 1, 1967.

class 20 property <Canada> class 3 or 6 property acquired from Dec 5, 1963 to Apr 1, 1967.

class 21 property <Canada> class 8 or 19 property acquired from Dec 5, 1963 to Apr 1, 1967.

class 22 property <Canada> property acquired after Mar 16, 1964 and before 1988 or 1990.

class 23 property <Canada> leasehold interest to expire not later than Jun 15, 1968 with a 100% capital cost allowance.

class 24 property <Canada> property acquired after Apr 26, 1965 and before 1971.

class 25 property <Canada> property acquired before Oct 23, 1968 with a 100% capital cost allowance.

class 26 property <Canada> a catalyst or heavy water acquired after May 22, 1979 with a 5% capital cost allowance.

class 27 property <Canada> property acquired before 1999 that would otherwise be included in another class.

class 28 property <Canada> property located in Canada acquired before 1988 or 1990 that would otherwise be included in another class.

class 29 property <Canada> property not included in class 41.

class 30 property <Canada> unmanned telecommunication spacecraft owned by a taxpayer.

class 31 property <Canada> multiple-unit residential building with 5% capital cost allowance.

class 32 property <Canada> multiple-unit residential building that would otherwise be included in class 6 with 10% capital cost allowance.

class 33 property <Canada> timber resource property with 15% capital cost allowance.

class 34 property <Canada> property that would otherwise be included in class 1, 2 or 8.

class 35 property <Canada> railroad car acquired after May 25, 1976.

class 36 property <Canada> depreciable property acquired after Dec 11, 1979.

class 37 property <Canada> property used in connection with amusement park with 15% capital cost allowance.

class 38 property <Canada> property not included in class 22.

class 39 property <Canada> property acquired after 1987 and before Feb 26, 1992.

class 40 property <Canada> property acquired after 1987 and before 1990.

class 41 property <Canada> property not included in class 41.

class 42 property <Canada> property that is fiber-optic cable.

class 43 property <Canada> property acquired after Feb 25, 1992 that is not included in class 29.

class 44 property <Canada> a patent for a limited or unlimited period.

class A share mutual fund share with identical features, such as *front-end load.*

class A stock one class of common stock that has advantage over class B stock in terms of voting power. ***See***: *voting stock.* (In UK, *A share* has no voting power, while in the USA class A stock has voting power). ***See***: *series A.*

class B share mutual fund share with identical features, such as *back-end load.*

class B stock one class of common stock which ranks behind class A stock in terms of voting power. ***See***: *nonvoting stock.* (In UK, *B share* has voting power, while in the US class B stock has no voting power).

class costing accumulation of cost data by class. ***Also***: lot costing.

classical variables sampling audit sampling that uses normal distribution theory to evaluate selected characteristics of a population on the basis of a sample.

classification separation of assets or liabilities into several groups.

classification method a method under which plant assets are categorized by function with differing depreciation ratios applied to each class. ***Also***: depreciation by kind.

classification of accounts = *chart of accounts.*

classification of fixed and variable costs = *determination of cost behavior.*

Classification Settlement Program (CSP) program that will allow businesses and tax examiners to resolve worker classification cases as early in the administrative process as possible, thereby reducing taxpayer burden.

classified asset an asset segregated according to function without regard to useful life, e.g. machinery and equipment, furniture and fixtures, or transportation equipment, grouped for depreciation purposes.

classified balance sheet a balance sheet with assets and liabilities classified into significant groups: current assets, long-term investment, plant assets, intangibles, current liabilities, long-term liabilities, and owners' equities. ***Also***: sectional balance sheet.

classified capital structure = *complex capital structure.*

classified financial statement a statement which groups all accounts in classifications in order to present more meaningful information.

classified, multiple-step income statement a classified income statement on multi-step approach. ***Also***: multi-step classified income statement.

classified stock equity securities divided into categories which have different rights, e.g. class A stock has voting power and class B stock does not. ***Also***: multiple voting share.

class life = *guideline life.*

class life period a component of the reserve ratio test for depreciation of pre 1971 assets to determine if the retirement and replacement practices for assets are within the guidelines for the class life used.

class of intangible assets <UK> a category of intangible assets having a similar nature, function or use in the business.

clawback = *dividend clawback.*

clawback tax <Canada> a tax on federal Old Age Security benefits.

clean balance sheet balance sheet of a company with very little or no debt.

clean bill of health by auditor = *unqualified opinion.*

clean-burning fuel deduction = *credit for qualified hybrid vehicles.*

clean opinion = *unqualified opinion.*

clean surplus concept = *all inclusive concept.*

clearing account <1> an account for recording the credit difference after the balance of trade between two countries is offset against each other. <2> = *suspense account.*

clearing fee a fee charged by clearing corporations for services provided to investment firms.

clearing house statement report on a security broker's trading activity.

client a person or company that consults a CPA or tax professional.

climate change levy (CCL) <UK> a levy on energy products such as electricity, natural gas, petroleum, coal, oil heat, etc.

clinging cost = *product cost.*

clinical testing expense any expense for testing certain drugs in a clinic.

clogged loss <UK> loss that can only be set against the gains of certain type.

close combination the merger of companies, whereby stockholders relinquish their stock to a board of trustees who then issue certificates and cash dividends. ***Also***: trust.

closed account = *account in balance.*

closed company = *private company.*

closed transaction a transaction the amount on a sale can be established, so that a gain or loss can be viewed as realized.

close investment holding company <UK> a closed-end investment holding company that does not have lower tax rates available.

close period the time period between the completion of a company's financial statements and the announcing of the results to the public.

closing account a method by which foreign trade balances between two countries are offset. ***Also***: final account.

closing balance = *ending balance.*

closing balance account an account with no balance carried forward from the last period. ***See***: *opening balance account.*

closing cost the cost associated with the purchase of a real estate, including attorney's fee, title recording fee, title insurance, and points paid to the bank, etc.

closing entry an entry made to close and clear all the revenue and expense accounts and to transfer net income or cost to a capital account or to the retained earnings account.

closing inventory = *ending inventory.*

closing rate the exchange rate on the date when the financial statements of multinational companies are combined.

closing rate method a method of converting foreign subsidiary statements by using the exchange rate of the closing date.

closing statement = *final statement.*

closing the accounts the act of transferring the balances in the expense and revenue accounts to the income summary account and then to the owners' equity account.

closing the books the act of trial balance and adjusting entries and post-adjustment trial balance, after closing the accounts. *Also*: closing the ledger.

closing the ledger = *closing the books.*

closing trial balance = *after closing trial balance.*

closing work-in-process the value of the work-in-process at the end of an accounting period. *Also*: ending work-in-process; final goods-in-process; work in process at close.

CLTV combined loan to value ratio

CM <1> contribution margin. <2> credit memorandum.

CMA Certified Management Accountant

CMA sampling cumulative monetary amount sampling

CMS cost management system

CNI consolidated net income

CNIL cumulative net investment loss

C.O. carried over

c/o carried over

Cobra Consolidated Omnibus Budget Reconciliation Act

COD cancellation of debt

code of accounts = *account code number.*

COD income = *cancellation of debt income.*

COE cost of equity

Cohan rule a rule under which deductible expenses may be allowed based on an estimate even when there is no documentation.

coin-operated employee an employee hired for a particular project or for a given period of time. *See: temporary helper.*

cola cost of living adjustment

cold review the review of audit working papers by a second partner from another CPA firm. *Also*: second-partner review. *See*: *peer review.*

collapsible corporation a corporation that is liquidated or sold before the expiration of three years after the manufacture, construction or purchase of certain property is completed, and before it realizes 2/3 of the income derived from that property.

collapsing a transaction = *step transaction doctrine.*

collateral investment account (CIA) = *cash collateral account.*

collateral security asset given in addition to a collateral to guarantee the performance of a contract.

collateral transaction agreement between tax payer and the IRS regarding a matter related to the disposition of a pending case.

collection float <1> the total amount presented for payment, or the conversion of any accounts receivable into cash. *Also*: bank collection float. <2> = *float period.*

collection fraction percentage of a month's sales collected during the month and the sales of each following month.

collection gain the gain realized when a creditor is paid by the debtor in an amount greater than the adjusted basis of the debt.

collection of taxes the procedure by which the IRS collects taxes imposed by law.

collection period = *number of days' sales in receivables.*

collection period ratio = *number of days' sales in receivables.*

collection ratio = *number of days' sales in receivables.*

collective account = *controlling account.*

collective fund a fund that combines tax exempt assets of various individuals and organizations in order to create a well diversified portfolio.

college credit = *education credit.*

college prepaid tax plan a program created by certain states that enables a taxpayer to defer earnings from the plan's assets until withdrawn for tuition payments.

college savings tax plan a tax-deferred plan under which a taxpayer can accumulate funds for a child's education through investment in securities and mutual funds.

columnar account an account with an extra column called the analysis column. ***Also***: divided account; multicolumn account.

columnar book a book designed to analyze the sales, expenses, etc. with columnar accounts. ***Also***: dissection book; tabular book.

columnar budget a budget having analysis columns for the semi-variable overhead.

columnar journal a journal having columns for entering specific data about each transaction of a group of like transactions. ***Also***: analytical journal; divided-column journal; multi-column journal; special-column journal; split-column journal.

columnar method a flexible budgeting method whereby several budget allowances are set under actual investigations. ***Also***: physical inspection method.

columnar work sheet a work sheet having analysis columns. ***Also***: analytical worksheet.

column-total posting the posting of the column totals of a special journal to ledger account.

combat pay tax-free payment received by members of the US Armed Forces and support personnel in combat zones, including peace keeping efforts.

combination basis of distribution a basis under which the fixed costs are distributed by the capacity of consumption, and the variable costs are distributed by the actual service consumed. ***Also***: dual basis of distribution.

combination cash journal the journal for recording all the cash transactions and their related transactions.

combination of the production and the straight line method a method under which half of the fixed assets are depreciated by the production method, and the other half by straight line method.

combination program a method of profit sharing under which half of the profit is shared by cash method and the other half is shared by deferral method.

combination report an auditor's report for both credit and management purposes.

combined approach combining constant dollar accounting and current cost accounting for financial reporting purpose.

combined balance sheet a balance sheet of all fund types and account groups of a government based on GAAP.

combined cost = *joint cost.*

combined costing method a combination of the absorption and variable cost methods.

combined depreciation and upkeep method a depreciation method whereby the upkeep costs are added to the asset costs to be depreciated in the asset life.

combined entry = *compound journal entry.*

combined financial statement a statement including the data of both head and branch office or of two or more companies or of companies under common control. ***Also***: composite financial statement. ***See***: *consolidated financial statement; group financial statement.*

combined income and earned surplus statement = *statement of income and retained earnings.*

combined income and retained earnings statement = *statement of income and retained earnings.*

combined journal a journal which has special columns for the same kind of transactions.

combined journal and ledger a journal used in old bookkeeping systems having the function of a ledger. *See*: *Boston ledger.*

combined loan to value ratio (CLTV) the ratio of the combined principal on a homeowner's first mortgage and a home equity loan to the value of the home.

combined national balance sheet = *national balance sheet.*

combined overhead rate combination of the fixed and variable overhead rates.

combined overhead rates method a method under which different overhead rates are applied to different overheads in the same center.

combined ratio of an insurance company, the sum of the loss ratio and the expense ratio, with a combined ratio of 100%, indicating breakeven, above 100% a profit. *See*: *exchange ratio; loss ratio.*

combined statement of cash flows cash flow statement of all proprietary and nonexpendable trust funds of a government.

combined statement of income and retained earnings = *statement of income and retained earnings.*

combined statement of income and surplus = *statement of income and retained earnings.*

combined statement of receipts and expenditures, balances etc. the statement showing cash receipts, disbursements and balance. *Also*: statement of cash receipts, disbursements and balance.

combined variance = *joint variance.*

combining statement individual fund statement presented side by side in adjacent columns, with a total column.

comfort letter a letter from an independent auditor required in the securities underwriting agreements to assure that information in the SEC registration statement and prospectus is correctly prepared and that no material changes have occurred since its preparation date. *Also*: accountant's letter; accountant's opinion; letter for underwriters.

comment letter <1> a letter from a CPA to an underwriter as part of that underwriter's due diligence. <2> a letter from the SEC which describes deficiencies or requests additional information be included in the prospectus.

commercial domicile the principal place from which the trade or business of a taxpayer is directed or managed.

commercial property real property used in income-producing activities.

commercial year <1> a year treated as having 12 months of 30 days each. <2> = *accounting year.*

commission <1> an entry that is posted to another account by mistake. *Also*: error of commission. <2> compensation based on a percentage of sales or a fixed amount.

commitment fee a fee paid to a commercial bank for commitment to lend funds that have not been advanced.

committed asset = *trade asset.*

committed cost = *capacity cost.*

commodity quota = *declared period quota.*

commodity tax straddle a strategy in which an investor profits from a commodity trading, then looks for a capital loss with which to offset income.

common-base-year analysis = *common-size analysis.*

common cost <1> = *irrelevant cost.* <2> = *joint cost.* <3> = *overhead.*

common denominator = *equivalent production.*

common depreciation method = *composite depreciation method.*

common dividend a dividend paid to the stockholder of common stock. *Also*: common stock dividend; discretionary dividend. *See: preferred dividend.*

common dollar accounting = *constant dollar accounting.*

common dollar financial statement = *constant dollar financial statement.*

common equity percent ratio of common stock and surplus to total capital.

common expense = *overhead.*

common fixed cost = *fixed overhead.*

common-law partner trust <Canada> = *joint spousal trust.*

common law trust <1> = *business trust.* <2> = *pure trust.*

common paymaster an agent who handles the payroll for two or more companies that hire the same individual. (FICA and FUTA taxes are paid based on the combined wages).

common period cost = *fixed overhead.*

common plant overhead = *general overhead.*

common production expense = *factory overhead.*

common reserve fund = *appropriated retained earnings.*

common-size analysis selecting accounts on financial statements, such as fixed assets, cost of goods sold and various overhead expense accounts, and expressing them as percentages to allow comparisons between different firms. *Also*: common-base-year analysis.

common-size balance sheet a balance sheet in which total assets are set as the base amount and is expressed as 100%, other items will be expressed as a percentage of the total assets. *Also*: 100% balance sheet; percentage balance sheet.

common-size comparative statement comparative financial statement in which each item is expressed as a percentage of a base amount.

common-size income statement an income statement in which net sales is set as the base amount, and other items will be expressed as a percentage of the base amount. *Also*: income statement, 100% ; 100% income statement; 100% profit and loss statement; percentage income statement.

common stock a stock that represents an equity in a corporation. *Also*: equity share; junior equity. *See*: *preferred stock.*

common stock dividend = *common dividend.*

common stock equivalent = *convertible security.*

common stockholders' equity = *residual equity.*

common stock ratio <1> ratio of the value of common stock to total capitalization. <2> = *equity-to-assets ratio.*

communal organization = *congregation.*

community income the income from *community property* held by a married couple.

community property a property that belongs to both husband and wife.

commutation payment <Canada> lump-sum payment from a registered retirement savings plan that is equal to the current value of all future payments.

commuting cost the commuting cost between taxpayer's home and work site regardless of the mode of transportation.

company = *corporation.*

company by-laws = *by-laws.*

company car a car provided to an employee by the company.

company doctor an executive hired from outside to solve the company problems.

company limited by guarantee <UK> a company the liability of shareholders is limited by the amount needed to be contributed to the company by the memorandum of association.

company limited by shares <UK> a company that liability of shareholders is limited by the unpaid share capital.

company secretarial budget a budget which includes registration expenses, legal fees, pension fund, insurance etc.

company secretary <UK> = *corporate secretary.*

company tax <New Zealand> a tax on the profit of domestic companies, superannuation funds and unit trusts.

company-wide overhead application rate = *single overhead allocation rate.*

comparability concept a concept which states that accounting data in different periods are comparable.

comparability principle a principle which requires every subsidiary in the same group should use the same accounting procedures.

comparable companies the companies that are similar to a subject company under analysis.

comparable profits method (CPM) a technique for transfer pricing that compares net margins between two or more companies and tries to evaluate them to arrive at a transfer price for profit and tax allocation purposes.

comparative analysis the process of evaluating the same data for two or more different dates or periods, or for two or more companies, so that their similarities and differences may be evaluated to reveal useful insights and trends in past and future performance.

comparative budget and actual income statement an income statement containing both the actual and budgeted figures.

comparative financial statement a financial statement with data for 2 or more successive periods placed in columns side by side in order to better illustrate changes in the data. *Also*: comparative statement.

comparative negligence a negligence that is allocated to one of the parties in a tort case. *See*: *contributory negligence.*

comparative sales approach a method of appraising an asset by reviewing and analyzing a number of arms-length sales of properties.

comparative schedule of actual and standard overhead cost a statement with both actual and standard overhead cost figures, and variance if any.

comparative statement = *comparative financial statement.*

comparative statement approach a method which looks at all items of revenue and cost under two alternatives, and compares the net income or contribution margin. *Also*: total project approach.

comparative statement of product cost a statement which shows the products cost figures of different periods.

comparison rule a rule which states that cost should only be compared with the allowed cost rather than with the budgeted cost.

compensated absence vacation or sick leave with pay.

compensating account = *accommodating account.*

compensating balance <1> an excess balance left in a bank account to avoid a bank service charge. *Also*: free balance. <2> deposit that a bank can use to offset an unpaid loan.

compensating error = *offsetting error.*

compensating interest compensation of the interest earned on a customer's account with the interest charge on loans made to that customer.

compensating use tax = *use tax.*

compensation expense the expense incurred in compensating the company's top management officials, such as stock options at a low price.

compensation package total amount of money and derivative securities values that a company pays to a top executive.

compensation related loan the excess of the amount borrowed over the present value of all payments required to be made under the terms of the loan to employees or officers.

compensation stock <UK> the government guaranteed stock given to shareholder as compensation when certain industries were nationalized.

compensatory error = *offsetting error.*

compensatory financing = *deficit financing.*

compensatory plan an employee stock options plan that involves additional compensation to the employee, usually to be issued at below fair value or at no cost to the employee.

compensatory stock option an employee stock option with a low price as a compensation to its holders. ***Opp***: *proprietary stock option.*

Competency Assessment Tool (CAT) a web-based tool designed to allow CPAs to assess their knowledge, skills and abilities.

compilation <1> public accounting service to prepare financial statements for a client. <2> presentation of financial statement information by the entity without certification of a CPA.

complete audit a thorough examination of a corporation's financial records and the system of internal control. ***Also***: unqualified Audit. ***See***: *partial audit.*

complete-contract method a method under which income or loss on a contract is not recognized until the completion of the contract. ***Also***: completed job method. ***See***: *percentage of completion method.*

complete cost <1> = *absorption cost.* <2> = *job order cost.*

completed crop pool method a method under which gain or loss is computed separately for each crop year pool in the year in which the last of the products in the pool are disposed of.

completed film tax shelter a tax shelter whereby investors buy a completed film claiming the investment tax credit, provided it is a new qualified film. ***Also***: movie shelter.

completed gift a gift after paying gift tax. ***Also***: taxable gift.

completed job method = *complete-contract method.*

completed product = *finished goods.*

complete equity method a method under which the amortization of goodwill reduces the share of income in the subsidiary. ***Also***: full equity method. ***See***: *partial equity method.*

complete inventory = *wall-to-wall inventory.*

complete liquidation shareholders' transfer of their stock to the issuing company in exchange for the its property.

completeness all transactions are included in the financial statements.

completeness control internal control in order to assure that all the transactions are entered in the books. ***Also***: integrity control.

complete pay-out period a period that ends when the gross income from a wasting asset is equal to all costs and development expenditures, plus the cost of operating the asset to produce that gross income.

complex capital structure capital structure of a public company with dilutive securities issued. ***Also***: classified capital structure; multiple capital structure.

Complex Personal Returns (CPR) <UK> a tax office dealing with wealthy taxpayers.

complex trust a trust that does not distribute or set aside all annual income. ***Also***: accumulation trust. ***Opp***: *simple trust.*

compliance audit internal audit for assuring that all divisions and employees are complying with a defined set of rules and regulations. ***See***: *financial statements audit; operational audit.*

compliance test audit test that focuses on the performance of prescribed procedures. ***See***: *substantive test.*

complimentary a gift from the managers of a hotel to favored customers.

component cost = *element cost.*

component depreciation a depreciation method that fragments an asset, often a building, into its elements and applies individual useful lives and salvage value to each such component.

component percentage the ratio of one item in a financial statement to the total that includes that item.

components approach an approach under which notes receivable transferred without recourse are removed from the books but a liability for recourse provision is recognized. ***Also***: financial components approach.

composite account the account for a group of assets for depreciation purposes regardless of their character or useful lives.

composite break-even point break-even point when there are more than one product or service involved.

composite depreciation the depreciation calculated under the *composite depreciation method*. ***Also***: group method.

composite depreciation method a method of depreciation which arranges the service lives of dissimilar assets as if they were a single asset. ***Also***: common depreciation method; composite life method. ***Also***: group method. ***Opp***: single-asset depreciation method.

composite entry = *compound journal entry*.

composite financial statement = *combined financial statement*.

composite life method = *composite depreciation method*.

compound accreted value = *accreted value*.

compound annual growth rate (CAGR) a measure of the growth rate of a business of a portfolio year over year, which equals (current value/base value) × (1/number of years) - 1.

compound annual return = *internal rate of return*.

compound closing entries closing entries used when the partnership income and expense are not reported separately among partners.

compounding earnings increase in the earnings rate of a company over each year.

compounding period = *conversion period*.

compound interest (CI) interest created by adding simple interest periodically to principal, the new base being the principal for the next interest. ***Also***: interest on interest. ***See***: *simple interest*.

compound interest method a method under which the depreciation amount of a period equals the straight-line depreciation amount minus the interest that the asset should earn. ***Also***: interest method.

compound journal entry an entry that contains 3 or more account titles. ***Also***: combined entry; composite entry. ***Opp***: single journal entry.

comprehensive allocation the allocation of income tax expenses for a period including accruals, deferrals, and estimates, necessary to adjust the income taxes actually payable for the period in order to recognize the tax effects. ***See***: *partial allocation*.

comprehensive audit an audit that is to provide an independent professional opinion about the company's financial status. ***See***: *limited audit*.

comprehensive budget = *master budget*.

comprehensive income change in equity from transactions and circumstances from non-owner sources, usually net income computed under GAAP and other comprehensive income.

comprehensive tax allocation method of measuring the tax effects of all transactions includible in accounting income for the period irrespective of the fact that they may be shown as income in the tax return in another year.

compression risk the potential loss from a decline in yields that triggers call features on corporate debt or prepayment on mortgaged debt, and causes an issue to behave like a short-term note.

compromise offer = *offer in compromise*.

comptroller = *controller*.

Comptroller and Auditor General <UK> an official appointed under the National

Audit Act of 1983 to carry out audits into the government departments and bodies. *See: Auditor General; Comptroller General.*

Comptroller General the head of the General Accounting Office. *See: Auditor General; Comptroller and Auditor General.*

compulsory audit = *legal audit.*

compulsory books = *statutory books.*

compulsory liquidation the winding up of a company by a court. *See: voluntary liquidation.*

compulsory loan = *forced loan.*

compulsory payroll tax automatic tax collected from employers and employees to finance specific projects.

compulsory reserve = *foreign exchange reserve.*

computation year the year for which income averaging is claimed.

computer-based accounting the accounting data processing with the assistance of a computer.

Computerized Accounting Tool Services (CASTA) series of software tools for CPAs used in providing accounting and auditing services to clients.

concealment of asset hiding assets from creditors in bankruptcy.

concentration account a centralized account where regional lock-box collections are sent.

concentration of credit risk = *off-balance-sheet risk.*

concept of cost transformation and allocation a concept that distinguishes cost transformation (e.g. the machine oil that is transferred to the final product), and cost allocation, (e.g. car oil that should be allocated to the car).

concept of distinguishing asset from expense a concept that an expenditure should be treated as an asset if it has a long-term benefit, and as an expense if it has a short-term benefit.

concept of distinguishing equity from revenue a concept that unrealized revenue should be treated as equity, and realized revenue should be recognized as current income. *Also*: concept of recognition of revenue.

concept of matching costs with revenue = *matching concept.*

concept of matching revenue with expense = *matching concept.*

concept of recognition of revenue = *concept of distinguishing equity from revenue.*

concern = *stock.*

concession adjustment of the difference in book value between redeemed shareholders and residual shareholders.

concessional rate = *bank prime interest rate.*

concurrent testing = *continuous testing.*

condemnation award the award received in excess of the adjusted basis of the condemned property.

condensed balance sheet a balance sheet that shows only the major items. *Also*: abbreviated account. skeleton balance sheet.

condensed financial statement a financial statement which contains major items only. *Also*: abbreviated financial statement; summary financial statement; unorthodox financial statement.

conditional liquidity international liquidity that can only be used on certain conditions.

condition of affairs = *statement of affairs.*

conduit concept principle applied to partnership that preserves the character of income, losses, gain, expenses, and credits in the hands of the partners, and partnerships are viewed as pure conduits in that they are mere reporting entities and not taxpayers.

conduit IRA an IRA established pursuant to a rollover from a qualified retirement plan.

conduit tax theory = *conduit theory.*

conduit theory the idea that qualifying investment companies and REITS should be treated like a partnership, since the earnings and capital gains will pass through to shareholders. *Also*: conduit tax theory.

confidence level the level of sampling risk that an auditor is willing to accept. *Also*: level of confidence; reliability level.

confidential client information confidential information obtained by a CPA from the clients.

confirmation an audit procedure that enables auditors to obtain information directly from an independent source.

conflict of interest unethical profiteering by a corporate officer having a financial interest in two or more companies dealing with each other.

conformance cost = *control cost.*

conglomerate financial statement = *consolidated financial statement.*

conglomerate merger combination of two or more firms with virtually unrelated activities.

congregation <Canada> a community, society or body of individuals that adheres to and operates according to the practices and beliefs of a religious organization. *Also*: communal organization.

connected company <UK> = *affiliated corporation.*

connected person a person who is making a disposal of an asset and is connected with the person acquiring the asset.

connecting account an account used to balance the gaps between ledgers, if separate ledgers are maintained under the general ledger.

consecutive audit IRS audit performed on a consecutive basis.

consent dividend preferred dividend declared and followed by an imaginary contribution of such amounts back to the company to avoid accumulated profits tax.

consent stock a stock that is entitled to residual earnings, e.g. a preferred stock with consent dividends or participating preferred stock.

consequential loss value of loss resulting from loss of use of property.

conservatism a concept which maintains that financial information should provide for all possible liabilities and losses but should anticipate no gains.

consideration value that passes in exchange for something promised or done.

considered married a taxpayer is considered married if separated from the spouse for less than 6 months or the spouse died during the year and the taxpayer did not remarry.

considered unmarried taxpayers are considered unmarried if on the last day of a tax year they are legally separated.

consignment in = *goods-in on consignment.*

consignment out = *goods-out on consignment.*

consistency concept a concept that there should be consistency of accounting treatment of the same items within each period of account and from one period to the next.

consistency period the period beginning one year before an acquisition period, including the acquisition period plus one year.

consistency principle the rule requiring a persistent application of a selected method or procedure period after period. *Also*: continuity principle; principle of consistency.

consistent formulas method a method which applies the same depreciation formula period after period.

consolidated balance sheet balance sheet in which are found figures of the parent company itself and those of all its subsidiaries. *Also*: aggregate balance sheet; amalgamated balance sheet; summarized balance sheet.

consolidated bond the bond issued to retire two or more outstanding issues.

consolidated excess = *credit differential.*

consolidated financial statement financial statement bringing together all accounts of a controlling corporation and its subsidiaries. *Also*: conglomerate financial statement. *See*: *combined financial statement; group financial statement.*

consolidated goodwill = *debit differential.*

consolidated income statement an income statement of both a parent company and its subsidiaries. *Also*: group profit and loss account; statement of consolidated income; summary income statement.

consolidated national balance sheet = *national wealth statement.*

consolidated net income net income shown on the consolidated income statement after eliminating inter-company transactions.

consolidated net operating loss an operating loss incurred during a consolidated return year determined by taking into account the separate taxable income of each member of an affiliated group.

consolidated net operating loss deduction consolidated net operating loss of an affiliated group, plus such net operating losses sustained by members of the group in separate return years as can be carried over or carried back to a taxable year.

consolidated retained earnings (CRE) retained earnings shown on the consolidated balance sheet.

consolidated return a federal income tax return filed by an affiliated group of corporations.

consolidated return year a 12-month period covered by a consolidated return. *Also*: consolidated year.

Consolidated Revenue Fund <Canada> the general pool of all income of the federal government.

consolidated security issue of securities large enough to provide the funds to retire 2 or more outstanding issues of debt securities.

consolidated surplus a surplus shown in the consolidated balance sheet.

consolidated tax return a federal income tax return filed by an affiliated group of corporations.

consolidated year = *consolidated return year.*

consolidation a new company is formed to issue stock in exchange for the stock of two or more combining companies. *Also*: consolidation merger; fusion; integration; statutory consolidation. *See*: *merger; acquisition.*

consolidation excess = *credit differential.*

consolidation goodwill = *debit differential.*

consolidation merger = *consolidation.*

consolidation of capital = *split down.*

consolidation of shares = *split down.*

constant cost = *fixed cost.*

constant dollar a unit of measurement that translates monetary units into equivalent units the currency at some reference period by comparing their general purchasing power. *Also*: dollar of constant value; purchasing power unit.

constant dollar accounting the accounting which uses a general price index to convert the historical cost of non-monetary assets to dollar of current purchasing power and to find the holding gain or loss on monetary items. *Also*: accounting for changes in general and specific prices; accounting for changes in the purchasing power of money; accounting for changing money value; accounting for price changes; accounting for price level changes; common dollar accounting; constant dollar inflation accounting; current purchasing power accounting; general price-level accounting; general price level adjusted accounting; general purchasing power accounting; money unit adjusted accounting; present dollar accounting; price-level accounting; purchasing power unit accounting; stabilized accounting. *See*: *inflation accounting.*

constant dollar estimates = *constant dollar financial statement.*

constant dollar financial statement financial statement showing items adjusted for the changes in the purchasing power of money. *Also*: adjusted financial statement; common dollar financial statement; constant dollar estimates; general price-level adjusted financial statement; index-linked financial statement; price-level-adjusted statement; price-level financial statement; supplementary financial statement.

constant-dollar formula = *constant-dollar plan.*

constant dollar inflation accounting = *constant dollar accounting.*

constant dollar plan a method that invests a fixed amount of dollars in securities at set intervals. ***Also***: averaging; constant-dollar formula; dollar averaging; Pound cost averaging. ***See***: *constant-ratio formula; variable-ratio formula.*

constant expense = *fixed expense.*

constant-growth model a dividend discount model that assumes a fixed growth rate for future dividends and a single discount rate. ***Also***: Gordon-Shapiro model.

constant-ratio formula a *formula investing* plan under which the dollar ratio between stocks and fixed-income assets is adjusted periodically to predetermined percentages. ***See***: *constant-dollar plan; variable-ratio formula.*

constant standard cost = *basic standard cost.*

constant yield method a method for the allocation of annual interest on a zero-coupon security for income tax purpose.

Constitutional pure trust = *pure trust.*

Constitutional trust = *pure trust.*

constraint-based costing costing that assigns resource costs to products and services based on the existence and location of a capacity constraint.

constructive auditing the auditing that yields constructive suggestions to the management for improving organization operations, or accounting.

constructive closing the closing of the accounts where income is determined artificially.

constructive dividend the dividend which is treated for tax purposes as a distribution of property even though a distribution has not been formally declared. ***Also***: disguised dividend.

constructive fraud a fraud that does not involve misrepresentation with intent to deceive. ***Also***: fraud in law; legal fraud. ***See***: *actual fraud; gross negligence.*

constructive gain a gain realized on the constructive retirement of bonds. ***Also***: gain on constructive retirement.

constructive loss a loss realized on the constructive retirement of bonds. ***Also***: loss on constructive retirement.

constructive ownership rule an IRS rule which holds that an asset owned by a trust or a related person will be deemed owned by the holder of that trust.

constructive receipt a tax doctrine to the effect that a cash method taxpayer can not postpone the reporting of income when the income is credited to his account or made available to him without any restriction.

constructive retirement issuing company's purchase of bond or treasury stock with no intent of reissue.

constructive retirement method a method used when treasury stock is treated under *face value method*, and gains resulting from a repurchase price less than the original issue price should be credited to the capital account and not to the retained earnings account. ***See***: *cost price method; face value method.*

constructive sale appreciated financial position deemed sold by the IRS when all the possible risk and award have been hedged away.

constructive short-term capital gain amount of capital gain in a period that is to be eliminated against the capital loss carryovers.

constructive trust a trust created by operation of law. ***Also***: implied trust; statutory trust. ***Opp***: *express trust.*

consulting services (CS) services provided by CPA firms in addition to the traditional audit, accounting, and tax services.

consumed cost = *expired cost.*

consumer expenditure spending by consumers to satisfy personal demands.

consumer interest = *personal interest.*

consumer price index (CPI) a measure of price changes in consumer goods and services.

consumption method a method of accounting for business supplies under which purchases are recorded as inventory, charged to expense only when they are used. ***See***: *purchase method.*

consumption tax a tax levied directly on a specified item or commodity, e.g. electricity.

container deposit a deposit made by the customers for the use of packing containers.

contemplation-of-death rule a rule under which gifts made within 3 years of death were figured back into the taxable estate.

contemporaneous reserve accounting (CRA) the method used by US federal reserve banks to determine weekly legal reserve by that week's liabilities.

contested liabilities deduction a deduction allowed to taxpayers for payments made but which may be returned in later years because of contest.

contested tax real property tax that has been contested by the taxpayer.

continental shelf income net income from wells, mines, and employment arising from the exploration of a country's continental shelf.

contingency reserve certain amount of profits set aside to meet unanticipated needs of the business or some unexpected loss. ***Also***: reserve for contingencies.

contingent annuity an annuity the terms of which depend on some uncertain future events.

contingent asset an asset right whose existence is conditional on the happening of some future event. ***Opp***: *real asset.*

contingent cost a cost that may occur if certain events occur.

contingent fee a fee based on the outcome of a professional service.

contingent interest additional amounts paid to partners by the firm with respect to capital contributions in the event of an economic success.

contingent liability potential liability that may become an actual liability if certain events occur. ***Also***: potential liability. ***See***: *determinable liability.*

contingent pension liability the contingent liability out of a pension plan.

contingent rental the rental payment based on factors other than the passage of time.

contingent share the issuable share that does not require cash consideration and depends on some future events or certain conditions being met.

contingent surplus note a note issued by an insurance company to obtain capital, which will not be shown on the balance sheet until capital is obtained.

continual redemption sinking fund = *sinking fund.*

continuing account an account for recording items that are to be transferred to other accounts at the end of a period. ***Also***: transfer account.

continuing accounting significance significant information contained in the permanent audit working paper.

continuing concern concept = *continuity concept.*

continuing multiple asset accounts the accounts used for depreciation purposes, kept open as long as the accumulated depreciation is less than the cost of the assets.

continuity concept a concept that a business is a going concern which will continue to operate, using its assets to carry on its operations and, with the exception of goods, not offering the assets for sale. ***Also***: continuing concern concept; going-concern concept; postulate of permanence.

continuity principle = *consistency principle.*

continuous allotment method a method under which service department costs are allocated one service department at a time, to all other departments served, the last department's costs are allocated to production departments only. ***Also***: attrition method; method of continued distribution; sequential method; sequential-step procedure; specified order of closing method; step allocation method; step distribution method; step-down method; step-ladder method; step method; step-wise allocation; two-step allocation. ***See***: *direct method; reciprocal service cost allocation.*

continuous audit annual audit that is performed on a recurring basis throughout the accounting period.

continuous budgeting a method of budgeting whereby figures of the 12th month are added and that of the first month are subtracted after one month has passed.

continuous compounding accumulating the time value of money forward in time on a continuous basis.

continuous cost system = *process cost system.*

continuous inventory = *perpetual inventory.*

continuous physical inventory = *cycle inventory.*

continuous process costing = *process costing.*

continuous process cost system = *process cost system.*

continuous process lot cost system a cost accounting system under which total costs are accumulated lot by lot in every process.

continuous return the rate of return that, when compounded continuously, will cause an investment to grow by a factor equal to 1 plus the periodic return.

continuous stock taking = *perpetual stock taking.*

continuous testing the testing by an auditor to capture the audit data while the transactions are being processed. ***Also***: concurrent testing.

continuous value at risk the worst cumulative outcome that could incur from inception to any point throughout the entire investment horizon.

contra account (con. acct) account representing modifications and the balance of which will be subtracted from the balance of an associated account to show more proper amount for the item recorded in the associated account. ***Also***: absorption account; offset account; per contra account. ***Opp***: *adjunct account.* ***See***: *calculation account.*

contra asset an item that should be subtracted from a fixed asset in order to show more proper amount of that asset. ***Also***: offset against asset.

contra balance the balance of an a/c contra to those accounts of the same kind.

contract allowance the limit set within a contract as to what the maximum amount of an item would be.

contract amount = *contract value.*

contract auditing examination of contracts to provide assurance that the terms are being carried out.

contract cost the cost allocated to a long-term contract that are not reported until the contract is completed.

contracted in <UK> an employee who is not a member of a contracted-out pension scheme and does not contribute to a personal pension plan.

contracted out pension scheme <UK> a pension scheme that provides benefits in place of a *state second pension.*

contracted value = *contract value.*

contract out <UK> to opt out the state second pension either through a membership of a contracted-out pension scheme or by joining an appropriate personal pension plan.

contract research expense research expense incurred inside the company. ***See:*** *in-house research expense.*

contract trust = *pure trust.*

contractual settlement day accounting (CSDA) a securities custody or safe-keeping accounting between an investor and a custodian under which the investor is credited for all payments due and debited for all payments required on the nominal settlement day.

contractual trust = *pure trust*

contract value the face value of a futures or options contract. ***Also***: contract amount; contracted value; lot size.

contrast account = *calculation account.*

contributed capital the capital resulting from amounts invested in the corporation by its shareholders. ***Also***: paid-in capital; paid-up capital; vested capital. ***See***: *permanent capital; unpaid capital.*

contributed capital from retirement of stock excess of stock value over their redemption value when retired.

contributed capital in excess of par value the amount by which contributed capital exceeds the book value of the stock. ***Also***: additional paid-in capital in excess of par value; paid-in capital in excess of par value; paid-in surplus.

contributed capital in excess of stated value excess of the capital paid-in from the non-par value stock over its stated value. ***Also***: additional paid-in capital in excess of stated value; paid-in capital in excess of stated value; paid-in surplus.

contributed surplus = *additional paid-in capital.*

contribution <1> = *charitable contribution.* <2> = *contribution margin.*

contribution approach a pricing method for special order of products based solely on the contribution margin.

contribution base the amount used to calculate contribution deduction of a taxpayer, which equals to the AGI computed by disregarding net operating loss carry-backs.

contribution margin (CM) excess of sales revenue over variable cost, which represents contribution to fixed costs and profit. ***Also***: basic profit; contribution; cover; marginal contribution; margin contribution; net cash inflow; performance margin; positive contribution margin. ***See***: *marginal profit.*

contribution margin approach method in which the income statement shows only contribution margin and not the gross profit.

contribution margin effect variance that portion of the difference in the total product line contribution margins, it is the difference between planned contribution and actual contribution multiplied by actual sales or production units.

contribution margin per unit contribution margin divided by the number of units sold.

contribution margin ratio contribution margin divided by sales. ***Also***: marginal income ratio.

contribution margin variance the difference between actual contribution margin per unit and the budgeted contribution margin per unit multiplied by the actual number of units sold.

contributory negligence a negligence on the part of the plaintiff that has contributed to his or her having incurred the loss. ***See***: *comparative negligence.*

contributory plan a pension plan under which employees contribute part of the cost.

control ownership of at least 80% of the voting stock and at least 80% of all other classes of stock of a corporation.

control account = *controlling account.*

control accounting that phrase of accounting that renders information to management for planning and control. ***Also***: performance control accounting.

control cost category of quality cost, including cost of prevention and cost of appraisal. ***Also***: conformance cost; cost of conformance; quality control cost.

controllability principle the principle that information concerning performance should be reported to the manager who has authority and capability to significantly influence the items being reported.

controllable cost <1> the cost over which a manager has control as to amounts incurred. <2> that portion of quality cost in order to provide quality products and determine the quality level and find out the failure. ***See***: *resultant cost.*

controllable expense overhead expense over which the manager of the cost center has control as to the amount incurred.

controllable overhead variance = *overhead controllable variance.*

controllable variance <1> difference between overhead actually incurred and the overhead budgeted at the operating level achieved. <2> part of the total factory overhead variance not attributable to the volume variance in two-way analysis.

controlled account a part of a controlling account. ***Also***: underlying account.

controlled adjustable rate preferred stock = *adjustable rate preferred stock.*

controlled company a company for which a majority of the voting stock is owned by another company. ***See***: *subsidiary.*

controlled foreign company <UK> a company that is resident outside the UK and owned by UK residents.

controlled foreign corporation (CFC) a corporation in a foreign country and owned by US citizens, the income of which is not taxed until it is distributed to the US shareholders.

controlled group a group of corporations more than 50% of the shares are controlled by a common shareholder. ***See:*** *affiliated group.*

controlled processing = *parallel simulation.*

controlled reprocessing a variation of *parallel simulation*, reprocessing of actual client data through a copy of the client's program.

controlled sale the sale of tangible property between members of a commonly controlled group.

controller <1> a person who supervises the accounting department and assists the management in interpreting and utilizing the accounting information. ***Also***: comptroller. <2><Canada> = *controlling corporation.*

controlling account <1> *general ledger account* that controls the accounts in a detailed ledger. ***Also***: collective account; control account; main account; master control account; organization account; total account. <2> an account used in a self-balancing ledger for recording the contra amounts of all other accounts so that it can produce a trial balance. ***Also***: adjustment account ; ledger adjustment account; ledger controlling account.

controlling company = *controlling corporation.*

controlling corporation a firm set up for the purpose of controlling other companies by buying 51% or more of their voting stocks. ***Also***: controller; controlling company; dominant company; holding company; proprietary; proprietorship company. ***See***: *parent company.*

controlling interest = *majority interest.*

controlling ledger = *general ledger.*

control of controls internal auditor's control of the controls.

control person an individual or an entity in a position to exert direct influence on the policy or action of a corporation. ***Also***: affiliate; affiliated person.

control risk the likelihood that a material misstatement will not be detected or prevented timely by internal control.

controls a set of guidelines expressed in dollar amounts or in percentages not to be exceeded, designated to assist management in monitoring progress and taking corrective actions as plans are executed.

control share a share owned by the controlling shareholders of a company.

conventional absorption costing = *absorption costing.*

conventional accounting <1> accounting by hand written bookkeeping. ***Also***: orthodox accounting. <2> = *historical cost accounting.*

conventional costing = *absorption costing.*

conventional cost system = *absorption cost system.*

conventional depreciation = *straight-line depreciation.*

conventional financial statement = *unit-of-money financial statement.*

conventional income statement = *absorption costing income statement.*

conventional interest an interest at the rate agreed upon and fixed by the parties.

conventional retail method = *lower of average cost or market retail method.*

convention expense travel expense incurred while at a business convention.

convention statement an annual statement that must be filed by life insurance companies in each state where they do business.

convergent acquisition the acquisition of related business. ***See***: *divergent acquisition.*

conversion <1> change from a C corporation form to an S corporation form. <2> change from a traditional IRA to a Roth IRA.

conversion cost <1> cost of converting material to products, it is the sum of labor costs and factory overhead. ***Also***: cost of conversion; factor cost; finishing cost; processing cost. <2> expense incurred when converting financial statements in foreign currency back to home currency.

conversion cost method a process costing method under which the conversion costs are accumulated in each process, and the total material costs are added at the end.

conversion of cost of sales to cash disbursement conversion of cost of goods sold to cash disbursements to determine cash flow.

conversion parity price the price paid for a common stock by buying a convertible security and then exercising the option. ***Also***: market conversion price. ***See***: *conversion price.*

conversion percentage = *percentage of completion.*

conversion period time interval for calculating compound interest. ***Also***: compounding period; interest period; period of conversion.

conversion premium amount by which the conversion price of a convertible security exceeds the market price. ***Also***: bond conversion premium; gain on bond conversion; premium; premium over conversion value.

conversion price the fixed price at which a convertible security can be converted into one share of common stock. ***See***: *conversion parity price.*

conversion price index an index used to convert base year cost to dollar lifo inventory cost at year end, calculated as price divided by ending inventory at base year price.

conversion rate = *conversion ratio.*

conversion ratio the number of shares one receives for each convertible unit he turned in. ***Also***: conversion rate; exchange rate; rate of conversion.

conversion transaction a transaction the gain of which is due to the time value of money, and involves offsetting positions on the same asset.

conversion value the value of a convertible security if exchanged for the common stock immediately, usually the conversion ratio multiplied by the market price of the common stock. ***Also***: parity value.

convertible = *convertible security.*

convertible currency US Treasury and Federal Reserve holdings of foreign currencies that are counted as part of official US reserve assets.

convertible discount the amount below the conversion value for which a convertible security is selling.

convertible exchangeable preferred stock the *convertible preferred stock* exchangeable at the issuer's option for other convertible debts with identical yield and identical conversion terms.

convertible floating rate preferred stock a *convertible preferred stock* with the dividend indexed to a floating interest rate.

convertible monthly income preferred shares the *monthly income preferred securities* convertible into the shares of the issuer.

convertible preferred stock preferred stock that can be changed into the common stock of the issuing company.

convertible security a bond or preferred stock that is convertible into common stock at a given price at the option of the holder. ***Also***: common stock equivalent; convertible.

convertible stock note a debt instrument that pays coupons and principal in the common stock of the issuer.

conveyance tax a tax imposed on the transfer of real estate property.

COO chief operating officer

cook accounts to alter the financial statement figures.

cookie jar accounting practice of taking reserves against losses during profitable years and using them in unprofitable years to smooth out the earnings and make the company's operations seem more consistent. ***See***: *voodoo accounting*.

cooking the book = *window dressing*.

cooling off period <1><Canada> 3 years during which a taxpayer can not claim the labour-sponsored fund credit if a share is redeemed, acquired or canceled by the corporation. <2> = *cooling period*.

cooling period the time between the filing of a registration statement for a security issue and the date when the SEC authorizes it to be released for sale, often 20 days. ***Also***: cooling-off period; 20-day period; waiting period. ***See***: *quiet period*.

coordinate audit the audit taken by both internal auditors and public accountants.

COQ cost of quality

COR cost of risk

core capital the capital required of a thrift institution, at least 2% of the total assets.

core earnings revenue derived from a firm's main or principal business less all associated expenses.

core statement = *first statement*.

corporate accounting the accounting that distinguishes between stockholder's equity resulting from investment and that resulting from earnings.

corporate acquisition indebtedness a bond issued after October 9, 1969, for the purpose of acquiring either the stock or two-third's of the non-cash operating assets of a target company through *leveraged buyout*.

corporate capital = *stockholder's capital*.

corporate capital gains tax a tax on the capital gains of a corporation. ***See***: *income tax*.

corporate equivalent yield = *equivalent bond yield*.

corporate finance a financial or monetary activity that deals with a company and its money.

corporate income tax a tax on the net income of a corporation subject to tax. ***Also***: corporate tax; corporation tax; tax on corporations.

corporate income tax audit the audit on the income tax and withholding of a corporation. ***Also***: income audit.

corporate inversion US company's switching registration with their offshore subsidiary in order to take advantage of foreign tax benefits.

corporate level taxation tax paid at corporate level of the S corporation, e.g. excess capital gains, lifo recapture, built-in gain.

corporate minimum tax 15% tax imposed on the items of tax preference of a company.

Also: minimum tax on items of tax preference.

corporate processing float = *float period.*

corporate reacquisition a company's buying back its own securities through a tender offer. *See*: *direct repurchase.*

corporate secretary an officer dealing with the daily running of a company and the general administration. *Also*: company secretary.

corporate social accounting that area which includes social economic accounting, social cost accounting, environmental accounting, ecological accounting, social audit, and social responsibility accounting.

corporate surtax <Canada> a tax applied to Part 1 tax otherwise payable after deduction of 10% of taxable income.

corporate tax <Canada> = *corporate income tax.*

corporate taxable equivalent rate of return required on a par bond to produce a safe after-tax *yield to maturity* that a quoted premium or discount bond would generate.

corporate tax return the tax return filed by a corporation. *Also*: Form 1120. *See*: *individual tax return; tax return.*

corporate tax view the argument that *double taxation* of equity returns makes debt a cheaper financing method.

corporate trust the function of maintaining records for debt securities issued by a corporation.

corporation <1> an entity formed under laws, having shareholders, directors, officers and limited liability. *Also*: company; incorporated company; incorporated partnership. <2><UK> one or more persons united together so as to be considered as one person in law.

corporation aggregate <UK> a company consisting of many persons. *See*: *corporation sole.*

corporation for profit = *business corporation.*

corporation sole <UK> a corporation consisting of one person only. *Also*: one-man company. *See*: *corporation aggregate.*

corporation's stock = *stock.*

corporation tax <UK> = *corporate income tax.*

corporation tax on chargeable gains <UK> a tax on capital gains realized by companies. *See*: *capital gains tax.*

corpus = *principal.*

correcting journal entry a journal entry for correcting errors. *See: auditor's adjusting entry; worksheet entry.*

correction of an error the correction of a deviation from a permissible method of accounting that does not require IRS approval.

correction of prior year's depreciation the adjustment of last year's errors in estimation of asset life, salvage, over- or under-estimation of depreciable value, etc.

correction period a statutorily fixed period during which some particular wrong doing can be reversed thereby avoiding penalties.

corrective return = *amended return.*

correct tax the tax determined by the IRS for tax deficiencies purposes.

correlation degree of relationship between business and economic variables such as cost and volume.

correlation method a method for determination of fixed and variable cost behavior.

correspondence audit an audit undertaken by the IRS using the mail. *See*: *interview audit.*

correspondent account = *nostro account.*

corridor approach a method under which the minimum amount of cumulative unrecognized gain or loss to be amortized is determined by computing, at the beginning of the year, the excess of the cumulative unrecognized gain or loss over 10% of the greater of PBO or the market related asset value.

corridor option = *accrual option.*

corroborating document = *corroborating evidence.*

corroborating evidence audit evidence used to verify the underlying evidence or other events, the supporting documentation that is the basis for a transaction being recorded in the journals and ledgers. ***Also***: corroborating document.

co-sale rights = *tag alongside rights.*

cost sacrifice of resources in order to achieve an object. ***Also***: cost price.

cost absorption <1> the attrition of costs to the cost units. ***Also***: absorbing cost; absorption; eating cost. <2> transfer of expense to the period.

cost accounting that area which deals with collecting and controlling the manufacturing costs of a given product or rendering a certain kind of service.

cost accounting by elements cost accounting that accumulates costs by elements (e.g. direct materials, labor, and overhead).

cost accounting by products cost accounting that accumulates costs by units of product.

Cost Accounting Standards Board (CASB) the 5-member federal body responsible for setting cost accounting standards for all government contractors.

cost accumulation collection of cost data by job costing or by process costing.

cost added = *added cost.*

cost adjusted for fair value method a method for recording investments whereas original investment is recorded in the Investment a/c, dividends received that exceeds earnings since the acquisition date is treated as a return of capital and recorded as reduction in Investment account. ***Also***: cost method; mark-to-market method. ***See***: *equity method.*

cost adjustment ratio a ratio to bring estimated labor hours and direct costs up from theoretical values to the actually achievable values, by dividing actual hours spent doing a job by the hours budgeted.

cost allocation assignment of indirect cost to cost centers in the productive sequence in the proportions in which they have attracted. ***Also***: apportionment; cost apportionment; cost distribution; cost reapportionment; distribution of cost. ***See***: *cost tracing.*

cost allocation method a method of funding a pension plan, either through individual level cost basis or aggregate level cost basis.

cost analysis determining the relationship between costs and the factors that effect them.

cost application assigning costs to an output unit on the basis of a budgeted rate. ***Also***: application.

cost apportionment = *cost allocation.*

coat approach a method for estimating the value based on current construction costs, less depreciation, plus land value. ***See***: *income approach; market data approach.*

cost assignment includes *cost tracing* and *cost allocation.*

cost assignment path link between a cost and one of its two or more cost objects.

cost atom a cost unit that can not be divided further.

cost attachment assignment of manufacturing cost to the raw material inventory, work-in-process, and finished goods.

cost avoidance concept a concept stating that the fixed cost that will not incur in the future should not be included in the ending inventory.

cost-based price internal transfer price based on variable cost or full cost.

cost basis <1> a method under which short-term bond investment is carried at cost, ignoring the accumulation of discount or amortization of premium. ***Also***: systematic accumulation and amortization basis. <2> = *tax basis.*

cost behavior analysis = *determination of cost behavior.*

cost behavior classification = *determination of cost behavior.*

cost-behavior pattern the fixed or variable behavior of a cost. *Also*> behavioral cost pattern; cost pattern.

cost-benefit analysis (C/B analysis) an analysis used by nonprofit organizations to determine whether the favorable results of an action are sufficient to justify the cost of taking that action. *Also*: benefit cost analysis; benefit-to-cost test.

cost-benefit ratio = *present value profitability index.*

cost center a business unit that incurs costs but does not directly generate revenue.

cost company a company owned by 2 or more manufacturers to extract minerals or to carry on some other functions, the profit of which are taxed to the owners rather than to the company. *See*: *joint venture.*

cost company arrangement the arrangement whereby the shareholders receives output free of charge but agree to pay all operating and financing charges of a project.

cost control the control of the incurrence or amount of cost, and the variance.

cost control account <1><UK> under integral accounts, an account in the financial ledger for recording entries made in the cost ledger. <2> <UK> under interlocking accounts, an account in the cost ledger simply acting as a receptacle for those double entries which would cross the line for entry into a financial account. *Also*: dustbin account; general ledger account.

cost depletion method a method that depends upon the unrecovered cost of the asset and depletion ends when the entire cost is written off. *See*: *percentage depletion method.*

cost difference the difference between the cost reported in the financial statements and the cost allowed by tax regulations.

cost distribution = *cost allocation.*

cost distribution sheet a statement that shows departmental cost distribution data.

cost driver <1> a factor that causes a cost to be incurred. <2> single measure of the frequency and intensity placed on the activities by cost objectives, such as part number, order number, etc. *Also*: activity cost driver; activity driver.

cost-effectiveness analysis the analysis of the benefit of a particular expenditure to establish whether the same expenditure could he used more effectively or whether the same benefits are attainable with less expenditure.

cost element material, labor or overhead.

cost escalation = *escalation.*

cost estimating approximating the probable cost of a specific activity based on past cost data. *Also*: cost measurement.

cost expiration = *depreciation.*

cost factor a factor used for ascertaining standard cost.

cost finding = *costing.*

cost flow changing of cost from inventory to manufacture to current assets. *Also*: flow of cost.

cost flow assumption the assumption of the flow of costs rather than the physical flow of goods, such as lifo, etc.

cost function a method for classifying cost accounts showing the nature of the output for which costs are incurred, such as product, packaging, sales, and production.

cost hierarchy framework for classifying production-related activities according to the level at which their costs are incurred.

cost increases in steps = *step-variable cost.*

costing procedure that aims at presenting management with cost information needed. *Also*: cost finding; cost system.

costing method a method which depends on the nature of production, derived from accounting principles for arranging and reporting cost information.

costing technique a technique of arranging cost data which depends on the purpose for which management requires the information, such as direct costing, standard costing, etc.

costing unit = *cost unit.*

cost judge <UK> an officer appoint to settle taxation of costs. *Also*: taxing master.

cost leadership a business strategy by which a company seeks to earn adequate profits by keeping costs low enough to support a very competitive price in the market.

cost less depreciation = *written-down value.*

cost less scrap = *depreciable cost.*

cost management system (CMS) cost and management accounting, control and reporting system.

cost matching income principle = *matching principle.*

cost me in OTC trading, the price of the security that I bought was.

cost measurement = *cost estimating.*

cost method <1> a method for recording raw materials issue and inventory at their cost price. <2> a method under which the costs of stock investment are recorded in one account, and dividend will be recorded in a separate account. *Also*: cost price method. <3> = *cost adjusted for fair value method.* <4> = *cost price method.* <5> = *legal basis method.*

cost module convention used to classify cost by location where incurred, its use and its ultimate user.

cost object the nature of the input used to make a product or provide a service, e.g. material, electricity, etc.

cost of appraisal cost of quality incurred to find defects by inspection audit, calibration, test and measurement.

cost of capital <1> cost of debt and equity capital of a company, usually the weighted average of cost of debt, cost of preferred stock, cost of common stock and cost of retained earnings. *Also*: capital cost; cost of funds; money cost. <2> asset betterment cost that is deductible by tax regulations.

cost of carry <1> finance charge incurred while an investor has a position, such as interest on long positions in margin account, dividends lost on short margin positions and incidental expenses. <2> = *carry.*

cost of carrying inventory = *carrying cost.*

cost of common stock calculated as common stock dividend ÷ (average market value of common stock + expected growth rate in dividend).

cost of conformance = *control cost.*

cost of conversion = *conversion cost.*

cost of debt capital the cost for obtaining debt capital, which equals interest × (1 - income tax rate). *Also*: debt capital cost.

cost of default the cost to the holder of a swap if the counterpart failed to perform.

cost of depreciation = *depreciation cost.*

cost of direct inputs = *prime cost.*

cost of doing business = *business expense.*

cost of equity (COE) the return that stockholders require for a company, expressed by the *dividend capitalization model.* *Also*: cost of equity capital.

cost of equity capital <1> = *accounting rate of return.* <2> = *cost of equity.*

cost of failure the cost that could have been avoided if the product had been made to an acceptable level of quality. *Also*: cost of non-conformance; failure cost; nonconformance cost. *See*: *external failure cost; internal failure cost.*

cost of flotation the expenses of issuing new securities. *Also*: capital structure expenditure; cost of issue; floatation cost; floating charge; flotation cost; issuance expense; issue cost.

cost of foreign adoption foreign adoption cost.

cost offset expenditure that a business is able to avoid, e.g. purchase discount for paying cash. *Also*: cost saving.

cost of fund = *interest.*

cost of funds = *cost of capital.*

cost of goods available for sale beginning inventory cost plus purchase cost of the current period.

cost of goods completed = *cost of goods manufactured.*

cost of goods manufactured direct material, labor and overhead transferred from work-in-process inventory to finished goods inventory. *Also*: cost of goods completed; cost of manufacture; cost of production; manufactured product cost.

cost of goods manufactured and sold cost that should be shared by the goods sold. *See*: *cost to make and sell.*

cost of goods on hand = *inventory cost.*

cost of goods purchased the price of the goods plus freight and storage cost. *Also*: cost of purchases.

cost of goods sold (CGS) cost of the products sold by a company, calculated as beginning inventory + net purchases - ending inventory. *Also*: cost of sales; expense of goods sold; gross cost; sales cost.

cost of goods sold budget a budget about the cost of goods sold.

cost of having = *carrying cost.*

cost of hedging = *premium.*

cost of initial partner's capital the discount rate that equates the after-tax inflows with outflows for capital paid by limited partners.

cost of installment sales the cost of goods sold under installment sales.

cost of issue = *cost of flotation.*

cost of lease financing the internal rate of return of a lease.

cost of limited partnership capital the discount rate that makes the after-tax inflows equal to the outflows for capital raised from limited partners.

cost of living = *living cost.*

cost of living adjustment (cola) <1> upward change in an employee's compensation because of inflation. <2> = *tax indexing.*

cost-of-living index an index issued by US Department of Labor, reflecting the changes in the cost of living.

cost of long-term debt calculated as interest on long-term debts × (1 - tax rate).

cost of manpower = *labor cost.*

cost of manufacture = *cost of goods manufactured.*

cost of materials = *materials cost.*

cost of money = *interest.*

cost of new external common equity cost of newly issued common stock, including floatation cost.

cost of nonconformance = *cost of failure.*

cost of not carrying lost of profit because of not carrying the goods demanded by customers. *Also*: opportunity cost; out of stock cost ; shortage cost; stock-out cost; underage cost.

cost of overhead = *overhead.*

cost of plant renovation cost of improving, renewing or replacement of plant asset. *Also*: plant modernization cost.

cost of prediction error cost of a failure to accurately predict a certain variable, such as sales, earnings or cash flow.

cost of preferred stock cost of raising capital by issuing preferred stock, calculated as annual dividend on preferred stock divided by market price net of cost of issuance.

cost of prevention *cost of quality* incurred to avoid defects, planning, preparation, training, preventative maintenance and evaluation.

cost of procuring = *ordering cost.*

cost of production = *cost of goods manufactured.*

cost of production report = *manufacturing statement.*

cost of purchases = *cost of goods purchased.*

cost of quality (COQ) = *quality cost.*

cost of replacement-new = *replacement cost-new.*

cost of reproduction = *reproduction cost.*

cost of reproduction-new value = *reproduction cost.*

cost of retained earnings cost of retaining earnings rather than distributing them, which equals estimated EPS × (1 - income tax rate of stockholders) ÷ current market value per share.

cost or rework additional cost for rework.

cost of risk (COR) quantitative measurement of the total costs associated with a risk.

cost of sales = *cost of goods sold.*

cost of sales adjustment (COSA) the amount that must be added to the historical cost of stocks consumed by a business in order to arrive at the value to the business of the stocks.

cost of service = *service cost.*

cost of spoilage = *spoilage cost.*

cost of subsidiary stock in excess of book value = *debit differential.*

cost of tender the total charges associated with the delivery and certification of commodities underlying a futures contract.

cost of the oldest stock method = *base stock method.*

cost of units uncompleted the costs shared by the units uncompleted.

cost of work performed (CWP) actual or budgeted cost of the job finished as of the measurement date.

cost or less principle a principle that asset cost should use the original cost or the lower.

cost or market, the lower = *cost or market, whichever is lower.*

cost or market, whichever is lower the lower of what each item actually costs or what it would cost to replace it on the inventory date. ***Also***: at the lower of cost or market; cost or market, the lower; lower of cost or market.

cost or market, whichever is lower method a method of pricing inventory at the lower of what each item actually costs or what it would cost to replace each item on the inventory date.

cost pattern = *cost behavior pattern.*

cost performance <Canada> a ratio of Canada's total labor income to its real gross domestic products. ***Also***: unit labor cost.

cost performance index (CPI) a ratio of earned value and the actual costs of work preformed of a project. ***See***: *cost variance; schedule performance index.*

cost per thousand (CPM) the cost it takes to reach one thousand people by advertising.

cost per unit (CPU) <1> under process costing, total cost of production incurred by a company in a given period divided by the number of units. ***Also***: average cost; per unit cost; product unit cost; unit cost. <2> in job order costing, cost of the job divided by the number of units produced on the job.

cost plus a policy under which the insurance company agrees to provide the insured with a series of benefits on a benefit-paid basis plus administrative service on a fee basis.

cost-plus basis a method of adding a percentage to cost to obtain the selling price.

cost-plus price transfer price computed as the sum of cost plus the agreed-on profit.

cost pool <1> = *activity cost pool.* <2> = *overhead.*

cost prediction forecast of cost data for decision making.

cost price = *cost.*

cost price method <1> a method under which cost of acquiring treasury stock is debited to Treasury Stock account which is treated as a deduction from the stockholders' equity and no reduction in the legal or stated capital will be made. ***Also***: cost method. ***See***: *constructive retirement method; face value method.* <2> = *cost method.*

cost principle a rule which requires assets and services plus any resulting liabilities to be recorded at historical cost.

cost profit and loss account an account used in interlocking accounts, for recording profit and loss in the production process.

cost profit and loss statement a statement showing only the revenue, expenses and profit and loss of the production department.

cost purchase accounting system that permits a company that owns less than 20% of the stock of another to include in its own income only the cash dividends received from its investment in that subsidiary. *Opp*: *equity purchase accounting.*

cost rate = *overhead rate.*

cost reapportionment = *cost allocation.*

cost recording classifying and assigning costs to the appropriate ledger account.

cost records the records maintained by an investor for the cost prices and commission on securities transactions.

cost recovery = *depreciation.*

cost recovery basis a basis under which the asset cost must be written off before profit and loss is determined when disposing an asset. *Also*: cost-recovery-first method.

cost-recovery-first method = *cost recovery basis.*

cost recovery method installment sales method under which no profit is recognized until the cumulative receipts exceed the cost of sales. *See*: *installment sales method.*

cost recovery period = *payback period.*

cost reduction actions taken to reduce cost.

cost reference source to determine the price of a product or service, such as supplier's price list.

cost reporting summarizing, communicating, interpreting cost information to interested parties.

cost saving = *cost offset.*

cost sheet a form prepared for each job or department.

cost split the break-down of cost associated with the production, usually into material, labor and overhead.

cost stream = *expense asset.*

cost subject to capitalization = *Section 236A cost.*

cost summary schedule a schedule used under process costing to determine the costs to be transferred to the finished goods inventory.

cost synergy the savings in operating costs expected after two companies merged into a new company.

cost system = *costing.*

cost theory a theory which states capital should be ascertained by the acquisition cost, normal working capital, and amortization, etc.

cost-to-cost method = *percentage-of-completion method.*

cost to government government's purchase cost of goods and services from private sector multiplied by (1 - sales tax rate).

cost to make = *manufacturing cost.*

cost to make and sell total cost incurred to make and sell a given product. *See*: *cost of goods manufactured and sold.*

cost to replace = *replacement cost.*

cost to sell = *selling cost.*

cost to society = *social cost.*

cost to the environment a cost to the society such as pollution. *Also*: environmental cost.

cost tracing assignment of direct cost to a cost object. *See*: *cost allocation.*

cost transformation the transformation of one kind of cost, e.g. cost of engine oil, to another kind, e.g. overhead.

cost-type accounting system = *business-type accounting system.*

cost unit an item or quantity of output, a period of time, an area of activity, a process, etc. in relation to which a cost may be ascertained or expressed. *Also*: costing unit.

cost-utility analysis a type of cost-effectiveness analysis in which outcomes are measured in terms of social value, e.g. cost per quality-adjusted life years gain.

cost value method = *legal basis method.*

cost variance <1> in actual costing, difference between actual cost and estimated cost. <2> difference between the earned value and the actual costs of work performed of a project. ***Also***: job project-performance cost variance. ***See***: *cost performance index; scheduled variance.* <3> = *standard cost variance.*

cost variance statement a statement showing the cost variance and the analysis of that variance.

cost-volume formula a formula used in cost prediction: $y = a + bx$, where y = mixed cost, x = volume, a = total fixed cost, and b = variable cost per unit. ***Also***: flexible budget formula.

cost-volume-profit analysis (CPV analysis) a method of predicting the effect of changes in costs and/or in the sales level on the net income of a business.

cost-volume profit chart (CVP chart) = *breakeven chart.*

cost with indirect benefit indirect cost which does not benefit the cost unit.

cost with traceable benefit indirect cost which benefits the cost unit.

"cotermination plant" plan depreciation plan which assumes that plant assets of a public utility have a stated life. ***See***: *"repeated plant" plan.*

council tax <UK> a local tax on domestic property collected by local authorities. ***Formerly called***: rate.

counter balance = *offset balance.*

counter balancing error = *offsetting error.*

counterclaim a defendant's answer to the plaintiff's complaint that includes a cause of action against the plaintiff.

counterpart item in the balance of payments, an item that is analogous to unrequited transfer in the current account.

countervailing duty additional duty imposed by the importing country to offset government subsidies in the exporting country.

country beta the covariance of a national economy's rate of return and the rate of return of the world economy divided by the variance of the world economy.

county auditor an official who is responsible for the examination of accounts and financial records of the county.

county tax lien a tax levied by the county for nonpayment of county tax.

coupon bond a bearer bond with an interest coupon attached.

coupon bond method method of determining taxable portion of OID, which applies only to Treasury inflation protected securities. ***See***: *discount bond method.*

coupon equivalent rate = *equivalent bond yield.*

coupon rate interest rate on the face amount of a debt. ***Also***: bond interest rate; nominal interest rate; nominal rate; normal rate.

coupon stripping tax avoidance by detaching interest coupons from a bond and soon selling the bond at a loss and recognizing an ordinary loss. ***Also***: bond stripping.

Court = *Tax Court of Canada.*

covariance a measure of the degree to which returns on 2 risky assets move in tandem. (A positive covariance means that asset returns move together, a negative covariance means returns vary inversely.)

cover <1> total profits divided by profit distributed. <2> = *contribution margin.*

coverage of fixed charges pre-tax accounting income + fixed charges such as interest, rent, etc. - fixed charges.

coverage ratio measure of a corporation's ability to meet a particular expense or liability.

Coverdell Education Savings Account (ESA) investment arrangement to help taxpayers fund their children's education, under which the contributions are taxed, but earnings used to pay education expenses are not. ***Also***: education IRA. ***See***: *lifelong learning plan.*

cover for dividend profit available for distribution ÷ dividends declared. *Also*: dividend cover.

covering entry <1> an entry with detailed explanations. <2> a false entry to cover a fact.

CP <1> capacity planning. <2> commercial paper. <3> community property.

CP 2501 = *income verification notice.*

CPA <1> certified public account. <2> chartered public accountant.

CPAC CPA candidate

CPA candidate (CPAC) a person who has passed the CPA exam and seeks to become a licensed CPA.

CPA firm = *public accounting firm.*

CPA/SEA Certified Public Accountants' Society Executives Association

CPE Continuing Professional Education

CPFA <UK> designation used by members of the Chartered Institute of Public Finance and Accountancy.

CPI <1> consumer price index. <2> cost performance index.

CPM <1> comparable profits method. <2> cost per thousand. <3> critical path method.

CPP Canada Pension Plan

CPR Complex Personal Returns

CR <1> cash receipts journal. <2> cash reserve. <3> current ratio.

CRA contemporaneous reserve accounting

crash cost the highest cost incurred to finish a job in the shortest time allowed.

CRAT charitable remainder annuity trust

CRE consolidated retained earnings

creative accounting management's attempt to overstate income or understate expense.

creator = *trustor.*

credential documentation maintained by the IRS about the authorized e-file providers.

credit (Cr)(crd)(cred)(ct) <1> to place an entry in the right hand side of an account. <2> = *credit side.* <3> = *tax credit.*

credit against tax = *tax credit.*

credit balance <1> balance of account on the credit side. <2> = *active balance of payments.* <3> = *tax credit.*

credit balance account <1> an account the balance of which is a credit balance under normal condition. <2> an account used when preparing the input-output table, into which the reduction in current liabilities will be debited with a credit to the current liability account.

credit carryback unused tax credit carried back to previous tax years.

credit carryforward unused tax credit carried to future tax years.

credit-debit plan = *debit-credit plan.*

credit differential the excess of the parent company's equity in the subsidiary's books over the investment cost. *Also*: amalgamation surplus; book value of subsidiary stock in excess of cost; capital from consolidation; consolidated excess; consolidation excess; excess of book value over investment cost; excess of fair value over cost; negative goodwill; profit from consolidation; surplus from consolidation. *Opp*: *debit differential.*

credit entry an entry to be posted in the credit side of an account.

credit equivalent value (CEV) the value of the credit risk exposure represented by an off-balance sheet transaction.

credit for adoption expenses = *adoption credit.*

credit for interest on student loan <Canada> a tax credit allowed for interest paid in a year or any of the previous five years on a student loan.

credit for low-income housing = *low-income housing credit.*

credit for producing electricity from certain renewable resources = *renewable electricity production credit.*

credit for qualified electric vehicles a tax credit (up to $5,000 in 2003) allowed to a taxpayer who purchased an electric vehicle.

credit for qualified hybrid vehicles a tax credit (up to $2,000 in 2003) allowed to a taxpayer who purchased a new car with hybrid gas/electric engines. ***Also***: clean-burning fuel deduction.

credit loss ratio the ratio of credit-related losses to the value of loans outstanding.

credit memorandum <1> memo sent to notify its recipient that the sender has credited the account of the recipient. <2> a notice from a bank indicating the balance has been increased due to some event other than a deposit.

creditor's equity = *exterior liability.*

creditors' equity ratio = *debt ratio.*

creditors' ledger <1> = *accounts payable ledger.* <2> = *purchase ledger.*

creditors' voluntary liquidation <UK> *voluntary liquidation* of a company following a resolution by the creditors. ***See:*** *members' voluntary liquidation.*

credit period a period qualified for the low-income housing credit.

credit sharing two or more tax payers sharing a tax credit.

credit-shelter trust a trust the assets of which does not exceed the *unified credit exemption* amount. ***Also***: bypass trust; empty bypass trust.

credit side <1> right-hand side of an account. ***Also***: credit; creditor side. ***See***: *right side.* <2> in the balance of payments of a country, the autonomous and compensatory transactions resulting in the purchase of the home-country currency.

credit variance = *favorable variance.*

credit voucher a voucher by which an entry is made in the credit side of an account

credit year tax year that an investment tax credit is being determined.

creeping acquisition the acquisition of a company by another in a series of steps, such as buying major amount of the stock followed by an exchange of shares.

criminal investigation IRS investigation of a criminal tax evasion case.

criminal tax penalty tax fines for violation of revenue laws enforced only by prosecution. ***See***: *civil tax penalty.*

critical audit an audit for giving critical opinions. ***Opp***: *instructional audit.*

critical event basis a basis for recognizing income, such as sales basis, and cash collection basis, accrual basis.

critical mass the level of sales or cash flow that a business unit must attain to be viable as an ongoing business.

critical path the path of a series of activities which requires the greatest time in a network.

critical path method (CPM) method that uses critical path for forecasting, planning, and controlling cost.

CRJ cash receipts journal

CROGI cash return on gross investment

crop basis a basis for recognizing revenue by the market value of the crop.

crop method a method by which farmers raising a crop that requires one year or more between the time of planting and disposal, may defer expenses until realization the crop income.

crop year the 12-month period during which the planting or harvesting of a crop occurred.

cross-border merger <Canada> the merger of two or more corporations that are resident in different jurisdictions to form a single corporation.

cross charging = *transfer pricing.*

cross entry an entry in the ledger that is opposite to another entry in the same amount, thus would not affect the trial balance.

cross footing adding the column totals of a journal or a report and comparing the two to see if they agree.

cross holding a listed company's holding of the securities issued by another *listed company.*

cross reference procedure used to check the accuracy of a journal by the cross footing.

cross reference number a number used by an auditor to link together the ledger and the journal, such as folio. *Also*: folio reference; posting medium; posting reference.

cross-sectional approach an approach that uses a statistical formula for a set of companies at a particular point in time.

cross-section analysis the analysis of the financial statements of several companies in different industries at the same time.

cross shareholding two or more companies holding shares of stock in each other.

cross subsidy improper assignment of costs among objects, e.g. more costs are allocated to some objects.

cross the line point of time at which typical tax shelters become financially burdensome to investors. *See*: *burned-out tax shelter*.

Crown gift <Canada> a gift made to the Crown by a taxpayer.

cruise ship convention a deduction of up to $2,000 per individual per year is allowed for attending a business convention held on board a cruise ship.

cruising an auditor's inspection of a tract of forestland for the purpose of estimating the total lumber yield.

CRUT charitable remainder unit trust

CRY consolidated return year

crystallised gain <UK> a gain that is subject to capital gains tax.

CS <1> capital stock. <2> common stock.

CSDA contractual settlement day accounting

CSP Classification Settlement Program

CSV cash surrender value

ct credit

CTA cumulative translation adjustment

CTT capital transfer tax

culmination of earnings process method of recognizing revenue, usually at the time of sale or rendering of a service.

cultural gift <Canada> a gift of cultural property made to institutions designated under the Cultural Property Export and Import Act.

cultural property <Canada> a property that the Canadian Cultural Property Export Review Board has determined meets the relevant criteria and disposed of to an institution or a public authority in Canada.

cum distribution = *cum dividend*.

cum dividend (c.d.) a share that is sold with a dividend declared out but not yet paid. *Also*: cum distribution; dividend in; with dividend.

cum drawing of bonds, soon due to be drawn with rights that may come with the drawing such as profit or premium.

cumulative abnormal return (CAR) sum of the difference between the expected return on a stock and the actual return, used to evaluate the impact of news on a stock price.

cumulative activity cost the cost of two or more activities added together.

cumulative amount = *year-to-date amount*.

cumulative and average income statement a comparative income statement which shows both the average and cumulative amounts.

cumulative dividend the dividend on preferred stock which must be paid before dividends to common shareholders are made.

cumulative effect the total effect on the retained earnings since a change in accounting methods occurred as if the new accounting methods had been used in the prior years.

cumulative effect method = *current approach*.

cumulative eligible capital = *undepreciated capital cost*.

cumulative monetary amount sampling (CMA sampling) = *probability-proportional-to-size sampling*.

cumulative net investment loss (CNIL) <Canada> net investment loss incurred after 1987 that is not yet covered by investment income.

cumulative preferred stock preferred stock issued under a provision that if dividends are omitted, the omitted dividends will be paid before any dividend is paid on any stock.

cumulative return total return over several periods calculated by compounding the rates of return in each year. ***Also***: cumulative total return.

cumulative total return = *cumulative return.*

cumulative translation adjustment (CTA) an entry in a translated balance sheet for the translation gain or loss accumulated over a period of time.

curable depreciation depreciated asset that is still considered to be economically useful.

currency accounting risk the risk of loss in the value of a firm's foreign currency denominated accounts due to a change in exchange rates.

currency appreciation = *revaluation.*

currency exchange risk = *exchange risk.*

currency risk = *exchange risk.*

currency transfer tax a tax on the international transfer of capital.

current account (C/A)(c/a)(cur. acct) <1> an account used for recording accounts payable or receivable with another party. <2> an account used in partnership accounting for recording items with the partners except the capital. <3> a country's international payments arising from exports and imports of goods and services, together with unilateral transfers.

current account deficit a deficit in the current account section of the balance of payments of a country.

current approach cumulative effect of the adjustment on prior years is reported on the current income statement net of related tax effect. ***Also***: cumulative effect method. ***See***: *retroactive method.*

current arrangement the arrangement of assets and liabilities in the balance sheet whereby the current assets and current liabilities precede the fixed assets and fixed liabilities. ***Also***: current first order of arrangement. ***Opp***: *capital arrangement.*

current asset (CA) asset that may reasonably be expected to be realized in cash or be consumed in one year, it is quick assets plus inventory. ***Also***: circulating asset; floating asset; fluid asset; immediate asset; short-term asset.

current asset short term capital gain capital gain from the sale or exchange of assets held for not more than one year.

current assets ratio = *acid-test ratio.*

current balance <1> the new balance of an account immediately after an entry has been entered. <2> the balance regardless of the capital movement.

current capital = *working capital.*

current cash debt ratio a ratio that measures the ability to pay current liabilities with cash derived from operations.

current cash equivalent = *current exit value.*

current cost (CC) <1> replacement cost of an asset at the balance sheet date. ***Also***: current replacement cost; economic cost; market replacement cost; recent cost; true cost. <2> the amount that has to be paid to obtain the resources consumed at the income statement date. ***Also***: current period cost; present cost.

current cost accounting the accounting that shows the current replacement cost of assets in the balance sheet. ***Also***: accounting based on value-to-the-firm; fair value accounting; replacement cost accounting; specific price-level adjusted accounting. ***See***: *current value accounting; inflation accounting.*

current cost/constant dollar method a method under which non-monetary assets are reported at current cost, but the measuring unit is restated dollar.

current cost depreciation = *replacement cost depreciation.*

current cost/nominal dollar method a method under which non-monetary assets are reported at current cost only.

current cost of goods sold number of units sold multiplied by average current cost per unit.

current cost of supplies income (CCS income) net income of a commodity trading company after taking into account increase (or decrease) in expenses. *Also*: adjusted current cost of supplies earnings; CCS earnings.

current cost or recoverable amount, the lower a basis for asset valuation with the lower of its current cost or recoverable amount.

current distribution a distribution other than a liquidating distribution.

current dividend a dividend paid out of profits and earnings from normal course of operation. *Opp*: *liquidating dividend.*

current dollar actual cost of goods and services each year measured by accounting.

current earnings rate investment income of a life insurance company divided by the average of the beginning and ending balance of assets.

current exit value what a company can sell an asset for in today's market. *Also*: current cash equivalent.

current expenditure the expenditure of the current fiscal year of a college. *Also*: current operation expenditure.

current expense an expense treated as an immediate cost, rather than a capitalized cost.

current exposure method a method of calculating the cost of default by using the replacement cost of all marked to market contracts currently *in the money*, plus the credit exposure of potential changes in future prices or volatility of the underlying asset.

current-first order of arrangement = *current arrangement.*

current fund = *general fund.*

current fund revenue money received by a college in the current fiscal year that can be used to pay current obligations.

current income <1> the taxable income plus items not taxable but that increase wealth and plus deductions that do not deplete wealth and minus items that are not deductible but that reduce wealth. <2> income routinely received from an investment or other sources.

current investment short-term investment in marketable securities.

current liability (CL) a debt which must be paid within one year. *Also*: circulating liability; floating liability; immediate liability; liquid liability; short-term financial liability; short-term liability.

current liquidation price = *exit value.*

currently attainable standard cost = *expected standard cost.*

current margin *operating margin* based on the replacement cost of materials.

current market value = *fair market value.*

current market value depreciation difference between selling value of the asset at the beginning and at the end of a given period.

current maturity <1> long-term liability that is maturing in the current fiscal year. <2> the time interval between the present date and the maturity date of a bond issue. *See*: *original maturity.*

current-noncurrent approach an approach under which the current items of the foreign subsidiaries' statements are converted at the current exchange rate, and non-current items are converted at the historical exchange rate.

current obligation the liability of a college that needs to be paid in the current fiscal year.

current operating income statement an income statement deducting from revenue the cost of goods and other expenses based on current values.

current operating performance concept = *current operating performance theory.*

current operating performance income statement income statement showing the current revenue and current cost.

current operating performance theory a theory which holds that an income statement should show current income only. ***Also***: current operating performance concept. ***Opp***: *all inclusive concept.*

current operation expenditure = *current expenditure.*

current outlay cost = *out-of pocket cost.*

current period average cost current production cost minus cost of the equivalent units.

current period cost = *current cost.*

current profit = *operating income.*

current purchasing power accounting (CPP acc) = *constant dollar accounting.*

current rate method a method that translates foreign currency financial statements using the exchange rate at the financial statement date. ***Also***: temporal accounting; temporal method. ***See***: *historical rate method.*

current ratio (CR) relation of current assets to current liabilities. ***Also***: working capital ratio.

current receivable account receivable that can be collected in the current period.

current replacement cost = *current cost.*

current replacement method = *replacement method.*

current report a report filed 10 days after the end of the month when certain significant events have occurred. ***Also***: Form 8-K.

current return <1> annual income of a bond or EPS of a stock divided by its current market price. ***Also***: dividend return; dividend yield; earnings price ratio; earnings yield; income yield; yield to shares. <2> = *current yield.*

current revenue the revenue realized in the current period.

current section a part in the construction-in-process a/c for recording current contract costs.

current service cost the cost of prospective retirement benefits accrued during any year. ***Also***: normal cost. ***See***: *prior service cost.*

current specific-price index replacement cost a replacement cost based on specific price index.

current standard cost an index used only for a certain period under certain circumstances. ***Also***: practical standard cost; present standard cost.

current use value a price that a property or land will realize if it is to continue to be put to its existing use. ***Also***: existing use value; user value.

current value <1> a price that a willing and well-informed buyer and an equally willing and well-informed seller would reach through negotiation. ***Also***: up-to-date value. <2> asset value expressed in current cost. ***See***: *historical value.*

current value accounting (CVA) periodical revaluation of the current value of assets and liabilities. ***See***: *current cost accounting.*

current value approach an approach for reporting balance sheet assets in their current value. ***See***: *historical cost approach.*

current value costing accounting which provides up-to-date current cost data.

current value depreciation the depreciation calculated when assets are restated in current value.

current value financial statement a statement where assets are reported at their current value.

current value income the result of adding unrealized holding gains to realized income.

current year basis a tax basis that income should be based on the revenue, profit, gains, etc. for the taxable year.

current year cost the cost of inventory at current year prices used in the lifo method.

current yield (CUR YLD)(curr y/d) yield of investment which equals the annual income of an investment divided by the price actually paid for it. ***Also***: actual yield; current return; running yield. ***See***: *indicated yield.*

curtailment reduction in the expected years of future service of present employees or elimination for a significant number of employees the accrual of defined benefits for some or all of their future services.

curt. y/d current yield

curvilinear semivariable cost a variable cost not in linear relationship with the volume, e.g. utility cost.

CUR YLD current yield

cushion amount by which a revenue bond's revenues exceed the operating costs and the maintenance cost and debt service, usually 20%. ***Also***: 20% margin.

custodial account an account in which assets are held under a safekeeping agreement on behalf of one or more customers.

custodial accounting = *financial accounting.*

custody cost charge by a custodian for safekeeping and some record-keeping services. *See*: *holding cost.*

customer costing = *operating costing.*

customers' ledger = *accounts receivable ledger.*

customer's net debit balance total amount of credit given by a NYSE member firm to its customers.

customs cost accounting the accounting procedures for customs duties.

customs duty = *tariff.*

cut-off <1> to cease the posting of entries in the account for audit purposes. <2> discrepancy between financial statements and the actual conditions.

cut-off date <1> an artificial cessation date of the flow of cash, goods, or other items for audit purposes. <2> the last day for switching from a joint return to a separate return.

cut-off point = *cut-off rate of return.*

cut-off rate of return in capital budgeting, the minimum rate of return accepted by investors. ***Also***: base interest rate; cut-off point; discount rate; hurdle rate of return; limit rate; lowest acceptable rate of return; minimum acceptable rate; minimum attractive rate of return; minimum cut-off criterion; minimum required rate of return; required rate of interest; required rate of return; vest charge.

cut-off statement a statement of account prepared at the cut-off date.

cut-off test a test made by an auditor several days after the year end balance sheet date by cut-off method.

cut-off yield the bond yield at which or below which the bids are accepted

cutting a melon declaration of a large stock or cash dividend that is in addition to the regular distribution.

CVA current value accounting

CVP cost-volume-profit

CVP **analysis** cost-volume-profit analysis

CWP cost of work performed

cybercash = *electronic money.*

cyberlaundering money laundering carried out through the Internet or electronic banking channels.

cycle billing sending bills to the customers at different time intervals.

cycle count = *cycle inventory.*

cycle inventory physical stock-taking of the assets daily, or month after month throughout the year. ***Also***: continuous physical inventory; cycle count.

cycle of accounting = *accounting cycle.*

cycle posting the posting of banking transaction entries within a month by classifying them into several groups according to nature.

D d

D <1> cash disbursements journal. <2> data. <3> deficit. <4> depreciation charge. <5> dividend.

D&O directors and officers

D&O insurance = *entity insurance.*

D/A <1> depletion allowance. <2> discretionary account. <3> dormant account.

DAC deferred acquisition cost

daily audit the audit performed daily by internal auditors. ***Also***: running audit.

daily basis a system of daily posting of entries into the ledger.

daily posting = *day-to-day posting.*

daily report a report prepared daily.

daily trial balance a trial balance prepared on daily basis after posting.

damage claim a claim for a damage.

DAN depositor account number

data mining a type of database application that looks for hidden patterns in large groups of data. ***Also***: data snooping.

data snooping = *data mining.*

data warehouse large database of information, which is often gathered from multiple back-office systems and other sources and structured in a way that facilitates *data mining.*

dated retained earnings retained earnings in the financial statements after the reorganization.

date of acquisition the date on which control of the acquired entity passes to the acquirer.

date of record date on which holders of record in a company's stock ledger are entitled to receive dividends or stock rights. ***Also***: record date. ***See***: *declaration date; payable date.*

daybook (D/B)(d. bk) = *journal.*

daybook cash journal = *cash journal.*

day count number of days in the calculation of interest payable. ***Also***: day count period.

days cash on hand the number of days cash assets are on hand, calculated as cash on hand ÷ [(operating expense - depreciation)] ÷ 365.

days in receivables = *number of days' sales in receivables.*

days' inventory = *number of days' sales in inventory.*

days of average inventory on hand = *number of days' sales in inventory.*

days payable = *days purchases in accounts payable.*

days payable outstanding (DPO) = *days purchases in accounts payable.*

days purchases in accounts payable ratio measuring the extent that accounts payable represent current debt rather than overdue obligations, which equals accounts payable divided by the cost of sales. ***Also***: accounts payable days; days payable; days payable outstanding.

days receivable = *number of days' sales in receivables.*

days sales outstanding (DSO) a measure to determine if a corporation is attempting to disguise weakness in sales, usually *accounts receivable* divided by quarterly sales times 91. ***See***: *number of days' sales in receivables.*

days sales uncollected = *number of days' sales in receivables.*

days to sell inventory = *number of days' sales in inventory.*

day-to-day posting the posting of entries into a ledger each day. *Also*: daily posting.

DB declining balance

D/B daybook

DBA doing business as

d. bk daybook

DB plan defined benefit plan

dbt <1> debit. <2> debt.

dbt acct doubtful account

DC direct costing

DCA distribution cost accounting

DCF discounted cash flow

DCL dual consolidated loss

DCN declaration control number

DC plan defined contribution plan

DDB double declining balance

DDB method double declining balance method

DDM <1> discounted dividend model. <2> dividend discount model.

dead account = *bad debt.*

dead capital the capital held in some unproductive investment or lying idle.

dead hand poison pill a provision in some *poison pill* plans to dilute an acquirer's position that permits continuing directors to redeem the poison pill rights.

dead hand provision a defense mechanism used by companies in order to protect against a merger or takeover by another company.

dead loan = *bad debt.*

dead stock = *stale inventory.*

deadweight loss the costs to society created by an inefficiency in the market.

deadwood effect taxpayers tends to contribute stocks they do not want, so the mutual fund may contain weak shares.

deathbed transfer the transfer of property by the transferor when he or she is terminally ill. *See*: *lifetime transfer.*

death benefit tax exempt proceeds of a life insurance policy as opposed to investment value.

death tax a tax imposed upon the death of an individual, e.g. *estate tax, inheritance tax.*

deb. bal. debit balance

debenture capital the capital obtained through the sale of unsecured bonds.

debenture stock <1> stock of a company with all or part of its assets promised as security. <2><UK> a bond that refers to debt issues as stock with a stock certificate issued.

debenture stock certificate <UK> a certificate that represents portion of a debt issued, e.g. if a holder of a certificate for 100, he can transfer units of 1 to another investor.

debit (deb.)(dbt)(Dr.) <1> to place an entry on the left hand side of an a/c. <2> = *account receivable.* <3> = *debit side.* <4> = *minus item.*

debit and credit convention an accounting convention that an entry must be debited to one account and be credited to another. *Also*: duality.

debit balance (deb bal.) <1> the balance of an account when the total sum of the debit entries exceeds the sum of the credit entries. <2> the balance of a current account representing money owed to the lender or seller.

debit-credit-balance form account = *balance-column account.*

debit-credit plan a method for recording the transactions by debiting and crediting the accounts. *Also*: credit-debit plan.

debit differential excess of a parent company's investment cost over its equity in a subsidiary. *Also*: consolidated goodwill; consolidation goodwill; cost of subsidiary stock in excess of book value; excess of cost of subsidiary stock over book value; excess of cost over fair value; goodwill; goodwill from consolidation; lost from consolidation; positive goodwill; purchased goodwill. *See*: *credit differential.*

debit entry an entry entered in the debit side of an account.

debit item <1> an item in the debit side of an account. <2> an item in the debit side of the international balance of payments, such as imports.

debit memorandum <1> a memo sent to notify its recipient that the sender has debited the account of the recipient. *Also*: charge notice. <2> a notice from the bank indicating that the balance has been decreased due to some event other than payment of a check.

debit note a notice to the seller for the undercharged amount in a former invoice.

debit side <1> the left-hand side of an account. *Also*: charge side, debit. *See*: *left side.* <2> in the balance of payments, transaction resulting in the sale of the home country currency.

debit-variance = *unfavorable variance.*

debit voucher a voucher for transactions to be debited into an account.

debt <1> money owed by a debtor. <2> = *tax liability.*

debt/asset ratio = *debt ratio.*

debt cancellation = *cancellation of debt.*

debt capacity the maximum amount of long-term debt that a company may borrow. *Also*: borrowing power.

debt capital loan to a firm on which a fixed annual interest is paid. *Also*: borrowed capital; debt financed capital; loan capital.

debt capital cost = *cost of debt capital.*

debt ceiling the maximum amount of money that a bond issuer can owe. *Also*: debt limit.

debt consolidation fund special account an account for the issuance, interest payment and redemption of a government debt.

debt coverage = *ratio of cash flow to debt.*

debt coverage ratio = *debt service ratio.*

debt discount = *bond discount.*

debt-equity ratio financial relationship between debt to outsiders and the owners' capital. *Also*: debt-net worth ratio; debt-to-capital ratio; debt-to-equity ratio; debt-to-net worth ratio; ratio of debt to capital; ratio of liabilities to net worth. *See*: *debt ratio.*

debt factor = *leverage ratio.*

debt-financed capital = *debt capital.*

debt-financed income net income from debt-financed property subject to income taxation

debt-financed property an income producing property, held by an exempt organization, on which there is an acquisition indebtedness.

debt forgiveness = *cancellation of debt.*

debt indicator an indication of whether a debt offset of a taxpayer's refund will occur.

debt limit = *debt ceiling.*

debt-net worth ratio = *debt-equity ratio.*

debt offset amount taken by the IRS from a tax refund against a current or previous tax liability.

debtor (dr.) <1> a person who owes money to another. <2> = *account receivable.*

debtor control ratio the accounts receivable from debtors at the weekend × 52 + annual average sales.

debtor's ledger <1> = *accounts receivable ledger.* <2> = *sales ledger.*

debtors to sales ratio = *ratio of accounts receivable to net sales.*

debt-paying ability = *solvency.*

debt ratio <1> the ratio of debt capital to debt capital plus contributed capital. <2> ratio of total liabilities to total assets of a company. *Also*: creditors' equity ratio; debt/asset ratio; debt to assets ratio; debt/total assets ratio; debt to total assets ratio; financial leverage; liabilities to assets ratio. **See**: *debt-equity ratio.*

debt receivable = *account receivable.*

debt reducing exchange offer (DREO) an offer of equity securities to holders of a company's bonds or other debt to extinguish the debt and reduce the debt portion of the capital structure.

debt repayment payment of principal, interest and other costs made to pay off an obligation. ***Also***: acquittance; payment of debt; settlement of debt.

debt restructure settlement of debt at less than the carrying amount or a continuation of the debt with a modification of terms.

debt schedule a schedule detailing the timing and magnitude of annual loan repayments, or amortization, along with the mix of specific debt instruments and their interest rates.

debt security any security representing a creditor relation with an enterprise.

debt service cash required for the payment of interest and current maturity of principal on the outstanding debt.

debt service coverage ratio of cash available to pay for debt to the total debt payments to be made. ***Also***: debt service coverage ratio.

debt service coverage ratio = *debt service coverage.*

debt service fund a fund used in government accounting to account for the accumulation of resources for the payment of long-term debt principal and interest.

debt service ratio <1> ratio of net operating income to total debt service. ***Also***: debt coverage ratio. <2> the *debt service* payments to gross household income.

debt-serving capacity = *solvency.*

debt-to-assets ratio = *debt ratio.*

debt-to-capital ratio = *debt-equity ratio.*

debt-to-equity ratio = *debt-equity ratio.*

debt-to-GDP ratio a ratio of national debt to a country's gross domestic products.

debt-to-net worth ratio =*debt-equity ratio.*

debt/total assets ratio = *debt ratio.*

debt-to-total assets ratio = *debt ratio.*

decimal amount a tax rate in decimal value.

decision accounting that phase of accounting which provides information for decision making. ***Also***: operational accounting.

decision cost = *programmed cost.*

decision facilitating that function of accounting which provides information before a decision is made.

decision influencing that function of accounting that provides information for appraisal after a decision has been made.

declaration announcement to pay dividends by the board of directors of the company. ***Also***: dividend announcement; dividend declaration

declaration control number (DCN) a number assigned to a tax return filed online.

declaration date the date on which a company declares it will pay dividend on a certain date. ***Also***: announcement date. ***See***: *date of record; payable date.*

declared capital = *stated capital.*

declared dividend the dividend declared by the board of directors to be paid. ***Also***: dividend declared.

declared period <Australia> period determined by the ATO prior to a change in the rate of excise duty where declared period quotas have been imposed.

declared period quota <Australia> a limit on the quantity of goods a taxpayer can buy at a particular rate of excise duty during a *declared period.* ***Also***: commodity quota; quota; tariff rate quota.

declassified cost manufacturing cost that is represented as material cost, labor cost, or any other basic expenditures.

decline in value <Australia> the decline in value of a depreciable asset, which a taxpayer can deduct from income to the extent the asset is used for taxable purpose.

declining balance method a way of providing for depreciation of an asset by writing off each year a fixed percentage of its value at the end of the previous year, so that its book value will be equal to its scrap value at the end of its life. ***Also***: decreasing charge method; diminishing balance method; diminishing value method; fixed percentage method; fixed percentage of declining balance method; fixed percentage of diminishing value method; reducing balance method; reducing installment method; service-capacity method; uniformity varying amounts method.

declining book value = *written down value.*

declining carrying value = *written down value.*

decommissioning cost the cost of decommissioning a discontinued plant.

decomposition analysis the analysis of an investment by using the *Du Pont formula.*

decoupling a departure from the typical relationship between two assets or asset class returns.

decreasing-charge interest method a method under which the depreciation is the difference between the book value of the asset and the present value of its estimated income in the future years.

decreasing charge method = declining balance method.

decreasing cost a cost which decreases as the production volume increases. ***Also***: degressive cost; diminishing cost.

decreasing return a drop in the rate of return because of over investment or lower earnings.

decremental cost the cost saved by adopting a less cost proposal.

decremental revenue the revenue lost when adopting a low income proposal.

dedicated capital = *nominal capital.*

deductible business expense business expense that can be deducted from revenue to arrive at net income. ***Also***: allowable business expense.

deductible charitable contribution charitable contribution made to a *qualified charitable organization.*

deductible expense = *tax deductible expense.*

deductible gift <Australia> a gift made by a taxpayer that can be deducted from the taxable income. ***Also***: income tax deductible gift; tax deductible gift.

deductible gift recipient (DGR) <Australia> an entity entitled to receive a tax deductible gift.

deductible IRA an IRA the contributions of which are tax deductible. ***See***: *nondeductible IRA; Roth IRA; traditional IRA.*

deductible loss a loss that arises when a taxpayer loses money, property or rights or when these items lose value as a result of an identifiable event. ***Also***: allowable loss.

deductible mortgage interest = *mortgage interest deduction.*

deduction <1> *bank discount.* <2> = *tax deduction.*

deduction for AGI = *above-the-line deduction.*

deduction for exemption = *tax deduction.*

deduction from gross income = *income deduction.*

deduction year a year in which a taxpayer chose to deduct foreign taxes rather than claiming the benefit of a foreign tax credit.

deemed acquisition <Canada> the acquisition of a property even though a taxpayer did not actually buy it.

deemed benefit <Canada> amount by which the actual cost of a share or mutual fund unit under the option is less than the FMV of the share or unit on its date of acquisition.

deemed disposition <Canada> the transfer of a property that is deemed to be sold by the tax law, such as transfer of securities from a non-registered retirement pension plan to a registered plan.

deemed dividend amount of dividend deemed to be paid to the shareholder on redemption, acquisition or cancellation of the share.

deemed gain <Canada> amount which is deemed to have been a gain of the taxpayer from the disposition of property is added in computing its adjusted cost base.

deemed inclusion rule a rule under which a deduction may be taken by an employer if he complies with the applicable information reporting requirements timely.

deemed IRA a separate retirement plan that meets the requirements of a traditional IRA. *Also*: sidecar IRA.

deemed non-resident <Canada> a resident of Canada who under a tax treaty is considered a resident of another country.

deem sale taxpayer's election of treating a security as sold so the gain can be taxed at a lower rate if he expects the tax rate will increase next year.

def <1> deferred. <2> deficit.

def. a/c deferred account

defalcation = *embezzlement.*

default failure of the company to pay interest on bonds.

default adjusted price the present value of actual default impaired cash flows discounted at the nominal yield of a bond or loan.

defaulted security the fixed income security unable to make interest rate payments and/or unable to repay its principal.

defaulting subscriber a subscriber to a stock issue but fails to pay the later installments.

default interest a higher interest payable after default.

defective product a product that may cause injury due to flawed design or poor quality.

defense cost the cost of defending a lawsuit.

defense surtax = *excess profits tax.*

defensive interval = *defensive-interval ratio.*

defensive-interval ratio number of days that the business can meet its basic operational costs and its debts without additional revenue, often the quick assets divided by average daily cash expenditure. *Also*: defensive interval. *See*: *burn rate.*

defensive stock a stock issued by a company with earnings, even when market is weak.

deferrable cost a cost that can be treated as a deferred asset which is to be amortized in the later periods.

deferral carrying forward of items in the current period to subsequent periods. *Opp*: accrual.

deferral election <Canada> a taxpayer's election of deferring employment benefits. *Also*: election to defer.

deferral method <1> a method showing the deferred tax as a liability in the balance sheet. *Also*: liability method. <2> a method which recognizes revenue in the subsequent periods. *See*: *net-of-tax method.*

deferral of tax postponement of tax payments from the current year to a later year.

deferred account (def. a/c) an account that postpones taxes until a later date.

deferred acquisition cost (DAC) deferred costs from acquiring new insurance policies.

deferred amount <Canada> amount that a taxpayer has a right to receive after the end of a tax year.

deferred annuity an annuity the payment does not begin until the future date chosen by the investor. *Also*: annuity in arrears; deferred payment annuity. *See*: *annuity due; ordinary annuity.*

deferred asset an amount receivable more than 12 months after the date of the balance sheet. *Also*: fictitious asset.

deferred charge expense or cost incurred for benefits that will be enjoyed at a future time and will be charged against future operations. *Also*: deferred charge to future income; deferred cost. *See*: *deferred debit item.*

deferred charge to future income = *deferred charge.*

deferred compensation a compensation paid to an employee in a tax year subsequent to when it was earned.

deferred compensation plan arrangement designed to save taxes by postponing receipt of some employee's compensation from one year into another.

deferred contribution payment at a future date for work done in an earlier period.

deferred cost = *deferred charge.*

deferred credit <1> = *deferred revenue.* <2> = *negative goodwill.*

deferred credit item favorable variance and other items shown as liability and will increase income in the future, e.g. *deferred revenue.*

deferred debit item items shown as assets and will decrease income in the future, e.g. *deferred charge.*

deferred debt a debt that can only be paid when other debts are paid.

deferred deficit = *deficit brought forward.*

deferred dividend a dividend declared but due to be paid at some future date.

deferred equity an expectation that the bond will be converted into shares of common stock.

deferred gain = *rollover deferral.*

deferred gross profit the profit not collected under installment sales and thus deferred on the balance sheet pending cash collection from the customer.

deferred income tax amounts of income tax delayed or put off until later years because of accelerated depreciation or timing difference.

deferred installments receivable = *installment accounts receivable.*

deferred interest income earnings from deferred interest.

deferred liability the liability that represents deferred income and deferred revenue. ***Also***: *fictitious liability.*

deferred method a method under which income tax effects of current timing differences are computed using tax rates in effect when the deferral of taxes takes place. ***See***: *liability method.*

deferred overhead charge overhead that is deferred to be absorbed by future products.

deferred payment annuity = *deferred annuity.*

deferred payment obligation a market discount bond, short-term obligation, US savings bond, annuity or similar obligation.

deferred-payment sale = *installment sale.*

deferred posting a mechanized system whereby one day's events are posted in one comprehensive alphabetical run on the following day. ***Also***: delayed posting.

deferred premium a premium that should be paid following the policy's statement date, but prior to the next policy anniversary.

deferred profit sharing portion of company profits allocated to employee's trust.

deferred profit-sharing plan (DPSP) <Canada> a savings plan which requires an employer to contribute at least 1% of the employee's earnings per year regardless of the profitability of the business.

deferred revenue cash received before delivery of products and the performance of service. ***Also***: deferred credit; income in advance; income received but unearned; prepaid income; revenue received in advance; unearned revenue. ***See***: *deferred credit item.*

deferred share <1> a share that receives no rights to a company's remaining assets in the event of liquidation until all common and preferred shareholders have been paid. <2><UK> = *founder's share.*

deferred start swap a swap where some or all payments are delayed for a specific period after their magnitude is determined, usually for tax purposes.

deferred stock a stock the dividends of which are not paid until the expiration of a stated date or until a specified event has taken place.

deferred tax a tax postponed for allocation to income tax expense of future period.

deferred tax accounting the accounting that makes adequate provision for any future tax liabilities in the accounts of a business.

deferred tax asset amount expected to be refunded in the future as a result of reversal of temporary difference existing at the balance sheet date.

deferred tax credit a potential tax benefit that will be carried forward into future tax years.

deferred tax expense non-cash tax-deductible expense which provides a source of cash flow.

deferred tax liability amount of tax expected to be paid in the future as a result of the turn around of temporary difference existing at the balance sheet date.

deficiency <1> excess of liabilities over assets. *Also*: accounting insolvency; accumulated deficit; deficit; deficit net worth; negative net worth. <2> tax assessed by the IRS in excess of the tax reported by the taxpayer. *Also*: tax deficiency. ***Opp***: *overpayment.* <3> of an insurance company, a situation where valuation premium is greater than the gross premium.

deficiency account <UK> = *liquidation account.*

deficiency dividend a tax rule which permits the corporation to distribute a dividend when it has a loss, and to use it to reduce retroactively the personal holding company tax liability.

deficiency letter <1> a letter from the SEC to a prospective issuer, stating that the preliminary prospectus needs revision or addition. <2> = *90-day letter.*

deficiency relief <UK> tax relief given on the maturity, surrender or sale of a life insurance policy.

deficiency reserve a reserve created by an insurance company as required by state laws when valuation premium is greater than gross premium.

deficiency statement <UK> = *liquidation account.*

deficit <1> = *budget deficit.* <2> = *deficiency.*

deficit adjustment a short-term adjustment to the trade deficit by the manipulation in the foreign exchange market.

deficit brought forward a deficit brought forward from last period to this period. ***Also***: deferred deficit; loss brought forward; loss forwarded.

deficit financing the funding of expenditures by borrowing. ***Also***: compensatory finance; pump priming.

deficit net worth = *deficiency.*

defined asset an asset which has a defined name in the balance sheet.

defined benefit pension plan = *defined benefit provision.*

defined benefit plan (DB plan) a pension plan that defines the amount of benefit employees will receive when they retire. ***Also***: 412(i) plan; fixed benefit plan. ***See***: *target benefit plan.*

defined benefit provision <Canada> a pension plan which calculates a specified level of pension income by a set formula. ***Also***: defined benefit pension plan. ***See***: *money purchase provision.*

defined benefit scheme <UK> a retirement plan where the benefits are defined independently of the contributions, and not related to the investment.

defined contribution plan (DC plan) a pension plan providing benefits in return for services rendered, and specifies how contributions to the individual account are to be determined.

defined contribution scheme <UK> a pension plan under which benefits are defined by the value of contributions paid in respect of each member.

deflating calculating constant dollar by dividing current dollar by an index.

defrauding the revenue = *tax evasion.*

degree of completion method = *percentage of completion method.*

degree of financial leverage (DFL) percentage change in earnings available to the common shareholders that is associated with a given percentage change in net income. ***See***: *financial leverage.*

degree of financial risk = *gearing ratio.*

degree of freedom (DF) number of data items that are independent of one another.

degree of operating leverage (DOL) change in net income before interest and taxes resulting from a percentage change in revenue.

degree of relative liquidity (DRL) percentage of a company's cash expenditures that can be secured from beginning fund and cash flow generated from normal operations.

degree of total leverage (DTL) percentage change in net income that is associated with a give percentage change in sales.

degressive cost = *decreasing cost.*

delayed costing = *back flush costing.*

delayed debit charge to a customer's account of the purchases at the end of a month.

delayed income the income of a previous period that is delayed to later periods.

delayed posting = *deferred posting.*

delayed recognition method a method applied to the sale of receivables on a recourse basis for more than the carrying value of accounts receivable, deferred financing charges be amortized as interest expenses over the periods during which the receivables are collected.

delayed remittance delayed remittance of foreign income or capital gains back to the taxpayer's resident country due to foreign exchange control.

delayed variable cost = *semi-variable cost.*

deleverage the reduction of financial instruments or borrowed capital previously used to increase the potential return of an investment. ***See***: *deleveraging.* ***Opp***: *leverage.*

deleveraging the process of decreasing the proportional use of debt in the capital structure. ***See***: *deleverage.*

deliberate audit = *selective audit.*

delinquent tax = *back tax.*

deliverable stock inventory of commodities located in an exchange-approved storage, for which receipts may be used in making delivery on futures contracts.

delivery basis a basis under which revenue is recognized when goods are delivered.

Deloitte & Touche LLP one of the big 4 accounting firms.

Delphi method qualitative forecasting method which seeks to use a collection of independent judgement of experts systematically.

demat dematerialization

demat account an account to hold the dematerialized securities.

dematerialization (demat) a process by which physical stock certificates held by an investor are converted to an equivalent number of shares in electronic form and credited in his account. ***See***: *rematerialization.*

dematerialzed securities the securities in electronic form rather than traditional paper certificates.

demerger to sell off subsidiaries or divisions of a company. ***Opp***: *merger.* ***See***: *reverse merger.*

de minimis aid grant in small amount.

de minimis amount the amount that equals ¼ of 1 percent.

de minimis fringe a nontaxable fringe benefit since its value is so small that accounting for it is not reasonable.

de minimis rule a rule that gains on the sale of a municipal bond bought at a discount is capital gain if the amount of the discount was less than the *de minimis amount.*

demolition loss a loss sustained by the property owner on demolition of the building.

denial of opinion report auditor's report where the auditor refused to give his opinion.

denied applicant an applicant who is denied in participating the IRS e-file program.

denied deduction <Canada> a tax deduction not allowed by the CCRA.

denomination = *face value.*

denominator level annual budgeted activity, e.g. direct labor hours, used to calculate predetermined overhead rate.

denominator variance <1> = *fixed overhead volume variance.* <2> = *overhead volume variance.*

departmental accounting the accounting matter for the sections or sub units of a business.

departmental costing the costing that accumulates cost data by departments.

departmental gross profit gross profit of a department.

departmental overhead cost other than direct material and direct labor incurred in a specific department.

departmental overhead variance difference between actual and standard departmental overhead.

departmental rate predetermined overhead rate for a particular department.

departure tax <Canada> tax on a corporation that ceases to be a resident of Canada.

dependency exemption a *tax exemption* that entitles the individual taxpayers to a deduction of $3,050 (for the year 2003) per dependent. *Also:* amount for an eligible dependent; equivalent-to-spouse amount; exemption for dependents.

dependency ratio a ratio indicating the number of dependents (aged 0-14 and over the age of 65) to the total population (aged 15-64).

dependent a person who relies on someone else for financial support. *See: eligible dependent.*

dependent cash flow cash flow of this period that is dependent of the results of the last period.

dependent child the child who can be claimed as a dependent of a taxpayer.

dependent income taxable income of a person while being claimed as a dependent of another taxpayer. *Also*: separate net income.

depletable asset = *wasting asset.*

depleted cost original cost of the wasting asset less accumulated depletion.

depletion accounting treatment available to corporations in the business of extracting oil and gas, coal or other minerals in the form of allowance that reduces taxable income.

depletion accounting methods for calculating, distributing, recording and reporting asset depletion

depletion allowance deduction from corporate gross income for exhaustible mineral deposits.

depletion asset = *wasting asset.*

depletion base cost of a wasting asset less scrap plus disposal expenses.

depletion cost the cost of the wasting asset that has been depleted under depletion.

depletion unit a taxpayer's basis in wasting asset divided by the volume of wasting asset subject to depletion.

depletion unit method = *production-unit basis method.*

depletive asset = *wasting asset.*

depn depreciation

deposit in transit cash deposits that arrive at the bank too late to be credited and shown in the statement of the current month.

deposit method <1> an inventory method under which returnable containers are considered fixed assets, the income from which is deferred until they clearly will not be returned. <2> a method of recognizing real estate profit, under which payments received are recorded as a liability until the sale is completed.

depositor account number (DAN) an account number to which a direct deposit tax refund is to be routed.

depository preferred stock an issue of high par value preferred stock deposited with a bank, which in turn issues more shares of a lower par value.

depository receipt a negotiable financial instrument issued by a bank to represents a foreign company's publicly traded securities.

deposit taker <UK> a financial institution that takes withholding tax deposits for the US Treasury.

depr depreciation

depreciable amount = *depreciable cost.*

depreciable asset an asset which by its nature loses its value through exhaustion, wear, tear, and obsolescence, thus subject to depreciation. ***Also***: character subject to depreciation; depreciable amount; depreciating asset. ***See***: *wasting asset.*

depreciable cost the original cost of a depreciable asset less salvage value. ***Also***: asset cost; cost less scrap; depreciation base; depreciation base value.

depreciable interest an interest in asset that allows the holder to claim depreciation.

depreciable life the time period in which an asset is depreciated.

depreciated cost the fixed asset cost that has been transferred to depreciation expenses a/c.

depreciated current cost original cost of an asset less accumulated depreciation based on the current replacement cost.

depreciated original cost = *written down value.*

depreciated replacement cost = *written-down replacement cost.*

depreciated value = *written-down value.*

depreciating asset <Australia> = *depreciable asset.*

depreciation (depn)(depr) the decline in value or the quantity of usefulness of a plant asset. ***Also***: asset expiration; cost expiration; cost recovery; expiration of assets; expired utility; impaired serviceableness. ***Opp:*** *appreciation.* <2> = *capital consumption allowance.* <3> = *depreciation cost.*

depreciation account an account in which the depreciation on an asset is entered on the debit side, and the same amount is also credited to the contra account of the asset associated. ***Also***: depreciation expense account.

depreciation accounting the procedures for the measuring, recording and reporting of asset depreciation. ***Also***: accounting for investment properties.

depreciation adjustment the amount that has to be added to a depreciation expense in order to arrive at the value to the business of the part of fixed assets consumed.

depreciation agreement an agreement between the IRS and a taxpayer in which the economic lives, salvage values, and depreciation methods are agreed upon.

depreciation allowance <1> a tax allowance to business on the cost of new machinery, spread over several years. <2> = *allowance for depreciation.*

depreciation and diminution provision = *allowance for depreciation.*

depreciation base = *depreciable cost.*

depreciation base value = *depreciable cost.*

depreciation by kind = *classification method.*

depreciation cost the cost resulting from the expiration of a plant asset's usefulness. ***Also***: capital recovery cost; cost of depreciation; depreciation, depreciation expense.

depreciation expense (depr. exp) = *depreciation cost.*

depreciation expense account = *depreciation account.*

depreciation fund method a depreciation method which debits the profit and loss a/c each year with a fixed amount equal to the depreciation of the asset and crediting the amount to a depreciation allowance account.

depreciation on current cost basis = *replacement cost depreciation.*

depreciation on market price = *replacement cost depreciation.*

depreciation on replacement value = *replacement cost depreciation.*

depreciation per unit of product depreciation calculated under units-of-output method.

depreciation rate the percentage applied to the cost or other basis of asset in order to calculate the amount of depreciation for a particular year. ***Also***: rate of depreciation.

depreciation recapture = *recapture of depreciation.*

depreciation reserve = *allowance for depreciation.*

depreciation schedule a list of depreciation of various assets in a given accounting period. *Also*: lapsing schedule; value-decrease schedule.

depreciation tax shield the value of the tax *write-off* on depreciation.

depr. exp. depreciation expense

deprival value <1> asset value which equals the loss that the firm would incur if it were deprived of the asset. <2> = *replacement cost.*

deprival value accounting system accounting system that shows the deprival value of assets in financial statements.

DEPS diluted earnings per share

derivative a security or transaction that derives its value from the value of an underlying asset. *Also*: derivative product; financial derivative.

derivative accounting convention a convention which requires that the balance sheet should represent the actual balances of the ledger, and should not show the present value adjustments.

derivative method a method under which assets and liabilities are shown on the balance sheet at their book balances. *Also*: inductive method. *See*: *inventory method.*

derivative product = *derivative.*

derivatives implementation group (DIG) a group of largely accounting practitioners and derivatives specialists established by the FASB to help implement FAS 133.

derivatives policy group (DPG) a group of people representing six large non-bank OTC derivatives dealers who worked with the CFTC and SEC to design oversight procedures for OTC derivatives activities of unregulated securities firm affiliates.

derived market value = *replacement cost.*

derived tax revenue a revenue that results from taxes assessed by governments on exchange transactions, e.g. sales tax based on exchange between merchant and consumers.

description <1> the explanation of the entry in an account. *Also*: extract. <2> = *interpretation.*

descriptive accounting that phase of accounting which argues that accounting should be limited to the disclosure of actual business transactions.

designated beneficiary <Canada> a beneficiary of a trust who is a non-resident alien or a non-resident-owned company.

designated income <Canada> earnings of a designated beneficiary from a trust.

designated insurance property <Canada> a property used or held in the ordinary course of carrying on an insurance business.

designated person <Canada> a beneficiary of a trust who is related to the grantor.

design-to-cost technique a method that provides a work-output based on resources available for estimating cost. *Also*: estimating-to-cost technique.

desk audit <1> a review of a job or jobs to see if the duties fit the assigned pay and rank and possibly to see if the person filling the job has the right qualifications. *Also*: job audit. <2> the review of a federal income tax return by an IRS official. *Also*: office audit.

desperate debt = *bad debt.*

detailed account an account in a subsidiary ledger for recording details of the general ledger account. *Also*: detailed ledger account; subsidiary account; subsidiary ledger account.

detailed audit careful examination of all or most of the transactions and related records of a business. *Also*: full audit.

detailed audit report = *long form report.*

detailed ledger = *subsidiary ledger.*

detailed ledger account = *detailed account.*

detailed principle a principle which concerns the application of broad operating principle and pervasive principle.

detection risk the likelihood that an auditor's procedures lead to an improper conclusions that no material misstatement exists in an assertion when in fact one does exist.

deterioration cost cost that results from the loss in the quality of materials, products, or the finished goods inventories.

determinable liability a liability the amount and time of repayment of which are known and reasonably precise. ***See***: *contingent liability.*

determination of cost behavior separation of costs into their fixed and variable components. ***Also***: classification of fixed and variable costs; cost behavior analysis; cost behavior classification; fixed variable cost analysis; fixed-variable split of cost; resolving of cost; segregation of fixed and variable costs.

development cost = *research and development cost.*

deviation <1> a sample item which does not have one or more of the attributes. <2> = *exception.*

deviation rate in audit sampling, it equals number of observed deviations divided by sample size.

DF degree of freedom

DFL degree of financial leverage

DGR deductible gift recipient

DI disability income

DIF Discriminant Income Function

DIF **score** a score assigned to a tax return by the *Discriminant Income Function.*

difference between cost and book value <1> = *accumulated depreciation.* <2> = *differential.*

difference estimation a variable sampling technique that uses the average difference between the audited amounts and the recorded amounts to estimate the total audited amount of a population and an allowance for sampling risk. ***See***: *mean-per-unit estimation.*

difference in books = *error in books.*

different activities approach an approach by which budget allowances or factory overhead application rates under different activity levels are determined.

differential the difference between investment cost shown in the parent company's book and its equities recorded in the subsidiary's book. ***Also***: difference between cost and book value; investment elimination adjustment. ***See***: *credit differential; debit differential.*

differential accounting the accounting methods that render differential income and differential cost data.

differential analysis = *relevant cost approach.*

differential cost = *relevant cost.*

differential costing = *relevant costing.*

differential disclosure <1> preparing different statements for different users. <2> reporting of conflicting or significant information in official statement such as annual reports, 10-Ks and 10-Qs by a public company.

differential income excess of differential revenue over differential cost.

differential revenue the revenue which differs between the alternative courses of action which are being considered.

difficult asset an asset the actual quantity of which is difficult to count.

DIG derivatives implementation group

digital money electronic money that can be used to pay for goods and services.

diluted earnings per share (DEPS) = *fully-diluted earnings per share.*

diluted shares the new number of shares outstanding after all dilutive shares have been accounted for. ***Also***: diluted shares outstanding.

diluted shares outstanding = *diluted shares.*

dilution reduction in earnings per share that would occur if the convertible securities were converted or if outstanding options and warrants were exercised.

dilution protection a provision that changes the *conversion ratio* in the case of a stock dividend or extraordinary distribution to avoid *dilution* of a convertible bondholder's potential equity.

dilutive security stock warrant, stock right, convertible bond, preferred stock, etc. the exercise or conversion of which would lower the EPS. ***Also***: residual security.

diminishing asset = *wasting asset.*

diminishing balance method = *declining-balance method.*

diminishing cost = *decreasing cost.*

diminishing marginal returns a theory which holds that as the amount of any one input is increased, holding all other inputs constant, the amount of output for each additional unit of the expanding input will generally decrease.

diminishing return a point beyond which the application of additional resources yields less than proportional increases in output.

diminishing value method = *declining-balance method.*

diplomatic concession <Australia> limited quantity of tariff-free goods granted to foreign embassies, consulates and other diplomats. ***Also***: diplomatic privilege.

diplomatic privilege <UK> = *diplomatic concession.*

dipping into lifo layers = *lifo liquidation.*

direct allocation = *one-step allocation.*

direct attribution a method that seeks to capture accurately the volume and cost of resources used by particular activities.

direct charge-off method = *direct method.*

direct cost the cost that is easily traced to or associated with a cost object. ***Also***: direct expense; directly related cost; direct traceable cost; identifiable cost; separable cost; specification cost; traceable cost.

direct costing the costing that charges direct costs to the product inventory. ***Also***: activity costing; cause and effect costing; marginal costing. ***See***: *variable costing.*

direct costing income statement an income statement prepared under unit-block system or multi block system, which shows the direct costs, contribution margin, etc. ***See***: *absorption costing income statement.*

direct cost method a method which charges only the direct cost to the product inventory and treats fixed overhead costs as expenses.

direct cost of financial distress cost incurred as a result of bankruptcy or liquidation.

direct credit a tax credit allowed as to the effectively connected income from sources outside the USA.

direct debit a withdrawal by the US Treasury from a taxpayer's checking or savings account for the tax payment.

direct department cost direct materials and direct labor of a department.

direct deposit the deposit of funds directly into a bank account as a form of payment, used by employers to deposit payroll or by IRS to send tax refund.

direct distribution = *one-step allocation.*

directed shares = *friends and family shares.*

direct estimate method <1> a method of determining fixed and variable cost behavior by inspecting its historical records. ***Also***: inspection of accounts method. <2> a method of cash budgeting based on detailed estimates of cash receipts and cash disbursements category by category.

direct expense = *direct cost.*

direct financial interest a personal investment under the direct control of the investor. ***See***: *indirect financial interest.*

direct financing type lease a leasing company purchased the desired asset from the seller and leases it to the buyer, only interest expense arises, no profit results from lease. ***See***: *sales-type lease.*

direct-fixed cost that part of a direct cost that does not change at different activity levels, e.g. manager's salaries. *Also*: traceable fixed cost.

direct inventory the inventory of direct materials, work-in-process, and finished goods.

direct investment the flow of US capital into foreign enterprises in which US residents have significant control.

direct labor work directly involved in making the product.

direct labor budget a budget that shows the number of the labor hours and the hourly rate of the different types of labor, which comprise the total cost.

direct labor cost a cost associated with personnel activity in the production process. *Also*: productive labor cost.

direct labor-cost method a method of applying overhead that uses direct labor costs as basis.

direct labor cost variance = *labor cost variance.*

direct labor efficiency variance = *labor efficiency variance.*

direct labor hour (D. labor hr)(DLH)(DL hr) hours taken in the actual production of goods.

direct labor hour method a method of allocating overhead costs using direct labor hours as the basis of distribution. *Also*: labor hour method; man hour method; productive labor hours method.

direct labor mix variance the cost variance caused when standard mix of different grades of direct labor has not been achieved.

direct labor price variance = *labor rate variance.*

direct labor rate variance = *labor rate variance.*

direct labor variance = *labor cost variance.*

direct loss property loss in which the insured peril is the proximate cause of the damage.

directly related cost = *direct cost.*

direct material a material that becomes an integral part of the finished product.

direct materials cost a cost associated with materials used to produce goods or service.

direct materials cost method a method of distributing overhead cost that uses direct materials cost as the basis.

direct materials cost percentage rate the rate of overhead costs as a percentage of the total direct materials costs. *Also*: percentage on direct materials.

direct materials efficiency variance = *direct materials usage variance.*

direct materials mix variance cost variance caused by the difference in cost of an actual mix and the standard cost of the standard mix.

direct materials price variance difference between the actual material price per unit and the standard price multiplied by the actual number of units of materials used.

direct materials purchase budget the budget about the direct materials cost.

direct materials purchase price variance the difference between the actual materials price and the standard price, multiplied by the actual number of units of materials purchased.

direct materials quantity variance = *direct materials usage variance.*

direct materials usage budget the budget about the direct materials usage.

direct materials usage variance the difference between the actual quantity of direct material consumed and the standard quantity allowed, multiplied by the standard price per unit of material. *Also*: direct materials efficiency variance; direct material quantity variance.

direct materials variance the difference between the actual direct material cost and the allowed cost.

direct materials yield variance cost variance caused when output is less than the input.

direct method <1> a method whereby uncollectible accounts are written off by a debit to a doubtful account expense a/c. *Also*: charge off method; direct charge-off method; direct write-off method; specific charge-off method; write-off method. **See**: *allowance method.* <2> a method under which service department costs are allocated directly to operating departments only. **See**: *continuous allotment method.* <3> a method under which the lower of cost or market amount is used directly in the cost of goods sold computation with no separate disclosure of LCM loss. <4> a method used to report major classes of gross cash receipts and gross cash payments and their net total, the net cash flow from operating activities. **See**: *indirect method.* <5> procedure of calculating cash flow from operations by adjusting each item of the income statement from an accrual basis to a cash basis.

director diagram = *breakeven chart.*

director's fee a fee paid by the company to its directors.

direct overhead the factory cost, selling or other expenses related to a specific product directly and resulting in a direct cost.

direct participation program (DPP) program enabling investors to receive the cash flow and tax benefits as passive income directly through a limited partnership.

direct percentage method = *arbitrary percentage method.*

direct posting = *bookless accounting system.*

direct product cost = *prime cost.*

direct product profitability a retailer's measure of the profit of a particular product taking into consideration the cost of handling and storage.

direct profit sales minus direct cost associated with a particular product.

direct relevant cost direct cost that is relevant to a future decision.

direct repurchase a company's buying back its own shares from the marketplace to reduce the *number of shares outstanding.* **See**: *corporate reacquisition.*

direct rollover a distribution from qualified pension plan, 401(k) plan, or 403(b) plan that is remitted directly to the trustee or the IRA owner and reported to the IRS as a rollover.

direct share program (DSP) plan designed to allow employees, their relatives, and other parties with a relationship to the company to buy stock as part of a public offering.

direct standard costing the costing where the actual overhead rather than standard overhead costs are used. ***Also***: integrated cost system; standard direct costing.

direct tax <1> tax cannot be shifted to others, such as *federal income tax.* <2> a tax on land. <3> = *income tax.* <4> = *poll tax.*

direct traceable cost = *direct cost.*

direct transfer the transfer of money directly to a new IRA by a taxpayer's spouse.

direct trust = *express trust.*

direct valuation a way of determining the fair value of a business by computing net present value of all its future revenue and expenditures. ***Also***: capitalization of net cash inflows method.

direct variable cost portion of the direct costs that tends to change in amount according to the change in the volume of production.

direct verification the verification of income statement items by analyzing the revenue and expense accounts. **See**: *indirect verification.*

direct wage rate variance = *labor rate variance.*

direct write-off method = *direct method.*

disability income (DI) insurance payment to a person who has been disabled for at least six months.

disability tax credit <Canada> a credit that reduces federal income tax up to $960 for a taxpayer with physical or mental disability.

disabled access credit a tax credit, 50% of the amount of eligible access expenditures that is over $250 but not more than $10,250.

disabled person a person who can not engage in any substantial gainful activity because of a physical or mental condition.

disallowable expense <UK> = *nondeductible expense.*

disappearing basis rule a rule the gist of which is that original investment in a stock can not be treated as taxable distribution when that stock is redeemed.

disaster loss an unreimbursed loss caused by loss or damage to a property in an area the President has declared eligible for federal disaster assistance. ***See:*** *casualty loss.*

disbursement payment of cash for expenditures.

disbursement float decrease in book cash but no immediate change in bank cash, generated by checks written by the firm and still outstanding. ***See:*** *collection float.*

disbursement voucher = *payment voucher.*

DISC domestic international sales corporation

dischargeable debt a debt that can be cancelled through bankruptcy. ***See***: *nondischargeable debt.*

discharge of debt = *cancellation of debt.*

disclaimer <1> statement made to free oneself from responsibility. ***Also***: *hedge clause.* <2> auditor's statement to express no opinions, or unable to express an opinion. ***Also***: disclaimer of opinion.

disclaimer of opinion = *disclaimer.*

disclosure to present financial data in accounting statements in accordance with GAAP.

disclosure principle a principle that accounting statement should show necessary information.

disclosure risk a risk of loss that the disclosure of financial information will put the company at a disadvantage in the future.

discontinued operation segment of business that is no longer part of the ongoing operations of the company.

discount = *bank discount.*

discount basis = *discount yield.*

discount bond method a method which requires the bond holders and issuers to make current adjustments to their OID accruals to account for inflation and deflation. ***See:*** *coupon bond method.*

discounted accounts receivable = *accounts receivable factored.*

discounted bailout period = *discounted payback period.*

discounted cash flow (DCF) future cash flows multiplied by discount factor.

discounted cash flow rate of return = *internal rate of return.*

discounted dividend model (DDM) = *dividend discount model.*

discounted earnings future earnings discounted to present value.

discounted expected value the present value of an expected future value.

discounted gross benefit cost = *present value profitability index.*

discounted net benefit-cost ratio (present value of annual cash inflows - asset depreciation)/present value of annual cash outflows.

discounted payback period time required to recover initial cash outflow from discounted cash flow. ***Also***: discounted bailout period.

discounted payback period method a method under which the cash flow is discounted before the payback period is computed.

discounted payback period rule an investment decision rule in which investment with shortest payback period will be chosen.

discounted rate of return = *internal rate of return.*

discounted rate of return method = *internal rate of return method.*

discounted security = *relevant discounted security.*

discounter = *tax rebate discounter.*

discount factor present value of $1 received at a stated future date. ***Also***: present value factor. ***See***: *annuity factor; future value factor.*

discount from asset value of an investment trust, the difference between the asset and price of the stock expressed as a percentage of the asset value.

discount interest = *bank discount.*

discount lost cash discount offered by the seller but not taken by the buyer. ***Also***: lost discount; purchase discount lost.

discount margin the return earned in addition to the index underlying the floating rate security.

discount method a method of paying interest by issuing a security at less than par and repaying par value at maturity.

discount on purchase = *purchase discount.*

discount on sales = *sales discount.*

discount on stock difference between the par value of stock and the amount below par value contributed by stockholders. ***Also***: excess of par value over issuing price of stock.

discount rate <1> the interest rate used in the calculation of the present value of a future amount. ***Also***: capitalization rate. <2> interest rate charged by the Federal Reserve Bank to its member banks. ***Also***: rediscount rate. <3> = *cut-off rate of return.*

discount risk the risk of loss to an investor when the discount on mutual fund shares widens.

discount yield actual yield on a bond sold at a discount, calculated as discount ÷ face amount × 360 ÷ days until maturity. ***Also***: discount basis.

discovery assessment <UK> the assessment of tax when the Revenue makes enquiry into a tax return. ***See***: *self-assessment.*

discovery sampling a procedure for determining the sample size required to have a stipulated probability of observing at least one occurrence when the expected population deviation rate is at a designated level.

discovery value the value of a wasting asset expressed by its newly discovered future income.

discovery value accounting the procedure which presents wasting assets at discovery value. ***Also***: dry hole accounting.

discovery value depletion the depletion allowance based on discovery value.

discrete compounding the process of calculating interest and adding it to existing principal and interest at finite time intervals, such as daily, monthly or yearly.

discrete presentation method presentation of most component units in the government-wide financial statement in a separate column. ***See***: *blended presentation method.*

discrete view each interim period in a separate accounting period stands on its own. ***See***: *integral view.*

discretionary account (D/A) account giving a broker the power to buy and sell securities without the client's prior consent.

discretionary cash flow cash flow available for paying cash dividends, repurchasing common stock, retiring debt, etc.

discretionary cost = *programmed cost.*

discretionary deduction tax deduction from adjusted gross estate to arrive at taxable estate, e.g. charitable contribution.

discretionary dividend <1> a dividend based on the operating results of a company. ***See:*** *nondiscretionary dividend.* <2> = *common dividend.*

discretionary expenditure an item of expenditure that can be postponed or eliminated.

discretionary expense center = *expense center.*

discretionary fixed cost fixed cost for which management has a significant choice as to whether the payments are made, their amounts and timing. ***Also***: managed fixed cost.

discretionary income a taxpayer's income available for spending after essentials (such as food, clothing, and shelter) have been deducted.

discretionary reserve balance sheet account that represents temporary accumulation of earnings from the current or the previous years.

discretionary trust <UK> a trust under which the trustees have a discretion to apply the net income and the capital of the trust as they wish. *See: fixed interest trust.*

Discriminant Income Function (DIF) an IRS scoring system for assigning a score to each tax return.

disguised dividend = *constructive dividend.*

dishonored check = *bad check.*

disinvestment decision of whether to terminate an investment or an operation.

dismissal pay = *severance pay.*

dispensation <UK> a notice from the Inland Revenue to an employer that payments made in accordance with arrangements that have been specified may be omitted from the tax return. ***Also***: notice of nil liability.

disposable capital = *idle money.*

disposable income personal income left to a taxpayer after income tax and other payroll deductions. ***Also***: disposable personal income; take-home pay.

disposable personal income = *disposable income.*

disposal discharging, selling or exchanging an old asset. ***Also***: *disposition.*

disposal cost the cost incurred when disposing an asset.

disposal date the date on which an asset is sold or discarded. ***Also***: disposition date.

disposal value = *residual value.*

disposition <1><Canada> a surrender, a dissolution of interest, a policy loan after 3/31/1978 and a lump-sum proceeds from a life annuity after 11/10/1978 and before 11/13/1981. <2> = *disposal.*

disposition date <Canada> = *disposal date.*

disposition of variances closing of immaterial variances to cost of goods sold or income summary.

disqualified debt instrument any corporate debt (or debt issued by a partnership to the extent of its corporate partners) that is payable in equity.

disqualified person a person subject to excise tax.

disqualifying equity the equity that may cause a leased property transferred to be regarded as the owner of the trust, so the rent payments are not deductible.

dissection book = *columnar book.*

distress termination a situation that arises when a pension plan lacks funds needed to continue to pay out the benefits earned by employees.

distributable funds concept a going concern has distributable funds available only after it makes provision to maintain that portion of its operating capacity financed by equity.

distributable income = *operating income.*

distributable net income (DNI) the amount used to limit the deductions allowed to estates and some complex trusts for the amounts paid, credited, or required to be distributed to the beneficiaries.

distribution = *dividend.*

distribution and use of income = *income distribution.*

distribution cost <1> the cost incurred after the product is manufactured and before it is sold, e.g. advertising. <2> a cost for the promotion of mutual fund shares.

distribution date = *payment date.*

distribution of cost = *cost allocation.*

distribution of net income the distribution of net income among participants in a joint venture.

distribution of shares = *allotment of shares.*

distributive share partner's share of partnership income, loss, deduction and credit.

district inspector <UK> the head of a tax office.

DIT double income tax

DITC double income tax credit

diurnal = *journal.*

div dividend

divd dividend

divergent acquisition the acquisition of new or unrelated business for diversification of investment. ***See***: *convergent acquisition.*

diversifiable risk = *unsystematic risk.*

diversity condition at which cost objects place different demands on activities, activities place different demands on resources, or processes place different demands on resources.

divided account = *columnar account.*

divided-column journal = *columnar journal.*

dividend (d.)(div)(divd) <1> a distribution of cash or other assets to the stockholders. ***Also***: capital interest; distribution; stock interest. <2> = *interest.*

dividend announcement = *declaration.*

dividend appropriation *retained earnings* appropriated for dividend paying only.

dividend capitalization model the formula to calculate *cost of equity*. COE = (dividend per share ÷ market value of stock) + growth rate of dividend.

dividend capture strategy = *dividend rollover plan.*

dividend carryovers that allows deductions for dividends paid in the 2 preceding years to the extent dividends exceed taxable income in those prior years.

dividend claim requesting the registered holder for the amount of the dividend for the trade made before the ex-dividend.

dividend clawback the arrangement under which sponsors of a project agree to contribute as equity any prior dividends received from the project to the extent necessary to cover cash deficiencies. ***Also***: clawback.

dividend clientele those shareholders who want the company to follow a specific dividend policy, for tax reasons.

dividend cover = *cover for dividend.*

dividend credit = *dividends received deduction.*

dividend crossover method a technique used to estimate the date on which the rising common stock dividend will equal the convertible's coupon.

dividend declaration = *declaration.*

dividend declared = *declared dividend.*

dividend discount model (DDM) a formula to estimate the intrinsic value of the common stock of a company by the present value of all expected future dividends. ***Also***: discounted dividend model.

dividend distribution mutual fund's distribution of cash dividends that it receives from other companies.

dividend drag an SEC rule which requires that cash dividends received by a trust not to be reinvested in the portfolio stocks, and must be accumulated and paid out to investors.

dividend equalization tax <UK> a tax on dividends paid out of income that has not been fully taxes. ***Also***: equalization tax; shareholder equalization tax.

dividend equivalent dividend imputed on stock options, if vest, charged to retained earnings, if not vest, to compensation expense.

dividend exclusion portion of dividend not subject to tax. ***See***: *85% exclusion*; *nontaxable dividend.*

dividend exclusive = *ex dividend.*

dividend growth model a model of estimating cost of equity by dividing expected dividend by the difference between the required rate of return and the expected dividend growth rate.

dividend in = *cum dividend.*

dividend in arrears unpaid dividend on preferred stock that must be paid before any dividends can be paid to common stockholders. ***Also***: arrearage; passed dividend. ***See***: *accumulated dividend; omitted dividend.*

dividend income gross income derived from dividend distribution and subject to tax.

dividend in kind a dividend paid by companies in tangible assets. ***Also***: non-cash dividend; property dividend. ***See***: *cash dividend.*

dividend in scrip = *scrip dividend.*

dividend off = *ex dividend.*

dividend out of capital = *capital dividend.*

dividend paid deduction = dividends paid deduction.

dividend paid on short sales = *in lieu of dividend.*

dividend payable dividend declared but not due for payment.

dividend-paying stock a stock that pays dividends regularly.

Dividend Payment Incentive Act of 2003 a bill that amends the US Internal Revenue Code of 1986 about the dividends paid deduction and dividend received deduction.

dividend payout proportion of earnings available for common stock that is paid to common stockholders in the form of dividend.

dividend payout ratio cash dividend per common share divided by earnings per share. ***Also***: dividend-to-earnings ratio; payout ratio.

dividend play = *dividend rollover plan.*

dividend policy the policy a company uses to decide how much and how often it will pay out to shareholders in dividends.

dividend rate a fixed or adjustable rate paid on *common stock* or *preferred stock.*

dividend received deduction (DRD) = *dividends received deduction.*

dividend record book a reference book published monthly by investment advisory service firms reporting detailed dividend information about all listed companies.

dividend return = *current return.*

dividend right a shareholder's right to receive per-share dividends.

dividend rollover plan buying stock 2 weeks before its ex-dividend date, after that, selling above the purchase price to collect dividend, and realize a capital gain. ***Also***: dividend capture strategy; dividend play; dividend trade; dividend trade roll.

dividend scrip = *scrip.*

dividend share = *bonus share.*

dividends paid deduction a deduction that permits diminution of the base on which the corporate accumulated earnings tax or the personal holding company tax is imposed. ***Also***: dividend paid deduction.

dividends per share (DPS) dividends paid-out per share of stock. ***Also***: dividends/share.

dividends received deduction (DRD) a tax deduction allowed to the shareholders of a corporation for dividends received from domestic corporations. ***Also***: dividend credit; dividend received deduction.

dividends/share = *dividends per share.*

dividend stock = *bonus share.*

dividend stock scrip = *scrip.*

dividend stripping a practice by which one company buys control of another and declares and pays dividends and then sells the company. ***Also***: dividend washing; stripping.

dividend tax <UK> notional tax on UK dividend income.

dividend tax credit <Canada> a non-refundable tax credit equal to 2/3 of ¼ of the dividend received from a taxable Canadian corporation. ***See***: *gross-up.*

dividend tax rate <UK> a 10% rate of notional tax on UK dividend income.

dividend to co-op patron = *patronage dividend.*

dividend-to-earnings ratio = *dividend payout ratio.*

dividend trade = *dividend rollover plan.*

dividend trade roll = *dividend rollover plan.*

dividend warrant an order by a company to its bank to pay a stated sum as dividend, often the dividend in arrears, to a named stockholder. ***Also***: sub-share.

dividend washing = *dividend stripping.*

dividend withholding tax (DWT) <New Zealand> income tax withheld on dividends paid to New Zealand taxpayers.

dividend within gain principle a notion that boot distributed in a corporate reorganization should give rise to dividend treatment only to the extent the shareholders have recognized gain on the transaction.

dividend yield = *current return.*

divisive D reorganization company A's transfer of assets to B, followed by A's distributions to its shareholders the stock and other assets received from B. (Both A and B continue in operation.) *Also*: butterfly transaction. *See*: *acquisitive D reorganization; type D reorganization.*

DM debit memorandum

DN debit note

DNI distributable net income

doctoring = *window dressing.*

doctrine of merger a rule if the trustee and beneficiary become one person due to the death of other beneficiaries, then the trust automatically terminates.

documentary tax stamp a stamp affixed to a deed showing the amount of transfer tax.

documentation <1> auditor's presentation of documents which authorize transactions to occur. <2> = *supporting document.*

documentation due date <Canada> = *tax return due date.*

dog = *promissory note.*

DOL degree of operating leverage

dollar accountability an emphasis upon the flow of liquid assets in accounting for nonprofit organizations.

dollar accounting the accounting that uses dollar as a unit of account.

dollar-and-cents difference = *net worth.*

dollar asset <1> = *cash asset.* <2> = *quick asset.*

dollar cost averaging = *constant dollar plan.*

dollar of constant value = *constant dollar.*

dollar sign rule a rule of adding the dollar sign $ in front of all amounts.

dollar unit sampling (DUS) sampling that sets dollar amount for units in order to show that a given attribute has been exceeded.

dollar value lifo the lifo that uses conversion price index to apply base year price to pools of inventory items rather than individual items. *See*: *traditional lifo.*

dollar value lifo method a method under which inventory can be priced at current costs which eliminates the need for the identification of specific costs of units in inventory. *Also*: lifo dollar value method.

dollar value method a method that determines the costs by using a base-year cost expressed in total dollar amounts rather than the cost based on the quantity and price of specific goods. *See*: *specific goods method.*

dollar value retail lifo method the same as the *dollar value lifo method* but using the retail price.

dollar-weighted rate of return the rate of return that would make the present value of future cash flows plus the final market value of an investment equal the current market cost of the investment. *See*: *internal rate of return.*

dollar year method a method of determining the average depreciation rate by dividing total depreciable costs by the total investment in all plant assets.

DOM 1 <UK> Inland Revenue questionnaire that helps determine a taxpayer's domicile.

domestic asset protection trust a trust created in a state that has laws to protect assets from creditors. *Also*: self-settled spendthrift trust.

domestic employer tax = *nanny tax.*

domestic international sales corporation (DISC) a US corporation that receives a tax incentive for export business.

domestic trust a trust set up within the home country. *See: offshore trust.*

domicile a country where the taxpayer intends to live permanently.

domicile of choice <UK> a country chosen by the taxpayer as domicile.

domicile of dependency <UK> the domicile of a dependent child.

domicile of origin <UK> the domicile of a taxpayer's father when the taxpayer was born.

dominance test a test to approve or deny a merger, which centers on whether the new company will have an excessive market share after a merger of two old companies.

dominant company = *controlling corporation.*

dominion register = *stockholder's ledger.*

domino theory a notion that a financial stress or default at one firm will precipitate defaults or financial stress within other firms, causing a ripple effect throughout the financial system.

donated capital a corporation's own stock by shareholders given freely to the corporation. *Also*: capital from donation; paid-in capital from donation; surplus from donated stock.

donated stock fully paid up stock donated by the stockholder to the issuing company without any consideration.

donated surplus credit in a stockholder's equity account when the stockholder donates shares back to the issuing company.

donation cash or other property given to a charity. *Also*: gift.

doomsday ratio = *acid-test ratio.*

dormancy period a period of time before a property can be deemed abandoned.

dormant account = *inactive account.*

dormant capital = *idle money.*

dormant partner = *silent partner.*

dot-com = *dot-com company.*

dot-com company a company that embraces the Internet as the key component in its business. *Also*: dot-com.

dot-com stock a stock issued by a *dot-com company.*

double account form balance sheet a balance sheet form that is divided into two sections the capital section and the operations section each is in the account form.

double accounting double counting of assets or liabilities in order to mislead the users of the financial statements.

double account system a system in which the balance sheet items were separated into fixed and current items, which were recorded and reported separately. *Opp*: *single account system.*

double category method a method under which shares bought at different prices of a mutual fund are broken into two categories by holding period, more than-a-year and one-year-or-less, the basis in each category is determined by dividing total cost in each category by the numbers of shares held. *See*: *single category method.*

double declining balance method (DDB method) a method the rate of depreciation of which is two times of that in the straight-line method. *Also*: double-rate declining balance method; 200%-declining balance method.

double-dip lease a cross-border lease in which the different rules of the lessor's and lessee's countries let both parties be treated as the owner of the leased property.

double distribution the distribution of overhead costs by 2 methods one after another.

double entry an entry with debit and credit amounts. *Opp*: *single entry.*

double entry accounting a universal system that produces equal debit and credit entries for every transaction.

double exemption bond = *double tax exempt municipal bond.*

double extension method a method for computing the base year cost and the current year cost of a dollar-value pool, under which quantity of each item in the pool is extended at both base-year unit cost and current year unit cost, then these costs are separately totaled to yield the base year and current year costs. ***See***: *link chain method.*

double gearing a situation where 2 companies are using shared capital to buffer against risk occurring in separate entities without the proper documentation of exposure.

double income relief the relief given to a taxpayer the income tax who has already paid in another country.

double liability of audit the liability shared by the auditor and his client.

double net lease = *net net lease.*

double posting <1> posting of the same entry into the general and the sub-ledger. <2> the posting of the same entry into one account by mistake.

double-rate declining balance method = *double declining balance method.*

double ruled lines = *double ruling.*

double ruling the two red lines crossed up and down the column totals. ***Also***: double ruled lines. ***See***: *single ruling.*

double T-account a T account in which there is a horizontal line under which is recorded the changes in the balance of the account.

double taxation a tax law that results in the same earnings being subjected to taxation twice. ***Also***: *double taxing.*

double taxation agreement an agreement between two countries for the elimination of double taxation.

double taxation relief <UK> a relief given against a UK tax liability in recognition of a liability to a foreign tax.

double tax exempt municipal bond municipal bond with interest exempt from state as well as federal taxes. ***Also***: double exemption bond.

double taxing = *double taxation.*

double unit sampling = *probability-proportional-to-size sampling.*

doubling up after buying a first lot of securities, then buy an equal amount of securities with unrealized loss and holding them along with the first lot for 30 days to avoid wash sale.

doubtful account (dbt. acct.) an account that may or may not be uncollectible. ***Also***: bad account. ***See***: *inactive account.*

doubtful asset an asset appeared in the balance sheet but which may not exist.

doubtful debt a definite indebtedness that may not be satisfied by the debtor.

dower the rights of a widow to a portion of her deceased husband's property.

downgrading engagement audit engagement from higher level to lower level, such as from audit to review, or from review to compilation.

down market a market with low price and low buying volume.

downside case a method of projecting the financial performance of a company on the basis of pessimistic operating and financial projection assumptions. ***See***: *base case.*

downstairs merger = *downstream merger.*

downstream exchange a company's exchange of its outstanding bond for new common stock or preferred stock, the accumulated interest on bonds may be tax free.

downstream merger the merger of the parent company into its subsidiary. ***Also***: downstairs merger. ***See***: *inverted takeover.*

downstream sale the sale of goods from parent to subsidiary, profit must be eliminated in preparing consolidated financial statements. ***See***: *upstream sale.*

down under bond a bond denominated in Australian dollar and New Zealand dollar.

DPG derivatives policy group

DPO <1> days payable outstanding. <2> direct public offering.

DPP direct participation program

DPSP deferred profit-sharing plan

Dr. <1> debit. <2> debit side.

dragon bond a Eurobond denominated in Asian dollar.

drain the IRS scheduled time for processing tax returns filed electronically.

drawback a refund of import duty on imported goods that are later exported in essentially the same condition or used in the manufacturing of exported goods.

drawdown a decline in account value after an investment is made.

drawing account <1> an account for recording personal withdrawal of capital from a sole proprietorship. ***Also***: owner's withdrawal account. <2> a credit available to salespersons paid on commission basis, in anticipation of future sales.

DRC dual resident corporation

DRD <1> dividend received deduction. <2> dividends received deduction.

DREO debt reducing exchange offer

DRL degree of relative liquidity

drop <1> amount lost on the table or slot machine in a casino. <2> an electronic filing identification number is no longer valid due to inactivity or administrative oversight.

drug testing credit a tax credit allowed up to 50% of certain clinical testing expenses related to the use of a drug for rare diseases.

dry hole accounting = *discovery value accounting.*

dry powder <slang> cash reserves kept on hand to cover future obligations.

dry trust = *passive trust.*

DSO days sales outstanding

DSP direct share program

DSS <1> decision support system. <2> Department of Social Security.

DTL degree of total leverage

dual basis of distribution = *combination basis of distribution.*

dual classification bookkeeping system a system in which all transactions are classified into debit and credit transactions. ***Also***: two-dimensional bookkeeping system.

dual class stock dual stock issued for a single company with varying classes indicating the different voting rights and dividend payments.

dual consolidated loss (DCL) net operating loss of a domestic corporation that is subject to the income tax of a foreign country.

dual index floater a floating rate note the interest rate of which is periodically reset in line with more than one index.

duality <1><UK> a tax rule which prohibits a deduction of expense not related to a trade or business. <2> = *debit and credit convention.*

dual plan a plan where the work-in-process account is recorded both in standard cost and in actual cost.

dual-purpose sampling audit sampling designed to both assess control risk and substantive test.

dual purpose testing <1> simultaneous searching for the exceptions to prescribed control procedures and monetary errors in the client's books. ***Also***: test of transactions. <2> audit test in which a single sample is used to test a control and to serve as a substantive test.

dual resident <UK> a taxpayer who is resident in two or more countries at the same time.

dual resident corporation (DRC) a US corporation that is also a resident of a foreign country for tax purposes.

dual-status taxpayer an alien who is a resident part of the tax year and a nonresident the rest of the tax year.

dual tax a tax on the foreign income of an overseas subsidiary on which a tax has been levied by that country which has no double-taxation agreement with the US.

dud cheque = *bad check.*

due care the degree of care that an ordinary person would exercise under the given circumstances. ***Also***: due professional care;

ordinary care; reasonable care. *See*: *utmost care.*

due date <1> the date on which a debt must be paid. *Also*: law day. *See*: *maturity date.* <2> = *tax return due date.*

due diligence <1> taking all necessary steps to ensure that the financial statements are correct. <2> close examination the financial statements and operations of a target company. <3> IRS requirements that income tax preparers must follow when preparing tax returns, especially those that involve earned income tax credits.

due from balance = *nostro account.*

due from bank account = *nostro account.*

due from other funds an account used to record advances to other funds in a non-profit organization.

due professional care = *due care.*

due to balance = *vostro account.*

due to bank account = *vostro account.*

due to other funds an account used to record advances from other funds in a non-profit organization.

dummy account a transit account for recording the flow used when it is difficult to distribute the sources among sectors.

dummy corporation a company the existence of which is disregarded and the income will be taxed on the owners. *Also*: sham corporation.

dummy shareholder a person who holds shares in his or her name, but the shares are really owned by someone else.

dunning the process of communicating with customers to ensure the collection of accounts receivable.

duplicating system a system under which the ledger sheets are not kept in loose-leaf books but are stored in deep boxes or drawers, entries are made directly to the ledger sheet, and a carbon copy is made on a journal or control sheet.

Du Pont equation an expression breaking down return on equity (ROE) into three parts: profit margin, total asset turnover, and financial leverage.

Du Pont formula a formula used to calculate return on investment, ROI = asset turnover × income as a percentage of sales.

duration gap an interval that measures the magnitude of the exposure to stockholders if interest rates move in an adverse direction. *Also*: maturity gap.

DUS dollar unit sampling

dustbin account = *cost control account.*

Dutch auction rate transferable security = *auction rate preferred stock.*

duty a tax on imports, exports or consumer goods.

duty remission waiver of import duty on imported goods.

DVP delivery vs. payment

DVR delivery vs. receipt

DWT dividend withholding tax

dynamic analysis an analysis that focuses on the income statement. *See: static analysis.*

dynamic balance sheet a balance sheet where the items that increase the equity are recorded on the left hand side and those that decrease the equity are recorded on the right hand side.

dynamic ratio = *income sheet ratio.*

dynamic statement = *income statement.*

dynasty trust = *perpetual trust.*

E e

E <1>earnings. <2> equity. <3> expense.

E&OE errors and omissions excepted

E&P earnings and profit

E&Y Ernst & Young LLP

EA enrolled agent

EAC estimate at completion

EA Exam = *Special Enrollment Exam.*

earliest acquisition cost method a method of valuing inventories under the dollar value method whereby current year costs of items in closing inventory are determined on the basis of the earliest costs of products purchased or manufactured during the year.

early closing the closing of books before the normal closing date.

early distribution the premature withdrawal of money from a tax-deferred investment. *Also*: premature distribution.

early distribution penalty a 10% penalty assessed on distributions from a qualified retirement plan before the participant attains age 59½. *See*: *premature distribution tax.*

early financial statement = *half-yearly financial statement.*

early withdrawal the premature withdrawal from a savings account or from a CD.

early withdrawal penalty the penalty paid to the bank for premature withdrawal from a savings account or a certificate of deposit. *Also*: premature withdrawal penalty.

earned capital = *retained earnings.*

earned depletion <Canada> a 33.33% tax deduction from the gross income of certain exploration and development expenditures and other investments prior to 1990.

earned-depletion basis <Canada> one third of the sum of specified resource-related expenses incurred by a taxpayer.

earned income <1> an individual's income from wages, salaries, tips or fees. ***Opp***: *unearned income.* ***See***: *active income.* <2><Canada> = *gross income.*

earned income credit (EIC) a credit that can be paid to low-income taxpayers, even if no income tax was withheld.

earned income tax credit (EITC) introduced in 1975, a refundable tax credit equal to 10% of earned income up to $5,000 that is available to eligible individual taxpayers. ***See***: *working families tax credit; working income supplement.*

earned on net worth = *return on stockholders' equity.*

earned surplus (ES) = *retained earnings.*

earned value (EV) the planned costs of the work allocated to the completed activities, it is calculated as percentage project completed × project budget. ***Also***: budgeted cost of work performed. ***See***: *planned budget.*

earned value management (EVM) business management to measure and communicate the real physical progress of a project taking into account the work complete, the time taken and the costs incurred to complete that work.

earning asset = *active asset.*

earning-capacity value the value of an asset expressed by the present value of its estimated future earnings.

earning power = *internal rate of return.*

earning power concept = *all inclusive concept.*

earning retention = *retained earnings.*

earnings (E) net change in resources resulting from operating activities over a period of time. *Also*: interest; proceeds; savings. <2> = *gross profit.* <2> = *retained earnings.*

earnings & profit (E&P) current and accumulated earnings used to determine if distribution is dividend or return of capital.

earnings available for ordinary shareholders <UK> = *income available for common stockholders.*

earnings before interest after taxes (EBIAT) = *income before interest and after taxes.*

earnings before interest and after taxes (EBIAT) net income of a business before deduction of interest but after income tax. *Also*: earnings before interest after taxes.

earnings before interest and taxes (EBIT) = *net income before interest and taxes.*

earnings before interest, less adjusted taxes (EBILAT) earnings before interest but after deduction of *adjusted taxes.*

earnings before interest, taxes and depreciation (EBITD) earnings of a company before deduction of interest, income taxes and depreciation.

earnings before interest, taxes, depreciation, amortization and rent (EBITDAR) earnings of a company before deduction of interest, income taxes, depreciation, amortization and rental expenses.

earnings before interest, taxes, depreciation and amortization (EBITDA) earnings of a company before deduction of interest, income taxes, depreciation and amortization.

earnings before taxes (EBT) = *pretax accounting income.*

earnings center = *profit center.*

earnings estimate projection of earnings or earnings per share of a public company by an analyst.

earnings forecast projection of earnings or earnings per share of a public company by its management or an independent analyst.

earnings growth rate the average annual rate of growth in earnings per share over the past five years.

earnings momentum an increase in the earnings per share growth rate from one reporting period to the next.

earnings multiple = *price/earnings ratio.*

earnings multiplier a company's estimated P/E ratio, adjusted for the current level of interest rates, used for purposes of valuation.

earnings per share (EPS) amount of earnings applicable to each share of common stock. *Also*: earnings/share. *See*: *primary earnings per share; fully-diluted earnings per share.*

earnings per share fully diluted = *fully diluted earnings per share.*

earnings price ratio (EPR)(EP ratio) = *current return.*

earnings rate of stock price calculated as [(estimated dividend + stock discount - stock premium) ÷ redemption period] ÷ 0.5 × (present value + face value).

earnings report an official quarterly or annual report published by a public company, showing earnings, expenses, and net income.

earnings retained = *retained earnings.*

earnings retention reinvesting earnings in a business rather than paying dividends. *Also*: plowback; profit reinvestment.

earnings retention ratio percentage of earnings reinvested in the business. *Also*: plowback ratio. *See*: *reinvestment rate.*

earnings season the months where a majority of quarterly corporate earnings are released to the public.

earnings/share = *earnings per share.*

earnings statement = *income statement.*

earnings surprise earnings report of a public company that differs from what the analysts were expecting.

earnings warning announcement made by a public company in advance of its earnings announcement indicating that profits will fall short of previous expected levels. ***Also***: profit warning.

earnings yield = *current return.*

earn-out arrangement in which sellers of a business receive additional future payment, usually based on future earnings.

earn-up an arrangement in which an acquirer of a company provides financial incentives to the existing management to encourage strong future performance.

EAT earnings after tax

eating cost = *cost absorption.*

EBIAT <1> earnings before interest after tax. <2> earnings before interest and after tax.

EBILAT earnings before interest, less adjusted taxes

EBIT earnings before interest and taxes

EBITD earnings before interest, taxes and depreciation

EBITDA earnings before interest, taxes, depreciation and amortization

EBITDAR earnings before interest, taxes, depreciation, amortization and rent

EBITDA volatility the change of EBITDA as a result of the operating performance of the company.

EC Examinations Committee

eCash = *electronic money.*

ECI Employment Cost Index

ecological accounting the accounting for rendering information to the ecology.

ecological gift <Canada> a gift of ecologically sensitive land.

economic accounting <1> the appraisal of a business by the net cash flow based on the current assets and the current cost of capital. <2> = *national economic accounting.*

economical depreciation the depreciation of the assets caused by technological obsolescence. ***Also***: capital replacement. ***See***: *technological obsolescence.*

economic basis method a method under which the consolidated subsidiary's earnings after combination are transferred to the parent's investment account, net income or loss of the unconsolidated subsidiary is combined to the parent's net income. ***Also***: actual value method; adjusted cost method; book value method; equity method; soak up method. ***See***: *legal basis method.*

economic cost <1> economist's view of cost as compared with the accountant's view and it is based on the acquisition cost. <2> the sum of the reported cost and the opportunity cost. <3> = *current cost.* <4> = *opportunity cost.*

economic depreciation = *functional depreciation.*

economic earnings real flow of cash that a business can pay out forever in the absence of any change in productive capacity.

economic exposure the risk of loss arising from changes in the market prices of interest rates, currencies, commodities or equities which is not directly tied to any single item in a firm's financial statements.

economic gain = *real gain.*

economic growth rate the annual rate of change in the gross national products.

economic income <1> amount that a person can consume during a period and still be as well off at the end of the period as at the beginning. ***Also***: sustainable income. <2> cash flow plus change in present value.

economic life the period during which a plant asset will provide its services. ***Also***: effective life; useful life; working life.

economic order quantity (EOQ) order size that minimizes the sum of carrying and ordering costs.

economic production run size particular size of production that can minimize the total annual cost of setting up and carrying inventory.

economic profit <1> residual profit after explicit and implicit costs have been paid. <2> = *excess profit.*

economic pure profit = *pure profit.*

economic rent <1> the rent a real estate property would generate if leased. <2> profit in excess of the competitive level.

economic surplus <1> profit after deduction of operating expenses, income taxes, interest and insurance. <2> excess of the market value of the assets of a business over the market value of its liabilities. <3> = *net worth.*

economic value <1> a current value based on the discounted future cash flow expected from the use of an asset during its useful life. <2> = *capitalized value.*

economic value added (EVA) calculated as: income after tax - (cost of capital × capital invested).

economy and efficiency audit the audit in order to find out if the organization is managing its resources efficiently.

ED Exposure Draft

EDF <1> estimated default frequency. <2> expected default frequency.

EDIT excess deferred income tax

edit control audit control used to identify incomplete, misleading or invalid input data.

EDMAX Educational Management Exchange Subcommittee

EDPA electronic data processing accounting

EDP **audit** electronic data processing audit

educational assistance payment to an employee for continuing education purpose, tax free up to $2,500 per year.

educational expense deduction tax deduction allowed to individuals for the costs undertaken to improve a skill.

educational travel deduction the cost of transportation between a taxpayer's place of work and school, deductible if the education improves skills.

education credit a tax credit available for education expenses, such as hope credit or lifetime learning credit. ***Also***: college credit; tuition credit.

education IRA = *Coverdell Education Savings Account.*

education tax credit <Canada> a tax credit allowed to a taxpayer who incurred qualified educational expenses.

EETC Equity in Education Tax Credit

effective debt total debt of a company including the principal value of annual leases and other fixed obligations.

effective income tax rate = *average tax rate.*

effective interest method <1> a method used to amortize lease liability, under which interest expense equals carrying value multiplied by *effective interest rate.* <2> = *interest method.*

effective interest rate <1> rate of interest of a loan equal to the nominal interest divided by the proceeds of the loan. ***Also***: effective rate. <2> = *yield to maturity.*

effective life <Australia> = *economic life.*

effectively connected income = *taxable income.*

effective margin (EM) the net earned surplus on assets in excess of financing costs for a given interest rate and prepayment rate scenario.

effectiveness audit an audit made to see if the firm's actual performance agree with targeted performance.

effectiveness variance calculated as: standard unit overhead × (actual hours - allowed hours at actual output). ***Also***: overhead effectiveness variance.

effective net worth net worth plus *subordinated debt,* as viewed by senior creditors.

effective par the par value of preferred stock that would ordinarily correspond to a given dividend rate.

effective rate <1> = *effective interest rate.* <2> = *effective yield.*

effective tax rate <1> tax after reconciliation of temporary difference divided by the pre-tax accounting income. <2> = *average tax rate.*

effective yield rate of return realized by an investor who buys a security and subsequently sells it. *Also*: effective rate.

effect of a dividend a standard for determining whether boot distributed in a reorganization should be treated as capital gain or as dividend.

efficiency = *yield.*

efficiency accounting accounting that provides information for the increase of management efficiency, such as management accounting, internal control accounting, etc.

efficiency audit = *operating audit.*

efficiency ratio a measurement of a bank's efficiency, it is calculated as <a> operating expenses divided by fees income plus tax equivalent net interest income; <b> the non-interest expense divided by total revenue less interest expense; <c> non-interest expense divided by net interest income before provision for loan losses; or <d> non-interest expense divided into revenue. The lower the ratio the better.

efficiency variance (eff var) difference between actual activity level and the standard activity level for the actual output, any unfavorable variance represents poorly motivated or poorly skilled workers. *Also*: physical variance.

eff var efficiency variance

EFILE <Canada> a system for transmission of tax returns designed for tax preparation services. *See*: *e-file.*

e-file process of submitting tax forms through the use of telephones, computers and tax software. *Also*: electronic filing. *See*: *EFILE.*

EFIN electronic filing identification number

EFT electronic fund transfer

EFTPS Electronic Federal Tax Payment System

EGM extraordinary general meeting

EI earned income

EIC earned income credit

EI deficit <Canada> the excess of program costs over premium revenue of an employment insurance plan.

eight-column worksheet form = *8-column worksheet form.*

EIN employer ID number

EI plan employment insurance plan

EI surplus <Canada> the excess of premium revenue over program costs of an employment insurance plan.

EIR earned income relief

EIS enterprise investment scheme

EIS deferral relief <UK> deferred gains from the sale of shares issued by a private unlisted company. *See: enterprise investment scheme.*

EITC earned income tax credit

EITC recertification a process under which a taxpayer must provide additional information on Form 8862 before they can claim *earned income tax credit.*

EITF Emerging Issues Task Force

elapsed time method a method of determining an employee's period of service for the purpose of accrual of benefits by reference to the employee's total period of service, rather than actual or equivalent hours of service.

elastic accounting = *windows dressing.*

electing large partnership (ELP) a partnership with 100 or more partners in preceding tax-year that elects the simplified flow-through provisions.

electing small business trust (ESBT) a trust with the ability of accumulating income for more than one beneficiary, limited to 75 for S corporation shareholders. **See**: *qualified subchapter S trust*.

election <UK> taxpayer's choice of being taxed in an alternative way.

election to defer = *deferral election*.

elective deferral an employer's contribution towards an employee's 401(k) plan on the employee's behalf that could have been accepted as cash, but was deferred by the employee. ***Also***: salary reduction contribution.

Electronically Transmitted Documents (ETD) a system for processing electronically filed documents other than tax returns.

electronic brainstorming the brainstorming through e-mail and a network.

electronic data processing audit (EDP audit) audit of accounting information system that is based on electronic data processing programs. ***Also***: paperless audit.

electronic document supporting document in electronic format.

Electronic Federal Tax Payment System (EFTPS) a service provided free by the US Treasury which enables a taxpayer to pay federal tax by phone, Internet, or a bank.

electronic filing = *e-file*.

electronic filing identification number (EFIN) a number assigned by the IRS to an applicant participating in the e-file program.

electronic fund transfer (EFT) arrangement by which the US Treasury transfer tax refunds to a taxpayer's bank account.

electronic money cash existing as debit and credit transfers over a network such as the Internet. ***Also***: cybercash; eCash.

electronic postmark the date and time the electronic tax return is received by the IRS.

electronic preparation the preparation of a tax return by a computer.

electronic return a tax return filed electronically.

electronic return originator (ERO) an IRS authorized e-file provider that originates the electronic submission of returns to the IRS.

Electronic Tax Administration (ETA) a department within the IRS for administering the electronic activities.

Electronic Tax Administration Advisory Committee (ETAAC) an advisory group established by the IRS Restructuring and Reform Act of 1998.

electronic transmitter identification number (ETIN) a number assigned by the IRS to a participant of the e-file program.

element cost the cost of a specific element of input, such as direct material, or labor. ***Also***: component cost; factor cost.

eligible account the account receivable that satisfies the lender's criteria as collateral. ***Also***: prime account. **See**: *ineligible accounts*.

eligible asset <1> a short-term asset such as treasury bill, money at call, gilt-edged security, etc. with one year or less to run. **See**: *bankable asset*. <2> retirement asset eligible for rollover to another retirement plan. <3> asset eligible for use as collateral in dealing with the Eurosystem.

eligible capital amount <Canada> amount by which proceeds from the disposition of the eligible capital property exceeds the costs incurred for the disposition.

eligible capital property <1><Canada> a property upon disposition of which would be an eligible capital amount. <2><Canada> = *intangible asset*.

eligible child a child eligible for child care expense.

eligible dependent <Canada> a *dependent* that can make a taxpayer qualify for one personal tax credit. *Formerly called*: equivalent-to-spouse.

eligible dividend a dividend paid out of a company's earnings for a taxable year. **See**: *qualifying dividend; 85% exclusion*.

eligible educational institution a school that qualifies for education credit. ***Also***: eligible post-secondary institution.

eligible employer plan = *qualified employer plan.*

eligible expense = *tax deductible expense.*

eligible goods <Canada> certain products the GST and HST paid on which can be claimed by a foreign visitor.

eligible gross wage the first fixed amount of wage subject to some state taxes.

eligible housing loss <Canada> housing loss in respect of an eligible relocation of the employee, spouse or family member.

eligible individual <1> an individual who has a qualifying child. <2> a person aged 18 or more who can contribute to an IRA.

eligible intangible an intangible asset eligible for using 15-year straight-line amortization.

eligible liability a liability included in the calculation of a banker's reserve asset ratio.

eligible post-secondary institution = *eligible educational institution.*

eligible production corporation <Canada> a corporation that carries on a business that is primarily a film or video production business or production service business.

eligible property Section 1245 property eligible for the expense election.

eligible relocation <Canada> a taxpayer's relocation the expense of which is deductible.

eligible retiring allowance <Canada> = *retiring allowance rollover.*

eligible rollover distribution the distribution from an IRA, qualified plan, 403(b) plan or 457 plan that is eligible to be rolled over to another eligible retirement plan.

eligible scholarship a scholarship that is excludable from gross income.

eligible small business a business with gross receipts for the preceding tax year not exceeding $1 million.

eligible stock a stock in which charities and financial institutions can invest.

eligible student a student who meets the requirements to get an education credit.

eligible withdrawal <Canada> a withdrawal from a registered retirement plan that meets the requirements.

elimination combining the credit balance against the debit balance of the same item when preparing consolidated statements. ***Also***: inter-company elimination. ***See***: *multilateral netting system.*

elimination entry = *reversing entry.*

Elliott Committee a committee of AICPA, responsible for analyzing and reporting on the current status and future of the audit assurance function and trends shaping the function's environment. ***Also***: Special Committee on Assurance Services.

ELP electing large partnership

EM effective margin

embedded loss = *unrealized loss.*

embedded value a value based on the sum of tangible book value plus the present value of the in-force block.

embezzlement wrongful use, for one's own selfish ends, of the property of another when that property has been legally entrusted to one. ***Also***: defalcation; misappropriation; misappropriation of assets; peculation.

emergency amortization = *accelerated depreciation.*

emergency fund a reserve of cash kept available to meet unexpected expenses of any emergencies.

emergency tax code <UK> the code applied by an employer for a new employee who does not produce Form P45 from a previous employer.

Emerging Issues Task Force (EITF) a team formed in 1984 by the *Financial Accounting Standards Board* as a response to guidance upon timely financial reporting.

emoluments <UK> a taxpayer's total earnings from an employment. ***Also***: employment income; income from employment.

employed <Canada> performing the duties of an office or employment.

employee a person who works for an employer.

employee advance a loan made to an employee. ***Also***: advance to employees.

employee benefit plan <Canada> an arrangement under which contributions are made by an employer for the benefit of current and former employees.

employee business expense an expense incurred by employees who are engaged in the trade or business of being employees.

employee contribution payment to a pension plan by the employee.

employee death benefit death benefit paid by an employer to survivors of a dead employee.

employee discount a discount from the listed price of products and service granted to an employee.

employee leasing firm a firm that leases its employees to another firm. ***See:*** *agency worker.*

employee loan a low- or no-interest loan to an employee from the employer.

employee profit sharing plan <Canada> an arrangement under which the employees share some profits of the business.

Employee Retirement Income Security Act (ERISA) a law enacted in 1974 that regulates the operation of private pension plans.

employee share ownership scheme <UK> = *employee stock ownership plan.*

employee share ownership trust (ESOT) <UK> a trust established by a company to acquire shares in a trust company.

employee stock option = *option grant.*

employee stock ownership credit a tax credit available to a business that maintains an employee stock ownership plan.

employee stock ownership plan (ESOP) a plan giving employees an ownership interest in the employer who contributes employer securities to this plan, and the plan will allocate securities to the employees. ***Also***: employee share ownership scheme; stock purchase plan.

employee stock purchase plan a plan that gives employees options to buy stock fixed at a price as low as 85% of the market value of the stock.

Employee's Withholding Allowance Certificate a formed given to the employer by a new employee to report information for federal and state tax withholding purpose. ***Also***: Form W-4; W-4 form. ***See***: *TD1.*

employee trust <Canada> a trust set up for the benefit of current and former employees.

employer a person or organization that hires an employee.

employer ID number (EIN) = *Federal ID number.*

employer matching contribution the amount that a company contributes to its employees' retirement accounts, typically in proportion to each employee's contribution.

employer provided child care credit a tax credit equal to 25% of qualified child care expenditures and 10% of the resource and referral expenses.

employer's liability insurance = *workers' compensation insurance.*

employer social security credit a credit for the excess social security tax paid by an employer.

employer's pension <UK> benefit received from a former employer.

employer's retirement benefits scheme <UK> a pension scheme set up by a company for its employees.

employment <Canada> the position of an individual in the service of some other person.

employment cost wage or salary paid to an employee plus the related payment for insurance, pensions, etc.

employment income <UK> = *emoluments.*

employment insurance plan (EI plan) <Canada> a system of income benefit based on hours worked, earnings, previous service and new employment benefits. ***See***: *unemployment insurance tax.*

employment-related expense an expense incurred in order to take care of a child while the taxpayer is working.

employment tax social security tax, federal unemployment tax and other payroll taxes.

employment zone employment credit a tax credit for a year equal to 20% of the *qualified zone wages* paid during the calendar year that ends with or within that year.

empty bypass trust = *credit-shelter trust.*

enacted tax rate a tax rate used to measure deferred tax liabilities and deferred tax assets.

encircled balance = *negative account balance.*

encroachment auditing work of one independent accountant over another.

encumbrance control of budget appropriation of a government when a transaction is entered into that requires performance on the part of another party, representing future expenditure.

encumbrance system a budget control system under which when a purchase order is issued or a contract is signed the amount is entered into Encumbrances a/c.

ending balance account balance at the end of a period after closing the books. ***Also***: closing balance; end-of-the-period balance.

ending inventories budget a budget about the cost of ending inventories.

ending inventory the inventory at the end of a period. ***Also***: closing inventory; final inventory; stock at close.

ending work-in-process = *closing work-in-process.*

end-of-period adjusting entry adjusting entry made at the end of a period.

end-of-period balance = *ending balance.*

end of year December 31 for tax purpose.

end-of-year convention a practice of treating cash flows as if they occur at the end of year instead of the actual date.

endowment assets of a nonprofit organization the principal of which can never be spent. ***Also***: permanently restricted net assets.

endowment benefit the proceeds received by the insured from an endowment policy.

endowment fund a fund used by a non-profit organization for recording endowment and related transactions. ***Opp:*** *expendable fund.*

endowment policy a life insurance that pays a sum of cash to the insured if he or she is still alive on the maturity date.

endowment policy method = *insurance method of depreciation.*

end-point costing = *back flush costing.*

energy credit a tax credit relating to business energy savings, 10% on the energy property placed in service during the tax year.

engagement letter a letter for establishing understanding of the engagement between the auditor and the engaging firm, usually signed by both the auditor and the client. ***Also***: letter for auditor; letter of engagement. ***See***: *letter of representation.*

engineered cost a cost the amount of which can be estimated precisely. ***Also***: operating cost.

engineering cost estimates method a technical method of estimating fixed and variable costs.

English audit standpoint an audit standpoint that focuses on accounting books. ***See***: *American audit standpoint.*

English form of closing the ledger a simplified form of closing the books in which there are no closing accounts.

English system of bookkeeping a bookkeeping system in which there are some special journals.

enhanced oil recovery credit (EOR credit) a credit that is 15% of the taxpayer's qualified enhanced oil recovery costs for the tax year.

enrolled agent (EA) a tax practitioner who, by passing an exam given by the US Treasury, can represent taxpayers before the IRS.

Enrolled Agent Exam = *Special Enrollment Exam.*

entering to the register = *journalization.*

enterprise accounting the accounting for the whole business rather than a department.

enterprise fund a government fund that provides goods or services to the general public for a fee that can cover the entity's cost. *See: internal service fund.*

enterprise investment scheme (EIS) <UK> a reduction in the income tax liability equal to 20% of the amount invested in subscribing for newly-issued shares in an unlisted company.

enterprise multiple a ratio used to determine the value of a company. It equals the *enterprise value* divided by EBITDA.

enterprise theory = *business entity principle.*

enterprise value (EV) a measure of what the market believes a public company's ongoing operations are worth, calculated as company's market capitalization + debt + preferred stock - cash and cash equivalents. *Also*: total company value.

enterprise zone trust <UK> a trust, approved by the Inland Revenue, that builds and lends commercial property in certain areas.

entertainment tax a state or local tax on entertainment such as cinema tickets.

entity accounting = *micro accounting.*

entity concept a concept which holds that both the parent company and the subsidiary's revaluation amounts should be shown in the consolidated financial statements. *See*: *parent company concept.*

entity insurance an insurance covering the liability of the act of directors and officers of a business or a government agency. *Also*: D&O insurance.

entity piercing doctrine = *piercing the corporate veil.*

entity theory <1> a theory under which a partnership is viewed as an entity separate from its participants. <2> = *business entity principle.*

entry accounting record of the amount, debit or credit side, and account title of a transaction. *Also*: accounting entry; bookkeeping entry; journal entry.

entry age normal method method applied to the defined benefit plans by which the age at which service credits begins for each employee is recorded and a level annual contribution is calculated, payable to normal retirement age in an amount sufficient to provide his benefit at retirement. *See*: *projected benefit cost.*

entry book = *book of original entry.*

entry price <1> the price at which an asset or a liability is first recorded in the books. <2> = *reproduction cost.*

entry value = *replacement cost.*

environmental accounting accounting that measures, evaluates and reports the operating environment of an organization and the effect of its activities to the environment.

environmental cost = *cost to the environment.*

environmental impact statement a statement which shows the effects of an organization's activities to the environment.

environmental pollution control cost the cost that society suffers due to pollution. *Also*: abatement cost; pollution prevention cost.

environmental remediation cost expense paid in connection with the control of hazardous substance at a qualified contaminated site.

environmental tax 0.12% tax on a corporation with modified alternative minimum taxable income over $2 million.

EOI economic order interval

EOQ economic order quantity

EOR credit enhanced oil recovery credit

EP European plan

EPR earnings price ratio

EP ratio earnings price ratio

EPS earnings per share

equ equity

equal annual payment method <1> *annuity method.* <2> = *sinking fund method.* <3> = *straight-line method of depreciation.*

equal gross margin percentages method a method of sharing joint costs by the proportion of the gross profits of the joint products.

equal installment method = *straight-line method of depreciation.*

equalization = *tax equalization.*

equalization reserve a long-term reserve set aside by an insurance company in order to equalize operating results from certain catastrophe risks.

equalization tax = *dividend equalization tax.*

equalizing dividend a special dividend declared and paid in order to correct unequal dividend benefits among stockholders.

equalizing the dividends supplementing a dividend payment from reserves, or deducting a possible dividend so as to permit a transfer to reserves in order to maintain a dividend at a consistent level.

equation method a method that uses an equation to find the break-even point or target income volume.

equipment leasing partnership a limited partnership which receives tax benefits by purchasing and leasing equipment to other parties.

equity (equ.) <1> a claim, right, or interest in asset. ***Also***: stake; total equity. <2> = *account equity.* <3> = *stock.*

equity accounting the accounting procedures and methods for the measurement, reporting and equalizing of equities. ***Also***: capital accounting.

equity capital the sum of a corporation's money and the adjusted basis of its other property, less its indebtedness.

equity carve-out = *partial spinoff.*

equity claim = *residual claim.*

equity concept a concept under which the net assets of a subsidiary would be included in the consolidated balance sheet at 100% of their fair value at the date of acquisition and minority interest is reported at its ownership share in the subsidiary. ***See***: *parent company concept.*

equity-debt ratio the ratio of equities to total liabilities. ***Also***: equity-to-debt ratio; net worth to debt ratio; ratio of capital to liabilities; solvency ratio.

Equity in Education Tax Credit (EETC) <Canada> a credit allowed to a qualifying taxpayer who incurred qualified education expenses in a tax year.

equity investment an investment in any stock other than nonqualified preferred stock in a corporation.

equity method <1> a method under which the investment is recorded at costs, investor's equity in subsequent earnings of the investee increases the investment a/c and subsequent dividends reduce the investment account. ***See***: *cost-adjusted-for-fair-value method; complete-equity method; partial equity method.* <2> = *economic basis method.*

equity money = *owner's capital.*

equity multiplier ratio of a company's total assets to the common stockholder's equity. ***See***: *asset/equity ratio.*

equity of residual claimants = *residual equity.*

equity option = *stock option.*

equity purchase accounting a system that permits a company holding 20% or more of another's stock to include in its own income the same percentage of the subsidiary's income. ***Opp***: *cost purchase accounting.*

equity-rate return a reasonable rate of return used in determining shareholder benefit that would have been earned by the corporation had it invested the capital at this rate.

equity ratio = *equity-to-asset ratio.*

equity redeemable bond = *participating equity preferred stock.*

equity security ownership interest or rights to acquire ownership interest and rights to dispose of ownership interest. ***See***: *equity-type security.*

equity share <1> a share in a credit union representing an equity interest. *See: non-equity share.* <2> = *common stock.*

equity spread calculation of equity value by multiplying beginning equity capital by the difference between the return on equity and the percentage cost of equity.

equity substitute amount added to or subtracted from the reported common equity to reflect the actual economic value invested in a company or business segment from the perspective of a shareholder.

equity-to-assets ratio the ratio of the owners' equities to total assets. *Also*: common stock ratio; equity ratio; solvency ratio.

equity-to-debt ratio = *equity-debt ratio.*

equity turnover a company's annual sales divided by its average stockholders' equity. *Also*: capital turnover; capital turnover rate; net worth turnover.

equity-type security a security that is neither a common stock nor a preferred stock but is capable of conversion, subscription, or exercise for either of them. *See*: *equity security.*

equity value = *market capitalization.*

equivalent annual annuity the amount per year for a number of years that has a present value equal to a given amount.

equivalent annual benefit the annual annuity with the same value as the net present value of an investment.

equivalent annual cash flow an annuity with the same annual cash flow as the company's proposed investment.

equivalent annual cost the cost per year of owning an asset over its entire life.

equivalent bond yield a yield on government bonds sold at a discount calculated by the comparison with yields on corporate coupon bonds. *Also*: bond equivalent yield; corporate equivalent yield; coupon equivalent yield.

equivalent finished unit a measure of cost accounting expressed as the number of units that may have been manufactured from start to finish during a period given to the amount of materials or labor used during the period.

equivalent foreign income <UK> income from investment in foreign securities.

equivalent loan the maximum amount of conventional loan that the same after-tax debt service stream is capable of supporting.

equivalent production in fifo process costing, the output produced during a production run or time period, computed for each input element for which unit cost information is desired. *Also*: common denominator; equivalent units of output. *See*: *output divisor.*

equivalent shares the new number of common shares recalculated if the convertible securities are converted to stock.

equivalent taxable yield the taxable yield on the corporate bond, calculated as the exempt yield divided by (1 minus marginal tax rate). *Also*: yield equivalence.

equivalent-to-married credit <Canada> a tax credit allowed to a taxpayer who is single, widowed, divorced or separated and has a dependent to support.

equivalent-to-spouse = *qualified dependent.*

equivalent-to-spouse amount <Canada> = *dependency exemption.*

equivalent uniform annual cost annual sum of all relevant costs.

equivalent units of output = *equivalent production.*

ERB Examinations Review Board

e-reporting disclosure of corporate financial information on the Internet.

ERISA Employee Retirement Income Security Act of 1974

Ernst & Young LLP (E&Y) one of the big 4 accounting firms.

ERO electronic return originator

erosion a negative impact on an asset.

ERP enterprise resource planning

error unintentional misstatement, omission of item or disclosure in the financial statements.

error in books a book error that makes a trial balance out of balance. ***Also***: difference in books; suspense.

error in posting error made in posting that may cause errors in books. ***Also***: misposting.

error of commission = *commission.*

errors and omissions <1> entries caused by an error or omission. <2> an insurance policy which covers losses resulting from financial institutions failing to effect insurance coverage. <3> an item in the balance of payments, which represents discrepancies that arise in gathering data. ***Also***: net errors and omissions.

errors and omissions excepted (E&OE) words printed on publication meaning it may contain error and omissions and will not be held liable.

ESA Coverdell Education Savings Account

ESBT electing small business trust

escalation the time oriented increase in costs brought about by increases in man-hour wage rates and in non-productive labor encountered in providing a given work output. ***Also***: cost escalation.

escalator clause a clause in a contract allowing cost increases to be passed on to other parties.

escapable cost = *avoidable cost.*

escapable expense an expense which will not incur if an unprofitable segment is eliminated.

escheat transfer of property to the government because the owner dies without a will or heir.

escheat property the property reverted to the government in the absence of legal owner or claimant. ***Also***: abandoned property.

escrow account = *impound account.*

ESOP Employee Stock Ownership Plan

ESOT employee share ownership trust

essential basic expenditure of an individual, e.g. food, clothing, and shelter. ***See***: *support.*

essential/nonessential approach an approach under which assets are divided into two groups essential and nonessential, the first group will be valued at the replacement cost, and the latter will be valued at net realizable value.

establishment charge = *business expense.*

establishment cost the cost incurred to support the existence of an organization of a given size for a given period of time. ***Also***: indirect cost.

estate accounting record keeping and the preparation of reports by the administrator of an estate.

estate administrator = *administrator.*

estate duty = *estate tax.*

estate executor = *executor.*

estate income earnings from the properties of an estate in a tax period.

estate inventory a detailed list of all properties of an estate. ***Also***: estate list.

estate list = *estate inventory.*

estate settlement cost the cost incurred to resolve an estate, such as medical expenses, funeral expenses, estate taxes, legal fees etc.

estate tax the *inheritance tax* imposed on the privilege of a decedent to transfer his or her property. ***Also***: estate duty; inheritance tax. ***See***: *accession tax.*

estate tax exemption = *unified credit exemption.*

estate tax return a tax return filed on behalf of anyone who died having a gross estate that exceeds the life time exclusion.

estimate at completion (EAC) estimate of the final costs of a project, calculated as actual cost of work performed + (original budget - earned value)/cost performance index. ***See***: *budget at completion.*

estimated cost <1> cost projected for a decision alternative. <2> an expense to be made after a sale.

estimated cost system a system in which estimated unit costs of a product are used to price inventories of work-in-process and finished goods shown in the ledger account.

estimated default frequency (EDF) the number of defaults of a company in a particular period. *See*: *expected default frequency*.

estimated future superior earnings expected earnings in excess of those which constitute normal earnings on the current fair value of identifiable tangible and intangible net assets.

estimated liability an obligation that exists but which is uncertain as to amount and due date, such as product warranty.

estimated life the estimated *economic life* of a plant asset. *Also*: estimated service life; estimated useful life.

estimated percent uncollectible estimated amount of bad debt as a percentage to net sales.

estimated receipts method a method used for amortizing movie production cost by applying a percentage of the current period receipts to the estimated total receipts.

estimated revenue a forecast of the source of fund working capital.

estimated salvage value the estimated *salvage value* of a plant asset.

estimated service life = *estimated life*.

estimated tax amount of tax that the taxpayer is expected to pay over the next tax year, minus tax credits.

estimated tax payable estimated tax due to be paid on future due dates.

estimated tax penalty an IRS penalty for underpayment of estimated tax.

estimated total audit value (ETAV) it equals population size multiplied by average audit value.

estimated useful life = *estimated life*.

estimate method a method of determining the fixed and variable portions of a cost item by estimation.

estimating-to-cost technique = *design-to-cost technique*.

estimation days the days on which estimated taxes are due, generally the 15th of April, June, September, and January of the following year.

estimation year the computation period for personal estimated taxes.

ETA Electronic Tax Administration

ETAAC Electronic Tax Administration Advisory Committee

ETAV estimated total audit value

e-tax <Australia> a program developed by the Australian Taxation Office enabling taxpayers to prepare a personal tax return.

ETD Electronically Transmitted Documents

ETFS electronic fund transfer system

ethical wall = *Chinese wall*.

ETIN electronic transmitter identification number

Eurocurrency <1> a deposit in a bank located outside the country but denominated in that country's currency. <2> = *Eurodollar*.

Eurodollar <1> high rate loan from foreign holders of dollars. <2> money held outside the USA by non-US residents.

European plan (EP) a hotel billing plan under which meals are separated from the room price. *See: American plan*.

EV <1> earned value. <2> enterprise value.

EVA economic value added

evasion of tax = *tax evasion*.

even daybook a journal daybook for recording transactions incurred on the even days, the 2nd, the 4th, the 6th, etc. *See*: *odd daybook*.

event subsequent to balance sheet date an event that incurs after the balance sheet date. *Also*: post-balance-sheet-date event; post-balance-sheet event.

evergreen option an employee option plan that grants additional shares to the plan every year.

evidential matter audit material that supports the financial statements, such as the underlying information and all corroborating information available to the auditor. **See**: *audit evidence.*

EVM earned value management

exact interest = *New York interest.*

exact method a method of determining the tax on accumulation distributions from complex trusts under which the beneficiary's income was redetermined for each year to which such a distribution was allocated.

examination <1> a report prepared by a revenue agent following an audit designed to inform taxpayers and IRS of the details of the audit. <2> an audit report which provides a positive opinion with reasonable assurance on whether assertions follow GAAP. ***Also***: inspection examination report. <3> = *inspection.*

ex ante income = *present-value income.*

ex ante return expected return of a portfolio, calculated from a proportional weighting of the expected returns of its component assets.

ex bonus (x.b.) = *ex capitalization.*

ex cap. ex capitalization

ex capitalization (ex cap.)(x.c.) without the bonus stock about to be issued. ***Also***: ex bonus; ex scrip.

excepted asset an asset which is not for the purposes of the business concerned throughout the whole or the last 2 years of the relevant period or required at the time of the transfer for future use for those purposes.

excepted dividend <Canada> a dividend received by a corporation on a share of the capital stock of a foreign affiliate.

excepted gift <Canada> a share of stock made as a gift to a person dealt with at arm's length.

except-for opinion a type of qualified opinion, attesting that the financial statements present fairly except for some reasons, such as unable to confirm accounts receivable. ***Also***: exception. ***See***: *subject-to opinion.*

exception <1> the client's failure to perform a required procedure or the failure to perform it properly. <2> a standard cost variance which has been over $50 for more than one week or over $30 for more than three weeks. <3> a tax provision that allows a corporate taxpayer to avoid the penalties for underpayment of the estimated tax. ***Also***: deviation; exception to estimated tax; safety zone. <4> = *except-for opinion.* <5> = *occurrence.*

exceptional item a charge incurred that must be noted upon a company's balance sheet according to GAAP.

exceptional return residual return plus benchmark return.

exception principle a policy by which management devotes its time to investigating only those situations in which the actual results differ significantly from planned results.

exception report <1> a report generated when a purchase order contains errors or missing information. <2> a report when the variance exceeds 10%.

exception to estimated tax = *exception.*

excess accelerated depreciation on the sale or disposition of property, the difference between the total depreciation taken since the property was acquired and the depreciation that would have taken if the straight-line depreciation method is used.

excess alimony = *front-loading.*

excess alimony payment = *front-loading.*

excess amount <Canada> amount contributed into a registered education savings plan in excess of the amount allowed by law.

excess burden a situation when some taxes are more onerous than others.

excess capacity = *spare capacity.*

excess cash accumulation = *undue retention.*

excess contribution penalty a 6% excise tax on the excess contribution to Roth IRA.

excess deduction amount in excess of a limit used to denote total portion of an otherwise deductible amount.

excess deduction account a cumulative account established by farmers for federal income tax purposes which recorded pre 1976 farming losses, as offset by gains.

excess deferred income tax (EDIT) excess contribution to tax-deferral plans, subject to 10% penalty.

excess depletion the excess of percentage depletion deducted for the year over the adjusted basis of the property at the end of the year.

excess FICA tax employee paid more than the FICA ceiling for the taxable year.

excess foreign tax foreign income tax paid in excess of the amount that may be credited for the tax year.

excess itemized deduction an itemized deduction in excess of the taxpayer's standard deduction and the personal and dependent exemptions.

excessive alimony = *front-loading.*

excessive depreciation the depreciation in excess of legally allowable depreciation.

excessive liability the excess of deficiency over net worth.

excess liability excess of liability to income tax over what it would be if all income tax were chargeable at the basic rate to the exclusion of any other rates.

excess loss account a negative balance in the investment account in the stock of a subsidiary held by a parent corporation where they file consolidated returns.

excess net passive income net passive income of an S corporation that exceeds 25% of gross receipts of that year.

excess of book value over investment cost = *credit differential.*

excess of cost of subsidiary stock over book value = *debit differential.*

excess of cost over fair value = *debit differential.*

excess of fair value over cost = *credit differential.*

excess of par value over issuing price of stock = *discount on stock.*

excess of revenue over expenses <of a nonprofit organization> = *net income.*

excess parachute payment an amount by which a *golden parachute payment* exceeds the *base amount* allocated to it.

excess present value index = *present value profitability index.*

excess profit <1> net earnings derived from extraordinary sources. <2> profit above the normal profit of competitors. ***Also***: economic profit; pure profit; super profit.

excess profits credit a level separating the normal and the excess profits.

excess profits tax additional tax on business income under national emergency, such as a war. ***Also***: defense surtax.

excess reserve actual reserve that exceeds *required reserve.*

excess return the difference between the return on a portfolio and the return that could have been raised by investment of the same amount of funds in a risk-free investment.

excess revenue = *retained earnings.*

excess shares new shares in a rights issue, allotted to a shareholder with rights.

excess umbrella policy = *umbrella policy.*

exchange adjustment = *translation of account balances.*

exchange charge fee paid to a bank for buying or selling foreign exchange.

exchange cover = *foreign exchange reserve.*

exchange gain = *translation gain.*

exchange loss = *translation loss.*

exchange of assets = *acquisition of assets.*

exchange offer <1> offer to acquire a target company through a *Type B reorganization.* <2> a method that allows limited partners to exchange their interests for marketable securities of a listed corporation on a tax-free basis. <3><UK> an offer to exchange one equity security for another.

exchange of shares acquisition = *Type B reorganization.*

exchange rate = *conversion rate.*

exchange rate risk = *exchange risk.*

exchange reserve = *foreign exchange reserve.*

exchange risk the risk that movement in exchange rates between home currency and the currency in which the assets are held moves against the investor. ***Also***: currency exchange risk; currency risk; exchange rate risk; foreign exchange risk.

exchange transaction <1> a transaction among assets, liabilities or capitals that would not cause changes in the profit and loss account. <2> government transaction in which goods or services of equal or approximately equal value are expected. ***See***: *non-exchange transactions.*

excise <Australia> = *excise duty.*

excise assessment <UK> an assessment of additional excise tax by the UK Customs.

excise collection <Australia> the collection of revenue in regard to excise business.

excise duty <Australia> a tax on domestic production of alcohol, tobacco, and light petroleum products. ***Also***: excise.

excise equivalent <Australia> customs duty on imported alcohol, tobacco, and light petroleum products.

excise tax <1> a tax imposed on manufacturing, selling or using goods or on an act, occupation or activity. <2> any tax other than income tax and property tax.

excludable fringe benefit fringe benefit not included in taxable income under specific tax code.

excluded addition an expenditure of more than $1,000 for property which is for an additional unit which substantially increases productivity or capacity of an existing unit by at least 25% or adapts it for a substantially different use.

excluded dividend <Canada> a dividend paid by a corporation to a shareholder that has a substantial interest in the corporation.

excluded property <1> a property that is exempt from inheritance tax. <2><Canada> any property on which the tax collection procedures do not apply.

excluded receipt the receipt of a domestic international sales corporation that is not qualified export receipt.

excluded stock the share of stock not counted in determining whether a shareholder owns 50% or more of the total voting power.

exclusion = *unified credit exemption.*

exclusion amount = *unified credit exemption.*

exclusion from income a receipt or accrual that is excluded from a taxpayer's gross income, e.g. gifts and inheritances.

exclusion ratio a portion of the return on investments or annuities that is income tax exempt.

ex d ex dividend

ex/d. ex dividend

ex date = *ex dividend.*

ex distribution (x dis) = *ex dividend.*

ex div. ex dividend

ex dividend (ED)(e.d.)(ex d)(ex/d)(ex div.)(x.d.) not including the next dividend soon due. ***Also***: dividend exclusive; dividend off; ex date; ex distribution; without dividend.

executed trust a fully established trust.

execution cost unfavorable difference between the price at which an order is executed and the market price at the time of decision.

execution gain favorable difference between the execution and the market price at the time of decision.

execution price the price at which an order is executed.

executive share option scheme <UK> a plan under which stock options are granted to the employees chosen by the management.

executor a person named in a will to administer the estate of a decedent. ***Also***: estate executor. ***See:*** *administrator.*

executory cost the cost excluded from minimum lease payment, e.g. insurance, maintenance and property taxes etc.

executory trust a trust that requires further transactions to establish fully.

exempt asset <UK> an asset free from capital gains tax when sold.

exempt business tax exempt business.

exempt corporation a corporation that is free from income tax.

exempt from withholding not having to pay a certain amount of federal income tax if the taxpayer meets certain income, tax liability, and dependency requirements.

exempt income amounts of earnings which would otherwise be considered gross income but which are not included therefrom, e.g. interest on municipal bonds, and life insurance proceeds. *Also*: nontaxable income; tax-exempt income; tax-free income; untaxed income.

exempt income expense the expense allocable to earning tax-exempt income, usually not deductible.

exempt interest <Canada> an interest in a partnership that was carrying on business or earning income from the rental or leasing of property on a regular basis on Feb 25, 1986. <2> = *tax-free interest.*

exempt interest dividend the dividend treated as interest paid by a regulated investment company from investment in private activity bonds to the extent of its proportionate share of the interest on such bonds.

exemption = *tax exemption.*

exemption amount <1> = *AMT exemption* <2> = *tax exemption.*

exemption for dependents = *dependency exemption.*

exemption for spouse = *spousal exemption.*

exemption of debt = *cancellation of debt.*

exemption trust a trust set up to drastically reduce or eliminate federal estate taxes for a married couple's estate.

exempt property <1> a debtor's property which can not be taken by creditors in bankruptcy. <2><Canada> a trust property not subject to *21-year deemed disposition rule.*

exempt security a security not required to be registered under the provisions of the SEC, e.g., governmental and municipal bond.

exempt wage the wage that is not subject to withholding, such as fringe benefit, reimbursed expense, domestic service, etc.

ex int. ex interest

ex interest (ex int)(x int) without the next interest payment soon due, such as a bond in default. *Also*: flat; selling flat; with no interest; without interest. *See*: *with interest.*

existence asset, liabilities and owners' equity reflected in the financial statement.

existing credit claimant a US corporation that was operating a business in a US possession on Oct 13, 1995 and had elected to use *possession tax credit.*

existing use value = *current use value.*

exit charge <UK> a charge to inheritance tax when property leaves a discretionary trust.

exit cost = *back-end load.*

exit fee = *back-end load.*

exit load = *back-end load.*

exit value non-discounted amount of cash an asset will bring into the firm either through sale or through holding and using it. *Also*: current liquidation price.

exit value method a method for the determination of the fair value of an asset by using current exit value or expected exit value.

exp. <1> expenditure. <2> expense.

expanded accounting equation the expanded form of accounting equation: assets = capital + liabilities + revenue - expenses - dividends. *See*: *basic accounting equation*

expatriation a citizen's departure from his home country and renunciation of a citizenship in order to avoid paying tax.

expected activity the rate of activity that is expected to prevail over the next year.

expected annual capacity the planned activity levels for a given year.

expected cash flow approach an approach that uses all expectations about possible cash flows instead of the single most-likely cash flow.

expected cost <1> the mean of the expected costs under different probabilities. <2> = *target cost.*

expected default frequency (EDF) a measure of credit weakness, focusing on the probability an entity will default. ***See***: *estimated default frequency.*

expected deviation rate estimate of a deviation rate in advance.

expected dividend yield total amount of dividends received for holding a particular stock one year.

expected earnings the earnings of a public company reported by an analyst for the upcoming quarter or year. ***See***: *forecasted earnings.*

expected exit value non-discounted amount of cash that a company expects to realize from holding a particular asset.

expected future cash flow the projected future cash flows associated with an asset.

expected future return the return that is expected to be earned on an asset in the future.

expected future years of service method a method for amortizing prior service cost under which total number of employee service years is calculated by grouping them according to the time remaining to their retirement, and then multiplying the number in each group by the number of periods remaining to retirement. ***Also***: straight-line basis over the average remaining service period method.

expected idle capacity variance excess of practical capacity over the master budget sales forecast capacity that is expressed in physical or dollar value.

expected population deviation rate an estimate of the deviation rate in the entire population. ***Also***: expected rate of occurrence.

expected rate of occurrence = *expected population deviation rate.*

expected rate of return <UK> the average rate of return expected on the remaining life of a related obligation on the actual assets held in a pension plan.

expected return <1> the profit anticipated from a business venture or a risky asset, usually the *benchmark return* multiplied by the beta of that investment. <2> an amount that the annuitant expects to receive under an annuity contract.

expected standard cost a cost that can be achieved under efficient conditions, which allows for normal loss of labor time due to machine breakdowns and similar work stoppages and normal spoilage of materials. ***Also***: actual expected standard cost; actually expectable standard cost; attainable good performance standard cost; attainable standard cost; currently attainable standard cost; good attainable standard cost.

expected value <1> amount that a company expects to realize from the future sales of assets in their ultimate form. <2> in audit sampling, the weighted average of all the values the variable can take, with respective probabilities as weights.

expected value approach an approach under which income for a period is considered to be the change in the total net assets of a business.

expected yield the amount of money an investor expects to earn from a specific security divided by the total investment.

expendable fund a fund the principal of which can be accessed. ***Opp:*** *endowment fund.*

expendable trust a trust both the principal and earnings of which could be expended for authorized purpose. ***See:*** *non-expendable trust.*

expendable trust fund a governmental fund restricted by an expendable trust agreement.

expenditure (exp.) <1> a disbursement made in order to obtain an asset or service. ***Also***: outgo; outgoing; outlay; payout. <2> cost deferred to future periods for matching future benefits. <3> an increase in liabilities of a fund.

expenditure approach a method under which national income is the sum of the market value of all goods and services.

expenditure method a method under which expenditures in excess of known sources of funds is treated as unreported income.

expenditure on revenue account = *revenue expenditure.*

expenditure variance = factory overhead expenditure variance.

expense (exp.)(expse) <1> a charge for a good or service received. ***Also***: outgo. <2> = *overhead.*

expense account budgeted money advanced to salespersons for daily expenses.

expense and revenue summary account = *income summary account.*

expense asset the asset invested that must be recovered from future revenue. ***Also***: cost stream; expired cost asset.

expense audit auditing of the amount and computation method of expense.

expense budget a budget for the planning of expenses in a given period.

expense burden = *factory overhead.*

expense center an activity, a group of persons, etc. which has outlay or expenditure. ***Also***: discretionary expense center.

expense control budget = *flexible budget.*

expense loading = *factory overhead.*

expense method a method of recording advance payments as expenses and at the end of the period transferring the portion of expense that was not consumed to an asset account. ***Opp***: asset method.

expense of goods sold = *cost of goods sold.*

expense ratio <1> for a mutual fund, operating costs divided by its average net assets for a given period. ***Also***: management expense ratio. <2> of an insurance company, the difference between the incurred insurance and related expenses divided by total written premium. ***See***: *combined ratio; loss ratio.* <3> ratio of general and administrative expense to total income of an investment trust.

expense reserve insurance company's liability for incurred but unpaid expenses.

expense variance = *budget variance.*

expensing practice of writing off an item immediately rather than capitalizing it.

experience account the ratio of premium to claims for a plan, coverage, or benefits for a stated time period.

experience effect improvement in efficiency and reduction in cost resulting from experience.

experience method <1> a method which determines practical capacity on the basis of actual output at practical capacity. <2> method for the additions to reserves for bad debts for banks under which the addition is calculated on the basis of actual bad debt experience over a six-year period. ***See***: *theoretical capacity method.*

experimental expense = *research and development cost.*

experimental test audit the test audit made by the auditor's experience and his direct observation.

expiration of assets = *depreciation.*

expired cost <1> cost the contribution of which to future revenue has passed. ***Also***: consumed cost. <2> = past cost.

expired cost asset = *expense asset.*

expired utility = *depreciation.*

explanation brief description of an entry in the journal.

explanatory note = *footnote.*

explicit cost production cost that needs outlay of cash. ***See***: *implicit cost.*

explicit interest the interest that is paid in cash.

explicit reinvestment rate of return method a method of computing rate of return in which the ROR = (annual income - the annual sinking fund balance required to recover investment at the end of period)/original investment cost. ***Also***: Hoskold's method.

exploration cost the cost incurred in exploring a mine or other mineral resources.

ex post income = *accounting income.*

Exposure Draft (ED) a proposed statement of financial accounting standards issued by the FASB for public comment, representing the FASB's considered judgment on a specific accounting issue.

express trust a trust established intentionally and explicitly. ***Also***: direct trust. ***Opp***: *constructive trust.*

expropriation take-over of foreign assets by a government without compensation.

expropriation loss the loss caused by take-over of assets by a foreign government without compensation.

ex scrip = *ex capitalization.*

extend indicating a figure has been transferred to another column.

extended IRA retirement plan that can be rolled over into the name of a spouse or child after the original IRA owner dies.

extended normal costing the costing that assigns direct costs using budgeted rates and actual quantities of inputs.

extension time period for filing a tax return that is extended beyond the due date.

exterior failure cost the cost incurred when nonconforming products are discovered after shipment to the customer, e.g. cost of settling claims. ***Also***: external failure cost. ***See***: *interior failure cost.*

exterior liability the company's liability owe to outside parties. ***Also***: creditor's equity; liability to outsider; liability to the public.

external account an account that is open to the public.

external accounting = *stewardship accounting.*

external audit annual audit of the accounting records of a business performed by a CPA. ***Also***: annual financial audit; professional audit; public audit.

external auditor = *independent auditor.*

external cost the cost of an activity that must be absorbed by other units. ***See***: *frictional cost.*

external document the document needed for record keeping generated by outside parties.

external expansion a company's growth by acquiring other companies. ***See***: *internal expansion.*

external failure cost = *exterior failure cost.*

external financing raising capital by new borrowing or new issue of shares. ***Opp***: *internal financing.*

external growth expansion of business through external opportunities or acquisition. ***Opp***: *internal growth.*

externally created document a supporting document prepared by the third parties.

external rate of return a rate of return one can expect to earn in lieu of making a particular proposed investment. ***Also***: opportunity cost; taxpayer's opportunity cost.

external transaction a transaction between the business and another entity.

extinguishment fund = *sinking fund.*

extra = *extra dividend.*

extra cost = *marginal cost.*

extract = *description.*

extra depreciation amount in excess of legally allowable depreciation. ***Also***: over-depreciation.

extra dividend a dividend paid in addition to the regular or usual dividend. ***Also***: bonus dividend; extra; special bonus dividend; special dividend.

extraordinary care = *utmost care.*

extraordinary cost = *nonrecurring cost.*

extraordinary depreciation = *abnormal depreciation.*

extraordinary gain or loss (X/O gain or loss) the gain or loss generated by unusual and infrequent events and transactions.

extraordinary general meeting (EGM) <UK> a meeting of shareholders other than an annual general meeting.

extraordinary item income statement item that is unusual in nature, infrequent in occurrence and nonrecurring but has material effects.

extraordinary repair any repair work that extends the life of a fixed asset more than one year and is capitalized rather then expenses. *See*: *ordinary repairs.*

extrinsic value the component of an option value which comes about purely by virtue of the time remaining before expiration. *Also*: time value. *See*: *intrinsic value.*

eye test the examination of some unimportant items by looking at them.

F f

F <1> favorable variance. <2> fixed cost.

FA <1> fixed asset. <2> floating asset. <3> frozen asset.

face amount <1> amount printed on a bond, which is paid when it is retired. <2> amount stated on the face of the policy that will be paid in case of death.

face capital = *nominal capital.*

face par = *face value.*

face value nominal value of a note or security as distinguished from the market value. ***Also***: denomination; face par; nominal price; nominal value; par; par value; principal; principal of instrument.

face value method a method by which the acquisition of treasury stock will be treated as reduction in capital stock, and reissuance would be treated as original issue of capital stock. ***Also***: par or stated value method; par value method; stated capital method. ***See***: *constructive retirement method; cost price method.*

facility fee the fee paid by the borrower on the total amount of the credit facility, irrespective of any usage.

factor = *accounts receivable factor.*

factorage <1> the commission or fee paid to a factor. <2> = *accounts receivable financing.*

factor analysis method a method of analyzing the factors that cause variance, under which each factor is substituted to calculate the portion of variance caused by that factor.

factor cost <1> price paid by a consumer for the goods or services minus the tax based on that price. <2> = *conversion cost.* <3> = *element cost.*

factor cost method method of valuing product cost and income in terms of the factors of production rather than the market price.

factoring = *accounts receivable financing.*

factory burden = *factory overhead.*

factory cost = *manufacturing cost.*

factory cost of sales = *manufacturing cost of goods sold.*

factory ledger group of accounts used to record factory-related transactions.

factory overhead the manufacturing cost other than direct material and direct labor. ***Also***: common production expense; expense burden; expense loading; factory burden; general overhead of mill; indirect expense; indirect factory cost; indirect overhead cost; manufacturing burden; manufacturing expense; manufacturing overhead; overhead; production overhead; shop burden; works overhead.

factory overhead allocation rate the rate of factory overhead on a chosen basis of distribution.

factory overhead budget a budget about the factory overhead costs. ***Also***: manufacturing overhead budget.

factory overhead expenditure variance the variance of actual factory overhead from the allowed amount based on actual activity. ***Also***: expenditure variance; spending variance.

factory overhead variance the variance of actual factory overhead from standard factory overhead.

factory service cost = *service cost.*

factory shut-down cost = *shut-down cost.*

factory supplies = *indirect material.*

factual resident <Canada> a taxpayer who remains residential ties with Canada while traveling or living abroad.

FAF Financial Accounting Foundation

failure cost = *cost of failure.*

fair market value (FMV) amount of cash or its equivalent that could be obtained by selling an asset in orderly market. ***Also***: current market value.

fair value accounting = *current cost accounting.*

fair value based method method of recognizing compensation expense of an employee stock ownership plan by using a fair market value. ***Also*** fair value method. ***See***: *intrinsic value based method.*

fair value hedge the hedge against the fair value of asset and liability. ***See***: *cash flow hedge.*

fair value method <1> a method of recording asset acquired via non-monetary exchange, under which acquisition is recorded at fair market value of asset surrendered or received whichever is more determinable. ***See***: *book value method.* <2> = *fair value based method.*

fair value reserve a reserve for unrealized gain or loss on investments classified as available-for-sale in the stockholders' equity section.

fairway option = *accrual option.*

false account any account that provides misleading information. ***Also***: fictitious account.

false entry = *fictitious entry.*

false return = *fraudulent return.*

false statement an assertion that is not true.

falsification of accounts defrauding, destroying, altering, multilating or falsifying book, writing, document or accounts, or making false entry in such book or account willfully and with intent.

family coverage health insurance that covers the taxpayer and the family members.

family credit <UK> tax credit available for working families with at least one full-time worker. Replaced by *working families tax credit* from October 1999.

family farm property <Canada> land or depreciable asset used in a family-own farm.

family incentive trust = *incentive trust.*

family income <Canada> = *household income.*

family income splitting a tax planning method that focuses on shifting taxable income, from family members in high income tax brackets to those in lower brackets through such devices as short-term trust and interest-free loans.

family owned business exclusion the exclusion of estate from tax if the family owned business interest passed to qualified heirs comprise of more than 50% of a decedent's adjusted gross estate not exceeding 1.5 million.

family strategist an expert in estate planning.

family support allowance a deduction from the estate paid to support the widow or dependent. ***Also***: widow's allowance.

family tax initiative <Australia> financial assistance provided to families with dependent children.

family trust a trust the beneficiary of which is the member of the family. ***Also***: B trust; bypass trust.

fancy accounting = *window dressing.*

FAR free asset ratio

FARE Financial Accounting & Reporting

farmer's averaging <UK> a tax relief that allows farmers to even out fluctuations in income.

farmer's optional computation method a method under which a farmer can use 2/3 of gross income as self-employment income if gross income from farming is $2,400 or less.

farm loss operating loss from running a farm.

farm price method an adjusted selling price method for pricing inventories of live stocks and other farm products, using their market value minus the direct costs of disposing the items.

FAS Financial Accounting Standards

FASAB Federal Accounting Standards Advisory Board

FASB Financial Accounting Standards Board

FASB No. 8 FASB's statement on foreign exchange standards issued in 1975.

FASIT financial asset securitization trust

fast-pay preferred stock a high-coupon stock designed to pay a tax-sheltered dividend that, in effect, liquidates the principal before the payment declines to a nominal level and the issuer is recapitalized. *Also*: step-down preferred stock.

favorable balance = *active balance of payments.*

favorable standard cost variance a standard cost variance occurred when the actual cost is less than the standard direct material cost.

favorable variance (fav var) amount by which the actual costs are less than the planned cost, or an excess of actual income over planned revenue. *Also*: credit variance.

FAVR method fixed and variable rate method

fav. var. favorable variance

FBT fringe benefits tax

FCA fellow member of the Institute of Chartered Accountants in England and Wales.

FCF free cash flow

FD full disclosure

FDWP foreign dividend withholding payment

feature audit the audit that focuses on the special events.

Federal Accounting Standards Advisory Board (FASAB) group authorized by the accounting profession to establish generally accepted accounting principles applicable to federal government entities.

federal fund accounting the procedures for the federal grants and awards used in a non-profit organization.

federal gift tax = *gift tax.*

federal highway use tax a tax on highway motor vehicles having a *taxable gross weight* of 55,000 lbs or more. *Also*: heavy highway vehicle use tax. *See: highway use tax.*

federal ID number (FIN) a number assigned to a business for tax reporting purposes. *Also*: employer ID number. *See: business number.*

federal income tax the tax levied by the federal government on personal and corporate income.

Federal Insurance Contributions Act (FICA) a legislation that provides benefits for retired workers, disabled workers and the dependents.

federal money = *hard money.*

federal/state e-filing the e-filing of both federal and state taxes at the same time.

federal surplus the extent to which government revenues exceed government spending.

federal tax clearance certificate = *certificate of tax clearance.*

federal tax identification number (FTIN) a number assigned to an individual who does not have a social security number for tax purpose. *Also*: tax identification number.

federal tax lien a *tax lien* against all assets of a taxpayer for nonpayment of federal tax.

federal tentative minimum tax = *tentative tax.*

federal unemployment tax = *FUTA tax.*

feed ratio the relationship of the cost of feed, expressed as a ratio to the sale price of animals.

FEI Financial Executives International

fertilizer cost the cost of applying chemical fertilizers to the land.

FF&E furniture, fixtures and equipment

FFO funds from operations

FICA Federal Insurance Contributions Act

FICA tax a tax levied by the Federal Insurance Contribution Act, equal amounts from both the employer and employees. *Also*: social security tax.

fictitious account <1> = *false account*. <2> = *nominal account*.

fictitious asset <1> an asset which has to appear in the balance sheet because of double entry bookkeeping but which has no present value or could not be realized. *Also*: nominal asset. <2> = *deferred asset*.

fictitious capital the capital in the form of valuable securities that can produce income.

fictitious entry an entry for the purpose of falsification of the account. *Also*: false entry.

fictitious liability = *deferred liability*.

fictitious profit the profit that exists in the income statement but not realized. *Also*: bookkeeping profit; book profit; nominal profit; phantom profit.

fidelity bond an insurance against loss caused by embezzlement.

fiduciary accounting the maintaining of property accounts in the hands of a trustee, executor or administrator.

fiduciary duty an obligation to act solely in the best interest of another party.

fiduciary estate the estate or interest of a trustee in property or cash. *See*: *beneficiary interest*.

fiduciary fund a fund used by government accounting to account for its responsibility for handling the assets placed under its control, e.g., *agency fund* and *trust fund*.

fiduciary income tax return a tax return filed by the fiduciary for a domestic estate or trust with income of $600 or more.

fiduciary liability federal tax liability of the property held as fiduciary.

fiduciary principal = *principal*.

fiduciary tax return tax return prepared by the trustee for a trust.

FIE foreign investment entity

field = *population*.

field audit an audit of the client's books and records, undertaken outside the office of the auditor. *Also*: on-site audit; on the spot audit; site audit. *See*: *traveling audit*.

field auditor a CPA who conducts audit at a client's location.

field work audit work done at the client's place.

fifo first-in, first-out

fifo cost the cost of materials inventory under the fifo method.

fifo cost flow assumption under process costing, an assumption that items transferred from last process were the first to be finished.

fifo method first-in, first-out method

file posting = *bookless accounting system*.

filing date <UK> = *tax return due date*.

filing-due date <Canada> = *tax return due date*.

filing status the format of tax return filed by a taxpayer, such as single, married filing jointly (MFJ), married filing separately (MFS), surviving spouse (SS), head of household (HH), etc. *Also*: tax status.

filing threshold the minimum income amount above which a taxpayer must file a tax return. *Also*: minimum requirements for filing.

FILO first-in, last-out

FIN Federal ID number

fin. <1> finance. <2> financial.

fin. acc. financial accounting

final account = *closing account*.

final audit an audit undertaken at the end of an accounting period. *Also*: audit of returns.

final CPU the cost per unit of good products after the exclusion of lost units.

final dividend the dividend declared by the company in the annual meeting in addition to interim dividends.

final entry = *ledger entry*.

final goods-in-process = *closing work-in-process*.

final inventory = *ending inventory.*

final products approach an approach under which the gross national product equals the products sold to consumers plus those sold to producers, government and foreign buyers.

final prospectus final approved *prospectus* issued to the public. ***Also***: statutory prospectus. ***See***: *preliminary prospectus.*

final return the last tax return filed for a deceased person for the part of the year up to the date of death.

final salary pension <UK> an *occupational pension scheme* the contribution under which relates to the plan's accrual rate and the member's earnings at retirement age. *See: money purchase scheme.*

final sales portion of GNP sold to ultimate users.

final salvage value = *salvage value.*

final statement <1> a statement prepared after the annual closing of books. ***Also***: closing statement. <2> the statement prepared after liquidation by liquidator.

final value = *future value.*

finance charge interest charge on the unpaid balance of revolving charge accounts.

finance cost = *financing cost.*

financial accounting (fin. acc.) accounting that provides financial information concerning a firm's financial position and operating results to external users, such as creditors, owners and the government. ***Also***: custodial accounting; financial reporting accounting; general accounting.

Financial Accounting Standards Board (FASB) the member board which replaced the APB and has the authority to formulate rules governing the practice of accounting in 1973.

financial asset a fixed amount of foreign currency and securities held for less than six months. ***See***: *non-financial asset.*

financial asset securitization trust (FASIT) a pass-through entity used to securitize debt obligations, such as mortgage receivables.

financial audit examination of accounts and records undertaken by internal auditors.

financial budget a budget that includes cash budget, budgeted financial statement, budgeted funds statement, and capital budget.

financial capital maintenance a concept under which the effects of the price changes in assets and liabilities are considered holding gain and losses, and are included in computing return on capital. ***See***: *physical capital maintenance.*

financial components approach = *components approach.*

financial corporation a corporation that deals primarily in money in substantial competition with banks.

financial cost the cost related to financial activities, such as interest, sales discount, bank service fee, etc.

financial derivative = *derivative.*

financial distress cost legal and administrative cost of liquidation or reorganization.

financial expense any expense on such items as interest on long-term debts, director's fee, audit fee, etc.

financial forecast the prospective financial statements, which present the management's beliefs about the entity's expected financial position, results of operations and cash flows based on future events and operating results. ***See***: *financial projection.*

financial gearing = *leverage.*

financial income = *book profit.*

financial institution a state or national bank, savings and loan association, or a credit union. ***Also***: banking institution.

financial interrelation ratio the ratio of financial assets to national wealth in the national wealth account.

financial lease = *capital lease.*

financial ledger = *general ledger.*

financial leverage <1> ratio of debt capital and contributed capital to net worth. <2> financial ratio showing the relationship between a firm's EBIT and its earnings per share, calculated as EBIT ÷ (EBIT- interests on bonds - dividend on preferred stock). *See*: *capital leverage*; *degree of financial leverage*. <3> = *debt ratio*.

financial leverage principle a principle the gist of which is that the higher the leverage is, the higher the stockholders' expected rate of return will be when the expected rate of return is higher than the interest rate.

financial leverage ratios = *capitalization ratios*.

financial liability a liability that requires cash payment, e.g. note payable, account payable, accrual expense, deferred income, etc.

financially dependent <Canada> at the time of an annuitant's death, a dependent resided with the annuitant and has gross income of less than certain threshold amount.

Financial Management Service (FMS) a department in the IRS for processing payments to and from the government.

financial planning evaluating the investment and financial alternatives available.

financial position the source of funds and their application at certain time. *Also*: capital position; financial standing; position.

financial position form a balance sheet form in which current assets are listed and totaled, the current liabilities are listed next and the total deducted from the total of current assets to derive an amount for working capital, other assets are then added and other liabilities deducted, leaving a residual amount as the stockholders' equity. *See*: *account form*; *report form*.

financial position statement a balance sheet in the financial position form. *Also*: statement of position; vertical balance sheet.

financial projection prospective financial statements that present expected results of a hypothetical event to the best of the company's knowledge and belief given one or more hypothetical assumptions. *See*: *financial forecast*; *pro forma financial statement*.

financial rate of return = *accounting rate of return*.

financial ratio a measure of the relationship between one financial statement item and another.

financial records income and spending records kept for tax purposes.

financial reporting accounting = *financial accounting*.

Financial Reporting Exposure Draft (FRED) <UK> an official statement of the Accounting Standards Board.

Financial Reporting Standard (FRS) <UK> a document issued by the Accounting Standards Board setting forth the guidelines of financial reporting for all businesses.

Financial Reporting Standard for Smaller Entities (FRSSE) <UK> a document of financial reporting guidelines for small businesses.

financial resources budget a plan that includes a budgeted balance sheet showing the effects of planned operations and capital investments on assets and equities, and a cash budget.

financial risk the risk that the returns to the owner of the equity of a firm will decrease because of the necessity to pay interest to suppliers of debt capital.

financial S corporation a financial corporation elected to be an S corporation.

financial service income earnings from delivering financial service.

financial solvency = *solvency*.

financial standing (fin. stndg) = *financial position*.

financial statement (fin stat) final product of accounting that conveys a concise picture of the profitability and financial position of an entity. *Also*: accounting statement.

financial statement account an account the balance of which must appear in the financial statements.

financial statement analysis evaluation of the past, current and projected conditions and performance of a business. ***Also***: analysis of financial statements.

financial statement method = *mercantile method.*

financial statement projection = *pro forma financial statement.*

financial statements audit the audit which focuses on financial statements for the purpose of expressing an opinion as to the fairness of the information presented. ***Also***: audit of financial statements. ***See***: *compliance audit; operational audit.*

financial tariff = *revenue tariff.*

financial transaction account social accounting statement which shows the circulation of currency and the credits in a stated period.

financial year = *accounting year.*

financing account = *accommodating account.*

financing activities transactions including distribution, acquisition, movement, and management of money.

financing cost the cost of borrowing to purchase and hold a specified asset position. ***Also***: finance cost.

financing cost saving a source of competitive advantage by being able to access to low cost capital.

financing lease = *capital lease.*

financing receivables = *accounts receivable financing.*

finder's fee the fee paid to someone who acts as an intermediary for a client in a transaction.

fine rate = *bank prime interest rate.*

finished goods (FG) product in its completed state ready for sale. ***Also***: completed product; manufactured goods.

finished goods inventory products that have been completed through the production process and are now available for sale to customers.

finished goods ledger a detailed ledger for each finished goods.

finished parts ledger = *work-in-process ledger.*

finishing cost <1> = *conversion cost.* <2> = *joint cost.*

fin. stat. financial statement

fin. yr. financial year

firewall = *Chinese wall.*

firm-on-firm review (FOF) review of a CPA firm conducted by another CPA firm. ***See***: *peer review.*

firm-wide cost <1> cost that relates to the whole company. <2> = *administration cost.*

first base amount a threshold amount in the calculation of inclusion in income 50% of the social security benefit. ($32,000 in 2003). ***See***: *second base amount.*

first cost <1> = *original cost.* <2> = *prime cost.* <3> = *target cost.*

first cost method = *original cost method.*

first credit year the tax year that includes the date that a qualified employer plan becomes effective.

first entry = *original entry.*

first-in cost the cost of the goods bought firstly.

first-in, first-out <1> an assumption that the first items bought or received were the first items sold or used. ***Also***: last-in, last-out; last-in, on-hand; last-in, still-here. <2> unused tax credit carried forward to future years will be treated as used against the first available expense, then the next expense.

first-in, first-out method (fifo method) <1> a method of pricing an inventory under the fifo assumption whereby issues of materials or finished units sold are measured at the costs of the units purchased or produced earlier. <2> a method for computing unit costs of a process by which the costs and equivalent units, included in beginning inventory are omitted in computing unit costs of work done in the current period. *Also*: last-in, on-hand method; last-in, still-here method. <3> a method under which the shares sold are assumed to be the earliest shares acquired for computation of capital gains. <4> a method under which money is considered to be withdrawn from an account in the order in which is was deposited.

first-in, last-out = *last-in, first-out.*

first-in, on-hand = *last-in, first-out.*

first-in, still-here (FISH) = *last-in, first-out.*

first mortgage loan a mortgage loan made to the homeowner at the time the house is bought.

first rate the tax rate on the first tax bracket. *See: middle rate; top rate.*

first stage the generation of income (*primary income*) from the production and distribution between production factors and government.

first statement the core financial statement, it was the income statement formerly but it is now the balance sheet. *Also*: core statement.

first tax bracket the first income range in a tax table with the lowest rate. *Also*: initial bracket. *See: bottom bracket.*

first-term shared-use equipment <Canada> depreciable property used by the taxpayer from the time of acquisition to the end of the first taxation year ending at least 12 months after the acquisition date for scientific and research and experimental development.

first-tier deduction miscellaneous deduction not subject to 2% AGI floor limit. *Also*: tier 1 deduction. *See: second-tier deduction.*

first time homebuyer a taxpayer who has no ownership of a house before the purchase of the present home.

first time homebuyer credit a tax credit allowed to first time home purchasers in Washington D.C.

first year allowance <UK> capital allowance given to a trader who purchased plant assets.

first year expense cost associated with the selling of a new insurance policy.

first year expensing deduction for up to $25,000 in 2004 a depreciable business asset other than real estate in the year purchased.

fiscal month = *income tax month.*

fiscal period <1> time lapsed when the business is being incorporated, liquidated or when there are any changes in the accounting periods. <2> = *accounting period.* <3><of a trust of estate> = *fiscal year.*

fiscal year (FY)(FYR) <1> a period of 12 consecutive months, other than a calendar year ending on the last day of a particular month. *Also*: fiscal period. *See*: *natural business year*. <2> = *accounting year.*

FISH first-in, still-here

fisher equation nominal rate of interest = real rate of interest + inflation.

fixed age allowance = *age allowance.*

fixed and variable rate method (FAVR method) a method of reimbursing employee auto expenses under which a periodic fixed payment is made to cover fixed costs such as depreciation, coupled with a variable payment to cover variable cost such as gasoline.

fixed annuity an annuity in which the payments to the annuitant are fixed. *Also*: period-certain annuity.

fixed asset (FA) = *plant asset.*

fixed asset to equity capital ratio = *fixed ratio.*

fixed asset turnover sales divided by fixed assets, a measurement of the productivity and efficiency of fixed assets. *Also*: sales to fixed assets.

fixed asset unit element making up the fixed asset account.

fixed base proportional method = *production method.*

fixed benefit payment to a beneficiary that is in fixed amount.

fixed benefit plan = *defined benefit plan.*

fixed budget a budget based on a single sales estimate that gives no consideration to the possibility that the actual sales volume may differ from the assumed amount. ***Also***: non-flexible budget; static budget. ***Opp***: *flexible budget.*

fixed capital (FC) <1> an investment, in assets intended for use over a long period. <2> capital the sum of which remains unchanged.

fixed capital method a method of partnership accounting under which capital of each partner is entered in a separate account distinguishing from the profit and withdrawals. ***Opp***: *capital account method.*

fixed charge <1> expense charge that must be met on a certain date, such as interest. <2> that part of the overhead that must be allocated to upper administration. <3> = *setting up cost.*

fixed charge coverage = *times fixed charges earned.*

fixed charge holder <UK> mortgage lender or a bondholder of a person being liquidated.

fixed charges earned = *times fixed charges earned.*

fixed cost (FC) a cost that tends to remain unchanged in total amount over a wide range of production level. ***Also***: constant cost; invariable cost; on cost; overhead; standing cost; supplementary cost. ***See***: *non-variable cost.*

fixed cost spending variance difference between actual fixed costs and the budgeted fixed costs.

fixed costs per unit fixed costs divided by the number of units of output. ***Also***: average fixed cost; unit fixed cost. ***See***: *variable unit cost.*

fixed cost variance difference between actual fixed costs and the budgeted or standard amount.

fixed deduction <UK> = *flat rate expense.*

fixed entry a journal entry for recording recurring transaction. ***Also***: recurring entry.

fixed expense an expense that remains constant irrespectively of the business volume or level of activity. ***Also***: constant expense; standing expense.

fixed factory overhead = *fixed overhead.*

fixed-first-order of arrangement = *capital arrangement.*

fixed income the income from sources such as bonds, that does not change in total amount.

fixed installment method = *straight-line method of depreciation.*

fixed interest cover ratio of profit before fixed interest to fixed interest and dividends payable.

fixed interest trust <UK> a trust the nominated beneficiary of which has an interest in income, but the capital will pass to another beneficiary at termination. ***Also***: life interest trust. ***See***: *discretionary trust.*

fixed investment trust = *unit investment trust.*

fixed liability an amount owed that will remain on the book during the remainder of the period.

fixed manufacturing cost manufacturing cost that remain unchanged for a given period.

fixed order interval system an inventory control system the order intervals are equal. ***Also***: periodic inventory system; periodic review system; p-system; time-based inventory system; T-system.

fixed order size system an inventory control system the order sizes are equal. ***Also***: Q-system; reorder point system.

fixed overhead (F o'h'd) overhead the amount of which tends to be fixed. ***Also***: common fixed cost; common period cost; fixed factory overhead; F overhead; inflexible burden; non-separable fixed cost. ***Opp***: *variable overhead.*

fixed overhead absorption rate calculated as standard fixed overhead/budgeted direct labor hours.

fixed overhead allowed multiplied the actual number of output units by the standard fixed overhead rate.

fixed overhead budget variance = *fixed overhead expenditure variance.*

fixed overhead calendar variance that part of fixed overhead variance caused by the difference between actual days and the calendar days.

fixed overhead capacity variance difference between fixed overhead costs budgeted at practical capacity and those at normal capacity.

fixed overhead efficiency variance a variance calculated as: (actual number of input hours - standard number of output hours) × standard overhead costs per hour.

fixed overhead expenditure variance the difference between the actual fixed overhead costs and those allowed under flexible budgets. ***Also***: fixed overhead budget variance; fixed overhead spending variance.

fixed overhead idle capacity variance a variance calculated as: (units of product at practical capacity - planned production to satisfy the sales forecast) × fixed overhead costs per unit.

fixed overhead marketing variance a cost variance calculated as: (units in the sales forecast - units actually produced and sold) × fixed overhead cost per unit of output.

fixed overhead normal activity variance a cost variance that is calculated as: (budgeted activity - normal activity) × fixed overhead costs per unit of output.

fixed overhead price variance difference between actual fixed overhead and standard fixed overhead.

fixed overhead spending variance = *fixed overhead expenditure variance.*

fixed overhead variance difference between the actual fixed overhead costs and the fixed overhead allowed.

fixed overhead volume variance difference between the budgeted fixed overhead based on the activity volume allowed and the standard fixed overhead cost applied to the units of output. ***Also***: denominator variance.

fixed percentage depreciation rate used under the *declining balance method*, calculated as: $1 - \sqrt[n]{(R/A)} \times 100$, where A is the asset cost, R is the residual value, n is the number of years of useful life.

fixed percentage method = *declining balance method.*

fixed percentage of cost method = *straight-line method of depreciation.*

fixed percentage-of-declining balance method = *declining balance method.*

fixed percentage of diminishing value method = *declining balance method.*

fixed price <1> price for the valuation of certain inventory accounts in standard costing. <2> the price charged under a contract. <3> the price that investment bankers agree to sell the issue to the public in a public offering.

fixed profit car scheme <UK> a scheme under which employers can pay the employee a mileage allowance for the business use of the employee's car. ***See***: *mileage allowance.*

fixed ratio the ratio of fixed assets to the owners' equities. ***Also***: fixed asset to equity capital ratio; ratio of fixed assets to net worth.

fixed reorder point method an inventory control method under which all stocks are reordered when reducing to a certain level.

fixed sample size approach audit sampling the sample size does not change. ***See***: *sequential sampling.*

fixed unit cost the *cost per unit* figure that remains constant., that is *variable costs per unit.* ***See***: *unit fixed cost; variable unit cost.*

fixed variable cost analysis = *determination of cost behavior.*

fixed-variable split of cost = *determination of cost behavior.*

fixing-up expense an expense incurred to physically prepare a house for sale.

fixture fixed asset whose utility is derived from its attachment to land or building.

FL folio

flash report a report which conveys the highlights of key information promptly to the responsible managers.

flat = *ex interest.*

flat benefit <Canada> a pension benefit the amount of which is fixed.

flat benefit formula a method used to determine a participant's benefits in a defined benefit plan by multiplying months of service by a flat rate.

flat cost = *prime cost.*

flat rate <1><Canada> a fixed rate used in calculating flat benefit . <2> = *flat yield.*

flat rate expense <UK> tax allowances for the cost of replacement, repair, cleaning of tools, overalls or the other protective clothing or uniform. ***Also***: fixed deduction.

flat rate scheme <UK> a plan that charges small business *value added tax* at a flat rate.

flat tax = *proportional tax.*

flat tax system a tax system under which all income levels are taxed at the same rate.

flat yield a yield earned by a fixed-interest bond expressed as a ratio of the amount invested, without recognition of the gain or loss on redemption. ***Also***: flat rate.

flexible accounting system an accounting system that uses flexible budgeting.

flexible auction rate preferred stock = *auction rate preferred stock.*

flexible budget a budget that provides budgeted amounts for all levels of production within the relevant range. ***Also***: expense control budget; formula budget; semi-variable budget; sliding budget; sliding scale budget; step budget; variable budget. ***Opp***: *fixed budget.*

flexible budget formula = *cost-volume formula.*

flexible budget performance report a report designed to analyze the difference between actual performance and budget performance, where the budgeted amounts are based on the actual sales volume or level of activity. ***Also***: performance report.

flexible budget variance = *budget variance.*

flexible cost fixed cost plus variable cost under flexible budget.

flexible expense an expense that can be adjusted or eliminated, e.g. luxury car, brand-name clothing or DVD player. ***Opp***: *inflexible expense.*

flexible spending account (FSA) a benefit offered to an employee by an employer which allows a fixed amount of pre-tax wages to be set aside for qualified expenses, such as child care. ***Also***: reimbursement account; salary reduction plan.

flight of capital = *capital flight.*

floatation cost = *cost of flotation.*

floater = *bearer stock.*

floating asset (FA) <1> = *current asset.* <2> = *variable capital.*

floating capital <1> = *idle money.* <2> = *working capital.*

floating charge <1> creditor's right extends to all the company's assets. <2> = *cost of floatation.*

floating cash reserve = *idle money.*

floating debt <1> continuously refinanced *short-term debt* for a company's ongoing operations. <2> short-term obligations of a government, e.g. Treasury bills.

floating liability = *current liability.*

floating lien general attachment against a company's assets.

floating money = *idle money.*

floating rate preferred = *adjustable rate preferred stock.*

float period time between the check is drawn and the time it is cashed. ***Also***: collection float; corporate processing float; mail float.

floor limitation net selling price of an inventory item less cost, cost to complete and normal profit. ***See***: *ceiling limitation.*

floor planning a financing plan under which a finance company buys the inventory and has it held in trust for the user.

floor record keeping record keeping required to be made on the floor of a stock exchange in connection with the disposition of an order or the execution of a trade.

flotation cost = *cost of flotation.*

flow account an account used by social accounting for recording the flow of goods or funds.

flow of cost = *cost flow.*

flow of current financial resources a concept which implies that each year is treated as a distinct event and the only measurement that is important is the source and use of fund. *See*: *flow of economic resources.*

flow of economic resources a concept under which governments would not be able to defer payment of expense into the future and avoid recognition in the current year. *See*: *flow of current financial resources.*

flow of entries = *posting.*

flow of funds <1> figures showing inflows or outflows of funds. *Also*: fund flow. <2> difference between inflows and outflows of funds in a given period.

flow of funds account (FoF a/c) account used in social accounting for recording transactions that involve the transfer of money between sectors in an economy. *Also*: money circuit account; money flow account.

flow of funds accounting the procedure for flow of funds operations. *Also*: fund flow accounting.

flow of funds statement <1> a statement showing the movement of fund over a given time. *Also*: fund flow statement. <2> = *statement of changes in financial position.*

flow statement = *cash flow statement.*

flow-through accounting = *flow-through basis.*

flow-through basis accounting for investment credit to show all income statement benefits of the credit in the year of acquisition, rather than spreading them over the life of the asset. *Also*: flow-through accounting.

flow-through entity <Canada> an entity the gains and losses of which are transferred to the owners.

flow-through method <1> a method used by public utility companies to pass tax savings on to their customers in the form of reduced rates. *See*: *normalization method.* <2> a method that uses straight-line depreciation in reporting to shareholders but accelerated depreciation in the tax return.

flow-through mining expenditure <Canada> exploration expense incurred after Jul 30, 2001 and before Jan 1, 2004 that can flow-through to investors.

flow-through share <Canada> a share of capital issued by mining, petroleum and certain energy corporations to finance exploration and project development activities, the tax-deductions will flow-through to the investors.

flow-through share investment tax credit <Canada> a 15% (20% in BC) non-refundable tax credit on flow-through mining expenditures.

FLP family limited partnership

fluid asset = *current asset.*

fluid capital = *working capital.*

FMS Financial Management Service

FMV fair market value

fo. folio

focal date artificial commencing date of interest fixed by a factor.

fo'd forward

FOF firm-on-firm review

FOF a/c flow of funds account

F o'h'd fixed overhead

fol. folio

folio (f.)(FL)(fo.)(fol.) <1> number of a single page in a journal or of a pair of facing pages in a ledger. *Also*: folio number. <2> unstructured basket of common stock that may represent an index or an actively-managed portfolio, but which may be modified by an investor to meet the tax and spending needs.

folio number = *folio.*

folio reference (F.) = *cross reference number.*

footing the adding of a column of figures and the recording in pencil of the temporary totals.

footnote explanatory words at the bottom of financial statements. ***Also***: accompanying note; annotation; appeared footnote; explanatory note; marginal note.

forced loan a loan that a government requires from its citizens, such as payment of estimated tax. ***Also***: compulsory loan.

forcing allocation the allocation of cost of sustaining activity to a cost object even though that cost object may not clearly consume or causally relate to that activity.

forecasted earnings the earnings of a future period reported by the company. ***See***: *expected earnings.*

forecasted financial statement an accounting statement that is prepared by forecasted figures. ***Also***: forward financial statement.

forecast variance = *marketing variance.*

foreclosure termination of an owner's right in a property that is subject to a mortgage or other security interest when he or she failed to make payments on time.

foreclosure gain excess of the sum paid to the owner over the owner's basis in the property foreclosed.

foreclosure loss excess of the basis in the property foreclosed over the sum paid to the owner.

foreign branch a branch located in a foreign country.

foreign corporation a company operating in a country other than the one of its incorporation. ***See***: *alien corporation.*

Foreign Corrupt Practices Act a law that prohibits bribes of foreign government officials for the purpose of securing business.

foreign currency translation = *translation of account balances.*

foreign currency translation reserve = *translation adjustment.*

foreign dividend withholding payment (FDWP) <New Zealand> withholding payments on dividends paid to New Zealand companies from overseas.

foreign earned income exclusion income of up to $80,000 a year in 2002 that can be excluded from gross income if a taxpayer lives and earns income in a foreign country. ***Also***: foreign earnings deduction.

foreign earnings deduction <UK> = *foreign earned income exclusion.*

foreign exchange accounting the translation of the foreign financial statement for financial exposure purpose. ***Also***: translation exposure accounting.

foreign exchange gain = *translation gain.*

foreign exchange loss = *translation loss.*

foreign exchange reserve foreign exchange assets held by a country. ***Also***: compulsory reserve; exchange cover; exchange reserve.

foreign exchange risk = *exchange risk.*

foreign income the income from foreign sources. ***Also***: foreign source income; gross income from source without the US.

foreign move expense of moving to a new principal place of work outside the US.

foreign plan <Canada> pension plan maintained to benefit non-residents for services performed outside Canada.

foreign premium the difference in price between shares owned by foreign investors and shares that must be held by domestic investors.

foreign resource expense (FRE) <Canada> expense incurred to acquire or operate a resource property in another country.

foreign resource pool expense <Canada> a taxpayer's foreign resource expense and foreign exploration and development expense.

foreign resource property <Canada> a right, license or privilege to explore petroleum, natural gas or hydrocarbons abroad.

foreign sales corporation (FSC) an export corporation created by the Tax Reform Act of 1984 eligible for some tax incentives.

foreign share-for-share exchange <Canada> exchange of shares issued by a foreign corporation for shares issued by another foreign corporation.

foreign source income = *foreign income.*

foreign tax levy imposed by a foreign government.

foreign tax credit tax credit allowed against US income taxes for foreign taxes paid. *Also:* tax credit relief.

foreign tax credit limitation the maximum amount of foreign tax credit that can be claimed against US income tax liability.

foreign tax redetermination a change in foreign tax liability that may affect US foreign tax credit claimed. *Also*: redetermination of foreign tax.

foreign tax year tax year of a subsidiary in respect of a foreign country.

foreign transaction account a statement showing transactions between the foreign investing sector and other domestic sectors.

foreign trust = *offshore trust.*

forensic accounting court procedure that utilizes accounting, auditing, and investigative skills to conduct an examination into a company's financial statements.

foreseeable party any party that an accountant could reasonably foresee would receive the financial statements and use them.

forfaiting factoring large, medium to long-term receivables to buyers who are willing to bear the costs and risks of credit and collection.

forfeited amount <Canada> the benefit amount a member no longer has the rights to under a deferred profit-sharing plan.

forfeited share the share of stock forfeited by the issuing company when the holder of which cannot meet the call on any unpaid amounts.

forfeiture reallocation of a forfeiture in a money purchase plan to other participants under non-discriminatory formula or reducing future employer contribution.

forfeiture of shares an expropriation by a company of a shareholder's share.

forgiven debt = *cancelled debt.*

forgoing interest = *forgone interest.*

forgone interest the interest at the applicable federal rate over actual interest payable. *Also*: forgoing interest.

forgone revenue = *opportunity cost.*

Form 3 a document required by the SEC to announce the holdings of directors, officers and shareholders owning 10% or more of the company's outstanding stock.

Form 4 a document required by the SEC to announce changes in the holdings of directors, officers and shareholders owning 10% or more of the company's outstanding stock.

Form 8-K = *current report.*

Form 10K a detailed *annual report* of a public company, to be filed 90 days after the end of the fiscal year. *Also*: 10K.

Form 10Q the required quarterly reports to the SEC. *Also*: 10Q; quarterly report.

Form 709 = *gift tax return.*

Form 870 a form for a waiver of restrictions on assessment and collection of tax deficiency.

Form 940 Employer's Annual Federal Unemployment Tax Return

Form 941 Employer's Quarterly Federal Tax Return

Form 945 a form used by employers to report annual income taxes withheld from non-payroll payments. *Also*: annual non-payroll tax return.

Form 970 a form used to elect lifo.

Form 990 an information return filed by an exempt organization or a private foundation. *See*: *information return.*

Form 1040 = *individual tax return.*

Form 1040EZ simplified form of *individual tax return* designed for taxpayers who meet certain requirements.

Form 1099-DIV required statement from a broker or a company that summarizes dividends paid to a taxpayer.

Form 1099-INT required statement from a bank, a broker or a company that summarizes interests paid to a taxpayer.

Form 1065 = *information tax return.*

Form 1120 = *corporate tax return.*

Form 1120F a form used for reporting foreign branch profits tax.

Form 1127 a form used to apply for extension of time for paying income tax.

Form 1128 a form used to change a taxpayer's accounting period.

Form 1138 a form used to apply for extension of time for paying corporate tax if loss carryback is expected.

Form 2290 a form used to declare *federal highway use tax.*

Form 2553 an IRS form for the election of an S corporation status.

Form 2758 a form used to apply for an automatic extension for filing an estate return.

Form 3115 a formed used to change a taxpayer's accounting method.

Form 4562 a form used to claim depreciation deduction.

Form 4797 a form used for recapture of depreciation.

Form 4810 a form used to request a *prompt assessment.*

Form 4868 a form used to file an extension of time for filing individual returns.

Form 5500EZ a form for reporting on a Keogh plan.

Form 7004 a form used to apply for extension for filing corporate returns.

Form 8109 a form used for depositing estimated taxes.

Form 8283 a form for substantiating charitable contribution of $250 or more.

Form 8736 a form used to apply for a 3-month automatic extension for filing partnership or trust returns.

Form 8800 a form used to apply for more than 3-month extension for filing partnership returns.

Form 8809 a form used to apply for an extension for filing information returns.

formal tax legislation process strict steps (that involve the President and Congress) that a proposed tax bill must pass through before it becomes a law.

formation expense = *organization cost.*

former business property <Canada> capital asset ever used by a taxpayer in a business.

form field number a number to identify the sequence of a tax return. ***Also***: form sequence number.

form of account = *account form.*

Form S-1 registration statement filed with SEC in the initial public offering of securities. ***Also***: Registration Statement; S-1.

form sequence number = *form field number.*

Form SS-5 Application for Social Security Number

Form T3 = *Statement of Trust Income.*

Form T4 = *Statement of Remuneration Paid.*

Form T5 = *Statement of Investment Income.*

Form T10 = *Pension Adjustment Reversal.*

Form T5007 = *Statement of Benefits.*

Form T5008 = *Securities Transactions.*

formula budget = *flexible budget.*

Form W-4 = *Employee's Withholding Allowance Certificate.*

Form W-2 = *Wage and Tax Statement.*

for-profit corporation = *business corporation.*

fortuitous loss the loss occurred by accident or chance, not by anyone's intention.

forward accounting that field of accounting such as standard cost, budgeting, estimating cash flow, pro forma financial statement etc. ***Also***: future accounting.

forward averaging a method of calculating tax on a lump-sum distribution from a qualified retirement plan, enabling the taxpayer to pay less than his current tax bracket, *5-year forward averaging* and *10-year forward averaging*. ***Also***: special averaging.

forward financial statement = *forecasted financial statement.*

forward looking statement a statement made with respect to the business or operations of an issuing company.

forward P/E price/earnings ratio using earnings estimates for the next 4 quarters.

forward pricing an SEC rule that requires open-end investment companies base all incoming buy and sell orders on the next asset valuation of fund shares.

forward purchase underwriting underwriting under which a corporation can raise capital by issuing stock at a price that is higher than prevailing levels if the company is willing to defer revenue until a later day.

forwards spreading <UK> tax relief that allows authors and artists to spread their lump-sum income forwards. ***See:*** *backwards spreading.*

foster child a child a taxpayer cares for as his or her own child.

founder a person who established a business. ***Also***: promoter.

founder's share the share taken up by founders of a company that ranks after the common stock which carries a fixed rate of interest, and receives residual earnings only. ***Also***: deferred share; promoter's share.

four-percent pricing method a method under which the DISC earns 4% of the export sales plus 10% of the DISC's export promotion costs and expenses attributable to the export sales.

fourth stage distribution of income through personal consumption, resulting in savings.

four-variance method an analysis method that divides variance into 4 parts, namely variable spending, fixed spending, volume, and efficiency variance.

FOVAR fixed overhead absorption rate

F overhead = *fixed overhead.*

FPA Financial Planning Association

fractional elimination method a method under which only part of the inter-company profits and losses are eliminated. ***Also***: partial elimination method; percent elimination method.

fractional-period depreciation less than one year depreciation computed on a proportional basis under accelerated depreciation.

fractional share unit of stock less than one full share.

franchise intangible asset from a privilege for the exclusive right to conduct business in a certain area.

franchise tax a state tax on banks and business entities.

franked dividend a dividend on which a tax has been paid.

franked income corporate income that is derived from the after-tax profits of another company, thus not taxable again.

fraud <1> deliberate action to cheat another, usually causing damages. <2> intentional act that causes a misstatement of the financial statements. ***Also***: irregularity. <3> = *actual fraud.* <4> = *tax fraud.*

fraud examination detection process to resolve allegations of fraud.

fraud in fact = *actual fraud.*

fraud in law = *constructive fraud.*

fraud in the execution = *fraud in the factum.*

fraud in the factum a misrepresentation as to the nature of a contract, will or other instrument being signed. ***Also***: fraud in the execution; fraud in the making.

fraud in the inducement misrepresentation upon which a person relies in entering into a contract about the subject of the contract or the surrounding circumstances. ***Also***: fraudulent inducement.

fraud in the making = *fraud in the factum.*

fraud penalty a penalty imposed by the IRS on a tax fraud.

fraud risk factor a factor whose presence often has been observed in circumstances where frauds have occurred.

fraud triangle a triangle comprising of three elements: opportunity, rationalization and incentive.

fraudulent conveyance the transfer of property for less than its full value to avoid creditor's attachment.

fraudulent financial reporting = *management fraud.*

fraudulent inducement = *fraud in the inducement.*

fraudulent return a tax return which contains false information, such as name or social security number. ***Also***: false return; incorrect return.

FRE foreign resource expense

FRED Financial Reporting Exposure Draft

free asset an asset that is neither pledged nor earmarked to the stated liabilities. ***Also***: unmortgaged asset.

free asset ratio (FAR) the market value of an insurance company's assets in excess of its policy liabilities.

free balance = *compensating balance.*

free capital <1> the capital in the form of money. ***Also***: capital in cash; liquid capital; monetary capital; money capital; nonspecific capital. <2> = *authorized capital stock.*

free cash flow (FCF) cash that remains after deducting the funds a company must commit to continue in operation. (earnings before interest less capital expenditures less the change in working capital.) ***Also***: free cash flow for the firm.

free cash flow for the firm = *free cash flow.*

free cash flow per share free cash flow divided by number of shares outstanding.

free depreciation the depreciation calculated at a rate chosen by the taxpayer.

free reserve the margin by which excess reserves exceed the Federal Reserve Bank's borrowings. ***Also***: non-borrowed reserve.

free surplus = *unappropriated retained earnings.*

free working capital = *working capital.*

freight transportation charge on goods.

freight allowance reserve for the freight that will be incurred.

freight-in transportation charge the company pays when it receives goods from a supplier. ***Also***: transportation in.

freight-out cost of transporting goods to a customer.

frictional cost <1> the difference between an index fund return and the index that it represents. <2> *external cost* of doing business.

friction cost the cost, implied or direct, associated with a securities transaction.

friendly takeover a *takeover* which is supported by the management of the *target company*. ***See***: *hostile takeover.*

friends and family shares the shares in an initial public offering or secondary offering that are allocated to certain persons at the request of the issuer. ***Also***: directed shares.

fringe benefit form of compensation other than an employee's basic earnings, such as overtime premiums, vacation pay, pensions and free stocks. ***Also***: payroll fringe; perks; perquisite.

fringe benefits tax (FBT) <New Zealand> a tax imposed on the non-salary fringe benefit provided to an employee.

frivolous income tax return a tax return that does not contain information on which the correctness of the tax liability may be judged. ($500 penalty.)

front-door approach a partnership audit method that begins with audits of the partnership and ends with audits of the partner.

front-end fee = *front-end load.*

front-end load a fee charged by open-end mutual funds at the time new securities are purchased by the investor. ***Also***: front-end fee; load; load charge; loading charge; purchase fee. ***See***: *back-end load; up front fee.*

front-end loading practice of mutual funds in which administrative, selling, brokerage and other fees are deducted from initial deposit.

front-end payment a single payment made at the beginning of a new contract.

front loading first year's alimony payment that exceeds the average of the payments made in the 2nd and 3rd years by more than $15,000. ***Also***: excess alimony; excess alimony payment; excessive alimony.

front money = *seed capital.*

frozen account a bank account the funds of which may not be withdrawn until a condition is satisfied or an ownership dispute is resolved. ***Also***: blocked account.

frozen credit the credit balance in a frozen account.

frozen plan a retirement plan to which no new contributions are being made.

FRS Financial Reporting Standard

FRSSE Financial Reporting Standard for Smaller Entities

F/S <1> funds statement. <2> fund statement.

FS financial statement

FSA <1> Federation of Schools of Accountancy. <2> Field Service Advice. <3> flexible spending account.

FSC foreign sales corporation

FTII fellow of the Chartered Institute of Taxation

FTIN federal tax identification number

full absorption accounting the accounting method in which direct and indirect production costs are included in ending inventory by an appropriate method.

full absorption cost = *absorption cost.*

full audit = *detailed audit.*

full cost = *absorption cost.*

full costing = *absorption costing.*

full cost method a method used by mining industry under which direct and indirect costs are both included in the production cost. ***Opp***: *successful efforts method.*

full cost plus pricing the pricing of a product by adding a markup to total manufacturing cost per unit.

full cost profit margin difference between total revenue and total costs traceable to a product.

full cost rule a rule by which the price is determined by adding a markup to full cost.

full depreciation the depreciation that is equal to the total depreciable amount of the asset.

full disclosure (FD) the requirement that each company listed on the stock exchange files a report relevant to financial and other data. ***Also***: accounting disclosure. ***See***: *Regulation FD.*

full disclosure principle a rule which requires that financial statements and footnotes disclose all material information relating to the financial position and operating results of the company.

full equity method = *complete equity method.*

full faith and credit all the resources of a government, including its taxing and borrowing power that back the debt issued by that government.

full partner = *general partner.*

full payout lease = *capital lease.*

full-price costing = *absorption costing.*

full product cost = *absorption cost.*

full rate <UK> a tax rate on profits of a company that is above a specified limit. ***See:*** *small company rate.*

full standard costing = *standard absorption costing.*

full-time education credit <Canada> a tax credit that is 16% of $400 per month in 2002 for the individual enrolled as a full-time student at a qualified educational program.

full-time gambler a taxpayer who spends significant amount of time gambling.

full-time student <1> a college student who enrolls 12 units per semester for two semesters per year. <2><UK> a college student for one academic year that runs for at least 24 weeks and involves at least 21 hours of study per week. <2><Canada>

post-secondary student who takes 60% or more of the usual course load.

fully depreciated asset an asset the carrying value becomes zero after depreciation.

fully diluted earnings per share the earnings per share calculated after all convertible bonds, options and warrants are assumed to have been converted or exercised in order to reflect the maximum potential dilution. ***Also***: diluted earnings per share; earnings per share fully diluted. ***See***: *primary earnings per share.*

full-year convention a convention by which annual depreciation of an asset is recognized as expenses in the first half of the acquisition year and no depreciation will be recognized in the second half of the year. ***See***: *half-year convention.*

fully fixed cost = *intrinsically fixed cost.*

fully funded plan = *funded pension plan.*

fully participating preferred stock preferred stock that in addition to receiving dividends, will participate in the excess dividends on a pro rata rate basis. ***See:*** *partially participating preferred stock.*

fully secret trust = *secret trust.*

fully tax-exempt security = *triple tax-exempt security.*

fully variable cost = *intrinsically variable cost.*

fully vested employee an employee who will be completely entitled to a pension plan benefits at retirement.

function accounting = *responsibility accounting.*

functional accounting the accounting and reporting by activity.

functional classification the classification of costs that refers to how the cost was used, such as manufacturing, administration or selling.

functional costing a system that classifies costs by allocating them to the various functions performed such as delivery, and warehouse.

functional currency the currency of the primary economic environment in which the company operates, generates and expends cash. ***Also***: non-base currency. ***See***: *reporting currency.*

functional depreciation the loss in usefulness of an asset because of technical inadequacy or obsolescence. ***Also***: economic depreciation; invisible deterioration. ***See***: *physical depreciation.*

functional reporting presenting expenses by major activity.

function audit = *operating audit.*

function cost a cost classification which shows the nature of the output for which costs are incurred, such as packing or sales promotion.

function form income statement = *absorption costing income statement.*

fund <1> cash or other assets designated for a specified purpose. <2> government entity with a self-balancing set of accounts.

fund accounting the accounting for receipts and disbursements of funds in a nonprofit organization.

fundamental accounting concept <UK> = *accounting concept.*

fundamental analysis an analysis of the stock of a public company by examining its financial statements.

fund assets value of a portfolio's assets minus outstanding debts.

fund balance the residual equity that balances the asset and liability accounts of a governmental fund.

funded debt = *long-term debt.*

funded liability source of fund that a firm must carry and bear interest cost.

funded pension plan a pension plan in which all liabilities are completely funded. ***Also***: fully funded plan.

funded reserve a liability that is offset by a reserve account funded by cash or other liquid assets. ***See:*** *unfunded reserve.*

fund flow = *flow of funds.*

fund flow accounting = *flow of funds accounting.*

fund flow statement <1> = *flow of funds statement.* <2> = *statement of changes in financial position.*

fund for replacement = *replacement fund.*

funding ratio the ratio of a pension plan's assets to its liabilities.

funds-flow-adequacy ratio a ratio showing the extent to which an entity can generate enough cash from operations to meet budgeted capital expenditure, calculated as cash from operation divided by capital expenditures.

funds-flow-fixed-charge coverage ratio of funds provided by operations plus fixed charges to fixed charges.

funds flow statement = *statement of changes in financial position.*

funds from operations (FFO) *cash flow from operations* of an investment trust. ***Also***: funds provided by operations.

funds lying idle = *idle money.*

funds provided by operations = *funds from operations.*

fund statement = *statement of changes in financial position*

fund theory a theory that accounting unit should be the fund other than the owner or the entity, and accounting equation should be: assets = fund commitment, and consolidated financial statements should be prepared by using *poly-corporate accounting.*

funeral expense an expense incurred to bury a deceased person.

funnel sinking fund a sinking fund in which the issuer has combined payments from several issues so the profits can be used to retire the most expensive of the issues.

furniture, fixtures and equipment (FF&E) a considered permanently attached to the real property.

fusion = *consolidation.*

FUTA Federal Unemployment Tax Act

FUTA tax a tax levied only on certain employers under the provisions of the FUTA. ***Also***: federal unemployment tax. ***See***: *unemployment insurance tax.*

future accounting = *forward accounting.*

future amount = *accumulated amount.*

future benefit the death benefit or endowment benefit under a life insurance policy.

future cost a cost incurred for the achievement of some future goals. ***Also***: prospective cost.

future cost avoidance theory a theory that states variable costs are not avoidable, and fixed costs can be saved, and inventory assets should be valued by direct cost.

future depreciation the depreciation that should be calculated in the future in order to cover investment cost.

future estate an estate to take effect in possession at a future date.

future interest reversion, remainder and other interest that is limited to use, possession, or enjoyment at some future date or time.

future taxable amount the amount postponed to future period that results in taxable income, e.g. gain included in financial statement but not recognized until future period under tax basis.

future tax deductible amount the amount that is deductible in future periods, e.g. warranty expenses included in the financial statements but only deductible when they actually incur.

future value amount to which an investment will grow at a future time if it earns an interest that is compounded annually. ***Also***: final value.

future value factor future value of $1 at a stated compound interest rate. ***See***: *annuity factor; discount factor.*

FV future value

FVO for valuation only

FY financial year

FYI for your information

FYR financial year

G g

G <1> general journal. <2> general ledger.

G&A cost general and administrative cost

GA <1> general account. <2> gross asset.

GAAP generally accepted accounting principles

GAAP basis statement financial statement of a government fund or agency based on GAAP. *See*: *budgetary basis statement.*

GAAS generally accepted auditing standards

GAGAS Generally Accepted Government Auditing Standards

GAI guaranteed annual income

gain <1> under revenue expense view, excess of reward over expense. <2> under asset-liability view, the increase in net asset. *Also*: increase in net assets; increase in owners' equity.

gain and loss the difference between a taxpayer's amount realized on the disposition of asset less the adjusted basis in that asset.

gain by trading = *retained earnings.*

gain contingency a condition, situation, or a set of circumstances, involving uncertainty as to possible gain. *Opp*: *loss contingency.*

gain from operation income a life insurance company earns from all sources including the company's share of investment yield and the income derived from the conduct of the underwriting operations.

gain from realization the excess of assets sold over liabilities at liquidation.

gain from reduction of capital stock gain when the capital reduced is greater than the amount paid to the stockholders. *Also*: surplus from deduction in capital stock.

gain from translation = *translation gain.*

gain in market value realized appreciation in the value of marketable securities.

gain of purchasing power = *monetary gain.*

gain on bond conversion = *conversion premium.*

gain on constructive retirement = *constructive gain.*

gain on disposal = *book gain.*

gain on exchange = *translation gain.*

gain or loss of a pension plan, a change in the value of either the PBO or the assets resulting from experience different from that assumed or from a change in actuarial assumption.

gambling income includes any money earned playing slot machines, bingo, or the lottery.

gambling loss a loss resulting from games of chance or wagers upon events with uncertain outcomes.

gambling loss rule a rule under which gambling loss can only be claimed against *gambling income.*

gaming duty <New Zealand> tax paid on the net income of gaming activities.

GAO General Accounting Office

garage transfer of assets to a place with little connection with the underlying transaction in order to shift profits into a low tax area.

garnishment withholding from an employee's paycheck and remitting it to another party, usually a creditor or a government agency.

GAS Government Auditing Standards

GASB Governmental Accounting Standards Board

gas guzzler tax an additional tax on vehicles sold which have a poor fuel economy.

gasoline excise tax an excise tax paid by consumers when purchasing gasoline.

GDP gross domestic products

GDS general depreciation system

GE gross earnings

GEAP generally elastic accounting principle

gearing = *gearing ratio.*

gearing adjustment the adjustment of monetary assets by a gearing ratio which equals the net monetary assets ÷ (monetary liability + capital stock).

gearing ratio the relationship between the capital and fixed interest capital, derived by dividing (preferred stock + loan capital) by common stock. ***Also***: degree of financial risk; gearing. ***See***: *leverage ratio.*

general account = *general ledger account.*

general accountant an accountant who has the authority to handle all kinds of accounting affairs in an organization.

general accounting <1> social accounting that views all economic activities in a country as a whole when budgeting and accounting. <2> that phase of accounting that deals primarily with recording transactions and preparing financial statements. ***See***: *special accounting.* <3> = *financial accounting.*

General Accounting Office (GAO) an official agency established in 1921, responsible to the Congress, for auditing and reviewing federal financial transactions and examines the expenditures of appropriations by federal units

General Accounting Office auditor an auditor from the *General Accounting Office.*

general administration cost = *administration expense.*

general administrative and selling expense = *selling and administrative expense.*

general and administrative expense = *administration expense.*

general and administrative overhead = *overhead.*

general average a contribution, by all parties toward a loss occasioned by the voluntary sacrifice of the property.

general balance sheet presentation of assets, liabilities and equities of a governmental, religious, charitable, educational, and social entities, in a standard commercial form. ***See***: *all-purpose financial statement.*

general budget = *master budget.*

general business credit a credit that combines several business inventive credits, such as investment, work opportunity, welfare-to-work, alcohol fuel, incremental research, etc.

general capital reserve fund <Canada> a municipal fund reserve for capital expenses.

general cash book a book for recording cash receipts and cash disbursements in a life insurance company.

general contingency reserve appropriation of retained earnings for general purposes rather than for a specific item of future loss or expense.

general depreciation system (GDS) most commonly used system for calculating depreciation, personal property is using the declining-balance method.

general expense = *administrative expense.*

general factor <Canada> a factor when multiplied by the federal or provincial amount yields the value of the federal or provincial credit.

general fixed asset account group self-balancing set of accounts to account for fixed assets of a government.

general fund a fund used to account for assets and liabilities of a nonprofit organization, or a government unit. ***Also***: current fund; general reserve fund.

general interest charge (GIC) <Australia> an interest charged by the Australian Taxation Office on an unpaid tax.

general interest method of depreciation the depreciation method that includes interest, cash inflows etc.

general journal (GJ) journal in which are recorded transactions other than those that must be entered in special or sub journals. ***Also***: ordinary journal; proper journal. ***See***: *special journal.*

general ledger <1> a ledger containing the financial statement accounts of a business. ***Also***: controlling ledger; financial ledger; key ledger. <2> = *impersonal ledger.*

general ledger account <1> an account in a general ledger. ***Also***: general account. ***See***: *controlling account.* <2> = *cost control account.*

general ledger worksheet = *summary worksheet.*

general liability business liability for bodily injury or property damage resulting from operations of the business. ***Also***: operations liability; primary liability.

general long-term debt account group self-balancing set of accounts used to account for the outstanding principal on all long-term debt except for that payable from an assessment, proprietary, or trust fund.

generally accepted accounting principles (GAAP) any conventions, procedures and rules that define accepted accounting practice, including broad guidelines as well as detailed procedures. ***Also***: recognized principle.

generally accepted auditing standards (GAAS) the audit standards proposed by the Auditing Standards Board of the AICPA, which are generally accepted by the public accounting profession.

Generally Accepted Government Auditing Standards (GAGAS) = *Government Auditing Standards.*

general meeting = *annual meeting.*

general obligation bond a municipal bond backed by the full faith and credit of the issuing municipality, without specific charge. ***Also***: GO bond.

general operating reserve fund <Canada> a municipal fund reserve for operating expenses, which can not exceed 5% of the total budget.

general overhead the overhead that benefits all over the firm. ***Also***: common plant overhead.

general overhead of mill = *factory overhead.*

general partner a partner in a general or limited partnership who has unlimited liability. ***Also***: full partner.

general partnership a partnership in which all partners have unlimited liability. ***See***: *limited partnership.*

general price-level accounting = *constant dollar accounting.*

general price-level-adjusted accounting (GPLA acct.) = *constant dollar accounting.*

general price-level-adjusted current value accounting the accounting procedures that restates the current value financial statements by general price level index.

general price-level-adjusted financial statement = *constant dollar financial statement.*

general price-level-adjusted historical cost accounting = *neoclassical school.*

general price-level gain = *monetary gain.*

general price level loss = *monetary loss.*

general price-level net realizable value accounting the accounting for measuring net realizable value of an asset by the purchasing power unit.

general price-level present value accounting that phase of accounting for measuring the present value by purchasing power unit.

general price-level replacement cost accounting the accounting for measuring the replacement cost by the purchasing power unit.

general purchasing power accounting = *constant dollar accounting.*

general purchasing power gain = *monetary gain.*

general purchasing power loss = *monetary loss.*

general purpose financial statement (GPFS) = *all-purpose financial statement.*

general reserve fund = *general fund.*

general revenue the sum of taxes, charges, and income taken in by a government.

general revenue sharing unrestricted funds provided by the federal government to the fifty states and to local governments.

general standards generally accepted auditing standards served as a guideline for the general planning of an audit.

general use report audit report not for specific parties. *See*: *restricted use report.*

generation skipping transfer (GST) transfer of property to beneficiaries who are more than one generation below the transferor.

generation skipping transfer tax (GSTT) a 55% flat rate tax on the properties under a generation-skipping transfer. ***Also***: tax on generation skipping transfers.

generation skipping transfer tax exemption an exemption allowed in determining the estate tax inclusion ratio. ($1.1 million in 2003.)

generation skipping trust a trust created by will in such a way that one's children will be the beneficiaries during their lives, then ownership of the properties will pass to their children.

gen. led. general ledger

getting cost = *ordering cost.*

GFOA Government Finance Officers Association

GIC general interest charge

gift <1> cash or other property given to another person free. <2><Australia> = *donation.*

gift aid an income tax relief for cash gifts to a charity.

gift loan a below-market-rate loan the forgone interest of which is in the nature of a gift.

gift splitting a gift-tax avoidance method in which a large gift to be given by the parents to a child is halved and given to the each child separately.

gift tax a tax imposed on the donor of a gift, applied to individual only. ***Also***: federal gift tax.

gift tax exclusion = *annual exclusion.*

gift tax return a tax return filed by a taxpayer who made a gift that is not fully excluded under the $11,000 annual exclusion (2003). ***Also***: Form 709.

gift to employee <Canada> a tax deductible gift to an employee.

Ginnie Mae pass-through = *pass-through security.*

GIS guaranteed income supplement

give as you earn <UK> = *payroll giving.*

given cost amount appropriated to achieve the requirements of the marketing plan.

giving account an account for recording disbursements. ***Also***: account to give; account to pay.

GJ general journal

global accounting = *international accounting.*

GNP gross national product

GNPIPD gross national product implicit price deflator

GO bond = *general obligation bond.*

going concern a business that is operating and expected to continue operations in the future.

going concern concept = *continuity concept.*

going concern value excess of the value of an operating enterprise over the value of its parts considered separately. ***Also***: going value.

going value = *going concern value.*

gold account the account used by balance of payments accounting for recording buying and selling transactions in gold by a government.

golden handcuffs rewards and penalties designed to discourage key employees from leaving a company.

golden handshake large payment made by a company to a senior executive upon termination of employment before his/her contract ends.

golden parachute payment money paid to the high officials of the company being acquired.

golden parachute rule a tax rule under which no deduction is allowed for *excess parachute payment.*

good attainable standard cost = *expected standard cost.*

goods and services tax (GST) <1><Canada> a 7% tax imposed on the sales value of goods and services. ***Also***: taxe sur les produits et services; TPS. <2><Australia> a 10% tax on most supplies of goods and services consumed in Australia.

goods and services tax credit <Canada> a tax credit for low income taxpayers (less than $29,000) who paid GST in a taxation year, replaced refundable federal sales tax credit. ***Also***: GST credit.

goods-in on consignment the merchandise received on consignment basis. ***Also***: consignment in.

goods in process = *work in process.*

goods in transit merchandise purchased but not received yet.

goods-out on consignment the merchandise sent out to a consignee on consignment basis. ***Also***: consignment out.

goodwill <1> that portion of the value of a business due to its ability of earning a rate of return greater than the average in its industry. <2> = *debit differential.* <3> = *positive goodwill.*

goodwill from consolidation = *debit differential.*

goodwill impairment the decrease in value of goodwill calculated as the difference between the expected future cash flow and the fair value of the net asset. ***See***: *recovery test.*

goodwill method a method under which the amount contributed and the corresponding percentage of the initial capital balance are used to calculate the value of the partnership and the presence of goodwill. ***See***: *bonus method.*

Gordon-Shapiro model = *constant-growth model.*

government accounting the accumulating, reporting, and auditing of income, payroll, taxes of government units as indispensable as in a business. ***Also***: budget accounting.

governmental fund a fund used to finance general government activities.

Government Auditing Standards (GAS) audit standards issued by the Comptroller General as audit guidelines for government audits. ***Also***: Generally Accepted Government Auditing Standards; Yellow Book.

Government Auditing Standards Board (GASB) group authorized by the accounting profession to establish GAAP applicable to state and local governmental entities.

government fund a fund except for the profit and loss fund.

government-mandated nonexchange transaction exist when providing government requires the receiving government to expend funds for a specific purpose.

government-sponsored retirement arrangement (GSRA) <Canada> an unregistered retirement plan that provides benefit to individuals who are not government employees but who paid for public funds for their services.

GP gross profit

GPFS general purpose financial statement

GPLA general price level adjustment

GPM gross profit margin

GPP general purchasing power

GR <1> gross receipts. <2> gross revenue.

graduated pension <UK> earnings-related pension benefit, £392 per year for a man and £328 per year for a woman.

graduated tax = *progressive tax.*

grandfather debt a mortgage debt taken out before 10/13/1987.

grandfathered share <Canada> a share issued after Jun 18, 1987 and before 1988.

grandfather exemption an exempt condition existing prior to the effective date of new laws.

grandfather rule a provision included in a new FASB rule adopted in 1970 which exempts goodwill acquired before 1970 from the required amortization.

grant date the date on which an employee receives a stock option.

grant of option <UK> = *option grant.*

grantor = *trustor.*

grantor trust a trust in which the grantor conveys property to a trustee to be held and managed for the grantor's own benefit. *Also*: grantor type trust. *See*: *bare trust.*

grantor trust rule a rule under which if a trust is deemed a grantor trust the income will be the grantor's taxable income.

grantor type trust = *grantor trust.*

graphic method <1> a break-even analysis that uses a graph. <2> a method of selecting an economic order quantity by plotting the costs on a graph.

gratuities = *tip income.*

great loss = *accounting bath.*

green baize door = *Chinese wall.*

greenmail payment payoff given to a potential acquiring company by the target company to buy back its own shares.

gross asset = *total asset.*

gross capitalized cost in car leasing, the agreed price, plus any service costs, insurance, and other items for which the buyer has to pay.

gross cost = *cost of goods sold.*

gross cost of production total manufacturing costs of the whole factory. *Also*: total work cost.

gross domestic products (GDP) the total value of all goods and services produced within a country in a given year.

gross earnings an individual's taxable income before any deductions and adjustments.

gross earnings method a method under which depreciation of each period is based on the proportion of the gross earnings of that period to the total expected earnings of the plant asset.

grossed-up basis the basis of company A's asset when its shares had been purchased by another company and went through a hypothetical liquidation.

grossed-up redemption yield net yield adjusted by adding back all taxes to which the recipient is subject. *Also*: net redemption yield.

gross equipment and plant of airlines, consists of original cost of planes, related equipment, buildings and other fixed assets owned.

gross equity method an equity method under which the investor's share of the aggregate gross assets and liabilities underlying the net amount included for the investment is shown on the balance sheet, and the share of the investee's income is also noted.

gross estate total estate valued at time of death or six months later.

gross federal debt total amount the federal government owes. *See*: *net federal debt.*

gross for common percent the ratio between balance available for common equity and operating revenues of utilities companies.

gross income the *income* from whatever source derived, unless expressly excluded from tax by law. *Also*: earned income.

gross income from source without the US = *foreign income.*

gross income test a test a person must meet to be claimed as a dependent, the annual gross income can not exceed the exemption amount.

gross investment lease receivable when there is an unguaranteed residual value, usually equals net investment plus unearned interest revenue.

gross investment income = *investment income.*

gross lease property lease in which the landlord agrees to pay all expenses which are normally associated with ownership, such as utilities, repairs, insurance, and sometimes taxes. ***See***: *net lease; net net lease; net net net lease.*

gross loss excess of the cost of goods sold over sales.

gross margin <1> the result of subtracting all components of cost of goods sold, including fixed and variable manufacturing costs from sales revenue. <2> = *gross profit.*

gross margin ratio = *gross profit on sales.*

gross method <1> a method under which the undiscounted total of the minimum lease payments and unguaranteed residual value are recorded in one or more asset accounts, credit for unearned interest is recorded in a contra-asset account. ***See***: *net method.* <2> a method used to record the purchase of goods, discount taken is shown as purchase discount which is netted against the Purchases a/c in determining cost of goods sold. <3> method used to record forward exchange contract under which the total forward contract receivable is recorded.

gross national income (GNI) total income of all sectors of economy of a country in a specific period of time, which equals gross national product in amount. ***Also***: aggregate income; gross revenue.

gross national product (GNP) the retail market value of all items and services produced in a country during a specific period of time.

gross negligence the *negligence* that results when an accountant recklessly disregards established accounting, reporting and auditing standards. ***Also***: wanton negligence; willful negligence. ***See***: *constructive fraud; negligence.*

gross operating spread = *gross profit.*

gross payroll = *payroll.*

gross premium <1> net premium receipts of an insurance company plus miscellaneous and operating expenses and agent's commission. <2> premium of life insurance company before dividends are subtracted.

gross premiums tax = *insurance tax.*

gross price the price before deduction of discounts or allowance.

gross price method a method which records the invoices at the full amount of the sale price without deducting offered discounts. ***See***: *net price method.*

gross proceeds the total amount raised from an initial public offering of stock.

gross production tax a state tax imposed primarily on mining companies for each unit mined.

gross profit (GP) net sales minus cost of goods sold and manufactured. ***Also***: earnings; gross margin; gross operating spread; gross profit from sales; gross spread; margin; sales margin; spread; trading profit.

gross profit from sales = *gross profit.*

gross profit margin (GPM) = *gross profit on sales.*

gross profit method a method for estimating an ending inventory in which an estimated cost of goods sold based on past gross profit rates is subtracted from the cost of goods available for sale to arrive at an estimated ending inventory. ***Also***: gross profit test.

gross profit on sales ratio of gross profit to sales. ***Also***: gross margin ratio; gross profit margin; gross profit ratio; gross trading profit.

gross profit ratio = *gross profit on sales.*

gross profit test = *gross profit method.*

gross receipts total receipts from the sales, lease, or rental of the property held primarily for sale, lease, or rental in the ordinary course of business of a firm seeking to be a DISC.

gross residual value = *salvage value.*

gross revenue (GR) <1> of a firm, total receipts before deduction of expenses. <2> = *gross national income.*

gross sales total sales at invoice values, not reduced by customer discounts, returns, or allowances or other adjustments.

gross sales value method = *relative sales value method.*

gross salvage value the amount realized on the sale or disposition of property when it is no longer useful, without reduction of the cost of removal, dismantling, or demolition.

gross savings and investment account a form that shows gross domestic investment and net foreign investment on left hand side, and all of the saving items on the right hand side.

gross spread (GS) = *gross profit.*

gross trading profit = *gross profit on sales.*

gross up <1><Australia> to add the taxable value of fringe benefits to calculate *fringe benefits tax.* <2> to add the amount of associated tax imposed on the transfer to the value of the property or income received. <2

gross-up <Canada> ¼ of the dividend received from a Canadian corporation to be added to the dividend to compute the *dividend tax credit.* ***Also***: gross-up amount.

gross-up amount = *gross-up.*

gross up method a method under which stockholders' personal income tax is subtracted from the corporation's total tax liability and paid separately.

gross variance = *total variance.*

gross working capital = *working capital.*

gross yield the rate of return on a stock or bond before tax.

gross yield to redemption <UK> the interest yield on a security plus the annual capital gain if the security is held to redemption.

ground rent money for the privilege of using other's land.

ground-up approach = *industrial engineering method.*

group account <1> account used under group method which shows assets similar in kind with approximately the same economic lives. <2><UK> system of financial statements that links companies engaged in similar business. <3> = *group financial statement.*

group annuity an annuity that covers all members of a group.

group costing the costing method that divides the cost units into several groups by their nature, and accumulates costs data separately.

group depreciation = *composite depreciation.*

group financial statement financial statement of two or more companies sharing the same ownership and having similar operational structure. ***Also***: group account. ***See***: *combined financial statement; consolidated financial statement.*

grouping financial statement method of preparing work sheets in consolidating financial statements.

grouping sheet = *lead schedule.*

group IRA an IRA established by an employer for its employees or by a group representing employees for its members.

group method = *composite depreciation method.*

Group of 100 prestigious cross functional group of accounting profession thought leaders.

group profit and loss account = *consolidated income statement.*

group term life insurance <Canada> a term life policy that covers a group of current and former employees.

growth accounting the accounting procedure for measuring growth of economic resources.

growth rate the annual percentage at which an investment or cash flow is expected to increase in value, expressed on a compounded basis.

GRV guaranteed residual value

GS gross sales

GSRA government-sponsored retirement arrangement

GST <1> generation skipping transfer. <2> goods and services tax.

GST credit goods and services tax credit

GST-free supply <Australia> a supply of goods or services that is free of GST.

GST input tax credit <Canada> a tax credit for GST paid on goods or services consumed in a business. *Also*: GST rebate; input tax credit.

GST rebate <1><Canada> a return of GST to foreign visitors. <2> = *GST input tax credit.*

GSTT generation skipping transfer tax

guaranteed annual income (GAI) the annual income guaranteed by a labor union.

guaranteed income supplement (GIS) <Canada> a non-taxable monthly benefit paid to lower-income old-aged security recipients on the basis of family income.

guaranteed payment a payment made from a partnership to partners that is made without regard to income.

guaranteed replacement cost coverage insurance a policy that covers the full cost of replacing damaged property without deduction.

guaranteed residual value (GRV) specifically determinable amount payable by lessee at termination of the lease.

guaranty fund a fund of last resort set up by local government to protect consumers interest.

guardian IRA an IRA for children under the age of 18 - 21.

guideline life the anticipated useful life of certain assets under Revenue Procedure 62-71, 1962-2C. B. 418. *Also*: class life; midpoint life.

H h

HA house account

half-finished goods = *work-in-process.*

half-month convention a rule under which real properties are treated as placed in service or disposed of in the middle of a month, resulting in a half-month of depreciation of the month placed in service or disposed of. *Also*: mid-month convention.

half secret trust <UK> a trust named in a will but the objects are not specified. *Also*: semi-secret trust. *See*: *secret trust.*

half-year convention a depreciation rule under which personal properties placed in service during the taxable year is deemed placed in service on the first day of the last half of the year. *Also*: mid-year convention. *See*: *full-year convention.*

half-yearly financial statement financial statement prepared at the end of the first half of the year. *Also*: early financial statement; semi-annual statement.

Hall of Fame an organization founded in 1950 at Ohio State University to honor individuals who have made significant contribution to accounting. *Also*: Accounting Hall of Fame.

hand-posted account an account that is posted by hand and ink.

haphazard sampling = *nonstatistical sampling.*

harbor due fee paid for the use of a harbor.

hard asset an asset such as a plant asset, which has physical existence. *See*: *soft asset.*

hard cost <1> = *original cost.* <2> = *prime cost.*

hard dollar cash money given in exchange for an equity in a transaction for real estate. *See: soft dollar*

hard money political contribution that meets certain requirements set by federal law. *Also*: federal money; regulated money.

harmonised sales tax (HST) <Canada> a 15% combined federal and provincial sales tax.

hashing a technique used to find an accounting record within a computer file.

hash total summation of numbers having no practical meaning as a control precaution, used by auditors primarily in a computer application.

HCA historical cost accounting

head book = *main book.*

heading the name, date, etc. at the top of a financial statement. *Also*: statement heading; title of statement.

headline the account title, folio and number, etc. at the top of a ledger sheet.

headline earnings reported earnings including all the tax-adjusted profits and losses from disposal of assets and sale or discontinued operations.

headline earnings per share (HEPS) the headline earnings divided by the number of shares outstanding.

head of household (HH) a filing status, to qualify, taxpayer must not be married or a surviving spouse at the year end, and must maintain his or her home that is the principal place of residence for more than 50% of the year for the dependents. *See*: *caregiver.*

head tax = *poll tax.*

heavy highway vehicle use tax = *federal highway use tax.*

HECS higher education contribution scheme

hedge accounting the accounting for investment hedge transactions.

hedge clause = *disclaimer.*

hedging reserve a reserve for the unrealized gain or loss arising from the revaluation of investments designated as *cash flow hedge.*

HEL home equity loan

held-over gain the chargeable gain which would have accrued on a disposal apart from a claim.

held-to-maturity (HTM) debt security intended to be held to maturity. **See**: *trading securities.*

HEPS headline earnings per share

herd basis <UK> a basis under which the value of animals in the herd is not taken into account in calculating trading profits, the cost of adding animals to the herd is not deductible, and the proceeds of the sale of animals are not brought into assessment.

HH head of household

hidden asset = *off-balance sheet asset.*

hidden cost the cost that is hidden in some larger items which must be considered in cost estimating.

hidden reserve = *secret reserve.*

hidden tax indirect tax levied on goods and/or services at some point in the manufacturing cycle and paid unknowingly by the consumer.

hidden value the value of an asset not shown on the balance sheet.

hierarchy of cost an approach to group activity costs as they vary with external and internal volumes, batch-related volumes, and cost object diversity-sensitivity.

HIFO highest-in, first-out

high-and-low points method = *high-low points method.*

higher education contribution scheme (HECS) <Australia> a system that allows a taxpayer to contribute certain amount each year to pay for educational expenses of the children.

higher rate <UK> tax rate on income above the basic rate band. **See:** *lower rate; starting rate.*

highest degree of care = *utmost care.*

highest-in, first-out (HIFO) accounting for mutual fund shares, under which the shares with the highest costs are sold first.

high-low method <1> = *high-low-points method.* <2> = *simplified method.*

high-low-points method a method of estimating the fixed and variable behavior of a cost by computing how much the cost increased from a recent period of the lowest activity to a recent period of highest activity. **Also**: high-and-low points method; high-low method; variable cost rate method.

highly condensed form a financial statement form which lists the material items only.

high-risk audit an audit of a public company with special scrutiny.

highway tax = *highway use tax.*

highway use tax (HUT) a tax charged by some states on some heavy motor vehicles. **Also**: highway tax. **See:** *federal highway use tax.*

HIPPAA Health Insurance Portability and Accountability Act

hire-purchase contract <UK> = *lease to purchase.*

historical absorption costing absorption costing restricted to actual data only. **Also**: actual absorption costing.

historical cost <1> a measurement of the economic sacrifices which have already been made based on actual prices paid. **Also**: old cost; out-of-date cost; past cost. <2> cost of an item to the first user in public utilities. <3> = *original cost.*

historical cost accounting (HCA) accounting on reporting assets on balance sheet at their original purchase costs. **Also**: conventional accounting; post mortem cost accounting.

historical cost approach a method of reporting balance sheet assets at historical cost. *Also*: acquisition cost method. *See*: *current value approach.*

historical cost/constant dollar method a method under which monetary assets will be reported at historical cost, but the measuring unit is constant dollar.

historical cost convention <UK> accounting policy adopted when assets appear on the balance sheet at the cost, and never revalued.

historical costing recording and analysis of costs after they have occurred. *Also*: actual costing. *See*: *standard costing.*

historical cost/nominal dollar method a method under which monetary assets will be reported at historical cost only.

historical cost or recoverable amount, the lower the FASB Statement 33 requires that constant dollar accounting should report assets at the lower of their historical cost or their recoverable amount.

historical exchange rate the exchange rate at the time an asset was purchased.

historical financial statement the financial statement based on historic cost data.

historical method an approach of accumulating and distributing the overhead costs based on their actual amount.

historical percentage method a method of forecasting next period income statement data by the fixed percentage of each item to total revenue in this period.

historical rate method a method of translating foreign statements by the rate of exchange at the date assets were acquired. *See*: *current rate method.*

historical standard cost target cost based almost wholly on past results of comparable operations.

historical summary a section in the annual report of a company in which significant items such as income, EPS, dividends are presented over a period of at least 5 years.

historical value asset value expressed in historical cost. *See*: *current value.*

historic preservation deduction a deduction for the depreciation of certain historic structures if the taxpayer had spent a significant amount on rehabilitating the structure.

hobby an activity not engaged in for profit. *Also*: not-for-profit activity.

hobby income <UK> income from hobby, not taxable.

hobby loss rule a rule that requires losses that may be deducted from an investment or an activity not engaged in for profit cannot exceed associated income, after deducting casualty loss, taxes, and interest.

holder for value the holder of a negotiable instrument who has performed the consideration in exchange for it.

holder in due course the holder of a negotiable instrument who takes value in the ordinary course of business without knowledge of any default.

holding company <UK> = *controlling corporation.*

holding company bailout practice under which the stock of corporations with substantial earnings were transferred to a newly formed holding company, which could not make distributions for lack of earnings so the stock can be treated as Section 306 stork.

holding cost <1> annual expenses associated with maintaining an ongoing position in a security or market, including *custodian cost* and tax. <2> = *carrying cost.*

holding gain <1> = *inventory profit.* <2> = *monetary gain.*

holding loss = *monetary loss.*

holding period the period of time an asset is held for the purposes of determining whether profit or loss on its sale is a short- or long-term capital gain or loss.

holding period return the total return received from holding an asset, usually the total income plus price appreciation during a specified time period, divided by the cost of the investment. ***Also***: holding period yield.

holding period yield = *holding period return.*

holdover relief <UK> relief on a gift that the gain that would otherwise be chargeable to tax is held over so that the gain may be eliminated.

holiday pay <UK> salary or wage received by a taxpayer on national holidays.

home acquisition debt a debt to buy, build or improve a residence. ***Also***: acquisition borrowing; acquisition indebtedness; home purchase loan. ***See:*** *home equity debt.*

home audit review of the records of the purchase of specified goods kept by an individual consumer.

home equity debt a loan backed by the borrower's equity in a house. ***Also***: home equity indebtedness; home equity loan. ***See***: *home acquisition debt.*

home equity indebtedness = *home equity debt.*

home equity loan (HEL) = *home equity debt.*

home equity option an option that allows a borrower to secure the existing home loan with the equity in his home, the interest paid on the loan is tax-deductible.

home office deduction deduction arising from having a place of business in the home.

home purchase loan = *home acquisition debt.*

homogeneity cost of an activity that has a similar cause-and-effect relationship with a cost object.

hope credit tax credit up to $1,500 per year per student and is available for the first two years of vocational school or college. ***Also***: hope scholarship credit. ***See***: *lifetime learning credit.*

hope scholarship credit = *hope credit.*

horizon analysis the analysis of returns using total return to assess performance over some investment horizon.

horizon return investment return over a given horizon.

horizontal analysis calculation of dollar and percentage changes from year to year by each expense item.

horizontal audit examination of the internal control work or system of an organization.

horizontal balance sheet = *account form balance sheet.*

horizontal equity a tax policy concept that people with a similar ability to pay taxes should pay the same amount. ***See***: *vertical equity.*

horizontal merger a merger between two or more competing firms in the same industry. ***See***: *vertical merger.*

Hoskold's formula a formula to calculate the rate of return, under which ROR = (annual net income - annual sinking fund balance required to recover the investment at the end) ÷ original investment cost.

Hoskold's method = *explicit reinvestment rate of return method.*

hospital accounting the accounting and reporting procedures for hospitals.

hostile takeover a takeover not supported by the target company. ***Also***: unfriendly takeover. ***See***: *friendly takeover.*

hot asset the asset that triggers the collapsible partnership rules upon the sale or exchange of a partnership interest or a disproportionate distribution of partnership property.

hour rate variance = *labor rate variance.*

house account a business' earliest customers who have grown along with it.

household bookkeeping the bookkeeping for household affairs.

household employment tax = *nanny tax.*

household expense amount paid for lodging, food consumed within the home, utilities paid, and other expenses.

household income the combined income of both spouses, not including the income of children. ***Also***: family income.

housing cost amount deductible amount equaling the excess of the taxpayer's actual housing expense over 16% of the salary shown on the W-2.

housing expense the expense paid or incurred during the taxable year by or on behalf of an individual for housing of that individual, his or her spouse, and any dependents in a foreign country.

housing loss <Canada> excess of the adjusted basis of the residence over its fair market value or the proceeds of its disposition.

housing trust a trust for the purpose of providing housing accommodation.

hovering deficit rule a tax rule that deficits in earnings and profits inherited from a transferor in a reorganization offset the transferee's post-acquisition earnings.

HRA human resource accounting

HR-10 plan = *Keogh plan.*

HST harmonised sales tax

HST **rebate** <Canada> a return of HST to foreign visitors.

HTM held-to-maturity

human capital the value of future labor earnings.

human cost = *labor cost.*

human resource accounting measuring the value of the human factor in business in an attempt at identifying the economic and social impact of business policies on employees, and through them, on the company.

hurdle rate of return = *cut-off rate of return.*

HUT highway use tax

hybrid accounting methods combination of acceptable methods of accounting permitted by the regulations.

hypothecated asset an asset that has been pledged but physical possession and title have not been transferred. *Also*: pledged asset; property pledged.

hypothecated stock a stock pledged as collateral on a loan.

hypothesis testing a testing to see if the recorded amount is materially misstated. *Also*: audit hypothesis testing.

hypothetical cost = *imputed cost.*

I i

i interest

IA <1> inactive account. <2> intangible asset.

IAAA Inter-American Accounting Association

IAC income available for common stockholders

IAFP International Association for Financial Planning

IANC method interest-adjusted net cost method

IAPC International Auditing Practices Committee

IAS <1> Instalment Activity Statement. <2> Institute of Accounting Staff. <3> international accounting standards.

IASB International Accounting Standards Board

IASC International Accounting Standards Committee

IBC international business company

IBNR incurred but not reported

IBOP international balance of payments

I/C internal control

ICA International Congress of Accountants

ICAEW Institute of Chartered Accountants in England and Wales

ICS issued capital stock

ID instructor dependent

Idaho Power rule a rule that depreciation on machinery used to produce a capital improvement must be added to the taxpayer's basis of property improved, rather than deducted as period depreciation.

IDC intangible drilling cost

IDEA interactive data extraction and analysis

ideal activity maximum number of operating hours which could be available ignoring the stoppage due to downtime, repairs, etc.

ideal standard cost unit costs that reflect the best conceivable production performance with the use of existing product specifications and equipment. *Also*: perfect standard cost; theoretical performance standard cost; theoretical standard cost.

identifiable asset and liability the asset and liability of the acquired company that are capable of being identified.

identifiable cost = *direct cost.*

identifiable fixed cost = *separable fixed cost.*

identification method = *specific identification method.*

identified cost method = *specific identification method.*

idiosyncratic risk = *unsystematic risk.*

idle capacity portion of the capacity not being used.

idle capacity cost that part of capacity cost due to the idle capacity of the equipment.

idle capacity variance = *overhead volume variance.*

idle cost the cost incurred because of the idleness of machine or workers.

idle fund = *idle money.*

idle money any money held in idle balance, such as uninvested available funds, inactive bank deposit, etc. *Also*: disposable capital; dormant capital; floating capital; floating cash reserve; floating money; funds lying idle; inactive money; unemployed capital.

idle time nonproductive time that is out of the control of labors.

idle time cost the cost incurred in the idle time.

idle time variance cost variance due to idle time.

IE <1> incidental expense. <2> instructor dependent plus experience.

IET interest equalization tax

IFA independent financial adviser

IFAC International Federation of Accountants

if-converted method a method of computing diluted EPS, which assumes that potentially all convertible securities are converted. *See*: *treasury stock method.*

I-F cost irrelevant future cost

IG inspector general

IHT inheritance tax

IIA Institute of Internal Auditors

illegal act violation of laws or regulations.

illegal profit gain from illegal activities.

illiquid asset an asset that is unable to be converted into cash.

image audit assessment of the perception of a company by selected group of persons.

IMAPI Improved Machinery and Allied Products Institute

IMAPI method a method established by the IMAPI which attempts to determine how much saving there would be in the next year with the proposed investment.

imbalance debit does not equal the credit, or income does not cover expenditures.

immaterial asset = *intangible asset.*

immaterial capital = *variable capital.*

immediacy cost the cost associated with the decision to trade a security quickly, rather than taking a chance on a better (or worse) price by entering a limit order away from the market.

immediate annuity an annuity paid for in a lump-sum and commences at once.

immediate assessment deficiencies that are promptly assessed without the usual formalities.

immediate asset <1> = *current asset.* <2> = *quick asset.*

immediate cost a cost the amount of which can be raised by planning.

immediate liability = *current liability.*

immediate recognition expensing of the costs that are deemed to provide no future benefits. *See*: *associating cause-and-effect; systematic & rational allocation.*

immovable = *immovable property.*

immovable property real property or personal property attached to it. *Also*: immovable. *See*: *movable property.*

immunization the construction of an asset and a liability of a portfolio to offset changes in its value. *Also*: income immunization.

impact of taxation = *tax impact.*

impaired capital reduction in a company's stated or par value capital brought about often by losses.

impaired long-lived asset long-lived asset the sum of the expected future cash flows of which is less than its carrying amount.

impaired serviceableness = *depreciation.*

impairment loss if the expected future cash flow is less than the carrying amount of an asset, loss is recognized, it equals the carrying amount minus the fair market value.

impairment of capital <1> amount by which stated capital has been decreased by distribution of dividends or losses. <2> excess liabilities over assets due to loss.

impairment of value permanent decline in the value of an asset.

impairment test = *recovery test.*

impersonal account an account not connected with persons that records all transactions of a particular type as they affect a firm. *Also*: nominal account; non-personal account.

impersonal ledger a ledger which contains real accounts and nominal accounts. ***Also***: general ledger; nominal ledger.

implicit cost <1> extra cost to the main costs, usually hidden and unrecorded, e.g. owner's time. ***See***: *explicit cost.* <2> = *alternative cost.* <3> = *opportunity cost.*

implicit price deflator the price index associated with the gross national product.

implicit tax rate (ITR) = *average tax rate.*

implied trust = *constructive trust.*

import duty = *tariff.*

imposed nonexchange transaction taxes and other assessments by governments that are not derived from underlying transactions, e.g. *property tax.*

impound account an account held by a lender for payment of taxes, insurance, or other costs. ***Also***: escrow account.

imprest cash fund = *imprest fund.*

imprest fund a fund of fixed amount used for making small expenditures that are most conveniently paid in cash. ***Also***: imprest cash fund; petty cash; petty cash fund; ready money.

improvement = *betterment.*

improvement curve = *learning curve.*

imputation <1> estimates which make possible the inclusion in the National Income & Product Accounts of some types of income and product flows which do not take measurable monetary form. <2> method of calculating the present value of a note by reference to the incremental borrowing rate of the company.

imputation tax system arrangement by which investors who receives a dividend also receives a tax credit for tax that the company has paid.

imputed cost <1> cost estimated because of the difficulty in finding the actual figure. ***Also***: assumed cost; book cost; hypothetical cost; pro forma cost. <2> = *opportunity cost.*

imputed income <1> the amount deemed to have earned by a taxpayer even though no cash was received.<2> the value of the consumption of self-produced goods, crops, and services. <3> the use of personally or family owned property.

imputed interest <1> interest charged to an investment center for using the company's own asset. <2> the interest on a loan assumed to be paid by the IRS if the stated rate of interest is below a minimum. ***Also***: interest imputed; unstated interest. <3> interest that has been effectively paid to a bondholder through OID, even though no cash bas actually been paid.

imputed negligence a negligence attributed to one person because of the negligent act of another with whom the first has a special relationship.

imputed principal amount the sum of the present values of all payments of principal and interest due under a debt instrument.

imputed underpayment netting the adjustments to the income and loss items of the partnership multiplied by the highest personal or corporate tax rate.

imputed value the value of an asset, service, or company that is not physically recorded in any accounts.

IMR interest maintenance reserve

in. <1> income. <2> interest.

inactive account ledger account with little or no entries. ***Also***: dormant account. ***See***: *doubtful account.*

inactive asset an asset not continually used in a productive way, such as auxiliary generator.

inactive bad debt account bad debt that can not be recovered.

inactive money = *idle money.*

inactive subsidiary an 80%-or-more controlled subsidiary that is inactive.

inactivity fee a bank charge on inactive accounts.

inadequacy effect of growth and changes in the scale of a firm's operations in determining the economic life of its assets.

inadmissible asset = *inadmitted asset.*

inadmitted asset an asset that has no liquidation value. *Also*: inadmissible asset; nonadmitted asset; unadmitted asset.

inavoidable cost a cost that would continue even though cost center were eliminated. *Also*: inescapable cost; unavoidable cost.

incapacity benefit <UK> a government benefit paid to a person who is unable to work due to an accident or illness.

incentive fee a fee paid to the general partner of a hedge fund, based on the performance.

incentive stock option (ISO) stock option as part of an executive compensation package, that is not included in the employee's taxable income when granted.

incentive tax rate a tax rate lower than *regular tax rate.*

incentive trust a trust created to make reward payment to a family member who makes certain achievement, e.g. college graduation. *Also*: family incentive trust.

incestuous share dealing buying and selling each other's shares by two companies to create a tax or financial advantage.

in-charge accountant = *in-charge auditor.*

in-charge auditor the one who is in charge of the field audit. *Also*: accountant in charge; in-charge accountant. *See*: *senior auditor.*

incidence of tax the party on whom a tax burden falls.

incidental cost = *miscellaneous cost.*

incidental expense (IE) expenses for laundry, cleaning and pressing of clothing, and fees and gratuities for services, such as for waiters and baggage handlers.

incidental item = *nonrecurring item.*

inclusion amount reported as part of a taxpayer's gross income.

inclusion amount the amount a taxpayer must add back to gross income if the fair market value of a leased car is above a certain amount.

inclusion rate <Canada> portion of the capital gains that is taxable, 50% in 2002. *Also*: capital gains inclusion rate.

inclusion ratio the ratio of taxable estate to the total estate value.

income <1> money made by a taxpayer. *See*: *gross income; net income.* <2> = *net income.*

income account <1> = *income statement.* <2> = *revenue account.* <3> = *revenue and expense account*

income adjustment debiting or crediting an income account in order to adjust the balance of income account.

income after interest income minus interest charges.

income and expense statement = *income statement.*

income and retained earnings statement = *statement of income and retained earnings.*

income approach <1> a method of calculating national income by adding up all incomes such as wages, interest, rent and profit, etc. <2> a procedure for property appraisal in which the value equals the total net income produced by the property. *See*: *cost approach; market data approach.*

income assignment = *assignment of income.*

income at liquidation = *liquidation income.*

income audit = *corporate income tax audit.*

income available for common stockholders (IAC) net income after income taxes and dividends paid to preferred stockholders. *Also*: earnings available for ordinary shareholders.

income averaging a method whereby personal income tax is roughly stated as the sum of the tax on 12% of average base period income plus 5 times the increase in taxes caused by adding 20% of averageable income to 120% of *base period* income. *Also*: averaging.

income basis a way of figuring out the rate of return of a security by dividing the price paid for it by the income paid that year.

income bearing asset <UK> = *income generating asset.*

income before bad debts income before deduction of bad debts.

income before depreciation income before deduction of depreciation cost. *Also*: pre-depreciation profit.

income before income taxes = *pre-tax accounting income.*

income before interest income before deduction of the interest expense.

income before non-cash expenses net income plus depreciation expense and amortization charges.

income before taxes = *pre-tax accounting income.*

income beneficiary a beneficiary who is entitled to income from trust property.

income bond a bond on which the payment of interest is made only when earnings are available. *Also*: income debenture.

income capitalization = *capitalization of earnings.*

income debenture <Canada> = *income bond.*

income deduction <1> an item that reduces the gross income. *Also*: charge on income; charge to income; deduction from gross income; other deduction. <2> non-operating expenses of a company that are listed in the final section of the income statement before arriving at net income.

income depressing "purchase" method the purchase method used when there has been a huge amount of income to be recognized when realized.

income distribution the separation of national income into meaningful categories. *Also*: distribution and use of income. *See: first stage; second stage; third stage; fourth stage.*

income duty = *tariff.*

income effect when prices are lowered, consumers with the same amount of income can buy more goods or services.

income equalization distribution of realized capital gains to shareholders of a mutual fund when redeeming the shares, thus capital gains can be shared between the leaving shareholders and the remaining shareholders.

income exclusion rule a rule under which gross income does not include interest on municipal bonds and returns of capital from annuities and pensions.

income for assessment = *assessable income.*

income forecast method = *revenue method.*

income for financial accounting purpose = *pre-tax accounting income.*

income for tax purposes = *taxable income.*

income from continuing operations income after tax arising from the ongoing operations of the business.

income from discharge of indebtedness = *cancellation of debt income.*

income from discontinued operations income after tax from a discontinued segment.

income from employment <UK> = *emoluments.*

income from estate <UK> income received by a legatee from the estate of a death person.

income from operations = *operating income.*

income from property = *property income.*

income from S corporations the income of a shareholder derived from an S corporation.

income generating asset an asset that can generate income for the owner. *Also*: income bearing asset.

income generating unit a group of assets and liabilities that generates income independently.

income immunization = *immunization.*

income in advance = *deferred revenue.*

income in respect of a decedent (IRD) income not included in the decedent's return due to the accounting methods used.

income interest <Canada> interest in a trust or partnership that has the right to income only. *See*: *residual interest.*

income investment company an investment fund that tries to provide the highest income possible to its fund holders.

income limit <UK> the maximum amount that a taxpayer can claim for some tax allowances and relief.

income limited partnership a limited partnership designed to achieve high income, which then uses tax shelters to protect its profits from taxes.

income maintenance insurance <Canada> an insurance that covers the loss of income from an office or employment.

income per books = *net income per books.*

income per dollar of sales = *profit on sales.*

income period = *conversion period.*

income phase-out amount = *threshold phase-out amount.*

income property real estate purchased for generating income.

income received but unearned = *deferred revenue.*

income replacement income received when an insured wage earner becomes injured or ill.

income replacement ratio the percentage of working income that an individual needs to maintain the same standard of living when retiring, usually 60-90%.

income return either the annual gain from an investment or the percentage figure found by dividing the annual gain by the initial price.

income risk the possibility that the income provided by a fund or a floating rate instrument will fluctuate due to changing interest rates.

income share one of the 2 classes of shares issued by a dual purpose fund, which pays both dividends and interest income of the fund to its holders. *See*: *capital share.*

income sheet = *income statement.*

income sheet ratio a ratio based on the income statement. *Also*: dynamic ratio.

income shifting moving the incidence of taxable income from one taxpayer to another.

income smoothing presenting income figures as management wishes. *See*: *accounting cushion.*

income splitting <1> fragmenting income among numerous taxpayers in order to minimize overall taxes. <2><Canada> = *pension assignment.*

income statement (IS) a statement showing revenues and expenses incurred in earning the revenues, and the resulting net income or net loss. *Also*: account of business; dynamic statement; earnings statement; income account; income and expense statement; income sheet; loss and gain statement; operating statement; profit and loss account; profit and loss statement; profit statement; statement of activities. statement of earnings; statement of income; statement of loss and profit; statement of profit and loss; statement of profit calculation; statement of revenue and expense; trading, profit and loss account.

income statement account an account for recording revenue or expense from which the income statement is prepared. *Also*: loss and gain account.

income statement and statement of retained earnings = *statement of income and retained earnings.*

income statement approach a method that makes an estimate of bad debts cost by an average percentage of credit sales not collected in the past period as soon as credit sales are recorded. *Also*: sales percentage method. *See*: *balance sheet approach.*

income statement audit an audit that focuses on the income statements. *Also*: stock exchange audit.

income statement charge = *revenue expenditure.*

income statement, 100% = *common-size income statement.*

income statement view = *revenue-expense view.*

income stream = *cash flow.*

income subject to tax = *taxable income.*

income summary account an account used in the closing procedures to summarize amounts of revenues and expenses, and, from which the net income or loss is transferred to the owners' equity or retained earnings. ***Also***: expense and revenue summary account.

income support <Australia> pension, benefit and allowance paid by the government.

income tax (IT) <1> tax on all kinds of income. ***Also***: direct tax; Part 1 tax. <2><UK> tax on the investment income of a company. ***See***: *corporate capital gains tax.*

Income Tax Act <UK> enactment relating to income tax.

income tax allocation the allocation of income tax liabilities. ***See***: *inter-period income tax allocation; intra-period income tax allocation.*

income tax basis a method under which the effects of events on business are recognized when taxable income or deductible expense is recognized, nontaxable income and expenses are included in the determination of income.

income tax deductible gift <Australia> = *deductible gift*

income tax exempt charity (ITEC) <Australia> a charity endorsed by the Australian Taxation Office as exempt from income tax.

income-tax exemption amount of an employee's annual earnings not subject to income tax. ***Also***: withholding allowance.

income tax expense account an account used to record income tax expense. ***Also***: provision for income tax account.

income tax method a method of recording cost of a traded-in new asset by adding accrual paid out sum of money to the book value of the original asset.

income tax month <UK> from 6th of a month to 5th of the next month. ***Also***: fiscal month.

income tax rate the rate applied to calculate income tax.

income tax return the form filed in each year reporting earnings and indicating amount of income tax being paid to the government by a person or business.

income tax return preparer = *tax preparer.*

income tax rule a rule under which the gain or loss on asset exchange must be absorbed into the cost of the new asset.

income tax table = *tax table.*

income tax withholding a mandatory practice of having employers and other entities act as collectors of income taxes by deducting taxes from salary and distribution to the taxpayers. ***Also***: pay-as-you-earn; source deduction; tax withholding; withholding of tax at source; withholding tax; withholding taxation.

income-tested benefit <Canada> a tax credit reduced when the recipient's income reaches a threshold amount.

income-testing <Canada> reduction in tax benefits or credits when a taxpayer's income reaches certain level.

income velocity a measurement of the rate at which money circulates in the economy, which is calculated as total sales divided by income. ***See***: *transaction velocity.*

income verification notice a notice from the IRS requesting support of income from a taxpayer. ***Also***: CP 2501.

income warrant a warrant that pays interest as well as carrying an exercise right.

income yield = *current return.*

incoming partner a partner joining the partnership.

incoming profit = *retained earnings.*

incomings = *revenue.*

incomplete work = *work in process.*

incorporated company = *corporation.*

incorporated partnership = *corporation.*

incorporated pocket book tax planning device to avoid progressive tax whereby an individual taxpayer would organize a corporation to hold the investment in securities, so the dividends and interest received would be taxed at the low corporate income tax rate.

incorporated talent tax planning device to avoid progressive tax imposed on individual taxpayers whereby a highly paid individual providing personal service would organize a corporation and contract to work for it at a relatively small salary.

incorporated yacht tax planning under which a wealthy taxpayer would organize a corporation and transfer to it a yacht, then rents the yacht from the corporation, the latter would then claim depreciation deduction for the yacht and the deduction would exceed the rents received.

incorporation the creation of a corporation.

incorporation relief <UK> a capital gains tax relief given to the company for disposal of its assets.

incorporeal capital = *variable capital.*

incorporeal property = *intangible asset.*

incorrect return = *fraudulent return.*

increase and decrease method = *asset method.*

increase in net assets = *gain.*

increase in owners' equity = *gain.*

increase of capital increase of the capital stock of a corporation often by issuing more shares. *See*: *reduction of capital.*

increasing charge depreciation = *sinking fund depreciation.*

increasing charge method = *sinking fund method.*

increasing cost the cost that increases as the volume of activity increases. *Also*: progressive cost.

incremental allowance amount reserved for projected misstatement by auditors, calculated by using only errors that are less than sampling interval ranked from highest to lowest in terms of tainting, considering incremental changes in reliability factors for actual errors found.

incremental analysis = *relevant cost approach.*

incremental audit risk a risk that misstatements or errors existing at balance sheet date will not be detected by the auditor.

incremental borrowing rate direct rate the lessee would pay in the lending market to buy the asset leased.

incremental capital-output ratio increase in capital stock derived by the increase in output of goods and services in a particular period.

incremental cash flow the difference in cash flow with or without a project.

incremental contribution margin increase in the contribution margin derived by the one unit increase in production output. *Also*: added contribution margin.

incremental cost <1> the excess of total cost of equipment over the amount that would have been expended if the equipment were not used for a qualifying purpose. <2> increase in cost caused by producing one additional unit of output. *Also*: added cost; addition cost. <3> = *relevant cost.*

incremental costing = *relevant costing.*

incremental cost of capital the average cost incurred for each additional unit of debt or equity issued.

incremental income <1> income derived by the increase in output or sales. *Also*: negative incremental cost. <2> excess of income over cost derived by further processing of the joint products.

incremental internal rate of return the internal rate of return on the incremental investment from choosing a larger project instead of a smaller one.

incremental loss excess of cost over income derived by further processing of the joint products.

incremental overhead factory overhead caused by increase in production output.

incremental research credit a tax credit, 20% of the excess of the qualified research expenses for the tax year over a base amount, plus 20% of the basic research payments.

incremental revenue <1> increase in sales derived by increase in output. <2> additional revenue derived by further processing of the joint products.

incremental revenue allocation procedure under which primary product is assigned 100% of its stand-alone revenue, with the remaining revenue from the bundle assigned to other products. ***See***: *stand-alone revenue allocation.*

incremental share under *treasury stock method*, the number of shares converted by the option minus number of treasury stock that can be bought by the proceeds.

incremental variable cost variable cost that tends to increase as the output increases.

incurred but not reported (IBNR) losses which have occurred during a stated period but have not yet been reported to the insurer.

incurred cost = *actual cost.*

incurred loss a deduction taken by insurers that is the discounted value of loss including those paid during the year and the discounted value of the loss reserve.

indefinite payment a payment to the creditor by a debtor who owes more than one debt.

indefinite reversal a condition in which interperiod income tax allocation is not required for the undistributed profits of a foreign subsidiary when there is sufficient evidence that those profits will be undistributed indefinitely.

independence condition of a public accountant acting as an auditor solely for the interests of clients and without any intervention or control from other parties. ***Also***: auditor independence.

independent accountant = *independent auditor.*

independent auditor an auditor in public practice who is independent of audit client. ***Also***: external auditor; independent accountant. ***See***: *external auditor.*

independent contractor a contractor who is self-employed and has the right to control the means and methods of performing work.

independent cost the cost that does not relate to a cost unit.

independent cost ledger a cost ledger maintained independently under interlocking accounts.

independent public accountant = *public accountant.*

independent taxation <UK> taxation on husband and wife separately since Apr 6, 1990.

in-depth audit an extensive examination made after preliminary audit has been completed and some problems have been found out.

index the combination of numbers and/or letters given to a work paper page for identification and organization purposes.

indexation allowance <UK> capital gains tax allowance adjusted by the retail price index between the date a capital asset is bought and the date sold. ***Also***: allowance for inflation; capital gains indexation allowance.

indexation loss <UK> loss created by applying indexation allowance to the cost of an asset in computation of capital gains tax.

indexed debt obligation <Canada> a debt the terms of which provide for an adjustment to an amount payable for a period during which the debt was outstanding.

indexed gain or loss <UK> the gain or loss on the sale of a capital asset after deducting the indexation allowance. ***See:*** *unindexed gain or loss.*

indexed security investment plan (ISIP) <Canada> an investment plan that offers savings of capital gains by adjusting the cost basis in listed shares by inflation.

indexing automatic adjustment of *standard deduction* and *tax exemption* for increase in the consumer price index.

indexing method a method of determining the asset replacement cost by the book value and a specific index.

index-linked financial statement = *constant-dollar financial statement.*

index method a method for computing the base year cost and the current year cost of a dollar value pool in a lifo system, either by extending a representative portion of the inventory by both current year unit cost and base year unit cost and comparing the two.

index of cost an index reflecting fluctuation of costs, especially inventory costs.

index of return index created by Dr. Fredolsten, calculated as 1% of the production cost savings in 1 year + 3% of the value of new products in 3 years + 2% of the value of improved product in 2 years.

index standard cost = *basic standard cost.*

Indian employment credit 20% tax credit of the sum of qualified employee wage and health insurance costs paid or incurred to qualified Indian employees.

indicated dividend dividends that would be paid on a share of stock throughout the next year if each dividend is the same amount as the previous payment.

indicated yield the yield that a share of stock would return, it equals indicated dividend divided by current price.

indifference analysis = *breakeven analysis.*

indirect cost <1> cost that can not be clearly identified with specific units of product or subdivisions of the entity, without arbitrary allocation. <2> = *establishment cost.* <3> = *overhead.*

indirect cost allocation the allocation of indirect costs to products under full absorption accounting for inventory valuation.

indirect cost rate = *overhead rate.*

indirect earnings income of a subsidiary which has not been shown in the consolidated income statement. ***Also***: unreported earnings.

indirect expense <1> that part of the factory overhead except indirect material and indirect labor. <2> = *factory overhead.*

indirect expense cost = *overhead.*

indirect factory cost = *factory overhead.*

indirect filer an authorized e-file provider that submits returns via another transmitter.

indirect financial interest an investment which is not under the direct control of the investor. ***See***: *direct financial interest.*

indirect-fixed cost fixed component of the indirect costs, e.g. rents. ***Also***: untraceable fixed cost.

indirect labor cost a cost that relates to the payment of an indirect worker. ***Also***: labor burden; labor overhead cost.

indirect loss a loss that is not a direct result of a peril, such as loss of business earnings due to damage to the business building.

indirect material raw material the relationship to the end product of which is indirect, e.g. lubricate oil. ***Also***: factory supplies.

indirect material cost indirect cost of materials and components. ***Also***: material burden.

indirect method <1> a method of recording depreciation whereby original cost of an asset remains unchanged in the balance sheet, and the accumulated depreciation is recorded in a contra asset account. <2> method of reporting net cash flow from operating activities by adjusting net income to reconcile it to net cash flow. ***Also***: reconciliation method. ***See***: *direct method.* <3> = *allowance method.* <4> = *appraisal method.*

indirect overhead cost = *factory overhead.*

indirect product costs = *overhead.*

indirect stockholding a subsidiary owns a controlling interest in a third company.

indirect tax a tax that can be shifted to others, such as *sales tax*. ***See***: *direct tax.*

indirect-variable cost the variable component of indirect cost, e.g. repairs.

indirect verification the verification of income statement items by substantiating the changes in the asset and liability accounts. ***See***: *direct verification.*

individual depreciation = *single asset depreciation.*

individual depreciation method = *single asset depreciation method.*

individual financial statement = *personal financial statement.*

individual level cost basis a basis of allocating pension cost under which future benefits for the employee are estimated and contributions are made periodically while the employee is working to fund these future benefits. ***See***: *aggregate level cost basis.*

individual level-premium method projection of costs for each individual in a pension or insurance plan. ***See***: *aggregate method; projected benefit cost.*

individual method of inventory valuation = *unit method of inventory valuation.*

individual pension plan (IPP) <Canada> a registered pension plan established for a qualifying individual.

individual posting = *individual transaction posting.*

individual retirement account = *IRA.*

individual retirement annuity an annuity that is established in connection with an individual retirement arrangement.

individual retirement arrangement = *IRA.*

individual savings account (ISA) <UK> an arrangement that allows individual taxpayers to hold various investments free of income tax and capital gains tax.

individual's tax <New Zealand> = *personal income tax.*

individual surtax <Canada> 3% surtax on personal income. (eliminated after 1999). ***Also***: Part 1.1 tax.

individual taxpayer identification number (ITIN) a taxpayer identification number assigned by the IRS to nonresident taxpayers or resident foreign nationals who may not be eligible for a social security number.

individual tax return a tax return filed by an individual. ***Also***: Form 1040; return of income. ***See***: *corporate tax return.*

individual transaction posting the posting of each entry from the journal to the ledger. ***Also***: individual posting.

inducement payment amount received by a taxpayer as an inducement or contribution in respect of the cost of a property.

inductive method = *derivative method.*

industrial accounting the accounting procedures and methods for the manufacturing industry.

industrial buildings allowance <UK> a balancing allowance applicable to industrial buildings.

industrial death benefit pension <UK> a benefit paid by the Department of Social Security to a widow if her husband died as a result of an accident at work.

industrial engineering method (IE method) a method that requires the estimating of man-hours and materials of each element and sub-element of work or job, and the pricing and accumulation of all the costs of the elements and sub-elements into a total cost estimate. ***Also***: ground-up approach. ***See***: *parametric approach.*

industrial rate of return = *internal rate of return.*

industry averages = *industry ratios.*

industry ratios financial ratios for a particular industry. ***Also***: industry averages.

ineligible account the account receivable that does not satisfy the lender's criteria as collateral. ***See***: *eligible account.*

ineligible corporation = *C corporation.*

ineligible retiring allowance <Canada> portion of retirement benefit that can not be transferred to a registered retirement plan, subject to tax.

inescapable cost = *inavoidable cost.*

infant industry a new or developing industry the production cost of which is higher than the established firms in the same industry.

inference the inference made by an auditor through comparisons, ratios, and trends.

inflated cost fictitious cost that exceeds the actual cost.

inflated price method a method under which the materials issue price being inflated slightly to ensure that some loss will be covered.

inflation account statement that shows the effect on the value of the inventories caused by inflation.

inflation accounting the accounting that tries to evaluate and compensate for the falling value of money, and adjust financial statement items according to the retail price index or the CPI. *See*: *constant-dollar accounting; current cost accounting.*

inflexible burden = *fixed overhead.*

inflexible expense an expense that cannot be adjusted or eliminated, such as a monthly car payment. ***Opp***: *flexible expense.*

inflow of capital = *capital inflow.*

influx large amount of money flowing into a company or a country.

InfoBytes Online library developed by the AICPA, which provides members with more than 1200 hours of continuing profession courses.

informal IRS notice an unofficial notice published by the IRS.

informal tax legislation process individuals and interest groups expressing and promoting opinions about tax legislation.

information accounting the procedures and methods for collecting, processing, and reporting information to the decision makers. ***Also***: user originated accounting.

information audit review of the accuracy and efficiency of information provided by the accountant.

information cost the cost of obtaining, processing and evaluating information. ***Also***: IT cost.

information risk the risk that the financial information used to make a decision is materially misstated.

information ratio (IR) <1> ratio of expected return to risk. <2> ratio of a variable against a standard deviation. <3> the ratio of annualized *residual return* to *residual risk.*

information return an annual return filed with the IRS by an exempt organization, an estate, a trust, a private foundation, etc. *See*: *Form 990.*

information tax return tax return prepared by a partnership. ***Also***: Form 1065.

infraction an offense prohibited by the IRS e-file program.

infrastructure asset streets, sidewalks, highways, etc. owned by the government.

inherent risk the likelihood of material misstatement of an assertion, assuming no related internal control.

inheritance tax (IHT) <1> a tax against the estate of a dead person through *accession tax* or *estate tax.* <2><UK> = *estate tax.*

inheritance tax return a tax return filed for inheritance tax purpose.

in-house research expense research expense incurred inside the company. *See: contract research expense.*

in-house review = *internal audit.*

initial acquisition cost the cost to the person who firstly acquired an asset by purchase, production, or construction.

initial allowance an allowance given to the person incurring capital expenditure for the period in which the expenditure is incurred.

initial audit an audit of a client for the first time.

initial bracket = *first tax bracket.*

initial cost <1> cost incurred in the service department which must be allocated to other departments. <2> = *organization cost.* <3> = *original cost.*

initial cost of asset = *book value.*

initial cost of business = *organization cost.*

initial direct cost the cost such as commissions, legal fees and costs of processing documents incurred by the lessor which are associated with negotiating and completing the leasing transaction.

initial entry <1> = *opening entry.* <2> = *original entry.*

initial goods-in-process = *opening work-in-process.*

initial inventory amount inter-company profit amount of a member of an affiliated group for the separate return year that precedes the filing of a consolidated return.

initial market value the market value of the shares determined on the date on which the shares were appropriated to the participant concerned.

initial repair the repair of a newly-acquired asset before it is in a usable condition.

initial reserve the *self-insurance fund* at the beginning of a year. **See:** *terminal reserve.*

initial special depreciation special depreciation made at the initial period of the asset.

Inland Revenue (IR) <UK> the government agency responsible for the administration of national insurance contributions, stamp duties, and income, company, capital gains, petroleum revenue, and inheritance taxes.

in lieu depreciation = *policy depreciation.*

in lieu of dividend payment to the lender of borrowed stock to make a short sale in lieu of the dividends distributed while the short position is maintained, deductible if the short position has been maintained for 46 days or more. ***Also***: dividend paid on short sales; in lieu of payment; manufactured dividend; premium.

in lieu of payment = *in lieu of dividend.*

in lieu of tax the tax imposed in place of overseas taxes that would otherwise qualify for the foreign tax credit.

in lieu tax a property tax imposed in lieu of local property taxation on automobiles by some states in addition to license fee.

inner reserve = *secret reserve.*

innocent spouse rule a rule, a spouse may claim to not be jointly liable if he or she did not know about the errors and did not benefit from them.

in-process goods = *work-in-process.*

input cost the cost of the production factors input to a process.

input method a method of establishing a standard cost by the number of input units.

input-output table (I-O) a statement that traces the inter-relationship among industries and shows who bought how much of each industry's products in a given year. ***Also***: inter-industry table.

input tax <UK> the tax paid to the suppliers with the purchase of raw materials. ***See***: *output tax.*

input tax credit = *GST input tax credit.*

input taxed supply a supply that is exempt from input tax.

inquiry audit procedure that involves either oral or written inquiry by the auditor.

inside basis the basis of property in the hands of a partnership and correspondingly for each partner's share of the basis. ***See***: *outside basis.*

inside buildup the increase in a policy's cash value that has not been borrowed by the policy holder. ***Also***: unborrowed policy cash value.

inside holding an investment with built-in tax shelter, the distribution from which will be taxed as ordinary income. ***See***: *outside holding.*

insider viewpoint approach = *cash flow method.*

insolvency exception discharge of debt that is excluded from the bankrupt debtor's gross income.

insolvency reorganization the reorganization in connection with bankruptcy.

inspection an audit procedure that involves careful scrutiny or examination of documents and physical resources. *Also*: examination.

inspection examination report = *examination.*

inspection of accounts method = *direct-estimate method.*

inspection of past cost behavior patterns method determination of fixed and variable behavior of costs by examination of their past behavior.

inspector general (IG) the individual charged with conducting and supervising audits and investigations relating to the programs and operations of their departments or agencies, and reporting on these semiannually to the congress and the chief executive of their department or agency.

installation cost the cost to install a plant asset.

installment portion of tax liability paid at regular interval.

installment account <Canada> an account for paying income tax by installments.

installment accounts receivable accounts receivable that are to be collected in future periods. *Also*: deferred installments receivable.

installment distribution the distribution of partnership cash on the basis of a schedule if the sale of assets can not be done in a short period.

installment liquidation the liquidation of a partnership over several periods.

installment method a method of accounting for property with at least one payment to be made in a year after the taxable year the sale is made, as a result, gains or losses are reported as payments are made.

installment payment corporations paying income taxes in two installments, the first on the tax return's due date and the second 3 months thereafter.

installment sale the sale of goods and services with payments in future periods. *Also*: deferred-payment sale.

installment sales method application of the theory that revenue realization coincides with the receipt of cash, which allows the dealer to spread over the period in which payments are received, provided the payments must be made in 2 or more installments. *See*: *cash collection basis; cost recovery method.*

Instalment Activity Statement (IAS) <Australia> a statement used to pay PAYG by a person or business not registered for GST.

instant interest the interest paid in advance. *Also*: anticipated discount; interest expense prepaid; interest in advance; interest prepaid; prepaid interest; unearned interest.

Institute of Chartered Accountants in England and Wales (ICAEW) <UK> the largest professional accounting body in Europe. (www.icaew.co.uk).

Institute of Internal Auditors (IIA) an organization providing certification, education, research, and technological guidance for the internal audit practitioners.

Institute of Management Accountants (IMA) national membership organization of CPAs and others involved in accounting, financial and data processing work for industry, commerce and government. It issues the designation Certified Management Accountant. *Formerly called*: National Association of Accountants.

institutional accounting the accounting for the nonprofit organizations other than government units.

instructional audit an audit the purpose of which is providing instructional advice to the client. *Opp*: *critical audit.*

in-substance defeasance a situation where a debt remains outstanding, but the debtor places risk-free monetary assets in a trust that restricts the use of the assets to meeting all of the cash flow requirements on the debt.

insufficient fund = *non-sufficient fund.*

insurance method of depreciation a method under which an insurance policy is bought up to the amount of the depreciable cost of an asset, and the depreciation expense each period equals the net premium paid to the insurance company. ***Also***: endowment policy method; insurance policy method.

insurance payout money paid to the insured by an insurance company.

insurance policy method = *insurance method of depreciation.*

insurance premium fee paid to an insurance company under a policy. ***Also***: premium.

insurance premium tax (IPT) <UK> a 5% tax on the general insurance such as houses and cars, and 17.5% on travel insurance. ***Also***: tax on insurance premium.

insurance reserve portion of the *initial reserve* in a year in payment of losses.

insurance settlement the payment by an insurance company to the insured to settle a claim.

insurance tax a state tax on the premium receipts of an insurance company. ***Also***: gross premiums tax.

insured benefit <UK> retirement benefit paid under insurance policies.

insured plan a defined benefit plan that is guaranteed by life insurance products.

int. interest

intangible asset an asset which has no physical existence but has value because of the rights conferred as a result of the ownership and the possession of this asset. ***Also***: eligible capital property; immaterial asset; incorporeal property; intangible property; invisible asset; long-term intangible asset; long-term intangible resources; nonphysical asset; non-visible property.

intangible asset approach accounting analysis method that focuses on intangible assets, especially goodwill.

intangible cost tax deductible cost incurred in drilling, testing, completing and reworking oil and gas wells.

intangible drilling cost (IDC) all necessary intangible expenditures incurred in drilling from the surface to the natural resource deposit.

intangible fixed asset a fixed asset that has no physical existence, and is acquired or created by the company for use on a continuing basis in the course of the company's activities.

intangible property = *intangible asset.*

intangible property income the income attributed to certain intangible personal property, earned by possessions.

intangible tax a state tax on individual bank deposits, including stocks and bonds.

intangible value total value of an organization as a going concern less the total value of its tangible assets.

integral accounts <UK> accounts that relates to a single system that contains both the financial and cost accounts, and all of them are in one single ledger. ***See***: *inter-locking accounts.*

integral view each interim period is an integral part of an annual audit. ***See***: *discrete view.*

integrated cost system = *direct standard costing.*

integrated test facility (ITF) an audit technique that introduces dummy transactions into the client's system in the midst of live transactions.

integration <1> transfer of illicit money into a company to be merged into the regular revenue of that business. ***See***: *overstatement of reported revenues.* <2> = *consolidation.*

integrity control = *completeness control.*

intellectual capital intelligence of the employees of a firm.

intellectual property a right in the creation of the mind, e.g. copyright, patent, a literal work, painting or software. ***See***: *soft asset.*

intensity driver a cost driver used to directly charge cost to an activity.

interactive data extraction and analysis (IDEA) EDP audit tool that allows the transfer and analysis of data from other computers.

inter-company account general ledger account recording a transaction between related companies.

inter-company dividend dividend received by one member from another member of the same control group in a *consolidated return year.*

inter-company elimination = *elimination.*

inter-company note promissory note issued from one affiliate company to another or to the parent company.

inter-company profit net profit of a control group arising when the selling affiliate records a gain on the sale but the buying affiliate has not sold the merchandise. ***Also***: unrealized inter-company profit.

inter-company profit elimination the elimination of inter-company profits among companies when preparing the consolidated financial statements. ***Also***: profit elimination.

inter-company transaction a transaction in a *consolidated return year* between corporations that are members of the same affiliated group immediately after the transaction.

interdisciplinary approach accounting study method focusing on objective management, behavioral science, etc.

interest (i.)(in.)(int.) <1> the price paid for the borrowed use of money. ***Also***: charge for credit; cost of fund; cost of money; dividend; interest charge; interest on money; premium; price of capital; price of money. <2> = *cost of carry.*

interest accrued = *accrued interest.*

interest-adjusted cost the average annual cost of a policy and is calculated using premiums, dividends, and cash values.

interest-adjusted net cost method (IANC method) method of comparing the costs of life insurance policies that takes into consideration the time value of money. ***See***: *ledger cost method.*

interest annuity = *annual interest.*

interest capitalization rule a rule under which a taxpayer must capitalize interest he or she pays or incurs during a production period.

interest charge = *interest.*

interest cost an increase in the projected benefit obligation of a pension plan due to the passage of time. (It equals beginning balance of PBO multiplied by discount rate.)

interest coverage a calculation of a company's ability to meet its interest payments on debts outstanding, calculated as EBIT divided by interest expenses. ***Also***: interest coverage ratio.

interest coverage ratio <1> = *interest coverage.* <2> = *times interest earned.*

interest deduction an interest expense allowed as a deduction for tax purpose. ***Also***: interest subsidy.

interest distribution payment from a company or a mutual fund in the form of interest rather than dividend.

interest equalization tax (IET) a 15% federal income tax on interest received from foreign borrowers, designed to restrict foreign debt issues sold into the US market.

interest expense deduction interest expense as itemized deduction or corporation interest expenses paid or accrued in the taxable year.

interest expense prepaid = *instant interest.*

interest-free loan a loan without interest.

interest imputed = *imputed interest.*

interest in advance = *instant interest.*

interest income the income earned from a bank account or lending money to others.

interest-in-general depreciation method = *interest method in general.*

interest maintenance reserve (IMR) reserve to accumulate realized capital gains and losses resulting from fluctuations in the interest rate.

interest method <1> a method under which the accumulation of the bond discount (or the amortization of the premium) will be the difference between the periodic cash receipts and the computed interest revenue. ***Also***: effective interest method. ***See***: *straight-line method.* <2> = *compound interest method.*

interest method in general a method whereby possible future income of the depreciable asset is discounted to its present value which will be used as the depreciable cost of that asset. ***Also***: interest-in-general depreciation method.

interest method of allocation a reporting method that uses present value techniques to compute changes in the carrying amount of an asset or liability from one period to the next.

interest on interest = *compound interest.*

interest only strip (IO) <1> a contractual right to receive interest on a financial instrument. <2> a security with cash flows based entirely on the monthly interest payments received from a mortgage pool.

interest on money = *interest.*

interest on tax the interest on delinquent tax payments.

interest out of capital = *capital dividend.*

interest per annum = *annual interest.*

interest prepaid = *instant interest.*

interest rate of return = *present value profitability index.*

interest ratio interest expense as a percentage of income.

interest revenue the revenue from the bond or loan interest.

interest subsidy = *interest deduction.*

interest tax shield reduction in income taxes that results from the tax-deductibility of interest payments.

interest warrant a company's demand of payment of interest due on notes or debts.

interest yield the nominal rate of interest or dividend, divided by the price of the security.

interest yield equivalent rate of return on a security sold on a discount basis, that assumes actual days to maturity and a 360 day year.

inter-fund transfer movement of cash from one governmental fund to finance current period activities in another fund. ***Also***: operating transfer.

inter-governmental revenue amount received from other governmental agencies and municipalities.

interim audit an audit performed before the end of a financial year. ***Also***: intermediate examination; mid-term audit.

interim certificate = *scrip.*

interim dividend a partial dividend which could be declared by the board of directors before the final closing of accounts at the year end.

interim financial statement financial statement prepared in between the annual statements, e.g. monthly, quarterly or semi-annual.

inter-industry table = *input-output table.*

interior failure cost the cost incurred when a non-conforming product is discovered before shipment to the customer, e.g. rework. ***Also***: internal failure cost. ***See***: *exterior failure cost.*

interior liability = *owner's capital.*

interlocking accounts <UK> a system of cost accounting in which the cost accounts have no double-entry connection with the financial accounts, but using the same basic data. ***See***: *integral accounts.*

intermediate examination = *interim audit.*

intermediate ledger a ledger between the general ledger and the detailed ledger for entering subtotals of certain items.

intermediate service provider a tax return service provider between an ERO (or a taxpayer) and the transmitter.

internal accounting control = *accounting control.*

internal and external verification verification of accounting data through both internal and external review and inquiry.

internal audit examination of the records and procedures of a business by its own internal staff to determine if established procedures are being followed. ***Also***: administrative audit; in-house review; staff audit.

internal auditor employee of a business who performs internal audit. ***Also***: staff auditor.

internal check accounting procedure or physical control to safeguard assets.

internal check system arrangement of jobs in such a way that the work of one individual independently verifies that of another.

internal control a process designed to protect the accuracy and reliability of accounting data, assure operating effectiveness and efficiency, and compliance of laws and regulations. ***See***: *accounting control.*

internal control questionaire a form listing various points that have a bearing on the related internal control.

internal control system a system adopted by a company to control its operations and protect its assets from fraud, wastes, and theft.

internal cost the cost incurred by the manufacturer himself.

internal document = *internally created document.*

internal evidence the evidence found inside the business by the auditors.

internal expansion a company's growth by increasing its operations and retained earnings. ***See:*** *external expansion.*

internal failure cost = *interior failure cost.*

internal finance fund generated within a firm by retained earnings and depreciation.

internal financing raising money for projects by keeping earnings, by getting back money from taxes due to depreciation. ***Opp:*** *internal financing.*

internal growth expansion of business through internal efforts. ***Opp:*** *external growth.*

internal growth rate maximum rate a firm can expand without additional financing.

internally created document a supporting document prepared by the firm itself. ***Also***: internal document; intra-office document.

internal rate method a method under which depreciation is calculated as (depreciable value - internal profit) × internal rate of interest.

internal rate of return (IRR) an interest rate that would make the present value of future cash flows from a project equal to the cost of initial investment. ***Also***: actuarial rate; adjusted rate of return; compound rate of return; discounted cash flow rate of return; discounted rate of return; earning power; industrial rate of return; marginal efficiency of investment; time-adjusted rate of return; true rate of return. ***See***: *accounting rate of return; dollar-weighted rate of return.*

internal rate of return method a method of determining the acceptability of an investment proposal by examining its internal rate of return. ***Also***: adjusted rate of return method; discounted rate of return method; investor's method; time adjusted rate of return method.

internal report accounting = *management accounting.*

internal reserve = *retained earnings.*

internal revenue the revenue from taxation levied by a government within its country.

Internal Revenue Agent an auditor sent by the IRS.

Internal Revenue Code (IRC) that portion of the US Code that contains all federal tax laws.

Internal Revenue Service (IRS) the federal agency that administers most federal tax laws. *Also*: Service.

internal service fund a fund for providing goods or services to other government departments. *See: enterprise fund.*

internal statement a statement for internal use only.

internal transaction expiration or transfer of costs within the business.

international accounting the accounting methods and principles which are generally accepted by many countries all over the world. *Also*: global accounting, multinational accounting; transnational accounting; world accounting.

International Accounting Standards Board (IASB) an organization whose members represent 153 accounting bodies in 112 countries. The group is dedicated to bringing about the harmonization of international accounting standards.

International Accounting Standards Committee (IASC) a committee from 142 accounting organizations from 103 countries, founded in 1973 to formulate international accounting standards and promote worldwide acceptance and observation.

international balance of payments = *balance of payments.*

international boycott income the income deemed distributed to shareholders of a DISC as a result of participation in an international boycott.

international traffic <Canada> a non-resident alien's business of transporting passengers or goods from Canada to a place outside Canada or from a place outside Canada to Canada.

Internet Tax Freedom Act a three-year law effective 1/1/1999 that bans the imposition of tax on Internet access and online services, extended for two more years on 12/2/2001.

inter-period equity a concept under which government accounting focuses on evaluating government activity one period at a time, future periods are essentially ignored.

inter-period income tax allocation allocation of income tax expense between accounting periods because of the timing differences. *See*: *intra-period income tax allocation.*

interpretation description of the items in the financial statements or the purposes of the accounting behavior. *Also*: description.

interview audit an IRS audit of a face-to-face variety. *See*: *correspondence audit.*

inter vivos trust a trust established and effective during the grantor's lifetime. *Also*: living trust. *See*: *testamentary trust.*

intra-office document = *internally created document.*

intra-period income tax allocation the allocating of income taxes to income from operations, to extraordinary items and to other sources of income and loss which required separate presentation in the income statement. *Also*: tax allocation within a period. *See*: *inter-period income tax allocation.*

intrinsically fixed cost a cost that will not change under any conditions. *Also*: fully fixed cost.

intrinsically variable cost a cost which changes in direct proportion to the change in a certain type of activity. *Also*: fully variable cost.

intrinsic value <1> the value of a company or an asset based on an underlying perception of the value. It equals the earnings per share ÷ expected rate of return. *Also*: absolute value. <2> amount an option is in the money, or the value of the option if it were to be exercised right now. *See*: *extrinsic value.*

intrinsic value based method a method that uses the quoted market price of the stock at the grant date in the computation of compensation cost of an employee stock ownership plan. ***Also***: intrinsic value method. ***See***: *fair value based method.*

intrinsic value method = *intrinsic value based method.*

inv. inventory

invalid care allowance <UK> a tax allowance to a taxpayer who spends at least 35 hours per week caring for a disabled person who receives certain state benefits. ***See***: *additional personal allowance.*

invariable cost = *fixed cost.*

inventoriable cost = *product cost.*

inventoried goods = *merchandise inventory.*

inventory (inv.) <1> value of a firm's raw materials, work-in-process, supplies, finished goods, or merchandise. ***Also***: stock in trade; stock of goods. <2> a list of items on hand at a given date.

inventory account an account for recording the costs of inventory assets. ***Also***: stock account.

inventory accounting <1> procedure for the acquisition, consumption and inventory of assets. <2> a method under which income or loss is reported by determining sales revenues for the year and subtracting cost of goods sold.

inventory adjustment increasing and decreasing book inventory.

inventory allowance = *allowance for inventory price decline.*

inventory approach an audit used in examining current assets, once the balances of the asset accounts have been verified, subsequent audit has only to examine those transactions that took place during the intervening period. ***See***: *transaction approach.*

inventory asset a company's stock in trade or other property that would properly be included in the year-end inventory on hand.

inventory carrying cost = *carrying cost.*

inventory control the use of various techniques to optimize levels of all types of stock.

inventory cost the cost of the inventory items valued at the end of a period. ***Also***: cost of goods on hand.

inventory costing calculation or determination of the cost of inventory properties. ***Also***: stock costing.

inventory cushion = *buffer stock.*

inventory depreciation the depreciation calculated under appraisal method, it equals beginning inventory plus cost of acquisition minus ending inventory of assets.

inventory-flow assumption an assumption of the flow of inventory items, such as lifo.

inventory layer the amount by which the ending inventory cost exceeds the beginning inventory cost in lifo. ***Also***: layer; lifo inventory layer; lifo layer.

inventory liquidation under dollar value lifo, the decrease in inventory level at year-end compared to base year.

inventory loss <1> loss of goods in stock due to shrinkage, theft, evaporation, mis-issuing, etc. ***Also***: loss of stock; loss on inventory taking; loss through standing; stock deficiency. <2> the loss realized when the replacement cost exceeds the book value of inventory.

inventory method <1> a method under which assets and liabilities are reported in the balance sheet at their actual inventory amounts. ***See***: *derivative method.* <2> = *appraisal method.*

inventory methods method of identifying goods and of valuing them such as lifo and fifo.

inventory order point = *reorder point.*

inventory overage the excess of actual inventory over the book inventory.

inventory pool grouping of inventory items for the purpose of determining the costs as part of a lifo method. ***Also***: lifo pools.

inventory profit difference between historical cost of an inventory item charged to cost of sales and its current cost at the time of sale under inflation circumstance by using lifo. ***Also***: holding gain. ***See***: *operating income.*

inventory reconciliation adjustment made to reconcile actual inventory to perpetual inventory accounts.

inventory reserve <1> appropriation of retained earnings to reflect future declines in the price of inventory. <2> reserve for the liquidation of the lifo base, used in interim reporting.

inventory reserve account an account used to reduce inventory from cost to market value in applying the lower of cost or market value rule.

inventory shortage amount by which the actual inventory is lower than the book balance.

inventory status file account of how much inventory is on hand or on order.

inventory status report a report of the overage, shortage and reorder of inventories.

inventory taking act of calculating the actual quantities of the assets and preparing an inventory. ***Also***: physical inventory; stocktake; stock taking; taking a physical inventory.

inventory turnover the number of times the average inventory is sold. It equals annual sales divided by year-end inventories. ***Also***: sales to inventories; stock turnover; turnover of inventory.

inventory turnover period = *number of days' sales in inventory.*

inventory valuation calculating the proper cost of the inventory assets.

inventory valuation adjustment amount obtained by subtracting the change in the book value of inventories from the current value of the change in inventories.

inverted takeover a smaller company's taking over of a larger company which has suffered big losses. ***See***: *downstream merger; reverse takeover.*

invested capital <1> sum of a company's long-term debt, stock and retained earnings. ***Also***: capitalization. <2> = *net worth.* <3> = *owner's capital.*

invested cost = *acquisition cost.*

invested earnings = *retained earnings.*

investee a company some of the shares of which are held by another company.

investment basis adjustment an annual adjustment used by parent corporations to adjust the basis in common and preferred stock of the subsidiaries in order to account for the subsidiary's operations.

investment center a profit center which is evaluated on the basis of the return earned on the invested capital of the center.

investment contract <Canada> debt instrument excluding income bonds the income of which is included in taxable income annually.

investment credit = *investment tax credit.*

investment credit property any depreciable or amortizable property eligible for the rehabilitation, the energy and reforestation credit.

investment elimination adjustment = *differential.*

investment income <1> all earnings from an investment, e.g. capital gains, dividend, rent, and interest. ***Also***: gross investment income. ***See***: *passive income.* <2> = *unearned income.*

investment in net assets = *net worth.*

investment in securities purchase of bonds and stocks.

investment in subsidiary money invested in a subsidiary by the parent company.

investment interest deduction the deduction of interest expense on investment, limited to the extent of investment income.

investment multiplier the change in national income which would result from a unit change in investment.

investment ratio relationship of gains from investments resulting from insurance operations of an insurance company to earned premium.

investment reserve = *terminal reserve.*

investment savings account (ISA) <UK> a pool of investment funds for tax benefits, replaced *personal equity plan* on Apr 6, 1999.

investment tax credit (ITC) a 3-part (4-part before 1983) of non-refundable credits the components of which are the rehabilitation credit, the energy credit, the reforestation credit, and before 1983, employee plan credit. ***Also***: investment credit; job development credit.

investment theft loss the loss as a victim of unsuitable investments, fraud, churning, misrepresentation, or bankrupt investment.

investment trust <UK> an investment company that is exempt from tax on its gains.

investment trust fund government fund used to account for the investment activities.

investment value estimated price at which the preferred stock would be likely to sell if it were not convertible.

investment yield an amount equal to a life insurance company's gross investment income less real estate expenses, investment expenses, depreciation and non-insurance trade and business deduction.

investor control rule a ruling which holds if the policyholder has sufficient control over his segregated account in the insurance company, he will be taxed on the earnings on the account. ***See***: *segregated account.*

investor's method = *internal rate of return method.*

invisible account <UK> item of export trade that deals in intangibles and services.

invisible asset = *intangible asset.*

invisible capital = *variable capital.*

invisible deterioration = *functional depreciation.*

invisible item the items in the balance of payments such as banking, insurance and transportation.

invisible venture capital the capital provided by angel investors. ***See***: *angel investor.*

invoice billing a billing system in which invoices are sent off at the time of customer orders, and separated from the bills to be paid.

invoice discounting = *accounts receivable financing.*

invoice method a method under which sales allowances and partial payments are noted on the face of the invoice, but the invoices are retained in the open file until the total amount is paid or received. ***See:*** *sales invoice method; purchases invoice method.*

involuntary conversion sudden loss of an asset that does not occur in the ordinary course of business, such as destruction by fire.

involuntary cost the cost that arises from the nature of a firm's business, its scale of manufacturing, the types of processes used.

inv't inventory

invty inventory

IO interest only strip

I-O input-output table

iou = *promissory note.*

I-P cost irrelevant past cost

IPP individual pension plan

IPT insurance premium tax

IQEX International Qualification Examination

IR Inland Revenue

IRA a personal savings plan that allows a taxpayer to set aside money for retirement, while offering deferred tax. ***Also***: individual retirement account; individual retirement arrangement; registered retirement savings plan; retirement savings account. ***See***: *deductible IRA; nondeductible IRA: Roth IRA; traditional IRA.*

IRA commission the commission paid that is related to an IRA.

IRA contribution amount of money contributed into an IRA by a taxpayer. ***Also***: RRSP contribution.

IRA deduction IRA contribution allowed to be deducted from gross income. ***Also***: RRSP deduction.

IRA loss investment loss incurred in an IRA.

IRA plus = *Roth IRA.*

IRB Internal Revenue Bulletin

IRC Internal Revenue Code

IRC 263(a) a tax rule under which capital improvements and certain expenses are not deductible and must be capitalized.

IRD income in respect of a decedent

IRD deduction tax deduction allowed against the *income in respect of a decedent.*

Irish dividend = *split down.*

ironclad exemption an exemption from paying full estimated tax if the withholding amount or quarterly tax payments is equal to or greater than last year's tax liability. *See: safe harbor rule.*

IRR internal rate of return

irrecoverable cost = *sunk cost.*

irregularity <1> inconformity of the firm's accounting treatment with the generally accepted accounting principles. <2> = *fraud.*

irrelevant cost a cost that does not relate with the present decisions. ***Also***: common cost.

irrelevant future cost a cost that does not relate with the future decisions. ***See***: *relevant future cost.*

irrelevant past cost a cost that does not relate to past decisions.

irrevocable trust a trust that, once its setup, cannot be changed at all. ***See***: *revocable trust.*

IRS Internal Revenue Service

IRS master file a centralized database containing taxpayers' information.

IRS set rate the interest rate determined by the IRS.

IS income statement

ISA <1> individual savings account. <2> investment savings account.

ISB Independence Standards Board

ISIP indexed security investment plan

ISO <1> incentive stock option. <2> internet securities offering

issuance expense = *cost of flotation.*

issue cost = *cost of flotation.*

issued capital stock (ICS) capital stock from the shares which have been issued and delivered to the stockholders. ***Also***: outstanding capital stock; outstanding share capital.

IT income tax

ITAR income tax application rule

ITC <1> income tax credit. <2> investment tax credit.

IT cost = *information cost.*

ITEC income tax exempt charity

item accounting = *single-asset depreciation method.*

item-by-item method a method of comparing the costs and market value of inventories item by item.

item depreciation = *single asset depreciation.*

item depreciation accounting = *single-asset depreciation method.*

itemized deduction a limited group of expenditures by individuals allowed as deductions from adjusted gross income if and to the extent they exceed the zero bracket amount. ***Also***: personal deduction.

itemizer a taxpayer who itemizes deductions.

item method = *single-asset depreciation method.*

item of tax preference amounts excluded from gross income under the dividends received deduction and after 1984 the partial exclusion of interest received, depreciation, amortization, or cost recovery, the accelerated portion of depreciation on leased property, etc. ***Also***: tax preference; tax preference item.

iterative method = *trial and error method.*

ITIN individual taxpayer identification number

ITR implicit tax rate

ITF integrated test facility

IVA inventory valuation adjustment

J j

J journal

JA joint account

jamming the auditor corporate management giving its auditor inadequate time to complete the audit before announcing operating results.

Jarvis rule a rule that the difference between the redemption price and the par value of a redeemed stock can be charged to profit and loss a/c.

JDB journal daybook

JEEP Joint Ethics Enforcement Program

jeopardy assessment IRS action to make an immediate assessment without following the procedures required for ordinary assessment.

J/F journal folio

JGTRRA Jobs and Growth Tax Relief Reconciliation Act

JIT just-in-time

job audit = *desk audit.*

job connected educational expense tax deductible expense incurred on education that can improve a taxpayer's skills.

job cost = *job order cost.*

job costing = *job order costing.*

job cost ledger a sub-ledger to the goods in process account in which are kept the job cost sheets of unfinished jobs.

job development credit = *investment tax credit.*

job hunting expense deducible expense as a result of looking for a job.

job-in-process a job order in the process of manufacturing. ***Also***: unfinished job in process.

job lot = *batch.*

job lot costing = *batch costing.*

job method a method of costing under which costs are accumulated by jobs.

job order an order issued to the factory to produce a definitive quantity of a specific unit or article. ***Also***: work order.

job order cost the cost of a job consisting of a single order. ***Also***: complete cost; job cost; work order charge; works cost.

job order costing costing that traces production costs directly to specific orders as a basis for planning, controlling and decision making. ***Also***: job costing; specific order costing.

job order cost sheet subsidiary record for work-in-process inventory, which lists the costs of a job order.

job order cost system a cost system in which costs are assembled in terms of jobs or job lots. ***Also***: production order system; special order cost system.

job project-performance cost variance = *cost variance.*

job project-schedule cost variance = *scheduled variance.*

Jobs and Growth Tax Relief Reconciliation Act (JGTRRA) a law enacted in 2003 allowing the first year expensing of $100,000 for assets acquired in a tax year for under $400,000.

job-seeker's allowance <UK> a benefit paid by the Department of Social Security for an unemployed person who is still looking for a job.

jo. fo. journal folio

John Doe summons a court summons that does not identify the person with respect to whose liability it is issued.

joint account an account that concerns 2 or more entities or persons

joint and survivor annuity an annuity contract under which payments are made to two or more annuitants so long as one of them remains alive.

joint annuity an annuity contract under which payments are made to two or more annuitants but only so long as they all remain alive. ***Also***: joint life annuity.

joint audit audit of the same firm undertaken by two or more independent auditors.

joint control the control of a joint venture by two or more entities.

joint cost <1> single cost incurred to produce two or more essentially different products. ***Also***: combined cost; common cost; finishing cost; joint product cost; related cost. <2> = *overhead.*

joint cost per unit joint cost of a unit of product.

Joint Ethics Enforcement Program (JEEP) program of cooperation between the AICPA and the state CPA societies in the enforcement and interpretation of the AICPA Code of Professional Conduct.

joint life annuity = *joint annuity.*

joint manufacturing costs the costs of two or more produced goods that are made by a single process and are not identifiable as separate products.

joint product the products that have a relatively significant sales value when two or more types of products result from a single process.

joint product cost = *joint cost.*

joint products costing determination of the joint costs and the allocation of them to joint products.

joint products method a method of sharing joint costs by proportion of the value of joint products.

joint return a tax return filed together by husband and wife reporting their aggregate income, signed by both spouses. ***Also***: joint tax return. ***See***: *separate return.*

joint spousal trust <Canada> an inter vivos trust created after 1999 by a spouse aged 65 or over. ***Also***: common-law partner trust.

joint tax return = *joint return.*

joint tenancy property the property owned by joint tenants.

joint variance a variance caused by two or more factors, usually both price and quantity. ***Also***: combined variance; mixed variance; mix variance.

joint venture (JV) <1> a venture formed by two or more other companies. <2> a partnership formed by two or more persons or companies cooperating in some special business activity in which there is some risk of losses, but a reasonable hope of profit. ***See***: *cost company.*

jour. journal

journal (J.)(jour.) the book of original entry in which all business transactions are recorded in the order of their occurrence. ***Also***: daybook; diurnal; journal daybook; journal entry daybook; register.

journal daybook = *journal.*

journal entry = *entry.*

journal entry daybook = *journal.*

journal folio (J/F)(jo. fo) number of pages in a journal. ***Also***: journal page number.

journalization a process of recording the business transactions in the journal. ***Also***: entering to the register; journalizing.

journalizing = *journalization.*

journal ledger = *Boston ledger.*

Journal of Accountancy monthly publication of the AICPA.

journal page number = *journal folio.*

journal voucher = *voucher.*

judge a judge in the Tax Court.

judgmental sampling = *nonstatistical sampling.*

judgement approach a method of determining the scope of audit test by the auditor's personal judgement.

judgement creditor a creditor by a court judgement.

judgement sampling = *nonstatistical sampling.*

juggled cost a cost that is reported but does not exist.

junior accountant = *bookkeeper.*

junior common stock plan a plan under which a company issues common stock that is subordinate to its presently outstanding common stock, often to its high executives. These shares can become common stock on the occurrence of future events.

junior debt = *subordinated debt.*

junior equity = *common stock.*

junior partner a low-level partner in a firm with limited profit sharing ratio and management influence. *See*: *senior partner.*

junior security a bond or stock with lower priority claim than a senior security, e.g. a preferred stock is junior to a bond, and common stock is junior to other securities.

junior stock shares issued to employees, that are usually subordinate to common stock. *See*: *mixed shares.*

junk value <1> the salvage value of a fixed asset which has been broken down. <2> = *scrap value.* <3> = *spoiled material cost.*

just-in-time (JIT) inventory control system under which materials or merchandises are delivered from the vendor immediately right before they are needed. *See*: *balanced inventory.*

K k

Kaizan budgeting a budgeting that projects costs on the basis of improvements yet to be implemented rather than upon current condition.

Keogh plan a qualified plan or profit-sharing plan for self-employed individuals and their employees permitting the annual deductible contributions of the lesser of $3,000 or 25% of earned income, after Keogh deductions. *Also*: HR-10 plan.

Keogh tax deduction 20% of self employment gross earnings.

key ledger = *general ledger*.

key person insurance a life insurance policy that a company purchases on the life of the company's key executive.

kickback an illegal, secret payment made in return for a referral which resulted in a transaction or a contract.

kiddie tax a tax for children under age 14 who have investment income of more than $1,400. *See*: *parental tax*.

kinder and gentler program a program that allows taxpayers to wipe out for pennies on the dollar past due income taxes, and start again with a clean slate.

kite = *bad check*.

kiting illegal practice in which a bank account shortage is concealed by exploiting the time required for a check to clear. *Also*: check kiting. *See*: *lapping*.

KPMG LLP one of the big 4 accounting firms in the USA.

L l

L <1> general ledger. <2> ledger. <3> liability.

LA liquid asset

labor burden = *indirect labor cost.*

labor calendar variance that part of labor cost variance caused by difference between standard days and calendar days.

labor cost the cost incurred to acquire personnel resources to produce goods and services. *Also*: cost of man-power; human cost; payroll cost; wages cost.

labor cost audit an audit made to determine whether the services received for the salaries paid are adequate and that salary expenditures are applied correctly in determining the cost of manufactured goods.

labor costing rate = *labor cost per equivalent unit.*

labor cost per equivalent unit labor costs of one unit of equivalent production. *Also*: labor costing rate.

labor cost variance difference between actual labor costs and standard labor costs. *Also*: direct labor cost variance; direct labor variance; labor variance.

labor delay variance excess of the actual costs over standard costs because of the payment of labor delay wages.

labor efficiency variance calculated as (actual labor hours - standard labor hours) × standard rate per hour. *Also*: direct labor efficiency variance; labor time variance; labor usage variance.

labor hour basis a basis of distributing overhead costs by the proportion of man-hours consumed.

labor-hour method = *direct labor-hour method.*

labor idle time variance that part of labor efficiency variance caused by the idle time.

labor in process labor cost in the work in process.

labor overhead cost = *indirect labor cost.*

labor price variance = *labor rate variance.*

labor rate variance calculated as (actual labor cost per hour - standard labor cost per hour) × actual hours used. *Also*: direct labor price variance; direct labor rate variance; direct wage rate variance; hour rate variance; labor price variance; wage rate variance.

labor time variance = *labor efficiency variance.*

labor turnover the number of employees leaving during the year divided by the average number of employees in that year.

labor usage variance = *labor efficiency variance.*

labor variance = *labor cost variance.*

labour-sponsored fund <Canada> a mutual fund designed to provide venture capital to emerging companies.

labour-sponsored funds credit <Canada> a tax credit equal to 15% of the first $5,000 of an employee's investment in existing labour-sponsored fund shares.

LAC long-run average cost

Lady Godiva accounting principles (LGAP) a theoretical set of accounting principles under which corporations must fully disclose all information, including that which often doesn't get reported to investors under GAAP.

Laffer curve the curve created by Arthur Laffer conjecturing that as taxes increase from low levels, government tax revenue also increases, however if above a certain point it would cause people to work less or not to work, thereby reducing tax revenue.

lag payment of a financial obligation later than is expected or required, as in lead and lag.

lagged reserve accounting (LRA) accounting to determine a bank's weekly cash reserve by the average of cash reserves of the preceding two weeks.

laid-down cost <Canada> cost to make an equipment available for use, such as freight, installation etc.

LAMBRA local agency area military base recovery area

land, building, furniture and equipment = *plant asset.*

land, buildings and equipment = *plant asset.*

landed cost the cost of an asset that includes the cost of loading, transporting and unloading at a specific destination.

landfill tax <UK> introduced in 1996, a tax on the companies that generate waste disposed of in landfill sites.

landfill tax credit <UK> a tax credit available to landfill site operators.

lapping concealing a cash shortage by putting the next customer's payment into the first's account, and so on. ***Also***: Ponzi scheme; tearing and lading. ***See***: *kiting.*

lapsing schedule = *depreciation schedule.*

large cap over $5 billion capitalization. ***See***: *small cap; micro cap; mid cap.*

large corporation tax (LCT) <Canada> a tax levied on corporations with capital employed in Canada exceeding $10 million.

last day of field work the day upon which the auditors conclude their audit procedures on a client's location.

last-in cost = *last invoice cost.*

last-in, first-out (lifo) an assumption that the last items received were the first items sold. ***Also***: first-in, last-out, first-in, on-hand; first-in, still-here; last-in, first-served, lifo assumption.

last-in, first-out inventory pricing the pricing of an inventory item under the lifo assumption. ***Also***: lifo inventory valuation.

last-in, first-out method a method used for determining inventory costs, which presumes that inventory on hand consists of the earliest units required under lifo assumption.

last-in, first-served = *last-in, first-out.*

last-in, last-out (lilo) = *first-in, first-out.*

last-in, on-hand = *first-in, first-out.*

last-in, on-hand method = *first-in, first-out method.*

last-in, still-here (LISH) = *fist-in, first-out.*

last-in, still-here method = *fist-in, first-out method.*

last invoice cost unit cost of the last bought in goods determined by their invoice. ***Also***: last-in cost.

last invoice price method a method whereby current year costs of items in closing inventory are determined on the basis of the latest costs incurred. ***Also***: last price method; last purchase method; latest acquisitions cost method; method of price of last purchase; natural acquisitions cost method; recent purchase method.

last price method = *last-invoice price method.*

last purchase method = *last invoice price method.*

last twelve month (LTM) the period of the last 12 months.

late charge a penalty for failure to pay an installment on time. ***Also***: late payment charge. ***See***: *prepayment penalty.*

late-filed election <Canada> a taxpayer's election to file a tax return later than the due date.

latent asset <1> = *off-balance sheet asset.* <2> = *potential asset.*

late payment charge = *late charge.*

latest acquisitions cost method = *last invoice method.*

law day = *due date.*

law of large numbers the statistical fact that it becomes harder and harder to maintain a given level of percentage growth (in revenues for example) as time goes on because that fixed percentage represents a larger absolute amount each period.

lawyer's letter a letter of inquiry sent by the auditor to a client's attorney requesting his or her description and evaluation of pending lawsuits and other loss contingencies.

layer <1> the distance between the point of original source of illicit money and the deposit of that money in a bank. <2> = *inventory layer.*

layering depositing illicit money into more than one bank to keep the deposit away from its original source.

layman financial statement financial statements to laymen.

LCC life cycle cost

LCM lower of cost or market

LCT large corporation tax

lead schedule a schedule which summarizes like accounts, the total of which is transferred to the working trial balance. ***Also***: grouping sheet; summary schedule.

learning curve a curve for representation of the rate of progress of trainees. ***Also***: improvement curve; progress curve; skill acquisition curve.

learning rate 1 minus the percentage reduction due to learning.

lease acquisition cost payment made by a lessee to get a business lease.

lease bonus amount paid to the lessor to obtain better leasing terms.

lease cancellation payment money paid by the landlord to the lessee to cancel a lease.

lease cost a cost in the form of the payment of rent for a lease contract.

leasehold improvement improvement on a leased asset that increases its value.

leasehold interest <Canada> the interest of a tenant in any leased tangible property.

lease liability the liability incurred when acquiring plant assets by capital or financing lease.

lease option = *sale-leaseback.*

lease term the period for which the lessee has contracted to lease the asset.

lease to purchase a lease contract giving the lessee an option to buy the leased property. ***Also***: hire-purchase contract.

least cost the cost of the smallest amount. ***Also***: minimum cost.

least costing the technique of minimizing the aggregate costs of several constructions performed at the same time by using linear programming.

least-cost point the point at which cost is the least under the high-low points method.

least-square method statistical method for locating a line which reflects the relationship between total cost and variable cost, so that the sum of the squares of the vertical distances of the points to the line is less than this sum of squares would be from other straight lines. ***Also***: line of least minimum; line of regression method; method of least minimum.

leaving payment = *redundancy payment.*

led ledger

led. fo. ledger folio

led. fol. ledger folio

ledger (led.)(lgr) the complete set of accounts for a business entity.

ledger account summary of all transactions with a particular firm.

ledger adjustment account = *controlling account.*

ledger asset an asset that is contained in the ledger.

ledger cash the cash balance shown in the general ledger. ***Also***: book cash.

ledger controlling account = *controlling account.*

ledger cost method a method used to determine the cost of a policy by taking gross premiums paid and subtracting dividends and the cash value of the policy. ***Also***: net cost method; traditional method. ***See***: *Linton yield method; interest-adjusted net cost method.*

ledger entry record of transactions in the ledger accounts. ***Also***: final entry. ***See***: *original entry.*

ledger folio (led. fo.)(LF) page number of a ledger sheet.

ledger journal = *Boston ledger.*

ledgerless accounting = *bookless accounting system.*

ledger paper = *ledger sheet.*

ledger posting = *posting.*

ledger sheet a page in the ledger. ***Also***: account; ledger paper.

left-hand financing borrowing money with business assets (listed on the left-hand side of a balance sheet) as collateral.

left-hand side = *left side.*

left side the left hand side of a T-account. ***Also***: left-hand side. ***See***: *debit side.*

legacy = *bequest.*

legal asset that portion of the assets of a deceased party which by law is directly liable, in the hands of his executor or administrator, to the payment of debts and legacies.

legal audit an audit required by law. ***Also***: compulsory audit; obligatory audit; statutory audit.

legal-basis method a method of preparing consolidated statements, whereby the parent's investment in subsidiaries is reported at cost, and the dividends from the subsidiaries are reported as increase in its net income. ***Also***: cost method; cost value method. ***See***: *economic basis method.*

legal capital = *stated capital.*

legal expense cost incurred in a lawsuit, including attorney's fee and court costs.

legal fraud = *constructive fraud.*

legal representation letter a representation letter from the lawyer of the client to the auditor.

legal reserve minimum amount of funds which an insurance company must keep to meet its future claims and obligations. ***Also***: reserve asset.

legatee someone who receives assets from the estate of a dead person.

legislative overkill law enacted to stop or prevent abuse of a loophole but instead goes far beyond the prevention.

lending asset <Canada> a bond, debenture, mortgage, hypothecary claim, note, agreement of sale or a *prescribed security.*

length of operating cycle number of days' sales in average receivables plus number of days' supply in average inventory.

lessor's implicit rate lessor's interest rate implicit in the lease used in computing the present value of the minimum lease payment.

let property <UK> = *rental property.*

letter for auditor = *engagement letter.*

letter for underwriters = *comfort letter.*

letter of auditor a reply from the auditor to the client after he has received the engagement letter.

letter of comment a letter sent by the SEC to a company planning a public offering suggesting that the company make certain changes to its registration statement.

letter of engagement = *engagement letter.*

letter of recommendation auditor's letter to the client containing the auditor's conclusions regarding its accounting and operating policies and procedures as well as internal controls.

letter of representation a letter signed by the client and addressed to the auditor, stating the financial statements are the responsibility of the management. ***Also***:

management representation; written representation. *See*: *engagement letter; representation letter.*

letter of rights = *stock warrant.*

letter to management = *management letter.*

level of confidence = *confidence level.*

level premium insurance premium that remains fixed over the life of a policy.

leverage <1> the degree to which a business is utilizing borrowed money. *See*: *capital leverage, financial leverage, and operating leverage.* *Opp*: *deleverage.* <2> effect on the gross national product of the new expenditures of a government. *Also*: financial gearing.

leveraged lease an arrangement whereby a long-term creditor provides non-recourse financing for a lease usually provides maximum income tax benefits to the three parties.

leverage ratio measures of the degree to which the owners or the creditors have financed a firm, usually the total debt divided by the total assets. *Also*: debt factor. *See*: *gearing ratio.*

levy <1> to assess a property and set the rate of taxation. <2> enforced collection by the IRS of a tax previously assessed.

LF ledger folio

L&G loss and gain

LGAP Lady Godiva accounting principles

lgr ledger

liabilities to assets ratio = *debt ratio.*

liability (L.) <1> a debt owed, including lien which represents a debt to which property is subject. *Also*: obligation. <2> both interior liability and the exterior liability.

liability and net worth the total of all liabilities and net worth of a company.

liability dividend = *scrip dividend.*

liability for recourse provision liability recognized when a note is discounted with recourse.

liability insurance an insurance against liability to third parties.

liability letter = *representation letter.*

liability method <1> a method of treating advance receipts as liabilities and transferred to revenue account periodically. <2> the method under which if the tax rates in the year the tax deferral takes place, are different from the expected tax rates in the year in which the payment of taxes is anticipated the latter rates are used to measure the deferred income tax liability. *See*: *asset and liability method; deferred method.* <3> = *deferral method.*

liability out of book actual liability which has not been recorded in the books yet. *Also*: non-ledger liability; out of book liability; unrecorded liability.

liability reserve allowance for any possible incurrence of future liabilities.

liability to be liquidated balance of liabilities at the date when a trustee is found.

liability to outsider = *exterior liability.*

liability to the public = *exterior liability.*

liability to the shareholders = *owner's capital.*

liability without regard to fault = *absolute liability.*

liberalized depreciation method a depreciation method chosen by the taxpayer. *Also*: arbitrary method.

LIF life income fund

life annuity an annuity payable for the life of an annuitant.

life cycle cost <1> the total of direct, indirect, recurring, nonrecurring, and related costs incurred, or to be incurred in the design, development, production, maintenance and support of a major system over its useful life. <2> cost of a product from its design to its obsolescence. <3> cost of an asset from its acquisition to its retirement.

life cycle costing the costing that considers the acquisition cost, maintenance charge, useful life and other factors.

life expectancy rule a method of calculating the income component of an annuity, by dividing the investment in the contract by the life expectancy of the annuitant, and treating that portion of each payment under the contract as a nontaxable capital return.

life income fund (LIF) <Canada> a registered retirement fund that receives funds from a *locked-in registered retirement savings plan.*

life insurance corporation = *life insurer.*

life insurer <Canada> a corporation that carries on a life insurance business. ***Also***: life insurance corporation.

life interest trust = *fixed interest trust.*

lifelong learning plan (LLP) <Canada> a plan that allows a taxpayer to withdraw from the RRSP $10,000 per year up to $20,000 in 4 years to pay qualified education expenses. ***See***: *Coverdell Education Savings Account.*

life of lease or improvements, whichever is shorter a rule of amortizing improvement costs at the shorter of the lease life or the improvement period.

lifetime exclusion = *unified credit exemption.*

lifetime exemption <Canada> a $100,000 basic capital gains exemption, no longer available since Feb 22, 1994.

lifetime general property exemption limit <Canada> capital gains exemption allowed to taxpayers, no longer available since 1994.

lifetime learning credit tax credit for qualified post-secondary and job-training educational expenses. Up to $1,000 a year can be claimed for an unlimited number of years. ***See***: *hope credit.*

lifetime transfer the transfer of property when the transferor is in healthy condition. ***See***: *deathbed transfer.*

lifo last-in, first-out

lifo accounting the accounting that uses last-in, first-out method.

lifo assumption = *last-in, first-out.*

lifo conformity rule the requirement that a corporation which uses lifo for tax purposes should use it for financial purposes.

lifo cost period cost ascertained under lifo costing method.

lifo cost flow assumption under process costing, an assumption that the latest input items to the process will be finished first.

lifo costing = *lifo cost method.*

lifo cost method a method of costing of finished goods under lifo cost flow assumption. ***Also***: lifo costing.

lifo dollar value method = *dollar value lifo method.*

lifo inventory layer = *inventory layer.*

lifo inventory valuation = *last-in, first-out inventory pricing.*

lifo layer = *inventory layer.*

lifo liquidation removal of old lifo inventory layer from the calculation of dollar value lifo, when sales exceed purchase, more earnings is resulted from decrease in inventory, because earlier, lower valued layers are included in the inventory. ***Also***: dipping into lifo layers.

lifo pools = *inventory pools.*

lifo recapture amount = *lifo reserve.*

lifo reserve the excess of the inventory cost of a company's assets over the inventory amount of such assets determined under lifo inventory. ***Also***: allowance to reduce inventory to lifo basis; lifo recapture amount.

lifo retail method retail method of inventory pricing under lifo assumption. ***Also***: lifo valuation retail method.

lifo taxation treatment of gain on fixed annuity investments whereby the earliest purchased annuities are to be withdrawn first.

lifo valuation retail method = *lifo retail method.*

lifting the veil <UK> = *piercing the corporate veil.*

like-for-like sales the portion of current sales achieved through activities that are comparable to the activities of the previous year.

like-kind exchange the exchange of property of the same nature or character, used in a trade or business. ***Also***: tax-free exchange.

like-kind property a property of the same nature or character, used in a trade or business, the exchange of them is tax-free.

lilo last-in, last-out

limited assurance = *negative assurance.*

limited audit <1> audit of only specific accounts or transactions. ***See***: *special audit.* <2> audit performed when a third party requires an independent report on the financial and operational status of the company in the short term, or when the owners seek objective assistance in the assessment of their own operational results. ***See***: *comprehensive audit.*

limited company <UK> a company in which the liability of each shareholder is limited by the share capital owned or the limit stated by the memorandum of association. ***See***: *company limited by guarantee; company limited by shares.*

limited interest <UK> a beneficiary's interest in only the income of trust assets. ***See***: *absolute interest.*

limited liability company (LLC) a legal entity that enjoys limited liability and is taxed like a partnership.

limited liability partnership <UK> a partnership treated like a company but taxed like a partnership. ***See***: *limited partnership.*

limited partner a partner in a limited partnership who has limited liability.

limited partnership (LP) a partnership in which there is at least one general partner who has unlimited liability, and all other partners' liabilities are confined to their contributed capital only. ***See***: *general partnership; limited liability partnership.*

limited review CPA engagement consisting of procedures and inquires that provide a basis to express limited assurance that no material changes are needed to the financial statements to bring them in conformity with GAAP.

limited scope audit scope that concentrates on one or two significant items on a tax return.

limited tax bond a bond secured by a special tax, a group of taxes or a specified percentage of the real estate tax.

limited-tax general obligation bond a *general obligation bond* of a government backed by specified or constrained revenue sources.

limited trust a trust created for a limited period of time. ***See***: *perpetual trust.*

limit of liability (LOL) the maximum amount for which an insurer is liable as set forth in the contract.

limit rate = *cut-off rate of return.*

linear programming the optimal allocation of scarce resources.

line of business reporting = *segmented reporting.*

line of least minimum = *least-square method.*

line of regression method = *least-square method.*

line sheet = *trial balance.*

link-chain method a method for computing the base-year cost and the current-year cost of a dollar-value pool, which involves double extending a portion of the pool and using two totals to compute a yearly index, which is then multiplied by the cumulative index from the beginning of the year, to arrive at the new current year's cumulative index. ***See***: *double extension method.*

linked asset an asset held for, or committed to, the payment of specific liabilities or obligations.

Linton yield the rate of return that makes the savings fund equal to a whole life policy's cash value.

Linton yield method a method of inputting Linton yield to a cash value policy to measure the cost of a life insurance. ***See***: *ledger cost method.*

liquid asset (LA) = *quick asset.*

liquidating dividend the dividend in excess of total profits as a return of part or all of the stockholder's investment. ***Opp***: *current dividend.* ***See***: *non-dividend distribution.*

liquidating trust a trust to which assets of a company undergoing liquidation are transferred.

liquidating value realizable value of an asset of a company that is going out of business. ***Also***: auction value. ***See***: *break-up value; liquidation value.*

liquidating value per share of an insurance company, the capital funds, plus special and conditional reserves plus allowance for equity in the unearned premium reserve divided by the number of shares outstanding.

liquidation the winding up of a business by converting its assets into cash and distributing cash to the proper parties.

liquidation account a statement prepared by a liquidator which shows the process and results of the liquidation. ***Also***: deficiency account; deficiency statement; realization and liquidation profit and loss account; statement of liquidation; statement of realization and liquidation.

liquidation accounting = *accounting for liquidation.*

liquidation income excess of scrap value of the assets over their book value at liquidation. ***Also***: income at liquidation.

liquidation value <1> value per share that will be paid to preferred stockholders upon liquidation of the corporation. ***Also***: liquidation value per share. ***See***: *liquidating value.* <2> = *abandonment value.*

liquidation value per share = *liquidation value.*

liquidation year a taxable year in which a qualified liquidation occurs.

liquidator a person appointed to conduct the winding up of a company.

liquid capital = *free capital.*

liquid deficiency = *working capital deficit.*

liquidity ability to convert an asset into cash. ***Also***: accounting liquidity.

liquidity index number of days in which current assets are removed from cash.

liquidity ratio <1> measure of a firm's ability to meet the maturing short term obligations, such as the acid-test ratio; cash ratio, current ratio etc. <2> = *acid-test ratio.*

liquid liability = *current liability.*

liquid ratio = *acid-test ratio.*

liquor tax a federal tax on liquor manufacturers.

LISH last-in, still-here

List A a schedule attached to the statement of affairs listing the names and addresses of all creditors.

List B a schedule attached to the statement of affairs listing the names and addresses of creditors who have been fully guaranteed.

List C a schedule attached to the statement of affairs listing names and addresses of creditors who have been partly guaranteed.

List D a schedule attached to the statement of affairs listing the names and addresses of creditors of note discounted.

List E a schedule attached to the statement of affairs listing names and addresses of creditors of contingent liabilities.

listed personal property (LPP) <Canada> a personal property that increases in value over time.

listed personal property loss <Canada> amount by which the aggregate of losses for the year from dispositions of listed personal property exceeds the aggregate of the gains for the year from dispositions.

listed property a property used by a tax payer for communication, transportation, recreation, entertainment, or amusement, and subject to special depreciation rules if used 50% or less for business purposes.

listed security a security that has been admitted for trading on a stock exchange and complied with the listing requirements. ***Also***: admitted to dealings; on-board security; quoted security.

listed shell company = *shell company.*

List F a schedule attached to the statement of affairs listing names and addresses of creditors in leasehold and their amounts.

List G a schedule attached to the statement of affairs listing the names and amounts of the creditors of taxes payable and wages payable.

List H a schedule attached to the statement of affairs listing the names and amounts of the property creditors.

List I a schedule attached to the statement of affairs listing the names and amounts of the real estate creditors.

List J a schedule attached to the statement of affairs listing the names of creditors of bills and promissory notes.

List K a schedule attached to the statement of affairs listing the cause and reasons of deficiency.

List L a statement prepared by a small business that contains information from List A to List J.

literary income <UK> income received by an author.

live asset = *active asset.*

living accommodation <UK> place in which a taxpayer can live, including the house, house boat and holiday villa.

living cost the cost of purchasing one basket of consumer goods at today's price compared with what the same basket would cost in previous or base period. ***Also***: alimony; cost of living; subsistence cost.

living expense = *personal expense.*

living trust = *inter vivos trust.*

LLC limited liability company

LLP <1> lifelong learning plan. <2> limited liability partnership.

load = *front-end load.*

load-adjusted return the return on a mutual fund adjusted downward to reflect sales fees.

load charge = *front-end load.*

load factor = *passenger load factor.*

loading charge = *front-end load.*

loan capital = *debt capital.*

loan discount = *bank discount.*

loan ledger a ledger for entering advances made by a bank to each customer.

loan loss provision = *allowance for bad debts.*

loan-to-cost (LTC) the ratio of the price paid for a property to the value of the loan that will finance the purchase.

loan to shareholder a loan made to its shareholders by a company. ***Also***: *quasi-distribution.*

loan-to-value (LTV) ratio of the fair market value of an asset to the value of the loan that will finance the purchase.

loan-value ratio the amount borrowed divided by the appraised value of the collateral.

loan written off <UK> a loan that has been cancelled by the lender. ***See:*** *cancelled debt.*

lobbying cost amount spent to influence legislation.

local tax a tax in addition to federal and state taxes. Usually collected in the form of property taxes. ***Also***: municipal tax.

lockbox a mail box in a bank used to facilitate collection of customer remittances. ***Also***: bank lockbox.

locked-in a situation in which an investor who wants to benefit from favorable capital gains tax treatment can not sell a security until it has been held long enough to qualify.

locked-in registered retirement savings plan <Canada> a registered retirement savings plan set up to receive funds transferred from a registered pension plan on the condition that it be used solely for retirement income purpose.

locked-in yield profit or yield on securities that have been protected through hedging.

log an auditor's record of certain processing activities.

logging tax <Canada> provincial tax on logging operations in a province.

LOL limit of liability

longer-dated receivable account receivable resulted from a change in credit policy.

long form report a report prepared in addition to a *short form report*, which includes detailed comments analyzing the financial position and results of operations or setting forth the major audit procedures followed. ***Also***: detailed audit report; management-type report.

long life asset <UK> = *plant asset.*

long-lived asset = *plant asset.*

long period variable cost variable cost measured for a long period.

long run cost the cost that is to be matched with the revenue in future. ***See***: *short run cost.*

long run incremental cost (LRIC) the forward-looking incremental cost that can be accounted for by a company.

long run marginal cost (LRMC) cost with all inputs fully adjusted to additional outputs. ***See***: *short run marginal cost.*

long schedule self-employment tax schedule in detailed format.

long-term asset = *plant asset.*

long term audit program an audit program for more than one year.

long term capital gain the gain realized from the sale or exchange of investments that have been held for more than one year.

long term capital gain deduction a deduction from gross income of 60% of the net long-term gains from capital asset sale or exchange.

long term capital loss the loss realized when capital assets that have been held for longer than 12 months are sold or exchanged at a loss.

long-term debt (LTD) debt maturing in more than one year. ***Also***: funded debt.

long-term debt offset = *sinking fund.*

long-term debt ratio the ratio of long-term debt to total capitalization.

long-term debt-to-equity ratio a ratio which compares long-term debt to shareholders' equity.

long-term expenditure = *capital expenditure.*

long-term gain or loss a capital gain or loss on an investment which was held for at least one year. ***See***: *short-term gain or loss.*

long term intangible asset = *intangible assets.*

long term intangible resources = *intangible assets.*

long term investment securities investment held for long term, not realizable in a short period.

long term liability a liability which is not due within one operating cycle or one accounting year.

long term tangible resource = *plant asset.*

long term timing difference timing difference that must be eliminated over a long period of time.

look-ahead bias the use of information in a simulation that would not be available during the time period being simulated, resulting in an upward shift of the results, such as earnings forecast.

look-back method a method used to compare actual tax and previously paid taxes on a completed long-term contract.

look-through earnings investment strategy that looks at the earnings of the company rather than judging the market price.

look thru a method for calculating tax liability on income from controlled foreign corporations.

loophole = *tax loophole.*

loose-leaf book an accounting book in loose-leaf form.

loro account the account of a third party. ***Also***: third-party account.

loss <1> expense over revenue, or gross receipts. <2> decrease in net assets for which no revenue is obtained.

loss adjustment expense cost involved in an insurance company's adjustment of losses under a policy.

loss and gain account = *income statement account.*

loss and gain statement = *income statement.*

loss appropriation statement a statement showing net loss and the appropriation of it. *Also*: statement of absorption of deficit.

loss area = *loss wedge.*

loss brought forward = *deficit brought forward.*

loss carry-back a provision that operating losses may be carried back against the taxable income of the 3 preceding years. *Also*: carry-back.

loss carry-forward a provision that operating losses may be carried forward against taxable income earned in the 7 years following the loss. *Also*: carry forward; tax loss carry-forward.

loss constant surcharge added to the basic premium rate charged to reflect fixed cost of settling loss.

loss contingency a condition involving uncertainty as to possible expense. *See*: *gain contingency.*

loss control activity action that an insured company takes in order to prevent accidents or losses.

loss deferral rule a rule to prevent deferral of income and to prevent conversion of ordinary income and short term capital gain on straddle transactions.

loss forward = *deficit brought forward.*

loss from business = *business loss.*

loss from consolidation = *debit differential.*

loss from realization amount by which cash receipt from the sale of properties is less than the liabilities in liquidation.

loss from reduction of inventory to market value loss when reporting inventories at their market value when the market prices are falling.

loss from translation = *translation loss.*

loss from uncollectible account = *loss on bad debts.*

loss harvesting taking advantage of unrealized loss and using it against investment income to lower the net gains. *Also*: tax-loss harvesting.

loss of income the insured's income prior to the disability minus income after the disability.

loss of purchasing power = *monetary loss.*

loss of stock = *inventory loss.*

loss of tax deduction loss caused when the actual tax deduction exceeds that amount estimated when there is no accounting records.

loss on bad debts loss incurred by recognition of a bad debt. *Also*: bad debt loss; loss from uncollectible accounts.

loss on bond conversion excess of the value of common stock over the carrying value of a convertible bond after conversion.

loss on constructive retirement = *constructive loss.*

loss on disposal of fixed assets the loss resulting from the disposal of a fixed asset. *Also*: business investment loss.

loss on inventory taking = *inventory loss.*

loss on inventory valuation the amount by which the appraised value of all assets at the end of an accounting period is less than the book value of them.

loss on involuntary conversion amount by which payment from the insurance company is less than the carrying value of an asset lost in involuntary conversion.

loss on redemption of stock excess of the price paid in the redemption of a stock over the market price.

loss on sale of assets the loss resulting from the sale of an asset.

loss on sales excess of cost over selling price. *Also*: sales loss.

loss on settlement loss realized by creditors on settlement of debt, it equals assets' fair value less than the carrying amount.

loss on tax sale loss realized on the foreclosure sale of property due to delinquent tax.

loss potential = *loss wedge.*

loss ratio <1> of an insurance company, ratio of losses incurred plus loss adjustment expense to the premiums earned for a twelve-month period. ***See***: *combined ratio; expense ratio.* <2> ratio at which partners share the losses. <3> ratio of loss to net sales.

loss reserve any accounts established to reflect, by means of a present deduction, anticipated future losses.

loss statement an income statement in which there is a net loss.

loss through standing = *inventory loss.*

loss wedge the area between the total revenue line and the total costs line when the revenue is less than the break-even point. ***Also***: loss area; loss potential.

lost account ratio a ratio of lost customers to the total number of accounts maintained by a particular salesperson.

lost capital = *reduction of capital.*

lost cost = *sunk cost.*

lost discount = *discount lost.*

lost units the physical units that are lost in the process of production.

lost units cost manufacturing costs, which should be allocated to lost units.

lot accounting = *aggregate accounting.*

lot costing = *class costing.*

lot method = *specific identification method.*

lot-midpoint method a method of determining the average costs of a lot by the costs at the midpoint of its output level.

lot size = *contract value.*

low cost any cost that is very small in amount.

lower of average cost or market retail method retail inventory method that uses the lower of the average cost or the market price for the basis of the cost percentage. ***Also***: conventional retail method.

lower of cost or market (LCM) = *cost or market, whichever is lower.*

lower-of-cost-or-market test audit test by comparing the recorded inventory cost with the net realizable value.

lower of cost or net realizable value concept a concept which holds that the asset should be valued at the lower of cost or the net realizable value.

lower of historic cost or net realizable value the lower of historic cost or net realizable value of an asset.

lower of investment value or current cost the lower of the investment value or current cost of a security or asset.

lower of original cost or replacement cost the lower of original cost or replacement cost of an asset.

lower of total cost or total market the lower of total cost or total market value of assets when using total inventory method.

lower rate <UK> tax rate on income subject to lower rate, such as *savings income*, foreign income etc. ***Also***: lower Schedule F rate.

lower Schedule F rate = *lower rate.*

lowest acceptable rate of return = *cut-off rate of return.*

low income annual household income that does not exceed 80% of the median household income for a given area.

low income allowance fixed minimum dollar amounts deductible that varied with the filing status.

low-income housing credit a tax credit allowed annually over a 10-year period beginning with the tax year the qualified building is placed in service. ***Also***: credit for low-income housing.

LP limited partnership

LPP listed personal property

LPR Business Law and Professional Responsibilities

LRA lagged reserve accounting

LRCM long-run marginal cost

LRIC long run incremental cost

LTC loan-to-cost

LTD long-term debt

LTM last twelve month

LTV loan-to-value

LUC lessor's unreimbursable cost

lump-sum acquisition the acquisition of several assets at the same time.

lump-sum charge off charging asset cost to expense for one time rather than amortizing it.

lump-sum distribution lump sum proceeds from a partnership liquidation after all assets have been sold and all creditors satisfied.

lump-sum method elimination of items of subsidiaries regardless of the acquisition dates.

luxury automobile limit maximum amount on the depreciation a taxpayer can take annually on an expensive automobile used for business purposes.

luxury car tax <Australia> 25% tax on a luxury car in additional to GST.

luxury tax a tax on products not considered essential, such as expensive cars.

M m

M&P income manufacturing and processing income

M&P tax credit manufacturing and processing tax credit

M a/c <1> my account. <2> merged account.

machine computation <Canada> calculation of tax by a computer.

machine-hour overhead rate the rate of overhead cost on the machine hours worked.

machine hour rate the rate at which the use of equipment is charged for estimating and costing purposes.

machine hours method a method of apportioning overhead costs on the proportion of machine hours.

machine posting the posting performed by bookkeeping machines.

machinery and plant <UK> = *plant asset.*

machinery ledger a subsidiary ledger for machines. *Also*: machinery register.

machinery register = *machinery ledger.*

macro-accounting = *aggregate accounting.*

MACRS modified accelerated cost recovery system

MAGI modified AGI

mail float = *float period.*

mail rule an internal control rule that requires all incoming mail to be opened in the mailroom.

main account = *controlling account.*

main book the book that must be kept under double entry accounting system. *Also*: head book; major book; principal book.

main material cost direct material costs minus cost of the purchased parts.

main product cost joint costs minus revenue from the sale of byproducts plus further processing cost.

maintenance cost <1> cost incurred in maintaining the equipment and plants. *Also*: upkeep cost. <2> = *operating cost.*

maintenance ratio of railroad companies, total expenses involved in the upkeep of road and equipment divided by gross revenue.

major book = *main book.*

majority holding ownership in a company by holding more than 50% of its voting stock.

majority interest the interest in a company by holding more than 50% of its voting stock. *Also*: controlling interest; parent's equity.

majority interest tax year the tax year of one or more of the partners having an aggregate interest in partnership profits and capital more than 50% on each *testing day.*

majority-owned subsidiary a subsidiary more than 50% of its controlling interests are owned by its parent company.

majority shareholder single shareholder who controls 51% or more of all outstanding shares. *See*: *interested shareholder.*

make-or-buy decision a decision of whether to make or buy a product (or a component) the firm needs to produce its products.

make up depreciation = *amortization gap.*

make-up money variance that portion of labor cost variance caused by the payment of make-up wages.

make-up wages payment to female employees who have left the workforce to have their children or to raise their children.

managed audit a self-audit of the books and records by a taxpayer under the guidelines set by some states.

managed capacity cost capacity cost the amount of which could be controlled by the management, such as salaries and staff wages.

managed cost = *programmed cost.*

managed fixed cost = *discretionary fixed cost.*

management accounting the accounting designed to provide information for the managers of a firm. ***Also***: accounting for internal reporting; internal report accounting; managerial accounting.

management advisory service accounting service dealing with the design, installation and improvement of a client's accounting system, plus advice on planning, budgeting, forecasting and all other fields of accounting.

management approach based on the way management organizes segments internally to make operating decisions and assess performance.

management assertion the representation of the management of a company.

management audit the assessment of all management functions and techniques to establish the current level of effectiveness.

management control report a report that summarizes the variance in standard costing and the effect on the gross profit.

management discussion & analysis (MD&A) first section of the financial statement of a government, a discussion by management of the significant activities of the government as a whole during the period and for the future.

management expense ratio (MER) = *expense ratio.*

management fee <1> a fee charged by a bank for managing a bond issue. ***Also***: manager's fee. <2> fee charged by mutual fund managers. <3> = *advisory fee.*

management fraud fraudulent reporting that makes the financial statements misleading. ***Also***: fraudulent financial reporting.

management letter a letter from the auditor to the managers which contains professional advice. ***Also***: accountant's report; letter to management.

management planning management's planning of the future operations of a firm.

management representation = *letter of representation.*

management review a review by an external auditor of management's performance.

management's discussion section in a quarterly or annual report in which the management describes the prior period operating results and the current outlook.

management statement a statement to stockholders and creditors prepared by the company's management.

management type report = *long form report.*

manager an executive in a public accounting firm who supervises two or more concurrent audit engagements.

managerial accounting = *management accounting.*

managerial audit = *operating audit.*

managerial control functions by measuring and evaluating the effectiveness of other controls.

managerial cost accounting that phase of accounting that provides cost information for control, planning, and decision making.

mandatory accrual a tax rule under which a taxpayer with *acquisition discounts* must use accrual basis.

mandatory conversion premium dividend preferred stock = *participating equity preferred stock.*

mandatory convertible = *participating equity preferred stock.*

maneuver = *windows dressing.*

man-hour method = *direct labor hour method.*

man-loading technique = *staffing technique.*

manufactured dividend <1><UK> a payment under a contract for the transfer of shares and may represent tax-free dividend to the recipient. <2> = *in lieu of dividend.*

manufactured goods = *finished goods.*

manufactured product cost = *cost of goods manufactured.*

manufacturers excise tax a federal tax on some manufacturers in gasoline, firearms and tires industries.

manufacturing account an account showing the direct cost of the production. ***Also***: production account; works account.

manufacturing and commercial expense = *overhead.*

manufacturing and processing income <Canada> income of a company in the business of manufacturing and processing.

manufacturing and processing tax credit <Canada> a federal tax reduction available to manufacturing and processing income not subject to the small business deduction. ***Also***: M&P tax credit.

manufacturing budget a statement of the estimated costs for materials, direct labor, and overhead associated with producing the number of units estimated in the production budget.

manufacturing burden = *factory overhead.*

manufacturing burden rate method a method requiring that a negative or positive difference between total budget overhead cost allocated to ending inventory and the total amount of such cost actually required to be allocated to such goods be treated as an adjustment to the ending inventory in the taxable year in which the difference arises.

manufacturing cost the cost incurred to produce goods for resale. ***Also***: cost to make; factory cost; works cost.

manufacturing cost of goods sold manufacturing cost that has been allocated to the goods sold. ***Also***: factory cost of sales.

manufacturing cost variance difference between the actual manufacturing cost and standard manufacturing cost.

manufacturing expense = *factory overhead.*

manufacturing expense-in process = *overhead in process.*

manufacturing labor the labor consumed in manufacturing, assembling, rework or testing of products.

manufacturing margin the excess of selling price over the manufacturing cost of a product. ***Also***: variable manufacturing margin.

manufacturing overhead = *factory overhead.*

manufacturing overhead budget = *factory overhead budget.*

manufacturing profit amount by which the cost of self-made asset is lower than the market price of the same asset. ***Also***: profit from manufacturing.

manufacturing statement a financial report showing the costs incurred to manufacture a product or products during a period. ***Also***: cost of production report; statement of cost of goods manufactured.

MAP Management of an Accounting Practice

March basis a convention of starting a fiscal or accounting year from the 1st of March.

marg margin

margin (marg) <1> = *gross profit.* <2> = *marginal profit.*

marginal contribution = *contribution margin.*

marginal cost (MC) the increase or decrease in cost as the result of producing one additional unit. ***Also***: extra cost. ***See***: *relevant cost.*

marginal cost accounting accounting which traces marginal cost to inventory, products, etc.

marginal cost equation revenue - marginal cost = fixed cost + profit.

marginal costing = *direct costing.*

marginal cost of acquisition extra cost of acquiring one additional unit of input. ***Also***: marginal factor cost.

marginal cost of ordinary share capital cost that is calculated as (expected dividends of new shares + growth rate of the company's profit) ÷ (the issue price - unit issuance cost).

marginal cost statement a statement showing the marginal cost and the marginal revenue of each product and the whole factory.

marginal cost variance the difference between actual marginal cost and the marginal cost allowed.

marginal efficiency of capital (MEC) annual percentage yield earned by the last additional unit of capital. *Also*: marginal efficiency of investment.

marginal efficiency of investment <1> = *internal rate of return.* <2> = *marginal efficiency of capital.*

marginal factor cost (MFC) = *marginal cost of acquisition.*

marginal income <1> personal income other than the regular wages and salaries. <3> = *additional income.* <3> = *marginal profit.*

marginal income ratio = *contribution margin ratio.*

marginal note = *footnote.*

marginal overhead additional overhead cost that will be newly incurred if it is decided to make another unit of output. *Also*: additional overhead.

marginal profit excess of marginal revenue over marginal costs. *Also*: additional net income; margin; marginal income; variable profit. *See*: *contribution margin.*

marginal rate = *marginal tax rate.*

marginal reserve accounting bank accounting for determining the legal reserve of this week by the sum of the liabilities of the previous two weeks and 100% of the change in deposits.

marginal revenue (MR) extra revenue from selling or producing one additional unit of product.

marginal tax rate the rate that applies to an additional dollar of income to be earned. *Also*: marginal rate.

margin contribution = *contribution margin.*

margin income = *spread income.*

margin of profit = *profit margin.*

margin of safety (M/S) <1> the difference between a company's current sales and sales at its breakeven point, when sales are above the break-even point. *Also*: safety margin. <2> excess of the expected market value of the equipment over the amount financed to buy it. <3> = *buffer stock.*

margin of safety ratio (M/S ratio) calculated as: (the actual sales - the breakeven sales) ÷ actual sales.

margin of solvency = *net worth.*

marital deduction a provision that permits the deceased to leave up to 50% of the estate to the spouse, with this amount deductible from the taxable estate.

marital deduction trust a trust that benefits the surviving spouse arranged to assure the estate tax base was reduced by the estate tax marital deduction. *Also*: A trust; marital trust.

marital transfer = *unlimited marital transfer.*

marital trust = *marital deduction trust.*

mark-down ratio a percentage of a price reduction to the original price.

marked-to-market <1> a treatment of section 1256 contracts held by a taxpayer at year end as if it has been sold for its fair market value on the last business date of the year. <2> the revaluation of stocks based on a decline in their market price.

market adjustment a/c an account used to record unrealized holding gain or loss of investment securities.

market auction preferred stock = *auction rate preferred stock.*

market-book ratio market price of a share divided by book value per share.

market cap = *market capitalization.*

market capital = *market capitalization.*

market capitalization the market price of the total number of shares outstanding of a public company. ***Also***: capitalization; equity value; market cap; market capital; market value; shareholder value.

market conversion price = *conversion parity price.*

market data approach an appraisal method under which the value of a property is based on the sales prices of comparable properties. ***See***: *cost approach; income approach.*

market discount <1> amount by which the market price of a security is below its issue price. ***See***: *original issue discount.* <2> the excess of stated redemption price of a bond at maturity over the taxpayer's basis for the bond immediately after acquiring it. ***See***: *acquisition discount.*

market discount bond a bond having a market discount, except: <a> short-term bonds having a fixed maturity dates of up to one year; <b> tax-exempt bonds bought before May 1, 1993; <c> US savings bonds; and <d> certain serial bonds.

market impact cost the result of a bid/ask spread and a dealer's price concession. ***Also***: price impact costs.

marketing activity variance the difference between the budgeted capacity and the sales volume of products of that period.

marketing audit auditor's analysis of market environment, objectives, strategies and marketing activities. ***See***: *sales audit.*

marketing budget details of advertising, and promotional activities, public relations, marketing research, customer services, and also selling costs, and distributing budget.

marketing cost variance difference between actual cost of marketing and the standard cost.

marketing mix cost variance calculated as: (the actual quantities sold - the target quantities sold) × (planned contribution margin - the average contribution margin). ***Also***: sales margin mix variance; sales mix variance.

marketing overhead = *selling overhead.*

marketing overhead expenditure variance the difference between the actual selling overhead and the budgeted selling overhead.

marketing premium = *original issue premium.*

marketing variance the difference between the ex ante and ex post budgeted activity level. ***Also***: forecast variance.

market portfolio = *market return.*

market price the price determined by buyers and sellers in the market. ***Also***: price.

market price basis <1> the basis of reporting assets at their market value in the balance sheet. <2> a method for determining intercompany transfer price by the market price of the same item.

market price method <1> a method of determining yield from stock investment by adding the market price effects to the dividends received. <2> a method of sharing joint costs based on the proportion of selling price of the joint products. <3> a method of estimating the property value by its market price.

market related value amount used to calculate expected return on pension plan asset, it can be either FMV or calculated value that recognized changes in the fair value in a systematic and rational manner.

market replacement cost = *current cost.*

market return the return on the market as a whole. ***Also***: market portfolio.

market risk <1> day to day potential for an investor to experience losses from fluctuations in securities prices. <2> = *systematic risk.*

market timing cost cost that arises from price movement of a stock during a transaction period but attributable to other activity.

market-to-book ratio = *price/book ratio.*

market value = *market capitalization.*

market value adjustment (MVA) increase or decrease in the surrender charge of a life insurance policy or annuity contract depending on the market.

market value method <1> a method of recording conversion of convertible bond to common stock, the difference between the fair market value of stock and the carrying amount of bond is recognized as gain or loss. *See*: *book value method.* <2> = *relative sales value method.*

market value ratio a ratio that relates the current market price of the common stock to a selected other financial statement item, such as *price/book ratio.*

markon amount added to the cost to arrive at the sales price. *Also*: markup.

mark-to-market method = *cost adjusted for fair value method.*

mark-to-market selection = *section 475(f) selection.*

mark-to-market system a method in which investors trading on the commodity futures exchanges are credited with unrealized gain or loss daily, losses require immediate cash deposits, and those unrealized gains can be withdrawn.

markup = *markon.*

marriage penalty consequence of the current tax system which results in most married people collectively paying more in taxes, whether they file jointly or separately, than they would if they weren't married. *Also*: marriage tax.

marriage tax = *marriage penalty.*

marriage value <UK> the amount by which the value of two companies, if merged, is greater than the sum of their separate values.

married age allowance <UK> an age allowance available to a married taxpayer.

married couple's allowance <UK> extra tax allowance for a married couple. (Withdrawn since Apr 6, 2000 except for people over 65.)

married filing jointly (MFJ) husband and wife file one tax return.

married filing separately (MFS) married individuals file their tax return separately, two returns.

marshalling the listing of assets and liabilities in a balance sheet according to their liquidation order.

marshalling of assets principle a doctrine the gist of which is that the equities of partners in the balance sheet are listed according to their liquidation order if there is not enough left over after all the debts have been paid.

MASEC Management Advisory Services Executive Committee

Massachusetts business trust = *business trust.*

Massachusetts trust = *business trust.*

mass assets a group of individual items of property not necessarily homogeneous each of which is minor in value relative to the total value of such group, usually accounted for only on a total dollar or quantity basis. *Also*: unitary assets.

mass asset theory a judicial concept that the elements of goodwill can not be broken down into distinct items.

massive statement a statement showing the performance of many projects concerning environmental impacts.

mass tax a broad tax that affects a majority of taxpayers.

master budget a comprehensive or overall plan for the business that typically includes budgets for sales, production, equipment, cash and a planned income statement and balance sheet. *Also*: across-the-board budget; comprehensive budget; general budget; overall budget; universal budget.

master control account = *controlling account.*

master limited partnership (MLP) a partnership that looks like a corporation in that it acts like one and is traded on a stock exchange, but is taxed like a partnership. *Also*: public limited partnership; publicly traded partnership.

master pension plan a qualified retirement plan sponsored by a financial institution. *Also*: prototype plan.

master's account an account used by the agency bookkeeping in which the operating capital of the corporation is finally entered.

master trust <1> a collection of funds from individual investors that are pooled together in order to obtain prices and rates that are not available for investors. <2><Canada> a trust that invests funds from a registered pension plan or a deferred profit sharing plan.

mat. material

matchable expenditure <Canada> deductible expenditure related to certain income.

matching concept a concept the gist of which is that when balancing cost against income to arrive at a net profit or loss during a period, the cost taken is accrued cost and income is accrued income. *Also*: accrual concept; concept of matching costs with revenues; concept of matching revenue with expense.

matching contribution a type of contribution an employer chooses to make to employee's employer-sponsored retirement plan.

matching cost with revenues the process under which items of income and expenses are associated in a manner designed to clearly reflect net income or loss.

matching principle a principle the gist of which is that all the expenses incurred in earning a revenue be deducted from the revenue in determining profit or loss. *Also*: cost matching income principle; matching rule; principle of matching costs with revenue.

matching rule = *matching principle.*

matching view = *revenue-expense view.*

material (mat)(mat'l)(mtl)(mtr) integral component of the finished goods.

material asset = *tangible asset.*

material audit internal audit that focuses on the cost of materials.

material burden = *indirect material cost.*

material information the information which would be likely to affect a stock's price once it becomes known to the public.

material in process material in the process of manufacturing and not yet finished.

material inventory material held in stock.

materiality <1> a concept that decision makers should take into account only those factors which will be significantly affected by their decision. <2> relative importance of a transaction or an account balance to the financial statements under audit. <3> in cost control, a situation whereby the percentage of cost variance on the budgeted cost is more than 10%.

material ledger the ledger for recording the receipts, issues and balances of every raw material item in stock. *Also*: stores-in-out book; stores ledger; stores received and issued book.

material participation the participation in a trade or business on a regular, continuous and substantial basis.

material price standard an estimate of what the average price of a unit of a given type of raw material should be for the coming period under economic purchasing conditions.

material quantity standard estimate of the quantity of a given type of material that should be used in manufacturing a unit of output under carefully controlled operating conditions.

material rate percent of material cost on the value of output. *Also*: materials-output ratio.

materials cost expense incurred to acquire the materials to be used in the production of the goods. *Also*: cost of materials.

materials cost method a method of apportioning factory overhead cost by the proportion of the materials cost.

materials cost variance the difference between the actual materials cost and the standard materials costs. *Also*: materials variance.

material scrap = *scrap.*

material scrap variance that portion of the materials usage variance due to the material scrap. ***Also***: scrap variance.

materials issued cost the cost of raw materials issued to the manufacturing departments.

materials mix variance that portion of the materials usage variance because of the variation in materials mix.

materials-output ratio = *material rate.*

materials price variance (MPV) difference between price actually paid for raw materials and those that should have been paid at standard.

materials purchases budget a budget which shows the quantity and cost of each material.

materials quantity variance = *materials usage variance.*

materials return journal (MRJ) a journal for recording material returns.

materials standard cost = *standard material cost.*

materials under-valuation adjustment book adjustment made when the actual materials cost exceeds the standard materials cost.

materials usage price variance a variance caused by the difference between the actual usage price and the standard price.

materials usage variance (MUV) difference between quantities of raw materials used and the quantities that should have been used when standards are applied. ***Also***: materials quantity variance; materials yield variance.

materials variance = *materials cost variance.*

materials yield variance = *materials usage variance.*

material variance = *significant variance.*

material weakness a condition that does not reduce to a relatively low level the risk that material misstatements might occur and not to be detected timely by employees in the ordinary course and performing assigned function.

mathematical solution allocation = *algebraic method.*

mat'l material

matrix bookkeeping old bookkeeping system that uses spread sheet to set the credit items (column) and debit items (row) into a matrix. ***Also***: bookkeeping in matrix form; only one entry bookkeeping; vector bookkeeping.

matrix form = *spread sheet.*

maturing liability a debt soon due to be paid.

maturity date the date on which a bill or note, an insurance policy, or a bond becomes due for payment or repayment. ***See***: *due date.*

maturity factoring an arrangement that provides collection and insurance of accounts receivable.

maturity gap = *duration gap.*

maturity value = *accumulated amount.*

maximum cost the maximum amount of cost that may incur. ***Also***: ultimate cost.

maximum foreseeable loss (MFL) maximum dollar that can be lost if a catastrophe occurs. ***See***: *maximum probable loss.*

maximum probable loss (MPL) maximum dollar amount that can be lost under realistic situation. ***See***: *maximum foreseeable loss.*

maximum tax rate tax rate that would apply to the various tiers of income subject to tax.

MC marginal cost

MCT mainstream corporation tax

MD&A Management Discussion & Analysis

meals and entertainment expense tax deduction up to 50% of the cost of meals and entertainment incurred in the ordinary course of business.

mean-per-unit estimation classical variables sampling that projects the sample average to the total population by multiplying the sample average by the number of items in the population. ***Also***: simple extension. ***See***: *difference estimation.*

mean return average expected return of an investment, when all possible outcomes are considered.

means of salvaging means used by an auditor for rendering piecemeal opinion when he can not provide either qualified or unqualified opinions.

measured income = *permanent income.*

measurement base <UK> the monetary attribute of the element of financial statements. *Also*: accounting base.

measurement date <1> the date at which employee knows both the number of shares granted and the options price. <2> date on which the company decides to discontinue a division of business. *See*: *phase-out period.*

measurement standard cost = *basic standard cost.*

measuring unit error an error that may happen when the financial statements have not been adjusted by the price level index.

MEC marginal efficiency of capital

median rule <Canada> a rule that uses the middle amount of the cost of acquisition, FMV on valuation day and the proceeds from disposition as the basis of the asset for capital gain purpose. *Also*: tax-free-zone method. *See*: *valuation day value method.*

medical expense a taxpayer's money spent for medical reason.

medical expense credit <Canada> a 16% tax credit on qualified medical expenses that are in excess of the lessor of $1,728 and 3% of the taxpayer's net income.

medical expense deduction an itemized deduction allowable to individuals for the unreimbursed payments for medical care and for certain drugs.

medical savings account (MSA) a trust account, like an IRA, that may be established by a taxpayer, under which earnings are not taxable, and distributions are not taxable.

Medicare program that funds the federal health program for people over 65.

Medicare levy <Australia> amount payable by a taxpayer to cover some cost of the public health system.

Medicare levy surcharge <Australia> additional Medicare levy when a taxpayer's taxable income exceeds a threshold amount.

Medicare tax portion of *FICA tax*, 1.45% for both employers and employees and 2.9% for *self-employed.*

members' voluntary liquidation *voluntary liquidation* of a company following a resolution by the shareholders. *Also*: shareholders' voluntary liquidation. *See: creditors' voluntary liquidation.*

memorandum column method a method for recording branch inventory at cost and the selling price is recorded in a memorandum column showing the gross profit.

memorandum entry a journal entry with description only, no debit or credit amounts are included.

memorandum of agreement (MOA) an agreement setting forth the rules of IRA e-file program. *See*: *request for agreement.*

memorandum of association <UK> a document filed with the Company Registrar by a new company, giving the title of the company, particulars of the business, amount of capital, address of the office, kinds of shares, etc. *See*: *by-laws.*

memorandum of audit (MOA) = *audit memo.*

mental accounting the tendency to categorize funds or items of value even though there is no logical basis for the categorization.

mental or physical impairment credit <Canada> a tax credit of $989 allowed to a taxpayer with a severe and lengthy mental or physical impairment.

MEP multi-employer plan

MER management expense ratio

mercantile method a method of determining the rate of return on a given investment by using the financial statements figures. *Also*:

accountant's method; accounting rate of return method; approximate rate of return method; book value method; financial statement method; unadjusted rate of return method.

mercantile rate of return = *accounting rate of return.*

merchandise inventory unsold merchandise on hand at a given time. ***Also***: actual articles; inventoried goods; stock goods; stock in trade.

merchandise ledger a detailed ledger for recording receipt, selling and the balance of each merchandise on hand.

merchandise purchases budget an estimate of the units and costs of merchandise to be purchased by a company.

merchandise trade balance the difference between the value of US goods exported to other countries and foreign goods imported into the US.

merged account (M a/c) an account which contains the balance carried forward from the last budget year.

merger one company acquires all assets and liabilities of one or more other companies in exchange for stock, cash or other consideration. ***Also***: absorption; amalgamation; amalgamation by absorption; business combination; combination. ***Opp***: *demerger.* ***See***: *acquisition; consolidation.*

MES marketable equity security

method of accounting = *accounting method.*

method of average price at the close of the preceding month a method under which the average price at the end of the preceding month is used as the average price at the close of this month.

method of continued distribution = *continuous allotment method.*

method of fixed percentage on cost = *straight-line method of depreciation.*

method of "ignoring" = *method of "neglect".*

method of least minimum (MLM) = *least square method.*

method of "neglect" a method under which the lost units are "neglected", and the manufacturing cost is distributed to the perfect units only. ***Also***: method of "ignoring".

method of price of last purchase = *last invoice price method.*

method of straight basis lines = *straight line method of depreciation.*

metric conversion cost <Canada> the cost of converting any measuring instrument or tool to the metric system.

mezzanine debt a debt that incorporates equity-based options, such as stock warrants, with a lower-priority debt.

mezzanine financing a preferred stock with a sinking fund to retire the issue within eight years.

MFJ married filing jointly

MFL maximum foreseeable loss

MFS married filing separately

micro accounting the accounting for a person, a company, or a government agency. ***Also***: entity accounting. ***See***: *aggregate accounting.*

micro cap under $250 million capitalization. ***See***: *large cap; mid cap; small cap.*

micropayment an electronic transaction consisting of the transfer of a very small sum of money.

mid cap $1 billion to $5 billion capitalization. ***See***: *large cap; micro cap; small cap.*

middle rate the tax rate on the middle tax bracket. ***See***: *first rate; top rate.*

mid-month convention = *half-month convention.*

mid-quarter convention a convention that applies to personal MACRS property, if more than 40% of the aggregate cost of the property is placed in service in the 4th quarter, then all properties are treated as mid-quarter.

mid-term audit = *interim audit.*

mid-term gain or loss profits from the sale of property owned more than one year but not more than 18 months.

mid-year convention = *half-year convention.*

mileage allowance <UK> a deduction of automobile expenses for people using their vehicles for business, charity, moving, medical, or any other allowable reason. ***See***: *fixed profit car scheme.*

millennium gift aid <UK> a plan that a taxpayer can make a gift of £100 or more to certain registered charities until Dec 31, 2000.

mill rate tax per dollar of assessed value of property, one mill is one-tenth of a cent.

mine development cost the cost incurred to develop minerals.

mine exploration cost the cost incurred before a mine has reached the development stage.

minimum acceptable rate = *cut-off rate of return.*

minimum amount <Canada> 16% of the amount by which a taxpayer's adjusted taxable income exceeds the basic exemption less the basic minimum tax credit.

minimum attractive rate of return = *cut-off rate of return.*

minimum cash balance safety cushion needed to avoid a possible cash shortage.

minimum cut-off criterion = *cut-off rate of return.*

minimum distribution the minimum annual required distribution amount for an IRA holder who reaches age 70. ***Also***: required minimum distribution.

minimum lease payment (MLP) regular rental payments excluding executory costs to be made by the lessee to the lessor in capital lease.

minimum legal capital amount that shareholders must invest in a company or be liable to its creditors.

minimum liability (ML) amount required when the accumulated benefit obligation exceeds the fair value of pension plan asset. ***Also***: minimum pension liability; unfunded accumulated benefit obligation.

minimum payment the smallest amount which can be paid on a revolving charge account to avoid penalty.

minimum pension liability = *minimum liability.*

minimum pension liability adjustment an element of other comprehensive income, it equals the excess of additional pension liability over unrecognized prior service cost.

minimum required rate of return = *cut-off rate of return.*

minimum requirements for filing = *filing threshold.*

minimum stock = *buffer stock.*

minimum stock method = *base stock method.*

minimum tax = *alternative minimum tax.*

minimum tax on items of preference = *corporate minimum tax.*

minimum value method a method used to calculate stock based compensation expense as the total of present value of exercise price and present value of expected dividend times the number of options granted.

minimum wage the smallest hourly wage that an employee may be paid as mandated by law.

minimum yield the yield to call or yield to maturity, whichever is lower.

mining reclamation trust = *qualifying environmental trust.*

min-max system = *optional replenishment inventory system.*

minority interest stockholders' equity in a subsidiary not owned by the parent company. ***Also***: noncontrolling interest.

minority shareholder a shareholder who owns less than 50% of the voting stock of a company. ***Also***: noncontrolling shareholder.

minus asset amount that must be deducted from the original cost of an asset to arrive at its net value.

minus item an item such as expenditures, increase in assets, decrease in liabilities, etc. appearing in the balance of payments. ***Also***: debit.

minus yield a condition in which a convertible bond is selling at a premium higher than the interest yield on the bond.

minutes book a formal record of the issues discussed and actions taken in meetings of stockholders and of the board of directors.

Miranda warning a warning issued by an IRS special agent when investigating criminal tax case, letting the taxpayer know that what he says may be used against him in court.

MIRR modified internal rate of return

misappropriation = *embezzlement.*

misappropriation of assets = *embezzlement.*

miscellaneous asset = *other asset.*

miscellaneous cost the cost that is not frequently incurred and small in amount. *Also*: incidental cost.

miscellaneous deduction = *miscellaneous expense deduction.*

miscellaneous excise tax federal excise tax on other items such as telecommunication, air freight etc.

miscellaneous expense <1> a nonrecurring expense that is very small in amount. *Also*: other incidental expense; out-of-pocket expense; sundry expense. <2> hospital charge in addition to room and board.

miscellaneous expense deduction tax deduction not specifically set forth on the tax return schedule, such as medical, interest, state tax, charitable, and union dues expense, etc. *Also*: miscellaneous deduction.

miscellaneous income <Canada> income not specifically listed as a single taxable item, such as personal service, student income, etc.

mischarge an error made in the process of charging an account.

misleading a wrong direction given to those who read the financial statements because of the mistakes and incompleteness of the statements.

misposted account an account into which an entry has been misposted. *Also*: principle.

misposting = *error in posting.*

misstatement an error, fraud or a direct illegal amount that has an immediate impact on reported figures.

mixed account an account having both nominal and real elements.

mixed business asset <UK> an asset used for both business and non-business purposes.

mixed cash-accrual basis = *modified cash basis.*

mixed cost the cost that is not clearly variable or fixed, but is a combination of both.

mixed curvilinear cost a cost that increases with activity, above a fixed increment, at an increasing or decreasing amount per unit.

mixed-dollar income = *monetary income.*

mixed fund <UK> a fund consisting of the proceeds of both real and personal property.

mixed income a balancing item in the income distribution account that equals value added minus salaries and wages, minus taxes and plus subsidies receivable. *Also*: operating surplus.

mixed linear cost a cost that has a fixed incremental and on top of that a variable increment that increases the same amount with each equal increase in activity.

mixed service cost the service cost portion of which must be capitalized under *capitalization rule.*

mixed shares the shares that have priority in dividend but have no or less priority in residual assets. *See*: *junior stock.*

mixed step cost = *step-variable cost.*

mixed variance = *joint variance.*

mix variance <1> cost variance caused by substitution of one factor of production for another factor. *Also*: rate composition variance. *See*: *joint variance.* <2> = *joint variance.*

ML <1> marginal loss. <2> minimum liability

MLP <1> master limited partnership. <2> minimum lease payment.

MOA <1> memorandum of agreement. <2> memorandum of audit.

MOAJ manufacturing overhead applied journal

modern internal audit = *operating audit.*

modified absorption costing absorption costing method by which fixed and variable costs are recorded in two separate accounts.

modified accelerated cost recovery system (MACRS) ADS modified by recent changes, it classifies depreciable assets into one of several recovery periods, each of which has a designated pattern of allowable depreciation.

modified accrual a method under which government revenue is recognized when it becomes available and measurable. ***Also***: cash flow accounting.

modified adjusted gross income adjusted gross income increased by any amount excluded from gross income.

modified aggregate method = *aggregate method.*

modified AGI (MAGI) AGI used to calculate provisional benefit tax amount, it equals AGI + foreign income, social security benefit, adoption assistance, US savings bond, IRA contribution, passive loss, and educational loan interest.

modified alternative minimum taxable income AMTI determined without regard to alternative tax net operating loss.

modified approach an approach under which infrastructure assets are reported in the government wide Statement of Net Assets at their cost without reduction for accumulated depreciation.

modified basis a custom that uses cash basis at daily bookkeeping, but uses accrual basis at the end of the period.

modified book value = *adjusted book value.*

modified cash basis a basis that treats an asset cost as one to be depreciated over its life, expenses such as rent or advertising paid in advance are also regarded as assets and are deductible only in the period to which they applied. ***Also***: mixed cash-accrual basis; obligation basis.

modified equity basis a basis under which investment in subsidiaries is adjusted through an account called the Unrealized Subsidiary Earnings, and subsidiary earnings are recognized only when the dividends from subsidiaries have been received.

modified internal rate of return (MIRR) internal rate of return adjusted for negative cash flow.

modified partial plan a partial plan under which costs based on the actual quantities and standard prices are debited to the Work-in-Process a/c, which also reflects every price variance.

modified percentage-of-completion method = *10% method.*

monetary approach an approach which uses money as a measure for the balance of payments.

monetary asset an asset the stated amount of which is fixed by contract or commitment regardless of price level changes.

monetary capital = *free capital.*

monetary gain any gain arises from holding monetary liabilities during a period where there has been a rise in the price level, or holding monetary assets during a price declining period. ***Also***: gain of purchasing power; general price-level gain; general purchasing power gain; holding gain; purchasing power gain; realizable cost savings.

monetary income net income adjusted by the purchasing power of money. ***Also***: mixed-dollar income. ***See***: *operating income.*

monetary liability any liability having money amounts fixed by contract or commitment regardless of the price level changes. ***Also***: money value liability.

monetary loss any loss arises from holding monetary assets during inflation, or from holding monetary liabilities during deflation. ***Also***: carrying loss; general price-level loss; general purchasing power loss;

holding loss; loss of purchasing power; purchasing power loss.

monetary measure accounting custom of using money for measuring transactions. *Also*: money measure.

monetary measurement unit principle a principle which holds that accounting should use money in measuring assets, capital, liabilities, revenue, expense, and profit or loss, etc. *Also*: monetary principle.

monetary/non-monetary approach accounting approach of translating foreign subsidiary statements to the home currency, the monetary items are translated at current exchange rate, and the non-monetary items are translated at historical rate.

monetary principle = *monetary measurement unit principle.*

monetary working capital working capital including trade debtor prepayments, trade bills receivable, stock out subject to a cost of sales adjustment, and sometimes minus trade creditors, accrued revenues, and trade bills payable. *Also*: net monetary working capital.

money balance sheet a balance sheet showing money receipts and disbursements during a period by social accounting.

money capital = *free capital.*

money circuit account = *flow of funds account.*

money cost <1> cost that can be measured in terms of money. <2> = *cost of capital.*

money flow account = *flow of funds account.*

money income the income measured in terms of money. *Also*: nominal income; relative income.

money market preferred = *auction rate preferred stock.*

money market preferred stock = *auction rate preferred stock.*

money measure = *monetary measure.*

money payment <UK> = *cash payment.*

money purchase = *money purchase plan.*

money purchase plan <Canada> a defined contribution plan under which the employer's contributions are mandatory based on each participant's compensation. *Also*: money purchase.

money purchase provision <Canada> a registered pension plan that provides each member with whatever level of benefit that the plan will buy. *See*: *defined benefit provision.*

money purchase scheme <UK> an occupational pension scheme the pension benefit of which is linked to the fund value, depending on the contribution and the investment return. *See: final salary pension.*

money unit adjusted accounting = *constant dollar accounting.*

money value liability = *monetary liability.*

monitoring IRS activities to ensure that e-file providers are in compliance with the IRS requirements.

monkey money = *scrip.*

Monte Carlo simulation an analytical method that randomly generates values for uncertain variables over and over to simulate a model.

month-end average cost method a method of determining this period's issue cost by the price at the close of the preceding period.

monthly basis a basis under which journal entries are posted into the ledger monthly.

monthly trial balance a trial balance prepared monthly.

morale audit an audit of the employee's morale in an organization.

more-than-50% test = *percentage test.*

mortgage interest deduction tax deduction allowed for interest paid out of the mortgage of the taxpayer's house. *Also*: deductible mortgage interest; qualified housing interest.

mortgage loan a loan for which repayment is secured by a mortgage.

mortgage pass-through = *pass-through security.*

mortgage pass-through security = *pass-through security.*

mortgage point = *point.*

Moti more-out-than-in

movable = *movable property.*

movable property a property that is not fixed in place or intended to be a permanent part of *immovable property. **Also***: movable.

movie shelter = *completed film tax shelter.*

moving annual total (MAT) a method under which budget amounts of the coming month will be added to the annual budget, and that of the first month will be subtracted.

moving average inventory method = *moving weighted average method.*

moving expense deductible expense that is related to moving the family, and possessions because of employment reasons.

moving expense deduction a deduction allowed to employees and self-employed individuals as an adjustment to gross income for the *moving expense.*

moving weighted average method a method used in perpetual inventory under which raw material issues are priced at the weighted average cost computed after each purchase. ***Also***: moving average inventory method.

MPL maximum probable loss

MPV materials price variance

MR marginal revenue

MRJ materials returned journal

M/S margin of safety

MSA medical savings account

mtl material

mtrl material

MU money unit

MUA money unit accounting

multi-block system a system under which the contribution and the marginal profit are calculated and reported separately according to the classification of the products or sales districts, and the income statement shows the direct costs. ***Also***: relative contribution approach.

multi-column account = *columnar account.*

multi-column journal = *columnar journal.*

multi-dimensional bookkeeping the bookkeeping that utilizes cost models or other decision models to provide information that satisfies the needs of every party.

multi-employer plan (MEP) <Canada> a registered pension plan in which a group of employers participate. ***See***: *single-employer plan.*

multilateral netting system elimination of offsetting cash flows between a parent and several subsidiaries. ***See:*** *elimination.*

multi-national accounting = *international accounting.*

multi-national netting elimination of offsetting cash flows within a multinational corporation's books.

multi-origin cost variance cost variance caused by more than one factor.

multi-party nontaxable exchange a deal under which party A wants to make a like-kind exchange of property with party B who does not own the property but will buy it from party C and will exchange it with A.

multiple = *price/earnings ratio.*

multiple asset account an account containing more than one asset, created for the purpose of depreciation or cost recovery deductions.

multiple asset depreciation accounting the accounting methods for the depreciation of the multiple assets, such as classification method, composite method, and group method. ***See***: *open-end account.*

multiple capital structure = *complex capital structure.*

multiple costing using different costing methods in the same factory.

multiple methods two accounting methods used by a taxpayer, one for the personal books and the other for business books.

multiple overhead rates a method under which a different predetermined overhead rate is set for each department.

multiple posting method the posting of entries into the subsidiary ledger as well as into the general ledger by carbon papers in one writing.

multiple recording government accounting under which entries are made in more than one fund, when there are two or more funds each having authority over the transaction.

multiple regression analysis a statistic method for determining fixed and variable behavior of cost used when the behavior of the costs is thought to be closely associated with two or more factors, e.g. the hours and temperature of a machine, etc.

multiple-step approach an income statement preparation method by which revenues and expenses are matched in several steps to obtain several interim totals.

multiple-step classified income statement = *classified, multiple-step income statement.*

multiple-step combined income and retained earnings statement a combined income and retained earnings statement prepared under multiple-step approach.

multiple-step income statement an income statement on which cost of goods sold and the expenses are subtracted in steps to arrive at net income.

multiple-straight-line method = *straight-line method of depreciation.*

multiple-support agreement an agreement under which two or more taxpayers, who together provide more than half the support for someone else, agree that one will claim that person as a *dependent* and the others will not.

multiple voting share <UK> = *classified stock.*

multiplier method a method under which the value of human resources of current period is determined by multiplying the value of the human resources of the previous period by the percentage change in the current income.

multi-product breakeven point breakeven point for a company selling a number of products determined by using a hypothetical unit made up of units of products in their expected units.

multi-section income statement an income statement on which the factory variable costs and the selling variable costs are reported separately to arrive at the manufacturing margin and the selling margin.

multi-step classified income statement = *classified, multi-step income statement.*

multi-step cost reassignment reassignment of cost that requires one or more intermediate activity cost reassignments prior to the cost assignment into the final cost object. *See*: *algebraic method; reciprocal service cost allocation.*

muni = *municipal bond.*

municipal accounting the accounting for city governments.

municipal bond debt obligation issued by a state or a local municipal entity. *Also*: muni; tax-exempt bond; tax-exempt security; tax-free bond.

municipal revenue bond a *municipal bond* supported by a pledge of revenue from a specified income generating facility such as a toll road or power plant. *Also*: revenue bond.

municipal tax = *local tax.*

mutual debts <UK> debts between two parties.

mutual fund trust <Canada> a unit trust in which all holdings and transactions comply with regulations.

mutual wills <UK> wills between two parties leaving estates reciprocally to the survivor.

MUV material usage variance

MVA market value adjustment

my account (M a/c) = *nostro account.*

N n

NAA National Association of Accountants

NAARS National Accounting Automated Research System

naked trust = *passive trust.*

name control the last four letters of a taxpayer's last name for identification purpose.

name of account = *account title.*

nanny tax various payroll or employment taxes assessed on wages paid to household employees. ***Also***: domestic employer tax; household employment tax.

narrative form <1> a form of reporting the operating results and the financial positions of a firm by descriptive words rather than the financial statements. <2> = *report form.*

narrative form balance sheet = *report form balance sheet.*

narrative form income statement = *report form income statement.*

NASBA National Association of State Boards of Accountancy

national account a major account for transactions of all locations throughout a country.

National Accounting Automated Research System (NAARS) computerized database for retrieving annual reports of the public companies and governmental entities, and authoritative promulgation of accounting and auditing of the AICPA, FASB, SEC etc.

National Association of Accountants (NAA) = *Institute of Management Accountants.*

National Audit Office <UK> the government office charged with examining government departments and local authorities.

national balance sheet the balance sheet that includes all sectors of a nation's economy. ***Also***: combined national balance sheet.

national child benefit (NCB) <Canada> a supplement to *child tax benefit*, $1,255 for the first child $1,055 for the second child and $980 for each subsequent child.

national economic accounting the reporting of the cost incurred in complying with anti-pollution, safety and health, and some other socially beneficial requirements and impact of the business entity on, and its endeavors to protect the society, its amenities and the environment. ***Also***: economic accounting; social accounting.

national income an income earned by a country's people, including labor and capital investment.

national income accounting the procedure which provides information about a nation's operation of the economic system in terms of specific activities such as capital formation, production, and consumption etc.

National Income and Product Account (NIPA) a statement prepared by the national economic accounting which shows the national income and national products for a given period.

national income and product accounts including the following 5 parts: consolidated business and product account; consolidated government receipts and expenditure a/c; personal income and expenditure account; the rest of the world account; and the gross savings and investment account.

national insurance contribution (NI) <UK> a tax levied on an employed or self-employed taxpayer for old age pension.

national insurance number <UK> a unique number (two letters followed by 6 numbers then another letter) used in identifying a person responsible for national insurance contributions.

National Society of Accountants (NSA) the national association for individuals with an interest in accounting. ***Formerly called***: National Society of Public Accountants

National Society of Public Accountants (NSPA) = *National Society of Accountants.*

national tax policy the way a country chooses to allocate tax burdens.

national wealth statement the modified form of the national balance sheet on which the obligations and credits among sectors of the economy have been eliminated. ***Also***: consolidated national balance sheet.

NAT number <Australia> a unique, 4-digit number allocated to each tax form and publication by the Australian Taxation Office.

natural acquisitions cost method = *last invoice price method.*

natural business year a year ending at the annual low point in business activity or at the end of a season. ***See***: *fiscal year.*

natural classification the classification of costs into labor, material, supplies, etc. that refers to the basic physical aspects of cost. ***Also***: natural grouping.

natural cost a cost classified according to its basic nature, such as salaries, material, expense, etc.

natural cost system a system under which all natural costs would be gathered together as a total for this item.

natural currency = *reporting currency.*

natural grouping = *natural classification.*

natural hedge foreign currency hedging that arises in the course of normal business.

natural resource long-term asset purchased for the physical substances that can be taken from them and used up rather than for the value of its location. ***Also***: resource property.

NAV net asset value

NCB national child benefit

NCGA National Council of Governmental Accounting

NDP net domestic products

N/E no effects

near-cash asset that portion of the liquid asset other than cash.

necessary expense = *tax deductible expense.*

necessary retained earnings retained earnings after the non-monetary items have been adjusted by the general price level index.

negative account balance credit balance in the accounts that normally have debit balances, or debit balance in accounts that normally have credit balances. ***Also***: encircled balance. ***See***: *red balance.*

negative amortization a gradual increase in mortgage debt that occurs when the monthly payment is insufficient to cover the interest due, and the principal balance owed keeps increasing.

negative asset a contra asset item or a liability.

negative asset distribution high level of fear of debt that the consumer will go to great lengths to avoid debt altogether or at the very least, decrease debt dramatically over a short period of time.

negative assurance the opinion made by an auditor stating that no material modifications should be made to the financial statements. ***Also***: limited assurance.

negative basis tax basis in property of less than zero.

negative carry condition in which the cost of borrowing money exceeds the return from it, usually implies a loss, except when some tax advantages may result. ***Also***: benefit of carry; negative cost of carry. ***See***: *carry.* ***Opp***: *positive carry.*

negative confirmation the confirmation of accounts payable and receivable balances by sending out letters which will be returned to the auditor's only when the balance differs from that of the recipient's. *See*: *positive confirmation.*

negative contribution margin excess of variable cost over revenue.

negative cost of carry = *negative carry.*

negative debt = *owner's capital.*

negative equity decline in the value of an asset after it is purchased to a level lower than the outstanding loan balance that financed the purchase.

negative gearing an investment strategy in which related costs such as interest exceed income from the asset, thus creating a deduction against other income.

negative goodwill <1> amount by which current fair value of the company is less than the carrying value of its net assets. *Also*: bad will; deferred credit. <2> = *credit differential.*

negative income tax <1> a program for a guaranteed minimum income, which provides income maintenance payments based on low income. *Also*: social dividend. <2> a payment from the state to the people with incomes below the subsistence level, usually amount by which the income tax liability is less than the tax credits.

negative incremental cost = *incremental income.*

negative monetary position a situation of holding an excess of monetary liabilities over the monetary assets.

negative net salvage value a case in which the cost of removal is expected to be greater than the salvage realized, or in which the demolition costs will be incurred without realizing any salvage value.

negative net worth = *deficiency.*

negative profit = *net loss.*

negative variance = *unfavorable variance.*

negative verification the verification of a bank statement if no difference is reported in 30 days the accounts will be considered correct.

negative working capital a situation in which the current liabilities of a firm exceed its current assets.

negligence an accountant or auditor's failure to conduct an audit with due care. *Also*: ordinary negligence; simple negligence. *See*: *gross negligence.*

negligence penalty the 5% to 20% penalty imposed by the IRS on a taxpayer for negligence.

negotiated price method a transfer pricing method that uses a price arrived at through negotiation.

neoclassical school a group of people who still comply with the historical cost principle, but do not use the money unit postulate in recognizing changes in the general price level. *Also*: general-price-level-adjusted historical cost accounting.

net accretion concept a concept under which net income should be measured by increases in an individual's wealth during a period. *See*: *asset-liability view.*

net adjusted present value the *adjusted present value* minus the cost of an investment.

net after-tax gain capital gain minus tax.

net amount payable <Australia> total amount of tax liability and Medicare levy.

net annual income <Canada> gross annual income less taxes, CPP, UIC.

net asset cover = *asset cover.*

net assets <1> active assets minus the negative assets. *Also*: capital. <2> the fixed assets plus net working capital. <3> = *net worth.*

net assets equation of an insurance company: premium income + investment income - dividends - policies surrendered for benefits - death claims - general expenses = net assets.

net assets per share = *book value per share.*

net assets released from restriction of a nonprofit organization, temporarily restricted net assets that became unrestricted during the year due to the expiration of time restrictions or the performance of purpose restrictions.

net asset value (NAV) calculated as (market value + cash in hand - debts) ÷ the number of shares the mutual funds has outstanding.

net asset value per share = *book value per share.*

"net" basis = *"net" method.*

net book value <1> face amount of bond minus issuance cost minus unamortized discount or plus unamortized premium, used to calculate gain or loss on redemption of bond. <2> = *written-down value.*

net capital it equals total capital - borrowed capital - deferred capital. *Also*: pure capital.

net capital employed all fixed and current assets less current liabilities.

net capital gain the excess of the net long-term capital gain for the year over net short-term capital losses for the year.

net capital loss net amount after combination of long-term capital loss and short-term capital loss.

net capital ratio SEC requirement that all broker-dealers maintain a ratio of no more than 15:1 debt to liquid assets.

net cash balance beginning cash balance plus cash receipts minus cash disbursements.

net cash flow net cash left after paying cash expenses and debt services, it equals net income plus depreciation less dividends paid.

net cash inflow = *contribution margin.*

net cash investment <UK> the fund invested in a lease by a lessor.

net company tax <New Zealand> *company tax* minus refunds.

net contribution this period to long period profit from operations contribution margin less capacity cost of the current period.

net cost <1> cost of an item before the expense of doing business are added. <2> gross cost less financial gain. <3><Canada> amount paid for the shares of a labour-sponsored fund less any assistance received.

net cost method = *ledger cost method.*

net current assets = *working capital.*

net current asset value per bond the value of the current assets alone applicable to a given bond after the deduction of all prior liabilities.

net current cost estimated current cost of an asset after deduction of accumulated depreciation.

net debt <1><UK> the borrowings of a firm together with related derivatives less cash and liquid assets. <2> the sum of fixed and existing liabilities less sinking fund and other assets that are earmarked for payment of the liabilities. *Also*: net long-term debt. <3> = *net federal debt.*

net deferred tax asset deferred tax asset net of related valuation account.

net direct interest expense interest expense on short-term government obligations after deduction of discounts.

net dividend <UK> a dividend excluding the tax credit enjoyed by shareholders.

net domestic products (NDP) the gross domestic products minus depreciation.

net earned surplus forward = *unappropriated retained earnings.*

net earnings = *net income.*

net earnings from self-employment = *self-employment profit.*

net errors and omissions = *errors and omissions.*

net estate the estate left to the beneficiaries after deductions for administering the estate.

net family income <Canada> net income of a taxpayer and spouse or common-law partner.

net federal debt the *gross federal debt* minus financial assets, such as loans, investments and foreign exchange accounts. ***Also***: net debt.

net financing cost = *carry*.

net float the total of *collection float* and *disbursement float*.

net free cash flow (NFCF) a measure of cash flow available after an enterprise meets its essential obligations, calculated as EBITDA minus cash taxes, cash interest, preferred dividends, and capital expenditures.

net income (NI) <1> excess of revenues over expenses of a business in a given period. ***Also***: excess of revenue over expenses; net earnings; net profit. ***See***: *profit*. <2> amount received by a taxpayer after deducting taxes, social security payments, and other expense. ***Also***: income. <3><Canada> = *adjusted gross income*.

net income after depreciation net income less capital consumption.

net income after tax net income less income tax. ***Also***: net operating profit after tax.

net income approach an approach under which the value of a business equals the capitalized net income plus the market value of the stock outstanding and minus market value of liabilities.

net income before income taxes = *pre-tax accounting income*.

net income before interest and taxes (NIBIT) net income before deducting interest expense and income taxes. ***Also***: earnings before income and taxes; operating income.

net income multiplier price of an asset divided by the net income it generates in a given period.

net income per books net income computed per GAAP. ***Also***: book income; income per books. ***See***: *net income per return*.

net income per return income shown on the tax return. ***Also***: taxable income. ***See***: *net income per books*.

net income per share of common stock = *primary earnings per share*.

net income stabilization account <Canada> an account under the net income stabilization account program.

net income stabilization account program <Canada> a program allowing manufacturers to put aside money in good years to draw in years when income is low.

net income to net worth = *return on equity*

net increase amount of the increase in the book value of an insurance company over a period of time.

net interest excess of interest payments made by the domestic business sector over its interest receipts from other sectors, plus net interest received from abroad.

net interest cost (NIC) total interest that will be paid on a debt.

net interest earned rate earned on an insurance company's average investments net of investment expenses but before income taxes.

net interest margin dollar difference between interest income and interest expenses.

net investment <1> investment in a project less depreciation. <2> in lease, present value of the sum of minimum lease payment and the unguaranteed residual value. <3><UK> net assets in a foreign subsidiary plus the equity stake in it.

net investment income <1> *investment income* less expenses associated with that investment. <2> investment income reduced by a child's itemized deduction for kiddie tax purpose.

net investment income per share investment income of a mutual fund less management fees and administrative expenses, divided by its total number of shares outstanding.

net invoice method a method of accounting for cash discounts under which such discounts are excluded from income until the discounted goods are sold.

net lease lease whereby the lessee undertakes to pay all the expenses of maintaining the leased property, such as insurance, taxes, utilities, repair, etc. ***See***: *gross lease*; *net net lease; net net net lease.*

net level premium life insurance premium that is constant from year to year.

net liquid assets liquid assets minus current liabilities.

net liquidation balance in the balance of payments, basic balance plus the noncurrent short-term capital plus errors and omissions.

net liquidation value the amount, after expenses and taxes, that can be realized for listed and readily marketable securities held by a corporation subject to accumulated earnings tax.

net long-term capital gains the excess of long-term capital gains or the taxable year over long-term capital losses for the taxable year. ***Also***: net section 1201 gain.

net long-term capital loss the excess of long-term capital losses for the year.

net loss (NL) <1> the excess of expenses over revenue. ***Also***: negative profit; red-ink entry. <2> loss absorbed by the insurance company minus reinsurance applicable to the loss.

net margin = *net profit margin.*

"net" method a method under which the minimum lease payments and unguaranteed residual value are debited in asset accounts, and unearned interest is credited in the same account. ***Also***: "net" basis. ***See***: *"gross" method.*

net method <1> a method of calculating the foreign tax credit for pre-1976 years and for distribution from less developed country corporations before 1979 to the extent such dividends were paid out of pre-1976 earnings and profits. <2> method used to account for purchase of goods, any purchase discounts offered are assumed taken and the purchase account reflects the net price, if subsequent to the recording of purchase, a purchase discount loss a/c is debited. ***See***: ***gross method.*** <3> a method for recording forward contract under which fair value from contract is not recorded.

net minimum tax minimum tax defined by Section 55 of the Revenue Code.

net monetary working capital = *monetary working capital.*

net national income = *real net national disposable income.*

net negative overhead variance excess of total actual factory overhead over total standard factory overhead.

net net income the amount that emphasizes the net income resulting in usable cash, after all costs and expenses have been paid.

net net lease a lease in which the lessee pays rent to the lessor, as well as insurance and taxes that arise from the use of the property. ***Also***: double net lease. ***See***: *gross lease; net lease; net net net lease.*

net net net lease a lease in which the lessee pays rent, as well as all expenses, insurance and taxes that arise from the use of the property. ***Also***: triple net lease. ***See***: *gross lease*; net lease; *net net lease.*

net-of-tax cost of capital calculated as capital cost × (1 - rate of tax). ***Also***: after-tax cost of capital.

net-of-tax method a method that treats the tax effect as an contra item to an asset or liability and not showing deferred tax in a balance sheet. ***See***: *deferral method.*

net operating earnings excess of gross profit from operations over operating expenses.

net operating income (NOI) income after deducting for operating expenses but before deducting for income taxes and interest. ***Also***: net operating profit.

net operating income approach a method of calculating the market value of stock issued by a corporation as (net operating earnings ÷ capitalization rate) - liabilities.

net operating loss (NOL) <1> the excess of operating expense over gross profit, provided that rate of capitalization remains unchanged when the financial leverage changes. *Also*: operating loss; revenue loss. <2> the excess of allowable deductions over gross income from a trade or business with adjustments.

net operating loss carryback net operating losses first carried back to the third year preceding the year of loss, and to the loss year, etc. until fully absorbed.

net operating loss carryovers net operating loss carried forward to 5 or 15 taxable years after the year of loss.

net operating loss deduction (NOL deduction) the aggregate of the net operating loss carryovers to such tax year plus the net operating loss carryovers or carrybacks to that year which is treated as a tax deduction. *Also*: operating loss deduction.

net operating margin net operating income divided by revenues.

net operating profit = *net operating income.*

net operating profit after tax (NOPAT) = *net income after tax.*

net operating profit less adjusted tax (NOPLAT) measure of the total cash available for distribution to financial capital contributors, which equals operating profits for a firm with adjustments made for taxes.

net passive income passive investment income reduced by deductions directly connected with the production of income.

net performance an increase or decrease in net asset value exclusive of additions, withdrawals and redemption.

net periodic benefit cost = *net periodic pension expense.*

net periodic pension expense excess of the sum of service cost-benefits earned, interest cost and net amortization and deferral over actual return on plan asset. *Also*: net periodic benefit cost.

net periodic pension income excess of actual return on plan assets of a pension plan over the sum of the following items: service cost, benefits earned, net amortization, deferral and interest cost.

net plant of utilities companies, the value of assets and facilities used in supplying utility service, taken at their original costs less depreciation.

net positive overhead variance excess of total standard, or anticipated factory overhead costs over total actual factory overhead.

net premium <Canada> gross premium on an insurance policy less dividends received or receivable and less premium returned.

net premiums written of an insurance company, the aggregate net amount of the premiums of all policies issued during the year, after deducting returns and reinsurance premiums.

net present value (NPV) present value of the future cash inflows from the project minus the cost of the initial investment.

net present value method a method for evaluating investment alternatives by comparing the present value of their expected cash inflows.

net price method recording invoices at the full amount of the sale price less offered cash discounts. *See*: *gross price method.*

net proceeds <1> amount received from the sale or disposal of property less all direct costs associated with the sale or disposal. <2> amount received from the issuance of securities less floatation cost.

net profit (n/p) <1> = *net income.* <2> = *pretax accounting income.*

net profit margin net profit divided by net revenues. *Also*: net margin. *See*: *profit ratio.*

net purchases total purchases minus purchase returns and allowances and discount, then plus freight-in.

net quick assets (NQA) quick asset minus current liability.

net realizable value <1> amount computed by subtracting expected additional costs of processing a joint product after the split-off point from the expected sales value of that product. <2> what an asset will bring into the firm when sold, after deduction of costs of sale. *Also*: resale value; settlement value.

net realizable value accounting the accounting method for restating the balance sheet assets by the net realizable value measured in money.

net realizable value method a method for assigning joint costs to the joint products in proportion to their net realizable values.

net realizable value operating income the sum of operating income from sales and the operating income of inventory.

net realized capital gains per share amount of long-term capital gains that an investment company realized on the sale of securities, less the long-term capital losses and divided by the number of shares outstanding.

net receivables accounts receivable less allowance for bad debts.

net recognized built-in gain the less of the amount that would be the S corporation's taxable income if only *recognized built-in gains* and losses are taken into account, or the taxable income determined without taking into account NOL carryovers or dividend-received deductions.

net redemption yield = *grossed-up redemption yield.*

net relevant earnings <UK> amount of a person's *relevant earnings* less the amount of deductions for income tax purposes.

net residual income the controllable residual value less uncontrollable interest expense.

net revenue <1> total revenue less unrealized revenue. <2> revenue less total costs of a responsibility center.

net sales total sales less discounts, allowances and returns.

net salvage value the excess of gross salvage value over the estimated cost of removal, permissible except under the asset depreciation range system.

net section 1201 gain = *net long-term capital gain.*

net short-term capital gain the excess of short-term capital gains for the taxable year over the short-term capital losses.

net short-term capital loss the excess of short-term capital losses for the taxable year over short-term capital gains for the year.

net state income tax deduction excess of amounts deducted from income for the payment of state taxes over the amounts included in income as a recovery of prior amounts paid through deductions.

net statutory income = *total income.*

net surplus profit remaining after subtracting for operating expenses, taxes, interest, insurance and dividends.

net tangible assets <1> net worth minus goodwill. <2> total assets minus intangible assets and liabilities.

net tangible assets per share calculated as (total assets - intangible assets - all liabilities - par value of preferred stock) ÷ number of common stock outstanding.

net tax-exempt income the excess of the interest on obligations of a state or political subdivision taxable under federal law over amounts of expense and interest that would be disallowed under the federal law plus any proper adjustment to the basis.

net tax liability tax liability minus tax credits available.

net terminal value terminal value of the cash inflows associated with a project minus the terminal value of the cash outflows at a specified time.

net total assets = *net worth.*

net unearned income adjusted gross unearned income reduced by the standard deduction for a child dependent and adjustments such as early withdrawal penalty.

net unrealized depreciation excess of the unrealized depreciation over unrealized appreciation in an asset.

net unrealized gain or loss on a portfolio, the difference between the aggregate market value and aggregate cost.

net value of debt total value of a business minus total debt.

net variance net amount after combining favorable variance and the unfavorable variance.

net working capital = *working capital.*

net working capital per share working capital divided by number of shares outstanding.

net world income <Canada> income from all sources both inside and outside Canada.

net worth (NW) a firm's total assets in excess of total liabilities. ***Also***: accounting capital; book equity; book value; capital; capital employed; capital liability; capital owned; dollar-and-cents difference; economic surplus; invested capital; investment in net assets; margin of solvency; net assets; net total assets; own capital; proprietorship; surplus; total equity.

net worth assessment <Canada> assessment of a taxpayer's net worth by the Minister.

net worth method <1> a method whereby the IRS provides that an individual understated taxable income by showing that individual has acquired more assets than would be bought by the stated income. <2> a method of reflecting foreign currency values, under which profits are determined by calculating the fixed assets at historical costs and net worth of current assets and liabilities at the beginning of the year at currency rates then prevailing, and adding remittances during the year and subtracting year-end current net worth at year-end rates.

net worth ratio net worth divided by total capital.

net worth to debt ratio = *equity-debt ratio.*

net worth turnover = *equity turnover.*

net yield rate of return on an investment after subtracting all expenses, such as commission and taxes.

neutrality quality of accounting information that requires freedom from bias.

new account-conversion ratio the ratio of new customers to total prospective customers.

new balance the current balance of an account immediately after a transaction has been entered in it.

new markets tax credit a tax credit on investment in shares issued by a qualified community development entity.

new section 38 property any property qualifying for the investment tax credit, that is first used by the tax payer.

new shareholder someone who was not a shareholder on the first day of the year when the company elected to be an S corporation, but bought the shares in later days.

newspaper technique a way of audit report, like a newspaper, completely showing a firm's financial position and operating results.

new surplus the surplus after reorganization. ***See***: *old surplus.*

New York interest the interest computed on the exact number of days in a month, not a 30-day month. ***Also***: exact interest. ***Opp***: *Boston interest.* ***See***: *365-day-per-year basis.*

New York method a method for amortizing the premium on mortgages that mutual savings banks and cooperative banks have purchased, acquired or originated at a premium payable in installments.

next-in, first-out method (nifo) a method under which the issue cost of raw materials or goods is calculated by the estimated price of the next purchase.

N/F no funds

NFCF net free cash flow

NG net gain

NI <1> national income. <2> national insurance contribution. <3> net income.

NIAT net income after taxes

NIBIT net income before interest and taxes

NIC net interest cost

nifo next-in, first-out

nimble dividend rule a state law rule that allows corporations to pay dividends out of current profits, despite cumulative losses.

nine-by-four layout = *9 by 4 layout.*

ninety-day letter = *90-day letter.*

ninety percent test = *90% test.*

NIPA National Income and Product Account

NIS not in stock

NIT negative income tax

NL net loss

NNO nongovernment, nonbusiness organization

no-action letter an SEC letter indicating that no civil or criminal action will be taken against an individual engaging in a particular activity.

no change letter a letter issued in a correspondence audit indicating that the tax return is accepted as filed.

nodal cost flow network source of the cost reassignment and downstream cost objects are thought of as sending and receiving nodes in a network.

no-dividend shares the shares the issuing company of which has never declared dividends for a long time.

no effects (N/E) = *non-sufficient fund.*

no funds (N/F) = *non-sufficient fund.*

NOI net operating income

NOL net operating loss

NOL deduction net operating loss deduction

nominal account <1> a temporary account used only for a single accounting period, and for which balances are closed out at the end of the period. ***Also***: fictitious account; provisional account; temporary account. <2> = *impersonal account.*

nominal asset <1> asset that has implicit value. <2> asset that is reported at its book value. <3> = *fictitious asset.*

nominal capital the sum of the face price of all shares authorized and issued. ***Also***: dedicated capital; face capital; nominal share capital. ***See***: *authorized capital stock.*

nominal cost an expenditure that has no character of cost but which is treated as a cost. ***Also***: quasi-cost.

nominal dollar financial statement = *unit of money financial statement.*

nominal income = *money income.*

nominal interest rate = *coupon rate.*

nominal ledger = *impersonal ledger.*

nominal price = *face value.*

nominal profit = *fictitious profit.*

nominal rate = *coupon rate.*

nominal reserve loss reserves which are not discounted for the time value of money.

nominal share capital <UK> = *nominal capital.*

nominal value = *face value.*

nominal yield amount of income earned from a fixed-income security divided by the par value.

nominee a person holding assets for another person.

nominee dividend the dividend that a person receives on behalf of someone else.

nominee interest the interest that a person receives on behalf of someone else.

nominee share a share held by a nominee company, e.g. a trustee for the true owners.

nominee shareholder <UK> a registered owner of shares in a company, but who holds the shares on behalf of another person.

nominee trust a trust the beneficiaries of which are not named, and to be selected by the trustee.

non-accredited investor individual who does not meet the SEC criteria of an *accredited investor.*

non-accrual asset an asset considered by a bank auditor as a slow-moving asset, or maybe a bad debt. ***See***: *accrual asset; slow loan.*

non-accumulation method a method under which total cost of a product is simply the sum of all the costs incurred in each process. *Also*: nonpyramid inventory method.

non-adjusting event <UK> a post-balance sheet event that concerns conditions which did not exist at the balance sheet date.

nonadmitted asset = *inadmitted asset.*

nonallocable receipts cash received from carryout sales or services to which a service charge of at least 10% is added, and which need not to be reported as gross income.

non-amortizable asset an asset the cost of which is not necessarily amortizable. *Also*: unamortizable asset.

non-arm's length <Canada> of a transaction between parties not dealing with each other at *arm's length.*

non-articulated view a view based on the belief that articulation leads to redundancy since all events reported in the income statement are also reported in the balance sheet prepared by using fifo while the income statement may use lifo.

nonassessable stock a stock whose owner cannot be assessed in the event of failure or insolvency. *Opp*: *assessable stock.*

nonaudit service an accounting service not related to audit.

non-base currency = *functional currency.*

non-borrowed reserve = *free reserve.*

non-budgetary transaction a transaction involving offsetting financial assets and liabilities thus leaving *net federal debt* unchanged.

non-business bad debt bad debt that qualifies for short-term capital loss treatment. *See*: *business bad debt.*

nonbusiness damage any damage not related to business, such as personal physical injury or personal physical sickness.

nonbusiness expense deduction expense not incurred in the course of a trade or business but nevertheless deductible.

nonbusiness income tax <Canada> income tax paid to a foreign government for income not generated from a business.

non-callable bond equivalent yield = *option-adjusted yield.*

noncapital expense = *revenue expenditure.*

non-capital loss <Canada> <1> the excess of expenses over income of a mutual fund, which can be offset against a shareholder's ordinary income. <2> = *business loss.*

non-CART any peer review not scheduled by AICPA or state CPA society staff.

non-cash dividend = *dividend in kind.*

non-cash expense an expense which does not require an outlay of cash e.g. depreciation. *See*: *out-of-pocket cost.*

noncash income income not in cash.

noncompensatory plan employee stock option plan created for an ordinary issue of stock and does not involve compensation expense.

nonconformance cost = *cost of failure.*

non-constant cost = *variable cost.*

noncontributory plan pension plan that employer makes no contribution.

noncontrollable cost = *uncontrollable cost.*

noncontrolling interest = *minority interest.*

noncontrolling shareholder = *minority shareholder.*

noncumulative = *noncumulative preferred stock.*

noncumulative preferred dividend preferred dividend that does not accumulate when unpaid.

noncumulative preferred stock a class of preferred stock on which the dividend does not accumulate if not paid every year. *Also*: noncumulative.

noncurrent asset an asset not expected to be sold or exchanged within the operating cycle of the business.

noncurrent liability claims against the assets of an entity that will become due in one year or more.

noncurrent receivable account receivable that can not be collected in the current period.

nondeductible contribution difference between total permitted contributions and total deductible contributions to an IRA.

nondeductible expense any expense not allowed by tax laws to be deducted from gross income. *Also*: disallowable expense; tax-unallowable expense.

nondeductible IRA an IRA the contributions are not tax deductible but the earnings are tax deferred. *See*: *deductible IRA; Roth IRA; traditional IRA.*

nondeductible tax state or local tax paid out but not allowed as a deduction in the federal tax return.

nondepreciable asset a fixed asset, such as land, which does not deteriorate with the passage of time, and not exhausted through use.

nondifferential cost = *sunk cost.*

nondischargeable debt a debt declared by the US Congress that can not be cancelled in bankruptcy, e.g. alimony. *See*: *dischargeable debt.*

nondiscretionary deduction a deduction from gross estate to arrive at adjusted gross estate, e.g. funeral expense.

nondiscretionary dividend <1> a dividend that is not based on the operating results of the company. *See: discretionary dividend.* <2> = *preferred dividend.*

nondiscretionary trust a personal trust the trustee of which has no discretion in deciding how income will be distributed.

nondistributable asset = *appropriated retained earnings.*

nondividend distribution a distribution that is not treated by tax laws as a dividend but rather as a return of capital if the distributing corporation lacks earnings. *See*: *liquidating dividend.*

non-equity dividend a dividend related to a non-equity share.

non-equity share a share issued by a credit union which represents a debt to the holder. *See: equity share.*

non-equity shareholder a holder of a non-equity share.

nonexchange transaction a transaction in which a government gives or receives value without directly receiving or giving equal value in exchange. *See*: *exchange transaction.*

nonexempt income any income that must be included in gross income.

nonexistent asset the asset that does not exist. *See*: *real asset.*

non-expendable trust a trust the principal of which can not be expended but the earnings can. *See: expendable trust.*

non-expendable trust fund a governmental fund restricted by a non-expendable trust agreement.

nonfarm option method a method used for determining Social Security tax for taxpayers who are self-employed, but with modest amounts ($1,600 or less) of income from nonfarm self-employment.

non-financial asset the asset with a physical value, such as real estate or personal asset. *See*: *financial asset.*

non-financial dollar financial statement = *unit of money financial statement.*

non-flexible budget = fixed budget.

nonforfeitable post-retirement benefit obligation = *vested benefit obligation.*

noninsured plan defined benefit plan not guaranteed by life insurance policies.

noninterest bearing note a note receivable or note payable that does not provide for interest.

noninterleaved form a form of accounting books without interleaved pages.

noninventoriable cost = *period cost.*

nonitemizer a taxpayer who does not itemize deductions.

nonledger asset <1> asset actually exists but not included in the books. *Also*: asset out of accounts; asset out of books; out-of-book asset; unlisted asset. <2> property of an insurance company that is due and payable in the current year but has yet to be received by the company.

nonledger liability = *liability out of book.*

nonliability statement <Australia> a statement of the items that do not relate to the liability statement, e.g. license fees, cash securities etc.

nonliquid asset an asset that is not readily convertible into cash without loss of principal.

nonmanufacturing cost a cost such as distribution cost, advertising cost and research cost.

nonmanufacturing expense = *operating expense.*

nonmonetary asset an asset whose money amount is not fixed by contracts or commitments.

nonmonetary exchange method of handling an exchange between one entity and another that results in the acquisition of assets or services or the satisfaction of liabilities by surrendering cash or service or issuing debt.

nonmonetary item any financial statement item stated in old dollars and therefore requiring direct adjustment in the price-level financial statements, e.g. depreciation.

non notification after assignment of accounts receivable, the debtor is not notified and payment still goes to the creditor who then remits the payment to the assignee.

non-operating asset assets that are unnecessary to the ongoing operations of a business.

non-operating gain or loss gain or loss not attributable to operations.

non-operating expense = *other deduction.*

non-operating income = *other income.*

nonopinion report = *unqualified report.*

non-par stock = *no-par-value stock.*

nonpassive income = *active income.*

nonperforming asset a bank's outstanding loan or lease that is not meeting its stated principal and interest payments.

nonperiodic distribution non-recurring distribution of funds to an employee from a retirement plan, including loans, rollovers, and lump-sum distributions.

nonpersonal account = *impersonal account.*

nonphysical asset = *intangible asset.*

nonprenotice audit = *surprise audit.*

nonprofit accounting the accounting policies, procedures, and methods employed by some nonprofit organizations.

nonprofit corporation a corporation organized for charitable, educational, religious and other purposes, and not to generate profit for the shareholders. ***Also***: not-for-profit corporation. ***Opp***: *business corporation.*

nonprofit sub-entity <Australia> a branch of a nonprofit corporation treated as if it is independent for GST purpose.

nonpublic company = *private company.*

nonpyramid inventory method = *nonaccumulation method.*

nonqualified option a stock option the income from which is ordinary income to the holder. ***Also***: non-qualifying stock option. ***See***: *qualified option.*

nonqualified retirement plan a retirement plan that does not meet the IRS (or ERISA) requirements for favorable tax treatment.

nonqualifying debt <Canada> testamentary debt other than death taxes in respect of a property or an interest in a trust.

nonqualifying real property <Canada> a real property disposed of after Feb 1992 and before 1996.

nonqualifying security <Canada> a donated share of a corporation with which the donor does not deal with at arm's length. ***Also***: prescribed security.

nonqualifying stock option (NSO) = *nonqualified option.*

nonquantifiable cost a cost the amount of which can not be measured in money.

nonreciprocal transfer <1> transfer of assets or services from a business to its owners or to another entity or vice versa. <2>

exchange of dissimilar assets in a nonmonetary transaction.

nonrecurring charge an extraordinary expense that will not recur in the future.

nonrecurring cost one time expense or write off appearing in a company's financial statement. ***Also***: extraordinary cost.

nonrecurring earnings business earnings from some special source not likely to appear again.

nonrecurring item income statement item that is either unusual in nature or infrequent in occurrence. ***Also***: incidental item.

nonrefundable credit a tax credit that can not go more than reducing a taxpayer's liabilities to zero. ***See***: *refundable credit.*

nonreproducible asset tangible asset with unique physical properties, like a parcel of land, a mine, or a work of art.

nonresident a person not maintaining residential ties in a country for tax purpose.

nonreviewable decision a Tax Court decision which becomes final in ninety days. ***See***: *reviewable decision.*

nonsampling error an error due to factors not directly caused by audit sampling.

nonsampling risk all aspects of audit risk that are not due to sampling.

nonseparable fixed cost = *fixed overhead.*

nonseparately stated income the income which is netted at the corporate level and then passed through to shareholders of an S corporation. ***See***: *separately stated income.*

nonspecific capital = *free capital.*

nonstatistical sampling a sampling whereby auditors judge risk by using professional judgement. ***Also***: haphazard sampling; judgmental sampling; judgement sampling. ***See***: *statistical sampling.*

nonstatutory options stock options that create ordinary income when exercised, to the extent of the spread between the value of the stock and the option price. ***Also***: nonstatutory stock options; unrestricted options. ***See***: *statutory stock options.*

nonstatutory stock options = *nonstatutory options.*

nonstock corporation a corporation which does not issue stock.

nonstrategic asset an asset that management considers nonessential in accomplishing business objectives.

non-sufficient fund (NSF) words on a returned check meaning there is not enough fund in the drawer's account to honor the check. ***Also***: insufficient fund; no effects; no funds; not-sufficient fund.

non sufficient fund check (NSF check) a check the drawer does not have enough fund to cover the amount. ***Also***: not sufficient fund check. ***See***: *bad check.*

non-systematic risk = *unsystematic risk.*

nontaxable = *tax exempt.*

nontaxable distribution = *nontaxable dividend.*

nontaxable dividend payment from a company, not from its earnings but as a return of investment in the stock. ***Also***: nontaxable distribution. ***See***: *dividend exclusion; return of capital.*

nontaxable exchange the exchange of properties, such as like-kind exchange and stock for stock exchange, the gain from which is not taxable.

nontaxable income = *exempt income.*

nontraceable cost = *overhead.*

nontrading asset an asset not used in the normal operations of the business.

nonvalue-added cost the cost of activities that can be eliminated without the customer perceiving and decline in product quality or performance. ***Also***: nonvalue-adding cost. ***See***: *value-added cost.*

nonvalue-adding cost = *nonvalue-added cost.*

nonvariable cost the cost that does not change in proportion to the volume of activity, such as capacity cost and programmed cost. ***See***: *fixed cost.*

nonvisible property = *intangible asset.*

nonvoting A ordinary share <UK> = *nonvoting stock.*

nonvoting stock a stock the holder of which does not have the right to vote on corporate matters. ***Also***: nonvoting A ordinary share. ***See***: *class B stock; voting stock.*

no-par stock = *no-par-value stock.*

no-par-value stock (NPV stock) a class of stock that does not have a par value assigned. ***Also***: non-par stock; no-par stock; share of no par value; stock without par value. ***See***: *par value stock.*

NOPAT net operating profit after tax

NOPLAT net operating profit less adjusted tax

normal absorption costing = *normal costing.*

normal account balance the balance of an account under normal condition, such as debit balance of an asset account.

normal-activity variance that portion of capacity variance caused by the difference between the budgeted activity level and a normal level of activity.

normal cost <1> cost that should be incurred in normal conditions. <2> = *current service cost.* <3> = *normal standard cost.*

normal costing the costing under which direct material and direct labor are actual cost, but overhead cost is normal overhead based on standard rate. ***Also***: normal absorption costing.

normal costing method a method under which the costs of a product is determined by the total of direct materials cost, direct labor costs and the normal overhead.

normal depreciation the depreciation caused by wear and tear and other natural factors. ***Also***: ordinary depreciation.

normal factory overhead rate the factory overhead rate under normal activity. ***Also***: average overhead rate; normalized overhead rate.

normalization method a method whereby the tax liabilities that would have been incurred had the utility not claimed a tax benefit are added to reserves for future taxes, thereby causing higher utility rates. ***See***: *flow-through method.*

normalization reserve a reserve set aside by some public utility companies to adjust sales to a level if the weather had been normal. ***Also***: weather normalization reserve.

normalization rule IRS rule requiring public utility companies to use normalization method.

normalized earnings <1> earnings adjusted for cyclical ups and downs in the economy. <2> on the balance sheet, earnings adjusted to remove unusual or one-time influences.

normalized overhead rate = *normal factory overhead rate.*

normalized pension the amount of lifetime benefits that would be payable immediately after the end of a year to an individual.

normalizing method a method that reports higher depreciation for tax and smaller depreciation for shareholders.

normal loss a loss that is expected by a business and for which provision is usually made in the budgeting process.

normal lost units physical units that are lost in production for the reasons that are expected during the productive process.

normal overhead <1> overhead cost that is expected to incur in normal conditions. <2> = *standard overhead cost.*

normal pension cost = *service cost.*

normal performance standard cost standard cost determined by the average of expected levels of activity for the coming periods.

normal profit the minimum return necessary to persuade capital suppliers to retain their investment in a firm.

normal rate = *coupon rate.*

normal spoilage loss of physical units that is an expected part of the production process.

normal standard cost an index expected to prevail over a period of time of sufficient length to level the effects of the seasonal and cyclical fluctuations. ***Also***: average standard cost; normal cost.

normal stock method = *base stock method.*

normal tax = *regular tax.*

normative accounting a theory which holds that accounting should be based on the events that have actually happened.

nostro account banking term to describe an account one bank holds with a bank in a foreign country, usually in the currency of that foreign country. *Also*: correspondent account; due from balance; due from bank account; my account; our account. *See*: *vostro account.*

note = *promissory note.*

note for a term = *promissory note.*

note of hand = *promissory note.*

note payable a liability evidenced by a formal written promise to pay.

note receivable a promissory note to be collected by a business from a customer.

notes receivable discounted the discounted proceeds received by the holder of a promissory note.

notes receivable journal a journal for recording notes receivable.

note to financial statements a descriptive note attached to the financial statements.

not-for-profit activity = *hobby.*

not-for-profit corporation = *nonprofit corporation.*

Notice 797 a notice to employees who have not had any tax withheld from wages because of earned income credit.

notice account a savings account in which the owner promises to tell the bank in advance before making a withdrawal.

notice of adjustment a notice from the IRS ordering the taxpayer to adjust the tax liability.

notice of assessment <Canada> an acknowledgment letter from the Canada Customs and Revenue Agency after it received a tax return from the taxpayer.

notice of deficiency = *90-day letter.*

notice of nil liability = *dispensation.*

notice of objection <Canada> a statement filed by a taxpayer who disagrees with the facts or tax levy in a notice of assessment.

notice of seizure letter or written notice from the IRS that authorizes them to liquidate a person's assets to cover income taxes due.

notional amount the referenced associated asset or liability in terms of units. *Also*: payment provision; settlement amount.

notional tax <Australia> equivalent of tax that would have been payable on business and investment income, excluding capital gains.

not ordinary resident <UK> not a resident in the UK year after year.

not posted (N/P) a term used in a column of a special journal meaning that the total amount of that column does not need to be posted to the ledger.

not sufficient fund (NSF) = *non-sufficient fund.*

not sufficient fund check (NSF check) = *non-sufficient fund check.*

not taxable = *tax exempt.*

not-taxable exchange the exchange of capital assets the gain or loss is recognized but deferred until the property is subsequently disposed of in a taxable transaction. *See*: *taxable exchange.*

n/p net profit

NPV net present value

NPV stock no-par-value stock

NQA net quick asset

NRO non-resident owned

NRV net realizable value

NSA National Society of Accountants

NSF <1> non-sufficient fund. <2> not-sufficient fund.

NSF check <1> non-sufficient fund check. <2> not sufficient fund check.

NSF charge a debit memo from the bank which is posted as a debit on the depositor's bank account statement to cancel the credit that was made when the bank receives NSF check from the customer.

NSO non-qualifying stock option

NSPA National Society of Public Accountants

NTA net tangible assets

nuisance value amount an insurance company will pay to settle a claim even though it is invalid.

nullification a state's refusal to recognize a federal law.

numbering system a system under which all the accounting documents and accounts are numbered.

number of days inventory is held = *number of days' sales in inventory.*

number of days' operations to cover working capital calculated as: (the number of days of this period × working capital deficit)/working capital from operations of the current period.

number of days' sales in average inventory number of days' sales in inventory calculated by the average inventory.

number of days' sales in ending inventory number of days' sales in inventory calculated by ending inventory

number of days' sales in inventory number of days needed to sell out the inventories, calculated as 365/(cost of sales/inventory). *Also*: average age of inventory; average inventory investment period; days' inventory; days of average inventory on hand; days to sell inventory; inventory turnover period; number of days inventory is held.

number of days' sales in receivables number of days needed to collect accounts receivable, it equals accounts receivable divided by annual sales and times 365. *Also*: accounts receivable days outstanding; average age of accounts receivable; average collection period ratio; average settlement period; average days' sales uncollected; average debtor collection period; collection period; collection period ratio; collection ratio; days in receivables; days receivable; days sales uncollectible. *See*: *days sales outstanding.*

number of shares outstanding of a company, number of share issued and held by shareholders. *Also*: shares outstanding.

number of times interest was earned = *times interest earned.*

number of times preferred dividends earned = *times preferred dividends earned.*

O o

OA old account

OAA other adjustment a/c

OAS <1> Old-Aged Security. <2> option-adjusted spread

OB opening balance

object classification the classification of ledger accounts into assets, liabilities, capital, etc.

object clause <UK> a clause in the memorandum of association setting out the object of the company.

object cost = *target cost.*

objective the purpose of an audit sampling.

objectives of financial reporting goal of presenting useful information to financial statement users so that proper decisions can be made.

objective statement cost statement expressed in direct costs or objectives of the expense.

objective value the value of an asset in terms of other assets in the market.

objectivity <1> a concept that focuses on the factual, unbiased information as a basis for a business decision. *Also*: verifiability. <2> the degree of disclosure of facts of an accounting measurement system

objectivity principle accounting rules requiring that wherever possible the amounts used in recording transactions be based on objective evidence rather than on subjective judgement. *Also*: principle of objectivity.

obligating event an event that creates a legal or constructive liability to an entity.

obligation = *liability.*

obligation basis = *modified cash basis.*

obligation bond a mortgage bond, the face value of which is greater than the value of the underlying property.

obligatory audit = *legal audit.*

OBS off-balance-sheet

obs obsolescence

observation an audit procedure pertaining to watching or witnessing the performance of some activity.

observation test physical and visual verification by inspection of financial statement items or activities.

observed depreciation amount by which the appraised value of a fixed asset is less than the acquisition cost or current replacement cost.

obsolescence (obs) a situation where because of new inventions and improvements, an old plant asset can no longer produce its product on a competitive basis.

obsolescence cost = *overage cost.*

obsolete asset an asset that is worth less on the market than it is on a balance sheet due to the fact that it has become obsolete in advance of complete depreciation. *Also*: stranded asset.

OBS risk off-balance-sheet risk

OCAR opportunity cost of revenue

OCBOA other comprehensive basis of accounting

occupational pension scheme <UK> pension plan available to salaried employees, the maximum contribution is 15% of the basic wage.

occupational tax = *special occupational tax.*

occurrence <1> the recorded transaction actually occurred. <2> = *exception.*

odd daybook a book of original entry for recording transactions occurred on odd days. ***See***: *even daybook.*

OE <1> operating expense. <2> owner's equity.

off-balance sheet accounting the contingent and contractual liabilities and assets of an organization which are not recorded on the balance sheet, such as derivative contracts, receivables sold and pension fund liabilities.

off-balance sheet asset an asset the owner of which assumes no liability that could affect his balance sheet. ***Also***: hidden asset; latent asset; off-the-book property.

off-balance-sheet financing the financing from sources other than debt and equity offerings, such as joint ventures. ***Also***: off-book financing.

off-balance sheet lease = *operating lease.*

off-balance sheet liability item not reported in the body of the financial statements as a liability but possibly requiring future payment or services.

off-balance-sheet risk (OBS risk) financial risk imbedded in instruments recognized as assets that entail conditional rights and obligations that expose the entity to a loss. ***Also***: concentration of credit risk.

off-balance-sheet transactions the contingent and contractual liabilities and assets of an organization which are not recorded on the balance sheet because of accounting convention.

off-book financing = *off-balance-sheet financing.*

offer in compromise (OIC) taxpayer's offer to settle tax liabilities for less than the total due. ***Also***: compromise offer.

offer-in-compromise fee a $150 non-refundable fee charged by the IRS for processing offer-in-compromise request.

office <Canada> the position that entitles a person to a remuneration.

office audit = *desk audit.*

office auditor IRS auditor whose job is to examine the individual tax returns. ***See***: *special agent.*

officer liability the officer's personal liability for underpayment of corporate tax.

official audit the audit of an insurance company by a government agency, such as the Department of Insurance.

official settlements account = *official settlements balance.*

official settlements balance an item in the balance of payments, which equals the sum of the net liquidating balance and the current short-term capital. ***Also***: official settlements account; overall balance; reserve transaction account; transactions in US official reserve assets and in foreign official assets in the US.

official unrequired transfer a variety of subsidies, aid, cancellation of debts, contributions to international organizations, taxes and fines.

offset reduction of private pension benefits to avoid duplication of social security benefits. ***Also***: social security offset.

offset account = *contra account.*

offset against asset = *contra asset.*

offset approach method of integrating an employee's retirement benefits with a qualified retirement plan, under which the employer offsets certain percentage of employee's Social Security benefit or disability income.

offset balance the balance after elimination of two or more items. ***Also***: counter balance.

offsetting error an error that is balanced by another mistake on the other side of the trial balance. ***Also***: compensating error; compensatory error; counter balancing error; self-correcting error.

offsetting loss a loss that is used to offset against gains.

offset to long-term debt cash and investment assets of sinking funds bond reserve, and other reserve funds held for redemption of long-term debt.

offshore trust a trust created in a foreign country to manage properties abroad on behalf of beneficiaries. *Also*: foreign trust. *See: domestic trust.*

off-site peer review a review of selected financial statements and accountant's compilation or review reports sufficient to provide a reviewer with a reasonable basis for expressing limited assurance that the reports do not depart in a material respect from professional standards. *See*: *on-site peer review.*

off-the-book property = *off-balance sheet asset.*

off the books payments for which no formal record is kept.

off-the-cuff method = *rule-of-thumb method.*

OH overhead

o'h'd overhead

OI operating income

OIC offer in compromise

OID original issue discount

OL operating loss

old account (OA) an account receivable collected after a long period of time.

Old-Aged Security (OAS) <Canada> a monthly payment to Canadians age 65 or over. *See*: *social security payment.*

old and cold transaction transactions so separated by the passage of time that they can not be integrated under the step transaction doctrine.

old and new balance proof method of proving the accuracy of account balances by adding debits to and subtracting credits from the old balance.

old balance the original balance of an account before credits and debits are entered.

old cost = *historical cost.*

old person's pension = *basic retirement pension.*

old surplus recorded surplus before the reorganization. *See*: *new surplus.*

OLS optimal lot size

omission from income a taxpayer's failure properly to include and report an amount of gross income.

omitted cost the cost that has not been included in the product cost.

omitted dividend a common stock dividend scheduled to be declared, but instead not voted for, by the board of directors. *Also*: passed dividend. *See*: *accumulated dividend; dividend in arrears.*

omnibus account a ledger account used by a futures dealer to record the transactions with more than one customer.

on account <1> payment made toward the settlement of an account. <2> = *partial payment.* <3> = *purchase or sale on credit.*

on-balance-sheet financial assets and liabilities which are recorded on the balance sheet of an organization.

on-board security = *listed security.*

once-a-year physical count physical inventory taking under perpetual inventory.

once-in-a-lifetime exclusion $125,000 exclusion available to a taxpayer who attained age 55 before the sale of a principal residence, in which he or she has lived in for at least 3 out of 5 years preceding the sale.

on-cost <1> = *fixed cost.* <2> = *overhead.*

one activity approach <1> approach under which only one predetermined allocation rate is set. <2> an approach under which the budget only includes figures at one activity level.

one and 20 an arrangement whereby mutual fund managers take 1% of the assets and 20% of profits as compensation.

one company-wide overhead rate = *single overhead allocation rate.*

one-examination rule a rule that a taxpayer's books of account may be inspected only once for each taxable year.

one-month liquidation = *section 333 liquidation.*

one-name paper = *promissory note.*

onerous contract <UK> a contract the cost of meeting the obligations exceed the benefits to be received under it.

one shot posting system a system in which debits and credits are posted to the ledger and statement sheets by 2 separate persons, duplicate record sheets are called back and agreed by total.

one statement approach a method that lists net income and other comprehensive income in one statement. ***See***: *two-statement approach.*

one-step allocation the allocation procedure under which service department costs are allocated to production departments in one step, with no intermediate allocation to other service departments. ***Also***: direct allocation; direct distribution.

one time expense an expense that incurred one time under one decision.

one-write journal the combination of sales journal and accounts receivable ledger, while entering data in the sales journal, a sheet of carbon paper and an accounts receivable ledger card underneath can create both kinds of records at once.

one write system a bookkeeping system in which several different forms are held in alignment so that a single writing on the top form produces the same entries on the forms beneath. ***Also***: pegboard system.

only one entry bookkeeping = *matrix bookkeeping.*

ONPO other nonprofit organization

on-site audit = *field audit.*

on-site peer review a review that examines a CPA firm's system of quality control over its accounting and auditing practice, and usually includes a review of selected accounting and auditing engagements. ***See***: *off-site peer review.*

on-the-spot audit = *field audit.*

OP operating profit

OPEB other post-retirement employee benefit

open account <1> account that has an unpaid balance. <2> account initiated by a creditor on the basis of credit rating.

open accounting system a system of external reporting by financial statements.

open book management a management philosophy that gets all employees involved in increasing financial performance and ensures that all workers have access to operational and financial information necessary to accomplishing performance improvements.

open-end account an account used to group similar or related assets in connection with the *multiple asset depreciation accounting* not under the class life asset depreciation range system. ***Also***: open-end multiple asset accounts. ***See***: *vintage account.*

open-end lease a lease wherein the lessee guarantees the residual amount structured into the lease and wherein, in the equipment is returned to the lessor at lease expiry and the lessor suffers a shortfall on disposal, the lessee pays the shortfall.

open-end multiple asset account = *open-end accounts.*

opening account the commencement of dealings in an account.

opening balance (OB) = *beginning balance.*

opening balance account an account with an opening balance carried forward from the last period. ***See***: *closing balance account.*

opening entry <1> an entry made at the time a business is organized to record the assets, liabilities, and capital of the new firm. ***Also***: initial entry. <2> an entry for adjusting the balances carried forward from last period. <3> an entry for adjusting balances when the firm uses a new accounting system.

opening expense = *organization cost.*

opening inventory = *beginning inventory.*

opening work-in-process the work-in-process inventory balance at the beginning of a period. *Also*: beginning goods-in-process; initial goods-in-process.

opening written-down value <UK> written-down value at the beginning of a period.

open ledger a ledger that is open to the external parties. *See*: *secret ledger*.

operating asset an asset which contributes to the regular income from a company's operations.

operating audit examining, analyzing and appraising the overall performance for searching ways of improving efficiency and effectiveness. *Also*: administrative audit; efficiency audit; functional audit; managerial audit; modern internal audit; performance audit; program audit; responsibility audit; system audit.

operating budget a budget that embraces the impact of operating decisions. *Also*: operational budget.

operating cash cycle the series of events that begin with taking cash, investing it in inventory, making credit sales and generating accounts receivable, and converting the accounts receivable back into cash.

operating cash flows = *cash flow from operations*.

operating charge that portion of overhead costs that should be allocated to management.

operating cost <1> non-capital expense of running a particular process, department, activity, or enterprise for a given period of time. *Also*: revenue cost; working cost. <2> = *engineered cost*. <3> = *operating expense*.

operating costing a unit costing used when costing a service. *Also*: customer costing; working costing.

operating cost statement a statement showing the operating costs in a particular period.

operating cycle average time period between buying inventory and receiving cash proceeds from its eventual sale.

operating day method a depreciation method based on the proportion of days used by the equipment, such as rotary oil drilling rigs, if obsolescence is not a material factor in causing its retirement.

operating decision a decision that involves routine tasks, such as planning production and sales, scheduling personnel and equipment, adjusting production rates, and controlling the quality of products.

operating efficiency ratio = *activity ratio*.

operating expense <1> expense incurred by a firm over a period in carrying out its normal operations, apart from financing expenses. *Also*: non-manufacturing expense; operating cost; outgo. <2> expense incurred to maintain the properties presently owned.

operating gain or loss gain or loss that are related to the business's central operations.

operating income <1> the result of selling a product or service at a price above current cost. *Also*: current profit; income from operations; operating profit; revenue profit; trading profit. <2> income available for distribution without impairment of capital. *Also*: distributable income. *See*: *inventory profit; monetary income*. <3> of an insurance company, it equals net investment income plus underwriting income plus other miscellaneous income. <4> = *net income before interest and taxes*.

operating income as percent of net interest income calculated as operating income before deducting loss on securities ÷ (interest income - interest expense - allowance for net loss on loans).

operating lease a lease other than a capital lease, the cost of the leased property is not included in the lessee's balance sheet. *Also*: off-balance sheet lease; short-term lease; tax lease. *See*: *capital lease*.

operating ledger a ledger that contains only the accounts that relate to the profit and loss from operations.

operating leverage measurement of the fixed costs in a company's operating structure, such as fixed costs to total costs, percentage change in operating income to the percentage change in sales volume, or net income to fixed charge. ***See***: *capital leverage; Wall Street leverage.*

operating loss (OL) = *net operating loss.*

operating loss deduction = *net operating loss deduction.*

operating margin <1> excess of selling price over the materials cost. <2> of a bank, ratio of pre-tax income to gross income. ***Also***: operating profit margin.

operating performance income statement income statement that includes only operating revenue and expenses of the period.

operating performance ratio measure of profitability to sales to determine the return earned on the revenue generated.

operating profit (OP) = *operating income.*

operating profit margin <1> operating income for a certain period divided by revenues for that period. <2> = *operating margin.*

operating rate the percentage of total production capacity of some entity, such as a country or a company, that is being utilized at a given time.

operating ratio <1> a company's operating expenses divided by its operating revenues. <2> a ratios measuring a company's operating efficiency, such as sales to cost of goods sold, net income to income, operating expenses to income, and net profit to net worth. <3> of railroad companies, operating expenses divided by gross revenue.

operating ratio based upon net sales total cost divided by net sales.

operating reserve allowance for costs such as repairs or maintenance which have not yet been incurred.

operating results = *bottom line.*

operating revenue net sales plus other regular income sources related to normal business operations of the entity, e.g. lease income of a major activity.

operating risk a risk caused by fluctuations of operating income.

operating statement <1> a summary of operating costs and the profit margin of the whole or part of the firm's activities. <2> = *income statement.*

operating surplus <1> = *mixed income.* <2> = *retained earnings.*

operating transfer = *inter-fund transfer.*

operational accounting = *decision accounting.*

operational asset an asset directly used by the enterprise in generating revenues, including tangible and intangible properties.

operational audit an audit performed by the internal auditors to evaluate the efficiency and effectiveness of an entity in achieving its specific goals. ***See***: *compliance audit; financial statements audit.*

operational audit standards those including budgets, goals, job descriptions, common business sense, industry averages, and various internal directives.

operational budget = *operating budget.*

operational cost driver higher order of an activity cost driver.

operational costing the accumulation and calculation of costs by operations.

operation costing hybrid of job order and process costing.

operations liability = *general liability.*

opinion audit an audit performed to prevent any material effects on financial statements.

opinion report = *auditor's report.*

opinion shopping a company's action of searching for an auditor who will give a positive opinion of the company's financial statements.

opportunity cost <1> any sacrifice made to gain some benefits. ***Also***: accounting price; alternative cost; alternative use cost; economic cost; forgone revenue; implicit cost; imputed cost; real cost; shadow price; tradeoff; transfer earnings. <2> = *cost of not carrying.* <3> = *external rate of return.*

opportunity cost approach an approach for appraising investment alternatives by considering their opportunity costs.

opportunity costing the process whereby opportunity costs are ascertained.

opportunity cost method the method for determining human resource value of an employee by the price the management is willing to pay that employee.

opportunity cost of capital expected rate of return from effectively employing of funds in the company. *Also*: pure return to capital; supporting cost of capital.

opportunity cost of revenue (OCAR) the revenue that can be produced if the money is being invested.

opportunity risk the risk that a better opportunity may present itself after an irreversible decision has been made.

opposite account the account of the opposite party of a transaction that is expected to be entered.

optimal capital structure capital structure with a minimum weighted-average cost of capital.

optimistic cost a cost that is expected optimistically. *See*: *pessimistic cost.*

optimum capacity the output level that creates the lowest cost per unit.

optimum inventory level right level balanced between the loss associated with tying up the capital unproductively in excess in products inventory, and the loss of profitable sales opportunities as a result of carrying too little inventory.

optimum leverage ratio the borrowing level that minimizes the cost of capital.

option a right, but not an obligation, to buy or sell a security, commodity or a real property within a stipulated time in accordance with the agreement.

optional dividend the dividend where stockholders have the choice of receiving either a stock dividend or a cash dividend.

optional gross income method the method for apportioning interest expenses on the basis of the ratio of the foreign source gross income to total gross income.

optional look-back method a method that calculates tax for the full 12 months starting at the beginning of the short year and prorates the tax according to the amount of income earned in the short year. *See*: *annualizing method.*

optional mileage deduction election that allows the taxpayer who incurs trade or business travel expenses to deduct 20 cents per mile on the first 15,000 miles of annual business travel and 11 cents per mile for actual mileage greater than 15,000 and 9 cents per mile for the purposes of medical, moving, and charitable travel.

optional replenishment inventory system a system under which the maximum and minimum stock levels are predetermined, when stock reduces to the minimum level, a replenishment order will be made. *Also*: min-max system.

optional standard deduction the larger of the percentage standard deduction or the low income allowance.

option grant the right given to the employee to obtain a certain number of shares of the employer's stock at a set price within a certain timeframe. *Also*: employee stock option; grant of option; stock option grant.

option to purchase shares = *stock option.*

order-filling cost part of distribution cost incurred to supply goods that a customer needs, such as processing expenses of orders, warehousing, billing, insurance, packing, loading, credit charge, collection, etc. *See*: *order getting cost.*

order getting cost part of distribution cost, incurred to obtain customer orders, such as market investigating, selling, advertising, distributing, etc. *See*: *order-filling cost.*

ordering cost a cost that varies with the number of purchase orders placed to acquire a given total quantity. *Also*: cost of procuring; "getting" cost; setting up cost; setup cost.

ordering rule a rule under which assets are distributed from a Roth IRA in the following order: <a> IRA participant contributions; <b> taxable conversions; <c> non-taxable conversions; <d> earnings.

order of permanence the order of assets in the balance sheet according to the length of their lives.

order on hand = *work-in-process.*

order point = *reorder point.*

ordinary and necessary expense a fully deductible expense that is both ordinary (i.e. current)and necessary (i.e. appropriate and helpful) for a business.

ordinary annuity a series of fixed payments made at the end of each period over a fixed amount of time. ***See***: *annuity due; deferred annuity.*

ordinary balance sheet balance sheet that must be prepared each year.

ordinary care = *due care.*

ordinary compensation income = *ordinary income.*

ordinary depreciation = *normal depreciation.*

ordinary dividend the dividend that is distribution of a company's profits, treated as ordinary income to the shareholder. ***Also***: regular dividend.

ordinary expense an expense that need not be capitalized.

ordinary gain = *ordinary income.*

ordinary gross income current ordinary income of a company, calculated as gross income minus gains from the sale of capital assets and minus section 1231 gain.

ordinary income gain that does not qualify for capital gains treatment. ***Also***: ordinary compensation income; ordinary gain.

ordinary interest = *Boston interest.*

ordinary IRA = *traditional IRA.*

ordinary journal = *general journal.*

ordinary loss a loss resulting from the sale or exchange of the property that is neither a capital asset nor a section 1231 asset.

ordinary negligence = *negligence.*

ordinary repairs expenditures, usually of a recurring nature, that are necessary to maintain an asset in good operating condition. ***See***: *extraordinary repairs.*

ordinary resident <UK> a resident in the UK year after year.

ordinary time earnings (OTE) <Australia> earnings from an employee's ordinary hours of work.

organization account = *controlling account.*

organizational expenditure = *organization cost.*

organization and system audit an audit focusing on the organization and system of a firm.

organization cost the cost of bringing a corporation into existence, such as legal fees, promoters' fees, and amounts paid to the state to secure a charter. ***Also***: business startup expense; formation expense; initial cost; initial cost of business; opening expense; organizational expenditure; preliminary expense; pre-opening expense; pre-operating cost; start-up cost.

original asset <1> asset such as bonds or stock received by the trustee when a trust is created. <2> estate on the hand of an administrator when it is being distributed.

original basis the basis of property in the hands of the taxpayer when first acquired by that taxpayer.

"original book" method a method under which the predetermined rate of return on investment is equal to the ratio of average annual profit after depreciation to original investment. ***See***: *"average book" method.*

original cost the cost associated with the acquisition of an asset, or the acquisition cost incurred by the entity that first devotes a property to public use. ***Also***: aboriginal cost; first cost; hard cost; historical cost; initial cost; primary cost.

original cost method a method under which costs of assets in the balance sheet are their original costs. ***Also***: first cost method.

original document = *supporting document.*

original entry initial record of transactions in the book. ***Also***: first entry; initial entry; preliminary entry; spot entry. ***See***: *ledger entry.*

original function of audit the function of checking internal fraud and errors of audit before the 13 century.

original IRA = *traditional IRA.*

original issue discount (OID) amount by which the issue price is less than the face amount of a stock or stated redemption price of a debt instrument. ***See***: *acquisition discount; market discount.*

original issue premium amount by which the original issue price of a bond or stock is above its face value. ***Also***: marketing premium.

original issue stock the stock issued when the company is first incorporated.

original maturity interval between the issue date and the maturity date of a bond. ***See***: *current maturity.*

original use the first use to which the property is put, regardless of by whom.

origination sending tax return electronically from an ERO to the IRS or from a taxpayer to a transmitter.

orphan's deduction estate tax deduction granted for certain property left to orphans and children under 21 years old whose parents had been dead.

orthodox accounting = *conventional accounting.*

o/s out of stock

OSHA Occupational Safety and Health Act

OTE ordinary time earnings

other adjustment <Canada> adjustment, such as investment tax credit, that reduces a taxpayer's *adjusted cost base* of a partnership interest.

other adjustment a/c account used by an S corporation to record tax exempt income and related expenses. ***See***: *accumulated adjustments a/c.*

other asset the asset in the balance sheet classified as an independent item not having specified names. ***Also***: miscellaneous asset.

other auditor who audits only a small portion of the company. ***See***: *principal auditor.*

other comprehensive basis of accounting (OCBOA) a basis of accounting, other than GAAP, that an entity uses to report its assets, liabilities, equity, revenues and expenses, e.g. income tax basis and cash basis.

other comprehensive income all income and gains not included in net income under GAAP, e.g. unrealized holding gain or loss on investment, additional pension liabilities, and foreign currency items etc.

other contributed capital = *additional paid-in capital.*

other current assets balance sheet item that includes the value of non-cash assets like prepaid expenses and accounts receivable due within one year.

other current liabilities balance sheet entry used by companies to group together current liabilities that are not assigned to common liabilities such as debt obligations or accounts payable.

other deduction <1> tax deduction from the sales revenue in the operating statement that is not an ordinary item. ***Also***: non-operating expense. <2> = *income deduction.*

other direct cost direct cost that does, not belong to a specified class.

other financing source non-revenue increase in a fund net assets.

other financing use non-revenue decrease in a fund net assets.

other incidental expense = *miscellaneous expense.*

other income <1> income from activities other than normal business operations, such as investment, rent, etc. ***Also***: non-operating income. <2> = *other taxable income.*

other liability a liability not classified in a major category.

other long term liabilities a balance sheet item that includes the value of lease, future employee benefits, deferred taxes and other obligations not requiring interest payments during the next year.

other nonprofit organization (ONPO) nonbusiness organization not covered by AICPA audit guides.

other pension <UK> pension paid by anyone other than the government.

other personal tax <New Zealand> tax on personal income that is not withheld at source.

other property any property that may not be received on a tax-free basis in what may be an otherwise non-taxable exchange.

other remuneration bonus, tip, and gratuity.

other taxable income personal income from hobbies, gambling, tips, etc. subject to tax. ***Also***: other income.

OTS Office of Thrift Supervision

our account = *nostro account.*

outflow concept a concept for recognizing the revenue by the outflow of goods or services, rather than the inflow of cash.

outgo <1> = *expenditure.* <2> = *expense.* <3> = *operating expense.*

outgoing = *expenditure.*

outlay = *expenditure.*

outlay cost = *out-of-pocket cost.*

outlays and expenses <Canada> amounts incurred to sell a capital asset.

out-of-balance-post-closing trial balance = *after-closing trial balance.*

out-of-book asset = *non-ledger asset.*

out-of-book liability = *liability out of book.*

out-of-cash date the future date at which the company will run out of cash if the current negative cash flow remains unchanged.

out-of-date cost = *historical cost.*

out-of-income profit net profit from income not including income deductions.

out-of-pocket cost a cost that requires a current outlay of cash. ***Also***: cash cost; current outlay cost; outlay cost; out-of-pocket expense. ***See***: *non-cash expense.*

out-of-pocket expense <1> expenditure by a taxpayer of his or her own funds for business or personal use. <2> = *cash charge.* <3> = *miscellaneous expense.* <4> = *out-of-pocket cost.*

out-of-pocket loss the difference between the value of what the buyer actually paid and the value of what he has received.

out-of-stock cost = *cost of not carrying.*

output approach an approach under which national income is equal to the sum of output (or added value) and the net property income from abroad. ***Also***: product approach.

output cost the sum of manufacturing cost and the cost of other non-manufacturing inputs.

output costing the costing where one commodity only is in question. ***Also***: single costing.

output cost statement a statement showing output costs for a given product.

output divisor in the weighted average process costing, the denominator for each input which is divided into the cost of the input to get a unit cost for the input. ***See***: *equivalent production.*

output method <1> a method for determining standard cost by multiplying a standard unit cost by actual output units. <2> = *production method.*

output tax <UK> tax on the products sold to manufacturers as raw materials. ***See***: *input tax.*

outside basis partner's basis in the partnership interest as distinct from his share of the partnership's basis in its asset. ***See***: *inside basis.*

outside earnings the amount of earnings an elderly individual under the age of 70 has earned outside of his or her Social Security benefits.

outside holding direct investment without any built-in tax shelters. *See*: *inside holding.*

outstanding capital stock = *issued capital stock.*

outstanding check a check issued by the company but not yet cleared by the bank. *Also*: check in transit; payment float.

outstanding share capital = *issued capital stock.*

over-55 exemption tax exemption allowing an individual over the age of 55 to exclude up to $125,000 in capital gains from the sale of his/her primary residence.

over-absorption credit balance in the Factory Overhead a/c that arises when the overhead costs applied to Work-in-Process a/c exceed the actual overhead incurred. *See*: *over-applied factory overhead.*

overage cost the cost incurred when all the inventory can not be sold out. *Also*: obsolescence cost.

overall balance = *official settlements balance.*

overall budget = *master budget.*

overall cost = *overhead.*

overall cost of capital = *weighted-average cost of capital.*

overall foreign loss excess of the expenses and deductions allowable over gross income from sources without the US.

overall limit maximum foreign tax credit that can be claim, usually equals tentative tax multiplied by foreign taxable income then divided by worldwide taxable income.

overall method <1> a method of accounting used for general purposes, such as the cash or accrual method, as compared with some special method relating to a particular item. <2> method of computing bond interest coverage whereby the number of times the total fixed charges are covered is determined.

overall opinion auditor's general opinion on the financial statements as a whole.

overall yield = *yield to maturity.*

over-applied factory overhead amount by which overhead applied on the basis of a predetermined rate exceeds overhead actually incurred. *See*: *over-absorption.*

over-assessment = *overpayment.*

overcapitalization a situation in which a company has too much capital for the needs of its business.

overcontribution allowance <Canada> an amount up to $2,000 of excess contribution permitted to a registered retirement savings plan to provide a margin of error without incurring a penalty tax of 1% a month.

over-costing a situation where the costs applied to the products exceed the actual costs.

over-depreciation <1> the excess of actual depreciation over that amount allowed by tax law. <2> = *extra depreciation.*

overdraft charge a fee charged by a bank for the overdraft of an account.

overhead (OH)(o'h'd)(o'head) <1> the cost that is not easily traced to a cost object. *Also*: burden; common cost; common expense; cost of overhead; cost pool; expense; general and administrative overhead; indirect cost; indirect expense cost; indirect product cost; joint cost; loading charge; manufacturing and commercial expense; non-traceable cost; on-cost; overall cost; overhead charge; overhead cost; overhead expense; pool expense; supplementary expense; untraceable cost. <2> = *factory overhead.* <3> = *fixed cost.*

overhead absorption computing and applying overhead cost rates for each production department to products passing through those departments. *Also*: absorption.

overhead accounting procedure for the calculation and allocation of overhead costs.

overhead allocation charging to a cost center those overheads that result solely from the existence of that cost center. ***Also***: apportionment; overhead apportionment.

overhead application rate a rate used in applying the overhead costs. ***Also***: applied overhead rate; attribution rate.

overhead applied overhead cost that has been assigned to the units of output on the basis of a predetermined rate. ***Also***: burden credit.

overhead apportionment = *overhead allocation.*

overhead assignment overhead cost applied to the products sold in order to calculate the net income of products.

overhead budget variance = *overhead expenditure variance.*

overhead capacity variance overhead variance caused by the difference between actual capacity and normal capacity. ***Also***: overhead utilization variance.

overhead charge = *overhead.*

overhead controllable variance the difference between actual overhead cost and the budget overhead cost based on actual activity level. ***Also***: controllable overhead variance.

overhead cost = *overhead.*

overhead cost summary = *overhead summary.*

overhead cost variance that portion of overhead variance caused by the difference between actual overhead costs and those predetermined based on the actual hours worked in the flexible budget.

overhead distribution sharing of overhead costs by all departments.

overhead distribution basis = *basis of distribution.*

overhead effectiveness variance = *effectiveness variance.*

overhead efficiency variance that portion of overhead variance caused by the difference between actual input and standard input.

overhead expenditure variance difference between actual overhead incurred and the budget allowance. ***Also***: overhead budget variance.

overhead expense = *overhead.*

overhead expense rate = *overhead rate.*

overhead fixed unit cost fixed overhead cost per unit of output.

overhead in process overhead cost applied to the work-in-process inventory. ***Also***: manufacturing expense-in-process; overhead on work-in-process.

overhead on work-in-process = *overhead in process.*

overhead pool = *burden pool.*

overhead price variance that portion of overhead variance caused by the difference between the actual overhead per unit and predetermined overhead rate.

overhead rate overhead per unit of cost basis. ***Also***: burden rate; cost rate; indirect cost rate; overhead expense rate.

overhead ratio operating expenses divided by the sum of taxable equivalent net interest income and other operating income.

overhead standard a predetermined standard of overhead for internal control purposes.

overhead summary a summary of all overheads incurred in the whole company. ***Also***: overhead cost summary; overhead distribution summary.

overhead unallocated overhead that has not been allocated to the cost center that incurred it. ***Also***: unallocated common expense.

overhead uncontrollable variance overhead cost variance the amount of which can not be controlled by management.

overhead utilization variance <1> that portion of overhead cost variance caused by the difference between the actual and budgeted volume of output. <2> = *overhead capacity variance.*

overhead variance difference between actual overhead costs and standard overhead costs.

overhead volume variance difference between the amount of overhead budgeted at the actual operating level achieved during the period and the standard overhead charged to production by a pre-determined rate. *Also*: denominator variance; idle capacity variance; production volume variance; volume variance.

overlapping debt the debt of a state government where its tax base overlaps the tax base of another political entity such as a city within the state.

overlap profit <UK> profit that has been taxed twice because part of the accounting period falls within the basis period for more than one year.

overlap relief <UK> tax credit for overlap profits carried forward.

overpayment taxpayer's payments to the IRS exceeds the actual tax liability. *Also*: overpayment of tax; over-assessment. *Opp*: *deficiency*.

overpayment of tax = *overpayment*.

overplus = *surplus*.

overseas employment tax credit <Canada> a tax credit allowed to an individual who has been working for a foreign employer for at least 6 months.

overstatement of reported revenues money laundering activity by mixing the illegal money with the regular revenues from a business. *See*: *balance sheet laundering; integration*.

overtime cost labor cost of overtime wage.

overtime wage payment of wage at higher rate for overtime hours.

over-withholding employer's withholding of income taxes in excess of the amount called for to meet the employee's actual tax liabilities.

own capital = *net worth*.

owner's account an account for recording transaction between the owner and his business.

owner's capital the capital invested in the business by its owner. *Also*: capital; capital invested; capital liability; equity money; interior liability; invested capital; liability to the shareholders; negative debt.

owner's equity the equity of the owner of a business in the assets of the business.

ownership equation = *accounting equation*.

ownership restriction the restriction on the ownership by certain buyers or of certain assets.

ownership-specific advantage a firm's advantage over other firms by possessing intangible assets such as patents, trademarks etc.

owner's withdrawal account = *drawing account*.

own work capitalized the value of work performed for own purposes and capitalized as assets.

P p

P <1> partnership. <2> present value. <3> profit. <4> purchase journal.

P&S purchase and sale statement

P9D <UK> a form sent by a company to its director or employee who receives less then £8,500 a year.

P11D <UK> a form sent by a company to its director or employee who receives more then £8,500 a year.

P45 <UK> a form sent by a company to its employee who left the company before year end.

P60 <UK> a form sent to an employee showing details of income and taxes withheld. ***See***: *Wage and Tax Statement.*

PA <1> pension adjustment. <2> professional corporation. <3> public accounting.

P/A private account

PAC pre-authorized check

paid check = *cancelled check.*

paid-in capital = *contributed capital.*

paid-in capital from donation = *donated capital.*

paid-in capital in excess of par or stated value = *additional paid-in capital.*

paid-in capital in excess of par value = *contributed capital in excess of par value.*

paid-in capital in excess of stated value = *contributed capital in excess of stated value.*

paid in dividend = *capital dividend.*

paid-in surplus <1> excess of an insurance company's admitted assets over the total value of its liabilities and minimum capital requirements.<2> = *additional paid-in capital.* <3> = *contributed capital in excess of par value.* <4> = *contributed capital in excess of stated value.*

paid loss monetary loss paid out within a given tax year.

paid up a situation in which all payments which are due have been paid.

paid-up capital = *contributed capital.*

paid-up policy reserve present value of future benefits.

paper asset an asset that is not readily usable or convertible to cash.

paper audit an audit that focuses on the books and financial statements. ***Also***: book audit.

paper expense = *book cost.*

paper gain or loss = *paper profit or loss.*

paperless audit = *electronic data processing audit.*

paper loss the loss which has occurred but has not yet been realized through a transaction. ***Also***: unrealized loss.

paper profit = *pre-tax accounting income.*

paper profit or loss unrealized capital gain or loss in an investment by comparing the market prices of the securities to the price they were originally bought. ***Also***: paper gain or loss; unrealized profit or loss.

paper trail = *audit trail.*

paper transaction = *accounting transaction.*

PAR pension adjustment reversal

par = *face value.*

parallel simulation a method of EDP audit whereby a client's data are reprocessed using auditor's controlled software program. ***Also***: controlled processing. ***See***: *test data.*

parametric approach a costing approach using historical data from previous work, and projects the cost of the new work based on increased or decreased size, quantity, weight, etc. *Also*: top-down approach. *See*: *industrial engineering method.*

parental tax the difference in tax on the parent's income figure with and without the child's investment income. *See*: *kiddie tax.*

parent company a company that holds enough voting stock in another company to control its management and operations. *See*: *controlling corporation; subsidiary.*

parent company concept a concept under which just the parent's share of the revaluation is shown and the minority interest is reported at it's share of the subsidiary's book value. *See*: *entity concept.*

parent's equity = *majority interest.*

parent-subsidiary controlled group = *parent-subsidiary group.*

parent-subsidiary group a group of companies one of them hold more than 51% of the ownership of all others. *Also*: parent-subsidiary controlled group. *See: brother-sister group.*

parity <1> an odd or even digit. <2> constant spread between two prices. <3> salary equality among workers.

parity value = *conversion value.*

parked cash the cash temporary invested in certificate of deposits.

par or stated value method = *face value method.*

parsonage allowance an allowance for designated church professionals such as clergy for the expenses of providing and maintaining a home.

Part 1 tax <Canada> = *income tax.*

Part 1.1 tax <Canada> = *individual surtax.*

Part 1.2 tax <Canada> tax on old age security benefits.

Part 1.3 tax <Canada> a tax on the income of large corporations.

Part 2 tax <Canada> a 50% surtax on tobacco manufacturer's income tax. *Also*: tobacco manufacturers' surtax.

Part 2.1 tax <Canada> a 45% tax on any distributions from a public company. *Also*: tax on corporate distributions.

Part 3 tax <Canada> additional tax on the excess of dividends distributed over the capital gains dividend. *Also*: additional tax on excessive elections.

Part 4 tax <Canada> tax on taxable dividends received by a taxpayer from another private corporation.

Part 4.1 tax <Canada> tax on dividends on certain preferred shares received by corporations.

Part 5 tax <Canada> a tax on the income of a revoked charity. *Also*: revocation tax.

Part 6 surtax <Canada> a 12% surtax on the capital tax of a financial institution.

Part 6 tax <Canada> = *capital tax.*

Part 6.1 tax <Canada> a tax on corporations paying dividends on taxable preferred shares.

Part 7 refund <Canada> = *Part 7 tax refund.*

Part 7 tax <Canada> a refundable tax on corporations issuing qualifying shares.

Part 7 tax refund <Canada> the excess of previous year's refund over the current year's Part 7 tax. *Also*: Part 7 refund.

Part 8 refund <Canada> = *Part 8 tax refund.*

Part 8 tax <Canada> a refundable tax on corporations that receives a scientific and experimental development tax credit.

Part 8 tax refund <Canada> the excess of previous year's refund over the current year's Part 8 tax. *Also*: Part 8 refund.

Part 9 tax <Canada> a 30% tax on the amount deducted in respect of a cumulative offset account.

Part 10 tax <Canada> a tax on deferred profit sharing plans and revoked plans.

Part 10.1 tax <Canada> a tax on over-contribution to an individual registered retirement savings plan.

Part 10.2 tax <Canada> a 1% tax on the fair value of property that is not a prescribed investment acquired by a taxpayer that is a registered investment.

Part 10.3 tax <Canada> a tax on labor-sponsored venture capital corporations.

Part 10.4 tax <Canada> a 1% tax on the taxpayer's share of the overpayments to registered education savings plans.

Part 10.5 tax <Canada> a tax on the contribution to a registered education savings plans.

Part 11 tax <Canada> tax in respect of certain property acquired by trusts governed by deferred income plans.

Part 11.1 tax <Canada> tax in respect of certain property held by trusts governed by deferred income plans.

Part 11.2 tax <Canada> a 30% tax on the fair value of dispositions of certain properties.

Part 11.3 tax <Canada> a tax on the amount by which the refundable tax on an RCA trust exceeds that of a previous year. ***Also***: tax in respect of RCAs.

Part 12 tax <Canada> tax on royalties, taxes, lease rentals etc. paid to a government by a tax exempt person.

Part 12.1 tax <Canada> a 45% tax on the income from carved-out properties. ***Also***: tax on carved-out income.

Part 12.2 tax <Canada> a 36% tax on the income of a designated beneficiary from certain trust.

Part 12.3 tax <Canada> a 15% tax on investment income from selling taxable life insurance policies.

Part 12.4 tax <Canada> a 28% tax on all income of qualifying environmental trusts.

Part 12.5 tax <Canada> a tax on the recovery of labor-sponsored funds credits.

Part 12.6 tax <Canada> a tax on corporations that issue *flow-through shares*. ***Also***: tax on flow-through shares.

Part 13 tax <Canada> a 25% tax on income from Canada of non-resident aliens.

Part 13.1 tax <Canada> a 25% additional tax on taxable interest expenses of authorized foreign banks.

Part 14 tax <Canada> a 25% additional tax on the income of non-resident corporations.

partial allocation a method where the income tax expense for the company will be the tax actually payable for the period, no deferred tax is considered, no tax allocation is necessary. ***See***: *comprehensive allocation*.

partial audit an audit that focuses on only a part of books. ***Opp***: *complete audit*.

partial bad debt deduction the deduction for partial worthlessness of a debt.

partial consolidated statement consolidated statement of a pool of companies within a multi-level, parent-subsidiary group.

partial cost <1> product cost that only includes manufacturing cost. <2> cost that includes only fixed or variable component. ***See***: *absorption cost*.

partial costing the costing, such as direct costing, whereby the product cost only includes partial cost. ***See***: absorption costing.

partial elimination method = *fractional elimination method*.

partial equity method a method used to record investment in subsidiary, the initial investment is in cost, the amortization of goodwill does not reduce the share of income. ***See***: *complete equity method*.

partial income statement an income statement that shows only some items.

partial loss damage of property that is not total.

partially approving opinion = *qualified opinion*.

partially controllable cost the cost only a part of which can be controlled by management.

partially funded plan a pension plan in which some liabilities are not funded.

partially nontaxable exchange an exchange of property in which a taxpayer receives unlike property or cash in addition to like property.

partially participating preferred stock preferred stock that in addition to preferred dividends, can participate in receiving common stock dividends on a pro rata basis up to a fixed rate specified on the stock certificate. *See*: *fully participating preferred stock.*

partially variable expense = semi-variable cost.

partial payment paying a portion of a debt. *Also*: on account.

partial presentation the presentation of prospective financial information that excludes one or more of the items required for prospective financial statements.

partial spinoff a situation in which a parent company sells a minority share of a child company, usually in an IPO, while retaining the rest. *Also*: carve-out; equity carve-out.

partial surrender the removal of a portion of the original cash balance of an insurance policy or annuity.

participant <Canada> a person who enrolls in a registered retirement plan and makes an eligible withdrawal.

participants acceptance testing (PATS) a testing of software by transmitters that participate in IRS e-file program prior to live processing.

participating dividend the dividend paid on *participating preferred stock.*

participating equity preferred stock (PEPS) a *convertible preferred stock* with an enhanced dividend.

participating preferred stock preferred stock that receives extra dividend in addition to preferred dividend. *See*: *fully participating preferred stock; partially participating preferred stock.*

participating trust = *unit investment trust.*

participation any work done by an individual in connection with the *activity.*

participation period <Canada> from January 1 of the tax year when a participant receives an eligible withdrawal till the date when the balance is zero.

participatory management staff participation in the setting of goals, and the establishing of the cost standards.

particular average the damage or partial loss happening to the ship, cargo or freight in consequence of an accident.

particular charge any expenditure incurred to protect the insured goods from loss within the cover of an insurance policy.

partly finished goods = *work-in-process.*

partly fixed cost = *semi-fixed cost.*

partly variable cost = *semi-variable cost.*

partner's basis = *basis.*

partner's capital = *partner's equity.*

partner's drawing withdrawal of money from the partnership by a partner.

partner's equity amount by which partnership assets exceed its liabilities. *Also*: capital equity; partner's capital; partnership equity.

partnership an unincorporated organization through which any business, financial operation or venture is carried on.

partnership accounting the accounting procedures for a partnership, the profit and loss are divided among partners.

partnership distribution a tax-free transfer of asset from a partnership to a partner.

partnership equity = *partner's equity.*

partnership income earnings of a partnership which will be passed through to each partner.

partnership item any item that must be taken into account for the partnership's tax year at the partnership level.

part-purchase and part-pooling accounting that uses purchase method for some items, and uses the pooling of interest method for other items.

parts cost the cost for obtaining parts.

part-time education credit <Canada> a 16% education tax credit on $120 per month in 2002 for an individual who enrolled in a qualified educational program for at least 3 consecutive weeks and 12 hours per month.

part-time employee an employee who works less than 40 hours a week.

part-time resident <Canada> a taxpayer who resides in Canada for less than a year.

par value = *face value.*

par value method = *face value method.*

par value stock a class of stock to which the issuer has assigned a par value. ***Also***: stock with par value. ***See***: *no-par-value stock.*

passed dividend <1> (common stock) = *omitted dividend.* <2> (preferred stock) = *dividend in arrears.*

passenger load factor of airlines, the ratio of passenger miles to available seat miles. ***Also***: load factor.

passive activity an activity in which a taxpayer does not physically participate in.

passive activity credit the amount the sum of all credits from passive activities allowable for the tax year exceeds taxpayer's regular tax liability allocable to all passive activities.

passive activity loss excess of expenses over the receipts from a passive activity. ***Also***: passive loss.

passive income the income from operations that a taxpayer does not actively participate in, such as royalties, dividends, interest, annuities, rents and the like. ***Also:*** passive investment income. ***See***: *active income; investment income*; *unearned income.*

passive income generating shelter (PIGS) = *passive income generator.*

passive income generator (PIG) an investment into a profitable business that is deemed passive by the IRS. ***Also***: passive income generating shelter.

passive investment income = *passive income.*

passive loss = *passive activity loss.*

passive loss rule a rule that a taxpayer can deduct passive loss only to the extent of passive income.

passive trust a trust the trustee merely holds title, but the beneficiary actually controls it. ***Also***: dry trust; naked trust.

pass through undivided interests are issued and the investors share in the cash flows. ***See***: *pay through.*

pass-through = *pass-through security.*

pass-through certificate = *pass-through security.*

pass-through coupon rate the interest rate paid on a pass-through security.

pass-through entity an entity that is taxed like a partnership or S corporation but with limited liability like a corporation.

pass-through security a security representing pooled debt obligations, that passes income from debtors to its shareholders, such as the mortgage-backed certificate. ***Also***: Ginnie Mae pass-through; mortgage pass-through; mortgage pass-through security; pass-through; pass-through certificate; pay-through security.

past cost <1> cost that has been paid out of cash. ***Also***: expired cost. <2> = *historical cost.*

past due account receivable an account receivable remained uncollected for a long time.

past due balance method a method for calculating finance charges (such as in a bank account, charge account, or credit account) in which no interest is charged if the balance is paid off within a period.

past due tax = *back tax.*

past service = *prior service.*

past service cost = *prior service cost.*

past service pension adjustment (PSPA) <Canada> benefit granted to an employee in a year with respect to past service reduced by certain PSPA transfer from other RRSPs, DPSPs and RPPs.

patronage dividend a taxable distribution made by a cooperative to its members or patrons. *Also*: dividend to co-op patron.

PATS participants acceptance testing

payable <1> = *account payable.* <2> = *bill payable.*

payable date the date on which dividend is paid to the holders of record. *See*: *date of record; declaration date.*

pay and file <UK> the corporation tax payment system from Oct 1, 1993 to Jun 30, 1999, under which a company had to report the corporation tax payable, but the Inland Revenue must raise an assessment before it can collect the tax. *See*: *self-assessment.*

pay-as-you-earn (PAYE) <UK> = *income tax withholding.*

pay-as-you-go (PAYG) <Australia> a practice of collecting GST at the time the consumer pays for the goods and services.

pay-as-you-go method a method under which pension cost or expense is recognized only when benefits actually are paid to retired employees.

pay-as-you-go profit-sharing profit sharing plans with current payouts according to company profits with no deferrals.

payback method a method for comparing investment alternatives under which the cash payback time is computed by dividing the additional investment required by each alternative by its estimated amount of additional periodic net cash inflows. *Also*: cash payback method.

payback period time period required to recover the original cost of investment. *Also*: bailout period; cost recovery period; pay off; period of cost recovery.

payback reciprocal a project's true rate of return when certain conditions are satisfied, calculated as 1 ÷ the payback period.

payback reciprocal method a method for comparing investment alternatives by which the internal rate of return is estimated for investments of relatively long duration by dividing 1 by the payback time period.

PAYE pay as you earn

PAYE settlement agreement (PSA) <UK> an arrangement under which an employer pays any tax due on certain benefits without deducting from the employee's payroll.

PAYG pay-as-you-go

payment date the date on which a dividend, mutual fund distribution, or bond interest payment is made. *Also*: distribution date.

payment float = *outstanding check.*

payment in kind (PIK) settlement of a charge for goods or services or satisfaction of obligation with similar or identical medium of exchange and value.

payment-in-kind program a 1983 program under which US Department of Agriculture issued certificates that could be redeemed for commodities, which then could be sold.

payment-in-kind security (PIK security) a bond which pays interest in the form of additional bonds, or preferred stock which pays dividends in the form of additional preferred stock.

payment of debt = *debt repayment.*

payment penalty = *prepayment penalty.*

payment provision = *notional amount.*

payments balance = *balance of payments.*

payment voucher (P/V) a voucher for the payment of cash. *Also*: cash voucher; disbursement voucher.

pay off = *payback period.*

payout <1> capital gains and profits paid from a mutual fund. <2> = *expenditure.*

payout journal = *cash disbursements journal.*

payout period <1> a period during which cash flow of an investment is negative. <2> period during which annuity or retirement withdrawals is negative. <3> the period of time for which guaranteed annuity payments may be made.

payout ratio = *dividend payout ratio.*

payroll (PR) total wages and salaries and other payment in a particular period. ***Also***: gross payroll.

payroll accounting the accounting for disbursements for wages, salaries and related payroll taxes.

payroll audit examination of the wage structure of the firm by an outside auditor. ***Also***: wage audit.

payroll cost = *labor cost.*

payroll fringe = *fringe benefit.*

payroll giving <UK> a program that allows employer to deduct charity contribution from employee's payroll. ***Also***: give as you earn.

payroll journal a special journal used to summarize the earnings and, deductions of all employees for a specific pay period.

payroll ledger a subsidiary ledger that contains wages accounts for each employee or cost department.

payroll register a summary of payroll information, including employee names, gross pay, withholding, etc.

payroll summary a statement of payroll and deductions of a pay period.

payroll tax a tax levied on the amount of a payroll or on the sum of an employee's gross pay.

pay through to use cash flows from the assets to pay off the debt securities. ***See***: *pass through.*

pay-through security = *pass-through security.*

PBC prepared by the client

PBO projected benefit obligation

PBR <1> payment by result. <2> price-book value ratio.

PC <1> petty cash. <2> prime cost. <3> professional corporation. <4> purchase commitment.

PCAOB Public Company Accounting Oversight Board

PCB petty cash book

PCF price/cash flow ratio

PCGE potential capital gains exposure

PCPS Private Companies Practice Section

p/e price-earnings ratio

pecking-order review a theory which holds the internally generated fund is the most preferred source of capital, followed by new debt, then debt-equity hybrids, and finally new equity.

peculation = *embezzlement.*

peer review a review by one auditor of the work done by another independent auditor, including a review of the firm's compliance with applicable membership requirements. ***See***: *cold review; firm-on-firm review.*

pegboard system = *one-write system.*

penalty tax <1> additional charges assessed against taxpayers who do not pay their taxes when due. $1,000 for individual and $10,000 for companies. <2> 10% on early withdrawal from retirement plans.

pencil footing a temporary total underneath a list of figures written by pencil.

pension adjustment (PA) <Canada> total pension benefits accruing to a taxpayer for a year under employer-sponsored RPPs and DPSPs of which the taxpayer is a member.

Pension Adjustment Reversal <Canada> a form used by Canadian taxpayers to report income earned under a pension adjustment reversal. ***Also***: Form T10; T10.

pension adjustment reversal (PAR) <Canada> amount that will restore RRSP deduction room to an individual taxpayer who receives a termination benefit which is less than the total pension adjustments and past service pension adjustments.

pension assignment <Canada> the transfer of pension benefit from a taxpayer to a spouse or common-law partner. ***Also***: income splitting.

pension carry back <UK> any unused tax relief because a taxpayer has not paid the maximum pension contribution, which can be carried back.

pension carry forward relief <UK> unused tax relief because a taxpayer has not paid the maximum pension contribution, which can be carried forward up to 6 years.

pension corporation <Canada> a corporation operated solely for the administration of a registered pension plan.

pension cost the cost of a pension plan, including 5 elements: interest on projected benefit obligation, actual return on plan assets, amortization of prior service cost, and gain or loss. ***Also***: annuity cost.

pension credit <Canada> the value of benefit that a taxpayer earns under a deferred profit-sharing plan or a money purchase or defined benefit plan.

pension fund resource set aside for an employee pension plan. ***Also***: superannuation fund.

pension fund blackout period = *blackout period.*

pension income <UK> payment that a taxpayer receives from a pension.

pension income credit <Canada> a tax credit available up to $1,000 on certain forms of pension income.

pension plan a contract between the company and its employees whereby the company agrees to pay benefits to employees upon retirement. ***Also***: pension scheme.

pension plan liability reserve liability recognized by the employer for the future liability to make annuity payments to employees.

pension reversion terminating an overfunded defined pension plan and replacing it with a life insurance annuity.

pension scheme <UK> = *pension plan.*

pension shortfall a situation wherein a company offering employees a defined benefit plan does not have enough money set aside to meet the obligations to employees who will be retired in the future.

pension trust <Canada> a trust governed by a registered pension fund or plan.

pension trust fund a government trust fund for the pension benefits of government employees.

PEP personal equity plan

PEPS participating equity preferred stock

PER price-earnings ratio

P/E ratio price/earnings ratio

per capita income the income per person in a population.

percentage balance sheet = *common-size balance sheet.*

percentage-completion of net sales method = *percentage-of-completion method.*

percentage depletion method a method under which depletion deduction may be computed as an arbitrary percentage of gross income received without regard to the cost of the asset or quantity produced, depletion will continue as there is income from the asset. ***Also***: statutory depletion method. ***See***: *cost depletion method.*

percentage income statement = *common-size income statement.*

percentage markup method a method, used by merchants of showing concealment of income assuming that sales are some percentage in excess of cost of sales, thus results in an inferred figure for the actual gross profit.

percentage method = *percentage of accounts receivable method.*

percentage of accounts receivable method accounting method of reporting allowance for bad debts, under which a specified percentage of eligible balance outstanding is used. ***Also***: percentage method; percentage of outstanding receivables method; percentage of outstanding loan method. ***See***: *aging method; percentage of net sales method.*

percentage of completion the percentage rate of goods-in-process or the construction-in-process to output, it equals cost incurred to date, less cost of unused materials, divided by the estimated total cost to complete the contract. *Also*: conversion percentage; percent completed.

percentage of completion method a method whereby the contract price of a construction contract is reported as income in accordance with the portion of the contract completed in the taxable year. *Also*: cost-to-cost method; degree of completion method; percentage completion of net sales method. *See*: *completed contract method; production basis method.*

percentage of net sales method a method under which a percentage of net sales is used to calculate the allowance for bad debts. *See*: *percentage of accounts receivable method.*

percentage of original cost method = *straight-line method of depreciation.*

percentage of outstanding loan method = *percentage of accounts receivable method.*

percentage of outstanding receivables method = *percentage of accounts receivable method.*

percentage of sales method a method under which the advertising allowance is computed as a percentage of sales.

percentage-of-taxable income method a method of reporting the additions to reserve for bad debts, under which a bank can increase its reserves, and deduct an amount sufficient to inflate the reserve up to the allowable percentage of taxable income.

percentage on direct materials = *direct materials cost percentage rate.*

percentage premium the premium over parity of a convertible bond divided by parity.

percentage rate method a method used to compute the required standard withholding as a percentage on the employee's gross income.

percentage standard deduction a deduction based on multiplying the adjusted gross income by a fixed percentage and subtracting the resulting number to a fixed ceiling.

percentage test the business use of a personal car must exceed 50% in order to qualify for accelerated depreciation. *Also*: more-than-50% test.

percent complete = *percentage of completion.*

percent-elimination method = *fractional elimination method.*

percent operating income to net plant of utilities company, ratio of operating income to net plant assets.

per contra self-balancing items in the balance sheet.

per contra account = *contra account.*

perfect standard cost = *ideal standard cost.*

performance accounting = *responsibility accounting.*

performance audit = *operating audit.*

performance control accounting = *control accounting.*

performance margin = *contribution margin.*

performance report = *flexible budget performance report.*

period = *accounting period.*

period-certain annuity = *fixed annuity.*

period cost a cost of service benefits that is excluded from the inventory costs and instead is treated as expense in the period that can be deducted from gross income. *Also*: non-inventoriable cost; periodic cost; time cost. *See*: *product cost.*

period depreciation charge depreciation charge as an expense in the period which can be deducted from gross income.

periodical audit an audit performed in a fixed period, usually one year. *Also*: periodic audit; regular audit.

periodic annual cost the sum of annual ordering cost and the annual cost of carrying stock under fixed order interval system.

periodic audit = *periodical audit.*

periodic average method a method under which the issue price of raw materials is determined by dividing the sum of beginning inventory quantity and the purchase quantity by the cost price. *Also*: total average method.

periodic budget a periodically prepared budget. *See*: *rolling budget.*

periodic cost = *period cost.*

periodic income = *accounting income.*

periodic inventory an inventory determined by a periodic inventory system. *Also*: physical inventory.

periodic inventory method a method in which at the end of each period the cost of the unsold goods on hand is determined by counting units of each product on hand, multiplying the count for each product by its cost, and adding together costs of the various products. *Also*: balance-of-stores system.

periodic inventory system <1> a system in which inventories and cost of goods sold are based on periodic physical inventories. <2> = *fixed order interval system.*

periodicity assumption = *accounting period assumption.*

periodic lease payment (PLP) fair market value of leased property in excess of present value of residual value divided by present value of an annuity factor using the lessor's implicit rate.

periodic loss excess of period cost over periodic income.

periodic return the percentage change in the value of an asset or investment, including reinvestment of income, and assuming no contributions or disbursements.

periodic review system = *fixed order interval system.*

period of conversion = *conversion period.*

period of cost recovery = *payback period.*

period of depreciation a period of time for full depreciation of assets.

perks = *fringe benefit.*

permanent account an account that must be kept permanently.

permanent asset = *plant asset.*

permanent book a book of accounts that must be kept permanently.

permanent capital the sum of common stock, preferred stock and retained earnings. *See*: *contributed capital.*

permanent difference the difference between income per book and the taxable income, caused by the deviation of the accounting methods and the tax law, which can not be eliminated in the periods. *See*: *temporary difference.*

permanent establishment a fixed place of business through which an entity's business is wholly or partly carried on.

permanent file audit working paper gathered during the first audit about the client's background information and summary of policies.

permanent income <1> income that is fixed or slightly variable. <2> national wealth multiplied by interest rate. <3> the income that an individual expects to earn from his work, and which can be consumed each year without reducing the overall wealth. *Also*: measured income.

permanently restricted net asset = *endowment.*

permanent standard cost = *basic standard cost.*

permitted asset any asset that can be put into a *financial asset securitization trust*, such as cash and cash equivalent, certain debt instruments etc.

permitted nonaudit service nonaudit service allowed to provide to a client that is being audited by the auditor. *See*: *prohibited nonaudit service.*

perpetual annual cost sum of the annual ordering cost and the annual cost of carrying under fixed order size system.

perpetual care fund = *cemetery care trust.*

perpetual inventory the inventory from adding the units and the cost of coming goods to previous inventory figures and subtracting the units and cost of outgoing goods. *Also*: book inventory; continuous inventory.

perpetual inventory method a method in which an individual record is kept for each product of the units on hand at the beginning, the units purchased, the units sold, and the new balance after each purchase or sale. *Also*: book inventory method; progressive inventory method.

perpetual inventory records the detailed records showing the receipts, issues, and balance in terms of physical quantities and costs for each type of material and each type of finished product.

perpetual inventory system an inventory system in which inventories and cost of goods sold are based on the book inventory records.

perpetual security a stock which is never called in for redemption, such as common stock.

perpetual stock = *buffer stock.*

perpetual stock method = *base stock method.*

perpetual stocktaking physical stock-taking of actual inventories continuously through out the year. *Also*: continuous stock-taking.

perpetual trust a trust that lasts as long as the need for it continues. *Also*: dynasty trust. *See: limited trust.*

perquisite = *fringe benefit.*

PERS public employee retirement system

personal account (PA)(p/a) a bank account the title of which is the name of a person.

personal age allowance = *age allowance.*

personal allowance <UK> a tax deduction introduced in July 2002 based on the age of a taxpayer.

personal capital asset = *capital asset.*

personal company a company own by an individual taxpayer.

personal consumption expenditures market value of goods and services purchased by individuals and non-profit institutions or acquired by them as income in kind.

personal deduction = *itemized deduction.*

personal equity plan (PEP) <UK> a tax-free share investment plan available before April 5, 1999. (Replaced by *investment savings account* on Apr 6, 1999).

personal exemption $3,050 in 2003 per individual taxpayer, used to offset adjusted gross income in arriving at taxable income. *See*: *dependency exemption; spousal exemption.*

personal exemption credit <Canada> a tax credit available since 1988 for personal items that were formerly deducted as personal exemptions.

personal exemption phase out reduction in personal exemption amount when adjusted gross income exceeds certain amount.

personal expense <1> an expense that is not deductible for income tax. *Also*: living expense. <2> personnel expense minus salaries.

personal financial statement financial statement prepared for an individual using the accrual basis. *Also*: individual financial statement.

personal holding company (PHC) a company 50% or more of its shares are held by less than 5%, and the net income of which is very high.

personal holding company tax a 39.6% penalty tax on the undistributed income of a personal holding company.

personal income (PI) the amount of current income received by individuals from all sources.

personal income tax a tax on an individual taxpayer's income. *Also*: individual's tax; tax on individuals.

personal income tax table = *tax table.*

personal interest non-deductible interest expense on personal loans other than home mortgage interest, investment interest, or business interest. *Also*: consumer interest.

Personal Liability Umbrella Security Plan (PLUS) AICPA insurance plan which provides members and their families with up to $5 million personal liability coverage.

personal living expense a taxpayer's cost of living.

personal loss losses that neither arise in a trade or business nor are a result of a business transaction.

personal outlay disbursement made by individuals.

personal pension <UK> a retirement pension set up by an individual taxpayer.

personal pension plan (PPP) <UK> a retirement plan available to self-employed taxpayers, or employees who are not a member of the employer's pension plan.

personal property a property other than *real property*. ***Also***: chattel.

personal property tax taxes paid on personal property, but only if based on value alone. ***See***: *real property tax.*

personal savings *personal income* in excess of personal outlays. ***Also***: savings.

personal service entity <Australia> a company, partnership or trust that provides personal service for a profit.

personal tax credit <Canada> a tax credit available to any taxpayer, $1,221 in 2002.

personal tax view a theory that holds that the difference in personal tax rates between income from debt and income from equity eliminates the disadvantage of the double taxation of income.

personal trust a trust the beneficiary of which is a family member of the grantor.

personal-use property any property owned by a taxpayer for personal use or enjoyment.

personnel cost all costs incurred to obtain employees services.

personnel expense such as salaries, wages, benefits, taxes, etc. ***Also***: staff expense.

per stirpes method for distributing the asset of an individual who dies without a valid will.

PERT program evaluation and review technique

PERT/cost establishing job, cost estimates directly from an activity or group of activities on a time network.

per unit cost = *cost per unit.*

per unit variable costs = *variable costs per unit.*

pessimistic cost a cost estimated pessimistically. ***See***: *optimistic cost.*

Petroleum Revenue Tax <UK> a tax charged on the profits of a licensed oil company from the exploitation of the oil field.

pet trust a trust established to provide funds to take care of a pet.

petty average small regular charge which occurs in the usual course of a voyage, e.g. port charge.

petty cash (PC)(p/c) = *imprest fund.*

petty cash fund = *imprest fund.*

petty cash voucher a form provided with spaces for recording data concerning disbursements from the petty cash fund.

PF <1> page footing. <2> pro forma.

P/FCF price/free cash flow ratio

PFP personal financial planning

phantom income reportable or taxable income which does not generate cash flow, such as income from a portfolio holding zero-coupon bonds.

phantom loss the loss resulting from a transaction without any economic purpose except to avoid tax.

phantom profit = *fictitious profit.*

phantom taxable profit the profit from one leg of a straddle, e.g. buy a call at $5.00 and sell a put at $5.00 to protect a stock position, when both expires, the profit from the put is taxable while the cost of the call is not deductible until the stock protected is sold.

phase 1 income lesser of taxable investment income or gain from operation of a life insurance company.

phase 1 tax the tax imposed on the phase 1 income.

phase 2 income half of any excess of the gain from operations over taxable investment income of a life insurance company.

phase 2 negative gains from operations are less than the taxable investment income of a life insurance company.

phase 2 tax a tax imposed on the phase 2 income.

phase 3 income amount deducted from the company's policyholders surplus account for the year.

phase 3 tax a tax imposed on the phase 3 income.

phase-in = *tax abatement.*

phase out reduction in tax exemption amount when adjusted gross income exceeds certain amount. ***See***: *personal exemption phase out.*

phase-out amount = *threshold phase-out amount.*

phase-out period from the date decision was made to discontinue a division of business to the date of final disposal. ***See***: *measurement date.*

phase out rate the amount per dollar of income deducted from the maximum benefit.

PHC personal holding company

PHSP private health service plan

physical asset = *tangible asset.*

physical capital = *real capital.*

physical capital maintenance a concept under which a return on physical capital results only if the physical product capacity at the end of a period exceeds its capacity at the beginning. ***See***: *financial capital maintenance.*

physical depreciation an asset's decline in usefulness because of physical wear and tear. ***Also***: wear and tear. ***See***: *functional depreciation.*

physical examination an auditor's physical inspection of the certificates or documents evidencing asset investments.

physical income the income other than money, such as safety, happiness in working, etc.

physical inspection an auditor's physical tour of the facilities in order to identify the areas which appear to merit special attention. ***Also***: physical walkthrough.

physical inspection method = *columnar method.*

physical inventory <1> inventory on hand after the actual inventory taking. ***Also***: actual inventory. <2> = *inventory taking.* <3> = *periodic inventory.*

physical life economic life under functional depreciation.

physical-service method a method of depreciation under which depreciation is computed according to the proportion of service (such as working hours, output, mileage, etc.) that the asset rendered.

physical standard a standard established from systematic observation, measurement, and controlled experimentation, or alternatively result from careful planning.

physical unit basis a method which assigns an equal share of the joint costs to each physical unit of joint product expressed in a common denominator such as pounds.

physical units method = *single asset depreciation method.*

physical variance = *efficiency variance.*

physical verification auditor's actual inspection of the assets to confirm their existence and value.

physical walk-through = *physical inspection.*

piece-meal opinion an auditor's opinion on only a limited event.

piece-work account an account for recording the completion of a construction work.

piercing the corporate veil a court's order to hold the shareholders of a limited liability company liable for wrong doing. ***Also***: entity piercing doctrine; lifting the veil.

PIG passive income generator

PIGS passive income generating shelter

PIK security payment-in-kind security

pilot program an approach used by the IRS to introduce new technology such as e-file, whereby the new technology will be tested in selected area by selected participants before it is offered to the general public.

PITI principal, interest, taxes and insurance

PJ purchase journal

PL purchase ledger

P&L profit and loss

P/L profit and loss

placed-in-service date the day on which an asset became available for use by a business.

placement depositing the laundered money in banks.

place of trade <UK> the location of a business for income tax assessment purpose.

plan asset an asset which has been segregated and restricted to provide benefit of a pension plan.

planned budget the budgets for all activities planned to be completed. ***Also***: budgeted cost for work scheduled; planned value. ***See***: *earned value.*

planned cost an estimate of the costs for a future period based on the assumption that management will consciously act in such a way as to affect the amount of the costs significantly.

planned value (PV) = *planned budget.*

plant = *plant asset.*

plant and building = *plant asset.*

plant and equipment = *plant asset.*

plant and equipment budget = *capital expenditures budget.*

plant and machinery <UK> = *plant asset.*

plant asset any tangible asset having a relatively long life used in the production or the sale of other assets or services. ***Also***: capital asset; fixed asset; land, building, furniture and equipment; land, buildings and equipment; long life asset; long-lived asset; long-term asset; long-term tangible resource; machinery and plant; permanent asset; plant; plant and building; plant and equipment; property, plant and equipment; plant and machinery; tangible capital asset; tangible fixed asset. ***See***: *hard asset.*

plant asset cost the cost of acquiring a plant asset and any additional expense to make it available for use. ***Also***: asset cost; capital cost.

plant fund a fund used to account for plant assets in a non-profit organization.

plant ledger a subsidiary ledger containing accounts for each plant asset.

plant modernization cost = *cost of plant renovation.*

plant rearrangement cost = *rearrangement cost.*

plant replacement reserve = *reserve for replacement.*

pledged asset = *hypothecated stock.*

plenty red = *accounting bath.*

plowback = *earnings retention.*

plowback ratio = *earnings retention ratio.*

PLP periodic lease payment

plugging adding the amounts to suitable credit or debit sides in a journal entry.

PLUS Personal Liability Umbrella Security Plan

plus item an increase in revenue, liability or a decrease in the asset.

PML probable maximum loss

PN promissory note

p/n promissory note

$p_{n|i}$ reads: small p angle n at i, present value of 1 formula.

PNW present net worth

PO purchase order

POB Public Oversight Board

point tax deductible fees paid to induce lenders to make mortgage loans at a lower interest rate. ***Also***: mortgage point.

policy cost <1> cost incurred because of the management policy, such as advertising cost. <2> that portion of the fixed cost other than capacity cost and organization cost.

policy depreciation the depreciation in asset's usefulness because of the fiscal or social policy of the state. ***Also***: in lieu depreciation.

policyholders' surplus a/c account maintained by a life insurance company in which taxes deferred are entered.

Polish dividend = *split down.*

political cost the cost of political actions, such as excess profit tax, antitrust actions, etc. of a government.

political organization taxable income the excess of the gross income over deductions directly connected with the production of income of a political organization.

poll tax a federal tax on everyone regardless of income. ***Also***: capitation; capitation tax; direct tax; head tax.

pollution prevention cost = *environmental pollution control cost.*

poly-corporate accounting the accounting which reflects the actual equities of each subsidiary in the financial statements. ***See***: *fund theory.*

Ponzi scheme = *lapping.*

pooled car <UK> a company car used by more than one employee.

pooled income fund a trust formed to pay income to one or more non-charitable beneficiaries and the remainder to charity.

pooled inventory program a process used to consolidate some financial assets such as residential mortgages into a structure which generates single or multiple payment streams which are then marketed as specific securities.

pool expense = *overhead.*

pool factor outstanding mortgage pool principal divided by the original principal balance, and expressed as a decimal between 0 and 1.

pooling of interest a merger under which the stockholders' equities of two companies are combined, old common stock is exchanged for the new common stock. ***Also***: tax-free acquisition; tax-free merger. ***See***: *purchase acquisition.*

pooling of interest method a method under which the consolidated balance sheets of affiliates are simply combined, disregarding goodwill. ***See***: *purchase method.*

pool of assets <UK> a group of plant assets the expenditures of which have been aggregated for capital allowance purpose.

population account balances and transactions of interest to the auditor in audit sampling. ***Also***: field.

pop up option a joint and survivor option that allows an employee to be reinstated to the basic pension if the spouse predeceases the retiree.

portability an employee's ability to convert an investment in one plan into another.

portfolio income the income from interest, dividends, annuities and certain royalties. ***See***: *capital gains.*

portfolio turnover rate of trading activity in a mutual fund's portfolio, that equals the lesser of purchases or sales divided by average total assets of a period usually one year.

position = *financial position.*

position audit = *situation audit.*

position bookkeeping self-balancing procedure for special transactions included in double entry bookkeeping.

positive carry condition in which the cost of an investment is less than the benefit or return obtained from it. ***Opp***: *negative carry.* ***See***: *appreciated financial position; carry.*

positive confirmation the confirmation of accounts receivable requesting the recipient to indicate whether the balance is correct. ***See***: *negative confirmation.*

positive contribution margin = *contribution margin.*

positive form a form sent by an auditor to confirm the accounts receivable, requesting the recipient to indicate whether the information provided is correct. ***See***: *blank form.*

positive goodwill <1> excess of cash flow over the book value of an asset or assets. ***Also***: goodwill. <2> = *debit differential.*

positive monetary position holding excess of monetary assets over liabilities.

positive pay a check fraud prevention system based on a requirement that the paying banks verify that the check is on a daily list of authorized checks furnished by the drawer.

possessions corporation a corporation with branch operation in a US possession and can obtain tax benefits as though the branch were operating as a foreign subsidiary.

possession tax credit a tax credit in lieu of foreign tax credit with respect to income from trade or business from US possessions.

post-acquisition charge <UK> a tax on the appreciated value of shares acquired by an employee.

post-acquisition earnings subsidiary income realized after it has been acquired. ***Also***: subsidiary earnings.

post audit IRS process of randomly selecting and reviewing settlements by its examining agents in the interest of evaluating the agent's acts and uniformity. ***Also***: post-audit review.

post-audit review = *post audit.*

post-balance-sheet-date event = *event subsequent to balance sheet date.*

post-balance-sheet event = *event subsequent to balance sheet date.*

post balance-sheet review audit applicable to the interval of time between the date of the financial statements and the completion date of the audit fieldwork.

post cessation expenditure expense that a taxpayer continues to pay related to a discontinued business.

post-cessation income <UK> = *post-cessation receipts.*

post cessation receipts money received after the permanent discontinuance of a trade, profession or vocation. ***Also***: post-cessation income.

post-closing = *after-closing.*

post-closing trial balance = *after-closing trial balance.*

post-combination earnings stockholder's earnings after the combination of companies.

post cost control cost control after the cost variances have been determined at the end of month.

post date placing a date on a document or a check a date that follows the date of drawing.

post-employment deduction <UK> deductible expense that a taxpayer continues to pay relating to a former employment.

postil a note made at the edge of a ledger sheet giving more details about the entries.

posting the process of transferring information from the journal to the ledger for the purpose of summarizing. ***Also***: flow of entries; ledger posting; posting of account.

posting medium <1> a book, such as a journal or a daybook, from which entries are posted into the ledger. ***Also***: book of posting entry. <2> = *cross reference number.*

posting of account = *posting.*

posting reference (p.r.) = *cross reference number.*

posting reference column a column that indicates which items have been posted and that provides a cross-reference system for tracing transactions from the book of original entry to the ledger accounts or vice versa.

posting rule a rule that the total sum of entries posted to subsidiary ledgers must be equal to the amount posted to their ledger controlling account.

post-liquidation return an after-tax return for a fund calculated as if the entire position had been liquidated and taxes paid at the end of the reporting period. ***See***: *pre-liquidation return.*

post list a list which shows new balances of all accounts after a run of posting.

post-money valuation the value of a company after external financing alternatives are added to its balance sheet. ***See***: *pre-money valuation.*

post-mortem cost accounting = *historical cost accounting.*

post-petition debt a claim against a bankrupt based on goods or services delivered to the debtor after the bankruptcy filing. ***See***: *pre-petition debt.*

postponable cost a cost that can be postponed to the future by a management decision, such as routine maintenance cost.

postponing income purposely delaying receipt of income to a later year in order to reduce current tax liability.

post. ref. posting reference

post-statement event an event occurred after the financial statements have been prepared. ***Also***: subsequent event.

postulate of permanence = *continuity concept.*

potential accounting irregularities the accepted way of referring to suspected fraud in reporting financial and managerial results, without opening oneself up to a lawsuit.

potential asset an asset which can be obtained in the future. ***Also***: latent asset.

potential capital gains exposure (PCGE) percentage of a portfolio's assets that would be subject to capital gains tax if it were liquidated at a particular point. ***Also***: capital gains exposure.

potential common stock options, warrants, convertible securities and contingent stock agreements.

potential liability = *contingent liability.*

potentially abusive return a tax return, not a fraudulent return, that contain inaccurate information that may lead to understatement of tax or overstatement of credit.

potentially dilutive securities stock options and convertible preferred stocks or bonds because of their potential to be exchanged for common stock and thereby dilute EPS.

potentially exempt transfer <UK> tax exempt gift that may be taxable if the transferor dies within 7 years.

potential sales loss = *present profit loss.*

Pound cost averaging <UK> = *constant dollar plan.*

pour-over trust a trust funded by assets from one or more identical sources.

PP <1> paper profit. <2> payback period.

PP&E property plant and equipment

PPP personal pension plan

PPS sampling = *probability-proportional-to-size sampling.*

PR <1> payroll. <2> purchase requisition.

pr. principal

P.R. posting reference

practical capacity the highest activity level at which the production center can operate with an acceptable degree of efficiency, taking into consideration unavoidable loss of productive time, e.g. the interruptions.

practical merger = *type C reorganization.*

practical overhead rate overhead application rate based on the practical capacity.

practical standard cost = *current standard cost.*

practice fee a fee imposed on practitioners admitted to practice before the Tax Court.

P ratio = *present sum to future sum ratio.*

PRC Peer Review Committees

preacquisition contingencies contingent assets or liabilities that are on existence before the consummation of a business combination.

preacquisition profit accumulated profit of a company before it is acquired by a parent company.

preadjustment balance the balance of an account before adjusting entries are entered.

pre-arranged trading fraudulent practice whereby commodities dealers carry out risk-free trades at predetermined prices to acquire tax advantages.

pre-audit = *pre-emptive audit.*

pre-authorized check (PAC) check that is authorized by a payer in advance, written either by the payee or by the payee's bank and then deposited in the payee's bank account.

preceding balance = *beginning balance.*

preceding year basis <UK> a basis whereby the income, profits or gains are charged to tax on the basis of the amounts arising in the year preceding the year of assessment, now replaced by *self-assessment.*

pre-change credit the excess of foreign taxes and alternative minimum tax credits to the extent attributable to ending on or before an ownership change.

precision = *allowance for sampling risk.*

preclosing trial balance the trial balance before the closing entries are entered.

predecessor auditor the one who audited the client before. *See*: *successor auditor.*

predepreciation profit = *income before depreciation.*

predetermined burden rate = *predetermined overhead rate.*

predetermined cost an estimate of the amount of a cost to be incurred in the future. *Also*: projected cost.

predetermined cost accounting the accounting that uses standard cost or estimated cost figures.

predetermined overhead rate a method for assigning factory overhead to jobs or to units of output on the basis of the number of units of activity performed on each job or unit. *Also*: predetermined burden rate.

predetermined standard cost a standard cost based on the pre-determined quantity of usage and the predetermined price.

predicted cost <1> an estimate of costs for a future period based on the assumption that management action will have little or no effect on the costs. <2> = *standard cost.*

predictive ratio a ratio that predicts the outcome of future conditions, such as Altman Z-Score.

predictive value a qualitative characteristic of information based on its relevance and its usefulness to a decision maker in forecasting a future event or condition.

pre-emptive audit an audit made before actual payment of an investment project costs. *Also*: administrative audit; pre-audit.

pre-emptive right the right of current stockholder to buy new shares on a pro rata basis before they are issued to the public.

preference equity redemption cumulative stock <UK> = *participating equity preferred stock.*

preference share = *preferred stock.*

preferential rate = *bank prime interest rate.*

preferred adjusted to common equity redeemable stock = *participating equity preferred stock.*

preferred bailout = *preferred stock bailout..*

preferred capital stock (PCS) capital obtained from the issuing of preferred stock.

preferred creditor a creditor having priority over another creditor when the company becomes bankrupt.

preferred dividend a dividend paid to preferred stockholders. *Also*: nondiscretionary dividend. *See*: *common dividend.*

preferred equity redemption stock = *participating equity preferred stock.*

preferred income participation security = *participating equity preferred stock.*

preferred preferred = *prior-preferred stock.*

preferred security a security issued by a bank, corporation, or foreign entity which has the fixed payment as bond and preference as preferred stock.

preferred stock a stock which entitles the holder to preferential rights to the dividend over other stockholders or to the assets in a liquidation. *Also*: preference share; prior stock; senior share. *See*: *common stock.*

preferred stock bailout tax avoidance method by which a company issues preferred stock tax free, later followed by stockholders' sales of such stock to outsiders, then the company will redeem the stock later. *Also*: preferred bailout. *See*: *section 306 stock.*

preferred stock dividend = *preferred dividend.*

preferred stockholder's equity the sum of preferred stock's par or stated value and cumulative preferred stock dividends in arrears.

preferred stock ratio preferred stock at par value divided by total capitalization.

preliminary audit <1> examination before the program is started. <2> the procedures in the preliminary stage of operating audit that includes physical walking tour of the facility, acquisition of written data, interviews with management, and certain financial analysis.

preliminary balance sheet = *tentative balance sheet.*

preliminary entry = *original entry.*

preliminary expense = *organization cost.*

preliminary prospectus the *prospectus* issued while it is being reviewed for fraudulent or misleading statements by the SEC. *Also*: red-herring. *See*: *final prospectus.*

pre-liquidation return an after-tax return for a fund calculated as if the position was still held at the end of a reporting period, leaving some unrealized tax consequences. *See*: *post-liquidation return.*

premature distribution = *early distribution.*

premature distribution tax a 10% tax on premature distribution from a Roth IRA. *See*: *early distribution penalty.*

premature withdrawal penalty = *early withdrawal penalty.*

premium (pm.)(prem.) <1> amount by which the selling price of a bond exceeds its face value. <2> = *conversion premium.* <3> = *in lieu of dividend.* <4> = *insurance premium.* <5> = *interest.*

premium income common stock = *participating equity preferred stock.*

premium on bonds = *bond premium.*

premium on capital stock = *additional paid-in capital.*

premium over bond value excess of the market value of a convertible bond over the price of another bond issued by the same company.

premium over conversion value = *conversion premium*

premium over theoretical value excess of the market price of a stock warrant over its theoretical value.

premium price an acquirer's offered price higher than the market price of a stock. *Also*: takeover premium.

premium-to-surplus ratio of an insurance company, ratio of premium income to surplus.

pre-money valuation the value of a company before external financing alternatives are added to its balance sheet. *See*: *post-money valuation.*

prenotice audit an audit the date, object and scope of which are known before it is performed.

prenuptial agreement <1> an agreement between two merging corporations that outlines certain events and preconditions. <2> a contract between a couple before marriage about how their assets and liabilities should be divided in the event of death or divorce.

pre-opening expense = *organization cost.*

pre-operating cost = *organization cost.*

prepaid asset an asset that appears in the balance sheet as prepaid advertising, prepaid expenses, etc.

prepaid expense current payment of expense that relates to future years.

prepaid income = *deferred revenue.*

prepaid interest = *instant interest.*

prepaid pension cost cumulative employer contributions in excess of accrued pension cost. *See*: *accrued pension cost.*

preparatory cost = *setting up cost.*

preparer's tax identification number (PTIN) a number used by a paid tax preparer to avoid disclosing the social security number.

prepayment a payment in advance.

prepayment credit tax credits allowed to individual taxpayers for the employers' withholdings of federal income tax withheld from wages over the course of the year.

prepayment penalty the penalty paid for prepaying a debt. ***Also***: acquisition charge; payment penalty. ***See***: *late charge.*

pre-petition debt a claim against a bankrupt based on goods or services delivered to the debtor before the bankruptcy filing. ***Also***: trade claims. ***See***: *post-petition debt.*

prescribed security <1><Canada> a bond or share issued by a corporation which derives most of its earnings from real estates. <2> = *non-qualifying security.*

present cost = *current cost.*

present dollar accounting = *constant dollar accounting.*

present interest unrestricted right to the immediate use, possession, or enjoyment of property or the income from property.

present profit loss the loss of present profit caused by out-of-stock. ***Also***: potential sales loss.

present standard cost = *current standard cost.*

present sum to future sum ratio the ratio of the present value to the future value of the same item. ***Also***: P ratio.

present value (PV) <1> value today of a future payment or stream of payments discounted at some appropriate compound interest rate. ***Also***: present worth. ***See***: *certainty equivalent.* <2> = *capitalized value.*

present value concept a concept which recognizes that one dollar obtained in the future is worthless than one dollar received today.

present value factor = *discount factor.*

present value income the estimated worth today of an amount of money to be received at a future date. ***Also***: ex ante income; subjective profit.

present value method <1> a method of evaluating the worth of property that creates a flow of income or is to be received outright in the future. <2> a method for determining the fair market value of a mineral deposit on the basis of its anticipated production, net of cost, discounted for the time required for risk and for extraction.

present value of 1 the decimal rate of the worth today of $1 of a future accumulation discounted to the present at compound interest.

present value of an annuity due the present value of an annuity due falls on the date the first rent is deposited or withdrawn.

present value of an annuity of $1 decimal ratio of the worth today of each dollar of a series of equal future payments discounted to the present at compound interest.

present value of an ordinary annuity present value of an ordinary annuity discounted at a compound interest rate.

present value of deferred annuity subtracting from the present value of an ordinary annuity the missing ordinary annuity for rents equal in number to the number of periods the annuity is deferred.

present value or net realizable value, whichever is greater concept a concept that asset value should be restated at the greater of their present value or their net realizable value.

present value profitability index ratio of the present value of future earnings to the current value of an investment. ***Also***: cost-benefit ratio; discounted gross benefit-cost ratio; excess present value index; interest rate of return; profitability index; solving rate of return.

present worth (PW) = *present value.*

present worth method = *sinking fund method.*

preserved benefit <Australia> benefit retained in the pension fund until the member has met a condition.

president the person in charge of an organization.

Presidentially declared disaster a disaster that occurred in an area declared by the President to be eligible for federal assistance, and deduction of *qualified disaster loss.*

pretax accounting income net income before income taxes as shown in the historical cost income statement. ***Also***: accountant's profit; accounting earnings; accounting income; accounting profit; book profit; earnings before taxes; financial income; income before income taxes; income before taxes; income for financial accounting purpose; net income before income taxes; net profit; paper profit; pretax book income; pretax financial income; pretax income; profit on paper; reported earnings.

pretax book income = *pretax accounting income.*

pretax contribution payment to a pension plan made with funds from an employee's paycheck before federal income taxes are deducted.

pretax financial income = *pretax accounting income.*

pretax income = *pretax accounting income.*

pretax rate of return yield on a particular security before taking into account an individual's tax situation.

prevention cost the cost of quality management that the company incurs in order to optimize its total quality cost. ***Also***: preventive cost.

preventive cost = *prevention cost.*

previous balance method a method for calculating finance charge on a charge account that takes the outstanding balance at the end of the previous billing period and applies the interest rate to that total.

previously taxed income (PTI) income of a DISC deemed distributed and therefore actually taxed to share holders.

previous process cost = *transferred-in cost.*

price = *market price.*

price/book ratio (P/B) market price of a stock divided by book value per share. ***Also***: market to book ratio; price to book ratio; valuation ratio. ***See***: *book to market ratio; price/earnings ratio.*

price/cash flow ratio (PCF) the market value per share divided by cash flow per share.

price-cost margin the difference between selling price and the total cost of a product.

price discount = *trade discount.*

price/earnings ratio (P/E)(PER) current price of a common stock divided by its dividends earnings per share. ***Also***: earnings multiple; multiple; P/E ratio; price-future earnings ratio; price to earnings ratio; ratio of market price to earnings per share. ***See***: *price/book ratio.*

price effect variance = *price variance.*

price/free cash flow ratio (P/FCF) market price per share divided by free cash flow per share.

price-future earnings ratio (PFER) = *price/earnings ratio.*

price gain or loss account an account for recording the difference when using lifo for pricing raw materials issues and fifo for pricing materials inventory.

price impact cost = *market impact cost.*

price index measure of the changes in prices of a particular market basket of goods or services.

price level accounting = *constant dollar accounting.*

price level adjusted statement = *constant dollar financial statement.*

price level financial statement = *constant dollar financial statement.*

price of capital = *interest.*

price of money = *interest.*

price risk difference between the current market price of a convertible preferred stock and its investment value.

price sales ratio (P/S) market value per share divided by annual sales per share.

price to book ratio = *price/book ratio.*

price to cash flow ratio the ratio of a stock's market price to its cash flow per share of the latest fiscal year.

price to earnings ratio = *price/earnings ratio.*

price to sales ratio market value of outstanding shares divided by sales in a 12-month period. Used only for unprofitable companies since they do not have a P/E ratio.

price variance a difference between actual revenue or cost caused by the actual price per unit being different from the budgeted price per unit. *Also*: price effect variance.

PricewaterhouseCoopers (PwC) one of the big 4 accounting firms in the world.

primary account an account in which transactions are first entered.

primary accounts = *eligible accounts.*

primary auditor = *principal auditor.*

primary cost = *original cost.*

primary earnings per share net income after allowing for tax but before extraordinary items attributable to the shareholders divided by the number of common stock issued. *Also*: basic earnings per share; basic net income per share; net income per share of common stock. *See*: *earnings per share; fully diluted earnings per share.*

primary income = *real primary income.*

primary liability <1> the seller's responsibility to pay stock transfer tax. <2> = *general liability.*

primary ratio apex of the ratio pyramids the rate of return.

primary reserve a bank's reserve of cash and demand deposits with the Fed and other banks.

primitive security = *underlying asset.*

prime account = eligible account.

prime cost (PC) direct materials and direct labor, and in UK, plus direct overhead cost. *Also*: cost of direct inputs; direct product cost; first cost; flat cost; hard cost; prime product cost; shut down cost.

prime costing a financial accounting concept which holds that costing is performed by including direct costs in inventory cost and deducting period cost.

prime cost method a method for distributing overhead costs based on the proportion of prime costs.

prime interest rate = *bank prime interest rate.*

prime product cost = *prime cost.*

prime rate = *bank prime interest rate.*

prime rate of interest = *bank prime interest rate.*

prin. principal

principal (pr.)(prin.) <1> sum of money, as opposed to the profits or interest made on that money. *Also*: amount at interest; corpus; fiduciary principal; principal sum; rest. <2> the person for whom a broker executes an order. <3> major party to a debt, as opposed to a guarantor. <4><of a bond> = *face value.* <5> = *promissory note.*

principal account the most important account used by bank bookkeeping.

principal and interest = *accumulated amount.*

principal auditor <1> the chief officer in the controlling company who is responsible for examining the subsidiaries. <2> an auditor retained by the parent company to perform most of the audits and known to the public. *Also*: primary auditor. *See*: *other auditor.*

principal book = *main book.*

principal establishment <Canada> the fixed place of business of a corporation.

principal of instrument = *face value.*

principal reduction method a method under which points paid in the form of discount is taxable income as stated principal payments on the loan are made.

principal residence the taxpayer's main residence. *Also*: abode; self-contained domestic establishment.

principal stockholder = *substantial shareholder.*

principal statements the most important financial statements: the balance sheet, the income statement and the statement of changes in financial position.

principal sum = *principal.*

principle = *misposted account.*

principle of allocation of costs a principle that the cost consumed should be treated as period cost and be matched with the current revenue.

principle of consistency = *consistency principle.*

principle of debit and credit principle the debit items always equal the credit items in amount.

principle of differential costing a principle that states only differential costs are considered in appraising investment alternatives.

principle of matching costs with revenues = *matching principle.*

principle of materiality a rule the gist of which is that a strict adherent to accounting principle is not required when adherence is relatively difficult or expensive and lack of adherence will not affect the reported net income materially.

principle of objectivity = *objectivity principle.*

principle of substitution <1> principle that the minimum cost or the, maximum profit mix should be chosen among input factors. <2> principle that the asset, liability or the operating accounts representing the head office should be eliminated with the goods shipped to the branches when preparing the combined financial statements.

prior charge the expenditure that is deducted from net earnings before the payment of common dividends, such as bond interest, preferred dividends, etc.

prior deduction method a method of computing bond interest coverage whereby the requirements of senior obligations are first deducted from earnings available for interest, and the balance is applied to the issue being considered.

prior department cost = *transferred-in cost.*

prior period adjustment revenue or expenses applicable to a previous period. ***Also***: retroactive adjustment.

prior-period profit and loss adjustment the adjustment to the errors in the previously issued financial statements.

prior preferred stock preferred stock ranking ahead of all other issues of preferred stock. ***Also***: preferred preferred.

prior service employee service before entry into the pension plan. ***Also***: past service.

prior service cost (PSC) estimated cost of prospective retirement benefits considered to have accrued in the years before the adoption of a pension plan. ***Also***: past service cost. ***See:*** *current service cost; retroactive benefit.*

prior stock = *preferred stock.*

pristine audit annual unannounced audit of every facility of HealthSouth by Ernest and Young LLP.

private account (P/A) = *secret account.*

private accountant an accountant that serves one organization only.

private annuity the transfer of money or property to an individual or organization in exchange for the transferee's promise to make lifetime payments to the transferor.

private audit the audit from 13 century to 17 century for protecting private assets only.

private cash book a book for recording spot cash and the balance of deposits only, other than the cash receipts or disbursements book.

private company a company owned by a few people. ***Also***: closed company; privately held company. ***See***: *nonpublic company; public company.*

private cost the cost of a specific item to an individual.

private ledger <1> a ledger of partnership that contains only capital accounts and the withdrawals accounts. <2> = *secret ledger.*

private ledger account = *secret account.*

private letter ruling a letter sent by the IRS in response to a request for clarification or interpretation of a tax law as it applies to a specific question or situation.

private limited company <UK> a limited company that has a restriction offering shares to the public.

privately held company = *private company.*

private medical insurance <UK> an insurance to cover the costs of private medical treatment.

private purpose trust fund a government fund used to account for all private activities.

private rate of return <1> financial rate of return anticipated by businessmen prior to investing their monies. <2> ratio of the annual investment income to the total investment.

private trust a trust created to benefit private individuals rather than the public at large. **See**: *charitable trust.*

private unrequited transfer the resident immigrant workers' transfer of money to their country of origin.

privity the relationship between parties to a contract.

PRJ purchase return journal

probability-proportional-to-size sampling audit sampling used to express a conclusion in dollar amounts. ***Also***: cumulative monetary amount sampling; dollar-unit sampling; PPS sampling. **See**: *variables sampling.*

probable cost the cost that may or may not incur.

probable maximum loss (PML) = *maximum probable loss.*

procedural audit an audit that focuses on the accounting policies, procedures, and internal control.

proceeds amount a taxpayer receives from the sale of a property.

proceeds of distribution <Canada> amount from a policy loan made after 3/31/1978 in excess of the unpaid policy loan or premium.

process account under process costing, an account used to take place of the work-in process account.

process audit social audit approach developed by Baner and Fenn of the Harvard University.

process cost manufacturing cost of a process.

process costing the costing procedure under which unit costs are computed by dividing the cost of a batch for a time period by units of output for that time period. ***Also***: batch costing; continuous process costing.

process cost report a report used in process costing system, including schedule of equivalent production, unit analysis schedule, and cost summary schedule.

process cost sheet a sheet listing total and unit cost figures under process costing.

process cost system a system in which costs are assembled in terms of steps or processes in manufacturing a product. ***Also***: continuous cost system; continuous process cost system.

processing cost = *conversion cost.*

product approach = *output approach.*

product contribution margin excess of the sales over the cost of a product or products.

product cost <1> cost that is associated with the product inventories which are expected to provide a future service benefit at the time of production. ***Also***: attributable cost; clinging cost; inventoriable cost. **See**: *period cost; variable cost.* <2> that portion of marketing cost that relates to the product and the marketing activities.

product costing the costing in which product costs are transferred from the asset inventory to cost of goods sold expense in the period in which the benefit is received by selling the goods.

product income statement income statement for a product or a group of products.

production account an account used by social accounting for recording output and costs of the production sector. ***Also***: manufacturing account.

production activity variance that portion of cost variance caused by the difference between the sales volume and production volume.

production available cost the sum of the beginning work-in-process costs and overhead costs.

production-based cost a cost that varies as the product changes.

production basis method <1> a revenue recognition method under which revenues are recognized at the point of production when product units are homogeneous, there is a relatively stable market and selling costs are normal. ***See***: *percentage-of-completion method*. <2> = *production unit basis method*.

production budget an estimate of the number of units to be produced during a budget period.

production capacity cost the cost of maintaining production capacity.

production cost the sum of factor cost and administration cost.

production costs per unit cost of production per unit of output. ***Also***: single cost; unit production cost.

production cost variance the difference between actual cost of production and the standard or budgeted cost of production.

production department expense that expense incurred in the production department other than materials and labor costs.

production hours method a method of depreciation based on the proportion of production hours.

production method <1> a method of recognizing revenue of a period based on the proportion of the production volume in that period to total production volume expected. <2> a method of allocating joint costs based on the proportion of production volume. <3> a method of separating byproduct at the time of production, the net realizable value of byproduct is deducted from the total cost of main products to obtain the cost of goods manufactured. ***Also***: fixed base proportional method; output method; productive output method; proportional method on fixed base; proportion on fixed base method; service unit method. ***See***: *sales method*. <4> = *production unit basis method*.

production order system = *job order cost system*.

production overhead = *factory overhead*.

production-unit basis method a method under which depreciation cost on a plant asset is allocated to products based on the relation of the units of product produced by the asset during a given period to the total units the asset is expected to produce during its life. ***Also***: depletion unit method; production basis method; production method; unit-of-output method.

production-unit depreciation depreciation allocated by the production unit basis method.

production variance the difference between ex post budgeted activity level and the standard activity level needed to produce the actual output.

production volume variance = *overhead volume variance*.

production yield variance = *yield variance*.

productive asset = *active asset*.

productive labor cost = *direct-labor cost*.

productive labor hours method = *direct labor-hour method*.

productive output method = *production method*.

productivity the efficiency with which people and capital are combined in the output of the economy. ***Also***: total factor productivity.

product line costing the costing under which costs of each product line are accumulated and distributed separately.

product line profit contribution margin for a defined product or group of products less the costs directly assignable to the segment.

product mix variance that portion of contribution margin variance caused by the variation in the product mix.

product unit cost = *cost per unit.*

product warranty cost a cost of providing product warranty.

professional accountant = *public accountant.*

professional association (PA) = *professional corporation.*

professional audit = *external audit.*

professional corporation (PC) an entity having some characteristics of a corporation but not offering limited liability. ***Also***: professional association.

professional ethics moral principles and standards of conduct guiding CPAs in performing their functions.

professional fee money paid for work done by a professional.

professional liability insurance coverage in various professional fields.

profit (prft)(prof) excess of revenue over cost. ***See***: *bottom line; net income.*

profitability average net income after taxes generated by investing funds in a project.

profitability accounting <1> the more popular name for financial accounting, performance evaluation accounting and accounting for decision making. <2> = *responsibility accounting.*

profitability index (PI) <1> a ratio of revenue to expenditure. <2> = *present value profitability index.*

profitability object level cost accumulation at which sales revenues are matched to cost to analyze profitability.

profitability ratio a ratio used to measure the profitability of a business, such as the profit on sales. ***See***: *basic earning power.*

profit after tax = *after-tax profit.*

profit and loss account (P/L a/c)(P&L a/c) <1> an account that shows gross profit and all expenses. <2> that part of an income statement which shows the gross profit, operating expenses and profit and loss. <3> = *income statement.*

profit and loss accounting the accounting for the revenue, expenditures and the profit and loss.

profit and loss adjustment a/c an account used by banks for recording profit and loss adjustment items, such as deferred revenue, deferred expense, accrual income and accrual expense, etc.

profit and loss appropriation account <1> the account for disclosing allocation of the balance of profit and loss among dividends, transfers, etc. <2> that part of an income statement showing the appropriation of net profit and loss.

profit and loss method a method of reporting currency gains and losses under which net profits or losses are first determined on the basis of a foreign currency, with the results determined when the currency is converted into dollars and repatriated to the US, with the unrepatriated balance determined at year end.

profit and loss on goods to arrive account under the gross price method, an account used to record profit and loss incurred in the process of transportation of goods.

profit and loss on realization = *realization profit or loss.*

profit and loss ratio a ratio at which partners share the profit and loss of a partnership.

profit and loss statement = *income statement.*

profit and loss statement equation revenue - expenditure = profit and loss. ***Also***: accounting profit equation; profit equation.

profit appropriation distribution of profit among all aspects.

profit appropriation statement a statement showing the appropriation of profits.

profit area = *profit wedge.*

profit budget a financial plan summarizing the projected revenues, expenses and net income for the coming period, together with supporting details, and also a sales budget, a production budget, a materials purchases budget, direct labor budget, factory overhead budget, cost of goods sold budget, selling and administrative expense budget and a budgeted income statement.

profit center a unit that incurs cost and also generates revenues. ***Also***: earnings center; profit responsibility center.

profit chart = *profit volume chart.*

profit contribution the contribution margin less fixed cost.

profit difference = *profit variance.*

profit drain decrease in profit because of the bad management, fraud, etc.

profit elimination = *inter-company profit elimination.*

profit engineering the analysis of breakeven point by using the profit volume chart other than the breakeven chart.

profit equation <1> income - target profit = allowed cost. <2> profit variance = revenue variance - cost variance. <3> an equation used in linear programming in order to find the highest profit point. <4> = profit and loss statement equation.

profit flow revenue expenditure + profit.

profit from business = *business income.*

profit from consolidation = *credit differential.*

profit from manufacturing = *manufacturing profit.*

profit in suspense the allowance made out of the profit for the retention monies that may incur in the future. ***Also***: profit reserved.

profit margin operating income divided by sales. ***Also***: margin of profit; profit rate.

profit maximization <1> maximizing the profit figure in the income statement. <2> maximizing the present value of assets.

profit maximization approach an approach under which the relationship of advertising costs and profits in the past is examined, and the advertising cost budget for the coming period is based on the highest profit level.

profit of stock the sum of interest in capital and the entrepreneur profit.

profit on paper = *pre-tax accounting income.*

profit on sales financial relationship of net income after taxes to the company's net sales for the accounting period. ***Also***: income per dollar of sales. ***See***: *return on sales.*

profit plan a summary of the projected revenues, expenses and income for the budget period.

profit planning chart = *breakeven chart.*

profit planning point sales calculated as (fixed cost + fixed capital × target rate of return) ÷ (1 - variable cost rate - variable capital rate × target profit on capital ratio).

profit rate = *profit margin.*

profit ratio a ratio, used for reporting gains from installment sales. It equals gross profit divided by the total contract price. ***See***: *net profit margin.*

profit reconciliation conversion of the profit ascertained under direct costing method to the profit under absorption method.

profit reinvestment = *earnings retention.*

profit-related pay <UK> income received by an employee under a *profit-sharing scheme.*

profit reserve = *profit in suspense.*

profit responsibility center = *profit center.*

profit retained = *retained earnings.*

profit sharing a plan maintained by an employer to provide deferred benefits from participation in profits by employees.

profit-sharing scheme <UK> a registered plan under which employees can receive tax-free profit related bonus. ***Also***: registered profit-related pay scheme.

profit-split method a method of setting hypothetical arm's length charges for the sales of goods between related parties, under which profit is divided between the parties so that each takes a realistic profit.

profit squeeze a smaller percentage of net profits caused by higher operating costs or lower selling price.

profit statement = *income statement.*

profit target = *target profit.*

profit variance a difference between actual profit and its planned amount. ***Also***: profit difference.

profit-volume chart (P/V chart) a graph of the total contribution margin expected at various levels of activity showing the effects of various changes in selling prices, variable costs, and fixed cost on expected total profit. ***Also***: profit chart.

profit-volume ratio (P/V) It equals sales revenue minus variable costs then divided by sales.

profit warning = *earnings warning.*

profit wedge the area between the total revenue line and the total costs line when the revenue exceeds breakeven point. ***Also***: profit area.

pro forma balance sheet when 2 companies are planning to combine, a balance sheet showing the planned new corporation and the relative position of each present company in the planned new company.

pro forma cost = *imputed cost.*

pro forma financial statement financial statement based on the results had a hypothetical event happened in the past. ***Also***: financial statement projection.

program accountability the accountability in connection of the economic effectiveness of a plan or program.

program approach an approach for preparing statement of activities of a government unit, the net program cost format provides cost information about the primary functions of the government and indicates the program's dependence on general revenues of the government.

program audit = *operating audit.*

program costing calculating cost of a specific program.

program evaluation and review technique (PERT) a method under which all tasks needed to complete a job are diagrammed in the network which is composed of events and activities and which shows relationship.

programmed cost the cost that results from a decision by management rather than from a change in the volume of activity. ***Also***: decision cost; discretionary cost; managed cost. ***See***: *capacity cost.*

progress billing account used to record billings to customers before completion of the construction contract, a contra account to Construction in Progress account.

progress curve =*learning curve.*

progressive cost = *increasing cost.*

progressive inventory method = *perpetual inventory method.*

progressive ledger = *Boston ledger.*

progressive tax income tax whose rates rise as the income increases. ***Also***: graduated tax. ***See***: *proportional tax; regressive tax.*

prohibited nonaudit service nonaudit service not allowed to provide to a client that is being audited by the auditor. ***See:*** *permitted nonaudit service.*

project accountant management accountant who is responsible for the accounting of projects.

project costing the costing that collects information on activities and costs associated with a specific activity, project or program.

projected balance sheet the balance sheet in projected data prepared when refinancing, merger or reorganization.

projected benefit cost a method under which the amount of pension expense assigned to the current year represents a level amount which will provide for the total projected benefits over the service lives of employees. ***See***: *aggregate method; attained-age-normal method; entry-age-normal method; individual-level-premium method; unit-credit method.*

projected benefit obligation (PBO) actuarial present value of the obligation determined under the benefit-years-of-service method.

projected cost <1> = *predetermined cost.* <2> = *standard cost.*

projected financial statement the financial statement used to assess the potential financial effects of the management decisions.

projected income <Canada> an estimate of a future pension benefit if a taxpayer is eligible to receive it now.

projected income statement an income statement based on cost analysis for use in profit planning in a service industry.

projected misstatement the *tainting percentage* multiplied by the *sampling interval.*

projected planning making special decisions, some of which may extend over many periods.

projected unit credit method = *benefits-years-of-service approach.*

projected unit method <UK> an accrued benefit valuation method under which the *actuarial liability* makes allowance for projected earnings. ***See***: *benefits-years-of-service approach.*

promise to pay = *acceptance.*

promissory note (PN)(p/n)(pro. note) written promise to pay a certain sum of money either on demand or by a certain time. ***Also***: bill obligatory; bill of debt; bill single; dog; iou; note; note for a term; note of hand; one-name paper; principal; time note.

promoter <1><Canada> a person who sells, issues or promotes the sale of a tax shelter or accepts consideration for it. <2> = *founder.*

promoter's share = *founder's share.*

promotion expense cost of samples or promotional items made available to the potential buyers.

prompt assessment the assessment of tax liability by the IRS immediately upon the request of a taxpayer.

pro. note promissory note

proofing machine a machine for combining two or more stages of the daily work of a branch and so affecting economies in time and staff, it lists and describes the day's credits and debits, and simultaneously records them on the appropriate sheets connected with the next stage of work.

proof of cash an audit procedure that reconciles the bank's record of cash activity with the client's accounting records.

proof of cost any evidence supporting the cost figure in the contract work.

proof of loss documentation of loss required by an insurance company.

proper journal = *general journal.*

property dividend a dividend paid in the form of securities of other corporations. ***Also***: asset dividend. ***See***: *cash dividend; dividend in kind.*

property income taxable income from property-related activities. ***Also***: asset income; income from property.

property, plant and equipment (PP&E) = *plant asset.*

property pledged = *hypothecated asset.*

property reserve = *allowance for depreciation.*

property tax <1> a tax imposed on the value of real and personal property. <2> = *real property tax.*

proportional cost a cost in direct proportion to the sales quantity or production volume.

proportional method on fixed base = *production method.*

proportional tax a system in which all levels of income are taxed at the same rate. ***Also***: flat tax. ***See***: *progressive tax; regressive tax.*

proportionate profits method a method for determining gross income from mining for depletion where representative market or field prices cannot be determined, which assumes that each dollar spent to produce, transport, and sell the first marketable product earns an equal proportionate profit.

proportion of inactive to total accounts ratio of inactive accounts to the total accounts receivable.

proportion on fixed base method = *production method.*

proposed adjustment an adjustment to a taxpayer's return, which the IRS proposes to make, following an examination of the taxpayer's tax return.

proprietary account <1> an account for recording actual transactions. <2> an account used in government accounting for recording asset, liability, revenue, expense, profit and loss.

proprietary company = *controlling corporation.*

proprietary current account an account for recording the transactions between owners and the business.

proprietary fund a fund that is used to finance a government's business-like activities, e.g. *enterprise fund* and *internal service fund.* ***Also***: quasi-business fund.

proprietary stock option an employee stock option designed to transfer stock ownership to its holders. ***Opp***: *compensatory stock option.*

proprietorship <1> unincorporated business owned by an individual. <2> = *net worth.*

proprietorship bookkeeping the bookkeeping for reporting earnings of the owners.

proprietorship equation = *accounting equation.*

prospective approach treatment of change in accounting estimates by reporting future financial statements based on the new basis, but not restating prior period statements.

prospective benefits method a valuation method in which the accrual value of liabilities relate to the benefits for current and deferred pensioners and their dependents and the benefits that members will receive.

prospective cost = *future cost.*

prospective financial statement either *financial forecast* or *financial projection,* including the summaries of significant assumptions and accounting policies.

prospective forecast financial statement or projection including summaries of significant assumptions and accounting policies.

prospective reserve amount designated as a future liability for life insurance companies to meet the difference between future benefits and future premium.

prospective trust <UK> a trust that gives a protected interest for life or any less period to a beneficiary.

prospectus a document accompanying a new offering of securities. ***See***: *preliminary prospectus; final prospectus.*

protective clothing <UK> tax deductible expense on clothing in order to protect a taxpayer's body while working.

protective tariff a tax levied on imported goods to protect domestic manufacturers.

protest check = *bad check.*

protest fee a bank charge for the protest of a dishonored bill.

protest letter a letter sent to the IRS by the taxpayer protesting an assessment or collection.

prototype plan = *master pension plan.*

provincial sales tax (PST) <Canada> a sales tax imposed by the provincial government.

proving the ledger the preparation of the trial balance and the conformity between the sum of the subsidiary account balances and the ledger controlling account balance.

provision an amount estimated for an expense or loss that is quite possible to incur in the future. ***Also***: allowance.

provisional account = *nominal account.*

provisional income modified AGI plus 50% of Social Security benefit.

provisional tax <New Zealand> a tax on income that has not been taxed or undertaxed at source.

provision for bad and doubtful = *allowance for bad debts.*

provision for bad debts = *allowance for bad debts.*

provision for depletion the practice of writing down the book value of a wasting asset, such as a coal mine or oil well until its value is taken as nothing when depleted.

provision for income taxes a/c = *income tax expense a/c.*

provision for repayments = *sinking fund.*

proxy tax a tax on lobbying and/or political expenses that exceed an allowable amount set by the IRS.

"prudence" convention a convention under which inclusion of revenue and profits in accounts only when they are realized and inclusion in profit of known liabilities whether their sum and timing are known or can only be estimated.

PS price/sales ratio

PSA PAYE settlement agreement

PSC prior service cost

PSPA past service pension adjustment

P/S ratio profit-sales ratio

PST provincial sales tax

p-system = *fixed order interval system.*

PTI previously taxed income

PTIN preparer's tax identification number

PTO pure trust organization

PTP publicly traded partnership

public accountant (PA) an accountant that provides serve to all kinds of organizations, and holding a license. *Also*: independent public accountant; professional accountant.

public accounting independent auditing and reporting on financial statements.

public accounting firm a firm engaged in the practice of public accounting and auditing. *Also*: CPA firm.

public accounts financial statements of the federal government.

public audit <1> = *external audit.* <2> = *voucher audit.*

public book a record kept by an exchange member of the limit orders that have not yet been filled because either the ask price is too high or the bid price is too low.

public company a company whose stock is traded in the stock exchange. *Also*: public corporation; publicly held company. *See*: *private company.*

Public Company Accounting Oversight Board (PCAOB) a private, non-profit body created by the Sarbanes-Oxley Act of 2002 to protect investors and to further the public interest by ensuring that public company financial statements are audited.

public corporation <1> an entity established to carry out specific governmental purposes. <2> = *public company.*

public corporation accounting the procedure and methods for public corporations.

public debt program <Canada> a program designed to raise funds for the government at stable and low cost.

public goods and services benefits that can not be withheld from those who do not pay for them, e.g. law enforcement.

public limited partnership = *master limited partnership.*

publicly held company = *public company.*

publicly traded partnership (PTP) = *master limited partnership.*

Public Oversight Board (POB) founded in 1977, a group of prominent nonaccountants who monitor the activities of SEC Practice Section to provide assurance that the section is serving the public's interest.

public relations audit research that measures the programs attempt to influence public opinions.

public shell = *reverse merger.*

public trust = *charitable trust.*

public trustee <UK> an official appointed as a trustee to deal with trusts where there is a difficulty in finding a trustee. *Also*: trustee of last resort.

public unit account an account that carries funds provided by the US Government.

public utility accounting the accounting method for public utilities corporations.

published financial statement financial statement that has been opened to the public. *Also*: circulated financial statement.

published price = *quoted price.*

pump priming = *deficit financing.*

pup company a small company that is a subsidiary of a very large company.

PuPU purchasing power unit

PuPU accounting purchasing power unit accounting

purchase accounting = *purchase method.*

purchase acquisition acquiring another corporation by buying its assets or stocks in cash. *Also*: taxable acquisition. *See*: *pooling of interests; Type B reorganization.*

purchase allowance reduction in price at the buyer's request.

purchase and sale statement (P&S) a statement prepared by a broker after the settlement of a futures contract which lists the price, quantity, fees and net income.

purchase cost the cost incurred in the purchase of merchandise. *Also*: acquisition cost; purchasing cost.

purchased goodwill = *debit differential.*

purchase discount a discount allowed for prompt payment of an invoice. *Also*: cash discount; discount on purchase.

purchase discount lost = *discount lost.*

purchased preacquisition earnings increase in the share of the earnings of subsidiary through the purchase of additional stock.

purchase fee = *front-end load.*

purchase journal a special journal in which all the purchases of goods on account are recorded.

purchase ledger (PL) a ledger that contains the accounts of suppliers or customers. *Also*: bought ledger; creditor's ledger.

purchase method <1> a method for business merger which essentially adds the actual amounts paid for the acquired company's assets to the assets of the acquiring company. *Also*: purchase accounting. *See*: *pooling of interest method.* <2> method of accounting for supplies by government units under which the purchase of supplies is recorded as expenditure, even though the supplies may not have been used. *See*: *consumption method.*

purchase order (PO) a formal order of goods or services placed by the buyer.

purchase or sale on credit arrangement under which merchandises are sold and payments are made after a credit period. *Also*: on account; time contract.

purchase price variance a cost variance that is calculated as actual usage of material × (standard purchase price - actual purchase price).

purchase rebate reduction in price for purchases above a certain amount in a given period.

purchase return the return of the bought-in goods back to the vendor. *Also*: returned purchase; return of goods bought.

purchase returns and allowances an account used to accumulate cash refunds and other allowances that the seller may have to make to its customers if the product sent to the customer is returned as being unsatisfactory.

purchase returns journal (PRJ) book of first entry in which a listing is made of goods returned to the suppliers. *Also*: returns outwards journal.

purchases audit an audit of the purchase procedures and records.

purchases invoice method an accounts payable method under which all the unpaid invoices are kept in an open file according to their due dates. *See*: *invoice method.*

purchasing cost <1> cost incurred in the process of purchasing. <2> = *purchase cost.*

purchasing power gain = *monetary gain.*

purchasing power loss = *monetary loss.*

purchasing power unit (PuPU) = *constant dollar.*

purchasing power unit accounting (PuPU accounting) = *constant dollar accounting.*

pure capital = *net capital.*

pure income profit a payment which, in the hands of the recipient, does not involve a condition or counter stipulation relating to the provision of goods.

pure loss cost = *burning cost ratio.*

pure operational audit operating audit that is only limited to searching for problems.

pure premium of an insurance, it equals total amount of loss divided by number of units of exposure.

pure profit <1> net income less capital return. ***Also***: economic pure profit. <2> non-contract cost less economic rent. <3> = *excess profit.*

pure return to capital = *opportunity cost of capital.*

pure trust a trust created by the contractual rights by Article 1, Section 10 of the US Constitution, without a named person with a beneficial interest in the trust assets. ***Also***: Constitutional pure trust; Constitutional pure trust; common law trust; contract trust; contractual trust; pure trust organization.

pure trust organization (PTO) = *pure trust.*

pure variable cost = *variable cost.*

purpose statement a form filed by a borrower that details the purpose of a loan backed by securities.

purpose trust <UK> a trust to carry out a purpose.

push-down accounting the valuation implied by the market price of the stock to the parent company is pushed-down to the subsidiary and used to restate its assets and liabilities in separate financial statements.

Putnam doctrine a generality that when a taxpayer lends money to his or her company and is not repaid, the result is a capital loss.

PV <1> par value. <2> planned value. <3> present value.

P/V <1> payment voucher. <2> profit volume ratio.

P/V chart profit-volume chart

PVF profit volume factor

PVR profit volume ratio

P/W present worth

PwC PricewaterhouseCoopers

pyramiding financial advantage that it needs to own only 51% the voting stock in all subsidiaries to be in control of them.

pyramiding of income tax arrangements under which a payer agrees to pay the payee's taxes, leading to potentially endless rounds of taxes.

pyramid ratios a concept that management and financial ratios are best realized in a hierarchical sequence starting with profits related to capital.

Q q

QA quick asset

OCIC Quality Control Inquiry Committee

QEE qualified education expense

QP quoted price

QPP Quebec pension plan

Q ratio <1> ratio of a company's physical assets to their current replacement cost. <2> a ratio created by Nobel Economics Laureate James Tobin of Yale University, whereby he hypothesized that the combined market value of all the companies on the stock market should be about equal to their replacement costs. ***Also***: Tobin's Q ratio.

QRPBI qualified real property business indebtedness

QSSS qualified subchapter S subsidiary

QSST qualified subchapter S trust

QST Quebec Sales Tax

QSub qualified S corporation subsidiary

Q-system = *fixed order size system.*

quadruple entry four-part entry of one transaction because both the buyer and the seller are using double entry.

qualification of the opinion addition to the opinion about the restrictions, doubt or adverse opinions.

qualified accounts = *certified financial statements.*

qualified acquisition the acquisition of land by means of a gift or death of a qualified transferor.

qualified acquisition cost the cost to buy, build or rebuild a home, including closing costs, that qualifies as exemption from early withdrawals penalty from an IRA.

qualified adoption expenses all the necessary expenses surrounding the adoption of a child.

qualified business indebtedness debt of the taxpayer if it was incurred or assumed by a corporation and the taxpayer makes an election to reduce the basis of depreciable assets or realty held as inventory.

qualified business use the use of a listed property in a trade or business more than 50%.

qualified charitable organization a charitable organization that fits into one of the categories specified in the tax law.

qualified child care expenditure expense incurred to acquire, construct, rehabilitate or expand child care facilities.

qualified clinical testing expense the expense for drugs for rare diseases before July 1999, 50% of which are deductible.

qualified contract a bona fide contract to acquire the non-low-income portion of a building.

qualified corporation <1> a company which is allowed accelerated cost recovery system deductions and the investment credits with respect to leased assets. <2> a corporation 100% of its stock is held by one or more qualified nonprofit organizations.

qualified cost amount of sales tax paid and included in the total cost of a plant asset.

qualified disaster loss a deductible loss from a disaster occurred in a Presidentially declared disaster area.

qualified disaster relief payment a federal payment to a person in a Presidentially declared disaster area.

qualified distribution <1> distribution made from a Roth IRA that are tax and penalty free. <2> amount paid by private foundations that has the effect of reducing the basis on which the 15%/100% excise tax on failures to make minimum distributions falls.

qualified dividend mutual fund dividend from shares held for more than 60 days, qualified for 15% tax rate.

qualified earned income earned income within the pension plan and foreign earned income exclusion definitions allowable as adjustments to the gross income that are properly allocable to or chargeable against such earned income.

qualified education expense (QEE) expense such as tuition and tuition related expense that an individual, spouse or child must pay to an eligible post-secondary institution. *Also*: qualified tuition and related expense.

qualified education loan a loan for educational purpose, the interest on which is deductible.

qualified electric vehicle a vehicle that is powered mainly by an electric motor.

qualified employee <1> an enrolled member of an Indian tribe or a spouse. <2><Canada> an employee qualified to participate in a pension plan.

qualified employee discount employee discount not included in the taxable income under a specific tax code.

qualified employer plan a pension plan that meets the requirements of Section 4972(d). *Also*: eligible employer plan; qualified plan.

qualified expenditure <Canada> expenditure of a taxpayer in respect of scientific research and experimental development.

qualified expense for education credit purpose, amounts paid for tuition and fees required for enrollment or attendance at an eligible educational institution.

qualified export asset in a DISC, inventory or rental property grown or produced, and held for sale or rental abroad, as well as operating assets used in the export, account receivable, working capital, obligations arising out of producers' loan, and certain other export-related investments.

qualified export receipt of a DISC, receipt from the sale of export property, related and subsidiary services, interest on obligations that are qualified export assets.

qualified farm indebtedness debt incurred directly in connection with taxpayer's farm business if at least 50% of his or her total gross receipts for the 3 years preceding the tax year is attributable to farming.

qualified farm property <Canada> real property owned by a taxpayer and used in the course of carrying on the business of farming in Canada.

qualified first-year wage qualified wage paid in the first year when a long-term family assistance receiving employee starts working.

qualified funding asset an annuity contract having payment periods corresponding to those of the liability, which the assignee purchased within 60 days before or after the date of the assignment, and uses to satisfy that liability.

qualified higher education expense for student loan interest deduction purpose, amounts paid for tuition, fees, room and board, and related expenses such as books and supplies.

qualified housing interest = *mortgage interest deduction.*

qualified individual a person aged 65 before the end of a tax year.

qualified investment expense tax deduction directly connected with the production of qualified investment income.

qualified investment income the sum of investment income but no short-term capital gains, net capital gains from the disposition of property held for investment, or amount of the items of tax preference.

qualified leased property new recovery property, leased within three months after its acquisition, or bought by the lessor within three months of the lessee's acquisition, that qualifies for the investment tax credit.

qualified liquidation a decrease in the closing inventory of the liquidation year from the beginning inventory of that year.

qualified low-income community investment equity investment in, or loan to an active low-income community business.

qualified military benefit allowance or in-kind benefit received by a member or former member of the uniform service of the US which is excludable from gross income.

qualified net capital gains capital gain of the lesser for the taxable year, or the net capital gain for the taxable year for post June 8, 1981 sales and exchanges.

qualified net investment income the excess of qualified investment income over qualified investment expenses.

qualified nonprofit organization a nonprofit organization which fits into one of the categories in Section 501(a) of the Internal Revenue Code.

qualified opinion an auditor's opinion stating "except for" or "subject to" the effects of the matter to which the qualification relates, the financial statements present fairly consistently applied. *Also*: partially approving opinion.

qualified option a stock option the income from which is capital gains to the holder. *See*: *non-qualified option.*

qualified plan = *qualified employer plan.*

qualified property any property that is contracted for, purchased and placed in service within a prescribed window of time. *Also*: qualifying property. *See*: *50% bonus property.*

qualified real property business indebtedness (QRPBI) a debt incurred or assumed by taxpayer in connection with real property used in a trade or business and secured by the real property.

qualified report an audit report holding qualified opinions in it. *See*: *unqualified report.*

qualified research expense research expense that meets the requirements of the Revenue Code 41(e)(1)(A).

qualified research expense credit tax credit granted to corporations with *qualified research expense*, limited to 100% of the first $25,000, plus 75% of the tax amount in excess of $25,000.

qualified residence a taxpayer's principal residence, or a property elected to be treated as qualified for the tax year.

qualified residence interest any interest paid or accrued during the tax year on acquisition indebtedness or home equity loan when the property is taxpayer's qualified residence.

qualified retirement plan a plan that meets requirements of the Internal Revenue Code and as a result, is eligible to receive certain tax benefits.

qualified sales a sale or exchange of land between an individual taxpayer and a member of his family.

qualified S corporation subsidiary (QSub) a 100%-owned subsidiary of an S corporation if the stock is held by its shareholders rather than by another S corporation.

qualified small business corporation <Canada> a Canadian-controlled private corporation with 90% or more of its assets being used mainly in an active business carried on in Canada. *Also*: small business corporation.

qualified small business corporation share <Canada> share issued by a qualified small business corporation.

qualified startup cost expense for the establishment and administration of an qualified employer plan.

qualified stated interest stated interest that is unconditionally payable in cash or property.

qualified state tuition program a program offered by 40 states that includes college savings plan and prepaid tuition plans. *Also*: 529 college savings plan; 529 plan; Section 529 program.

qualified stock a stock held by non-corporate shareholders if, during the shorter of the 5-year period ending with the distribution in partial liquidation or the whole period during which the distributing corporation was in existence, the shareholder held at least 10% by value of the outstanding stock.

qualified student loan any loan to pay the *qualified higher education expenses.*

qualified subchapter S trust (QSST) a trust the grantor can attach strings to the assets he/she places in the trust. *See*: *electing small business trust.*

qualified taxpayer a producer of agricultural commodities who received certificates in the 1983 *payment-in-kind program.*

qualified transferor a person who held a land before Feb 23, 1983 or acquired a land after Feb 23, 1983.

qualified tuition and related expense = *qualified education expense.*

qualified wage <1> wage paid to a qualified employee. <2> wage paid to individuals who are long-term family assistance recipients.

qualified zone wage the wage paid or incurred by an employer in a particular employment zone.

qualifying acquisition = *tax-free reorganization.*

qualifying child a taxpayer's son, daughter or a descendant of either, a stepson, a stepdaughter, or an eligible foster child. *Also*: qualifying individual.

qualifying corporation <Canada> a Canadian-controlled private corporation with taxable income of the previous year is less than the business limit ($200,000).

qualifying disposition a disposition that does not involve all the assets, or the last asset, and that takes place because of a casualty, charitable contribution, the cessation of a business, etc.

qualifying distribution <1> distribution from a tax-deferred annuity for educational and exempt organization employees. <2> amount paid out to accomplish a private foundation's exempt purpose and acquire assets used or held for use directly in carrying out an exempt purpose.

qualifying dividend the dividend qualifying for the 100% dividends received deduction available to affiliated corporations that do not file consolidated tax returns. *See*: *eligible dividend.*

qualifying employer premium <Canada> employer's UI premium attributable to remuneration paid in the period to qualifying employees.

qualifying environmental trust <Canada> a trust created to fund the reclamation of a site. *Also*: mining reclamation trust.

qualifying income interest, dividend, rents, capital gains, etc. to make a publicly traded partnership qualified as a corporation.

qualifying indebtedness mortgage and other debt encumbering asset sold plus unsecured debt.

qualifying individual = *qualifying child.*

qualifying loan <UK> a loan the interest paid is tax deductible.

qualifying merger = *tax-free reorganization.*

qualifying person a child, dependent or spouse who meet specific requirements set by the IRS for tax credit purposes.

qualifying property = *qualified property.*

qualifying reserve = *restricted surplus.*

qualifying share <1> common stock held in order to qualify as a director of the issuing firm. <2><Canada> a share issued by a corporation after May 22, 1985 and before 1987.

qualifying share option <Canada> stock option granted by a Canadian controlled private corporation to its employees the exercise of which is tax free.

qualifying stock option an option granted by a company to its employees to buy its shares at a discount.

qualifying taxpayer <Canada> a taxpayer who resides in Ontario on Dec 31 of a tax year, and qualified for Equity in Education Tax Credit.

qualifying transfer <Canada> the transfer of capital property to a joint spousal trust.

qualifying travel expense <UK> business travel expense allowed to be deducted for tax purpose.

qualifying widow = *surviving spouse.*

qualifying withdrawal <Canada> withdrawal from a pension or retirement plan that meets the requirements to be exempt from taxes.

quality audit review of the quality of an accounting system.

quality control cost = *control cost.*

quality control standards audit standards for establishing quality control policies and procedures that provide reasonable assurance that all of a CPA firm's engagements are conducted in accordance with applicable professional standards.

quality cost the cost or expense incurred in order to improve the quality of products. *Also*: cost of quality.

quality cost accounting the accounting that accumulates and reports quality cost information.

quality of earnings extent that earnings is realistic in portraying the operating performance of a business. The more conservative, the higher the quality.

quantifiable cost a cost that can be measured in money.

quantitative unit method a method under which joint costs are distributed on proportion of the quantity of joint products.

quantity discount = *trade discount.*

quantity effect variance a variance calculated as: average contribution margin × (planned quantity of units sold - the actual quantity of units sold).

quantity variance cost variance calculated as standard price for a given source multiplied by the difference between the actual quantity used and the total standard quantity allowed for the number of good units produced.

quarterly report = *Form 10-Q.*

quasi-business fund = *proprietary fund.*

quasi-capital assets property held for the requisite long-term holding period.

quasi-community property a community property acquired from a decedent.

quasi-cost = *nominal cost.*

quasi-distribution <UK> = *loan to shareholder.*

quasi-external transaction payment from one governmental fund to another for services or goods that are being provided in the current period.

quasi-liability item that appears as a liability in the balance sheet which is actually not a liability.

quasi-reorganization reorganization that occurs when a corporation in financial difficulty modifies its capital structure without being forced to do so by creditors and without coming under supervision of a bankruptcy court.

quasi subsidiary <UK> a company, trust, partnership that is directly or indirectly controlled by the reporting entity, though not fulfilling the definition of a subsidiary.

Quebec pension plan (QPP) <Canada> a pension plan that operates in Quebec.

Quebec Sales Tax (QST) <Canada> a provincial sales tax on goods and services in Quebec. *Also*: taxe de vente du Quebec.

quick asset (QA) highly liquid asset such as cash, marketable securities, note receivable and perhaps accounts receivable that may be converted into cash. (Quick assets plus the inventory equals *current assets*). ***Also***: dollar asset; immediate asset; liquid asset; realizable asset.

quick capital the capital that can be realized quickly.

quick liability current liability that must be met within one month.

quick method <Canada> a method of computing remittance of GST by applying a prescribed rate to taxable sales.

quick ratio = *acid-test ratio.*

quick test = *acid-test ratio.*

quid pro quo an arrangement whereby a brokerage firm provides free research reports to another firm in return for executing all of its trades. ***See:*** *soft dollar.*

quiet period the period during which an issuer is "in registration" with the SEC and may not promote any new issue. ***Also***: blacked-out quiet period. ***See***: *cooling period.*

quittance = *cancellation of debt*

quota <Australia> = *declared period quota.*

quoted price (QP) stated price at which the last sale and purchase of a particular security or commodity took place. ***Also***: published price.

quoted security = *listed security.*

R r

R <1> cash receipts journal. <2> rate. <3> ratio. <4> revenue.

rabbi trust a trust the assets of which are subject to the claims of the creditors.

R a/c revenue account

radical school group of people who prefer present value and constant dollar accounting.

railroad unemployment repayment tax a 4% tax on a railroad employee's wages per federal unemployment tax act.

RAL refund anticipation loan

random number sampling audit sampling that uses a random number table or computer program to generate random numbers so that every sampling unit has the same probability of being selected.

random variances differences that are due to chance. *Also*: chance variances.

RAP <1> regulatory accounting principles. <2> regulatory accounting procedures.

RAR revenue agent's report

RAROC risk adjusted return on capital

RARORAC risk adjusted return on risk adjusted capital

rate <UK> = *council tax.*

rateable value <UK> = *assessed value.*

rate composition variance = *mix variance.*

rate earned on common stockholders' equity = *rate of return on common stockholders' equity.*

rate earned on stockholders' equity = *return on stockholders' equity.*

rate earned on total assets = *return on total assets.*

rate of conversion = *conversion ratio.*

rate of depreciation = *depreciation rate.*

rate of profit on capital employed ratio of profit to the average capital employed.

rate of return (RoR)(RR) a rate at which the present value of cash inflows equals the present value of cash outflows. *See*: *yield.*

rate of return on assets calculated as (net assets + interest expense) ÷ assets.

rate of return on average investment the annual, after tax income divided by the average investment in assets to produce the income.

rate of return on book value equity calculated as: dividend income - book value of stock.

rate of return on common stockholders' equity net income after tax and preferred dividends divided by average common stockholders' equity. *Also*: rate earned on common stockholders' equity.

rate of return on investment = *return on investment.*

rate of return on total capital = *all capital earnings rate.*

rate of tax = *tax rate.*

rate of variable cost variable costs divided by total costs or total sales revenue.

rate variance the difference between the actual wages paid and standard wage rate multiplied by the total actual hours of direct labor used.

ratio analysis evaluating the financial strength or weakness of a company and its operating trend by various ratios.

ratio estimation a variables sampling technique that uses the ratio of audited amounts to recorded amounts in the sample to estimate the total dollar value of the population and allowance for sampling risk.

ratio method a method under which an auditor uses sampling results to estimate the ratio of audited value to book value, then applies this ratio to the population to get the estimated actual value.

rational & systematic method a method providing for periodic pension expense between the minimum and maximum range.

ratio of accounts receivable to net sales accounts receivable balance divided by net sales. *Also*: debtors to sales ratio.

ratio of accumulated depreciation to cost of fixed assets the accumulated depreciation balance divided by the acquisition cost of fixed assets.

ratio of advertising to additional contribution margin annual advertising expenditure divided by additional contribution margin.

ratio of average trade debtors to daily sales average trade account receivable balance divided by daily sales amount.

ratio of breakeven sales to actual sales breakeven sales divided by actual sales.

ratio of capital investment a partner's invested capital divided by total partnership capital.

ratio of capital to current liabilities capital divided by the current liabilities.

ratio of capital to fixed assets total capital balance divided by fixed capital.

ratio of capital to liabilities = *equity-debt ratio.*

ratio of cash flow to debt cash flow divided by average balance of debts. *Also*: debt coverage.

ratio of cash flow to sales = *cash flow ratio.*

ratio of cash in hand to creditors cash on hand divided by the accounts payable.

ratio of cash plus marketable securities to current liabilities calculated as: (cash on hand + marketable securities) ÷ current liabilities.

ratio of cash to current liabilities cash on hand divided by the current liabilities.

ratio of debt to capital = *debt-equity ratio.*

ratio of earnings distribution after consolidation ratio at which income will be distributed among each group of shareholders after consolidation.

ratio of earnings distribution before consolidation ratio at which net income was distributed before consolidation.

ratio of earnings to total assets = *asset earnings power.*

ratio of fixed assets to net worth = *fixed ratio.*

ratio of liabilities to net worth = *debt-equity ratio.*

ratio of market price to earnings per share = *price-earnings ratio.*

ratio of net income to net worth = *return on stockholders' equity.*

ratio of production of business equipment to production of consumer goods ratio of index of production in business and consumer industries of final products in the Index of Industrial Production.

ratio of sales to debtors = *accounts receivable turnover.*

ratio of sales to total assets = *asset utilization ratio.*

ratio of times covered calculated as: net income × (long-term interest + preferred dividend).

Raw-in-Process Inventory a/c inventory account in the just-in-time system that combines the materials inventory and the work-in-process inventory account.

raw material unprocessed material bought in by a business for manufacturing. *Also*: stock raw.

raw material ledger a subsidiary ledger containing accounts for each material.

RBL reasonable benefit limit

RCA retirement compensation arrangement

RCA trust a trust created and governed by an RCA.

RE retained earnings

reabsorbed costs cost absorbed again by the products.

reacquired stock = *treasury stock.*

readjustment entry <1> entry for adjusting cash basis figures to accrual basis figures. <2> = *reversing entry.*

ready cash the cash asset held ready for immediate use.

ready money = *imprest fund.*

real account an account for balance sheet items, such as asset, liability, and capital, having balance which will be carried forward from one period to another. *Also*: balance account.

real asset <1> a balance sheet asset that actually exists. *See*: *nonexistent asset.* <2> bonds, real estates, etc. **Opp**: *contingent asset.*

real capital the capital invested in physical plant assets for the production of goods. *Also*: physical capital; substantial capital.

real capital stock = *capital stock.*

real controlling account an account that contains no suspense or balancing items.

real cost <1> cost measured in tonnage, mileage, etc. <2> cost measured at the base period price. <3> = *opportunity cost.*

real cost of production the sum of wages and profit.

real earnings the earnings adjusted to exclude the effects of inflation.

real economic earnings (REE) earnings based on the fundamental underlying earning power of a company.

real estate = *real property.*

real estate investment trust (REIT) a trust that uses the pooled capital of investors to purchase and manage income properties and/or mortgage loans.

real estate limited partnership a limited partnership formed to build new structures and generate income from existing property, or profit from the capital appreciation of undeveloped land.

real estate syndication a corporation that invests in real estate and distributes income to each participant.

real estate tax shelter tax shelter involving investments in improved real estate.

real gain the gain adjusted to exclude the effect of inflation. *Also*: economic gain.

real gross national disposable income (RGNDI) real gross national income plus real secondary income receivable and minus real secondary income payable to the rest of the world.

real gross national income (RGNI) gross national income after deducting real primary income payable to the rest of the world and adding real primary income receivable.

real income the income of an individual, group, or country adjusted for changes in purchasing power caused by inflation. *Also*: absolute income; real wage.

real interest rate the current interest rate minus the current inflation rate.

realizable asset = *quick asset.*

realizable cost savings = *monetary gain.*

realizable values method a method under which the cost of joint products inventory contains only realizable value other than actual cost.

realization account an account maintained when a business is being wound-up or sold.

realization and liquidation profit and loss account = *liquidation account.*

realization concept a financial concept which maintains that, except for unusual cases, the unrealized profits should not be recorded.

realization principle a rule which defines revenue as an inflow of assets in exchange for goods or services, and revenue is to be recognized at the time, but not before it is earned. *Also*: recognition principle; revenue realization principle.

realization profit or lose the balance of the liquidation a/c after realization. *Also*: profit and loss on realization.

realized depreciation = *recapture of depreciation.*

realized gain or loss gain or loss arising from sales or other dispositions of the property.

realized income the sum of current operating income and realized holding gains.

realized loss the loss recognized when assets are sold for a price lower than the original purchase price.

realized profit net proceeds from a transaction in excess of cost.

reallocation of income IRS's reallocation of income shifted by the taxpayer.

reallowance amount paid to a broker/dealer who is not part of the underwriting syndicate but who still sells shares in the offering.

real net national disposable income (RNNSI) real gross national disposable income minus consumption of fixed capital. ***Also***: net national income.

real primary income labor income and property income of a country. ***Also***: primary income.

real profit earnings left after allowance has made for the impact of inflation.

real property an interest in land or things attached to it. ***Also***: real estate; realty. ***See***: *immovable property.*

real property tax a tax on the assessed value of a real property. ***Also***: property tax. ***See***: *personal property tax.*

real rate of return rate of return after adjusting for inflation.

real reserve <UK> = *self-insurance fund.*

real return actual payback on an investment after removing the effect of inflation.

real secondary income taxes and other transfers of a country. ***Also***: secondary income.

real-time posting the posting of ledger accounts immediately after the entry is made. ***See***: *batch posting.*

realty = *real property.*

real wage = *real income.*

real year dollar value that includes the impact of inflation.

rearrangement cost a cost incurred in order to rearrange the plant assets. ***Also***: plant rearrangement cost.

reasonable allowance depletion allowance equaling 5% of the gross income.

reasonable amount <Canada> amount of reserve for future proceeds calculated as a percentage of the proceeds not yet due multiplied by the capital gain.

reasonable benefit limit (RBL) <Australia> the maximum amount of retirement and termination of employment benefits that individuals can receive over their lifetime at reduced tax rates.

reasonable care = *due care.*

reasonable cost <1> the cost not more than the actual cost to the employer of the board, lodging, or other facilities furnished to the employees. <2> cost of prescription drugs not too high for the taxpayers. <3><UK> cost for each year of education in a college which can be afforded by a student.

reasonable criteria the criteria that yield useful information.

reasonableness test procedures to examine the logic of accounting information.

reasonably attainable standard cost target cost established at levels of performance expected to be achieved in the coming period.

reassessment <Canada> tax assessment made after a previous assessment.

reaudit after obtaining an independent auditor's opinion, the client engaged another independent auditor to give another opinion.

rebalancing making adjustments to counteract the fact that different assets have performed differently and having different percentages of the portfolio than they were intended to.

rebate = *bank discount.*

recalculation audit procedure involving a reperformance of calculations made by the client.

recapitalization <1> readjustment of capital and liabilities by general price level index, <2> accounting for the deficit by paid-in surplus, or the change of outstanding securities.

recapitalization capital the capital derived from the excess of the market value of new shares over the book value of original shares.

recapture increase in current tax liability, or an adjustment in a carryover rather than an adjustment to prior years.

recapture income that portion of a gain that would be ordinarily treated as long term capital gain, but is treated as ordinary income as a result of the application of a recapture provision.

recapture of depreciation amount by which the selling price exceeds the book value of an asset that is disposed of and subjected to recapture of the investment tax credit. *Also*: depreciation recapture; realized depreciation.

recapture rate tax rate used to compute recapture of depreciation.

recapture rule a rule that excess alimony made in the first year and second year must be recaptured in the third year.

recast earnings a recalculation of earnings of a target company and the acquiring company based on the assumption that certain costs could be eliminated through new forms of cost savings.

receipt ledger a ledger containing accounts for each kind of receipts.

receipts and payments statement a statement showing the receipts, disbursements of cash in a given period.

receivable = *account receivable.*

receivable account = *account receivable.*

receivables balance fractions percentage of a month's sales that remains uncollected.

receivables ledger = *accounts receivable ledger.*

receivables turnover = *accounts receivable turnover.*

Receiver General <Canada> the CFO of the Canada federal government.

receiving report document used within a firm, upon receiving the goods, to report the actual quantity received.

recent cost = *current cost.*

recent-purchase method = *last invoice price method.*

recharacterize to treat an IRA contribution to one type as made to another type. *See*: *reverse.*

reciprocal account an account that relates to another account in the counter party.

reciprocal allocation = *reciprocal service cost allocation.*

reciprocal service cost allocation cost allotment among service departments that serve each other. *Also*: reciprocal allocation. *See*: *algebraic method; continuous allotment method; multi-step cost reassignment.*

reciprocal stockholding a subsidiary company owns stock in the parent company.

reciprocal trust a trust that one person creates for the benefit of another who in turn creates another trust for the benefit of the first party.

reckonable date <UK> the date from which interest is calculated on late payment of tax.

reclassification change in the depreciation life of an asset.

reclassification adjustment reversal of unrealized amount that has been recognized and included in net income of prior period. *Also*: recycling adjustment.

reclassification entry an entry intended for the auditor's working paper pertaining to the proper financial statement presentation of a correct balance. *Also*: reclassification journal entry.

reclassification journal entry (RJE) = reclassification entry.

recognition recording a business occurrence in the accounting records.

recognition principle = *realization principle.*

recognized built-in gain any gain recognized during the recognition period on the disposition of any assets held on the first year the corporation becomes an S corporation. *Also*: built-in gain

recognized gain or loss taxable gain and deductible loss realized.

recognized principle = *generally accepted accounting principle.*

recommended entry an adjusting entry recommended to the client by an auditor.

recomputed basis adjusted basis of the asset, adding depreciation, or amortization, which was allowed or allowable, for the purposes of determining the amount of gain on the disposition of an asset.

reconciliation adjusting the difference between two items so that the figures agree.

reconciliation account an a/c used for reconciling the difference between flow amounts and stock amounts in the preparation of the national balance sheet. *See*: *accommodating account.*

reconciliation method = *indirect method.*

reconciliation of bank account accounting for the difference between the bank balance and the cash book balance of the depositor. *Also*: reconciliation of cash receipts and payments.

reconciliation of cash receipts and payments = *reconciliation of bank accounts.*

reconciliation of cost and financial accounts <UK> accounting for any difference between cost accounts and financial accounts under interlocking accounts.

reconciliation of financial and cost profit accounting for the difference between the profit figures in the cost accounts caused by the inventory pricing methods.

reconciliation of surplus reconciliation for the ending and the beginning surplus.

reconciliation statement of bank accounts a statement showing exactly what entries make up the difference at any time between the bank balance shown in the cash book and that shown in the bank statement.

reconciliation statement of surplus a subsidiary statement showing the reasons why the book surplus and the statement surplus differ.

reconstruction of income determination of a taxpayer's income by the IRS in the absence of adequate books and records.

record date = *date of record.*

recorded cost the cost recorded in the books. *Also*: book cost.

recording principle the rule that must be applied with when keeping records.

record keeping safe keeping and maintaining of the accounting records, books, accounts, evidence papers, etc. necessary for the tax and management purposes.

recoverability test = *recovery test.*

recoverable amount the greater of the net realizable value of an asset and its value in use.

recoverable cost the current value of inventory assets that is lower than their original cost. *Also*: reimbursable cost.

recovery <1> payback of investment costs in revenue. <2> the return to, or recoupment by a taxpayer of amounts previously deducted.

recovery of capital a concept the gist of which is that a taxpayer should not be viewed as having received income until the original investment is recovered.

recovery of uncollectible accounts written-off collection of the bad debts that have been written off previously.

recovery property a tangible asset acquired after 1980 from any unrelated persons that is of a character subject to depreciation and either used in a trade or business or held for the production of income. *Also*: Section 168 property.

recovery tax <Canada> a tax on payments to high-income pension receivers whose net world income exceeds a threshold amount. *Also*: social benefits repayment.

recovery test a test used to determine the impairment of the value of an asset or goodwill by comparing the fair value or undiscounted expected net future cash flows to the carrying value. *Also*: impairment test; test for impairment; test of impairment; recoverability test. *See*: *goodwill impairment.*

recovery value <1> = *residual value.* <2> = *salvage value.*

rectification account an account that is debited the rectification cost, credited the value of rectified units and the balance of which is transferred to factory overhead or profit and loss account.

rectification cost <1> cost incurred to rectify the spoiled unit. <2> fees paid by a shareholder whose name is wrongly entered on (or omitted from) a register to the keeper of the register to remove (or enter) his name.

recurring audit = *repeating audit.*

recurring cost a cost that incurs repeatedly under the same condition.

recurring income business income that occurs from normal operations and is likely to be repeated in future periods.

recurring journal entry = *fixed entry.*

recurring profit to sales ratio recurring profit divided by sales.

recycling adjustment = *reclassification adjustment.*

recycling income personal income received for recycling beverage containers. *Also*: recycling revenue.

recycling revenue = *recycling income.*

red balance account balance in red ink. *Also*: negative account balance.

redeemable preference share <UK> = *redeemable stock.*

redeemable stock a preferred stock that can be called in for redemption by the issuer. *Also*: redeemable preference share.

redeemed share = *treasury stock.*

redemption <1> purchase of bonds outstanding by the bond issuer. <2> mutual fund investor's selling of fund shares. <3> = *stock redemption.*

redemption cost the lesser of the amount of the discount provided by the terms of the coupon, or the amount incurred by the taxpayer for paying such discount plus the amount paid to the retailer.

redemption premium = *call premium.*

redemption reserve a reserve established by the manufacturers and merchants to account for future obligations to make payments to satisfy their trading stamp and premium coupons.

redemption value amount that a corporation must pay for the return of a share of preferred stock previously issued by the corporation.

redemption yield <1> internal rate of return of an investment that consists of buying a security that is redeemable, keeping it until it is redeemed and receiving the proceeds of a redemption. <2> = *yield to maturity.*

redetermination of foreign tax = *foreign tax redetermination.*

red-herring = *preliminary prospectus.*

red-ink entry <1> a record in the book in red ink. <2> = *reversing entry.* <3> = *net loss.*

rediscount rate = *discount rate.*

redistributed cost the cost, which was distributed from other departments, distributed again to other departments.

red-line method = *two-bin method.*

reduced profit method a method under which a real estate seller recognizes a portion of profit at the time of sale with remaining portion recognized in future periods.

reduced rate <UK> lower rate of value added tax on some supplies.

reduced value entry recording acquired property at its *written-down value.*

reducing-balance form = *report form.*

reducing-balance method = *declining balance method.*

reducing installment method = *declining balance method.*

reduction of capital <1> the reduction in total capital because the share value has risen far above the nominal value or because the share value has fallen so far below the nominal face value. ***See***: *increase of capital.* <2> capital amount that has been reduced. ***Also***: lost capital.

reduction rate <Canada> a reduction of 7% of tax in the form of a tax credit granted to a CCPC on its third $100,000 income from active business.

redundancy payment <UK> a payment to an employee who is leaving the company because there is no longer work available. ***Also***: leaving payment.

REE real economic earnings

referral fee a fee paid to a person for help in completing a transaction.

reforestation credit a 10% tax credit on the basis of qualified timber property attributable to reforestation expenditures.

refund = *tax refund.*

refundable credit a tax credit that can reduce tax liabilities to a negative amount that can be refunded. ***Also***: refundable tax credit. ***See***: non-refundable credit.

refundable investment tax credit <Canada> refundable amount of 40% of the investment tax credits earned in a taxation year.

refundable tax <Canada> a tax that can be returned to the taxpayer if certain conditions are met.

refundable tax credit = *refundable credit.*

refund anticipation loan (RAL) a loan lent to a taxpayer based on the anticipated refund on the return.

refund check a check used to pay tax refund to the taxpayer.

refund cycle the time between the date a tax return is submitted and the anticipated date on which a refund is issued by the IRS.

refund of premium <Canada> amount paid out of or under an RRSP to the spouse of an annuitant as a consequence of the annuitant's death prior to the plan's maturity.

refund of tax = *tax refund.*

register (reg)(regr) = *journal.*

registered auditor <UK> a member of a recognized supervisory body having granted an order to perform audit.

registered capital = *authorized capital stock.*

registered education savings plans (RESP) <Canada> a program that allows taxpayers to put aside some income for their children's educational use.

registered investment <Canada> a trust of corporation that has applied and been accepted by the Minister as a registered retirement savings plan or a deferred profit sharing plan.

registered pension plan (RPP) <Canada> a retirement plan that can be regulated by provincial and federal pension legislation, such as money purchase provision and defined benefit provision.

registered profit-related pay scheme <UK> = *profit-sharing scheme.*

registered public accounting firm a public accounting firm registered with the *Public Company Accounting Oversight Board.*

registered retirement income fund (RRIF) <Canada> a fund established with a carrier and registered with the Canada Customs and Revenue Agency. ***Also***: retirement income fund.

registered retirement savings plan (RRSP) <Canada> = *IRA.*

registered security <1> a security the owner of which is recorded by the issuing company. <2> public security registered with the SEC.

Registration Statement = *Form S-1.*

regression analysis measurement of the average amount of change in cost or expense that is associated with one unit of increase in production or other variables.

regression approach a method using both the average ratio and the average difference in calculating an estimate of the total amount for the population.

regressive tax a tax that takes a larger percentage of the income of low-income people than of high-income people. ***See***: *progressive tax; proportional tax.*

regular account <1> an account that must be kept under normal condition. <2> an account used to record the transaction affecting a fund. ***See***: *budgetary account.*

regular audit = *periodical audit.*

regular cost <UK> consistent ongoing cost under the *actuarial method.*

regular dividend = *ordinary dividend.*

regular income tax = *regular tax.*

regular IRA = *traditional IRA.*

regular tax <1> personal income tax liability calculated under normal exemption and deductions rather than AMT or surtax. ***Also***: normal tax; regular income tax. <2> income tax of a corporation when using straight-line depreciation.

regular tax deduction an alternative floor that must be exceeded for the minimum tax on items of tax preference to apply.

regular tax liability the tax liability less nonrefundable credit, penalty taxes, etc.

regular tax rate the rate of regular tax. ***See:*** *incentive tax rate.*

regulated money = *hard money.*

Regulation A an SEC regulation that governs the offerings of $5,000,000 or less, which qualify for simplified registration (an exemption).

Regulation D an SEC regulation that governs private placement exemption when there is no investment banker involved.

Regulation FD SEC regulation enforcing full disclosure of information by a publicly-listed corporation. ***See:*** *full disclosure.*

Regulation M <1> an IRS regulation that allows regulated investment companies to pass taxes from capital gains, dividends, and interest distributions directly onto individual investors. <2> the SEC regulation which became effective on March 4, 1997 and used Rule 101, 102, 103, 104 and 105 to replace Rules 10b-6, 10b-6A, 10b-7, 10b-8 and 10b-21.

Regulation S-X SEC regulation specifying the specific format and content of financial reports.

regulatory accounting principles (RAP) the requirements or methods of accounting and reporting specified by regulatory agencies for supervisory reporting purposes. ***Also***: regulatory accounting procedures.

regulatory accounting procedures (RAP) = *regulatory accounting principles.*

rehabilitation credit a 10% (20% for certain historic structure) special tax credit given for the qualified expenditures on the continued use and rehabilitation of historical buildings and old structures.

rehabilitation expenditure an expense in connection with the rehabilitation of historical buildings and old structures.

reimbursable cost = *recoverable cost.*

reimbursable entry an entry for replenishing petty cash or inventory transactions.

reimbursement <1> payment from one governmental fund to another for costs paid earlier on its behalf. <2> payment to the employee by the employer for company expenses paid in advance by the employee.

reimbursement account = *flexible spending account.*

reinstated account current account reopened after the writing off of the bad debts.

reinsurance fund <UK> = *self-insurance fund.*

reinvested distribution mutual fund distribution that has been reinvested.

reinvested earnings = *retained earnings.*

reinvestment rate the rate at which cash flows from fixed-income securities may be reinvested. ***See***: *earnings retention ratio.*

reinvestment relief <UK> a capital gains tax relief that enabled a gain on the disposal of an asset to be rolled over if shares from an unlisted company are acquired.

REIT real estate investment trust

rejected check = *bad check.*

related company = *affiliated corporation.*

related cost <1> cost that relates to the current period revenue. ***Also***: associated cost. <2> cost that relates to another cost. <3> = *joint cost.*

related party transaction a transaction between two parties one of whom can exercise control or significant influence over the operating policies of the other.

relative contribution approach = *multi-block system.*

relative fixed cost fixed cost that may be avoided.

relative income = *money income.*

relative market value method = *relative sales value method.*

relative return the return on an investment that is based on the income achieved by replacing the deteriorated or obsolescent facilities.

relative risk a risk that may happen in the financial statement audit because of the wrong test scope selected.

relative sales value <1> sales value of a joint product after the split-off point or after further processing. <2> the market value of the bonds.

relative sales value allocation <1> allocation of the joint cost of joint products by the proportion of their relative sales value. <2> allocation of the portfolio cost of securities by proportions of the relative sales value.

relative sales value method a method used to allocate joint cost or lump-sum cost based on their relative sales value. ***Also***: gross sales value method; market value method; relative market value method; sales value basis.

release = *abandonment.*

release from debt = *cancellation of debt.*

relevance accounting information capable of making a difference in a decision by helping users to form predictions about the outcomes of past, present and future events.

relevant accounting period accounting period of which any part enters into the basis year.

relevant cost future cost that differs in amount between two alternative courses of action, e.g. a plant costing $10,000 2 years ago, has accumulated $2,000 depreciation, now it is worth only $1,000 the relevant cost will become $8,000. ***Also***: differential cost; incremental cost. ***See***: *marginal cost.*

relevant cost approach decision making approach that utilizes the concept of relevant cost. ***Also***: differential analysis; incremental analysis.

relevant costing the costing which is concerned with long-run questions and shows differences between alternatives as a basis for decision. ***Also***: differential costing; incremental costing.

relevant discounted security <UK> a security the issue price of which is less than the redemption amount by more than 0.5% of the issue price times the number of years between the issue and the redemption. ***Also***: discounted security.

relevant earnings <UK> the personal income arising irrespective of remuneration from an office or employment held by the individual concerned other than a pensionable office or employment.

relevant future cost (R-F cost) the future cost that relates to the present decisions. ***See***: *irrelevant future cost.*

relevant income distributable income other than trading income for the accounting period concerned as can be distributed without prejudice to the requirements of the company's business.

relevant period months beginning on the day following the end of the period of account in which the sum in questions is charged as an expense.

relevant range (RR) the normal operating range for the business excluding extremely high and low levels of production which are not apt to be encountered.

reliability level = *confidence level.*

reliance strategy a strategy under which an auditor sets control risk below maximum and relies on internal control and performs less substantive test. *Also*: systems approach. *See*: *substantive strategy.*

relief <UK> = *tax credit.*

relief for blind person <UK> £1,480 additional tax allowance for a registered blind taxpayer. *Also*: blind person's allowance; blind person's relief.

remainder = *balance.*

remaining book value = *written down value.*

remaining principal balance amount of principal dollars remaining to be paid under a mortgage as of a given time.

remarketed preferred stock = *auction rate preferred stock.*

remeasurement changing local currency statements to functional currency statements. *See*: *translation.*

remeasurement gain the gain on remeasuring the account balances of a foreign subsidiary which does not maintain full set of financial statements. *See*: *translation gain.*

remeasurement loss the loss on remeasuring the account balances of a foreign subsidiary which does not maintain full set of financial statements. *See*: *translation loss.*

remission <Australia> waiver of a duty on dutiable goods.

remission of debt = *cancellation of debt.*

remission of tax = *tax exemption.*

renewable electricity production credit a 1.7 cents per kilowatt hour of electricity produced by taxpayers from wind or closed-loop biomass at a qualifying facility during the 10-year period after the facility is placed in service. *Also*: credit for producing electricity from certain renewable resources.

renewal <UK> reconstruction of the entire asset.

renewal expenditure the expense on the renewal of an asset.

renewals basis <UK> a basis of property measured at the assumption that it is going to be renewed.

rent <1> periodic payment under an *annuity* contract. <2> money for the privilege of using other's property.

rental expense deduction a deduction allowed for payments for the use of another's property for trading or business purposes.

rental property a property allowed to be used by someone in return for a rent. *Also*: let property.

rent-a-room relief <UK> a £2,125 tax deduction introduced in August 2002 available to taxpayer with rental income that exceeds £4,250 per year.

renter's credit state tax credit available to qualified renters.

rent-to-own property (RTO property) any consumer durable property rented and transferred to the renter at the end of the contract.

reorder point a predetermined signal that a replenishing order should be placed. *Also*: inventory order point; order point.

reorder point system = *fixed order size system.*

reorganization recapitalization of ownership only by a shake-up of management and organizational structure or both.

reorganization accounting the accounting for reorganization affairs.

repair allowance amount by which a taxpayer could elect to characterize a fixed amount of the annual expenses as being treated as deductible repairs.

repair cost the raw materials, labor and other expense incurred in the repair of an asset.

repair, maintenance and depreciation fund method a method under which repair costs and maintenance expenses are added to the depreciable cost of an asset for depreciation purposes.

repair reserve method a method under which repair costs are added to the depreciable cost of an asset for depreciation.

repeat audit = *repeating audit.*

"repeated plant" plan a method of depreciating new plant assets according to the past depreciation experience of the same asset. *See: "cotermination plant" plan.*

repeating audit an audit of the client that has ever been audited by the same auditor before. *Also*: recurring audit; repeat audit.

repetitive audit IRS's audit of the same item in a tax return for two consecutive years.

replaceable asset <1> an asset that can be replaced by a new asset. <2> asset the replacement cost of which could be measured in money.

replacement the substitution of an old asset by a new one to provide the same service.

replacement accounting the accounting method under which assets are depreciated when replaced, using the replacement cost of an asset as the measure of depreciation.

replacement cost <1> the amount that would need to replace the services lost by the sale or disposal of an asset. *Also*: cost to replace; deprival value; derived market value; entry value; replacing cost; replacement value. <2> = *swap replacement cost.*

replacement cost accounting = *current cost accounting.*

replacement-cost-adjusted earnings = *replacement cost income.*

replacement-cost approach an approach under which the total human resource value of a firm is determined by the cost that must be expended in order to reacquire the staff.

replacement cost based financial statement financial statement the assets in which are expressed in their replacement costs.

replacement cost depreciation a depreciation based on the replacement cost of plant assets. *Also*: current cost depreciation; depreciation on current cost basis; depreciation on market price; depreciation on replacement value; replacement depreciation.

replacement cost income distributable income plus realized holding gains less realized holding loss. *Also*: replacement cost-adjusted earnings; replacement cost net income.

replacement cost insurance an insurance which replaces lost, stolen or destroyed property by paying current market price, rather than depreciated value.

replacement cost less depreciation = *actual cash value.*

replacement cost method a method under which income is not earned until the current replacement cost of assets consumed in operations has been recovered.

replacement cost net income = *replacement cost income.*

replacement cost-new replacement cost of the newest asset. *Also*: cost of replacement-new.

replacement cost of sales cost of sales determined when the inventories are expressed at their replacement cost.

replacement cost-used cost to acquire a second-hand asset having the same serviceableness as that of the asset.

replacement cycle the frequency with which an asset is replaced.

replacement depreciation = *replacement cost depreciation.*

replacement fund a budget allocated to the replacement of asset depleted by wear and tear. *Also*: fund for replacement.

replacement method a depreciation method under which original cost of all items of plant is retained in asset accounts and the cost of replacements is charged to expense when they are acquired. *Also*: current replacement method; reproduction method.

replacement period taxable years following the liquidation year, unless a shorter period is specified.

replacement price method a method under which raw materials cost is determined by the replacement cost of the raw materials.

replacement ratio <1> the ratio of unused resources to total resources. <2> ratio used by agents and insurers to determine how many policies have been lost and how many new business premiums need to be written.

replacement ratio analysis (RRA) a comparison of one organization's retirement programs to programs of its competitors to show the percentage of preretirement income replaced by the expected retirement benefits at various ages.

replacement share a share bought back in less than 30 days after selling a similar one.

replacement value = *replacement cost.*

replacing cost = *replacement cost.*

rep letter = *representation letter.*

reportable condition a significant deficiency in the design or function of internal control that could adversely affect the organization's ability to record, process, summarize and report financial data.

reportable fringe benefit (RFB) <Australia> the fringe benefit that exceeds $1,000 in a tax year.

reportable payment any payment for which information returns are required.

reported earnings = *pre-tax accounting income.*

report form a form of financial statements in which all items are listed from top to the bottom. *Also*: narrative form; reducing balance form; running form; statement-form; vertical form. *See*: *account form; financial position form.*

report format = *statement.*

report form balance sheet a form of balance sheet in which the liabilities and capital sections are listed below the assets section. *Also*: narrative form balance sheet.

report form income statement a form of income statement in which the expenses and profit and loss sections are listed below the revenue section. *Also*: narrative form income statement.

reporting accountant <UK> an accountant hired by an individual or company to compile financial statements.

reporting currency the currency in which a company prepares its financial statements, e.g. US dollar for a US company. *Also*: base currency; natural currency. *See*: *functional currency.*

report of directors an annual report prepared by the board of directors, which lists the dividends, reserves, names of the directors, main operation of the company, fixed assets, issues of securities, etc.

report of independent CPA = *auditor's report.*

report of management by exception a report used by the management-by-exception system.

report on internal control an audit report on the internal control of a client.

report year the year that the financial statements are reported to the public or losses are reported to the insurance company.

repossession creditor's taking of property pledged as collateral.

repossession gain excess of the fair market value over the remaining balance receivable of an item repossessed.

repossession loss excess of the remaining balance receivable over the fair market value of an item repossessed.

representation contents of a *short-form report.*

representation letter the written representative from management in meeting the field auditor. *Also*: liability letter; rep letter. *See*: letter of representation.

reproducible asset an asset, such as inventory, that can be reproduced.

reproduction cost the cost to duplicate an asset identical to the asset owned without regard to technological changes. *Also*: cost of reproduction; cost of reproduction new value; entry price; reproduction value.

reproduction cost new, less depreciation approach the process of establishing the cost to reproduce the same item of property new as at the appraised date and reducing this result by the depreciation of actual property as compared to the new property.

reproduction method = *replacement method.*

reproduction value = *reproduction cost.*

request for agreement (RFA) a written request used to establish a *memorandum of agreement* with the IRS.

request for procurement (RFP) a written request used in negotiated acquisitions over $100,000 to communicate government requirements to prospective contractors.

required minimum distribution (RMD) = *minimum distribution.*

required rate of interest = *cut-off rate of return.*

required rate of return <1> the rate of return expected by the shareholders. <2> = *cut-off rate of return.*

required reserve the reserve that a bank is required to maintain on deposit at a Federal Reserve Bank.

resale price method a method under which the arm's length price of a controlled sale is determined by comparing the controlled sale to a later sale to an unrelated party.

resale value = *net realizable value.*

research and development cost the cost in order to discover and develop improved process and products. *Also*: development cost; experimental expense; research and development expenditure.

research and development credit a tax credit companies can deduct 20% of increased qualified expenditures for researching and developing new products. *Also*: research expense credit. *See*: *scientific research and experimental development investment credit.*

research and development expenditure = *research and development cost.*

research cost the cost incurred in the product research activities.

research expense credit = *research and development credit.*

reserve (res.) <1> something held for a specific purpose. <2> = *accrued liability.* <3> = *appropriated retained earnings.*

reserve account <1> an account for recording reserves. <2> an account for recording any difference occurred when translating foreign subsidiary statements to the home currency version.

reserve asset <1> an asset held by banks so that it can be treated as gold. <2> = *legal reserve.*

reserve assets ratio a ratio between a bank's eligible liabilities and its reserve assets.

reserved capital that portion of a company's share capital can not be called up except in the event of the company being wound up. *Also*: reserve liability.

reserved surplus = *appropriated retained earnings.*

reserve for asset valuation reserve for the future decline in assets value.

reserve for bad debts = *allowance for bad debts.*

reserve for compensation on assets premium excess of depreciation adjusted by a general price index over the original depreciation.

reserve for contingencies = *contingency reserve.*

reserve for doubtful debts = *allowance for bad debts.*

reserve for encumbrances account used in government accounting that reflects part of the fund balance that has been committed by a contract, purchase order, salary agreement, travel claim, etc.

reserve for estimated expenses amounts established for financial reporting purposes by accrual method taxpayers as a reduction from current income, designed to reflect future expenses.

reserve for guarantee amount set aside as a reserve for credit risk as guarantee.

reserve for obsolescence reserve for the future obsolescence of plant assets.

reserve for replacement reserve for the replacement of assets in the future. *Also*: plant replacement reserve.

reserve for retirement of preferred stock appropriated retained earnings for retirement of preferred stock, which has the effect of restricting common dividend declarations.

reserve for wear, tear, obsolescence and inadequacy = *allowance for depreciation.*

reserve lag accounting (RLA) accounting method under which a bank's reserve for the current week is determined by this week's liabilities, and the reserve for payment is still that of last week.

reserve liability = *reserved capital.*

reserve ratio <1> a bank's cash reserve divided by its total liabilities. <2> = *cash ratio.*

reserve ratio method setting up a bookkeeping account for each employer to which the taxes he pays are credited, and against which benefits charged are debited.

reserve recognition accounting (RRA) SEC's attempt to improve the reporting practices of oil and gas companies' valuations of natural resource reserves.

reserve transaction account = *official settlements balance.*

resident audit an audit performed when the auditor lives in the client's company.

resident withholding tax (RWT) <New Zealand> tax withheld on New Zealand resident's interest income.

residual approach an approach under which return to the residual stock is treated as an extra return to the stock holders.

residual asset the asset left to the owners after liquidation. *Also*: surplus asset.

residual beneficiary a beneficiary who is entitled to the assets in an estate after taxes.

residual claim a claim to a share of earnings after debt obligations have been met. *Also*: equity claim.

residual cost <1> that portion of asset cost that can be recovered from the residual value of the asset. <2> = *undepreciated cost.*

residual earnings net income after tax of a company less any preferred dividends.

residual equity assets less special equities such as preferred stock. *Also*: common stockholders' equity; equity of residual claimants.

residual equity theory a theory that common stockholders are considered to be the real owners of the business.

residual income (RI) <1> income minus interest on capital employed. <2> real estate income minus annual cost associated with the administration of that estate.

residual interest <Canada> interest in a trust or partnership with rights to income and the residual assets. *See*: *income interest.*

residual method a method of allocating the purchase price for the acquisition of another firm among the acquired assets.

residual net income net income minus preferred dividends.

residual return the return of an asset that is independent of the benchmark, calculated as *excess return* minus *beta* times *benchmark return.*

residual risk the risk (annualized standard deviation) of the *residual return.*

residual security = *dilutive security.*

residual value (re. v.) realized value of a plant asset less cost associated with the sale or disposal. *Also*: disposal value; recovery value.

residuary estate <UK> a testator's property not specifically devised or bequeathed.

resolving of cost = *determination of cost behavior.*

resource accounting the accounting for the consumption and measurement of the resources.

resource allowance <Canada> an annual deduction to mining and oil and gas producers, equal to 25% of the annual resource profit.

resource cost the cost of economic elements or inputs used to perform activities.

resource cost assignment process of assigning cost from general ledger accounts to activities using resource drivers.

resource cost driver single measure of the quantity of resources consumed by an activity.

resource profit a taxpayer's income from resource-related activities.

resource property = *natural resource.*

resource-related expense <Canada> an expense incurred in the resource-related activities.

RESP registered education savings plans

responsibility accounting a system designed to accumulate controllable costs in timely reports about a responsibility center to be given to each manager responsible for the costs, and also to be used in judging the performance of each manager. ***Also***: activity accounting; function accounting; performance accounting; profitability accounting.

responsibility audit = *operating audit.*

responsibility center a part of the organization which is headed by a person who is assigned certain duties and who must report to a higher authority.

responsibility cost a cost the amount of which is responsible for a person.

responsibility reporting system a system that is directed toward controlling costs at basic supervisory levels.

responsible official a person with authority over the IRS e-file operation in the office of a provider.

responsible person a person who is responsible for the company's tax liability.

rest <1> the time at which one period ends and the next begins in calculating interest on loans payable quarterly, half-yearly or annually. <2> = *principal.*

restated retained earnings retained earnings readjusted at the price level index or replacement cost.

RE statement = *retained earnings statement.*

restatement of balance sheet adjustment of balance sheet by current cost or general price level index.

restatement of income statement readjustment of the income statement by accrual basis or by replacement cost.

restatement of overhead rate approach implemented at the end of the period to calculate the actual overhead rates and then restate every entry involving overhead.

restatement of tort approach a defense approach based on the Second Restatement of the Law by the American Law Institute which holds that auditors are liable for ordinary negligence to a limited class of foreseen third parties.

rest of the world account a statement showing the receipts and expenditures of the rest of the world sector.

restricted account (RA) a broker account the balance of which exceeds the highest lending limit of the stock held.

restricted asset an asset that is transferred in exchange for services, but which is either not transferable or subject to a substantial risk of forfeiture.

restricted farm loss <Canada> loss of a taxpayer from a farm which has been found not the taxpayer's main source of income.

restricted fund the fund in a non-profit organization whose assets are limited to designated purposes as per donor or grantor request.

restricted stock a stock granted to the employee that can not be sold for a stated period after it is acquired. ***Also***: 144 stock; restricted stock grant. ***See***: *blackout.*

restricted stock grant = *restricted stock.*

restricted surplus earned surplus that can not be distributed as dividends. ***Also***: qualifying reserve.

restricted-use report audit report intended only for specific parties. *See*: *general-use report.*

restructuring charge a one-time deduction taken against earnings for expenses such as plant closings and severance payments.

resultant cost a failure cost caused by the bad quality. *See*: *controllable cost.*

resulting trust a trust inferred from a conduct or a transaction that normally evidences an intent that property in the hands of one person be held for the benefit of another.

resumption of dividends stockholder's acquisition of the company's surplus or assets after receiving dividends.

resyndication limited partnership the sale of existing properties to new limited partners, so that they can receive the tax advantages that are no longer available to the old partners.

retail cost the cost calculated as retail price × (1 - *markon* percentage).

retailers' excise tax federal excise tax on retailers such as jewelers.

retail inventory method a method for estimating ending inventory based on the ratio of the cost of goods for sale at the marked selling prices.

retail method a method for estimating the value of inventory which involves the maintenance of the records showing both costs and retail prices of purchases.

retail sales tax <Canada> <1> a provincial tax levy on retail sales of goods and services in Prince Edward Island, Ontario, Manitoba, Saskatchewan and BC. <2> = *sales tax.*

retained earnings stockholder's equity in a corporation resulting from earnings in excess of losses and the dividends declared. *Also*: earned capital; earned surplus; earning retention; earnings; earnings retained; excess revenue; gain by trading; incoming profit; internal reserve; invested earnings; operating surplus; profit retained; reinvested earnings; revenue profit; revenue surplus; seed capital; surplus; surplus from profits; surplus profit; surplus reserve; undistributed profit.

retained earnings-appropriated = *appropriated retained earnings.*

retained earnings statement (RE statement) a statement which reports the changes in a corporation's retained earnings in a period. *Also*: statement of changes in retained earnings; statement of retained earnings; statement of surplus analysis.

retained earnings-unappropriated = *unappropriated retained earnings.*

retention rate = *retention ratio.*

retention ratio <1> retained earnings, or net income minus dividend, divided by the net income. <2> percentage of present earnings held back or retained by a corporation, or one minus the dividend payout rate. *Also*: retention rate.

retirement a permanent withdrawal of depreciable property from its use in a trade or business or from being held for the production of income.

retirement accounting a system of depreciation under which tax deductions are claimed only when an asset is retired from use.

retirement annuity <UK> an annuity paid out of a retirement scheme to a taxpayer.

retirement benefit lump-sum payment to an employee by an employer upon retirement. *Also*: retiring allowance.

retirement compensation arrangement (RCA) <Canada> unregistered retirement plan established by a company to provide additional benefits to an employee, funded by and tax-deductible by the company.

retirement income fund (RIF) = *registered retirement income fund.*

retirement method a depreciation method whereby the cost of plant asset units (net of residual value) is charged to expense account in the year in which the asset is retired from service.

retirement of stock a company's purchasing of its stock not to be held as treasury stock but for cancellation.

retirement relief <UK> tax relief allowed on a material disposal of a business or shares of a company.

retirement savings account (RSA) <Australia> = *IRA*.

retirement savings plan (RSP) <Canada> a contract or arrangement under which an individual or his or her spouse pays certain periodic or other amounts for retirement income.

retiring allowance <Canada> = *retirement benefit*.

retiring allowance rollover <Canada> *retirement benefit* that can be transferred to a registered retirement plan to defer tax. ***Also***: eligible retiring allowance.

retiring partner a partner who leaves a partnership.

retracing an auditor begins with the documents created when the transaction is executed and proceeds to follow the evidence through the recording process.

re-transfer <Canada> the transfer of property to the parent on the death of the child.

retroactive adjustment = *prior period adjustment*.

retroactive allocation the allocation to a partner of profits or losses arising prior to the admission of the partner to the partnership.

retroactive benefit the benefit granted in a pension plan amendment that is attributed by the pension benefit formula to employee services rendered in periods prior to the amendment. ***See***: *prior service cost*.

retroactive method adjustment of the past financial statement data after a change in accounting principle has been adopted, all accumulated effect is entered in current retained earnings as prior period adjustment. ***See***: *current approach*.

retroactive statement financial statement presented as if it has originally been prepared using the new accounting principle.

return after tax = *after-tax return*.

returned check = *bad check*.

returned material (RM) material returned to the storage.

returned material journal (RMJ) a special journal for recording returns of raw materials.

returned purchase = *purchase return*.

returned sales = *sales return*.

returned value = *salvage value*.

return inward = *sales return*.

return item = *bad check*.

return of capital a payment, or a portion of a payment that is viewed as resulting in the recovery of the taxpayer's investment, rather than as a gain or loss-producing transaction. ***Also***: capital distribution. ***See***: *nontaxable distribution*.

return of goods bought = *purchase return*.

return of income <Canada> = *individual tax return*.

return on assets (ROA) = *return on total assets*.

return on assets managed (ROAM) sales minus the cost of goods sold as a percentage of assets managed minus liabilities.

return on assets pricing a pricing method in which the objective of price determination is to earn a profit equal to a specific rate of return on assets employed in the operation.

return on capital (ROC) income after taxes divided by capital.

return on capital employed (ROCE) earnings before interest and tax ÷ (capital employed + short term borrowings - intangible assets).

return on equity (ROE) retained earnings of the period divided by owner's equity. ***Also***: net income to net worth.

return on investment (ROI) dividing earnings by investment. ***Also***: capitalization rate; cap rate; rate of return on investment.

return on investment capital (ROIC) company's net income minus dividends, divided by all long term debt plus common and preferred shares.

return on net assets (RONA) net income divided by the sum of fixed assets and net working capital.

return on net capital employed (RONCE) a return calculation with *pretax accounting income* as the numerator and capital committed to the specific operation as the denominator.

return on net worth (RONW) = *return on stockholders' equity.*

return on operating assets operating income divided by operating assets.

return on operating assets minus the cost of capital (ROA-COC) an analysis that focuses on shareholder value creation. Shareholders demand an ROA in excess of a company's cost of capital.

return on pension plan assets income from the investment of pension plan assets.

return on plant investment rate of return being earned by a utilities company on the value of its property devoted to the public service.

return on revenue (ROR) = *return on sales.*

return on risk adjusted capital (RORAC) return divided by the capital released by offsets among risk factors. ***See***: *risk adjusted return on capital.*

return on sales (ROS) net income before interest and tax divided by revenue. ***Also***: return on revenue. ***See***: *profit on sales.*

return on stockholders' equity corporate net income divided by stockholders' equity. ***Also***: earned on net worth; rate earned on stockholders' equity; ratio of net income to net worth; return on net worth.

return on total assets net income divided by average total assets. ***Also***: rate earned on total assets; return on assets. ***See***: *all capital earnings ratio; asset utilization.*

returns inwards journal a book of prime entry in which details are entered of goods returned by customers. ***Also***: sales returns journal.

returns outwards journal = *purchase returns journal.*

re. v. residual value

revalorization = *revaluation.*

revaluation <1> restatement of an asset's value to current market value. <2> the restoration of the value of a depreciated currency that has been devalued previously. ***Also***: currency appreciation; revalorization.

revaluation account a stockholders' equity a/c for recording the increase or decrease in assets and liabilities after the revaluation.

revaluation reserve the difference between historical cost and current cost when assets are revalued in a current value accounting system. ***Also***: asset revaluation reserve; capital reserve.

revaluation surplus = *appraisal capital.*

revenue (rev.) the incoming of asset from all sources. ***See***: *sales.*

revenue account (R a/c) <1> an account that shows the revenue of a corporation and the expenditure chargeable to it. ***Also***: income account; temporary addition to capital account. <2> = *revenue and expense account.*

revenue agent person working for the Examination Division of the IRS, usually performs audit. ***See***: *revenue officer; special agent.*

revenue agent's report (RAR) a report prepared by a revenue agent for proposed adjustments.

revenue allocation occurs when revenues, related but not traceable to individual products are assigned to those individual products. ***See***: *revenue tracing.*

revenue and expense account accounts the balance of which are closed to income summary account when financial statements are prepared. ***Also***: income account; revenue account; temporary owner's equity account. ***See***: *balance sheet account.*

revenue asset intangible asset derived from the capitalized value of future excess profits.

revenue bond = *municipal revenue bond.*

Revenue Canada Taxation = *Canada Customs and Revenue Agency.*

revenue capital the capital from retained earnings rather than from paid-in capital.

revenue center unit in an organization in which a manager's responsibility is defined in terms of the ability to influence the revenues through decisions.

revenue charge = *revenue expenditure.*

revenue cost = *operating cost.*

revenue-cost graph = *breakeven chart.*

revenue deduction item that reduces revenue, such as municipal or utility expense, taxes, uncollectible accounts.

revenue duty = *revenue tariff.*

revenue expenditure an expenditure that should be deducted from revenue on the income statement. ***Also***: expenditure on revenue account; income statement charge; noncapital expense; revenue charge. ***Opp***: *capital expenditure.*

revenue-expense elimination the elimination of revenues and expenses of subsidiaries.

revenue-expense view a view which holds that revenues and expenses result from a proper matching. ***Also***: income statement view; matching view. ***See***: *asset-liability view.*

revenue from sales = *sales revenue.*

revenue fund a fund that accounts for all revenues from an enterprise financed by a *municipal revenue bond.*

revenue generated per dollar of investment = *asset turnover.*

revenue income <1> revenue generated per dollar of investment. <2> excess of actual tax revenue of government over the target tax revenue because of inflation.

revenue loss <1> amount by which actual tax revenue is less than the target tax revenue because of taxation or deflation. <2> = *net operating loss.*

revenue method a method of depreciation under which the basis of the depreciable property is written off in proportion to the total anticipated future income from the property taking salvage value into account. ***Also***: income forecast method.

revenue officer agent employed by the Collection Division of the IRS to conduct tax delinquency field investigations. ***See***: *revenue agent.*

revenue offset revenue which has never realized and which should be deducted from gross revenue in the income statement.

revenue passenger miles (RPM) how many seats were actually sold on an airline's flight. ***Also***: revenue seat miles.

revenue per employee sales divided by number of employees.

revenue per share = *sales per share.*

revenue principle the principle which holds that the revenue should be recognized before net income can be determined.

Revenue Procedure a published official statement of the IRS regarding a matter of federal tax procedure, published by the National Office of the IRS.

revenue profit <1> *operating income.* <2> = *retained earnings.*

revenue protection compliance programs designed to endure the collection of tax and disbursement in the form of refunds are accurate and timely.

revenue realization principle = *realization principle.*

revenue receipts <1> revenue under cash basis. <2> = *taxable revenue.*

revenue received in advance = *deferred revenue.*

revenue recognition the recording of revenue in the ledger at the time of sale of goods or rendering of service.

Revenue Reconciliation Act of 1993 = *Tax Reform Act of 1993.*

revenue reserve a sum built up out of favorable profit and loss balance in previous years. ***See***: *capital reserve.*

revenue ruling rule published by the IRS giving taxpayers guidance in the preparation of their tax returns. ***See***: *ruling.*

Revenue Ruling 94-38 an IRS ruling that states that clean up costs are deductible as ordinary and necessary business expenses, constructing groundwater treatment facilities are capital expenditures.

revenue seat miles = *revenue passenger miles.*

revenue sharing <1> splitting of profits and losses between the general partner and limited partners in a limited partnership. <2> a plan to relieve the state and local fiscal deficit by distributing general purpose, unearmarked grants from the federal government to sub-national governments.

revenue surplus = *retained earnings.*

revenue tariff a tax on imported goods levied to generate revenue for the government. ***Also***: financial tariff; revenue duty.

revenue tracing occurs where revenues can be identified with an individual product (service, customer etc.) in an economically feasible (cost-effective) way. ***See***: *revenue allocation.*

reversal cost method calculation of cost by subtracting gross profit from the retail price.

reversal entry = *reversing entry.*

reversal method a method for reporting the inflation effects on the stock price of the corporation under which adjustments are made under the same rules and procedures.

reversal of entries an error in bookkeeping that is not uncovered by a trial balance being due to a credit entry having been debited and the corresponding debit entry having been credited.

reverse to cancel a Roth IRA conversion and revert it back to a traditional IRA in order to claim the loss accumulated. ***See***: *recharacterize.*

reverse acquisition = *reverse merger.*

reverse charge <UK> charge on the company that buys materials from tax-exempt foreign suppliers.

reverse entry = *reversing entry.*

reverse merger the acquisition of a public company by a private company. ***Also***: public shell; reverse acquisition; reverse takeover; shell merger. ***See***: *demerger.*

reverse premium money paid by a landlord to a tenant at the beginning of a lease.

reverse split = *split down.*

reverse stock split = *split down.*

reverse takeover <1> buying a large corporation by a smaller one. ***See***: *inverted takeover.* <2> = *reverse merger.*

reversing entry an entry that reverses the adjusting entry for an accrued item. ***Also***: elimination entry; readjustment entry; red-ink entry; reversal entry; reverse entry.

reversion removal of assets from an overfunded defined benefit pension plan by the plan sponsor.

review a public accounting service, which provides a report that includes limited assurance, a phrase such as "I'm not aware of any material modifications that should be made." is usually used. ***Also***: accounting and review service.

reviewable decision a Tax Court decision that can be appealed in 90 days. ***See:*** *nonreviewable decision.*

revised accounting equation net asset = liability + owners' equity + revenue - expense.

revision variance cost variance caused by the revision of original standards.

revocable trust a trust whereby provisions can be altered or cancelled dependent on the grantor. ***See***: *irrevocable trust.*

revocation tax <Canada> = *Part 5 tax.*

revoked IRA an IRA revoked by the holder within 7 days after the IRA is established.

revolving account = *running account.*

revolving fund account that is repeatedly expended, replenished, and then expended again.

revolving period a period in which undivided interests are issued, but until liquidation, the net cash flows are split between buying additional assets and paying off investors.

rework *finished goods* that must be returned for reprocessing.

RFA request for agreement

RFB reportable fringe benefit

R-F cost relevant future cost

RFP request for procurement

RGDI real gross disposable income

RGNDI real gross national disposable income

RGNI real gross national income

RI residual income

RIC regulated investment company

RIF retirement income fund

right-hand side = *right side.*

right side (r.s.) the right hand side of a T-account. ***Also***: right hand side. ***See***: *credit side.*

rights letter = *stock warrant.*

risk accounting method and procedures for rendering information for risk management.

risk adjusted discount rate riskless rate plus a risk premium.

risk adjusted return a measure of how much an investment return in relation to the amount of risk it took on.

risk adjusted return on capital (RAROC) the return minus expected loss then divided by capital. ***See***: *return on risk adjusted capital.*

risk adjusted return on risk adjusted capital (RARORAC) return after deduction of expected loss divided by capital released offsets among risk factors.

risk adjustment the price that marketplace participants are able to receive for bearing the uncertainties in cash flows.

risk advisory service a service designed to identify, assess and manage risks of an entity and measure and monitor risk management strategies implemented by that entity.

risk analysis process of measuring and analyzing the risk associated with financial and investment decisions.

risk-based capital ratio *tier I capital* divided by total risk-weighted assets.

risk capital (RC) <1> common stock from a new company. ***Also***: venture capital. <2> long-term loans or capital invested in high risk business. ***Opp***: *security capital.*

risk-free asset = *riskless asset.*

risk-free rate a theoretical interest rate at which an investment may earn interest without incurring any risk. ***Also***: risk-free return; riskless rate of return.

risk-free return <1> = *basic yield.* <2> = *benchmark return.* <3> = *risk-free rate.*

riskless asset an asset the future earnings of which is known and certain. ***Also***: risk-free asset.

riskless rate of return = *risk-free rate.*

risk of assessing control risk too high = *alpha risk.*

risk of assessing control risk too low = *beta risk.*

risk of incorrect acceptance = *beta risk.*

risk of incorrect rejection = *alpha risk.*

risk premium compensation for accepting uncertainties, it equals the amount by which the required return on an asset or security exceeds the risk-free rate.

RJE reclassification journal entry

RLA reserve lag accounting

RMD required minimum distribution

RMJ return material journal

RNNDI real net national disposable income

ROA return on assets

ROA-COC return on operating assets minus the cost of capital

ROC return on capital

ROCE return on capital employed

ROE return on equity

ROI return on investment

ROIC return on investment capital

ROL reorder level

rolling budgets sequence of revised budgets prepared in continuous budgeting. *See*: *periodic budget.*

rolling capital = *working capital.*

rolling EPS *earnings per share* calculated by using the previous 2 quarters and adding them to the following 2 quarter's estimated EPS.

rolling start rule <Canada> a rule under which capital cost allowance is allowed on the second taxation year after the property was acquired by the taxpayer.

rollover <1> a transaction in which the cash or other consideration is received, followed or preceded by the reinvestments with tax-deferred results. <2> renewal of a short-term obligation by mutual agreement of debtor and creditor. <3> movement of funds from one investment to another. <4><Canada> deferral of any capital gain until the time of disposal of the property. Also: *tax-deferred rollover.* <5> = *rollover deferral.*

rollover deferral before May 7, 1997, deferral of gain from the sale of a principal residence reinvested in a new residence. *Also*: deferred gain; rollover.

rollover relief <UK> a capital gains tax to be deferred until the subsequent sale of the asset into which the gain has been rolled.

roll-up fund an investment fund that pays no dividends, with money concentrated in world currencies. Returns are considered capital gains and not income.

RONA return on net assets

RONCE return on net capital employed

RONW return on net worth

ROR <1> *rate of return.* <2> *return on revenue.*

RORAC return on risk adjusted capital

ROS return on sales

Rosenblum approach a defense approach based on a common law decision that holds CPAs liable for acts of ordinary negligence to reasonably foreseeable third parties not in privity of contract.

rotating-account system a plan for saving bookkeeping and reconciliation procedures under which 2 separate bank accounts are maintained, and the checks written against one account should be readily distinguished from those checks written against the other.

Roth IRA a new *IRA* established in the 1997 Taxpayer Relief Act, which allows taxpayers to make after-tax contributions, the earnings are tax free. *Also*: IRA plus. *See*: *deductible IRA; nondeductible IRA; traditional IRA.*

royalty income payment for the use and exploitation of certain kinds of property, such as artistic or literary works, patents, and mineral rights.

royalty owner's credit a credit of $2,500 granted to qualified royalty owners against the crude oil windfall profits tax imposed on their royalty oil in 1981.

royalty owner's exemption 2 barrel-per-day exemption (3-barrel-per-day after 1984) from the crude oil windfall profits tax available to qualified royalty owners with respect to qualified royalty production.

RPM revenue passenger miles

RPP registered pension plan

RR <1> rate of return. <2> relevant range.

RRA <1> replacement ratio analysis. <2> reserve recognition accounting.

RRIF registered retirement income fund

RRSP registered retirement savings plan

RRSP deduction <Canada> = *IRA deduction.*

RRTA Railroad Retirement Tax Act

RRTA tax federal income tax withheld from a railroad worker's wages.

RSA retirement savings account

RSP retirement savings plan

RTO rent to own

RTO property rent-to-own property

rubber check = *bad check.*

rubber cheque = *bad check.*

rubricated account = *special account.*

rule 504 exemption exempt issuance of securities up to 1 million dollars sold in 12-month period to any number of investors. *Also*: seed capital exemption.

rule 505 exemption up to 5 million dollars in 12-month period sales of securities to 35 unaccredited investors and unlimited number of accredited investors.

rule 506 exemption exempt private placement of securities of unlimited amount up to 35 unaccredited investors must be sophisticated.

ruled-bin system a variation of the two-bin system in which the inventory is kept in a container that has a line drawn inside it at a particular level.

rule off physical underscoring of a total or amount in a ledger to indicate that it should not be disturbed or altered because it represents a cumulative significant figure.

rule of 45 under which the qualified deferred compensation plans must provide that employer contributions for an unterminated employee with at least five years of service must vest when the sum of his or her age and years of service equals or exceeds 45.

rule of 72 a rule stating that in order to find the number of years required to double your money at a given interest rate, you divide the compound return into 72.

rule-of-thumb method a method for preparing the operating budgets and decisions by the use of average data adjusted to reflect the plans of the business. *Also*: off-the-cuff method.

ruling official interpretation by the IRS of the tax law as applied to specific situations. *See*: *revenue ruling.*

ruling an account drawing a red line underneath the last entry in an account, and another red line underneath the totals.

running account an account for transactions in an ongoing business relationship. *Also*: revolving account.

running audit = *daily audit.*

running balance account balance after the recording of each transaction under perpetual inventory.

running cost = *activity cost.*

running form = *report form.*

running margin = *carry income and loss.*

running yield = *current yield.*

RWT *resident withholding tax*

S s

S <1> sale. <2> sales journal. <3> salvage.

S&P core earnings the measurement of *core earnings*, including the exclusion of gains related to pension activities, net revenues from the sale of assets, goodwill impairment, prior-year charge and provision reversals, and settlements related to litigation or insurance claims.

SAB Staff Accounting Bulletin

safeguarding of assets protecting a firm's assets through a good internal control system.

safe harbor concept a provision which recognizes that the bases for current value information are inherently more subjective than traditional accounting methods.

safe harbor lease the transfer of tax benefits associated with machinery and equipment.

safe harbor rule <1> rule tax provision enacted as part of the Economic Tax Recovery Act of 1981 to guarantee sale-leaseback treatment to transactions if specific requirements are met. <2> amount of estimated tax that must be paid to avoid penalty. (in 2003, 110% of last year's tax). *See: ironclad exemption.*

safe payment approach distribution of a partnership where the amount of the payment to partners is computed at specific period in time.

safety audit examination of an organization's operations, and real and personal property to discover existing and potential hazard and the action needed to reduce the hazard.

safety inventory = *buffer stock.*

safety margin = *margin of safety.*

safety stock minimum balance carried in inventory to take care of irregularities in supply and rate of usage.

safety zone = *exception.*

salary deferral arrangement <Canada> a plan under which an employee has the right to receive salary in the next taxation year.

salary reduction contribution = *elective deferral.*

salary reduction plan <1> = *flexible spending account.* <2> = *401(k).*

sale accounting the choice between treating the merger as a purchase of assets or as a pooling of interests.

sale and leaseback = *sale-leaseback.*

sale and purchase inventory method an inventory method under which returnable containers are included in inventory until sold along with their contents.

sale-leaseback a lease when an owner of an asset sells it and immediately leases it back from that buyer. *Also*: lease option; sale and leaseback.

sales inflow of assets from the sale of goods of services. *See: sales revenue; top line.*

sales allowance reduction in the selling price of goods because of a particular problem.

sales and entertainment tax a state or local tax on the sales and entertainment activities.

sales audit analysis of sales by the production, size of product, geographical distribution, etc. *See*: marketing audit.

sales basis a basis under which revenue is recognized and matched with expenses when the sales are made.

sales budget an estimate of goods to be sold and revenue to be derived from sales.

sales cost = *cost of goods sold.*

sales cut-off a concept that the financial statements only include sales until the statement date.

sales discount the discount given on sales of merchandise. ***Also***: discount on sales.

sales forecast opportunity variance measure of the difference between scheduled capacity and the forecast capacity in a master budget, usually expressed in dollars.

sales invoice method an accounts receivable method under which sales invoices are kept in an open file organized by customer name until paid. ***See***: *invoice method.*

sales journal (SJ) a journal in which all the credit sales are recorded. ***Also***: sold daybook.

sales ledger (SL) a detailed ledger that contains the accounts for each credit sale. ***Also***: debtor's ledger.

sales loss = *loss on sales.*

sales margin <1> manufacturing margin less variable selling costs. <2>= *gross profit.* <3> = *unit contribution margin.* <4> = *unit profit.*

sales margin mix variance = *marketing mix cost variance.*

sales margin price variance = *sales margin selling price variance.*

sales margin quantity variance that part of the sales margin variance caused by the difference between actual sales quantity and planned sales quantity.

sales margin selling price variance that portion of the sales margin variance caused by the difference between the actual selling price and the planned selling price. ***Also***: sales margin price variance.

sales margin variance difference between actual sales margin and the budgeted sales margin.

sales margin volume variance difference between the actual number of units sold and the budgeted number multiplied by the budgeted selling price per unit.

sales method a method of separating byproducts costs at the time of sales, under which net realizable value of byproducts is reported as ordinary sales, other income or contra to cost of sales. ***See***: *production method.*

sales mix variance = *marketing mix cost variance.*

sales percentage method = *income statement approach.*

sales per share total revenue earned in a fiscal year by the weighted average of shares outstanding for that fiscal year. ***Also***: revenue per share.

sales price variance difference between the actual unit selling price and the budgeted unit selling price, multiplied by the actual number of units sold.

sales quantity variance = *sales volume variance.*

sales return the return to the seller by the buyer of goods sold previously. ***Also***: returned sales; return inward.

sales returns and allowances an account used to accumulate amount of cash refund granted to customers or other allowances related to prior sales.

sales returns journal = *returns inwards journal.*

sales revenue revenues that arise from sales of goods by a merchandising company. ***Also***: revenue from sales.

sales tax sate or local tax based on the selling price of goods or services, and paid by the buyer. ***Also***: retail sales tax.

sales to cash flow ratio a ratio that indicates whether or not a company's sales are high in comparison to its cash flow, usually equals sales per share divided by cash flow per share.

sales to fixed assets = *fixed asset turnover.*

sales to inventories = *inventory turnover.*

sales turnover sales less sales taxes. ***Also***: turnover.

sales-type lease a lease used by a manufacturer or dealers to sell the product on an installment basis. ***See***: *direct financing type lease.*

sales uncollectible account adjustment estimated amount that is deducted from gross sales as bad debts reserve under the direct charge off method.

sales value basis = *relative sales value method.*

sales variance difference between actual sales revenue and budgeted sales revenue.

sales volume variance a variance which results from the difference in unit sales prices or unit production costs. *Also*: sales quantity variance.

salvage charge expense of recovering property by a salvor.

salvage value the share of a plant asset's cost recovered at the end of its service life through the sale or a trade-in allowance on a new asset. *Also*: final salvage value; gross residual value; recovery value; returned value; scrap; scrap value; terminal salvage value; terminal value.

sample size number of samples required for the audit sampling.

sampling audit = *audit test.*

sampling error difference between the value obtained by sampling and the value that would have been obtained if the entire population had been investigated.

sampling interval the interval between corresponding points on two successive samples.

sampling risk a risk that the auditor's conclusion based on a sample, might be different from the conclusion which would be if the test were applied to the entire population.

sampling unit individual item in an audit sampling, such as a voucher.

sanction a measure that restricts the privilege of an e-file provider from the e-file program. *See*: *suspension.*

Sansome doctrine a doctrine to the effect that in order to prevent tax avoidance in a corporate fusion, the target corporation's earnings must be carried on the acquiring corporation's accounting records.

SAR stock appreciation right

Sarbanes-Oxley Act (SOx) law enacted in 2002 to improve quality and transparency in financial reporting and independent audits and accounting services for public companies. Public Company Accounting Oversight Board is created.

SAS Statements on Auditing Standards

Saskatchewan Pension Plan (SPP) <Canada> a voluntary retirement plan designed for taxpayers who have no access to private pension plans or other arrangements.

savable cost expense which can be saved under certain conditions.

save as you earn (SAYE) <UK> a plan that enables a taxpayer to set aside a regular sum from his or her salary for 3 years, and the sum will be paid tax-free at the end of the period.

savings = *personal savings.*

savings incentive match plan for employees (SIMPLE) a retirement plan with simplified procedures available to employers with less than 100 employees.

savings income <UK> dividend, interest and *equivalent foreign income* subject to a lower tax rate.

savings rate *personal savings* as a percentage of *disposable income.*

savings rate tax <UK> rate of tax on savings income. (20% in 2000.)

SAYE save as you earn

SBD small business deduction

SBIC small business investment company

SBIC stock small business investment company

SBIN service bureau identification number

SC standard cost

scale benefit charge <UK> tax on the benefit received by an employee from using a car or cell phone provided by the employer.

scatter diagram a graph which represents two variables for a series of the past observations or measurement to estimate the relationship between cost and activity.

SCFP statement of changes in financial position

schedular method by definition a method under which the equity in the consolidated balance sheet equals the parent corporation's owners' equity minus dividends income from subsidiaries and plus equity in them.

schedular method by residual calculation a method under which the total equity in the consolidated balance sheet equals the sum of the parent corporation's owners' equity and the subsidiary company's owners' equity.

schedular system <UK> the income tax system under which income is subject to tax if it falls into one of the 5 schedules: *Schedule A, Schedule B, Schedule C, Schedule D and Schedule E.*

Schedule A <1> listing of itemized deductions in a tax return. <2> <UK> listing of rental income from land and buildings.

Schedule B <1> listing of dividend and interest income in a tax return. <2> <UK> listing of income from farming and commercial forest.

Schedule C <1> listing of profit <or loss> from business or profession. <2> <UK> listing of income from public revenue.

Schedule D <1> listing of capital gains and losses. <2> <UK> a listing of income from business, profession or self-employment.

scheduled cost = *standard cost.*

scheduled debt a debt listed by a bankrupt on a schedule filed with the court.

scheduled property <1> a property listed by a bankrupt on a schedule filed with the court. <2> a property listed on a schedule attached to an insurance policy.

scheduled variance (SV) difference between the earned value and the planned budget of a project. ***Also***: job project-schedule cost variance. ***See***: *cost variance.*

Schedule E <1> listing of supplemental income. <2> <UK> listing of income such as wages, salary, fees, annuities, etc.

Schedule F <1> listing of farm income and expenses. <2> <UK> listing of income from dividends and other distributions.

Schedule G listing of income averaging.

Schedule M-1 imbedded in Form 1120, used to reconcile book income to taxable income.

Schedule M-2 imbedded in Form 1120, used to analyze changes in a corporation's unappropriated retained earnings per books between the beginning and end of the year.

schedule of account balances = *trial balance.*

schedule of accounts receivable by age = *aging schedule.*

schedule of equivalent production a schedule used in process costing in which a period's equivalent units are computed for both materials costs and conversion costs.

schedule performance index (SPI) the ratio of earned value to planned value. ***See***: cost performance index.

Schedule R listing of retirement income credit computation.

Schedule SE listing of the computation of the Social Security self-employment tax.

schedule variance the difference between actual production and scheduled production.

Schedule X listing of items other than that in the Schedule Y and Z of a single individual.

Schedule Y income tax table for married persons and certain widows.

Schedule Z tax rate table for unmarried persons and legally divorced persons.

scienter intent to deceive, manipulate or defraud.

scientific research and experimental development investment credit <Canada> = *scientific research and experimental development tax credit.*

scientific research and experimental development tax credit (SR&ED credit) <Canada> a 10% tax credit granted to qualifying corporations that carry on scientific research and experimental development projects. ***Also***: scientific research and experimental development investment credit.

scientific cost accounting the accounting in the Taylor times.

scientific method = *yield method.*

scientific tax-exempt organization an organization other than a private foundation that is exempt from tax.

scope limitation auditor is not allowed to or unable to perform an audit procedure.

scope paragraph = *scope section.*

scope section that part of an audit report listing the audit goal, standards, procedures, certification, etc. *Also*: scope paragraph.

S corporation a corporation treated for federal income tax purposes in a manner somewhat similar to a partnership. *Also*: subchapter S corporation; small business corporation; sub-S corporation; tax option corporation.

Scottish dividend = *split-down.*

scrap <1> results from the fact that the materials being processed is not of the exact length, width, or thickness required for the product being made. *Also*: material scrap; scrap material. <2> = *salvage value.*

scrap cost the cost of the scrap material.

scrap material = *scrap.*

scrap value <1> the excess of scrap sales over scrap cost. *Also*: junk value. <2> = *salvage value.*

scrap variance = *material scrap variance.*

scrip <1> a temporary promissory note for the payment of dividends deferred. *Also*: dividend scrip; dividend stock scrip; stock scrip. <2> a temporary certificate which entitles the holder or bearer to receive stock or a share of stock in a corporation. *Also*: interim certificate; monkey money. <3> = *stock certificate.*

scrip dividend the dividend declared that consists of promissory notes calling for payment at some future date. *Also*: dividend in scrip; liability dividend.

scrubbing the books reviewing accounting entries by management.

search cost expense associated with locating a counterpart for a trade.

seasonal company a company the sales of which vary due to seasonal effects, such as weather and holidays.

seasonal cost the cost that is high in one season, but low in another.

seating capacity rule a rule that requires at least 50% of the seating capacity is occupied for a noncommercial flight on employer-provided aircraft to be excluded as fringe benefit. *Also*: zero inclusion rule.

SEC Securities and Exchange Commission

SECA tax = *self-employment tax.*

secondary account the account into which the classified items from the book of first entry are entered.

secondary income = *real secondary income.*

secondary liquidation bank assets that can be liquidated within two or twelve months.

secondary ratios constituent elements of the primary ratios, namely capital turnover and profit on sales.

secondary reserve assets retained by banks other than *primary reserve.*

second base amount a threshold amount in the calculation of inclusion in income 85% of the social security benefit. ($44,000 in 2003). *See*: *first base amount.*

second-best evidence the substitute of the original receipt that may support a deduction.

second disposition rule a rule designed to prevent installment sellers from recognizing income slowly, while related installment purchasers promptly dispose of their acquisitions.

second examination an additional inspection of a taxpayer and his books of account for the same taxable year.

second mortgage loan a mortgage loan made to the homeowner in addition to the *first mortgage loan.*

second-partner review = *cold review.*

second stage income distribution through transfers, resulting in *disposable income.*

second statement, the balance sheet, which is deemed to be the second important statement by the APB in 1973.

second-term shared-use equipment <Canada> similar to a first-term shared-use equipment except that it must be used by the taxpayer from the time of acquisition to the end of the first taxation year ending at least 24 months after the acquisition date for scientific and research and experimental development.

second-tier deduction miscellaneous deduction allowable only to the extent that it exceeds 2% of AGI floor limit. ***Also***: tier 2 deduction. ***See***: *first-tier deduction.*

secret account the account kept by the owner and is not open to the public. ***Also***: private account; private ledger account.

secret ledger a ledger containing secret accounts. ***Also***: private ledger. ***See***: *open ledger.*

secret partner a partner whose identity is undisclosed.

secret reserve amount of reserve, which has not been shown in the balance sheet, because of the omission or under valuation of the assets, or over valuation of liabilities. ***Also***: hidden reserve, inner reserve; undisclosed reserve.

secret trust a trust created by a will and the trustee agreed to hold the property. ***Also***: fully secret trust. ***See***: *half secret trust.*

Section 8 deduction = *child care expense deduction.*

section 38 property asset that qualifies for the investment tax credit, e.g. tangible personal asset with 3 or more years of life used in a trade or business.

Section 83(b) election an election which converts future appreciation that would otherwise be taxable as ordinary income to capital gains.

Section 168 property = *recovery property.*

section 179 property tangible personal property that qualifies for the investment tax credit and the taxpayer is authorized to deduct the first $5,000 of such property in 1982, the $5,000 increases to $24,000 in 2001 and thereafter.

section 197 intangible = *section 197 property.*

section 197 property goodwill and other intangibles such as a going concern value acquired on the acquisition of a business, amortizable over 15 years for tax purpose, and 40 years for financial reporting purpose. ***Also***: amortizable section 197 intangible; section 197 intangible.

section 263A = *capitalization rule.*

Section 236A cost the cost which is subject to *capitalization rule.* ***Also***: additional 263A cost; cost subject to capitalization.

section 306 stock a stock issued as a stock dividend or in a corporate reorganization, which when redeemed or sold, will generally result in ordinary income to the shareholder. ***Also***: tainted stock. ***See***: *preferred stock bailout.*

section 333 liquidation a liquidation that can result in a substantial gain realized from the transfer of asset by the liquidating company. ***Also***: one-month liquidation.

section 338 acquisition an acquisition under which a purchasing company that has made a qualified stock purchase may elect within 75 days of the acquisition, to treat the target company as having sold and then purchased its properties, and as becoming a new company thereafter.

section 341 assets certain assets a potentially collapsible corporation holds for less than 3 years such as stock in trade, dealer property, section 1231 assets, unrealized receivables or fees.

section 351 transactions = *type C reorganization.*

section 367 transfer the transfer of property from a US corporation to its foreign subsidiary.

section 381 limit limitation of NOL of an acquired company that can be offset against acquiring company's ordinary income, often calculated as NOL multiplied by days after acquisition and divided by total days in taxable year.

section 382 limit limitation of NOL of an acquired company that can be offset against acquiring company's ordinary income, often calculated as fair market value of acquired company multiplied by federal long-term tax exempt rate.

section 383 limit limitation on the *pre-change credit* to be attributable to taxable income which does not exceed *section 382 limit.*

section 401(k) plan = *401(k) plan.*

section 403(b) plan = *403(b) plan.*

section 412(i) plan a defined benefit pension plan guaranteed exclusively by annuity contracts and life insurance.

section 457 plan = *457 plan.*

section 457(b) plan = *457 plan.*

section 471 cost material cost, direct labor and overhead included in inventory cost.

section 475(f) election the election by an active stock trader to treat gain and loss from stock trading as ordinary gain and loss for tax purpose. ***Also***: mark-to-market selection.

Section 501(c)(3) the Internal Revenue Code under which not-for-profit organizations are accorded tax-exempt status.

Section 529 program = *qualified state tuition program.*

section 751 assets a series of assets which create ratable ordinary income on the sale or exchange of a partnership interest, or on certain disproportionate distribution by the partnership.

section 1231 assets depreciable assets and realty used in a trade or business, and capital assets that were the subjects of an involuntary conversion.

section 1231 gains overall gains from dealing in section 1231 assets and certain casualties, etc.

section 1244 stock a stock the gain is considered a capital gain and loss is ordinary loss, up to 50,000 ordinary loss per year applied to first $1,000,000 of stock and must be sold by original purchaser. ***Also***: 1244 stock; small business corporation stock; small business investment company stock; small business stock.

section 1245 property = *section 1245 recovery property.*

section 1245 recovery property recovery property other than the residential 15-year real estate, 15-year realty used overseas, 15-year nonresidential real estate, with respect to which a taxpayer elected straight-line cost recovery. ***Also***: section 1245 property.

section 1248 amount earnings that would have been attributable to the stock of a foreign corporation where the stock was in fact exchanged.

section 1250 property depreciable property, other than section 1245 property and elevators and escalators.

section 1256 contract regulated futures contract, foreign currency contract, nonequity option, dealer equity option, or dealer securities future.

section 1256 property real estate that is or was of a character subject to depreciation under tax law.

sectional balance sheet = *classified balance sheet.*

sectional balancing dividing the general ledger accounts into several groups, each having a self-balancing trial balance.

sectional balancing ledger self-balancing ledger in the sectional balancing system.

sector balance sheet balance sheet of a specific sector of economy, such as financial, nonfinancial, governmental, household, etc.

secured creditor a creditor who holds some security for his debt.

secured debt a debt with collateral attached.

Securities Act of 1933 US law that requires a company intending to offer securities to the public to first file a registration statement with the SEC.

Securities Act of 1934 US law that requires all companies under SEC jurisdiction to file audited financial statements with the SEC.

Securities and Exchange Commission (SEC) federal agency monitoring and regulating corporate financial reporting and disclosure, use of accounting principles, auditing and trading activities.

Securities Transactions <Canada> a form used by a taxpayer to report income and losses on securities transactions. ***Also***: Form T5008; T5008.

securities transfer excise tax (STET) a proposed tax on the transfer of securities. ***See***: *stamp duty.*

securities transfer tax = *stamp duty.*

securities valuation reserve the reserve maintained by insurance companies to soften swings in value of securities they held in their portfolios.

security capital low risk capital such as government bonds, housing mortgages, etc. ***Opp***: *risk capital.*

security interest an interest in the property of another consisting of the right to sell that property when the owner defaults.

security specific risk = *unsystematic risk.*

SEE Special Enrollment Exam

seed capital <1> money used for the initial investment in a project or startup company, for proof-of-concept, market research, or initial product development. ***Also***: front money; seed money. <2> = *retained earnings.*

seed capital exemption = *rule 504 exemption.*

seed money <1> money put up by venture capitalists to finance a new business. <2> = *seed capital.*

segment a division of an enterprise.

segment accounting the accounting for the profit and loss of a department, an area, etc;

segment asset the asset that belongs to a segment.

segment contribution sales revenue of a segment, an area, etc. less its variable costs.

segmented reporting process of reporting activities of various segments of a firm, e.g. branches, product lines, or sales territories. ***Also***: line of business reporting.

segment reporting presentation required in the annual report when a reportable segment meets one or more of the following tests: <a> revenue is 10% or more of combined revenue; <b> operating profit is 10% or more of combined operating profit; or <c> the identifiable assets are 10% or more of the combined identifiable assets.

segregated account the account with an insurance company, the fund in which is not exposed to creditors' claims. ***See***: *investors control rule.*

segregated asset account asset account that is segregated from the general asset accounts. ***Also***: separate account.

segregation of duties internal control concept in which individuals should not have responsibility for incompatible activities. ***Also***: separation of duties.

segregation of fixed and variable costs = *determination of cost behavior.*

seigniorage the profit that results from the difference in the cost of printing money and the face value of that money.

selective audit an audit of a selected object. ***Also***: deliberate audit. ***See***: *automatic audit.*

selective control the techniques which apply the principle that the dollars and effort spent in controlling inventories should be in direct ratio to the value of the inventories being controlled. ***See***: *ABC method.*

selective disclosure the disclosure of financial information to a selected group of investors by a public company.

self-assessment <1><UK> a tax system that replaced *pay and file* since Jul 1 1999, under which taxpayers report their income to the Inland Revenue and pay the taxes due. ***See***: *discovery assessment.* <2><Australia> a tax system under which the ATO will send a letter to a taxpayer after a return is received and let the taxpayer assess the tax liability.

self-balancing ledger a ledger the trial balance of which balances itself. *Also*: balancing ledger.

self-constructed asset an asset constructed by a firm that intends to use it.

self-contained domestic establishment = *principal residence.*

self-correcting error = *offsetting error.*

self-directed IRA an IRA the account holder of which can make investment instructions.

self-employed a taxpayer who is not employed by any person or companies, e.g. individual in business or profession and certain partner.

self-employed health insurance deduction the deduction of health insurance cost of a self-employed tax payer.

Self-employment Contributions Act tax = *self-employment tax.*

self-employment expense a deductible expense from the business of a self-employed taxpayer.

self-employment income personal income from self-employment business.

self-employment loss the amount by which the self-employment income is less than the self-employment expenses.

self-employment profit the amount by which the self-employment income is greater than the self-employment expenses. *Also*: net earnings from self-employment.

self-employment tax a 2-part tax imposed on the earnings from self-employment at a rate of 15.3% in 2003. *Also*: SECA tax; Self-employment Contributions Act tax; tax on self-employment income.

self-insurance fund cash set aside by a bank or other financial institution for emergency use. *Also*: real reserve; reinsurance fund.

self-managed superannuation fund (SMSF) <Australia> a pension fund with fewer than 5 members, and all members are trustees. *See: small self-administered pension scheme.*

self-only coverage health insurance that covers the taxpayer only.

self-service cost the cost of rendering services to other departments in the same business.

self-settled spendthrift trust = *domestic asset protection trust.*

selling and administrative expense expense incurred in the selling and administration activity. *Also*: general administrative and selling expense.

selling and administrative expenses budget detailed plan of operating expenses needed to support the sales and overall operations of the organization for a future period.

selling and distribution overhead (S&D o'h'd) = *selling overhead.*

selling cost the cost incurred in the selling goods and services. *Also*: cost to sell.

selling expense the expense of preparing and storing goods for sale promoting sales, making sales, and if a separate delivery department is not maintained, the expenses of delivering goods to customers.

selling expense budget a budget about the selling expense of a future period.

selling expense variance the difference between the budgeted selling expense and the actual selling expense.

selling flat = *ex interest.*

selling, general and administrative expense (SG&A) operating expenses relating to the storage, promoting or selling of a product.

selling overhead the overhead cost incurred in inducing customers to place orders. *Also*: marketing overhead; selling and distribution overhead.

selling price method a method under which a segment's revenue is based on the selling prices and actual units sold.

semi-annual statement = *half-yearly financial statement.*

semi-direct expense an expense only a part of which relates to the product.

semi-finished goods = *work-in-process.*

semi-finished goods ledger = *work-in-process ledger.*

semi-fixed cost a cost which is essentially fixed over the relevant activity range, but which may have to be increased substantially at several activity levels if production is increased. ***Also***: partly fixed cost. ***See***: *step-variable cost.*

semi-secret trust = *half secret trust.*

semi-variable budget = *flexible budget.*

semi-variable cost a cost which is basically variable but the slope may change abruptly when certain activity level is reached. ***Also***: delayed variable cost; partially variable expense; partly variable cost.

senior accountant staff accountant in a CPA firm who supervises a client engagement.

senior auditor person who is responsible for the overall planning, directing, & reporting of a large audit project. ***See***: *in-charge auditor.*

senior partner a high-level partner in a firm with considerable influence on management. ***See***: *junior partner.*

senior share = *preferred stock.*

SEOS socio-economic operating statement

SEP <1> simplified employee pension. <2> single-employer plan.

separable cost <1> cost incurred after the split-off point in processing some of joint products further. ***Also***: separable processing cost. <2> = *direct cost.*

separable cost-remaining benefits method a method of sharing overhead costs based on the proportion of separable cost or remaining benefits.

separable fixed cost fixed cost that changes between alternatives. ***Also***: identifiable fixed cost; specific capacity cost.

separable processing cost = *separable cost.*

separate account = *segregated asset account.*

separate accounting tax law burdens imposed on employers or collectors of excise taxes, to designate a separate bank account as trustee for the IRS, to which deposit must promptly be made, or risk penalties.

separate factory ledger an independent ledger for a single factory.

separate income the income of a spouse in a community property jurisdiction.

separately stated income the income of an S corporation which retains original characters as is passed through to the shareholders. ***See***: *non-separately stated income.*

separately stated tax a state or local general sales tax paid by consumers, regardless of the legal incidence of the tax.

separate maintenance payment = *alimony.*

separate net income (SNI) <Australia> = *dependent income.*

separate property a property that belongs to the husband or wife, not both. ***Opp***: *community property.*

separate return <1> tax return filed by married persons who choose to state their own income and deductions. ***See***: *joint return.* <2> tax return of an affiliate in a group of companies.

separate return tax liability tax liability of a member of an affiliated group filing a consolidated income tax return, calculated as if the member had filed a separate return.

separate taxable income the taxable income of a corporation filing a consolidated return, disregarding gain or loss from transactions with respect to stock, bonds, or obligations between members of affiliated group.

separation of duties = *segregation of duties.*

SEP IRA an IRA created in connection with the simplified employee pension plan. ***Also***: simplified employee pension IRA.

sequence of accounts the order of accounts in the ledger.

sequential costing synchronous tracking methods attempt to time entries with physical production events sequentially.

sequential method = *continuous allotment method.*

sequential sampling a sampling plan for which the sample is selected in several steps with each step conditional on the results of the previous step. *Also*: stop-or-go sampling. *See*: *fixed sample size approach.*

sequential-step procedure = *continuous allotment method.*

SERP <1> state earnings-related pension. <2> supplemental executive retirement plan.

service employment taken into consideration under a pension plan.

Service, the = *Internal Revenue Service.*

service auditor the auditor who reports on the processing of transactions by the service organization.

service bureau an IRS center serving a particular area.

service bureau identification number (SBIN) a number assigned by the IRS to an ERO which performs the services of a service bureau.

service capacity method = *declining balance method.*

service center = *service department.*

service cost <1> a service department's cost incurred in rendering service to production departments and other service departments. *Also*: cost of service; factory service cost; service department cost. <2> actuarial present value of benefits attributed by the pension benefit formula to the employee's service. *Also*: normal pension cost.

service department a department that does not produce revenue but which supplies other departments with essential services. *Also*: service center.

service department cost = *service cost.*

service department overhead the overhead because of the allocated service costs from other departments.

service life method a method of calculating depreciation by the proportion of the time period a plant asset is used in the production and sale of other assets or services.

services budget a budget including boiler house, gate-keeping, night watchman, security, gardening, and similar activities.

service unit method = *production method.*

service-yield basis a method of calculating depreciation by the proportion of the volume of service rendered by the plant asset. *Also*: yield basis of depreciation.

servicing asset benefit that results in serving financial assets, e.g. collecting, paying taxes and insurance, investing, accounting, etc.

servicing liability the liability that results when the cost of servicing financial assets exceeds the compensation.

set of accounts group of ledger accounts that a particular firm adopts.

set-off <1> a tax collector's power to apply refunds and other amounts due the taxpayer to reduce tax liabilities. <2><Australia> the payment of a refund made by reducing a payment relating to a future excise liability.

set-on <Australia> additional payment made to cover an underpayment relating to a previous excise liability.

setting up cost <1> cost of setting up a production facility, or expense incurred each time a batch is produced. *Also*: fixed charge; preparatory cost; setup cost; starting load cost. <2> = *ordering cost.*

settlement <Australia> the process of lodging a liability statement and making a payment for excise duty.

settlement account <1> items in the balance of payments, including errors and omission, allocation of SDRs, official reserves, etc. *Also*: balancing account; balancing item. <2> notional account in terms of dollar value.

settlement amount = *notional amount.*

settlement of debt = *debt repayment.*

settlement period <Australia> a period, one week, for the settlement of excise duty.

settlement rate discount rate used to calculate the interest on projected benefit obligation of a pension plan.

settlement value = *net realizable value.*

settlor = *trustor.*

set up cost <1> = *ordering cost.* <2> = *setting up cost.*

seven-pay test premium a policy must be paid over at least seven years so that loans and withdrawals can be tax-free.

severance damage money paid to the property owner for loss of value in the part of property condemned.

severance pay payment made to employees upon separation from the employer. *Also*: dismissal pay; termination pay.

severance tax a state tax imposed on the act of extracting oil, gas, or minerals from the ground, often expressed in terms of cents per volume or weight, or on occasion on a percentage of the value of the resources.

SF sinking fund

SFAC Statement of Financial Accounting Concepts

SFFAS Statements of Federal Financial Accounting Standards

SFSS Student Financial Supplement Scheme

SG superannuation guarantee

SG&A selling, general and administrative expense

SGC superannuation guarantee charge

shadow director <UK> a person who acts like a director of a company.

shadow price = *opportunity cost.*

sham corporation = *dummy corporation.*

SHAR superannuation holding accounts reserve

share bonus = *stock dividend.*

share dividend = *stock dividend.*

shared responsibility opinion an audit report in which the principal auditors decide to share responsibility with other auditors who performed some segments of the client.

shareholder = *stockholder.*

shareholder equalization tax = *dividend equalization tax.*

shareholder's equity = *stockholder's equity.*

shareholder's fund <UK> the called-up shares plus all reserves minus minority interest.

shareholders' voluntary liquidation = *members' voluntary liquidation.*

shareholder value <1> the value that a shareholder is able to obtain from his/her investment in a company, e.g. capital gains, dividends, proceeds from buyback programs and other payout. <2> = *market capitalization.*

share of no par value = *no-par-value stock.*

share option = *stock option.*

share premium <UK> = *additional paid-in capital.*

share-purchase tax credit <Canada> a tax credit available to taxpayers who purchased shares in certain unit investment trusts.

share-related benefit <UK> benefit provided to an employee through share-related bonus items.

shares authorized = *authorized shares.*

shares outstanding = *number of shares outstanding.*

share split-up = *stock split.*

share warrant <UK> = *stock warrant.*

Sharpe ratio risk-adjusted measure of return calculated by dividing the annualized *excess return* of a portfolio by its *total risk.*

shell company a company with few or no assets, income, products, services, activities, business plan, management team, employees, or anything else that an ongoing business ordinarily has, except for registration with the SEC. *Also*: blank check company; listed shell company.

shell merger = *reverse merger.*

shelter cost = *storage cost.*

sheltered workshop school operated by certain tax-exempt organizations, or by a government agency, that provides special instruction or training designed to alleviate the disability of the individual.

shifting of income a practice of changing the flow of taxable income from one person to another in order to minimize aggregate income taxes.

S-H-M accounting principles accounting principles established by 3 American professors: Sanders, Hatfield, and Moore.

shock loss = *accounting bath.*

shop burden = *factory overhead.*

shop-loading method = *staffing technique.*

shopping by principles changing from one auditor to another in order to sanction a disputed accounting principle issue.

shortage cost = *cost of not carrying.*

short cut method one of two methods for computing throw-back tax. *See*: *throwback rule.*

short entry an entry in the customer's deposit book when a bank received an unmatured collection bill.

shortfall gain from the sale of investment in securities held for less than 6 months.

short form Form 1040A filed by individuals who do not identify their deductions.

short form report an audit report without detailed comments analyzing the client's financial position and results of operations. *See*: *representation.*

short-life asset an asset with a life shorter than it is expected.

short run approach a method for determining whether to accept a rate of interest by the capital cost of a project.

short run capacity cost capacity cost which remains constant in a short period.

short run cost the cost to be matched with the current revenue. *See*: *long run cost.*

short run marginal cost (SRMC) marginal cost where some input quantities are fixed by decisions. *See*: *long run marginal cost.*

short run variable cost a cost that is variable in a short period of time.

short sale rule = *30 % rule.*

short schedule self-employment tax schedule in simplified format.

short short rule = *30 % rule.*

short swing profit the profit taken by investors in trading securities in a 6-month period, especially profit made by insiders. *See*: *trading profit.*

short tax year tax period less than 12 months long, resulting from a business start-up or the transition to a tax year ending on a different date.

short-term defined for various tax and other financial purposes as less than a week, one month, six months, 9 months, and one year.

short-term asset <1> an asset that will change its form within one operating cycle. <2> = *current asset.*

short-term auction rate = *auction rate preferred stock.*

short-term capital losses (STCL) any losses from sales or exchanges of capital assets held for not more than one year.

short-term debt obligation payable by the debtor within one year.

short-term debt ratio the ratio of short-term debt to total debts.

short-term financial liability = *current liability.*

short-term gain or loss capital gain or loss on an investment which was held for less than one year. *See*: *long-term gain or loss.*

short-term lease = *operating lease.*

short-term liability = *current liability.*

short-term preferred share <Canada> a preferred share issued by a corporation after Dec 15, 1987.

short-term solvency ratio a ratio used to judge a firm's adequacy of liquid assets to meet short-term debts when due, e.g. *current ratio, acid-test ratio, inventory turnover,* and *accounts receivable turnover.*

short-term tax exempt a short-term security issued by states, municipalities, and quasi-government entities.

short-term tax-free income an investment style that seeks capital preservation while providing attractive tax-free income.

short-term trust a trust for a short period of time.

"should be" cost = *standard cost.*

should-cost = *standard cost.*

shut-down cost <1> cost incurred to stop a department, an operation or a factory. ***Also***: factory shut-down cost. <2> = *prime cost.*

SIC code Standard Industrial Classification code

sick pay payment to an employee while away from work due to sickness.

sidecar IRA = *deemed IRA.*

side transaction any transaction that will not affect the asset, liability, and capital, and need not to be recorded in the books.

sight test auditor's test without detailed analysis.

significant control influence over the operating, financial, or accounting policies of an entity. ***Also***: significant influence.

significant influence = *significant control.*

significant participation passive activity (SPPA) any trade or business in which a taxpayer significantly participates for the tax year but doesn't materially participate.

significant variance cost variance that exceeds certain limit and is significantly important to the person responsible. ***Also***: material variance.

silent partner a partner who does not participate in the management. ***Also***: dormant partner; sleeping partner.

SIM specific identifications method

SIMA Special Import Measures Act

similar bond a bond with the same yield, maturity date or credit rating as the one sold.

SIMPLE savings incentive match plan for employees

SIMPLE 401(k) a 401(k) plan for which certain of the usual requirements are simplified.

simple average method <1> a method for pricing the issued materials by the simple average purchase price of all purchased materials. <2> a method for forecasting under which the forecasted month figure is the simple average of the past several months.

simple cost accounting cost accounting that classifies the costs by nature.

simple extension = *mean-per-unit estimation.*

simple interest the interest calculated on a principal sum, and not on any interest that has been earned by that sum. ***Also***: ordinary interest; single interest. ***See***: *compound interest.*

SIMPLE IRA an IRA created in connection with a savings incentive match plan for employees. ***Also***: simple retirement account.

simple journal a journal that has only credit and debit columns.

simple journal entry an entry that includes only two accounts.

simple liquidation a liquidation at which all assets are realized.

simple liquidation method a liquidation method under which cash after liquidation will be distributed among partners at one time.

simple machine-hour method a method for apportioning overhead costs based on the proportion of total overhead costs to the total machine-hours worked.

simple negligence = *negligence.*

simple process costing a process costing used when there is only one product or repeat production.

simple rate of return = *accounting rate of return.*

simple retirement account (SRA) = *SIMPLE IRA.*

simple trust <1> a trust all current income of which must be distributed each year. ***See***: *complex trust.* <2><UK> a trust which requires no act to be done by the trustee.

simple yield return equal to the nominal dollar interest divided by the market value of a bond.

simplified dollar value lifo a method under which a taxpayer who deals in a large variety of products may value inventory by the use of the dollar value rather than natural units.

simplified employee pension (SEP) a type of pension plan that an employer can establish, contributions are tax deductible.

simplified employee pension IRA = *SEP IRA.*

simplified flow-through rules a rule under which the taxable income of an electing large partnership is computed in the same manner as that of an individual, except disallowing the deduction for personal exemptions, NOL and certain itemized deductions.

simplified look-back marginal-impact method a look-back method used by pass-through entities whereby the tax underpaid or overpaid under a long-term contract is found by multiplying the contract income over- or under-reported for the year by the top marginal tax rate applicable.

simplified method <1> a method used for per diem amount paid for travel by guidelines set by the IRS for the highest and lowest rates on designated cities. ***Also***: high-low method. <2> a method of computing input tax credit by calculating 1/107 or 15/115 of taxable purchases.

simulation a condensed case study section of the computerized CPA exam.

simultaneous allocation = *algebraic method.*

simultaneous equations method = *algebraic method.*

SIN social insurance number

single a filing status of an unmarried taxpayer.

single-account system <UK> a former system under which assets and liabilities are shown in the balance sheet and not classified into fixed and variable components. ***See***: *double account system.*

single all-inclusive unit-cost figure = *absorption cost.*

single asset depreciation the depreciation calculated under the *single asset depreciation method.* ***Also***: individual depreciation; item depreciation; unit depreciation.

single asset depreciation method accounting procedure for depreciation of assets where accounts are kept for each depreciable asset. ***Also***: individual depreciation method; item accounting; item depreciation accounting; item method; physical units method; unit approach; unit method of depreciation. ***Opp***: *composite depreciation method.*

single audit combination of financial statements audit and compliance audit relating to federal financial assistance program, governed by Single Audit Act & OMB Circular A-133.

Single Audit Act of 1984 law that establishes uniform requirements for audits of federal financial assistance provided to state and local governments.

single category method a method under which shares bought at different prices of a mutual fund are placed in one account and divided by total cost, sales on first-in, first-out cost assumption, regardless of the length of the holding period. ***See***: *double-category method.*

single cost = *production costs per unit.*

single costing = *output costing.*

single cost system a cost system that applies the same costing procedure to different products.

single debit a method of mortgage accounting under which all currently paid installments are reported as one single item, uncollectible installments are reported in details.

single-employer plan (SEP) <Canada> a pension plan that is sponsored by one employer only. ***See***: *multi-employer plan.*

single entry transactions are recorded in only one account. ***See***: *double entry.*

single entry bookkeeping the bookkeeping that applies the single entry plan.

single entry plan a system of bookkeeping in which each item is entered only once in the ledger, etc.

single journal entry a journal entry that has only one debit or credit. ***See***: *compound journal entry.*

single overhead allocation rate a single overhead rate computed for the entire factory. ***Also***: blanket overhead rate; company-wide overhead application rate; one company-wide overhead rate; single rate; total company wide overhead rate.

single plan a plan in the input method, under which standard costs are credited in the direct materials account and direct labor account, and the cost variances are shown as the balances in these accounts.

single posting system a bank system in which the deposit slips are posted to the deposit ledger at one time by carbon paper.

single premium a premium that substantially all of it is paid within four years from the purchase date.

single premium costing the costing of the single one time payment of pension by considering the costs to be an insurance premium in the life time. ***See***: *annual premium costing.*

single premium life insurance an insurance policy that substantially all the premiums are paid within the first four years from the purchase date.

single presentation the reporting of primary earnings per share only.

single-product process costing process costing for the repeat production of one product.

single rate = *single overhead allocation rate.*

single ruling the single line drawn underneath the last entry of an account. ***See***: *double ruling.*

single-step approach method that groups all revenues in one category, all expenses in another, and derives a single resultant net income figure.

single-step form an income statement form whereby revenue and expenses are matched in one step.

single-step income statement an income statement on which cost of goods sold and the expenses are added together and subtracted in one step from revenue to arrive at the net income.

single tax system a tax system suggested by Henry George, in which all net income from the ownership of land would be taxed for the total amount, thus eliminating the need to collect other tax.

sinking fund (SF) fund created by issuers for the purpose of redeeming bonds outstanding. ***Also***: continual redemption sinking fund; extinguishment fund; long-term debt offsets; provisions for repayments.

sinking fund depreciation the depreciation amount under the sinking fund method. ***Also***: increasing-charge depreciation.

sinking fund depreciation plus interest on first cost approach a method under which current depreciation expense is the sum of sinking fund depreciation, and the interest on original cost of the plant asset.

sinking fund method a method under which the amount of annual depreciation is equal to the increase in the asset replacement fund which would consist of the equal periodic deposits plus the interest revenue at the assumed rate on the sinking fund balance. ***Also***: equal-annual-payment method; increasing charge method; present worth method.

sin tax a tax levied on products considered vices, such as cigarettes.

sister corporation a corporation which is the same subsidiary of the same parent company.

site audit = *field audit.*

site direct expense direct expense incurred on the site of the construction.

sitting on a gain holding a stock which has been appreciated in value.

situation audit assessing a firm's performance in absolute terms or in comparison to a competing or parallel organization. *Also*: position audit.

six-column worksheet work sheet having 6 columns, e.g. both debit and credit columns for the trial balance, the balance sheet, and the income statement. *See*: *sorting process.*

six-tenths rule a rough guide to the cost of a new plant A, when a similar plant B of the same size has been constructed at a known cost C, the new plant cost = C × e × (A÷B) × 6/10, where e represents the amount of inflation between the dates of construction of the two plants.

size approach a method for deciding whether to report an item as a separate item in the income statement by the percentage of it to the net income in the income statement.

SJ sales journal

skeleton account = *T-account.*

skeleton balance sheet = *condensed balance sheet.*

skill acquisition curve = *learning curve.*

skip person a person who is two or more generations younger than the transferor in a generation-skipping transfer.

SL <1> sales ledger. <2> straight line.

slack path the path representing other series of activities that require less time.

slack time excess of the time reflected by the critical path over the time of any other paths.

sleeping account = *bad debt.*

sleeping partner <UK> = *silent partner.*

sliding budget = *flexible budget.*

sliding scale budget = *flexible budget.*

slip a document for recording transactions. *Also*: voucher.

slip daybook a book consisting of slips under bookless accounting system.

slippage <1> difference between estimated and actual transaction costs. <2> cost to the investors that results from buying at the asked price and selling at the bid price.

slip system = *bookless accounting system.*

SL method straight line method

slow asset an asset that can not be exchanged for cash without cutting price.

slow loan a short-term loan not repaid for more than 60 days, or long-term loan not repaid for more than 90 days. *See: nonaccrual asset.*

slow turning account an account receivable that needs a long time to collect it.

small a angle n at i = $a_{n|i}$.

small business bond <Canada> a bond issued by a *qualified small business corporation.*

small business corporation <1> corporation with capital receipts of less than $1 million. <2><Canada> = *qualified small business corporation.* <3> = *S corporation.*

small business corporation stock = *section 1244 stock.*

small business deduction (SBD) <1> taxable deduction allowed to an insurance company, the lower of 10% of its investment yield or $25,000. <2><Canada> reduction of tax rate from 28% to 12% available to Canadian-controlled private corporations for the first $200,000 taxable income.

small business investment company (SBIC) a privately-owned investment company which provides equity investments and management assistance to qualified small businesses.

small business investment company stock (SBIC stock) = *section 1244 stock.*

small business stock = *section 1244 stock*

small cap $250 million to $1 billion capitalization. *See*: *large cap; micro cap; mid cap.*

small cap stock a stock the total market capitalization is from $250 million to $1 billion.

Small Case Division a division of the US Tax Court for the case involving an amount not exceeding $50,000.

small companies' rate = *small company rate.*

small company <UK> a company with total asset less than £1.4 million, turnover of £2.8 million or less and no more than 50 employees.

small company rate tax rate applied to the profits of a company that is above the limit for a *starting rate* but bot exceeding an upper limit for a *full rate*. ***Also***: small companies' rate.

small disposal <UK> a disposal of asset that is free of capital gains if the taxpayer receives less than £3,000 or 5% of the total assets.

small issue exemption <1> issue of industrial development bonds the interest of which is exempt if the proceeds are used for acquisition, construction or improvement of land, or depreciable properties. <2> issues of securities of $1 million or less.

small p angle n at i = $p_{\overline{n}|i}$.

small self-administered pension scheme <UK> a pension scheme under which there are less than 12 members, and all members are trustees and all agreed to invest the assets by themselves. ***See:*** *self-managed superannuation fund.*

small tax case a case that involves an amount of less than $10,000.

SMEP specified multi-employer plan

SMSF self-managed superannuation fund

soak up method = *economic basis method.*

social accounting = *national economic accounting.*

social asset staff asset, organization resource, and the use of public properties.

social assistance <Canada> payment made to Canadians on the basis of need by provinces and municipalities with federal contributions under the *Canada Health and Social Transfer.*

social audit a study of the social impact of company or national policies, including how far they are realizing and being affected by the expectations.

social balance sheet a balance sheet showing social assets, social liabilities and social equities.

social benefit the increase in the wealth of the society resulting from a specific act or action. ***Also***: spill in.

social benefits repayment = *recovery tax.*

social capital all resources of the society used to produce goods and services. ***Also***: social goods; social overhead capital.

social cost decrease in social wealth measured in terms of effects on the social amenities, the lives and happiness of people with environmental factors such as pollution. ***Also***: cost to society; spill-out; spill-over cost.

social dividend = *negative income tax.*

social economic accounting taking social consequences of decisions into account in financial management information and accounting procedure.

social economic profit the excess of internalized social benefit over social cost of a firm.

social goods = *social capital.*

social impact statement detailed report to assess the effect and consequences of the public interest, nonprofit activities of an entity.

social income statement a statement that shows social benefits, social costs and social economic profit of a given organization.

social insurance number (SIN) <Canada> a number assigned to an individual taxpayer.

social liability staff liability, organization liability and public liability.

social opportunity cost the cost to the society when resources are transferred from the private sector to the public sector.

social overhead capital = *social capital.*

social overhead cost expenditure on the public construction of the society.

social performance accounting the accounting for measuring the relationship between a business and other organizations, between resources and environment, and also between products and all resources, etc.

social responsibility accounting the accounting that focuses on the measuring and reporting of the prevention, disposition, rectification and repayment of unfavorable impact to the society by the activities of a given business.

social security benefit = *social security payment.*

social security number an 8-digit number assigned to a person by the Social Security Administration.

social security offset = *offset.*

social security payment benefit paid to a qualified person from social security. ***Also***: social security benefit. ***See***: *Old-Aged Security.*

social security tax = *FICA tax.*

social-value-oriented accounting the measuring of the value of the society based on accounting data and the social benefit standards.

society's equity excess of social assets over social liabilities.

socio-economic operating statement (SEOS) the expenditures statement of a business on activities concerning the society, products, people, and environment.

soft asset an asset such as *intellectual property* and information. ***See***: *hard asset.*

soft cost architectural, engineering and legal fees, as distinguished from land construction costs. ***See***: *hard cost.*

soft currency debt <Canada> an obligation denominated in a foreign currency other than Canadian dollar.

soft dollar <1> the value of research services that brokerage houses supply to investment managers free of charge in exchange for the investment manager's business. ***See:*** *quid pro quo.* <2> dollar amount invested in the purchase or development of real estate that is deductible, e.g. prepaid fee. ***See:*** *hard dollar.*

sold daybook = *sales journal.*

solidity surplus additional amount of surplus generated by an additional amount of capital to be included in the surplus.

sollen amount the amount of assets shown in the books.

solvency the ability to repay debts when due. ***Also***: debt-paying ability; debt-serving capacity; financial solvency.

solvency ratio <1> = *equity-debt ratio.* <2> = *equity-to-assets ratio.*

solvency surplus additional amount of surplus generated by an additional amount of capital to be included in the book value surplus.

solving rate of return = *present value profitability index.*

S-1 = *Form S-1.*

S-1 review procedures carried out by auditors at the client's office on or close to the effective date of a registration statement.

SOP <1> statement of policy. <2> Statement of Position.

SORP Statement of Recommended Practice

sorting process the work sheet process of transferring items from the adjusted trial balance columns to the balance sheet or income statement columns. ***See***: *six-column worksheet.*

SOT special occupational tax

soundex code a code used in military accounting for the name of a person.

sound value replacement value, reproduction value or the value after depreciation or one of the above.

source and application of funds method = *cash expenditures method.*

source and application of funds statement = *statement of changes in financial position.*

source and disposition of working capital statement = *statement of changes in financial position.*

source-by-source basis <Canada> a tax basis under which income or loss from each trade, business and property is to be treated as a separate source of income.

source deduction <New Zealand> = *income tax withholding.*

source document = *supporting document.*

SOx Sarbanes-Oxley Act

SOYD sum-of-the-years'-digits

SOYD depr sum-of-the-years'-digits depreciation

SP2 state second pension

space available rule a rule of figuring out the taxable portion of the personal use of the commercial air flight provided to a taxpayer by the company. (25% of the actual carrier's highest unrestricted coach fare is taxable).

space cost the cost, such as rent and light, that relates to the space in use.

spare capacity amount of available plant and equipment not in use. *Also*: excess capacity.

SPD summary plan description

SPE special purpose entity

special account an account, such as variance account, that provides special information. *Also*: rubricated account.

special accounting the accounting that classifies a nation into several sectors for budgeting and accounting purposes. *See*: *general accounting.*

special agent a specialist employed by the IRS to conduct investigations involving criminal violations of Internal Revenue Law. See: *office auditor; revenue agent.*

special allocation the allocation of one or more items of income, gains, losses deductions or credits to a partner that depart from the partner's general allocation of profits and losses.

special assessment tax levied on those who benefited from a special service or project.

special assessment fund a fund used in government accounting to account for the financing of public improvements or services from the issuance of bonds or assessments levied against properties benefited.

special audit <1> audit on the specific events. <2> audit with a restricted, narrow scope to confirm with a governmental agency's regulatory requirements. *See*: *limited audit.*

special audit report audit report about special events. *Also*: special report.

special averaging = *forward averaging.*

special bonus dividend = *extra dividend.*

special-column journal <1> = *columnar journal.* <2> = *special journal.*

Special Committee on Assurance Services = *Elliott Committee.*

special cost the cost that relates to special problems in decision making, such as opportunity cost.

special cost investigation cost investigation for special purposes.

special daybook = *special journal.*

special depreciation = *abnormal depreciation.*

special disaster relief a relief available to taxpayers whose principal residence and/or contents are involuntarily converted as a result of a disaster.

special dividend = *extra dividend.*

Special Enrollment Exam (SEE) a 4-part examination one must pass to be licensed to practice tax before the IRS.

Special Import Measures Act (SIMA) <Canada> a legislation that provides for the imposition of anti-dumping and countervailing duties.

specialized journal = *special journal.*

specialized statement = *special-purpose financial statement.*

special journal a columnar journal for recording one kind of transaction. *Also*: auxiliary journal; special-column journal; special daybook; specialized journal; subsidiary journal. *See*: *general journal.*

special ledger a ledger consisting of special accounts.

special occupational tax (SOT) a special tax on a taxpayer engaged in a business, office or employment that requires a license. *Also*: occupational tax.

special order cost system = *job order cost system.*

special order decision a management accounting decision whether to accept an order at an offered price that is below the normal selling price.

special purpose entity (SPE) an entity that at least 3% of the capital has been invested from an independent shareholder.

special-purpose financial statement financial statement that provides special information for limited users. ***Also***: specialized statement.

special report <1> a financial report for special use, such as further investigation of cost variance by managers. <2> auditor's report issued on a special event. ***Also***: special audit report.

special revenue fund account for the proceeds of specific revenue sources that are legally restricted to expenditures for specific purposes.

special tax credit a tax incentive granted to businesses in targeted areas.

special trust a trust established to carry out a particular purpose.

specification cost <1> = *direct cost.* <2> = *standard cost.*

specific capacity cost = *separable fixed cost.*

specific charge-off method = *direct method.*

specific cost direct cost of a given department or product.

specific cost method = *specific identification method.*

specific goods method a method under which physical inventory units must be identified from year to year, thus decrease in any identifiable unit will produce an increased taxable income due to the earlier low costs being charged as cost of sales. ***See***: *dollar value method.*

specific identification method <1> method under which each item of inventory should be identified with its cost and the sum of these amounts should constitute the inventory value. ***Also***: identification method; identified cost method; lot method; specific cost method. <2> a method whereby the cost of specific acquisitions of bonds must be identified in matching with the resale prices.

specific invoice pricing the pricing of an inventory where each inventory item can be associated with invoice and be priced accordingly.

specific order costing = *job order costing.*

specific price level-adjusted accounting = *current cost accounting.*

specific reserve a provision for a specific or contingent liability, such as tax or dividend shortly to be paid.

specific risk = *unsystematic risk.*

specified investment business <Canada> a business other than a credit union, or a business the principal purpose of which is to derive income from property.

specified multi-employer plan (SMEP) <Canada> a *multi-employer plan* with certain conditions specified.

specified order of closing method = *continuous allotment method.*

specified partnership loss <Canada> the corporation's share of losses of a partnership of which it is a member from active business carried on in Canada.

specified retirement arrangement (SRA) <Canada> an unfunded or partially-funded plan that is regulated by federal or provincial legislation.

specified shareholder <Canada> a taxpayer who owns at least 10% of any class of the stock of a corporation.

spending variance <1> = *budget variance.* <2> = *factory overhead expenditure variance.*

spendthrift trust a trust created to provide some income to the beneficiary while preventing both the beneficiary and his or her creditors from having access to the asset.

spent overhead = *actual overhead.*

SPI schedule performance index

spill-in = *social benefit.*

spill-out = *social cost.*

spill-over cost = *social cost.*

spin-off a corporation sets up and funds a new subsidiary and gives the shares of this new company to the old company's shareholders on a pro rata basis, free of charge. *See*: *split-off; split-up.*

spin-off ruling an IRS ruling that legally binds a spin-off of a corporation.

spin-off share <Canada> the share in other company received on the eligible distribution in respect of the original share.

split = *stock split.*

split back = *split down.*

split-column journal = *columnar journal.*

split-dollar arrangement whereby costs and benefits of life insurance are split by employers and employees.

split down to increase the face value of a company's shares by issuing a new stock to replace each of 2 or more shares outstanding. *Also*: consolidation of capital; consolidation of shares; Irish dividend; Polish dividend; reverse split; reverse stock-split; Scottish dividend; share consolidation; split-back; stock split-down.

split election an election of S corporation status for federal tax purpose and not for state tax purpose.

split income <Canada> dividend received from private corporations by a family trust that has been allocated to a beneficiary under the age of 18.

split-interest agreement an arrangement where a donor makes an initial gift to a trust or directly to the not-for-profit organization, in which the organization has a beneficial interest but is not the sole beneficiary.

split ledger account ledger account that is controlled by two or more profit and loss accounts.

split-off occurs when a company sets up and funds a new one and gives the shares of this new company to the stockholders of the old company in exchange for their shares in the old company. *See*: *spin-off; split-up.*

split-off point the point in the productive process at which joint products are separated.

split-rate tax system tax system that taxes retained earnings at a higher rate than earnings that are distributed as dividends.

split share a share that is being or has been split or divided into a number of new shares. *Also*: split stock.

split stock <1> purchase or sale of stock shared with others. <2> = *split share.*

split up occurs when a company divides into two or more separate new companies, gives the shares of the new companies to its old shareholders, and goes out of business. *See*: *spin-off; split-off; stock split.*

split-year treatment <UK> if a taxpayer lives in UK for only part of a year, he is taxable for the time he stays in the UK.

spoilage loss that results either when the material being processed or the finished item is discovered to be unusable because of defects in workmanship or material.

spoilage cost the cost that must be absorbed by the spoilage. *Also*: cost of spoilage.

spoilage cost variance difference between actual spoilage cost and budgeted spoilage cost.

spoiled goods finished goods that can not be used due to the defects in workmanship.

spoiled material cost direct cost of materials spoiled. *Also*: junk value.

spontaneous current liabilities short-term obligations that automatically increase and decrease in response to financing needs, such as accounts payable.

spontaneous liabilities obligations that arise automatically in the course of operating a business when a company buys goods and services on credit.

spot asset = *cash asset.*

spot entry = *original entry.*

spousal exemption a tax exemption that a taxpayer is entitled to deduct for his or her spouse, $3,050 in the year 2003. *Also*: exemption for spouse.

spousal IRA an IRA set up by a married person in the name of his/her spouse who has an annual income of less than $2,000.

spousal remainder trust fixed-term trust from which income is distributed to the beneficiary to take advantage of a lower tax bracket, and that at the end of the term passes to the grantor's spouse.

spousal support = *alimony.*

spouse's allowance <Canada> a non-taxable monthly benefit paid to low-income taxpayer aged 60 to 64 who is a spouse of Old Age Security pensioner or widow(er).

SPP Saskatchewan Pension Plan

SPPA significant participation passive activity

spread <1> the difference between the highest and the lowest marginal tax rates. (38.6 - 10 = 28.6 in 2003). <2> = *gross profit.*

spread income of a bank, the difference between interest income from loans and the cost of funds. *Also*: margin income.

spread sheet <1> a ledger sheet with the data from the income statement, balance sheet and the sales statements laid out in columns and rows. *Also*: account matrix; matrix form. <2> = *articulation statement.*

springing trust a trust the beneficiary can not be a US citizen until at least one year after the death of the grantor.

sprinkling trust a trust that allows annual distribution of certain amount of principal and income to each beneficiary at the trustee's discretion.

SR special reserve

SR&ED credit scientific research and experimental development tax credit

SRA <1> simple retirement account. <2> specified retirement arrangement.

SR bk stores-received book

SRJ sales returns journal

SRM summary review memorandum

SRMC short-run marginal cost

SS surviving spouse

SSAE Statements on Standards for Attestation Engagements

SSAP Statement of Standard Accounting Practice

SSARS Statements on Standards for Accounting and Review Services

SSBIC specialized small business investment company

SSCE Statements on Standards for Consulting Services

SSTS Statements on Standards for Tax Services

stability of the measuring unit stability of money, the measuring unit in accounting.

stabilized accounting = *constant dollar accounting.*

stable-dollar assumption = *stable monetary unit assumption.*

stable monetary postulate = *unit-of-money postulate.*

stable monetary unit assumption the idea that the purchasing power of the unit of measure used in accounting, the dollar, does not change. *Also*: stable dollar assumption.

stable unit of measurement a concept that the measurement unit of accounting should be stable, not changeable.

staff asset in social accounting, the sum of human resources and the investments in training workers.

staff assistant = *staff auditor.*

staff audit = *internal audit.*

staff auditor <1> auditor in a CPA firm who examines a client's financial records. *Also*: staff assistant. <2> = *internal auditor.*

staff expense = *personnel expense.*

staffing technique a technique for estimating the man-hours required to finish a given job by envisioning the job, the work location, and the equipment or machine required, and estimating the number of people and skill that would be needed to staff a particular operation. *Also*: man-loading technique; shop-loading method.

staff liability the liability expressed as the wages and salaries payable to the employees.

stair-step cost = *step-variable cost.*

stair-stepped cost = *step-variable cost.*

stair-step semi-variable cost = *step-variable cost.*

stake = *equity.*

stakeholder <1> any party that has an interest in a firm, such as stockholder, creditor, employee, supplier, etc. <2><UK> a person holding a sum of money paid as a deposit on a contract for the purchase of a property.

stakeholder pension <UK> introduced in April 2001, a low-cost personal pension scheme for small companies with 5 or more employees.

stale inventory the inventory of merchandise that can not sell for a long time even with cutting price. *Also*: dead stock; stale stock.

stale stock = *stale inventory.*

stamp duty <1> <UK> a 0.5% tax on the purchase of equity shares, and 1.5% on depositary receipts. *Also*: securities transfer tax; stamp duty reserve tax. *See*: *securities transfer excise tax.* <2> = *stamp tax.*

stamp duty reserve tax = *stamp duty.*

stamp tax a tax imposed on a product or a transaction by means of a stamp to be affixed to the product or instrument. *Also*: stamp duty.

stand-alone cost method a method that allocates a portion of common costs to each user by applying a ratio equal to the stand-alone cost of providing benefits to that user divided by the sum of the stand-alone costs for all users.

stand-alone revenue allocation procedure that uses proportion of individual product selling price, cost, or units in bundle to total of all products in bundle to allocate revenues. *See*: *incremental revenue allocation.*

Standard & Poor's core earnings net earnings that focuses on a public company's core business, excluding litigation costs, but including cost of employee pension plans.

standard absorption costing standard costing using absorption method. *Also*: absorption standard costing; full standard costing; standard total absorption costing.

standard accounting procedures standard procedures established by the accounting profession. *Also*: accounting model.

standard audit report = *unqualified report.*

standard confirmation form a form used by auditors to obtain information from financial institutions and other accounts receivable customers. *Also*: standard form.

standard contribution margin excess of actual revenue over standard variable cost.

standard conversion cost conversion cost under standard cost system.

standard cost (SC) cost amount that should be incurred under normal conditions in producing a given product, or in performing a particular service. *Also*: predicted cost; projected cost; scheduled cost; "should be" cost; should-cost; specification cost; target cost.

standard cost allowed multiplying the units of output by the standard cost for each type of input, and for all inputs combination.

standard cost applied multiplying the determined standard cost per unit of output by the number of units of output produced.

standard costing cost accounting that focuses on developing the estimated future product costs as a basis for planning and control decisions. *See*: *historical costing.*

standard costing variance = *standard cost variance.*

standard cost method a method for apportioning indirect costs to closing inventory, under which the goods in ending inventory are allocated a ratable portion of any net negative or net positive overhead variances and any net negative or net positive direct production cost variances, ignoring insignificant variances unless they are allocated in the financial reports.

standard cost revision re-estimating of standard cost so that it might be closer to the actual cost.

standard cost sheet a sheet that illustrates how standard costs are developed and accounted for.

standard cost system a system in which goods in process and finished goods are all reported in standard costs.

standard cost variance difference between actual costs and standard costs arrived at by standard costing. ***Also***: cost variance; standard costing variance.

standard deduction tax allowance amount deducted from AGI to arrive at taxable income if itemized deduction is not chosen. ***Also***: zero bracket amount.

standard deviation a measure of the dispersion around the expected value, it equals the square root of the mean of the squares differences between the observed values and the expected value.

standard direct costing = *direct standard costing.*

standard direct labor cost = *standard labor cost.*

standard direct material cost = *standard material cost.*

standard fixed manufacturing overhead rate total budgeted fixed manufacturing overhead costs divided by an expression of capacity, usually normal capacity in terms of standard hours or units.

standard form = *standard confirmation firm.*

standard income statement income statement for internal use, in which standard costs are reported.

Standard Industrial Classification code (SIC code) a standard series of 4-digit codes that are used to categorize business activities.

standard labor cost labor cost based on the standard labor rate. ***Also***: standard direct labor cost.

standard labor rate direct labor rate that should be paid for each hour of labor time.

standard material cost material cost based on the standard unit cost and standard usage. ***Also***: materials standard cost; standard direct material cost.

standard mileage rate amount per mile, determined by the IRS, to calculate vehicle expense instead of keeping track of actual costs.

standard of control minimum ownership level (80%) required to identify an investee company as a controlled subsidiary and allow the preparation of consolidated tax return.

standard opinion = *unqualified opinion.*

standard overhead cost sum of the estimates for variable and fixed overhead costs in the next accounting period. ***Also***: normal overhead.

standard report = *unqualified report.*

standards of field work generally accepted auditing standards served as a guideline for the audit field work.

standards of reporting generally accepted auditing standards served as a guideline for the audit report.

standard total absorption costing = *standard absorption costing.*

standard unqualified report = *unqualified report.*

stand-by cost method a method under which idle costs are viewed as fixed costs, other costs are viewed as variable costs.

standing auditor one acting as an auditor for the same client for more than two consecutive periods.

standing cost = *fixed cost.*

standing expense = *fixed expense.*

starting-load cost = *setting up cost.*

starting rate <UK> the tax rate applied to the first range of all types of income above the personal allowance. *See: basic rate of tax.*

startup cost = *organization cost.*

stated account = *account stated.*

stated capital sum of capital calculated by its stated value. *Also*: declared capital; legal capital.

stated capital method = *face value method.*

state death tax death tax imposed by the state.

stated interest the interest on a debt as stated by a coupon or contract.

stated liability amount listed under liabilities in the various financial records and statements without audit or verification.

stated value artificial amount established by a corporation's board of directors, that is credited to the no-par stock a/c at the time the stock is issued.

state earnings-related pension (SERP) = *state second pension.*

state income tax state tax based on your income

statement a report that has a stated format. *Also*: account; report format.

statement billing a method in which the sales for a period are collected into one statement and the customer should pay all of the invoices at once.

statement form = *report form.*

statement heading = *heading.*

statement of absorption of deficit = *loss appropriation statement.*

statement of account a report indicating the account status of an agreement between creditor end debtor. *Also*: account rendered.

statement of accounting policies a statement attached to the financial statements giving details of accounting policies used.

statement of activities <non-profit entity> = *income statement.*

statement of affairs a statement setting out the assets and liabilities at a certain date of a bankrupt debtor or of a company in liquidation. *Also*: condition of affairs; statement of condition of affairs.

statement of assets and liabilities = *balance sheet.*

Statement of Benefits <Canada> a form used by a taxpayer to report workers compensation benefits. *Also*: Form T5007; T5007.

statement of cash flows = *cash flow statement.*

statement-of-cash-flows method a method of cash budgeting that is organized along the lines of the statement of cash flows.

statement of cash receipts and disbursements = *cash flow statement.*

statement of cash receipts, disbursements and balance = *combined statement of receipts and expenditures, balance, etc.*

statement-of-changes-in-equity approach method that lists net income, other comprehensive income and changes in stockholder's equities in one statement.

statement of changes in financial position (SCFP) a statement reporting the financing and investing activities of a business during a period, and indicating their effects on working capital. *Also*: capital reconciliation statement; flow of funds statement; fund flow statement; funds flow statement; fund statement; source and application of funds statement; source and disposition of working capital statement; statement of fund and its application; statement of variation of funds; where got, where gone statement.

statement of changes in net worth a statement that presents the major sources of increases and decreases in net worth of a person, household or a family.

statement of changes in plan net assets a statement of the year-to-date changes in the net assets of the pension plan.

statement of changes in retained earnings = *retained earnings statement.*

statement of changes in stockholders' equity a statement showing the increases and decreases in the stockholders' equity of a corporation in a given period.

statement of changes in working capital statement that shows the increases and decreases in working capital in a given period. ***Also***: statement of working capital changes; statement of working capital flows; working capital flow statement.

statement of condition = *balance sheet.*

statement of condition of affairs <1> = *balance sheet.* <2> = *statement of affairs.*

statement of consolidated income = *consolidated income statement.*

statement of consolidated income and retained earnings = *statement of income and retained earnings.*

statement of cost of goods manufactured = *manufacturing statement.*

statement of cost of goods manufactured and sold a statement showing the calculation of the cost of goods manufactured and sold and the total.

statement of cost of goods sold a statement showing all components of the cost of goods sold for a given period.

statement of earnings = *income statement.*

Statement of Financial Accounting Concepts (SFAC) definition of broad accounting principles or ideas used the US generally applicable worldwide.

Statement of Financial Accounting Standards (SFAS) = *Statement of Position.*

statement of financial condition a statement that presents the estimated current values of assets, liabilities, the estimated income taxes on the difference between the estimated current amounts of assets and liabilities and their tax basis and net worth at a specific date of a person.

statement of financial position <non-profit entity> = *balance sheet.*

statement of fixed and variable costs a schedule showing fixed and variable costs under flexible budgeting.

statement of functional expenses a statement required to report by a voluntary health and welfare organization, listing all expenses by functions

statement of fund and its application = *statement of changes in financial position.*

statement of income = *income statement.*

statement of income and comprehensive income an income statement with disclosure of comprehensive income. ***See***: *struggle statement.*

statement of income and profit and loss = *all inclusive income statement.*

statement of income and retained earnings income statement which shows the changes in retained earnings. ***Also***: combined income and earned surplus statement; combined income and retained earnings statement; combined statement of income and retained earnings; combined statement of income and surplus; income and retained earnings statement; income statement and statement of retained earnings; statement of consolidated income and retained earnings.

Statement of Investment Income <Canada> a form used by Canadian taxpayers to report income from investments in stocks, bonds, mutual funds, annuities, etc. ***Also***: Form T5; T5.

statement of liquidation = *liquidation account.*

statement of loss and profit = *income statement.*

statement of net quick asset flows statement that shows the changes in the quick assets.

statement of net worth = *statement of stockholders' equity.*

statement of plan net assets a statement of the fair value of the pension plan assets, liabilities and net assets.

statement of policy (SOP) a statement showing the equity of the controlling corporation, accounting methods for consolidation, condition of the controlled corporation, etc.

statement of position = *financial position statement.*

Statement of Position (SOP) Statements which provide guidance on practice or industry financial accounting or reporting problems until the FASB or GASB provides standards in those areas. *Also*: Statement of Financial Accounting Standards.

statement of profit and loss = *income statement.*

statement of profit calculation = *income statement.*

statement of realization and liquidation = *liquidation account.*

Statement of Recommended Practice (SORP) accounting professional guidelines for UK companies.

Statement of Remuneration Paid <Canada> a form used by Canadian taxpayers to report wages, salaries or commissions from an employer. *Also*: Form T4; T4.

statement of retained earnings = *retained earnings statement.*

statement of revenue and expense = *income statement.*

Statement of Standard Accounting Practice (SSAP) <UK> a statement created by the councils of the 6 major accounting bodies in 1990.

statement of stockholders' equity statement which shows the changes' in stockholders' equity. *Also*: statement of net worth.

statement of surplus analysis = *retained earnings statement.*

statement of surplus appropriation a statement showing the appropriation of surplus.

statement of the sources and composition of company capital = *balance sheet.*

Statement of Trust Income <Canada> a form used by Canadian taxpayers to report income from a trust. *Also*: Form T3; T3.

statement of value a letter from the IRS that a taxpayer may rely on to substantiate the fair value of an item of art appraised at $50,000 or more.

statement of variation in profit statement that shows the changes in net profit in comparison with the last period.

statement of variation of funds = *statement of changes in financial position.*

statement of working capital a statement that shows the current assets, current liabilities, and the working capital in a given period.

statement of working capital changes = *statement of changes in working capital.*

statement of working capital flows = *statement of changes in working capital.*

statement order the order of account titles in the financial statements.

Statements on Auditing Standards (SAS) statements issued by the ASB to provide CPAs with guidance regarding the application of GAAS.

Statements on Standards for Accounting and Review Services (SSARS) statements issued by the ARSC to provide CPAs with guidance regarding the reporting on the unaudited financial statements or other unaudited financial information of nonpublic entities.

Statements on Standards for Attestation Engagements (SSAE) Statements issued by the ASB, ARSC, or the MASEC to provide guidance to CPAs engaged to perform attest services.

Statements on Standards for Consulting Services (SSCS) Statements which provides behavioral standards for the conduct of consulting services.

Statements on Standards for Tax Services (SSTS) tax behavioral standards binding under the AICPA Code of Professional Conduct.

state pension <UK> pension paid to a person from the Department of Social Security.

state retirement pension <UK> a benefit payable to a man who has reached age 65 and woman aged 60, e.g. *basic retirement pension, state second pension* and *graduated pension.*

state second pension (SP2) <UK> a retirement pension from the state in addition to basic retirement pension, usually related to a taxpayer's former earnings. *Formerly called*: state earnings-related pension.

state tax a tax levied by the state government.

state tax lien a tax lien by the state government for nonpayment of state tax.

state unemployment tax a tax levied by a state, the proceeds from which are used to pay benefits to unemployed workers.

static analysis the analysis that focuses on the balance sheet. ***See***: *dynamic analysis.*

static budget = *fixed budget.*

static standard cost = *basic standard cost.*

static statement <1> the statement showing figures in a given period of time. <2> = *balance sheet.*

static theory a theory that the firm's capital structure is determined by a trade-off of the value of tax shields against the cost of bankruptcy.

statistical accounting application of probability theory and statistical sampling approaches to evolution of prime accounting information and auditing of accounting data.

statistical cost control procedure for distinguishing between random and other types of cost variances that need investigation.

statistical sampling audit sampling whereby auditors judge sampling risk by using statistical techniques. ***See***: *nonstatistical sampling.*

statistical test audit the test audit made under random sampling of statistics.

statute of frauds a law enacted in most jurisdictions requiring certain contracts to be in writing and signed by any party charged with failing to fulfill obligations under the contract.

statutory accounting the accounting, such as tax accounting, the procedures and statement format of which are set by legislation.

statutory audit = *legal audit.*

statutory books the books that must be kept by every limited company registered. ***Also***: compulsory books.

statutory consolidation = *consolidation.*

statutory depletion method = *percentage depletion method.*

statutory earnings revenue of an insurance company based on conservative reserve requirements of various states.

statutory exclusion the exclusion from income for certain fringe benefits or compensation.

statutory merger = *Type A reorganization.*

statutory notice of deficiency = *90-day letter.*

statutory profit of an insurance company, total earned premium minus total expenses and losses paid.

statutory prospectus = *final prospectus.*

statutory reserve the reserve required by state regulations.

statutory sick pay <UK> payment to an employee during times when he or she is unable to work because of sickness.

statutory stock options stock options with tax benefits made available under tax laws. ***See***: *nonstatutory options.*

statutory surplus insurance company's excess funds about the amount required to establish legal reserve for policies in force.

statutory trust <UK> = *constructive trust.*

STCL short-term capital loss

step allocation method = *continuous allotment method.*

step budget = *flexible budget.*

step-by-step approach = *block method.*

step cost = *step-variable cost.*

step distribution method = *continuous allotment method.*

step-down method = *continuous allotment method.*

step-down preferred stock = *fast-pay preferred stock.*

step-fixed cost = *step-variable cost.*

step function cost = *step variable cost.*

step ladder method = *continuous allotment method.*

step method = *continuous allotment method.*

stepped cost = *step-variable cost.*

stepped-down basis the basis on property acquired in a taxable transaction, which has declined in value in the previous owner's hand. ***See***: *stepped-up basis.*

stepped-up basis the basis on property acquired in a taxable transaction, that has appreciated in value in the previous owner's hand. ***See***: *stepped-down basis.*

step-transaction approach <UK> a method under which each step in series of transaction must be carried out primarily for bona fide non-tax purposes.

step transaction doctrine a doctrine under which separate steps of an overall transaction will be treated as part of a single transaction if the steps can fairly be integrated. ***Also***: collapsing a transaction.

step-up basis the value of a stock inherited on the decedent's day of death.

step-up in basis change in the value of an asset inherited upon the owner's death.

step-variable cost a cost that remains constant over a range then increases by a lump sum if production is expanded further, then remains constant over another range of production increases and so forth. ***Also***: cost increases in steps; mixed step cost; stair step cost; stair-stepped cost; stair-step semi-variable cost; step cost; step fixed cost; step function cost; stepped cost. ***See***: *semi-fixed cost.*

step-wise allocation = *continuous allotment method.*

STET securities transfer excise tax

stewardship accounting the accounting that prepares periodical financial statements to outside users. ***Also***: accounting for external reporting; accounting for stewardship; external accounting.

stk stock

stock (stk) <1> legal capital of a corporation divided into a number of shares. ***Also***: concern; corporation's stock; equity. <2> UK, a stock can be transferred in any value and divided into shares, while shares can only be transferred in units of face value. <3> a security representing the right in the marketable loan. <4> = *stock certificate.*

stock account <1> a report showing increase, decrease and book balance of goods of a branch when the goods shipped to which are not recorded at cost. <2> an account for recording capital stock. <3> an account for recording stock by social accounting. <4> = *inventory account.*

stock acquisition = *acquisition of shares.*

stock appreciation right (SAR) entitles employees to receive cash or stock in an amount equal to the excess of the market value of a stated number of shares over a stated price. ***See***: *stock right.*

stock at close = *ending inventory.*

stock at start = *beginning inventory.*

stock bonus = *stock dividend.*

stock bonus plan a plan under which the benefits are distributable in stock of the employer company at retirement death or termination of employment.

stock certificate an evidence of ownership of a company's shares. ***Also***: capital stock certificate; certificate; certificate of capital stock; certificate of stock; scrip; stock; stock trust certificate.

stock costing = *inventory costing.*

stock deficiency = *inventory loss.*

stock discount the amount a stock's par value exceeds its paid-in capital.

stock dividend a distribution by a company of its own shares to its common stockholders without any consideration being received in return thereof. ***Also***: capital bonus; share bonus; share dividend; stock bonus.

stock exchange account = *account period.*

stock for stock exchange <1> the exchange of common stock for other common or preferred stock for other preferred stock of the same corporation. <2> = *Type B reorganization.*

stock goods = *merchandise inventory.*

stockholder the owner of shares issued by a company or mutual fund. ***Also***: shareholder.

stockholder books set of books kept by the company for its annual report that follows GAAP. ***See***: *tax books.*

stockholders' capital the capital invested by stockholders. ***Also***: corporate capital.

stockholder's equity the equity of a stockholder in a corporation's asset. ***Also***: shareholder's equity.

stockholder's ledger a detailed ledger controlled by the capital stock account which shows the number of shares of stock held by each stockholder at any time. ***Also***: dominion register.

stockholders' meeting = *annual meeting.*

stockholder's report the annual report and other report sent to stockholders.

stockholding cost = *carrying cost.*

stock interest = *dividend.*

stock in trade <1> = *inventory.* <2> = *merchandise inventory.*

stock ledger a record of each shareholder's ownership in a corporation.

stockless purchase = *balanced inventory.*

stock of capital = *capital stock.*

stock of goods = *inventory.*

stock option (SO) <1> an option giving the holder the right to buy or sell the underlying stock at a specified price, by a specific date. ***Also*** equity option. <2> an option issued by a company to its employees giving them the right to buy the company's own stock at a favorable price. ***Also***: option to purchase shares; share option.

stock option grant = *option grant.*

stock-out cost = *cost of not carrying.*

stockpiling collection of tax returns from taxpayers or authorized e-file providers before transmitting to the IRS.

stock purchase plan = *employee stock ownership plan.*

stock purchase warrant = *stock warrant.*

stock raw <UK> = *raw material.*

stock reacquisition expense amount paid or incurred by a corporation in connection with the reacquisition of its stock.

stock redemption company's buying back of its own outstanding stock. ***Also***: *redemption.*

stock right a right to purchase a given quantity of a new stock at a discount, it is distributed to shareholders in proportion to their holdings. ***Also***: subscription right. ***See***: *stock appreciation right.*

stock scrip = *scrip.*

stock split the division of a company's outstanding shares into a larger number, without reducing the total value of the company's capital stock. ***Also***: share split-up; split; stock split-up; subdivision of shares. ***See***: *split up.*

stock split down = *split down.*

stock split-up = *stock split.*

stock statement a statement prepared by the social accounting showing the stock balance of each item.

stock subscription contractual commitment to buy unissued shares. ***Also***: subscription.

stocktake <Australia> = *inventory taking.*

stock taking = *inventory taking.*

stock transfer tax a tax levied on the transfer of stock.

stock trust certificate = *stock certificate.*

stock turnover = *inventory turnover.*

stock value ratio for bonds ratio of the total market value of the capital stock of a company to the principal value of its bond issued.

stock warrant a document the bearer of which has the right to buy certain sum of the stock of the company at a subscription price. ***Also***: letter of rights; rights letter; share warrant; stock purchase warrant; subscription warrant; warrant.

stock without par value = *no-par-value stock.*

stock with par value = *par value stock.*

stop-or-go sampling = *sequential sampling.*

storage cost the cost incurred in safekeeping the assets. *Also*: shelter cost.

storage time ratio the ratio of the daily or weekly usage of stores to the daily or weekly sales quantity of products.

stores-in-out book = *material ledger.*

stores issued book (SI bk) a memorandum book for recording the receipts, issues and usage of materials.

stores ledger = *material ledger.*

stores received and issued book = *material ledger.*

straddle rule IRS rule under which any loss realized from closing one leg is deferred to the extent there is any unrealized gain on the open leg, any gain realized must be reported immediately.

straddle sale the sale of assets at a loss by a company before its liquidation, followed by the sale of assets at a gain after liquidation, so the loss can offset the company's income and gains.

straight debt a form of debt of an S corporation that is assumed of not being classified as equity, hence cannot create a prohibited second class of stock.

straight exclusion $500,000 ($250,000 for single) exclusion of gain on sale of principal residence, available to a taxpayer who owned and occupied the house in 2 of the 5 years immediately preceding the sale.

straight-line amortization the amortization of intangible property in equal amounts each year.

straight-line basis over the remaining service period method = *expected future years of service method.*

straight-line depreciation the depreciation of tangible asset in equal amounts each year. *Also*: conventional depreciation.

straight-line depreciation plus average interest method a method under which the depreciation expense is the total sum of straight line depreciation and average interest on the asset.

straight-line depreciation plus interest on first cost a method under which the cost of depreciation is the total sum of straight line depreciation and interest on the original cost of the asset.

straight-line depreciation rate calculated as (1 - salvage rate) ÷ asset life estimated.

straight-line item depreciation accounting item depreciation accounting using straight line method.

straight-line method (SL method) a method under which the bond discount or premium is spread uniformly over the life of the investment. *See*: *interest method.*

straight-line method of depreciation a method that allocates equal share of depreciation to each year in a plant asset's life. *Also*: age-life method of depreciation; equal annual payment method; equal installment method; fixed installment method; fixed percentage of cost method; method of fixed percentage on cost; method of straight base lines; multiple straight-line method; percentage of original cost method. *See*: *fixed percentage of cost method.*

straight-line recovery of intangibles either equal monthly amortization of intangible drilling and development costs over 120 months beginning in the month production from the well begins or any method of cost depletion of the well that the taxpayer selects.

stranded asset = *obsolete asset.*

stranded cost = *sunk cost.*

strata a subgroup under *stratification.*

strategic alliance an alliance between companies for the purpose of achieving cost efficiencies and more competitive advantage.

stratification the technique of dividing a population into relatively homogeneous subgroups called *strata.*

stratified sampling audit sampling under which population is divided into groups and random sampling is applied to each group.

street certificate = *bearer stock.*

stress testing a technique used on asset and liability portfolios to determine their reactions to different financial stresses.

stretch-out IRA an IRA created as an estate-planning strategy which names one or more beneficiaries of the account's resources so that when its creator dies the tax-deferred distributions generated by the account will pass to them.

strict liability = *absolute liability.*

striking a balance the process of ascertaining if the final totals are correct.

stripped preferred stock preferred stock which does not have participating privilege, and has a fixed redemption price.

stripping = *dividend stripping.*

struggle statement <UK> a statement of unrecognized gains and losses that do not impact net income. *See*: *statement of income and comprehensive income.*

Student Financial Supplement Scheme (SFSS) <Australia> a voluntary loan scheme giving some students the option of borrowing money to finance their college study.

student loan interest deductible interest on student loans.

Subchapter F an IRS regulation dealing with unearned income that is currently taxed whether or not it is remitted into the US.

Subchapter M an IRS regulation dealing with investment companies and real estate investment trusts that avoid double taxation by distributing interest, dividends, and capital gains directly to shareholders, who are taxed individually.

Subchapter S IRS regulation that gives a corporation with 35 or fewer shareholders the option of being taxed as a partnership to escape corporate income taxes.

subchapter S corporation = *S corporation.*

subcontrol account controlling account used under block method for controlling small group of subsidiary accounts.

subdivision analysis method valuation method that uses the present value of the expected gross return (based on a gross profit of 100% on new land sales discounted for a ten year holding period).

subdivision of shares <UK> = *stock split.*

subfooting = *subtotal.*

subfund a fund accounted for under another fund.

sub group method a method used with respect to the filing of such returns by life insurance companies and their members, which involves creating 2 sub groups, with losses of each sub group carried back against prior sub group income.

subjective profit = *present value income.*

subjective value theory a theory which holds that the balance sheet should be based on the subjective value of assets.

subject to opinion an opinion issued by the auditor because of uncertainties about future events that cannot be resolved or the effect of which cannot be estimated or reasonably provided for at the time the opinion is rendered. *See*: *except-for opinion.*

subledger = *subsidiary ledger.*

submission cost the expenses needed to readjust financial statement in general price level.

sub-normal depreciation the depreciation below the normal level in the industry.

subordinated debt securities that have a claim on the firm's assets only after the claims of holders of senior debt have been satisfied. *Also*: junior debt; subordinate debt.

subordinate debt = *subordinated debt.*

subordinated ledger = *subsidiary ledger.*

Subpart F special category of foreign-source "unearned" income that is currently taxed by the IRS whether or not it is remitted to the US.

sub-part F income any income of a controlled foreign corporation which must be reported according to the IRS rules.

subperiod return the return of a portfolio over a shorter period of time than the evaluation period.

sub-S corporation = *S corporation.*

subscribed capital stock which individuals have agreed to purchase but for which stock certificates have not yet been issued.

subscribers' ledger a subsidiary detailed ledger that contains an account for each stock subscribers showing the amount owed for subscriptions to the stock.

subscription = *stock subscription.*

subscription right = *stock right.*

subscription warrant = *stock warrant.*

subsection (e) asset property held by a collapsible corporation that would result in ordinary income if sold by the entity or certain major stockholders.

subsection (f) asset noncapital asset that a potentially collapsible company holds or has an option over on the date of any sale of stock by a shareholder, including any interest in realty, other than a mortgage or other security interest, and unrealized receivables of fees.

subsequent adjustment an adjustment resulting from a preacquisition contingency made after the end of the allocation period.

subsequent cost = *after-separation cost.*

subsequent event = *post-statement event.*

subsequent processing cost = *after-separation cost.*

sub-share = *dividend warrant.*

subsidiary a company a majority of its voting stock is owned by a parent company. ***Also***: subsidiary company; subsidiary corporation. ***See***: *controlled company; parent company.*

subsidiary account <1> either a contra account or an adjunct account. <2> = *detailed account.*

subsidiary book of account = *book of original entry.*

subsidiary company = *subsidiary.*

subsidiary company accounting the accounting undertaken by a subsidiary for the recording of transactions with the parent company.

subsidiary corporation = *subsidiary.*

subsidiary earnings = *post-acquisition earnings.*

subsidiary journal = *special journal.*

subsidiary ledger a group of accounts other than general ledger accounts which show the details underlying the balance of the controlling account in the general ledger. ***Also***: auxiliary ledger; detailed ledger; subledger; subordinated ledger.

subsidiary ledger account = *detailed account.*

subsidiary ledger schedule a list of the balances of all accounts in a subsidiary ledger at the end of a given period.

subsistence <UK> meals, refreshments and accommodation taken while working away from a taxpayer's normal place of work.

subsistence cost = *living cost.*

substantial authoritative support accounting-related statements made by authoritative bodies requiring specified accounting, reporting and disclosure by entities.

substantial capital = *real capital.*

substantial improvement an improvement that exceeds 25% of the adjusted basis of a building.

substantial interest <Canada> 10% or a higher percentage of all voting shares of a company. ***Also***: absolute interest.

substantially appreciated inventory items inventory items held by a partnership that are worth more than 120% of their adjusted basis and more than 10% of the fair market value of all partnership property other than money.

substantial shareholder one who owns more than 40% of the stock of a corporation. ***Also***: principal stockholder.

substantive strategy a strategy under which an auditor sets control risk at maximum and performs more substantive test. *See*: *reliance strategy*.

substantive test audit test of details of transactions and balances, and analytical procedures. *See*: *compliance test*.

substituted basis <1> basis of property without considering the profit and loss. <2> basis of a property by referencing to the basis of another property.

substituted property a property acquired by a taxpayer in 30 days that is the same or identical to the one sold.

subtotal total of certain figures only. *Also*: subfooting.

subvariance a portion of the total variance.

subvention the provision of financial support from a government.

successful efforts accounting oil industry accounting for the capitalization of drilling costs of the well with oil reserve, capitalized exploration costs will be amortized based on the reserves produced.

successful efforts method a method under which drilling costs are capitalized rather than transferred to profit and loss account. *See*: *full cost method*.

successor auditor an auditor who has accepted an engagement or an auditor who has been invited to make a proposal for an engagement. *See*: *predecessor auditor*.

success tax 15% excise tax on "excess" distributions from tax-deferred retirement plans that was repealed by the Taxpayer Relief Act of 1997.

SUI State Unemployment Insurance

summarized balance sheet = *condensed balance sheet*.

summary account a temporary account maintained for revenues and expenses of a single proprietorship or partnership.

summary book a book for recording summarized data.

summary financial statement = *condensed financial statement*.

summary income statement = *condensed income statement*.

summary journal a special journal for adjusting entries and summarizing them.

summary of consolidated revenue and earnings a statement showing summarized figures of the parent and subsidiaries.

summary of financial position a summary of the uses and sources of funds in a given period.

summary of income and profit and loss a statement showing the accumulated profit and loss of several periods.

summary of overhead variances a summary of the cost variances of all departments.

summary of significant accounting policies a note attached to the financial statements that shows the main accounting policies adopted in the current year.

summary of variances a list of the variance and subvariances of an item.

summary plan description (SPD) document that explains the fundamental features of an employer's defined benefit plan or defined contribution plan, including the eligibility requirements, contribution formulas, vesting schedules, benefit calculations, and options of distribution.

summary posting recording the column total from a journal in a ledger account rather than recording the individual amounts in the column.

summary review memorandum (SRM) memorandum prepared at the conclusion of a peer or quality review which documents the planning, scope of work performed, and the findings and conclusions that support the report and letter of comments issued.

summary schedule = *lead schedule*.

summary worksheet a work sheet the trial balance of which contains the general ledger accounts only. *Also*: general ledger worksheet.

sum of parts valuation the valuation of a company by what its divisions could be worth if they were broken up and spun-off or acquired by another company.

sum of the years' digits (SOYD)(SYD) the total of the years' digits in the estimated useful life of a plant asset.

sum-of-the-years'-digits method a method of accounting for allocating depreciation in a fractional basis, denominator of the fractions used is the sum of the years' digits, and the numerators are the years' digits in reverse order. *Also*: years'-digits method.

sundry expense = *miscellaneous expense.*

sundry income = *windfall profit.*

sunk cost the cost incurred as a consequence of a past decision and that, therefore, cannot be avoided. *Also*: irrecoverable cost; lost cost; non-differential cost; stranded cost; unrecoverable cost.

super-absorption costing tracing costs from all links in the value chain as an inventory cost.

superannuation fund <Australia> = *pension fund.*

superannuation guarantee (SG) <Australia> a minimum required employer contribution to a pension fund set by the Superannuation Guarantee Act 1992.

superannuation guarantee charge (SGC) <Australia> a charge on an employer who failed to meet the minimum superannuation guarantee amount.

superannuation holding accounts reserve (SHAR) <Australia> a reserve account maintained by the ATO in case the employer failed to meet the superannuation guarantee.

superannuation surcharge a 15% surcharge on certain superannuation fund rollovers and termination payments.

superficial loss <Canada> loss incurred on the disposition of property where the taxpayer acquires the same or identical property in 30 days before or after the disposition and still owns it 30 days after the original disposition.

supermajority an amendment in a company's charter requiring a large majority (anywhere from 67%-90%) of shareholders to approve important changes, such as a merger. *Also*: supermajority amendment.

supermajority amendment = *supermajority.*

super profit <1> partnership profit after deduction of the partners' salaries and investment interest. <2> = *excess profit.*

super-variable costing the costing that treats only direct materials as the only variable cost.

supervision cost that part of indirect labor cost incurred to supervise the workers.

supplemental credit = *additional credit.*

supplemental executive retirement plan (SERP) a plan which provides highly compensated employees with retirement benefits that would otherwise be limited in amount, or subject to additional taxation, if provided through the qualified plan.

supplementary account an account that provides supplementary information.

supplementary cost <1> product cost other than prime cost and administrative cost. <2> product cost other than prime cost. <3> = *fixed cost.*

supplementary expense = *overhead.*

supplementary financial statement = *constant dollar financial statement.*

supplementary fixed factory overhead rate factory overhead rate used to adjust the product cost under variable costing to the product cost under absorption costing at the end of an accounting period.

supplementary rate <1> an allocation rate used when the predetermined rate differs significantly from the actual rate. <2> supplementary rate for scientific machine hour.

supplementary statement a statement giving additional information of price level changes, e.g. inflation-adjusted statement.

supplementary unemployment benefit plan = *unemployment benefit plan.*

supplement cost = *additional cost.*

supplies ledger a sub-ledger that contains accounts for each supply.

supply <Australia> a good or service sold by a company which may be subject to tax.

support for income tax purpose, including food, clothing, shelter, education, medical, recreation, and transportation. *See*: *essential.*

support costs the costs incurred for administration, marketing, research and development, occupancy, and others of a comparable nature.

supporting cost of capital = *opportunity cost of capital.*

supporting document basic written evidence of a transaction. *Also*: accounting document; business voucher; documentation; original document; source document; voucher.

supporting evidence all items of a given type or class that are used by an auditor.

supporting person <Canada> a person that incurs child care expenses in supporting a child.

supporting schedule a listing of the elements or details comprising the balance in an asset or liability account at a specific date.

supporting worksheet a work sheet that contains subsidiary accounts and their adjustments.

surcharge charge added on top of another charge, such as fuel surcharge on freight.

surplus <1> excess of assets over liabilities and capital stock. <2> excess of revenue over expenditure of a government. *Also*: budget surplus; overplus. <3> excess of supply over demand when the price exceeds the equilibrium price. <4> <Canada> a benefit not allocated to a member of a retirement plan. <5> = *book surplus.* <6> = *net worth.* <7> = *retained earnings.*

surplus accumulation tax = *accumulated earnings tax.*

surplus advance corporation tax advanced corporation tax of a company which can not be set against its corporation tax liability because the company has no income charged to corporation tax in that period.

surplus allowance <UK> unused married couple's tax allowance or blind person's allowance that arises because of low income.

surplus asset = *residual asset.*

surplus capital method a method in which the partner's capital contributions are geared to the profit and loss sharing ratio, and partners whose capitals are relatively surplus are ranked first to receive payment according to the degree of excess.

surplus earnings net income of a subsidiary company after payment of dividends.

surplus from consolidation = *credit differential.*

surplus from deduction in capital stock = *gain from reduction of capital stock.*

surplus from donated stock = *donated capital.*

surplus from profits = *retained earnings.*

surplus from revaluation = *appraisal capital.*

surplus on appreciation of capital assets = *appraisal capital.*

surplus principle an accounting principle that states capital transactions should be suspense account distinguished from profit and loss transactions.

surplus profit = *retained earnings.*

surplus ratio percentage of total assets set aside by an insurance company to provide for unexpected losses.

surplus reserve <1> = appropriated retained earnings. <2> = *retained earnings.*

surprise audit an audit performed occasionally. *Also*: casual audit; non-prenotice audit.

surprise count inventory taking made occasionally.

surrender of share <UK> giving up shares to a company for cancellation of membership.

surrender of stock return of the stock to the company for new stock after merger or for cash.

surrender value = *cash surrender value.*

surtax <1> an additional tax as a percentage on the income tax liability. <2> a tariff in addition to an existing tariff.

surtax exemption the portion of a taxpayer's income not subject to a surtax.

survey memorandum the summary of the results in preliminary audit.

surviving spouse (SS) person who had a marital relationship with the deceased for the month of death. ***Also***: qualifying widow.

survivorship annuity an annuity payable for the life of an annuitant and then to a specified survivor.

suspended loss a loss that a taxpayer can not deduct because of the loss limitation rule. ***Also***: suspended passive activity loss; suspended passive loss.

suspended passive activity loss = *suspended loss.*

suspended passive loss = *suspended loss.*

suspense = *error in books.*

suspense account <1> an account used temporarily for the items which for lack of detail or information at the time of posting cannot be placed into their regular accounts in the book. ***Also***: clearing account; transit account. <2> account in the general ledger used to hold over unposted items so that the business day can be closed in balance. <3> as applied to income tax, an account held open pending future events. <4> a bank account used to store short-term funds or securities until a permanent decision is made about their allocation.

suspension a measure of revoking an authorized e-file provider's privilege for participating in the e-file program. ***See***: *sanction.*

sustainable income = *economic income.*

sustaining activity cost the cost of an activity that benefits the organization but is not caused by any specific supplier, product, service, or customer cost object.

SV <1> scheduled variance. <2> surplus value.

swap <1> the sale of one security for the purchase of another. <2> = *barter.*

swap replacement cost the cost that would be incurred to replace a defaulted or canceled in-the-money swap with a comparable instrument. ***Also***: replacement cost.

sweat equity <1> increase in property value due to an owner's making improvements. <2> common stock acquired by a company's executives on favorable terms.

sweep-out dividend a dividend that an investment company may deduct for taxable year, provided that it is declared within that year or paid soon after the close of the company's tax year.

sweetheart deal a merger between two or more companies where one gives the other very attractive terms and conditions.

switching cost the cost incurred when a customer changes from one supplier or marketplace to another.

SYD sum of the years' digits

symbolization of accounts = *accounts code system.*

symbol system of account = *accounts code system.*

synergies economic gains resulting from a merger or acquisition.

synthetic put a tax elusion practice whereby a taxpayer sells stock at a loss, and immediately writes a naked in-the-money put, with the hope that it will be exercised.

systematic accumulation and amortization basis = *cost basis.*

systematic and rational allocation a method of expense recognition, under which costs are allocated on a systematic and rational basis among the periods benefited, if the direct association between cost and revenue is not apparent. ***See***: *associating cost and effect; immediate recognition.*

systematic risk a risk associated with the movement of a market as opposed to distinct elements of risk associated with a specific security. ***Also***: market risk; systemic risk. ***See***: *unsystematic risk.*

systematic sampling an audit sampling technique in which every n^{th} item is selected after a random start.

system audit <1> the audit of the efficiency, target, and benefit, etc. of the new system that substituted the old one. <2> = *operating audit.*

systemic risk = *systematic risk.*

systems approach = *reliance strategy.*

systrust an engagement in which a CPA considers availability, security, integrity and maintainability of a company's computer system.

T t

T total cost

T&E travel and entertainment

T3 = *Statement of Trust Income.*

T4 = *Statement of Remuneration Paid.*

T5 = *Statement of Investment Income.*

T10 = *Pension Adjustment Reversal.*

T5007 = *Statement of Benefits.*

T5008 = *Securities Transactions.*

TA tangible asset

TAB tax anticipation bill

Tab tax anticipation bill

Table A <UK> the regulations for the management of a company limited by shares.

Table B <UK> the memorandum of association of a company limited by shares

Table C <UK> the memorandum of association and articles of incorporation of a company limited by guarantee.

Table D <UK> the memorandum of association and articles of incorporation of a company limited by guarantee but having a share capital.

Table E <UK> the memorandum of association and articles of incorporation of a company limited by guarantee of a unlimited company with share capital.

Table F <UK> the memorandum of association of a public company.

tabular book = *columnar book.*

tabular ledger = *Boston ledger.*

tabular method a method that lists the costs at different order sizes for selecting the economic order quantity.

tabulated ledger = *Boston ledger.*

T-account a form of account which shows only the account title the debit and credit sides, like the letter T. *Also*: skeleton account; T form account.

T-account method a method that uses T-accounts to analyze transactions in preparing statement of cash flows.

tag alongside rights a procedure under which if a majority shareholder sells stake, then the minority shareholders have the right to join the transaction and sell their minority stake too. *Also*: co-sale rights.

tainted stock = *Section 306 stock.*

tainting in PPS sampling, using a *tainting factor* to apply the effect of misstatement on the projected error.

tainting factor (TF) a factor used in *tainting*, calculated as (BV - AV)/BV, where BV = book value, AV = audit value.

tainting percentage amount of misstatement divided by dollar amount of the sample.

take home pay = *disposable income.*

takeover premium = *premium price.*

takeover target = *target company.*

takeover tax treatment implications based on the terms of a takeover by one company of another.

taking a business approach an audit method under which the information obtained should be documented by the auditor and retained in a file for use in subsequent examination.

taking a physical inventory = *inventory taking.*

TAN tax anticipation note

tanden currencies two currencies other than a functional currency expected to move relative to an entity's functional currency.

tangible asset (TA) asset which can be seen and touched other than a financial asset. *Also*: material asset; physical asset; tangible property.

tangible asset value per share total assets less intangible assets less liabilities and par value of preferred stock then divided by common stock.

tangible capital asset = *plant asset.*

tangible cost the oil and gas drilling accounting phrase, meaning cost of items that can be used over a period of time.

tangible fixed asset = *plant asset.*

tangible loss a loss of an asset which has a physical form.

tangible movable asset an asset capable of being realized.

tangible net worth total assets less intangible assets and total liabilities.

tangible property = *tangible asset.*

TAO Taxpayer Assistance Order

taper relief <UK> a reduction in chargeable gains according to the length of time an asset has been held after Apr 5, 1998.

target benefit plan a pension the benefits provided to participants at retirement are based on the performance of the investments, and therefore are not guaranteed. *See*: *defined benefit plan.*

target company a company chosen as the target for takeover by an *acquiring company. Also*: acquisition target; takeover target; target firm.

target cost <1> a cost that is used as a target. *Also*: expected cost; first cost; object cost. <2> = *standard cost.*

target costing identifying the estimated cost of a new product that must be achieved for that product to be priced competitively and still produce an acceptable profit.

target firm = *target company.*

target income amount of income an organization is trying to achieve during a particular period.

target income sales amount required to attain a particular income level or target net income.

target profit the desired level of profitability of management, which is measured either in dollars or in terms of a financial ratio. *Also*: profit target.

tariff <1> tax on imports or exports. *Also*: customs duty; import duty; income duty; tariff duty. <2> schedule of rates or fares in the transportation industry.

tariff duty = *tariff.*

tariff item a specific type of goods to which a rate of duty is applicable.

tariff rate the rate of duty that applies to the tariff item.

tariff rate quota <Canada> = *declared period quota.*

TAROR time-adjusted rate of return

tax charge imposed by a government body on personal and corporate income, estates, gifts or other sources to obtain revenue for the public good.

tax abatement reduction of an assessment under a new tax. *Also*: abatement; phase-in; tax phase-in.

taxable subject to tax. *Opp*: *tax exempt.*

taxable acquisition = *purchase acquisition.*

taxable capital gain portion of realized capital gain subject to tax.

taxable combination the acquisition of stock or assets that results in a tax liability. *See*: *tax-free reorganization.*

taxable dividend <Canada> dividend received by a taxpayer that is subject to tax.

taxable equivalent yield = *tax-equivalent yield.*

taxable estate excess of *gross estate* over non-discretionary and discretionary deductions. *See*: *adjusted gross estate.*

taxable event a transaction that involves property that is considered sufficiently significant to justify finding that a gain or loss on the transaction can be said to be realized.

taxable excess the excess of alternative minimum taxable income over the *AMT exemption.*

taxable exchange the exchange of capital asset, the gain from which is taxable. *See*: *nontaxable exchange.*

taxable gain portion of a gain from distribution of mutual fund shares that is liable to taxation.

taxable gift = *completed gift.*

taxable gross weight the total of the unloaded weight of a vehicle, a trailer, and maximum load carried. *See: federal highway use tax.*

taxable importation <Australia> a merchandise imported into Australia that is not duty-free.

taxable income <1> income that a taxpayer has after exemptions, and deductions have been subtracted, that is subject to tax. ***Also***: calculated income; effectively connected income; income for tax purposes; income subject to tax; taxable profit. <2> = *net income per return.*

taxable interest income interest income subject to tax. *See*: *tax-exempt interest income.*

taxable investment income a life insurance company's share of each item of investment yield.

taxable life insurance policy <Canada> a life insurance policy subject to *Part 12.3 tax.*

taxable net gain <Canada> net gain on disposition of listed personal property.

taxable person <UK> a taxpayer that must be registered for value added tax.

taxable preferred share <Canada> a preferred share issued after Jun 18, 1987 or a *short-term preferred share.*

taxable profit <UK> = *taxable income.*

taxable revenue the revenue of a government from the collection of taxes. ***Also***: revenue receipt; tax income.

taxable stock dividend stock dividend taxable if the employee has the option to take cash or other property instead of the stock.

taxable supply <1><Australia> a product item that is subject to GST tax. <2><UK> anything subject to climate change levy, e.g. electricity, natural gas, petroleum, coal, oil heat, etc.

taxable transaction a transaction that is not tax-free to the parties involved.

taxable year = *tax year.*

tax accounting the accounting methods properly used for tax purposes, that is to reflect correct tax liability as oppose to financial accounting for commercial or personal purposes, that is to reflect correct income figure.

tax accrual work-paper the work-paper, e.g. memoranda generated by accountants to evaluate a taxpayer's contingent tax liability.

tax act <UK> = *tax law.*

tax agent <Australia> = *tax preparer.*

tax agreement = *tax treaty.*

tax allocation the allocation of tax revenues among different levels of government. ***Also***: allocation of tax dollars.

tax allocation method one of four basic methods of charging all or a portion of the consolidated tax liability of an affiliated group to individual member of that group.

tax allocation within a period = *intra-period income tax allocation.*

tax and loan account an account in a private bank, held in the name of the district Federal Reserve Bank, which holds operating cash for the business of the US Treasury. ***Also***: Treasury tax and loan account.

tax anticipation bill (TAB)(Tab) special bill that the US Treasury occasionally issues that matures on corporate quarterly income tax dates and can be used at face value by corporations to pay their tax liabilities.

tax anticipation note (TAN) a short-term note issued by a state or municipal government in anticipation of future tax collections. ***Also***: tax certificate.

tax arbitrage trading that takes advantage of a difference in tax rates or tax systems as the basis for profit.

taxation of costs <UK> the settlement by a cost judge of the amount payable by a party in respect of costs in a lawsuit.

taxation position approach a method under which taxable income is determined by the net income in the income statement.

taxation year <Canada> = *tax year*.

tax attorney an attorney specializing in tax.

tax audit an IRS audit that focuses on the calculation of taxable income.

tax avoidance legal means of preventing a tax liability from coming into existence or in a lesser amount. ***Also***: avoidance; avoidance of taxation.

tax avoidance motive something that causes a person to avoid tax.

tax avoidance transaction <Canada> a transaction that results in a tax benefit. ***Also***: avoidance transaction.

tax base the sum of taxable activities, collective value of real estate and assets subject to tax within a community.

tax basis purchase price used to determine capital gains and capital losses for tax purposes. ***Also***: basis; cost basis; tax cost.

tax benefit a reduction, diminution, avoidance or deferral of tax liability.

tax benefit of loss carryback benefit to the current period because of the carryback of deficits.

tax benefit of loss carryforward benefit to the future periods because of the carry-forward of current deficit against future income.

tax benefit rule a concept allowing a recovery of an item deducted in an earlier year to be included in current gross income to the extent that a tax benefit was derived from the prior deduction of the recovered item.

tax books set of books kept by a company for its tax return that follows IRS tax rules. ***See***: *stockholder books*.

tax bracket certain amount of income to be taxed at a particular rate of tax. ***Also***: bracket.

tax break reduction in taxable income or tax liability from an event, strategy or plan.

tax certificate = *tax anticipation note*.

tax clawback agreement an agreement to contribute as equity to a project the value of realized project-related tax benefits.

tax clearance certificate = *certificate of tax clearance*.

tax code the official body of the tax laws and regulations.

tax collection agreement an agreement enabling different governments to collect taxes through an administration or a collection agency on behalf of another government.

tax concession a tax credit or reduction in tax rates.

tax consequence <Canada> amount of income of, tax payable by or refund to a taxpayer.

tax cost = *tax basis*.

tax cost basis the basis of property that was not received in exchange for property or money but was reported as income.

Tax Court US administrative court where judges handle cases of dispute between the taxpayer and the IRS. ***Also***: United States Tax Court.

Tax Court decision a decision made by the Tax Court.

Tax Court of Canada <Canada> the court created by the Tax Court of Canada Act for settling the tax cases. ***Also***: Court.

tax credit <1> a direct, dollar for dollar, reduction in the amount of tax liability. ***Also***: credit; credit against tax; credit balance; relief; tax offset; tax relief. <2><UK> a reduction in tax allowed to a taxpayer for the dividend from a company.

tax credit relief <UK> = *foreign tax credit.*

tax cut reduction in tax rates.

tax deductible coupon loan interest coupon the payment of which is tax-deductible.

tax deductible expense an expense that can be deducted from gross income. ***Also***: allowable expense; deductible expense; eligible expense; necessary expense.

tax deductible gift <Australia> = *deductible gift.*

tax deduction an amount, whether paid in cash, in kind, or merely claimed on paper which is used as an offset in determining taxable income or a taxable estate. ***Also***: allowable deduction; deduction; deduction for exemption.

tax deduction certificate <UK> a document evidencing tax withheld from a taxpayer's income.

tax deed document evidencing the passage of title to a purchaser of property sold for taxes.

tax deferral a tax result or strategy under which reportable income is deferred until a future year.

tax deferral option an option that allows the capital gains tax on an asset to be payable only when the gain is realized by selling the asset.

tax deferred annuity (TDA) employee retirement plan for a public school system or a qualified charitable organization.

tax-deferred income ordinary income and capital gains from investments in a qualified retirement plan.

tax-deferred retirement plan employer-sponsored retirement plan that allows contributions and earnings to be made and accumulate tax free until they are paid out.

tax-deferred rollover = *rollover.*

tax deficiency = *deficiency.*

tax deflecting trust a trust set up to deflect income from the true earner.

tax deposit the deposit of withheld payroll taxes into bank accounts designated by the IRS.

tax depreciation the depreciation calculated by tax law. ***Also***: tax return depreciation. ***See***: *book depreciation.*

tax differential view a view that shareholders prefer capital gains over dividends, and hence low payout ratios, because capital gains are effectively taxed at lower rates than dividends.

Tax District Office (TDO) <UK> a tax office responsible for investigation of selected individual tax returns and processing business accounts.

taxed capital gains <Canada> amount of taxable gains for the year from disposition of property minus the aggregate of allowable capital losses from disposition of property and the amount of deductible net capital loss.

taxe de vente du Quebec (TVQ) = *Quebec Sales Tax.*

taxed profit = *after-tax profit.*

tax effect <1> the effect on the amount of tax by the application of any special accounting methods, it equals the difference between actual income taxes payable and the income tax expenses. <2> impact on taxes of a taxable revenue or expense item.

tax effect accounting the accounting for the calculation and distribution of tax revenue and expense.

tax efficiency characteristic of a financial instrument that permits a dealer or an end user to establish or modify a position in a way that requires lower tax payments from either or both parties to the transactions than an alternate similar position or instrument.

tax efficiency ratio the ratio of after-tax returns to pre-tax returns of a investment.

tax-efficient resulting in less tax liability than other similar investments.

tax election choice of an option with respect to tax treatments of specified situations, transactions, report form, and timing of report.

tax equalization <1> distributing property tax assessments evenly among property owners. ***Also***: equalization. <2> <Canada> a federal transfer program that allows all provinces to provide comparable levels of services at roughly comparable level of taxation.

Tax Equity and Fiscal Responsibility Act (TEFRA) 1982, legislation to increase tax revenue by eliminating various taxation loopholes and instituting tougher enforcement procedures in collecting taxes.

Tax Equity Center <UK> a tax office that provides personal assistance to taxpayers.

tax equivalent income tax-exempt income that, for comparative purposes, has been increased by an amount equal to the taxes that would be paid if this income were fully taxable.

tax-equivalent yield pre-tax yield required from a taxable bond in order to equal the tax-free yield of a municipal bond. ***Also***: taxable equivalent yield.

taxe sur les produits et services (TPS) = *Goods and Services Tax.*

tax evasion knowingly reporting tax that is less than the tax liability under the tax law. ***Also***: defrauding the revenue; evasion of tax.

tax exempt not subject to tax. ***Also***: non-taxable; not taxable; tax free. ***Opp***: *taxable.*

tax exempt bond = *municipal bond.*

tax exempt goods and services <Canada> taxable goods and services that are subject to a 0% rate of GST. ***Also***: zero-rated goods and services; zero-rated supplied.

tax exempt income = *exempt income.*

tax exempt interest = *tax-free interest.*

tax-exempt interest income interest income not subject to tax. ***See***: *taxable interest income.*

tax exemption deductions of a specified amount which a taxpayer can claim, e.g. personal exemption, dependency exemption; and spousal exemption. ***Also***: exemption; exemption amount; remission of tax.

tax exempt organization a nonprofit organization that is exempt from federal income taxation.

tax exempt security = *municipal bond.*

tax-exempt special savings account (TESSA) <UK> a tax deferred plan introduced in 1991 under which a taxpayer can contribute up to £9,000 in 5 years and the gains are tax free.

tax exempt trust <Canada> a trust that is exempt from income tax under Part 1.

tax expenditure revenue lost to government because of any form of legal tax reduction or tax forgiveness.

tax file number (TFN) <Australia> a unique number assigned to a taxpayer by the ATO.

tax fraud the illegal act of intentionally filing a fraudulent return. ***Also***: fraud. ***See***: *under reporting.*

tax free = *tax exempt.*

tax-free acquisition = *pooling-of-interest.*

tax-free bond = *municipal bond.*

tax-free capital dividend = *capital dividend.*

tax-free exchange = *like-kind exchange.*

tax-free income = *exempt income.*

tax free interest the interest on state and local bonds that is exempt from federal income tax. ***Also***: exempt interest; tax exempt interest.

tax-free merger = *pooling of interest.*

tax-free profit the profit under the exempt threshold amount.

tax-free reorganization practical merger, Type A, Type B, and Type C reorganization, section 333 liquidation, etc. the distributee of which can be free of immediate tax. ***Also***: qualifying acquisition; qualifying merger. ***See***: *taxable combination.*

tax-free slice <UK> a portion of income or gains which is covered by an exemption while the rest of the income or gain is taxable.

tax-free threshold <Australia> $6,000 per year threshold, all income above this amount must pay income tax.

tax-free yield a yield on tax-exempt securities.

tax-free-zone method = *median rule.*

tax haven a country or area which levies zero tax or at lower rates.

tax heaven an area where tax rates are lower. *Also*: tax paradise.

tax holiday a period in which a tax concession is available by law.

tax home a city or general area where an individual taxpayer works or resides.

TAXi TAXinteractive

tax identification number (TIN) = *federal tax identification number.*

tax impact the estimate of possible outcome of a decision after taking into account the tax. *Also*: impact of taxation.

tax income = *taxable revenue.*

tax indexation <Canada> = *tax indexing.*

tax indexing method using an indexation to decrease the overall impact of the erosion of purchasing power in periods of inflation. *Also*: cost-of-living adjustment; tax indexation.

tax information return a statement showing the gross income, deductible expenses, taxable income etc.

taxing master <UK> = *cost judge.*

tax in respect of RCAs = *Part 11.3 tax.*

TAXinteractive (TAXi) <Australia> a web-based training service provided by ATO.

tax invoice <Australia> a sales invoice with GST amount on it.

tax law legislation on tax. *Also*: tax act.

tax lease = *operating lease.*

tax levy taking of a taxpayer's property to satisfy unpaid tax liabilities.

tax liability total amount of tax that a taxpayer must pay based on the income and the current tax rates. *Also*: debt; total tax bill. *See*: amount due.

tax lien governmental claim on a taxpayer's property for delinquent or overdue taxes. *See*: *federal tax lien.*

tax lien certificate a certificate of claim against property that has a lien placed upon it as a result of unpaid property taxes.

tax loophole unintentional characteristic of the tax law which allows one to eliminate tax liability without actually breaking the law. *Also*: loophole.

tax loss <1> loss to the taxpayer because of the improper use of the accounting methods in calculating tax liability. <2> negative amount of taxable income. *See*: *cash loss.*

tax loss carry forward = *loss carry forward.*

tax-loss harvesting = *loss harvesting.*

tax lot accounting record keeping technique that traces the dates of purchase and sale, cost basis and transaction size for each security in a portfolio.

tax-managed fund a mutual fund that is designed specifically to minimize tax consequences for its investors.

tax matters partner (TMP) a partner who acts on behalf of the partners in the unified partnership proceedings.

tax minimization the minimization of tax liability and recovery of overpaid tax.

tax minimization service professional service to minimize tax liability and recover overpaid taxes.

tax month <UK> from the 6th day of a month to the 5th day of another.

tax neutrality characteristic that taxes do not interfere with the natural flow of capital toward its most productive use.

tax office <UK> an office headed by a district inspector to provide tax service.

tax offset = *tax credit.*

tax on carved-out income <Canada> = *Part 12.2 tax.*

tax on corporate distributions <Canada> = *Part 2.1 tax.*

tax on corporations = *corporate income tax.*

tax on flow-through shares <Canada> = *Part 12.6 tax.*

tax on generation skipping transfers = *generation skipping transfer tax.*

tax on individuals = *personal income tax.*

tax on insurance premium = *insurance premium tax.*

tax on scholarship tax levied on grants received by a degree candidate at a college.

tax on self-employment income = *self-employment tax.*

tax on undistributed profit tax levied on undistributed profits.

tax option corporation = *S corporation.*

tax paradise = *tax heaven.*

tax payable <Canada> tax liability of a taxpayer as fixed by assessment.

taxpayer a person that is liable to pay tax.

taxpayer advocate the official inside the IRS who is charged with helping individuals resolve their problems with the IRS.

Taxpayer Relief Act of 1997 a significant tax cut statute enacted by the US Congress in 1997.

taxpayer right the legal right of a taxpayer in the event of an IRS audit.

taxpayer's bill of rights a law enacted to protect a taxpayer's privacy and property rights during the tax collection process.

taxpayer's charter <UK> a document sent to a taxpayer by the Inland Service listing rights and obligations of the taxpayer and the Service.

Taxpayer Service Office (TSO) <UK> a tax office responsible for sending out and processing tax returns.

taxpayer's opportunity cost = *external rate of return.*

tax period <Australia> a month or a quarter for GST tax purpose.

tax phase-in = *tax abatement.*

tax planning arranging the affairs of a taxpayer in such a way as to incur the smallest possible tax liability.

tax point the date on which value added tax is chargeable.

tax preference = *item of tax preference.*

tax preference item = *item of tax preference.*

tax preparation expense <UK> expense incurred to have a tax return prepared.

tax preparation service professional service of preparing tax returns for a fee.

tax preparation software computer software designed to prepare tax returns.

tax preparer a professional that provides tax preparation service. ***Also***: income tax return preparer; tax agent; unenrolled preparer.

tax presence <UK> a taxpayer's presence in the UK long enough to have to pay income tax.

tax rate percentage at which tax is calculated based on taxable income. ***Also***: rate of tax.

tax rebate <UK> = *tax refund.*

tax rebate discounter <Canada> a person who acquires a right to a refund of tax from a taxpayer entitled there to. ***Also***: discounter.

tax receipt money collected by a government in the form of tax.

tax recovery tax refund that is included in computing AGI but not included in gross income for determining AMTI.

tax recovery service tax review service that can help recover overpaid taxes and unclaimed refunds.

Tax Reform Act of 1976 US legislation relating to taxation, including changes in the capital gains tax laws.

Tax Reform Act of 1984 US legislation enacted as part of the Deficit Reduction Act of 1984.

Tax Reform Act of 1986 a major change in the US tax code.

Tax Reform Act of 1993 US legislation enacted to reduce spending and increase taxes. ***Also***: Revenue Reconciliation Act of 1993.

tax refund return of tax previously paid or overpaid back to the taxpayer. ***Also***: refund; refund of tax; tax rebate.

tax refund income taxpayer's income from the refund of state or local taxes.

tax relief <UK> = *tax credit.*

Tax Relief Board <Australia> a committee that considers whether a taxpayer should be granted a release from tax liability.

tax return a report by taxpayers that sets forth the facts necessary to establish the amount of tax due in their capacities as the parties liable for paying the tax. ***See***: *corporate tax return; individual tax return.*

tax return depreciation = *tax depreciation.*

tax return due date the date when a taxpayer must file a return. ***Also***: documentation due date; due date; filing date; filing-due date.

tax return profit net income reported by corporations to the IRS in tax returns.

tax revenue the calculated revenue of a government in the form of tax.

tax risk tax provision that frustrates a reasonable business or economic transaction by making the economics unattractive after taxes or by injecting tax uncertainty.

tax roll a list of all taxable property within a given jurisdiction.

tax sale a judicial sale of property for the payment of taxes due.

tax schedule a scale published by the IRS, it is used for taxpayers with taxable income over $100,000.

tax season from December through April during which CPAs and tax professionals are busy. ***Also***: busy season.

tax selling the selling of securities near the end of the year in order to establish desirable tax gains or losses.

tax shelter publicly or privately distributed offering of the limited partnership interests or sometimes direct ownership interests, which offer significant tax benefits which can reduce taxes on income from other sources.

tax-sheltered annuity an annuity that permits employees of tax-exempt organizations or public educational organizations to make before-tax contribution via a salary reduction agreement to a tax-sheltered retirement plan. ***Also***: 403(b) annuity.

tax-shelter farm loss operating loss from a farm that is a passive activity.

tax-shelter ID a number assigned by the IRS to a registered tax shelter.

tax shield maximum deduction allowable in computing taxable income.

tax shield effect annual depreciation multiplied by tax rate.

tax shift a shift of a tax that one taxpayer is supposed to pay to someone else.

tax software computer software designed to help taxpayers prepare tax returns.

tax status = *filing status.*

tax status election a taxpayer's decision on his or her filing status.

tax straddle a straddle in which taxpayers simultaneously enter into a contract to deliver a commodity at a future date and a sale of a contract for delivery of the same item in a different month, such that they can close out the losing leg.

tax swap the sale of a security that has declined in price since its purchase and the simultaneous purchase of a similar but not identical security, in order to realize a loss for tax purposes while maintaining a position.

tax switch selling securities that have declined in value in order to deduct a tax loss for the current year, and using the proceeds to buy another depressed security.

tax table a table that shows the amount of tax payable depending on an individual's income bracket. ***Also***: income tax table; personal income tax table.

tax table income the adjusted gross income in excess of the zero bracket amount.

tax table method the calculation of individual federal income taxes on the basis of tables provided in instructions to Form 1040, which permit federal income tax liabilities to be determined his or her taxable income, filing status, and, number of dependents.

tax-timing option the option to sell an asset and claim a loss for tax purposes or not sell the asset and defer the capital gains tax.

tax transfer <Canada> the reduction of tax rates by the federal government to allow provinces to raise their tax rates by an equivalent amount.

tax trap an event that may end up paying more taxes.

tax treaty an agreement entered into by two or more nations for the avoidance of double taxation and prevention of tax evasion. *Also*: tax agreement.

tax umbrella tax loss carry forwards stemming from losses of a company in past years, which are to shield profits earned in the current and future tax years from taxes.

tax-unallowable expense = *non-deductible expense.*

tax withholding = *income tax withholding.*

tax written-down value <UK> original cost of an asset less accumulated depreciation reported for tax purpose.

tax year 12-month period that a tax return covers. *Also*: taxable year; taxation year.

tax-year spread forward tax law's demand for adjustments arising from a change of accounting method to be taken into account over the next decade following the change as a condition to allowing the change.

TB <1> Technical Bulletin. <2> trial balance.

TC team captain

TCCO total cost center overhead

TCD total cost approach to distribution

TCO total cost ownership

TD1 <Canada> a form filed with the employer about an employee's tax deduction and other information. *See*: *Employee's Withholding Allowance Certificate.*

TDA tax deferred annuity

TDO Tax District Office

TE tax exempt

T&E travel and entertainment

team audit an audit undertaken by a group of revenue agents in case where there are multiple related taxpayers or transactions.

team captain (TC) an individual responsible for organizing and conducting a peer review or quality review.

tearing and lading = *lapping.*

Technical Bulletin (TB) information issued by FASB which provides timely guidance on certain financial accounting and reporting problems.

technical cost the cost such as maintenance, depreciation, material, labor, fuel, power, etc.

technical form income statement = *account form income statement.*

technological obsolescence decrease in the efficiency of a plant asset due to the technological advance. *See*: *economic depreciation.*

technology cost a cost associated with the development, acquisition, implementation and maintenance of technology assets.

TEFRA Tax Equity and Fiscal Responsibility Act

telefile a program that lets a taxpayer to use a tone touch phone, but not a cell phone, to send tax information directly to the IRS computer.

Tele Tax an authorized telephone service which contains pre-recorded messages covering various tax topics.

temporal accounting = *current rate method.*

temporal method = *current rate method.*

temporary account = *nominal account.*

temporary addition to capital account = *revenue account.*

temporary asset current asset that fluctuates in response to seasonal or anticipated short-term.

temporary difference a difference between net income per book and the taxable income, because the period in which an income is taxable or an expense is deductible differs from the period in which it is recognized by GAAP. ***Also***: accounting timing difference; timing difference. ***See***: *permanent difference.*

temporary helper an employee hired temporarily to help finish a job. ***See***: *coin-operated employee.*

temporary owner's equity account = *revenue and expense account.*

temporary restricted net assets the balance of resources that a nonprofit organization is permitted to spend in accordance with the specific legal restrictions imposed by outside donors.

tentative balance sheet balance sheet that needs to be revised. ***Also***: preliminary balance sheet.

tentative deduction a tax deduction, usually the smaller of two deductions to be selected by a taxpayer.

tentative minimum tax 26% on the *taxable excess* not exceeding $175,000 plus 28% on that exceeding $175,000.

tentative tax a tax applicable if all the taxpayer's income were earned in the USA, it equals (foreign income + US source income) × US tax rate. ***Also***: federal tentative minimum tax.

term certain method a method for retirement plan, whereby the first year's distributions are calculated based on life expectancy, and the distributions in each successive year are calculated based on the life expectancy minus the number of years that have passed.

terminal account an account the balance of which is referenced when preparing financial statements.

terminal funding method a method whereby the provisions, funding and recognition of pension expense for future benefit payments is made only at the end of an employee's period of active service.

terminal loss the undepreciated balance in a class of depreciable property that a taxpayer no longer owns in that class.

terminal reserve the *self-insurance fund* at the end of a year. ***See***: *initial reserve*

terminal salvage value = *salvage value.*

terminal tax <New Zealand> tax paid at year end in settlement of underpayment of tax during the year.

terminal value <1> = *accumulated amount.* <2> = *salvage value.*

termination accounting = *accounting for liquidation.*

termination amount = *accumulated amount.*

termination pay = *severance pay.*

termination tax a tax levied on the termination of a private foundation status.

term out to transfer a debt within a company's balance sheet without acquiring new debt.

term preferred share <Canada> a share issued or acquired after Jun 28, 1982.

Territorial Formula Financing <Canada> *tax transfer* based on a formula that fills the gap between the expenditure requirements and revenue capacity of the territories.

territorial tax system tax system that taxes domestic income but not foreign income.

tertiary ratios the constituent elements of the secondary ratios, such as gross profit to sales, sales to overhead, sales to working capital, and sales to fixed assets.

TESSA tax-exempt special savings account

test = *audit test.*

testamentary debt amount payable as a consequence of death.

testamentary trust a trust created as a result of explicit instructions from a deceased's will or taking effect only upon the grantor's death. ***See***: *inter vivos trust.*

test audit = *audit test.*

test audit by experience test audit the scope of which is determined by the auditor's experience.

test basis examination = *audit test.*

test check substantiation of certain items in an account or financial record so the auditor can form an opinion as to the accuracy of the entire account or financial record.

test checking = *audit test.*

test costing the costing of the sample batch, the result of which is used to determine the average cost of all batches of products.

test data a method for EDP auditing whereby dummy data are developed by the auditor and processed under auditor's control by the client's computer. *See*: *parallel simulation.*

test for impairment = *recovery test.*

testing = *audit test.*

testing day the first day of the partnership's tax year as otherwise determined by the IRS.

test of completeness tracing from source documents to the ledger to determine the completeness of recording and to detect understatement. *Also*: tracing forward.

test of controls test of a client's controls over internal control by using test data or parallel simulation.

test of details examine the actual details making up the various account balances.

test of existence tracing from the ledger to the source documents to determine the existence of an account balance to detect overstatement. *Also*: tracing backward, vouching.

test of impairment = *recovery test.*

test of profitability measurement of profitability by the gross profit ratio and the rate of return.

test of transaction = *dual purpose testing.*

TEV total enterprise value

text book method <1> a method for calculating the depreciation rate. <2> method used under declining balance method, in which the $R = 1 - \sqrt[n]{L/P}$, where P means the asset cost, L means the salvage value.

TF tainting factor

TFC total fixed cost

TFN tax file number

T form account = *T-account.*

theft the unlawful taking and removing of money or property with the intent to deprive the owner of it.

theft loss the unreimbursed loss from a theft.

theoretical amount asset amount determined by an auditor after calculation and observation.

theoretical capacity method a method for estimating product costs which would result if the productive level were constant and at peak capacity, this figure is then reduced by estimated down time to determine practical capacity. *See*: *experience method.*

theoretical concept a concept accepted by accountants just because of its conformity with the principle of financial disclosure of private entities.

theoretical depreciation a method under which depreciation is equal to the present value of the future income when using internal rate of return as the discount rate.

theoretical performance standard cost = *ideal standard cost.*

theoretical standard cost = *ideal standard cost.*

theoretical value the value of an option calculated by Black-Scholes Option Pricing Model.

theory of accounts approach an approach for establishing the accounting theory, which holds that the equilibrium of the accounting equation should always be maintained.

thin capitalization a corporation's capital structure with more debt than equity capital.

thin corporation a corporation whose capital structure is so debt laden that a portion of the debt may be capitalized as equity, and interest expenses are not deductible.

third party account = *loro account.*

third party beneficiary a person who is named in a contract to receive benefits under the contract.

third party recovery delinquent accounts receivable recovered by a collection agency for a fee.

third stage redistribution of income via social transfers in kind, resulting in *adjusted disposable income.*

third statement the third important financial statement, that is the statement of changes in financial position.

thirty day letter = *30-day letter.*

thirty-percent tax = *30% tax.*

three-account system <1> inventory system that maintains three accounts, namely sales account, purchases account, and last period inventories account. <2> account system that classifies the accounts into three groups, assets and capital, revenue and expenditures, costs and income.

three-bin system a system that maintains a third bin for insurance purposes, while the other 2 bins function as those in the two-bin system.

three-column account = *balance-column account.*

three-column cash book a ledger that combines the cash and deposit accounts into one a/c which has three columns, namely, discounts, details and bank.

three-digit system a coding system that uses three digits.

three-dimensional analysis cost analysis in three elements, namely cost, department, and product.

three-dimensional variance analysis = *three-variance analysis.*

three-division horizontal working paper combined working paper that is divided into 3 columns the left column for the balance sheet, the middle column for the income statement, the right column for the statement of changes in financial position.

three-division vertical working paper a combined working paper that is divided into three stages, the upper for the balance sheet, the middle for the income statement, and the lower for the statement of changes in financial position. *Also*: vertical working paper.

three-ledger system a system that maintains 3 ledgers, the general ledger, the accounts receivable ledger end the accounts payable ledger.

three-variance analysis the analyzing of factory overhead variances into spending, efficiency and volume variance. *Also*: three-dimensional variance analysis; three-way analysis; three-way breakdown.

three-variance method a method of analyzing variance into three sub variances.

three-way analysis = *three variance analysis.*

three-way breakdown = *three-variance analysis.*

three-way classification <1> classification of costs into manufacturing, selling, and general administration costs. <2> classification of merchandise accounts into beginning stock, purchases and goods sold.

three-way separation the additional separation of inventory into raw materials, work in process, and finished goods.

three-year cooling-off period = *cooling-off period.*

threshold = *threshold phase-out amount.*

threshold phase-out amount the amount of adjusted gross income above which a tax credit begins to phase out. *Also*: income phase-out amount; phase-out amount; threshold.

thrift plan *defined contribution plan* in which an employee contributes, usually on a before-tax basis, toward the ultimate benefits that will be provided. The employer agrees to match all or a portion of the employee's contributions.

through-put accounting the accounting that recognizes costs by both the book of original entry and the balance sheet.

throwback rule an anti-tax avoidance plan in order to tax the beneficiaries of complex trusts on delayed distributions of earnings, other than capital gains as if the beneficiary had received the earnings on a current basis. *Also*: trust throwback rule. *See*: *short cut method.*

throw-back tax a tax imposed on income that was realized in the previous periods.

TI taxable income

tick mark a symbol used in working papers by the auditor to indicate a specific step in the work performed.

TIE times interest earned

tier 1 capital a bank's capital that can absorb losses without the bank being required to cease operations, including equity capital and disclosed reserves.

tier 1 deduction = *first-tier deduction.*

tier 1 RRTA tax RRTA tax withheld for a taxpayer who works for one railroad company.

tier 2 capital a bank's capital which can absorb losses in the event of a winding-up, including undisclosed reserves, general loss reserves, subordinated term debt, and more.

tier 2 deduction = *second-tier deduction.*

tier 2 RRTA tax RRTA tax withheld for a taxpayer who works for more than one railroad companies.

till money <1> cash kept by a cashier for daily disbursements. *Also*: vault cash. <2> = *cash reserve.*

timber preference income the untaxed capital gains from timber transactions that would be included as part of the tax preference.

time adjusted rate of return (TA RoR) = *internal rate of return.*

time-adjusted rate of return method = *internal rate of return method.*

time-adjusted revenue method a method for calculating depreciation cost based on the proportion of discounted revenue of each period. *See*: *cash proceeds approach.*

time apportionment <UK> apportionment of income and expenses between two periods before and after the effective date of a new tax legislation.

time-based cost the cost that increases as the time passes. *Also*: time cost.

time-based inventory system = *fixed order interval system.*

time contract = *purchase or sale on credit.*

time cost <1> = *period cost.* <2> = *time-based cost.*

timeliness the qualitative characteristic of accounting information that reaches the user in time to help in making a decision.

time note = *promissory note.*

time of supply <UK> for value added tax purpose, the time of occurrence of a supply of goods or services.

time-period concept the idea that the life of a business is divisible into time periods of equal length.

times-fixed charges earned net income before fixed charges and income taxes divided by fixed charges, e.g. interest. *Also*: fixed charge coverage; fixed charges earned.

times-fixed interest charges earned ratio = *times interest earned.*

time sharing accounting methods and procedures for recognizing each client, recording usage time, storage, controlling errors, etc. when using a computer on time sharing basis.

times interest earned (TIE) operating interest divided by annual interest expense. *Also*: interest coverage ratio; number of times interest was earned; times fixed interest charges earned ratio; times interest ratio.

times interest ratio = *times interest earned.*

times preferred dividends earned net income divided by annual preferred dividends. *Also*: number of times preferred dividend earned.

time value <1> excess of the price at which the company is merged over the price of its stock before merger. <2> = *extrinsic value.* <3> = *time value of money.*

time value of money the value the money can produce in a given period, often equals the *future value* in excess of *present value*. ***Also***: time value.

time weighted value of money the value of a sum of money taking into account the rate of return it will earn and the length of time for which it will be used.

timing classification classifying cost into period cost and product cost.

timing difference = *temporary difference.*

timing error an error incurred in one accounting period but the effect of which is reflected in another period.

TIN tax identification number

tip income money received over and above wages for services rendered. ***Also***: gratuities; tips; toke.

tips = *tip income.*

Title 26 Internal Revenue Code (Section 26 of the US Code.)

title of accounts method = *account method.*

title of statement = *heading.*

TL total loss

TLO total loss only

TMP tax matters partner

tobacco manufacturers' surtax <Canada> = *Part 2 tax.*

tobacco tax federal excise tax on tobacco manufacturers.

Tobin's Q ratio = *Q ratio.*

Tobin tax an international tax on foreign currency exchange, first proposed by James Tobin, a Nobel-Prize-winning economist.

toke = *tip income.*

tolerable deviation rate = *upper deviation rate.*

tolerable error = *tolerable misstatement.*

tolerable misstatement the maximum monetary misstatement that may exist without causing the financial statements to be materially misstated. ***Also***: tolerable error.

tolerable rate maximum rate of deviation from a control structure policy or procedure that an auditor is willing to accept without modifying the planned assessed level of control risk.

top-down approach = *parametric approach.*

top estate tax rate the highest estate tax rate. (48% in 2004.)

top-hat plan deferred compensation plan available to top executives only.

top line *sales* or *revenue* as it is shown at the first line of an income statement. ***See***: *bottom line.*

top office expense an expense incurred in the top office of a business, e.g. the president's salaries.

top rate the highest rate on personal income or estates. ***See***: *first rate; middle rate.*

top-slicing relief <UK> a tax relief that treats a lump sum income (e.g. proceeds from a life insurance policy) as if it was received over several year and only one year's portion is taxable.

total absorption cost = *absorption cost.*

total absorption costing = *absorption costing.*

total account = *controlling account.*

total assets total amount of the assets of an organization. ***Also***: gross assets.

total assets to equity ratio = *asset/equity ratio.*

total asset turnover = *asset turnover.*

total average method = *periodic average method.*

total brought forward total of a column brought from the previous page in a ledger.

total carried down column total brought forward to the next page in a ledger.

total cash flow the sum of cash flow from all sources. ***Also***: aggregate cash flow.

total company value = *enterprise value.*

total company wide overhead rate = *single overhead allocation rate.*

total consolidated asset sum of consolidated asset plus unamortized goodwill.

total cost (TC) <1> sum of costs including manufacturing cost and selling and distribution costs. ***See***: *all-in cost; cost of goods sold.* <2> purchasing cost + storage cost +

ordering cost + cost of not carrying. *Also*: aggregate cost. <3> = *absorption cost.*

total cost approach to distribution (TCD) a technique used to identify and aggregate the more obscure distribution related costs as well as the more obvious and commonly recognized distribution costs.

total cost center overhead (TCCO) sum of the overhead incurred by the cost center itself and that transferred from other cost centers.

total costing = *absorption costing.*

total cost of ownership purchase price plus the additional costs of owning an asset.

total cost ownership (TCO) tracing costs to a person or organization responsible for costs related to their designated products, services and/or customers.

total cost per unit sum of the average cost of each process or each element under process costing. *Also*: average total cost; unit total cost.

total cost system = *absorption cost system.*

total debt to total assets a ratio calculated by adding short-term and long-term debt, and then dividing by a company's total assets.

total depreciation = *accumulated depreciation.*

total direct labor cost variance difference between standard direct labor cost for the good units produced and the actual direct labor costs incurred.

total direct materials cost variance difference between standard cost for direct materials and the actual cost incurred for those items.

total enterprise value (TEV) calculated as market capitalization + interest bearing debt + preferred stock - excess cash.

total equity <1> = *equity.* <2> = *net worth.*

total factor productivity = *productivity.*

total fixed cost (TFC) <1> the sum of all fixed costs. <2> the a in the cost-volume formula: f = a + bx.

total income sum of all income subject to tax. *Also*: net statutory income.

total inventory method a method of applying the lower-of-cost-or-market method to inventory pricing.

total liabilities the sum of current liabilities and long-term liabilities as listed on the balance sheet.

total loss (TL) damage or destruction to such an extent that it cannot be rebuilt or repaired to equal its condition prior to the loss.

totally-held subsidiary a subsidiary more than 90% but less than 100% of controlling interests are owned by its parent company. *See: wholly-owned subsidiary.*

total manufacturing cost total cost of direct materials, direct labor, and manufacturing overhead incurred and charged to production during an accounting period.

total manufacturing overhead variance difference between the actual manufacturing overhead costs incurred and the standard manufacturing overhead costs applied to production using the standard variable and fixed manufacturing overhead rates.

total positive income (TPI) the sum of all positive income figures in a tax return.

total present value combination of present values of free cash flows over a projection horizon plus free cash flows from subsequent years, usually derived from capitalizing and discounting the terminal value.

total process cost the sum of the cost of each process under process costing.

total profit <1> the sum of profits of all departments or all subsidiaries. <2> the accumulated profits from the set-up of the business till now.

total project approach = *comparative statement approach.*

total return <1> investment return including income from dividends and interest, as well as appreciation in the price of the securities. *Also*: absolute return. <2> for bonds held to maturity, discount rate at which the initial investment in the bond will grow to the total value available at maturity with interim cash flows invested at an assumed reinvestment rate. *Also*: horizon return; realized compound yield.

total revenue total sales and other revenue for a particular period.

total risk the sum of *systematic risk* and *unsystematic risk.*

total shareholder return (TSR) <1> the total return of a stock to an investor (capital gain plus dividends). <2> internal rate of return of cash flows to an investor during the holding period of an investment.

total tax the sum of all taxes owe for the tax year after all credits, but not payments, have been applied.

total taxable income the portion of a lump-sum distribution from a qualified plan that qualifies for favorable tax treatment.

total tax bill = *tax liability.*

total unstated interest present value of all imputed interest from a deferred payment sales contract.

total variable cost a cost that varies in total in direct proportion to changes in activity.

total variance the sum of all subvariances. *Also*: gross variance.

total work cost (TWC) = *gross cost of production.*

Totten trust a bank account the balance in which will be left to a beneficiary should the account holder die.

TPI total positive income

TPS taxe sur les produits et services <Canada> = *Goods and Services Tax.*

trace <1> to determine if a financial statement item has been handled according to proper corporate or accounting policy. <2> to assign cost to an activity or a cost object using an observable measure of the consumption of resources by an activity.

traceability assignment of costs to a particular segment of the business based on a definable set of cause-effect relationships.

traceable cost = *direct cost.*

traceable fixed cost = *direct fixed cost.*

tracing backward = *test of existence.*

tracing forward = *test of completeness.*

tracking error = *active risk.*

tradeable asset <UK> an asset that can be sold easily on the market.

trade asset an asset used in or derived from the firm's activity. *Also*: committed asset.

trade balance = *balance of trade.*

trade certificate <UK> a certificate issued by the Registrar of Companies enabling a company to do business.

trade claim = *pre-petition debt.*

trade deficit negative balance of trade, i.e. exports exceeds imports. *Opp*: *trade surplus.*

trade discount reduction of the list price in return for the purchase of large quantities. *Also*: price discount; quantity discount.

trade fixture <UK> fixture installed in a premise for the trade or business.

trade-in allowance a price reduction for turning in an old item when buying a new item.

trade liberalization multilateral reduction in tariffs and other measures that restrict international trade.

trade-off = *opportunity cost.*

trade-off in cost a situation under which the cost of carrying increases while the cost of not carrying decreases.

trade payables turnover period calculated as (bills payable + accounts payable) ÷ daily sales.

trade surplus positive balance of trade, i.e. exports exceeds imports. *Opp*: *trade deficit.*

trade working capital the difference between current assets and current liabilities directly associated with daily business operations.

trading book the portfolio of financial instruments held by a brokerage or bank.

trading capital sum of fixed capital and liquid capital.

trading cost the cost of making a securities or futures trade including both the commission and the bid/ask spread.

trading difference = *balance of trade.*

trading loss <UK> expenses in a trade exceed receipts.

trading profit <1> profit on an investment position held for less than one year, taxed as ordinary income. *See*: *short swing profit.* <2> = *gross profit.* <3> = *operating income.*

trading, profit and loss account = *income statement.*

trading securities the securities that are not to be *held to maturity.*

traditional allowance <UK> allowance given to married women in 1990 if their husbands were on low income.

traditional breakeven chart breakeven chart with fixed cost line at the base. ***Opp***: *breakeven chart with variable costs at base.*

traditional cost allocation allocating indirect costs without using cost drivers.

traditional costing = *absorption costing.*

traditional cost system = *absorption cost system.*

traditional form of cost ascertainment a method for determining the fixed and variable behavior of cost by verifying the invoices.

traditional IRA an IRA the contribution into which is tax deductible. ***Also***: ordinary IRA; original IRA; regular IRA. *See*: *deductible IRA; nondeductible IRA; Roth IRA.*

traditional lifo lifo that applies to each unit of inventory items. *See: dollar value lifo.*

traditional method = *ledger cost method.*

trailing twelve months (TTM) the timeframe of the past twelve months (the past year) used for financial reporting.

transaction an event or exchange that affects the assets, liabilities, or the owners' equity of a firm.

transactional stage a period during which a company tries to acquire or establish another company, the expenses incurred are not deductible.

transaction approach an audit procedure that predominates in the examination of physical plant assets as a result of low turnover, all transactions have to be verified completely. ***Opp***: *inventory approach.*

transaction balance the balance of cash or other current assets that must be maintained for the need of operations.

transaction documents written records, either handwritten or prepared mechanically for every transaction taking place in a business.

transaction in securities a trade in securities.

transaction method a method for reporting the currency gains and losses under which each transaction is reported on the basis of currency exchange rates prevailing at the time of each transaction.

transaction review reexamination of transactions by auditors.

transactions cost the cost incurred in the performance of a transaction, e.g. cost of obtaining information about the price, quality, usefulness, etc.

transactions in US official reserve assets and in foreign official assets in the US = *official settlements balance.*

transaction system a system in which inventory taking is made only when there have been quite a number of transactions incurred.

transaction tax a tax that applies mainly to the transactions in domestic goods and services, and international equities trades.

transaction trail chains of evidence provided through coding, cross references, and documentation connecting accounting balances and other summary results with original transactions and calculations.

transaction velocity measurement of the rate at which money circulates in the economy, which equals total sales divided by total spending. *See*: *income velocity*

transaction-volume cost driver cost driver that draws on a measurement from a feeder subsystem that not only varies with cost magnitude but proportionately assigns the costs to its objects.

transfer movement of money between government fund and proprietary fund.

transfer account = *continuing account.*

transfer cost <1> the cost that a department accepts for items supplied by other departments. <2> = *book cost.*

transfer earnings = *opportunity cost.*

transfer-in cost = *transferred-in cost.*

transfer of rights to income = *assignment of income.*

transfer of share conveyance of share to another.

transfer of tax credit <Canada> the transfer of unused tax credit to a taxpayer's spouse, supporting parent, grandparent, child or grandchild.

transfer payment <1> <Canada> a funding by the federal government to the provinces and territories. <2> flow of income which represents a change in the distribution of national wealth but not compensation for current contribution to the production process.

transfer pricing the pricing where one service department within a company charges for the use of its services by other divisions of the company either at the cost or some agreed formula. *Also*: cross charging.

transferred basis the basis of property determined by reference to the basis of property in the hands of the transferee.

transferred-in cost the cost of the previous process transferred as an input into this production process. *Also*: previous process cost; prior department cost; transfer-in cost.

transferred-out cost the cost of this process transferred to the next process under process costing.

transferred property <Canada> depreciable property that is transferred from one class to another for tax purpose.

transfer slip a slip other than cash receipts and cash disbursements slips. *Also*: transfer voucher.

transfer tax <1> estate tax and gift tax. <2> a tax imposed by New York State when a security is sold or transferred.

transfer to other account amount of inventory transferred to another account for calculation of cost of goods sold.

transfer to spouse the transfer of property to a spouse.

transfer variance difference between actual cost and standard cost transferred to the next process under process costing.

transfer voucher = *transfer slip.*

transformation of cost fixed cost becomes variable cost, or vice versa.

transit account <1> an account for recording goods or accounts in transit when a branch is using independent accounting system. <2> = *suspense account.*

transition asset excess of the FMV of plan assets over the accumulated post retirement benefit obligation at the beginning of the fiscal year for which SFAS 106 is adopted.

transition obligation excess of accumulated post retirement benefits obligation over the fair value of plan asset at the beginning of a fiscal year for which SFAS 106 is adopted.

transitory income <1> current income minus permanent income. <2> = *windfall profit.*

translation changing functional currency statements back to home currency statements. *See*: *remeasurement.*

translation adjustment the amount to balance the accounts due to translation gain or loss. *Also*: foreign currency translation reserve.

translation exposure = *accounting exposure.*

translation exposure accounting = *foreign exchange accounting.*

translation gain the gain from translating of foreign subsidiary financial statements into home currency when the exchange rate is favorable. *Also*: exchange gain; foreign exchange gain; gain from translation; gain on exchange. ***See***: *remeasurement gain.*

translation loss the loss from translation of foreign subsidiary financial statements back to home currency due to fluctuation in the exchange rates. ***Also***: exchange loss; foreign exchange loss; loss from translation. ***See***: *remeasurement loss.*

translation of account balances translation of the foreign subsidiary's account balances back to the home currency. ***Also***: exchange adjustment; foreign currency translation.

transmit (TX) to send a tax return to the IRS electronically.

transmitter a service provider that sends electronic tax returns to the IRS.

transnational accounting = *international accounting.*

transportation in = *freight-in.*

transportation ratio of railroad companies, total expenses incurred in moving trains divided by gross revenue.

travel and entertainment expense deduction tax allowance for a percentage (50%) of travel and entertainment expenses.

travel expense an expense, such as meals and lodging, incurred while away from home. ***Also***: away-from-home expense.

traveling audit auditing of the branches, in which the auditor must travel to the places where the branches reside. ***See***: *field audit.*

traveling auditor <1> one who performs audit of branches. <2> a CPA who performs field audit for a client at a distant location on a continuous basis.

treasurer person in a firm who deals with financial and money matters.

Treasury bond US government long-term security having a maturity longer than five years

treasury bond a bond reacquired by its original issuer.

treasury stock issued stock that has been reacquired by the issuing corporation. ***Also***: reacquired stock; redeemed share.

treasury stock method a method of computing the number of common stock under the assumption that the money paid by those who have stock option in purchasing common stock will be used as a fund for purchasing the treasury stock. ***See***: *if-converted method.*

Treasury tax and loan account (TT&L a/c) = *tax and loan account.*

treaty-exempt income <Canada> income of a nonresident that is exempt from income tax.

treaty-protected business <Canada> a business the income from which is exempt from tax because of a tax treaty with another country.

Treynor ratio the returns earned in excess of those that could have been earned on a riskless investment per each unit of market risk assumed.

trial-and-error method a method of calculating the internal rate of return, under which a trial rate is selected which is expected to cause the sum of the discounted present value of the cash inflows to equal the cost of investment, if the discounted present value is higher, a higher rate must be use, and vise versa until the correct rate is found. ***Also***: iterative method.

trial balance a listing of all the assets, liabilities, capital, revenue, and expense account balances at a given time. ***Also***: abstract; line sheet; schedule of account balances.

trial balance account = *balance sheet account.*

trial balance after adjustment = *adjusted trial balance.*

trial balance after closing = *after closing trial balance.*

trial balance before adjustment = *unadjusted trial balance.*

trial balance ledger = *Boston ledger.*

trial balance of balances list of all the account balances of a self balancing ledger.

trial balance of footings = *trial balance of totals.*

trial balance of totals a list of the debit totals and the credit totals of all the accounts. *Also*: trial balance of footings.

trial balance of totals and balances a combination of the trial balance of totals and the trial balance of balances.

triggering event an event that allows participants in a qualified plan to be eligible to receive a withdrawal without suffering a tax or penalty.

trinsically fixed cost fixed cost that must be considered by accounting methods.

trinsically variable cost variable cost that must be considered by accounting methods.

triple entry bookkeeping a bookkeeping that views the capital and wealth as past, present, and additional entry of the wealth, as the derivative of capital, is made.

triple exemption a bond or bond fund whose dividends and interest are exempt from Federal, state and local income taxes for investors in the appropriate locations.

triple net lease = *net net net lease.*

triple tax-exempt security a municipal bond featuring federal, state, and local tax-free interest income to investors. *Also*: fully tax-exempt security.

TRO turnover ratio

true balance bank account balance after reconciling items are adjusted.

true cost = *current cost.*

true interest cost the coupon rate required to provide an identical return assuming a coupon-bearing instrument of like maturity that pays interest in arrears.

true lease a lease that qualifies as a valid lease agreement under the Internal Revenue Code.

true rate of return = *internal rate of return.*

true taxable income a standard used to determine what the controlled company's income would have been had it been independent of its affiliates.

true value rule a rule under which one who subscribes for and receives corporate stock must pay therefor the par or stated value thereof either in money or in its worth.

trust <1> the arrangement in which one person holds the property for the benefit of a named party. <2> = *close combination.*

trust company <Canada> a financial institution that offers fiduciary administration of estates, trust and pension plans.

trust corporation <UK> a company that acts like a *public trustee.*

trust distribution payment made to a taxpayer from a trust.

trustee <1> the person who holds the property in a trust. <2> a person with fiduciary duty to another.

trustee of last resort = *public trustee.*

trust fund a fund restricted by a trust agreement, such as pension trust fund, investment trust fund and private-purpose trust fund. *See: agency fund.*

trust grantor = *trustor.*

trust income tax return <1> Form 1041 filed by a trust with income of $600 and above. <2><Canada> an income tax return filed by a trust.

trustor the person who creates a trust. *Also*: creator; grantor; settlor; trust grantor.

trust protector someone appointed to audit the trustee's books and protect the trust assets.

trust throwback rule = *throwback rule.*

TSO Taxpayer Service Office

T-system = *fixed order interval system.*

TT&L a/c Treasury tax and loan account

TTM trailing twelve months

tuck-in acquisition the acquisition of a company with the sole purpose and intent of merging it into a division of the acquirer.

tuition credit = *education credit.*

turnover = *sales turnover.*

turnover of inventory = *inventory turnover.*

turnover ratio (TRO) = *activity ratio.*

turnover tax indirect tax, typically on an ad valorem basis, applicable to a production process or stage.

TVC total variable cost

TVQ taxe de vente du Quebec

TWC total work cost

twelve-month acquisition period any twelve-month period, beginning when an acquiring company first purchases stock of the target corporation.

twenty-one year deemed disposition rule = *21-year deemed disposition rule*

twice straight-line-declining balance method a depreciation method the rate under which is twice the straight-line rate of depreciation.

twin-track tax US tax system that imposes tax on one track of regular computation and another track of alternative minimum tax.

two-account system <1> the system for calculating sales cost, in which there are only a purchases account and a sales account. <2> a bookkeeping system that classifies account into active and passive groups.

two-bin method a method of controlling inventory, by using 2 bins, one for the safety stock, the other for normal inventory and replenishment order must be placed when the normal inventory bin is empty. *Also*: red-line method; white-line method.

two-bin system a system of inventory control in which a particular stock-keeping unit is divided into two parts, the first part is for normal use and the other part can only be used when the first is exhausted. *Also*: white line system.

two-class method a method of showing earnings per share, in which earnings per share of the preferred and ordinary stock are reported separately.

two-dimensional bookkeeping system = *dual classification bookkeeping system.*

two-dimensional variance analysis = *two-variance analysis.*

two-part accountability report accountability report that includes production quantity and cost amount.

two-payment rule an accounting provision, the gist of which is that installment sale reporting was impermissible unless there were at least two payments in two different taxable years.

two-rate system a taxation system under which retained earnings are taxed at a higher rate, while declared dividends are taxed at a lower rate.

two-section income statement an income statement that shows both contribution margin and net income.

two-sided balance sheet = *account form balance sheet.*

two-sided form = *account form.*

two-statement approach a method of listing net income and other comprehensive income in two separate statements. *See*: *one-statement approach.*

two-step allocation = *continuous allotment method.*

two-T-account method a method of showing foreign exchange gain or loss, or the price level changes by using two T accounts, one for actual figures, the other for adjusted figures.

two-tier tax system *See: 2-tier tax system.*

two-variance analysis a method of analyzing factory overhead variance into a budget variance and a volume variance. *Also*: two-dimensional variance analysis.

two-year rolling start rule <Canada> a rule under which capital can only be claimed in the third year if the taxpayer acquired a property and has not used it in two years.

two-year rule <1> a rule the gist of which is that if property is sold to a related party on installment method and is resold within two years, then the original seller's gain will be accelerated by the second disposition. <2> test of the condition of a merger for using pooling of interest method, the 2 companies must be independent within 2 years before the plan of merger is initiated.

TX transmit

type 1 error = *alpha risk.*

type 1 subsequent event an event which provides additional evidence about conditions that existed at the balance sheet date and affects the estimates.

type 2 error = *beta risk.*

type 2 subsequent event an event which provides evidence with respect to conditions that did not exist at the balance sheet date, but arose after that date.

Type A reorganization a reorganization pursuant to the laws, such as consolidation. *Also*: statutory merger.

Type B reorganization the acquisition by one company, in exchange solely for all or a part of its or its parent's voting stock, or stock of another company if, immediately after the acquisition, the acquirer has control of the other. *Also*: exchange-of-shares acquisition; stock-for-stock exchange. *See*: *purchase acquisition.*

Type C reorganization acquirer's acquisition of assets of the target company in exchange for acquirer's shares,. *Also*: practical merger; section 351 transactions.

Type D reorganization company A's transfer of its assets to company B, followed by A's distribution to its shareholders stocks, bonds, and other assets received from B. *See*: *acquisitive D reorganization; divisive D reorganization.*

Type E reorganization reshuffling of the capital structure where some or all the stockholders exchange some or all of their shares.

Type F reorganization a mere change in the identity or the place of organization.

Type G reorganization <1> in bankruptcy, the transfer by company A of some or all of its assets to company B, provided company B distributes its shares to its shareholders tax free or partially tax free. <2> = *bankruptcy reorganization.*

U u

UA unit of account

UBI unrelated business income

UBTI unrelated business taxable income

UCC <1> undepreciated capital cost. <2> Uniform Commercial Code.

UI unemployment insurance

UIC unemployment insurance contribution

UIC and CPP credit <Canada> a 16% tax credit on the premium paid on UI and CPP premium.

UI premium credit <Canada> a tax credit allowed to an employer for unemployment insurance premium paid.

ultimate cost = *maximum cost.*

Ultramares approach a defense approach based on a court decision under which auditors are liable to third parties not in privity of contract for acts of fraud or gross negligence but not for ordinary negligence.

umbrella liability policy an insurance policy that provides protection against damages not covered by standard liability insurance.

unabsorbed overhead the overhead cost remained unallocated and under applied.

unaccountable accounting that kind of accounting described in the book of the same name by Mr. Brioff, A. J. 1971, published by N.Y. Harper & Row.

unadjusted basis <1> cost or other basis of a property established under the class life ADRS, less *bonus depreciation*, and after the adjustments other than depreciation or amortization. <2> the base on which cost recovery is claimed in the year that recovery property is placed in service.

unadjusted exemption personal exemption before deduction of personal exemption *phase out* amount.

unadjusted gross profit gross profit before deducting the unrealized income and contra income item.

unadjusted rate of return = *accounting rate of return.*

unadjusted rate of return method = *mercantile method.*

unadjusted trial balance a trial balance prepared after transactions are recorded but before any adjustments are made. ***Also***: trial balance before adjustment.

unadmitted asset = *inadmitted asset.*

unagree case a case under which an agreement has not yet been reached between the taxpayer and the IRS.

unallocated common expense = *overhead unallocated.*

unallowable cost any cost not allowed to be treated as cost under the cost-plus contract.

unallowed cost any item that can not be treated as cost by law and regulations.

unamortizable asset = *non amortizable asset.*

unamortized bond discount the difference between the par value of a bond and the proceeds received by the issuing company, this amount will be written off to interest expenses periodically.

unamortized bond premium difference between the par value of a bond and the price paid by the investor.

unamortized cost = *written-down value.*

unamortized credit a tax credit not previously restored to rate base.

unamortized intangibles intangible assets not fully amortized when being liquidated.

unappropriated profit earnings not paid out as dividend but instead reinvested in the business or used to pay off debt.

unappropriated retained earnings retained earnings not marked for a particular use, so it can be used for paying dividend. ***Also***: accumulated earnings; accumulated income; available surplus; free surplus; net earned surplus forward; retained earnings-unappropriated. ***See***: *appropriated retained earnings.*

unapproved share option <UK> an option from an unapproved share option scheme.

unapproved share option scheme <UK> a share option scheme not approved by the Inland Revenue.

unasserted claim a possible legal claim of which no potential claimant has exhibited an awareness.

unaudited financial statement = *uncertified financial statement.*

unaudited opinion an opinion by a CPA who has not audited the relevant financial statements.

unavoidable cost = *inavoidable cost.*

unbalanced entry an entry the credit and the debit of which are out of balance.

unbilled receivable account receivable for which the customer has not been billed. ***See***: *billed receivable.*

unborrowed policy cash value = *inside buildup.*

uncalled capital that portion of *unpaid capital* not required to be paid. ***See***: *called-up capital.*

uncertificated share mutual fund share maintained on the transfer agent's records, no stock certificate is issued. ***Also***: book share. ***See***: *book entry security.*

uncertified financial statement a financial statement that has not been audited by a certified public accountant. ***Also***: unaudited financial statement.

unclaimed bank account a bank account without a deposit or withdrawal in 5 years. ***Also***: abandoned bank account.

uncollectible account = *bad debt.*

uncompleted transaction a transaction that has not been completed and may cause other accounting events to be happened.

unconfirmed profit the profit on subsidiary income statement that has not been certified by the parent company. ***Also***: book profit.

unconsolidated subsidiary a subsidiary showing individual financial statements that are not presented in the consolidated financial statements.

unconsumed cost = *unexpired cost.*

uncontrollable cost a cost the amount of which a specific manager can not control within a given period of time. ***Also***: non-controllable cost.

uncontrollable expense unavoidable expense of a government, such as long term contract cost, interest on public debts, etc.

uncontrollable overhead an overhead the amount of which can not be controlled by the manager.

uncontrollable variance cost variance not under the control of the manager.

undefined asset <UK> asset held by discount houses which is not defined asset.

undepreciated capital cost (UCC) <Canada> residual value of a fixed asset after *capital cost allowance* has been taken. ***Also***: cumulative eligible capital. ***See***: *unrecovered basis; written-down value.*

undepreciated cost asset cost remained after depreciation. ***Also***: residual cost.

undepreciated value = *written-down value.*

underage cost = *cost of not carrying.*

underapplied factory overhead amount of overhead by which the actual overhead incurred exceeds the overhead applied to production based on a predetermined application rate and evidenced by a debit balance in the overhead account

undercapitalization the situation in which a business does not have enough capital to carry out its normal business.

undercosting a costing process resulting in understatement of cost in the financial statements.

underdepreciation depreciation procedure the result of which is the accumulated depreciation being less than the depreciable cost.

underfunding excise tax excise tax on employers who fail to fund a qualified plan at minimum required level.

underground economy legal and illegal activities that people do not report to the IRS.

underlier = *underlying asset.*

underlying = *underlying asset.*

underlying account = *controlled account.*

underlying asset a financial instrument on which an option or futures contract is subject to delivery. ***Also***: primitive security; underlier; underlying; underlying security.

underlying security = *underlying asset.*

under/over stock report a report of the stock inventory level as compared with the maximum or minimum levels.

underpayment = *underpayment of estimated income taxes.*

underpayment of deposits = *underpayment of estimated income taxes.*

underpayment of estimated income taxes failure to pay 90% of the amount of income taxes due for a tax quarter, minus amounts actually paid for the quarter out of wage withholding and payments of estimated taxes. ***Also***: underpayment; underpayment of deposits.

underpayment penalty a penalty for not paying enough total estimated tax and withholding.

under reporting illegal practice where a person under states taxable income or a company understates earnings. ***See***: *tax fraud.*

understandability qualitative characteristic of accounting information that is presented in a form and in terms that its user can understand.

understated income an income reported in the tax return that is less than the actual amount.

understated product cost product cost in the income statement, which is less than the actual product cost.

understatement of income tax income tax shown on a return is less than the actual tax liability, caused by clerical errors or *under reporting.*

understocking a situation in which the inventory is not enough to fill the needs of production or sales.

underutilization cost a cost due to the underutilization of capacity.

underwater roll rollover of an investment position with a mark-to-market loss deferred.

underwithholding a situation when a taxpayer has withheld too little income tax and therefore owes tax when filing a return.

underwriting gain or loss profit or loss that remains after paying claims and expenses.

underwriting income earned premium of an insurance company minus incurred losses plus loss adjustment expense plus other incurred underwriting expenses plus policyholder dividends.

underwriting profit margin of an insurance company, the difference between the combined loss and expense ratio and 100%.

undisclosed income = *unreported income.*

undisclosed reserve = *secret reserve.*

undiscounted net benefit-cost ratio if I_1, I_2,......I_n are the forecasted cash inflows from an investment project in year 1, 2,......n, D_1, D_2,......D_n are depreciation expenses of the project Year 1, 2 ....n, and O_1, O_2,......O_n are the forecasted cash outflows, then the $\Sigma(Ii - Oi)/\Sigma Oi$ is the undiscounted net benefit cost ratio of the project.

undistributable reserve = *capital reserve.*

undistributed capital gain capital gain of a regulated investment company that has not been distributed and is proportionately includable in the shareholder's income and subject to taxation at the company level.

undistributed income <1> excess of equity in subsidiary over dividends received. <2> = *undistributed PHC income.*

undistributed net income (UNI) basis on which the throwback tax is imposed on distributions of prior accumulations of trust income, often equal to the distributable net income (DNI) minus taxes imposed on the trust with respect to the undistributed DNI and required and discretionary distributions for the year.

undistributed PHC income net income of a personal holding company not distributed to its shareholders. ***Also***: undistributed income.

undistributed profit <1> profit of a joint-venture, a syndicate, or a partnership before distributions to the related parties. <2> = *retained earnings.*

undistributed taxable income the taxable income of an S corporation minus the minimum tax imposed on the corporation, capital gains tax, and the amount of money distributed as dividend.

undivided profit <1> profit not transferred to the appropriated retained earnings account. <2> that portion of the unappropriated retained earnings which may be used to pay dividends, bad debts loss or any other special losses.

undrawn profit net income remained undrawn by the partner or owner of the firm.

undue retention excess of retained earnings over the present and future investment needs. ***Also***: excess cash accumulation.

unearned discount = *instant interest.*

unearned income an individual's income derived from sources other than employment, such as interest and dividends. ***Also***: investment income. ***Opp***: *earned income.* ***See***: *passive income.*

unearned interest the interest received on a loan but can not be treated as income since the principal has not been outstanding for a given interest period.

unearned interest income the difference between the lessor's gross investment in the lease and the cost or carrying amount of leased asset.

unearned premium reserve account of an insurance company, which consists of the unencumbered assets, equal to a minimum of 25% of the gross written premiums received by it from all warranty contracts in force.

unearned revenue = *deferred revenue.*

unemployed capital = *idle money.*

unemployment benefit plan <Canada> a plan under which benefit payments are made by an employer to a trustee exclusively for the periodic payments to employees or former employees who are laid off. ***Also***: supplementary unemployment benefit plan.

unemployment insurance tax state programs that uses taxes collected from employers to provide temporary income for unemployed workers. ***See***: *employment insurance plan; FUTA tax.*

unencumbered balance amount of resources that can still be obliged or expended without exceeding the legal or authorized limit.

unenrolled preparer = *tax preparer.*

uneven cash flow cash flow of each period that is not equal in amount to each other.

unexpired cost a cost the contribution to revenue of which will be made in the future. ***Also***: unconsumed cost.

unfavorable balance of payments the payments made by a country to other countries exceed payments received by the country. ***See:*** *active balance of payments.*

unfavorable standard cost variance cost variance that occurs when the standard cost is less than the actual cost.

unfavorable variance a variance where the discretionary is to the disadvantage of the firm as when actual profits fall short of budgeted profits. *Also*: adverse variance; debit variance; negative variance.

unfiled return a tax return which has not been sent to the IRS.

unfinished goods = *work-in-process.*

unfinished job in process = *job in process.*

unfinished work = *work in process.*

unfranked dividend <Australia> dividend paid out of corporate earnings which have not been subject to tax.

unfriendly takeover = *hostile takeover.*

unfunded accrued pension cost = *accrued pension cost.*

unfunded accumulated benefit obligation = *minimum liability.*

unfunded nonforfeitable post-retirement benefit obligation excess, if any, of the nonforfeitable post-retirement benefit obligation, including benefit eligibility as of the last day of the plan year, over the value of plan assets.

unfunded pension plan a pension for which there is no money put aside on a regular basis.

unfunded reserve a liability that is not offset by a reserve account funded by cash or other liquid assets. *See: funded reserve.*

unguaranteed residual value (URV) the excess of estimated value over guaranteed residual value (GRV) if the GRV exists.

UNI undistributed net income

Unicap uniform capitalization rule

unidentifiable asset an asset, e.g. managerial expertise, personal reputation, etc. contributed to the partnership by a partner.

unified credit amount that can be deducted from the estate tax liability, which equals unified credit exemption multiplied by estate tax rate. *Also*: applicable credit; unified tax credit; unified transfer tax credit.

unified credit exemption maximum exclusion from gift tax in the lifetime of a taxpayer. ($1.5 million in 2004, $2 million in 2006, but only $1 million can be used when the taxpayer is alive.) *Also*: applicable exclusion amount; estate tax exemption; exclusion; exclusion amount; lifetime exclusion. *See*: *annual exclusion.*

unified tax credit = *unified credit.*

unified transfer tax credit = *unified credit.*

uniform accounting the application of uniform principles, terms and systematic procedures in accounting.

uniform capitalization rule (Unicap) IRS rule that states that cost of tangible personal property must be capitalized, if average gross receipts for the 3 preceding years exceed 10 million dollars.

uniform cost accounting the use of a common set of accounting definitions, procedures, terms, and methods for the accumulation and communication of cost data.

uniformity varying amount method = *declining balance method.*

uniform reserve ratio method a method used by banks to increase reserves for bad debts up to the extent of 2.4% of the bank's outstanding loans at the end of the year.

unilateral account an account for recording gratuitous exports.

unilateral transfer an item in current account of the balance of payments that corresponds to gifts from or pension payment to foreigners who once worked in the country.

unincorporated association <UK> an association subject to corporation tax and not income tax.

unindexed gain or loss the capital gain or loss on the sale of an asset before deducting the indexation allowance. *See*: *indexed gain or loss.*

unissued stock shares that have been authorized but not yet issued.

unit approach = *single-asset depreciation accounting.*

unitary accounting the accounting system that views the whole nation as an entity.

unitary assets = *mass assets.*

unit block system a system under which contribution margin of all products is shown at one time, and income statement shows direct labor.

unit comparison approach a method of make or buy decision by comparing the unit costs of the alternatives.

unit contribution margin the dollar amount that the scale of one unit contributes toward the recovery of fixed costs and that toward profit. *Also*: sales margin.

unit cost = *cost per unit.*

unit cost analysis schedule a schedule used in process costing to accumulate all costs charged to the Work-in-Process Inventory a/c of each department or production process and to compute cost per equivalent unit for direct material costs and conversion costs.

unit costing a method of costing used when the cost units are identical, based on the basic computation: total cost number of units.

unit-credit method a method under which the sum of pension expense assigned to the current year is equal to the present value of the increase in the employee's retirement benefits resulting from the services in the current year. *Also*: accrued-benefit cost method. *See*: *projected benefit cost.*

unit depreciation = *single asset depreciation.*

United States Tax Court = *Tax Court.*

unit fixed costs = *fixed costs per unit.*

unit income statement income statement for a unit of product.

unit inventory an inventory item that exists as a whole unit such as a car, a boat, a house, etc.

unit investment trust (UIT) SEC-registered investment company which buys a fixed, unmanaged portfolio of income-producing securities and then sells shares in the trust to investors. (Mutual fund is actively managed, while a UIT is not managed at all). *Also*: authorized unit trust; fixed investment trust; participating trust; unit trust

unit labor cost = *cost performance.*

unit lifo method a method under which the goods are grouped into several units, the average cost of each unit is used for pricing that unit.

unit livestock price method a method of inventory valuation used by farmers under which livestock raised, or purchased before maturity or to be raised to maturity are grouped by age and class and then valued at normal cost for such groups.

unit loss excess of unit cost over unit selling price.

unit method of depreciation = *single-asset depreciation accounting.*

unit method of inventory valuation the method for inventory pricing, under which assets are grouped by natural class. *Also*: individual method of inventory valuation.

unit of account (UOA) artificial unit designed to provide a consistent reference value against the varying exchange rates.

unit of money financial statement financial statement based on the money unit at the historical cost. *Also*: conventional financial statement; nominal dollar financial statement; non-financial dollar financial statement.

unit of money postulate a postulate which holds that accounting statements should base on the unit of money. *Also*: stable monetary postulate.

unit of output method = *production-unit basis method.*

unit of product an item or quantity of output.

unit process cost unit cost of a given process under process costing.

unit product cost the cost of a group of products divided by the number of units.

unit production cost = *production costs per unit.*

unit profit the excess of unit selling price over the manufacturing cost per unit of output under absorption costing. *Also*: sales margin.

unit purchase price purchase cost divided by the number of units purchased.

units-of-general-purchasing power financial statement financial statement based on the general purchasing power of money.

units-started cost unit cost figure of the semi-finished goods at the beginning of a process under process costing.

unit summation method of depreciation a method of depreciation under which each asset is depreciated at its own rate of depreciation, and the over or under-depreciated amounts are adjusted at the end of the period.

unit total cost = *total cost per unit.*

unit trust (UT) <UK> = *unit investment trust.*

unit variable cost = *variable cost per unit.*

universal budget = *master budget.*

university basic research credit a 20% tax credit on the basic research expense of a university.

unjustified accounting change change in accounting principles that is not supported by management, auditor should express qualified or adverse opinion.

unknown liabilities hidden liabilities not known to the buyer of a business.

unlimited company <UK> a company the members of which have unlimited liability.

unlimited marital transfer the transfer of unlimited amount of assets to a spouse without paying tax. *Also*: marital transfer.

unlimited tax bond municipal bond backed by a full faith and credit commitment to tax at whatever rate and for whatever duration is necessary to fulfill the obligation.

unlisted asset = *nonledger asset.*

unmatched book the average maturity of a bank's liabilities is shorter than that of its assets.

unmortgaged asset = *free asset.*

unnecessary cost the cost incurred when producing goods of a quality that exceeds the relevant standard.

unorthodox financial statement = *condensed financial statement.*

unpaid capital amount of capital not paid by the shareholder, usually the total capital authorized exceeds the *paid up capital.*

unpaid dividend a dividend that has been declared by the board of directors but has not reached its payment.

unpaid expense an expense that has not been paid.

unpaid tax <UK> = *back tax.*

unpaid vouchers file a file in which unpaid vouchers may be filed either alphabetically or numerically or by due date.

unpostponable cost a cost that can not be postponed to the future periods.

unproductive asset <1> asset not used in the production of goods or services. <2> asset that can not produce income by itself.

unqualified audit = *complete audit.*

unqualified opinion an opinion in which the auditor absolutely agrees with the client's accounting records and behavior. *Also*: clean bill of health by auditor; clean opinion; standard opinion.

unqualified report an audit report with unqualified opinion. *Also*: auditor's standard report; non-opinion report; standard audit report; standard report; standard unqualified report. *See*: *qualified report.*

unrealized appreciation <1> increase in the value of property that the tax-payer has not been realized by sale or other disposition. <2> increase in the owner's equity resulted from the revaluation of assets in excess of historical cost.

unrealized appreciation from revaluation of assets = *appraisal capital.*

unrealized capital increment = *appraisal capital.*

unrealized depreciation adjusted bases of property in excess of the value of that property.

unrealized gain appreciation in the market value of property that has not yet been realized. ***See***: *appreciated financial position.*

unrealized holding gain excess of appraised value of assets over their book value, or the amount by which the appraised value of the liabilities is less than their book value.

unrealized holding loss amount by which the appraised value of assets is less than their book value or the appraised value of the liabilities exceeds their book value.

unrealized inter-company profit = *inter-company profit.*

unrealized loss <1> decrease in stockholder's equity resulting from decline in the market value of the equity securities held in a non-current investment portfolio. ***Also***: embedded loss. <2> = *paper loss.*

unrealized profit the profit that has not become actual.

unrealized profit or loss = *paper profit or loss.*

unrecognized net gain or loss cumulative net gain or loss that has not been recognized as a part of net periodic pension expense.

unrecognized prior service cost portion of prior service cost that is not recognized as a part of the net pension expense.

unreconciled difference the difference between cash account balance and the bank statement balance that has not been reconciled yet.

unrecorded expense an expense incurred but the applicable amount of which has not been recorded during the month.

unrecorded liability = *liability out of book.*

unrecoverable cost = *sunk cost.*

unrecovered basis portion of the basis in a property that has not yet been recovered through tax credit or depreciation.

unrecovered inventory amount the lesser of the inter-company profit amount in a consolidated return year or the initial inventory amount.

unrecovered losses the losses arising from breaches of contract, fiduciary duty, or anti-trust violations to the extent they do not create a tax benefit to the taxpayer.

unrelated business income (UBI) = *unrelated business taxable income.*

unrelated business taxable income (UBTI) unrelated trade or business income of an exempt organization, less direct related deductions typical of any trade or business. ***Also***: unrelated business income.

unrelated debt-financed income the same percentage of the gross income derived from debt-financed asset of exempt organizations characterized as the average acquisition indebtedness bears to the average adjusted basis of such property.

unremittable overseas income overseas income that is subject to income tax on accrual basis but which can not be remitted into the UK.

unremitted income earnings from a foreign subsidiary or divisions that are known but not yet transferred to the parent company.

unreplaceable asset an asset the replacement cost of which can not be calculated.

unreported earnings = *indirect earnings.*

unreported income the income not reported to the tax authority. ***Also***: undisclosed income.

unrestricted fund a fund that is available for current spending.

unrestricted net assets net assets of a government unit with no external restriction as to use or purpose.

unrestricted options = *non-statutory options.*

unseparable cost the cost that can not be separated as fixed or variable components.

unstated interest = *imputed interest.*

unsubscribed capital stock capital stock that has not yet been subscribed.

unsystematic risk a risk that affects a very small number of securities or portfolios.

Also: diversifiable risk; idiosyncratic risk; non-systematic risk; security specific risk; specific risk. *See*: *systematic risk*.

untaxed income = *exempt income*.

untraceable cost = *overhead*.

untraceable fixed cost = *indirect fixed cost*.

unused credit excess of a tax credit earned for the taxable year, over the limitation based on the amount of income tax for that year.

unused zero bracket amount zero bracket amount minus the greater of itemized deductions or earned income.

U/O under or over

UPA Uniform Partnership Act

upkeep cost = *maintenance cost*.

upper deviation limit the sample deviation rate plus an allowance for sampling risk. *Also*: achieved upper precision limit; upper occurrence limit.

upper deviation rate the maximum acceptable deviation rate. *Also*: tolerable deviation rate.

upper limit on misstatement = *upper precision limit*.

upper occurrence limit = *upper deviation limit*.

upper precision limit an estimate of the maximum amount of misstatement in the account. *Also*: acceptable upper precision limit; upper limit on misstatement..

upside capture fraction of the risky asset's terminal value that is captured by the overall portfolio insurance strategy.

upstream sale the sale of goods from subsidiary to parent company, profit must be eliminated in preparing consolidated financial statements. See: *downstream sale*.

up-to-date value = *current value*.

URV unguaranteed residual value

usable cost the cost data useful to the managers.

usage value in stock control, the total cost of the quantity of stock of a particular stock keeping unit used during a period of time.

usage-value classification the classification of inventory for the purpose of stock control, according to their usage value. *Also*: ABC classification.

usage variance cost variance caused by the difference between actual usage and standard usage.

useful life = *economic life*.

usefulness expenditure not expired in the current accounting period.

use-it-or-lose-it a tax rule under which unused credit or deductions can not be carried forward.

use method a method of depreciation based on the proportion of the usage.

user auditor the auditor who reports on the financial statements of the user organization, which uses a service organization in data processing.

user cost <1> the sum of depreciation cost and raw materials cost. <2> = *capital consumption*.

user fee an excise tax, in the form of a license, to fund a public service.

user need approach = *value approach*.

user-originated accounting = *information accounting*.

user tax a tax that is paid directly by the consumer.

user value = *current user value*.

use tax a state tax on the purchase of goods from outside the state for use within the state. *Also*: compensating use tax.

utilities cost the cost of providing public utilities.

utility cost the cost for the use of utility.

utility expenditures government expenditures for construction or acquisition for publicly owned utility facilities or equipment, etc.

utilization cost the cost incurred for the achievement of a goal.

utilization fee a fee charged on Eurocredits in lieu of a commitment fee.

utilization variance = *capacity variance*.

utmost care the standard of care that must be exercised by a trustee or other fiduciary in connection with fiduciary responsibilities. *Also*: extraordinary care; highest degree of care. *See*: *due care*.

V v

V variable cost

vacation pay payment to employees who are on a vacation.

vacation-with-pay trust <Canada> a trust created pursuant to the terms of a collective bargaining agreement for providing for the payment of the employees' vacation pay.

validity control the control of the validity of the internal behavior and accounting records.

valuation account <1> an account for recording adjustment to another account. *Also*: adjustment account. <2> account for accumulated depreciation.

valuation account practice = *appraisal method.*

valuation allowance <1> net realized loss in a marketable securities investment portfolio. <2> allowance for the loss incurred in the revaluation of some assets, e.g. an allowance for inventory price decline.

valuation assumption = *accounting assumption.*

valuation basis the basis of property determined according to the value of the property as of a certain date.

valuation day <Canada> the day on which the value of a property is taken into account for computing capital gains and losses.

valuation day value method <Canada> a method that uses the value of a property on the valuation day as the basis for capital gains purpose. *See*: *median rule.*

valuation loss the amount by which the appraised value of an asset is less than its book value. *Opp*: appraisal capital.

valuation method = *appraisal method.*

valuation opportunity cost the potential increase in business value associated with investments that are for gone due to capital rationing.

valuation premium amount required by state law that an insurance company must reserve to cover all of its liabilities.

valuation problem the difficulty of assigning a value to a business transaction; in general, determined to be original, or historical, cost.

valuation profit = *appraisal capital.*

valuation ratio = *price/book ratio.*

valuation reserve a reserve established for all items that wear out in order to reduce the value over time, usually viewed as a contra asset in the balance sheet.

value added attributes of a transaction or a process that increase the value of the transaction or process by their addition.

value-added cost the cost of activity that can not be eliminated without the customer perceiving a decline in product quality or performance. *See*: *non-value-added cost.*

value added tax (VAT) a tax imposed on the value increase of a product after a process.

value approach an approach under which the assets in the balance sheet are at their actual value. *Also*: user need approach.

value asset a measure calculated as: (assets - liabilities - liquidation value and the accrued dividend of preferred stock) ÷ number of shares of common stock.

value at risk (VAR) a method which uses the statistical analysis of historical market trends and volatilities to estimate the likelihood that a given portfolio's losses will exceed a certain amount.

value chain design, procurement, market, distribution and post-sale service of a product.

value chain costing activity-based costing that contains all of the activities in the value-chain of a business.

value-decrease schedule = *depreciation schedule.*

value index (VI) net income produced by one dollar of research expense on new products.

value in use present value of future cash flows expected to be derived from the use of an asset at an appropriate rate that allows for the risk of the activities concerned.

value variance the price variance and the rate variance.

VAR value at risk

variable annuity an annuity the rents vary in amount according to the value of the investments made by the funds.

variable budget = *flexible budget.*

variable capital <1> capital that varies as the volume of production changes. <2> capital represented by labor, which undergoes an alteration of value in the production process. ***Also***: floating asset; immaterial capital; incorporeal capital; invisible capital; wage capital.

variable component the variable portion of the cost.

variable cost (var cost)(VC)(vrble cost) a cost that changes in total amount proportionately with the production-level changes. ***Also***: non-constant cost; pure variable cost. ***See***: *product cost.*

variable costing the costing procedures by which only the variable costs are applied to the products. ***Also***: variable product costing. ***See***: *direct costing.*

variable cost rate method = *high-low points method.*

variable costs percentage total variable costs divided by total sales.

variable costs per unit cost of the variable inputs of production per unit of output. ***Also***: average variable cost; per unit variable cost; unit variable cost; variable unit cost. ***See***: *fixed unit cost.*

variable cost plus pricing determination of price by adding a markup to the variable cost.

variable cost to produce manufacturing cost under variable costing.

variable cost with a fixed-cost component cost such as maintenance cost, which may have an avoidable fixed component at very low levels of activity, but may vary directly with increases in activity at higher levels.

variable direct expense the direct expense that is variable.

variable expense the expense that varies as the volume of production varies.

variable factory overhead = *variable overhead.*

variable factory overhead price standard a weighted average of costs of the supporting factory services divided by the expected number of units.

variable factory overhead quantity standard the number of units of supporting factory services whose costs are variable, divided by the expected number of units.

variable manufacturing margin = *manufacturing margin.*

variable margin excess of revenue over short term variable cost.

variable overhead (var o'h'd)(V o'h'd) factory overhead the amount of which changes with the production output. ***Also***: variable factory overhead. ***Opp***: *fixed overhead.*

variable overhead absorption rate (VOAR) variable overhead divided by the number of units.

variable overhead allowed multiplying the actual number of output units by the standard variable overhead cost per unit of output.

variable overhead efficiency variance the difference between the actual units of activity and the standard units of activity allowed for the output produced, multiplied by the standard variable overhead rate per unit of activity.

variable overhead rate the variable overhead divided by the number of units of activity.

variable overhead spending variance the difference between actual variable overhead cost and budgeted variable overhead based on the actual units of activity multiplied by the standard variable cost per unit.

variable overhead variance difference between the actual variable factory overhead cost and the variable overhead allowed.

variable portion the variable portion of the mixed cost.

variable product costing = *variable costing.*

variable profit = *marginal profit.*

variable ratio formula a *formula investing* plan under which the ratio of stock in a portfolio is adjusted to maximize stock purchases at low prices and minimize their acquisition at high prices. ***See***: *constant-dollar plan; constant-ratio formula.*

variables estimation approach an audit approach based on the substantive audit test.

variables sampling a sampling that reaches a conclusion in dollar amounts. ***See***: *attributes sampling; probability-proportional-to-size sampling.*

variable standard costing variable costing that uses standard cost data.

variable unit cost <1> cost per unit figure that changes in proportion to the volume of output, that is *fixed costs per unit.* <2> = *variable costs per unit.*

variance difference of revenue, costs, expenses, and profits from the planned amount.

variance analysis = *analysis of variance.*

variance of estimated cost of materials difference between actual and estimated cost of the raw materials.

variety reduction a cost reduction method which cuts out all varieties that have less profits.

VAT value-added tax

VAT invoice an invoice from the seller with value added tax shown on it.

vault cash = *till money.*

VC variable cost

VCT venture capital trust

vector bookkeeping = *matrix bookkeeping.*

venture capital = *risk capital.*

venture capital firm a company that invests its money in startups and other risky but potentially very profitable ventures. ***See***: *angel investor.*

venture capital trust (VCT) <UK> an investment trust with both equity and loan features introduced in 1993.

verifiability <1> the possibility of being proved by other source of the documents of accounting data. <2> = *objectivity.*

verification of assets the work of an auditor in checking the existence and the value of the assets of a business.

vertical acquisition taking over a firm in the same industry.

vertical analysis financial analysis which deals with single-year financial statements.

vertical balance sheet = *financial position statement.*

vertical equity a tax concept which states that people in different income groups should pay different rates of taxes. ***See***: *horizontal equity.*

vertical form = *report form.*

vertical merger a merger of companies with vendor-customer relationship. ***See***: *horizontal merger.*

vertical working paper = *three-division vertical working paper.*

very low income annual household income that does not exceed 50% of the median household income for a given area.

vest charge = *cut-off rate of return.*

vested benefit a benefit for which the employee's right to receive a present or future pension benefit is no longer contingent on remaining in the service of the employer.

vested benefit obligation the actuarial present value of vested benefits. *Also*: nonforfeitable post-retirement benefit obligation.

vested capital = *contributed capital.*

VHWO voluntary health and welfare organization

victim company = *acquired company.*

vintage account an account that contains eligible assets placed in service during the taxable year and no others. *See*: *open-end account.*

visible balance = *balance of trade.*

visitor tax rebate <Canada> return of GST or HST to foreign visitors.

VITA volunteer income tax assistance

VOAR variable overhead absorption rate

V o'h'd variable overhead

volume cost low cost or special cost that represents effects of the quantity.

volume efficiency variance cost variance caused by the difference between the actual and standard labor efficiency.

volume of activity a percentage of capacity (where full capacity is equal to 100%).

volume variance <1> the difference between the allowed amount of each variable expense at the actual sales volume and the budgeted amount of that expense. <2> = *capacity variance.* <3> = *overhead volume variance.*

voluntary audit an audit made at the decision of the management.

voluntary compliance a system that relies on citizens to report their income, calculate tax liability and file tax returns on time.

voluntary contribution = *after-tax contribution.*

voluntary expenditures the expenditures that are not required and, therefor, may be denied deductibility.

voluntary health and welfare organization (VHWO) an organization that offers free or low-cost services to the public and supported by public contributions.

voluntary liquidation winding up of a company following a resolution by the shareholders or creditors. *See: compulsory liquidation.*

voluntary nonexchange transaction including grants and entitlements from one government to another where the providing government does not impose specific requirements upon the receiving government.

voluntary reserve a reserve decided by the articles of association or the stockholder's meeting.

voluntary trust a trust established by a deed of transfer of title made voluntarily by a person or other legal entity to a trustee for a specific purpose.

voluntary winding-up a winding-up settled without going to court.

voluntary withholding deducting taxes from social security benefits by filing form W-4V.

volunteer income tax assistance (VITA) a service program whereby people volunteer their time to help their neighbors prepare their tax returns at no charge.

voodoo accounting the accounting that does not follow principles of conservatism. *See*: *cookie jar accounting.*

vostro account an account maintained with a bank by a bank in a foreign country. *Also*: due to balance; due to bank account; your account. *See*: *nostro account.*

voting stock a stock the holder of which has the right to vote on corporate matters. *See*: *class A stock; nonvoting stock.*

voting trust a trust legally created to combine the voting power of shareholders through the transference of legal title and voting rights to a designated trustee for a set duration.

voucher (vch) <1> a paper for summarizing a transaction and approving it for recording and payment. ***Also***: journal voucher. <2> a document provided to an employee free that entitles him to cash or goods or services. <3> = *slip*. <4> = *supporting document slip*.

voucher audit inspection of vouchers and comparing them with the records. ***Also***: public audit; vouching.

voucher register a book of original entry in which approved vouchers are recorded.

voucher system a system used to control the incurrence and payment of obligations requiring the disbursement of cash.

vouching <1> = *test of existence*. <2> = *voucher audit*.

vouching account an account approved by the payment vouchers.

vrble cost variable cost

W w

W-2 = *Wage and Tax Statement.*

W-4 form = *Employee's Withholding Allowance Certificate.*

W-9 Form tax form which certifies an individual's tax identification number.

WACC <1> weighted average capital cost. <2> weighted average cost of capital.

wage employee compensation, including salaries, fee, bonus, commission and fringe benefit.

Wage and Tax Statement an annual form sent to the employee and the Social Security Administration by the employer reporting gross income and deductions for a calendar year. ***Also***: Form W-2; W-2 Form. ***See***: *P60.*

wage assignment an arrangement allowing the lender to deduct payments from a borrower's wage in case of default.

wage audit = *payroll audit.*

wage base level of earnings to which the full Social Security tax applies, $87,000 in 2003. ***Also***: wage base limit.

wage base limit = *wage base.*

wage-bracket method a method used by small businesses to compute the required standard withholding according to the wage bracket table.

wage-bracket withholding table a table showing the amount to be withheld from employees' wages at various levels of earnings.

wage capital = *variable capital.*

wage continuation plan a plan whereby salaries and wages are continued during an employee's illness or disability.

wage rate variance = *labor rate variance.*

wages cost = *labor cost.*

wages percentage overhead rate overhead rate based on the wage percentage.

wages variance that part of labor cost variance caused by having high payment workers.

WAI wealth added index

waiting period <1> a period of time a participant in a health insurance plan must pass before he/she is eligible to be covered. <2> = *cooling period.*

waiver of dividend majority shareholder's disclaimer of his right to receive dividends, while the remaining shareholders continue to receive dividends.

walk-in e-filing the e-filing offered by Volunteer Income Tax Assistance without charge to taxpayers who visit a VITA office.

walk-in service the tax service provided over a walk-in counter by the IRS.

walk-through test a procedure whereby the auditor looks at the supporting document for a transaction from its starting point and then proceeds to examine the accounting system steps thereafter until ultimate disposition of the item.

wallpaper = *worthless security.*

Wall Street leverage a profit increase will cause the stock of a public company to rise and thus increase the value of the company. ***See***: *capital leverage; operating leverage.*

wall-to-wall inventory the inventory taking of all items on hand. ***Also***: complete inventory.

wanton negligence = *gross negligence.*

warehouse expense an expense incurred in the process of storing goods.

warning written notice sent from the IRS to an authorized e-file provider requesting correction action to be taken to avoid sanction.

war profits tax a tax on corporations deriving income from war-related government contracts.

warrant = *stock warrant.*

wash sale rule an IRS rule prohibiting a taxpayer from claiming a loss on the sale of an investment if that same investment was purchased within 30 days before or after the sale date. ***Also***: 30-day wash rule.

wastage loss of materials in the production process.

waste residual material that has no resale or re-use value. ***Also***: waste material.

waste book (WB) <1> an old system of analysis of the daily transactions occurring in a bank office, superseded by the mechanized bookkeeping. <2> = *blotter.*

waste material = *waste.*

wasting asset real asset which is consumed on used over time. ***Also***: depletable asset; depletion asset; depletive asset; diminishing asset. ***See***: *depreciable asset.*

watered capital stock capital increased by way of paper entries only, or when new shares are issued without any provision being made to provide the yield thereon.

WB <1> warehouse book. <2> waste book.

W/C working capital

WDV written-down value

weak currency debt a debt in a non-Canadian currency.

wealth account a statement that shows privately owned reproducible tangible wealth.

wealth tax <1><Canada> a tax imposed on the net value of assets, such as property tax, gift tax, estate tax, etc. <2> a tax levied by some countries such as India on the annual net worth of a taxpayer.

wear and tear = *physical depreciation.*

wear and tear allowance <UK> allowance available to a taxpayer who rents out some properties such as furniture.

weather normalization reserve = *normalization reserve.*

webtrust attestation engagement in which CPAs assess a client's internet site for predefined criteria that are designed to measure transaction integrity information protection and disclosure of business practices.

weekly return = *bank return.*

weekly statement <1> a statement prepared weekly. <2> = *weekly trial balance.*

weekly trial balance trial balance prepared after weekly posting of entries. ***Also***: weekly statement.

weighted average borrowing rate interest rate that is the result of averaging rates of all financing sources to finance the construction of a plant asset.

weighted average capital cost (WACC) = *weighted-average cost of capital.*

weighted average cost the cost calculated by the weighted average of all elements.

weighted average cost flow assumption an assumption which holds that the beginning goods and those added this process are both finished at the end of the process.

weighted average costing = *average costing.*

weighted-average cost of capital (WACC) cost of capital computed by weighting the percentage cost of each component by the percentage of that component in the financial structure. ***Also***: overall cost of capital; weighted-average capital cost.

weighted average inventory pricing the pricing of ending inventory with the weighted average cost of beginning inventory and each purchase.

weighted average perpetual inventory method a procedure for keeping subsidiary inventory records by which the units issued and the units remaining on hand are both priced at the weighted average unit cost before the issue.

weighted average process costing method a procedure for computing the unit cost of a process by which the equivalent units and costs are included in computing the unit cost of work, completed during the period.

weighted average unit cost unit cost ascertained by weighted average method.

weighted cost driver technique of increasing or decreasing the cost consumption intensity of an individual cost object by weighting the measured quantity of the cost driver.

welfare-to-work credit a tax credit given to employers that hire long-term family assistance recipients before July 1, 1999.

WET wine equalisation tax

WFTC working families tax credit

where-got, where-gone statement = *statement of changes in financial position.*

whisper number rumored earnings number about to be reported by a public company.

white-collar crime a business or financial crime of a type engaged in by executives and professional people.

white-line method = *two-bin method.*

white-line system = *two-bin system.*

whole dollar accounting = *cents less accounting.*

whole-life cost life cycle cost plus after-purchase cost.

wholly-owned subsidiary a subsidiary 100% of its controlling interests are owned by its parent company. ***See:*** *totally-held subsidiary.*

widget synthetic basket instrument issued by an investment bank and usually listed on an exchange to permit one or more investors to avoid dividend withholding taxes.

widow a married woman whose husband has died.

widowed mother's allowance <UK> government pension paid to a widow aged 45 to 60 and with children or pregnant.

widower a married man whose wife has died.

widow's allowance = *family support allowance.*

widow's bereavement allowance <UK> extra allowance that a widow received in the tax year of her husband's death. (Abolished from Apr 6, 2000.)

widow's pension <UK> pension paid to a widow aged 45 to 65 who is not entitled to widowed mother's allowance.

willful negligence = *gross negligence.*

windfall = *windfall profit.*

windfall profit gain that requires no investment or effort. ***Also***: sundry income; transitory income; windfall.

winding up payment of the current account of a company.

window dressing taking steps just before financial statements are prepared to make current position appear better than it is. ***Also***: cooking the book; doctoring; elastic accounting; fancy accounting; maneuver.

window posting a procedure under which a cashier who receives the cash from the customer also posts the entry directly to the customer's account.

wine equalisation tax (WET) <Australia> a 29% tax on the wholesale price of wine.

WIP <1> work in process. <2> work in progress.

with cost the winning party of a lawsuit may recover costs.

with dividend = *cum dividend.*

withdrawal money withdrawn from the business by its owner.

withholding allowance = *income tax exemption.*

withholding of tax at source = *income tax withholding.*

withholding tax = *income tax withholding.*

withholding taxation = *income tax withholding.*

withholding tax reclaim reclaiming part of a tax withheld by a foreign government.

with interest meaning a security carries accrued interest. ***See***: *ex interest.*

with no interest = *ex interest.*

without dividend = *ex dividend.*

without interest = *ex interest.*

witness fee compensation paid to a person summoned to appear in the Tax Court.

workers' compensation insurance an insurance which provides payments to workers involved in job-related injuries. *Also*: employer's liability insurance.

working account profit and loss account of a construction work.

working asset <1> asset other than capital asset. <2> asset value calculated as: (asset value - liabilities - liquidation value of the preferred stock - accrued dividends) ÷ number of outstanding preferred stock.

working balance sheet and income statement method = *working trial balance method.*

working capital the capital in productive use represented by the amount by which current assets exceed current liabilities. *Also*: active capital; circulating capital; current capital; floating capital; free working capital; fluid capital; gross working capital; net current asset; net working capital; rolling capital.

working capital basis a basis for the statement of changes in financial position, based on the working capital.

working capital deficit excess of current liabilities over current assets. *Also*: liquid deficiency.

working capital expense an expense that may reduce the net working capital.

working capital flow statement = *statement of changes in working capital.*

working capital generated by operations calculated as: revenue - cost - operating expense - income tax - interest expense.

working capital management deployment of current assets and current liabilities so as to maximize short-term liquidity.

working capital ratio <1> working capital divided by net sales. <2> = *current ratio.*

working capital turnover rate sales divided by net working capital.

working condition fringe any property or services provided to an employee by the employer to the extent that the cost of the property or services would have been deductible by the employee.

working cost = *operating cost.*

working costing = *operating costing.*

working families tax credit (WFTC) <UK> a tax credit replacing family credit in October 1999. *See*: *earned income tax credit; working income supplement.*

working hours method a depreciation method used where the major depreciation is the hours of use rather than time periods.

working income supplement <Canada> introduced in 1993, a tax credit available to low-income taxpayers with children. *See*: *earned income tax credit; working families tax credit..*

working interest direct participation in the operations of a business.

working life = *economic life.*

working paper <1> memo, analysis, and other papers prepared by accountants and auditors and used as a basis for the more formal reports. *Also*: work paper. <2> = *work sheet.*

working ratio a ratio calculated by taking the company's total annual expenses (excluding depreciation and debt-related expenses) and dividing by the annual gross income.

working sheet = *work sheet.*

working sheet and income statement method = *working trial balance method.*

working trial balance a listing of ledger accounts with current year-end balances, with columns for adjusting and reclassifying entries as well as for final balances for the year.

working trial balance method a method consisting of a listing of each ledger account together with its balance at the end of the previous year under audit, its balance at the end of the current year under audit and columns for adjusting entries, reclassifying entries and final balance. ***Also***: working balance sheet and income statement method; working sheet and income statement method.

work-in-process (WIP) products in the process of being manufactured that have received a portion or all of their materials and have had some labor and, overhead cost applied but that are not completed. ***Also***: goods in process; half-finished goods; incomplete work; in-process goods; order on hand; partly finished goods; semi-finished goods; unfinished goods; unfinished work.

work-in-process at close = *closing work-in-process.*

work-in-process cost the cost applied to the work in process.

work-in-process inventory units that are partially completed in terms of materials, labor or overhead at the beginning or end of an accounting period.

work-in-process ledger a subsidiary ledger that contains accounts for each work-in-process. ***Also***: finished parts ledger; semi-finished goods ledger.

work-in-process deduction <Canada> work-in-progress not included in the gross income of a professional.

work-in-process turnover total cost divided by work-in-process cost.

work-in-progress <Canada> unfinished work of a professional that can bill the client.

work opportunity credit = *work opportunity tax credit.*

work opportunity tax credit (WOTC) a tax credit given to an employer that employs members of certain target group before Jul 1, 1999, up to $6,000 per employee. ***Also***: work opportunity credit.

work order (WO) = *job order.*

work order charge = *job order cost.*

work paper = *working paper.*

work-related expense <UK> a taxpayer's expense incurred in carrying out his or her employment.

works account = *manufacturing account.*

works cost <1> = *job order cost.* <2> = *manufacturing cost.*

work sheet a working paper used by an accountant to bring together in an orderly manner the information used in preparing the financial statements and adjusting entries. ***Also***: working paper; working sheet.

work sheet entry an entry never journalized, e.g. an entry used to adjust inter-company elimination or to adjust amounts reported in prior periods. ***See***: *auditor's adjusting entry.*

work sheet method a method that uses work sheets to analyze transactions in order to prepare statement of cash flows.

works overhead = *factory overhead.*

world accounting = *international accounting.*

world income <Canada> a taxpayer's income from all sources within or outside Canada.

world-wide income the sum of the parent's net income and that of the foreign subsidiaries.

worthless account = *bad debt.*

worthless check = *bad check.*

worthless security a security treated as if it had been sold or exchanged, which has no capital value to holders during the taxable year, except in the case of securities in affiliated corporations. ***Also***: wallpaper. ***See***: *blue-skying stock; junk bond.*

WOTC work opportunity tax credit

wrap account an account in which a brokerage helps an investor find a money manager in exchange for a flat quarterly or annual fee, which covers all administrative and management expenses.

wrap around annuity an investment that allows the annuitant the choice of underlying investments tax-deferred.

write-down <1> deduction of bad debts from the accounts receivable account. ***Also***: charge-off . <2> = *write-off.*

write-off <1> operating loss that can be reduced from the taxable income of the company. <2> an adjustment on the books that reduces the undepreciated value of a fixed asset. ***Also***: write-down.

write-off method = *direct method.*

write-up <1> increase in an asset's book value not resulting from added costs. <2> an adjustment of an asset account to correspond to an appraisal value.

write-up client one who gets the bookkeeping service from a public accountant.

write-up work = *bookkeeping.*

writing-down allowance <1> amount that a person or company deducts from taxable trading profits to represent depreciation of fixed assets or amortization of intangible assets. ***Also***: written down allowance. <2> = *capital allowance.*

written down allowance = *writing down allowance.*

written-down book value = *written-down value.*

written-down replacement cost replacement cost less accumulated depreciation. ***Also***: depreciated replacement cost.

written-down value (WDV) cost of the plant asset less any accumulated depreciation or accumulated depletion. ***Also***: book value; carrying value; cost less depreciation; declining book value; declining carrying value; depreciated original cost; depreciated value; net book value; remaining book value; unamortized cost; undepreciated value; written-down book value. ***See***: *tax written-down value; undepreciated capital cost.*

written representation = *letter of representation.*

wrong account the account that has been misposted.

W-2 Form = *Wage and Tax Statement.*

X x

X Roman numeral for 10.

x.b. ex bonus

x.c. ex capitalization

X-dis. ex distribution (in stock listings of newspapers).

X **div.** ex dividend

X **int**. ex interest

X/O gain or loss extraordinary gain or loss

Y y

yardstick standard cost = *basic standard cost.*

year-end adjustment process of adjusting the entry to an account at the end of a calendar or fiscal year to properly state it for financial statement purposes.

year-end audit the audit performed at the end of a year.

year-end dividend a dividend declared by the board of directors at the end of a fiscal year.

yearly accounting period = *accounting year.*

yearly interest <UK> interest expressed to be paid yearly, e.g., a 3-month loan does not carry yearly interest, but a loan without a fixed term carries yearly interest. ***See:*** *annual interest.*

year of service a 12-month period during which an employee has over 1,000 hours of service, or the equivalent.

year-over-year change <Canada> the change from one period to the same period a year later.

year's digits method = *sum-of-the-years'-digits method.*

year's maximum pensionable earnings (YMPE) <Canada> the earnings on which benefits from Canada pension plan and Quebec pension plans are based.

year to date (YTD) period beginning January 1st of the current year up until today's date.

year-to-date amount total amount accumulated from the beginning of the year. ***Also***: cumulative amount.

Yellow Book = *Government Auditing Standards.*

yield (YLD) income received by an investor from a security expressed as a percentage of the money invested or of the current price of the security. ***Also***: efficiency. ***See***: *rate of return.*

yield advantage extra amount of earnings an investor earns if he buys a convertible security instead of the common stock of the same company.

yield basis of depreciation = *service-yield basis.*

yield equivalence = *equivalent taxable yield.*

yield method a method of amortizing bond premium by the annual yield. ***Also***: scientific method.

yield on shares = *current return.*

yield to adjusted minimum maturity UK, a measure designed to give the yield to the shortest possible life of a bond. ***Also***: yield to crash; yield to worst.

yield to average life yield derived when the average maturity of the bond is substituted for the final maturity date of the issue.

yield to call (YTC) calculated on the assumption that the bond is called on the first permissible date, and redeemed at the price laid down in the indenture for the first call date.

yield to crash = *yield to adjusted minimum maturity.*

yield to maturity (YTM) a bond's composite rate of return off all payouts, coupon and capital gain or loss. ***Also***: effective interest rate; overall yield; redemption yield.

yield to put the return a bond earns assuming that it is held until a certain date and put to the issuing company at a specific price (put price).

yield to worst = *yield to adjusted minimum maturity.*

yield variance cost variance caused by the difference between actual and planned output. *Also*: production yield variance.

YMPE year's maximum pensionable earnings

your account = *vostro account.*

YLD yield

YTC yield to call

YTD year to date

YTM yield to maturity

Z z

ZBA <1> zero balance account. <2> zero bracket amount.

ZBB zero-based budget

zero balance account (ZBA) a checking account with which checks are written or deposits are made and the net balance is transferred to a concentration account.

zero balance system a system where the inventories are counted when the stock on hand balance drops to zero.

zero-based budget <1> a financial management method to redirect funds from lower priority current programs to the higher ones, to pinpoint opportunities for improving the efficiency and effectiveness, to reduce the budgets while raising the operating performance, and to improve profitability. <2> an approach of justifying the budget and its program for each year or two, instead of studying funding increases or decreases in the programs separately as the need arises.

zero bracket amount (ZBA) = *standard deduction.*

zero budgeting expenditure planning on the basis that no present commitments exist and no balance is carried forward.

zero inclusion = *seating capacity rule.*

zero proof proving of the posting of entries by verifying all the accounts.

zero rate <UK> value added tax rate that is zero for some materials.

zero-rated goods and services <Canada> = *tax-exempt goods and services.*

zero-rated supplies <Canada> = *tax-exempt goods and services.*

zero-rate preference share <UK> a share without dividend payments but will be redeemed on a payment higher than the issue price.

zero salvage value the salvage reduces to zero after the depreciation of a plant asset.

Z-score = *Altman Z-score.*

Z share mutual fund shares of a class available to employees of the fund.

[redacted]

978-0-595-31018-0
0-595-31018-4

WITHDRAW

Printed in the United States
29769LVS00001B/347

9 780595 310180